D0583907

DATE DUE

DEMCO 38-296

R

Celestial Sirens

Nuns and their Music in Early Modern Milan

ROBERT L. KENDRICK

CLARENDON PRESS · OXFORD
1996

Riverside Community College
Library
4800 Magnolia Avenue
Riverside, CA 92506

ML 290.8 .M4 K46 1996

Kendrick, Robert L.

Celestial sirens

...ess, Walton Street, Oxford OX2 6DP

...xford New York

...ckland Bangkok Bombay
Calcutta Cape Town Dar es Salaam Delhi
Florence Hong Kong Istanbul Karachi
Kuala Lumpur Madras Madrid Melbourne
Mexico City Nairobi Paris Singapore
Taipei Tokyo Toronto
and associated companies in
Berlin Ibadan

Oxford is a trade mark of Oxford University Press

Published in the United States
by Oxford University Press Inc., New York

© Robert L. Kendrick 1996

This publication has been supported by a subvention
from the American Musicological Society

All rights reserved. No part of this publication may be reproduced,
stored in a retrieval system, or transmitted, in any form or by any means,
without the prior permission in writing of Oxford University Press.
Within the UK, exceptions are allowed in respect of any fair dealing for the
purpose of research or private study, or criticism or review, as permitted
under the Copyright, Designs and Patents Act, 1988, or in the case of
reprographic reproduction in accordance with the terms of the licences
issued by the Copyright Licensing Agency. Enquiries concerning
reproduction outside these terms and in other countries should be
sent to the Rights Department, Oxford University Press,
at the address above

British Library Cataloguing in Publication Data
Data available

Library of Congress Cataloging in Publication Data
Kendrick, Robert L.
Celestial sirens : nuns and their music in early modern Milan /
Robert L. Kendrick.
p. cm. — (Oxford monographs on music)
Includes bibliographical references (p.).
1. Music—Italy—Milan—16th century—History and criticism.
2. Music—Italy—Milan—17th century—History and criticism.
3. Nuns as musicians—Italy—Milan. I. Title. II. Series,
ML290.8.M4K46 1996   781.71'2'0082—dc20   95-44937
ISBN 0–19–816408–4

1 3 5 7 9 10 8 6 4 2

Typeset by Hope Services (Abingdon) Ltd.
Printed in Great Britain
on acid-free paper by
Biddles Ltd
Guildford & King's Lynn

For Karel Kilimnik

Ma quantunque cessata sia la pena, non per ciò è la memoria fuggita de' benefici già ricevuti, datimi da coloro a' quali per benivolenza da loro a me portata erano gravi le mie fatiche; nè passerà mai, sì come io credo, se non per morte.

Boccaccio, *Decameron*, preface

ACKNOWLEDGEMENTS

MY first thanks are due to the Archivio Storico Diocesano Milanese (and its director, Dott. Piergiorgio Figini), the Archivi di Stato of Milan, Bergamo, and Florence, the Civico Museo Bibliografico Musicale of Bologna (Dott. Giorgio Piombini and Oscar Mischiati), the Archivio della Veneranda Fabbrica del Duomo di Milano (Dott. Roberto Fighetti), the Biblioteca Nazionale Braidense (Milan), and the Isham, Law, and Houghton Libraries of Harvard University. The Biblioteca dell'Arciginnasio (Bologna), the Biblioteca Capitolare della Metropolitana (Milan), the Biblioteca Trivulziana and Archivio Storico Civico (Milan), the Conservatorio di Musica 'Giuseppe Verdi' (Milan), the Istituto per la Storia dell'Arte Lombarda (Milan), the Istituti per l'Assistenza Beneficaria (Milan), the Università Cattolica del Sacro Cuore (Milan), the Biblioteca Nazionale (Turin), the Royal Conservatory of Music and Royal Library Albert Ier (Brussels), the Bayerische Staatsbibliothek (Munich), the Ratsbücherei (Lüneburg), the Bischöfliche Zentralbibliothek (Regensburg), the Zentralbibliothek (Zürich), the Bibliothèque Nationale (Paris), the British Library (London), the University Library (Glasgow), the University Library (Wrocław), the Newberry Library (Chicago), the Sibley Library (Rochester), the Archivio Segreto Vaticano (Rome), the Biblioteca Queriniana (Brescia), and the Archivi Capitolari of Novara (Don Angelo Stoppa), Vercelli, Aosta, and Asti provided generous access to sources; the Archivio Storico Civico, Civico Museo Bibliografico, and the Wrocław University Library all gave permission to reproduce materials. Count Luigi Antona-Traversi, Don Fausto Ruggieri, Don Agostino Borretaz, the Academy Library, and the National Library of Vilnius all kindly provided important information or documents. The work would have been impossible without the unstinting aid of Dr Louis Jordan, Curator of the Frank M. Folsom Ambrosiana Microfilm and Photographic Collection, The Medieval Institute, University of Notre Dame, which latter gave permission to reproduce materials. I thank Marc-Joachim Wasmer for permission to quote his excellent reconstructions of Rusca's motets, and Mary-Ann Winkelmes for her permission for photograph reproductions.

I owe much to my counsellors: Kay K. Shelemay, Gabriella Zarri, and E. Ann Matter. The comments of Elizabeth Rhodes, Ellen Koskoff, and David Burrows improved several chapters. Professor Stanislaw Baranczak guided me through seventeenth-century Polish. The splendid performances by Bologna's Cappella Artemisia and Boston's La Donna Musicale helped some of this music sound for the first time in three centuries. And I would never have been inspired were it not for the Concerto delle Donne: Candace Smith, Laurie Monaha.n, Nanneke Schop, and those who, sad to say, would not see this indirect result of their labours, Marc-Philippe Maystre, Trix Landolf, and Nikolaus deBrunner. The Dean's Dissertation Fellowship at New York University and the Charlotte W. Newcombe Foundation funded the writing of my initial approach to this repertory. I am deeply indebted to the Publications Committee of the American Musicological Society for a generous subvention for this book's publication costs.

One pleasure was to meet and learn from those who enriched my understanding of early modern Milan and its music: Franco Pavan, Alexander Blachly, Mary-Ann Winkelmes, Marc-Joachim Wasmer, Lislot Frei, John O'Malley, Pamela Jones, Danilo Zardin, Renée Baernstein, Wietse de Boer, and Gianvittorio Signorotto. To my fellow *seicentisti* Steven Saunders, Wendy Heller, Irene Alm, and Kathryn Welter I am indebted for several points, while Ann Gross, Kees Vlaardingerbroeck, and Liane Curtis helped with essential materials. Mariangela Donà and Francesco Degrada aided my understanding of local musical traditions. And I shall never forget the personal warmth of the country in which I worked, especially that of the *milanesi*, the *baristi*, and the library aides who helped me overcome, in some small way, the fogs of autumns and centuries. I owe special thanks to Candace Smith, Antonio Riccardi, and Craig Monson, collaborators in the study of nuns' music, for their limitless counsel, hospitality, and support. And the unerring eye of Bonnie Blackburn, my copy-editor, made this a far better book than it would otherwise have been. I am also grateful to Leofranc Holford-Strevens for many refinements to the Latin translations.

Much of the book was written in my first year at the Harvard Society of Fellows, which provided unparalleled resources for thought; my gratitude goes to its Secretary, Diana Morse. Senior and Junior Fellows—Bernard Bailyn, Herbert Bloch, Brad Gregory, and Augusta Reid Thomas—provided encouragement and advice. To

Lewis Lockwood, Thomas Walker, and Laura Benedetti I am indebted for trust and comments. The counsel of Jessie Ann Owens and Jane Bernstein helped focus my work and my spirits. Perhaps the happiest times were those spent among friends in Lombardy and Emilia-Romagna: Monica Chittò and the Riccardi family, Bruce and Elisa Dickey, Monica Romano, Andrea Luppi and Anna Cavadini, Jesse Rosenberg and Alessandra Visconti. Those to whom the book would have meant most—Richard, Catharine, and Alexander Kendrick—did not, alas, live to see it. The book's ultimate inspiration came from the gifted, courageous, and diverse musicians who form its subject, while its dedication, to the one person without whose love and support it would have been impossible, speaks for itself.

R.L.K.

Cambridge, Mass.
August, 1995

CONTENTS

Contents

LIST OF ILLUSTRATIONS

MAPS

GLOSSARY OF ECCLESIASTICAL TERMINOLOGY

Angelica: title of a nun belonging to the Angeliche, the congregation at S. Paolo

ascoltatrice: the nun assigned to be present in the parlour during discussions with outside visitors

Cassinese: the reformed congregation of Italian Benedictines (from Monte Cassino)

Clarissans: Franciscan nuns following one of two thirteenth-century Rules

clausura: Eng. 'enclosure', meaning both the obligatory physical walling-off of female monasteries after 1566 and the legal status of nuns as shut off from the external world

clausura pontificia: designation for female monasteries in the diocese of Milan subject to Roman jurisdiction (exercised through the archbishop)

clothing (or **investiture**): the ceremony for a nun's taking final vows (It. *vestizione*)

convent/monastery: throughout this study, female monastic houses subject to *clausura* (as well as male Benedictine houses) are called 'monasteries' (It. *monaster[i]o*); male mendicant houses and those Ursuline foundations not subject to *clausura* are called 'convents' (It. *convento*)

conversa: a nun who did not take final vows, usually with a lower *dote spirituale*. *Converse* functioned as servants inside monasteries

Donna: title of a *professa* in Benedictine houses

dote spirituale: Eng. 'spiritual dowry', the sum paid at final profession of vows to the monastery, usually by a nun's family or guardian. At the major patrician monasteries in the Seicento, the normal *dote* was 4,000 lire (at S. Radegonda, 2,709 lire); at the less prestigious houses, about half that. A patrician marriage dowry could reach 20,000 lire

double church: a typically Lombard architectural form of the church in female monasteries, with an exterior church (*chiesa esteriore*) for the public separated by some kind of wall from the interior church for the nuns (*chiesa interiore*)

educande: girls residing at a female house for education

ferrata: the grates set up between the external and internal parlours so as to restrict access to nuns

Humiliate (It. *Umiliate*): order of nuns found mainly in Lombardy; the larger, wealthier male branch was suppressed in 1571

licenza: an episcopal licence, usually for male doctors or repair workers, to enter a specific female monastery for a specific purpose and for a certain period (normally one year); also used for organ-builders and male music teachers

livello: annual sum over and above the *dote spirituale* paid by a nun's family for her personal use (food, books, etc.)

novitiate: post-Tridentine regulations (not always observed in practice) prescribed that girls wishing to profess vows be examined for sincerity and unforced vocation, that they spend a year of novitiate before final vows, and that no novice was to be allowed to profess before the age of 18. A senior nun was to be assigned as *maestra delle novitie*

office, monastic: according to the Tridentine reforms, the abbess and prioress were to be elected annually; this usually took place in conjunction with the visitation by the bishop or regular superiors

parlatorio: Milanese monastic parlours were divided into two parts, the exterior (for visitors) and the interior (for nuns), by grates; according to Carlo Borromeo's rules of 1577 only a small window for speaking was allowed. In practice the parlours were open, allowing for musical performances

professe (or **velate** or **coriste**): nuns who had taken the full vows of poverty, chastity, and obedience. This status required either a full *dote*, or an exemption (or reduction), the latter to be granted by the Sacra Congregazione dei Vescovi e Regolari

protectors: the four laymen in nominal charge of a female monastery. The term is also used for the Roman cardinal who looked after the affairs of a given congregation

ragionamento: term for Federigo Borromeo's sermons

regulars: male monks following a given rule

religione: monastic tradition or congregation (e.g. *religione cassinese, religione franciscana*)

renunciation: upon profession of final vows, nuns often signed a written, formalized statement renouncing any share in their inheritance

r(u)ota: the revolving enclosed wheel at the gate of a female monastery through which food and supplies were to be passed

Sacra Congregazione dei Vescovi e Regolari: Lat. *Congregatio Episcoporum et Regularium*, post-Tridentine Vatican jurisdictional body, founded 1601, successor to the *Congregazione de' Vescovi* (*Congregatio Episcoporum*, this latter founded 1586), with ostensibly ultimate authority over all monks, male and female, in the Catholic world

S(u)or: normal title for nuns, *professe* and *converse*, in Franciscan, Augustinian, Humiliate, Ursuline, and other congregations, also used for *converse* in Benedictine houses

vicario delle monache: Milanese diocesan official whose major task was to monitor the condition of female monasteries, an office instituted by Carlo Borromeo

vicario generale: Eng. 'vicar-general', the diocesan official responsible for the daily functioning and discipline of diocesan institutions as a whole

visitation: the Council of Trent established the norm of an annual visitation by the bishop or regular superiors to female monasteries; the proceedings and disciplinary orders were to be recorded in writing

voice, active and passive: the right to speak and be spoken to inside *clausura*, often rescinded as a disciplinary measure

LIST OF ABBREVIATIONS

AEM	*Acta ecclesiae Mediolanensis* (Milan, 1890–7)
ASC	Archivio Storico Civico, Milan
ASDM	Archivio Storico Diocesano Milanese (*olim* Archivio della Curia Vescovile)
ASF, MP	Archivio di Stato, Florence, Mediceo Principato
ASL	*Archivio storico lombardo* (Milan, 1889–)
ASM	Archivio di Stato, Milan
ASMod	Archivio di Stato, Modena
ASV, VR	Archivio Segreto Vaticano, Sacra Congregazione dei Vescovi e Regolari
BA	Biblioteca Ambrosiana, Milan
BT	Biblioteca Trivulziana, Milan
Cant.	Song of Songs (with chapter and verse)
DBI	*Dizionario biografico degli italiani* (Rome, 1962–)
DCA	*Dizionario della chiesa ambrosiana* (Milan, 1988–93)
fasc.	fascicle
JAMS	*Journal of the American Musicological Society*
MSDM	*Memorie storiche della diocesi di Milano* (Milan, 1954–68)
NG	*The New Grove Dictionary of Music and Musicians*, ed. S. Sadie (London, 1980)
p.a.	parte antica (in ASM, Fondo Religione and Fondo Culto)
pb	part-book
RISM	*Repertoire International des Sources Musicales*
RSCA	*Ricerche storiche sulla chiesa ambrosiana* (Milan, 1972–)
SCVR	Sacra Congregazione dei Vescovi e Regolari

I have not expanded the following conventional abbreviations:

R.V.	Reverenza Vostra
Sig.re(a)	Signore/Signora
V.R.	Vostra Reverenza
V.S. Ill.	Vos[tra] Signoria Illustrissima

Part-book and voice-type names are abbreviated as follows:

C	Canto, Cantus

S	Soprano
A	Alto, Altus
T	Tenor, Tenore
B	Basso, Bassus
5	Quintus
Bc	Basso continuo
Bp	Basso principale
BpO	Basso per l'Organo
Org	Organo
Part	Partitura

RISM sigla are used for music libraries. Clef names use the standard letter/line system (C3 = alto clef). Pitch names are designated by the Helmholtz system (middle C = c'). Expansions of abbreviations in documents are italicized; editorial additions or notes are in square brackets. I have neither modernized spellings nor changed consonantal *i* and *u* and vocalic *j*. I have used the Vulgate numeration of the Psalms. All translations and transcriptions, musical and documentary, are mine unless otherwise noted.

LIST OF MUSIC EXAMPLES

I

Religious Women in Milan: From 'Counter-Reformation' to 'Early Modern Catholicism'

<><

Church history from the Middle Ages to the modern era, seen
obsessively only through the eyes of the Reformation, appears
distorted . . . The basic problem was not one of the moral
reform of corruption but essentially a political problem . . . The
question [of decadence or shift in the late Cinquecento] . . . still
has great potential beyond the earlier response, namely that one
could not speak of a crisis but of a transition, from creativity in
the visual arts to creativity in music and scientific investigation.

(P. Prodi, 'Controriforma e/o riforma cattolica', 1989)

Any attempt to outline the musical world of nuns in an Italian city
between the Cinquecento and the Seicento must begin with context: their institutional traditions, the intellectual and musical background to the flowering of their work, their thought and spirituality,
and, on the broadest level, the interplay of ideology and expressive
culture in their society. The world-view of such everyday patrician
women as were the performers and composers in this study provided
the underpinnings for their art. In the less exalted circles of city and
cloister, far from the experiments of Florentine or Roman humanism, the survival and power of late medieval modes of thought have
become almost a historiographic commonplace, so much so that one
now must insist on both the essentially supernatural ideology of
urban society and on the almost universally shared norms of orthodox belief.[1] Several themes here—not least the long-standing

---

[1] Not least, one enlightened Swiss patrician's view of equality between the sexes in early

tradition of nuns' public and political role, but also the classical and transcendent conceptions of music itself—underline this point of continuity with the Middle Ages. In fundamental ways, the symbolic complexity and ideology of their world is reminiscent of the venues of modern musical ethnography. In this spirit, I hope to convey some of the flavour of daily life and music-making inside the often porous walls of female monasteries. If much of the story is necessarily structural, still individuals' daily encounters with the cultural and musical norms of their monastic and urban environments help us understand such ideology, one that included both consensus and discord.

The initial interest in the surviving music composed by several nuns (Claudia Sessa, Claudia Rusca, Chiara Margarita Cozzolani, and Rosa Giacinta Badalla) stemmed directly from the advances in women's history over the last two decades. Here the present study takes a tack different from some pioneering work.[2] In its terms and methods, its emphasis on large-scale trends, its focus on the individual, and its disregard for religious experience, this first wave of research proved influential. Indeed, one might even have concluded that the marginality of nuns—indeed of female religious activity in general—in post-Enlightenment Europe was also true earlier.

It was thus no surprise that the recognition of religious women's important role in late medieval and early modern Italy was tardy. The emergence of numerous figures—nuns, 'court prophetesses', locally venerated *beate*, holy widows, tertiaries—and their institutions as central players in the urban prestige and politics of northern Italian cities is largely due to the studies of Gabriella Zarri.[3] The for-

modern Italy has proved idealistic at best; cf. J. Burckhardt, *Die Kultur der Renaissance in Italien* (Basle, 1860), whose classic formulation read 'Zum Verständnis der höheren Geselligkeit der Renaissance ist endlich wesentlich zu wissen, daß das Weib dem Manne gleich geachtet wurde' (pt. 5, ch. 6). For the modern critique of Burckhardt, see P. Burke, *The Italian Renaissance: Culture and Society in Italy* (Princeton, 1986), 1–11; for musical re-evaluation, J. A. Owens, 'Music Historiography and the Definition of "Renaissance"', *Notes*, 47 (1990), 305–30.

[2] In a sort of reverse Burckhardtianism, Joan Kelly posited a drastic decline in European women's status, due to increased social restrictions and a narrowed public sphere; see 'Did Women Have a Renaissance?', in R. Bridenthal and C. Koontz (eds.), *Becoming Visible: Women in the European Past* (Boston, 1977), 137–64.

[3] 'I monasteri femminili a Bologna tra il XIII e il XVII secolo', *Atti e memoria della Deputazione di Storia patria per le provincie di Romagna*, NS 24 (1973), 133–224; 'Pietà e profezia alle corti padane: Le pie consigliere dei principi', in *Il Rinascimento alle corti padane: Società e cultura* (Bari, 1977), 201–37 (now in Zarri, *Le sante vive: Profezie di corte e devozione femminile tra '400 e '500* (Turin, 1990)); 'Le sante vive: Per una tipologia della santità femminile nel primo Cinquecento', *Annali dell'Istituto storico italo-germanico di Trento* (1980),

mal expression of their activity was varied; 'open' monasteries, independent lay communities, and tertiaries all existed together with cloistered orders, at least until the Council of Trent. Female monastic population waxed and waned with waves of reform from the Trecento through the Cinquecento; a major impetus was provided by the observant movements of the Quattrocento. Monastic foundations served as both spiritual and political focuses for civic sentiment. Nuns (along with the less formally organized *pinzochere*, *beate*, and devout women) were increasingly drawn from both the patriciate and wealthier merchant classes, to which their houses were linked by family ties of commerce and patronage. The sanctity of such institutions (considered as earthly manifestations of the Heavenly Jerusalem), along with local cults of female saints, played an important role in urban and even neighbourhood pride; sisters were seen as 'oratrici perpetue', perpetual intercessors, on behalf of their cities. At northern Italian courts, 'irregular' figures—women mystics, 'spiritual mothers', 'living saints'—enjoyed public and political prominence as intercessory figures backed by ducal support. In the Cinquecento, the female monastic population grew sharply as its public role was decreased, mirroring and encapsulating social tensions between newly empowered bishops and urban aristocracies inside houses. Finally, the Tridentine reforms, and the contemporary (re)introduction of monastic enclosure (It. *clausura*) to all orders except the Ursulines, attempted to divert such sanctoral and political traditions inside cloistered walls while hardly shattering nuns' patrician ties.[4] Zarri also noted the increased renown of liturgy and music at female houses from the late Quattrocento onwards.[5]

As a result of such work, interest in women's religious life in early modern Europe grew apace.[6] Even for such a late phenomenon as

---

371–445 (also in *Le Sante vive*); 'Aspetti dello sviluppo degli Ordini religiosi in Italia tra Quattro e Cinquecento: Studi e problemi', in P. Prodi and P. Johanek (eds.), *Strutture ecclesiastiche in Italia e in Germania prima della Riforma* (Bologna, 1984), 207–57; and, most crucially, 'Monasteri femminili e città (secoli XV–XVIII)', in G. Chittolini and G. Miccoli (eds.), *Storia d'Italia: Annali*, ix: *La chiesa e il potere temporale dal Medioevo all'età contemporanea* (Turin, 1986), 357–429. I use the term 'religious women' to underscore the point that many of these figures were not formally cloistered nuns.

[4] The older literature is now superseded by Zarri's works and the studies it has inspired; the essays in L. Scaraffia and Zarri (eds.), *Donne e fede: Santità e vita religiosa in Italia* (Rome, 1994), summarize and update the field.

[5] 'Monasteri femminili', 394–5.

[6] A. Benvenuti Papi, *'In Castro Poenitentiae': Santità e società femminile nell'Italia medioevale* (Rome, 1990) perceives, perhaps unjustifiably, a state of anarchy by the end of the Middle

nuns' musical expression of devotion, Caroline Walker Bynum's studies of nutritional and bodily behaviour of late medieval women in northern Europe are an important point of departure, explicating the influence of holy women over their ecclesiastical and social environment and their own self-presentation.[7] Her work has delineated the religious expression of gendered roles in society, with particular emphasis on women's association with food, especially the symbolic sustenance of every Christian, Christ's Body and its physical avatar in the Eucharist. Bynum also viewed several themes in late medieval piety concerned with the Real Presence and the Passion as most fully developed in the lives and writings of female mystics and visionaries. Certainly both famine and Eucharistic devotion shaped the Milanese Seicento, and it is no surprise that several aspects of the musical repertory represent later refashionings of similar points: feminized themes in Eucharistic spirituality, the emphasis on Christ's bodily suffering as a point of personal identification for nuns, and sisters' use of the affective bodily and erotic imagery of the Song of Songs as a polyvalent textual vehicle in the individual soul's search for its Redeemer.

Most recently, nuns' artistic activity in early modern Italy has started to emerge from the shadows; indeed it has enjoyed something of a recent boom.[8] The autobiographies of orthodox and heterodox figures, the institutional diversity of women's lives, the spirituality of religious orders, the reflections of the outside world in nuns' theatre, the iconographic themes of church decoration, and the close ties between sanctity and family prestige have all been placed in context,[9]

Ages; several essays in G. Calvi (ed.), *Barocco al femminile* (Rome, 1992), consider religious women in the 17th c., for instance S. Evangelisti's portrait of a Brescian Benedictine chronicler, 'Angelica Baitelli, la storica', 71–96.

[7] *Holy Feast and Holy Fast: The Meaning of Food to Medieval Religious Women* (Berkeley, 1987); *Fragmentation and Redemption: Essays on Gender and the Human Body in Medieval Tradition* (New York, 1991).

[8] On music, C. A. Monson, 'Elena Malvezzi's Keyboard Manuscript: A New Sixteenth-Century Source', *Early Music History*, 9 (1989), 73–128. For nuns' theatre, E. Weaver, 'Spiritual Fun: A Study of Sixteenth-Century Tuscan Convent Theater', in M. B. Rose (ed.), *Women in the Middle Ages* (New York, 1980), 173–206; Beatrice del Sera, *Amor di virtù*, ed. E. Weaver (Ravenna, 1990).

[9] Monson (ed.), *The Crannied Wall: Women, Religion and the Arts in Early Modern Europe* (Ann Arbor, 1992); E. A. Matter and J. Coakley (eds.), *Creative Religious Women in Medieval and Early Modern Italy: A Religious and Artistic Renaissance* (Philadelphia, 1994). For a recreation (in the tradition of microhistory) of the world of the 17th-c. Sicilian noblewoman, Benedictine mystic, and beatified nun Isabella Tomasi, see S. Cabibbo and M. Modica, *La santa dei Tomasi: Storia di Suor Maria Crocifissa (1645–1699)* (Turin, 1989). Much of her life is

accompanied by the critical restoration of these religious women's writings and thought.[10]

In the context of Italian ecclesiastical historiography, the delays in this recognition were in part due to the late arrival of the critical re-examination of religious life and thought in the early modern period. But the revision of Church history undertaken in the 1960s demolished the idea of a decadent Quattrocento for religious orders and public piety, rescued by the radical revolution of the Council of Trent. The new perspective weakened the verities of northern European historiography: monolithic and miraculously effective post-Tridentine policy, the 'secular' nature of pre-Reformation piety, and the universal corruption of the pre-conciliar Church.[11] The ongoing reform of devotional life initiated by urban aristocracies (not by the hierarchy) lasted from the Trecento up through the Cinquecento. These waves of renewal found institutional form in the observant movements of mendicant (and other) religious orders, beginning in the fourteenth century. Such efforts also enjoyed significant popular support, and were politically linked to the consolidation of dynastic city-states in northern Italy.[12] Many of their outstanding representatives were women in and out of cloisters: Catherine of Siena, Angela of Foligno, Catarina de' Ricci, Maria Maddalena de' Pazzi.

The study of monastic culture in the later sixteenth century benefited from the re-examination of Tridentine history begun by Hubert Jedin, which detailed the often impromptu nature of the Council's decisions, the bitter arguments in its sessions, and the vagueness of its prescriptions and proscriptions, especially for such

relevant here: nuns and their houses as emblems of patrician prestige; the slow or failed application of Tridentine decrees; the traditions of creative (and sometimes suspect) spirituality in Seicento monasteries. Tomasi had also learnt music as a girl (ibid. 112).

[10] F. Medioli, *L''Inferno monacale' di Arcangela Tarabotti* (Turin, 1990); C. Ferrazzi, *Autobiografia di una santa mancata*, ed. A. J. Schutte (Bergamo, 1990); L. Pioppi, *Diario 1541–1612*, ed. R. Bussi (Modena, 1982). Nuns' theatre has been elucidated by E. B. Weaver; cf. her summary, 'Le muse in convento', in Scaraffia and Zarri (eds.), *Donne e fede*, 253–76. The pioneering work on music is G. L. Masetti Zannini, 'L'educazione musicale', ch. 5 of *Motivi storici dell'educazione femminile (1500–1650)* (Bari, 1980) and 'Espressioni musicali in monasteri femminili del primo Seicento a Bologna', *Strenna Storica Bolognese* 35 (1985), 193–205. For a longer bibliography, see Kendrick, 'Genres, Generations, and Gender: Nuns' Music in Early Modern Milan, c.1550–1706' (Ph.D. diss., New York University, 1993), 14–20.

[11] The classic study of an individual amidst reform was P. Prodi, *Il cardinale Gabriele Paleotti (1522–1597)*, i (Rome, 1959).

[12] Zarri, 'Aspetti dello sviluppo'.

issues as life (and music) in the religious orders.[13] The by no means predetermined implementation of conciliar decrees—or, more precisely and crucially, of episcopal interpretations of Tridentine statutes, and of religiously motivated opposition to such interpretations—on a diocesan or local level also left traces in the documentary records.[14] The results of archival research undermined the idea that papal or conciliar directives were instantly and miraculously effective without divergence, debate, compromise, negotiation, and evasion in almost all institutions of the Catholic world.[15] Rather than viewing the Council's efforts primarily as an attack against Protestant heresy, the new historiographic consensus underlined the intellectually and culturally diverse ways in which Catholics sought first to renew the local structures and spiritual life of the faithful in the tradition of earlier efforts.[16]

Post-Tridentine Catholicism had thus reaped the harvest of a long line of popular devotional and reform movements, among which the Council represented an important and structural—but hardly apocalyptic—moment, and in which urban prestige was inextricably bound to spiritual fervour. A detailed examination of 'post-conciliar' sacred art—painting, literature, rhetoric—revealed far more diversity and stylistic pluralism than formerly considered, especially after the severe neo-classical experiments of the 1560s. And the new devotion enjoyed real popularity and support among a wide range of urban classes; the phenomenon seems to have accelerated towards the end of the Cinquecento.[17] A final historiographic consequence has been

[13] Jedin, *Geschichte des Konzils von Trient*, 4 vols. (Freiburg im Breisgau, 1951–75).

[14] Prodi, *Il cardinale*, and M. Marcocchi, *La riforma cattolica: Documenti e testimonianze* (Brescia, 1967–70). For female monasteries in Italy, the first archivally based local studies of post-Tridentine trends, detailing the real differences between nuns and bishops, were Marcocchi, *La riforma dei monasteri femminili a Cremona: Gli atti inediti della visita del vescovo Cesare Speciano (1599–1606)* (Cremona, 1966), and C. Russo, *I monasteri femminili di clausura a Napoli nel secolo XVII* (Naples, 1970); in both, nuns' polyphony emerges as an important and contested issue in daily claustral life.

[15] For one case in the Milanese hinterland in which orthodox and religiously active patricians physically attacked curial representatives of Carlo Borromeo's reform plans, see D. Zardin, *Riforma cattolica e resistenze nobiliari nella diocesi di Carlo Borromeo* (Milan, 1984). For the methodological importance of local studies in Church history, see Prodi, 'A proposito di storia locale dell'età moderna: Cultura, spiritualità, istituzioni ecclesiastiche', in C. Violante (ed.), *La storia locale: Temi, fonti e metodi della ricerca* (Bologna, 1982), 143–56.

[16] J. O'Malley, 'Was Ignatius Loyola a Church Reformer? How to Look at Early Modern Catholicism', *The Catholic Historical Review*, 77 (1991), 177–93.

[17] For one such case relevant here, the polystilism outlined in P. M. Jones, *Federico Borromeo and the Ambrosiana: Art Patronage and Reform in Seventeenth-Century Milan* (Cambridge, 1993).

the revision of the still-prevalent wisdom, dating from De Sanctis and Croce, in which the cultural 'decadence' of 'Baroque' Italy was due to the power of the post-conciliar Church and the lack of a strong secular State, a phenomenon supposedly epitomized by Milan.[18] There is a terminological corollary: the abandonment of the negative catch-all term 'Counter-Reformation', and its replacement with the more accurate and more inclusive 'early modern Catholicism'.[19]

Similar points are basic to this book. It would be an understatement to say that the concerns outlined here—beginning with female monastic music, but ranging to the broader considerations of sacred polyphony's cultural role in its time—have not been central to most research on these repertories. The assumption has been that the vague Tridentine decrees were immediately known to and accepted by composers, performers, and audiences over a century, without local policy changes, social opposition, divergent interpretations, and the continuation of earlier traditions. Stylistically, sacred music has been either subsumed under the rubric of an undifferentiated and timeless *stile antico*, or considered to have received its driving forces from secular repertories throughout the entire period. A further unquestioned point is that Italian composers across the peninsula produced remarkably similar compositional simplifications in conscious response to the Council, resulting in a 'Counter-Reformation' repertory defined primarily as clear in declamation and simplistic in technique, lasting well into the new century.[20]

[18] The traditional view of Seicento decadence still informs such works as G. Tomlinson, *Monteverdi and the End of the Renaissance* (Berkeley, 1987), along with less sophisticated studies. For its classic formulations, F. De Sanctis, *Storia della letteratura italiana* (Florence, 1870–1), ch. 18, 'Marino', and B. Croce, *Storia dell'età barocca in Italia* (Bari, 1929). To Croce's credit, he used the era of Spanish domination as a trope for the horrors of Mussolini's regime; but it is high time for a more balanced view of the era.

[19] For the interplay among philosophy, devotion, policy, and politics, see A.D. Wright, *The Counter-Reformation: Catholic Europe and the Non-Christian World* (New York, 1982), who noted (p. 48 and *passim*) female conventual life as the freest part of the post-conciliar Church, and remarked on the overall failure of the most restrictive Tridentine policies on nuns' lives. For the most recent historiographic synthesis, see Prodi, 'Controriforma e/o riforma cattolica: Superamento di vecchi dilemmi nei nuovi panorami storiografici', *Römische historische Mitteilungen*, 31 (1989), 227–37.

[20] This idea was due, not to the classic case-study (L. Lockwood, *The Counter-Reformation and the Masses of Vincenzo Ruffo* (Venice, 1970)) of the musical reflections of Borromeo's initial reform plans in Ruffo's Milanese masses, but rather to others' broad and undocumented generalizations from this one specific moment to several generations of pan-European Catholic repertories. For the first critical overview, see A. Borromeo, 'La storia delle

Unsurprisingly, serious consideration of Latin-texted music, liturgical and non-liturgical, on a par with vernacular repertories has suffered, even in a century noted for its musical concern with the expression of texts. And any considerations of possible polystilism have been lost in the teleological rush to separate 'modern' monodic from 'conservative' *stile antico* approaches, normally to the detriment of the latter, or to define 'progressive' trends in the Seicento motet.[21] Much work has relied on an explicitly evolutionist view, with 'minor figures' important only in so far as they strove towards the formal syntheses and expressive devices of either Monteverdi or the 'High Baroque'. The search for structural traits comprehensible to modern musical morphology led to a neglect of composers' responses to the variety of texts set in the early Seicento, and to an understatement of the text-generated inspiration of Seicento music.[22]

But an examination of the largely unpublished evidence, for instance the 100,000-odd post-conciliar documents concerning monks and nuns alone contained in the Archivio Segreto Vaticano, or of the wide variety of musical styles even in the immediate post-Tridentine generation of Italian sacred music, underlines the conflicts and differences—as well as the real popular devotion—found in daily practice. Seventeenth-century devotional life, the context for much of this book's repertory, has similarly suffered in its historiog-

---

cappelle musicali vista nella prospettiva della storia della chiesa', in O. Mischiati and P. Russo (eds.), *La cappella musicale nell'Italia della Controriforma* (Cento, 1993), 229–37. On the key issues, C. A. Monson, 'Catholic Reform, Renewal, and Reaction', in J. Haar (ed.), *The New Oxford History of Music*, rev. ed., iv (forthcoming).

[21] *Pace* J. Roche's helpful introduction, *North Italian Church Music in the Age of Monteverdi* (Oxford, 1982). The cross-cultural evidence (from Judaism, Islam, and Hinduism) also hardly justifies a strict correlation between religious orthodoxy and musical conservatism.

[22] Even the standard classification of Latin texts set to music into 'liturgical' and 'paraliturgical' categories reflects this difficulty. It does not distinguish among: (i) those items likely to be sung as part of an Office (Vesper or Compline Psalms, Magnificats); (ii) those items taken wholly from the (Roman, Ambrosian, or monastic) breviary but unlikely to have been sung in their liturgically correct place (Matins responsories, items from the Little Hours); (iii) those texts formed by a cento of breviary texts and new material; (iv) non-breviary but scriptural passages or centos (often Song of Songs settings); and (v) completely new texts, often written in rhymed (and prosodically Italian) verse. Furthermore, ever since the work of Stephen Bonta ('Liturgical Problems in Monteverdi's Marian Vespers', *JAMS* 20 (1967), 87–106, and 'The Uses of the *Sonata da Chiesa*', *JAMS* 22 (1969), 54–84), it has been apparent that the 'paraliturgical' texts were indeed used in services.

raphy.[23] Indeed, although the late medieval outlines of nuns' piety continued, the Seicento witnessed changes in Eucharistic, Marian, and sanctoral spirituality, trends evident in the music by and for nuns. Similarly, the historiographic miasma surrounding post-Tridentine liturgy, especially that of the religious orders, has obscured the origin of motet texts and the ceremonial use of polyphony, not to mention the central role that liturgical items played in the daily lives of nuns.[24]

From a traditional viewpoint, then, the musical culture of sisters, especially in such a supposedly reactionary city as Milan, could only have seemed marginal and curious, at best part of a princely *Wunderkammer* like the one that Mathias de' Medici would assemble in mid-Seicento Florence. But the rediscovery of the role that female religious played in music marks their polyphony as an important part of intellectual life and urban prestige, and the musical life of their orders as worthy of further study. Indeed, the sheer number of records on music inside Italian cloisters is remarkable, offering significant testimony to the cultivation of polyphony after 1550 in female houses of all the major (and some minor) urban centres: Turin, Monferrato, Asti, Vercelli, Novara, Milan, Bergamo, Brescia, Verona, Vicenza, Padua, Venice, Genoa, Piacenza, Parma, Reggio Emilia, Modena, Ferrara, Bologna, Florence, Siena, Lucca, Rome, Macerata, Naples, and Foggia.[25]

---

[23] In the small literature, one structuralist study of devotional thought is M. de Certeau, *La Fable mystique: XVIe–XVIIe siècles* (Paris, 1982). For affective Christological and Marian piety in Italy, see M. Petrocchi, *Storia della spiritualità italiana*, ii: *Il Cinquecento e il Seicento* (Rome, 1978). For female monastic spirituality after 1600, see now several essays in Scaraffia and Zarri (eds.), *Donne e fede*, notably S. F. Matthews Grieco, 'Modelli di santità femminile nell'Italia del Rinascimento e della Controriforma'; M. Caffiero, 'Dall'esplosione mistica tardo-barocca all'apostolato sociale'; and M. Modica Vasta, 'La scrittura mistica', at 303–26, 327–74, and 375–98 respectively.

[24] Work on the musical life of religious orders is only incipient, although some initial studies of the male branches have been suggestive: O. Mischiati, *La prattica musicale presso i canonici regolari del SS. Salvatore nei secoli XVI e XVII e i manoscritti polifonici della biblioteca musicale 'G.B. Martini' di Bologna* (Rome, 1985); also J. A. Owens, 'Music and the Friars Minor in Fifteenth- and Sixteenth-Century Italy', in *I Frati Minori tra '400 e '500* (Assisi, 1986), 169–88; Mischiati, 'Profilo storico della cappella musicale in Italia nei secoli XV–XVIII', in D. Ficola (ed.), *Musica sacra in Sicilia tra rinascimento e barocco* (Palermo, 1988), 23–46.

[25] The evidence is defined as one or more of the following: nun composers, nun dedicatees of polyphonic music, nuns whose musical abilities came to the attention of the Sacra Congregazione dei Vescovi e Regolari in Rome, nun musicians whose talents were the subject of 16th- or 17th-c. outsiders' reports, or female houses from which polyphonic manuscripts survive. The list is probably biased towards northern Italy, simply because most of the research for this study has been done there; the highly urban character of such music is noteworthy.

The disjuncture between the received wisdom and the sources for nuns' polyphony is striking. If the Renaissance, or the Counter-Reformation, represented a setback for women's non-domestic roles, why do the testimonies to the very public music of female monasteries begin precisely in the second half of the Cinquecento? If these women were marginal to musical life, why is there so much evidence for their skills, especially when compared with reports on music in parishes and male monasteries, or even in some cathedrals? Do the compositions by and for female religious evince some sort of untrained musical idiolect, or do they represent trends found among their male contemporaries? And what does the repertory tell us about their views of spirituality, of their institutions, and of other musical styles?[26] Until Craig Monson's studies on musical life in Bolognese houses, there was little discussion of the actual music produced by or for nuns, the urban and order-specific context of such a repertory, or performance practice.[27] In their wake, other cities' claustral polyphony has also slowly come under scrutiny.[28]

Perhaps ineluctably, another perspective has sometimes, implicitly or explicitly, undergirded the literature: the biologically essentialist view that the music of (i.e. composed by) women *qua* women partakes of certain formal and expressive features not found in music written by men and that, concomitantly, there exists a specifically female musical tradition in the West (and perhaps elsewhere) that

---

[26] I have thus attempted to reach beyond the important but sometimes general work of G. Stefani, 'Sirene nel chiostro', in *Musica e religione nell'Italia barocca* (Palermo, 1975), and J. Bowers, 'The Emergence of Women Composers in Italy, 1566–1700', in ead. and J. Tick (eds.), *Women Making Music: The Western Art Tradition, 1150–1950* (Urbana, Ill., 1986), 116–67, esp. 125–8 and 141–5. To the latter's checklist of printed music composed by women might be added other works by nuns: [Agata] Caterina Assandra, *Salve regina* in B. Re, *Motecta octonis vocibus* (Venice: Vincenti, 1611); Assandra, *Audite verbum Domini* in Re, *Sacrae cantiones* (Venice: Vincenti, 1618); and Alba Trissina's *Vulnerasti cor meum, Quemadmodum cervus, In nomine Jesu*, and *Anima mea liquefacta est*, all in Leone Leoni, *Sacri fiori*, book iv (Venice: Vincenti, 1622).

[27] Beginning with the manuscript intabulations owned by one nun in the 1560s, Monson documented the critical points: the strict episcopal policy of the Paleotti and nuns' resistance thereto; family influence and the traditions of music at the Camaldolese house of S. Cristina; and the social context, devotional world, and musical environment of the 1623 *Componimenti musicali* written by S. Cristina's Lucretia Vizzana; see 'La prattica della musica nei monasteri femminili bolognesi', in Mischiati and Russo, *La cappella musicale*, 143–60; and id., *Disembodied Voices: Music and Culture in an Early Modern Italian Convent* (Berkeley, 1995).

[28] For the remarkable musical life of Genoese houses (including the careers of nuns from the Ferrabosco family), see M. R. Moretti, *Musica e costume a Genova tra Cinquecento e Seicento* (Genoa, 1992), 131–3.

transcends cultural, historical, and stylistic divides.[29] In paradoxical concord with both 'great figure' musical historiography and Burckhardtian emphases, this line of analysis has sometimes sought gender-specific recurrent traits, or female 'voice', in the production of women composers.[30] This study will contribute some evidence on the issue for a local tradition, one that spawned the largest number of women composers—and boasted arguably the most renowned female musicians—of any seventeenth-century European city. The relationships among nuns, devotion, and musical style present broader theoretical implications for the study of music, gender, and socio-religious ideology.

For musical life, the cultural interpretation of nuns' womanhood was central for the outside world; in northern Italy, far more documentation of controversy concerning the propriety, aesthetic value, and disciplinary regulation of nuns' music has survived than is the case for their male monastic counterparts.[31] Partially, this was due to the linkage between their virginity and their polyphony, often with reference to the classic Mediterranean concepts: patrician *onore* represented by their status, and mediation to supernatural realms through the agency of virgins; as the text of a Marian motet by Chiara Margarita Cozzolani put it, 'cum virginitatis honore'.[32] At least one composer inscribed a 'pleasant' eight-voice Introit collection to the cousins Giacoma and Caterina dei Bossi at the monastery of S. Girolamo in nearby Brescia, explicitly drawing the connection between virginity and music as parallel habitats of the Holy Spirit; in

---

[29] In the final analysis, many strands of the argument are derived from French post-structuralist interpretations of Lacan's theories of psychosexual development.

[30] Owing to the views still present in the first wave of work, female monastic composers have not been the subject of this—or any—approach in the currents most strongly identified with essentialism. Ironically, in research claiming feminist inspiration, nuns have been 'de-gendered' precisely because of their lack of sexual activity.

[31] I have employed the more nuanced and historically informed understanding of the social interpretation of biology defined by J. W. Scott: 'Gender is a constitutive element of social relationships based on perceived differences between the sexes, and gender is a primary way of signifying relationships of power': *Gender and the Politics of History* (New York, 1988), 42. Cf. Burke's considerations on the anti-theoretical nature of much work in the field, *History and Social Theory* (Ithaca, NY, 1993), 52. For the varied evidence outside Western aristocratic culture, see E. Koskoff, *Women and Music in Cross-Cultural Perspective* (Westport, Conn., 1989), esp. 1–23.

[32] A. Blok, 'Notes on the Concept of Virginity in Mediterranean Societies', in E. Schulte van Kessel (ed.), *Women and Men in Spiritual Culture, XVth–XVIth Centuries* (The Hague, 1986), 27–33. The quote is from *Concinant linguae* (1642), in which Mary is addressed as 'gaudia matris habens, cum virginitatis honore'.

this dedication, musical sisters were compared to the unblemished choirs of the Apocalypse, singing eternal praise to the Lamb. For Valerio Bona, the Carmelites' unsullied music, its order and harmony, had the power to banish evil spirits and attract the sevenfold power of the third member of the Trinity.[33]

A broader concern is thus necessary in order to do justice to musicians' own intentions. Which were the contemporary aesthetic and spiritual values that nuns' music (both the philosophy of music and individual pieces) might have represented to its monastic and non-monastic audiences? Even to suggest answers involves several considerations: nuns' own statements of their spiritual states and of music's role in their lives; the musical implications of contemporary aesthetics; the models and practice of female spirituality, Christological devotion, and female sanctoral cults; the varying intellectual and musical traditions of the orders; and Seicento iconography. Most immediately present in the motet and Office repertory that was projected by polyphony into the urban world is the shared cultural meaning of the key texts read or memorized by sisters. This is to be found in contemporary scriptural exegesis, especially of the monastic (and increasingly universal) proof text, the Song of Songs; the breviary assignment and personalized use of other biblical passages; and even the late medieval handbooks of devotion (by Gerson, Bonaventure, and others) read by every nun. But it also depends directly on the revolutionary changes in Italian spirituality after Trent.

Several approaches to the musical repertory are thus present here: serious consideration of motet texts as both literature and devotional documents; the linkage of (or disjuncture between) musical philosophy and musical practice; and an evaluation of how female monastic musicians may have helped shape a local musical tradition. Not only did the Latin texts of the polyphonic repertory, however recherché

---

[33] Bona, *Li dilettevoli Introiti a otto*, op. 18 (Venice: Vincenti, 1611), dedication, p. [3]: '. . . a chi si poteua offerire più degnamente, che a chi stanni cittarizanti intorno al Sacrificato Agnello in incessabili canti? tanto più che la Musica, come l'intese bene il Profeta Dauide, che inuittò anco le Vergini à cantare le diuine lodi ne' musicali stromenti, virtù ha efficacissima, e di fugare i cattiui spiriti, e di attrarne lo spirito settiforme. Et in quella guisa, che virginità è habitacolo dello Spirito Santo, parimente la Musica, è il suo gratiosissimo Giardino, per la conueneuolezza, che è tra la musica e la virginità, atteso che se la virginità deue essere immaculata, con la musica è vn'ordine, & un concerto, quale ad ogni ben minima e immaginabile alterazione si disordina, e si sconcerta.' On the house, see G. Spinelli, 'Ordini e congregazioni religiosi', in *Diocesi di Brescia* (Storia religiosa della Lombardia, 3; Brescia, 1992), 327.

they may appear to modern sensibilities, incorporate the values and spirituality of patrician society, but they must have been intelligible to performers and audiences even across the walls that separated musical nuns from the world of their origin; indeed, the occasional battle over motet texts reflected the sacredness of the words and the high value placed on their polyphonic projection into the city. And the words' form and imagery had reflections in the musical settings; more precisely, since the texts did not circulate independently, the music was the only rhetorical medium in which they were presented to urban audiences.

Thus a more sophisticated consideration of sacred music is helpful, for instance the view of a given motet print as an artistically conceived whole, with its proem, conclusion, and hallmark pieces that exemplify artistic and musical conceits, much like madrigal collections. From this perspective, pieces function as their contemporaries might have heard them: an aural expression of devotional and intellectual ideas held by urban society as a whole. If social history provides the framework, still the importance of polyphony for both its female religious practitioners and their audiences underlines the crucial role of musical evidence in expanding and sharpening the view of this female monastic world present in the archival records.

This approach also credits the culture of early modern Italy with being more unified than musicology has normally allowed. The ease of movement back and forth between 'secular' and 'sacred' behaviour and even musical genres, the political role of religious orders, and the shared values of Catholicism that united all society should warn us against hasty attempts at separating an essentially secular and modern civil world (embodied in the urban ruling classes) from a theocratic and medieval Church, with corresponding implications for the interpretation of musical styles.[34] From an 'emic' point of

---

[34] The *locus classicus* for the interpenetration of religion and social life in early modern Europe is L. Febvre, *Le Problème de l'incroyance au XVIe siècle: La religion de Rabelais* (Paris, 1947), bk. ii, ch. 1. On the social violence but cultural unity of pre-capitalist society, see the works of N. Elias, especially *Die höfische Gesellschaft* (Frankfurt am Main, 1969), *passim*. Philip IV of Spain, the ruler of Milan for much of this study's period (1621–65), and the ultimate defender of sisters' rights against the diocesan curia, surrounded himself with such mystical nuns—who also played a political role—as Maria de Agreda and Luisa de Carrión; the latter founded a confraternity devoted to the Immaculate Conception with some 40,000 members, among them the king himself; C. Guilhem, 'L'Inquisition et la dévaluation des discours féminins', in B. Bennassar *et al.*, *L'Inquisition espagnole: XVe–XIXe siècle* (Paris, 1979), 200.

view, there is no evidence that musicians or audiences considered sacred repertories as inherently more marginal or conservative than secular music, the latter accorded greater study in modern times. As some of the documentation below indicates, the women and men who sang and composed such works believed passionately in the thaumaturgic efficacy and personal relevance of their music, 'sacred' or 'secular'. A view of nuns' polyphony as indicative of broader attitudes permits insight into a hierarchy of beliefs and values, not explicitly religious in its entirety, as articulated in aural expression. It follows that the overlap between secular and sacred musical genres and techniques might be broader than expected.

If the world which produced nuns' music was a system based on premisses foreign to modern Western society, some ethnomusicological methods might be helpful. Several themes here share much with the results of ethnographic approaches: music's relationship to rapture and ecstasy; the strongly oral character of some repertories; the musical definition of sacral space; claustral music in the public ritual life of a city; 'insider' versus 'outsider' accounts of music-making; status, role-playing, and authority in the regulation of female monastic musicians; and even currents in Seicento epistemology that differentiated between the perceptual or experiential capacities of men and of women. If the historically derived categories employed here be not without their own limitations, they at least avail themselves of some basis in the mental world and musical thought of the musicians studied, thus providing one avenue around the anachronisms of seemingly different modern heuristic tacks.[35] Of primary concern is not the recovery of selected pieces (or composers) for current consumption based on modern aesthetics.[36] Rather, I seek to examine the ways in which female monastic music might have expressed aspects of its culture, and how such a repertory might have been perceived and valued by its apparently many listeners. At the same time,

[35] Ironically, both traditional dismissals of this culture's 'quaintness' and postmodernist approaches derived from French interpretations of Freud undercut the historically conditioned meanings crucial for its composers and audiences. For the centrality of symbolic behaviour in early modern Italy, and the usefulness of historically based ethnographic categories in its study, see P. Burke, 'Historians, Anthropologists and Symbols', in E. Ohnuki-Tienney (ed.), *Culture Through Time: Anthropological Approaches* (Stanford, 1990), 268–83.

[36] Perhaps music historians err in concerning themselves at all with this task for cultures temporally or geographically remote from our own. In the same vein, the question of whether Milanese sacred music represents a 'provincial' stylistic current is largely irrelevant; of far more import is a synchronic view of the possible options available in monastic musical life in a given city at a given time.

nuns' repertories constituted an important part of the aural world of at least one major city in early modern Europe; as the importance of local musical practice becomes evident, their specificity helps focus issues of aesthetics and repertory.

Finally, this approach might advance us past the curiously symmetrical literatures of lament present in both earlier religious historiography and some recent scholarship: the former, which viewed sisters as a disciplinary problem solved by the great figures of Catholic reform; the latter, which concentrated largely on the very real restrictions and oppression suffered by female religious. In both perspectives, however, these women were seen as largely marginal and passive, for some critics even eccentric, figures. I shall attempt to tease out of the documents some ideas about the ways in which nuns might actively have operated so as to study, perform, and foster music in their institutions—one of the most contested, but also most effective, methods by which they might project their presence back into the world whence they had come.

This study treats one urban centre: Milan from roughly 1560 to 1706 (the end of Spanish rule), clearly one of the more important cities in Europe for polyphony, especially that associated with its nuns. Since episcopal decrees nominally affected nuns in an entire diocese, and because the extra-urban houses (S. Vittore in Meda) often drew their membership—and their music—from the metropolis, I have included all the female monasteries of the archdiocese (App. B). The renown of the repertory is no secret; most urban panegyric literature of the Seicento remarked on nuns' performances (while normally omitting or downplaying music in other institutions) and ecclesiastical historians have mentioned it repeatedly.[37] Pieces by Chiara Margarita Cozzolani and Rosa Giacinta Badalla circulated in Germany, France, and England, more widely than most local music; at least one of the former's motets was ascribed by a contemporary French copyist to Carissimi.[38] To any objective observer (of the seventeenth or twentieth century), some of the women studied here

[37] F. Cazzamini Massi, *Milano durante il dominio spagnolo* (Milan, 1947), 766–7, and E. Cattaneo, 'La religione a Milano dall'età della Controriforma', *Storia di Milano*, xi (Milan, 1958), 325.

[38] For the circulation of *Concinant linguae*, see App. C. Other post-1600 local composers whose works survive in transmontane transmission include Ignazio Donati, Serafino Cantone, Egidio Trabattone, and Francesco della Porta.

were among the most famous musicians of the city in early modern times. Yet there has not been a detailed study of the social background to their music-making, the give-and-take of their conflict with episcopal authority, the ways in which they might actually have performed polyphony, or the styles publicly associated with them.[39] Even general non-musical work on their institutions is very recent.[40]

The patrician origin of the women studied here, and their music's role in urban prestige, highlight the city's sometimes difficult political and economic status. The Duchy of Milan had fallen to Charles V in 1535; after 1554 it became part of the Spanish Habsburg domain until the Austrian conquest in 1706.[41] Yet the absentee character of Madrid's rule, exercised through a local Spanish governor, ensured that the various levels of the patriciate—the old-line families, newer clans coming to wealth, and even the descendants of the city's former rulers—would exert major and often effective influence over urban life through their institutions: the magistrates (the grand chancellor, the *capitano di giustizia*) and the collegial bodies. These latter, more indigenous formations included the Milanese Senate (composed of fifteen representatives chosen from among sixty families), the sixty decurions, and the *tribunale di provvisione*, the head of civic administration.[42]

---

[39] There are a number of pretexts for such exclusion: the presumed marginal status of nuns; their location in a 'provincial' Milan; and their curiosity value as token female composers and singers. The absence of any serious study of either their repertories or of the larger musical environment undermines any argument that female monastic music is unimportant on the basis of 'quality'.

[40] For the first overview, see L. Sebastiani, 'Monasteri femminili milanesi tra medioevo e età moderna', in C. H. Smyth and G. C. Garfagnini (eds.), *Florence and Milan: Comparisons and Relations* (Florence, 1989), ii. 3–15, followed by two well-documented and highly relevant case-studies: D. Zardin, *Donna e religiosa di rara eccellenza: Prospera Corona Bascapè, i libri e la cultura nei monasteri milanesi del Cinque e Seicento* (Florence, 1992), and P. R. Baernstein, 'The Counter-Reformation Convent: The Angelics of San Paolo in Milan, 1535–1635' (Ph.D. diss., Harvard University, 1993). Shorter articles based on *tesi di laurea* include G. Colturi, 'Monache a Milano fra Cinque e Seicento: La storia del monastero di Santa Maria della Consolazione, detto della Stella (1494–1778)' and R. Busnelli, 'Il tramonto di un monastero patrizio: Le benedettine di San Vittore di Meda nel Settecento', in *ASL* 116 (1990), 113–46 and 147–66 respectively.

[41] D. Sella, 'Sotto il dominio della Spagna', in id. and C. Capra, *Il ducato di Milano dal 1535 al 1796* (Turin, 1984), esp. 21–59.

[42] For one view of economic history, Sella, *Crisis and Continuity: The Economy of Spanish Lombardy in the Seventeenth Century* (Cambridge, Mass., 1979), esp. 30–2 on the patriciate's political role. For a detailed demography of urban classes and their spatial organization in the city, see S. D'Amico, *Le contrade e la città: Sistema produttivo e spazio urbano a Milano fra Cinque e Seicento* (Milan, 1994), the first extensive documentary study.

The city flourished during the second half of the Cinquecento, with a notable increase in population and material culture. But the tenor of life was starkly interrupted, and the limitations of the political order illuminated, by the crises: notably the apocalyptic experiences of the 1576 and 1629–30 plagues (the latter killed around a third of the population and two-thirds of the male clergy), but also the later economic stagnation of the State of Milan from 1630 to 1650. The ripples of European conflicts were also felt in the State and its monastic houses.[43] Obviously, and not only because of the political difficulties, the archdiocese and its institutions—including autonomous ecclesiastical judiciary and police—were principal actors in the city.[44] Owing to Carlo Borromeo's evolving efforts to implement his own personal and increasingly drastic interpretation of Tridentine decrees, and to the conflicts that thus arose between episcopal authority and patrician or Habsburg power, the lives of the women studied here were marked by a contested status and by repeated episcopal efforts, sometimes occasioned by music, to impose new, public, and post-medieval standards of behaviour upon them, a phenomenon not unknown in early modern Europe.

This period embraces some five generations of musical nuns, separated by thirty-year intervals. A first group took vows at the time of a sharp rise in female monastic population, contemporary with Carlo Borromeo's attempted reforms of the 1570s. A second received public musical testimony in the relatively peaceful and stable years at century's end and the beginning of Federigo Borromeo's tenure. A third came to maturity around the crisis of 1630. A fourth rose to musical prominence in the troubled 1660s. And a fifth carried the traditions into the Settecento.[45] The city itself housed many of the premier musical foundations: the Benedictines of S. Radegonda, S. Margarita, and the Monastero Maggiore (S. Maurizio); the Clarissans of S. Apollinare, S. Orsola, and S. Chiara; the Humiliate of S. Maria Maddalena al Cerchio and S. Caterina in Brera; the Augustinians of

---

[43] Most notably the passage of Spanish troops *en route* to Flanders, and the wars of the Mantuan succession (1613 and 1627–30).

[44] For an overview of diocesan history, A. Rimoldi, 'L'età dei Borromei (1560–1631)', and D. Zardin, 'L'ultimo periodo spagnolo (1631–1712): Da Cesare Monti a Giuseppe Archinto', in A. Caprioli *et al.* (eds.), *Diocesi di Milano* (Storia religiosa della Lombardia, 10; Brescia, 1990), ii. 389–466 and 575–613.

[45] Modern ethnography assumes a generational gap of roughly twenty-year intervals; but the rather unusual demography of Seicento Milanese nuns argues for a longer span.

S. Marta; and the Lateran Canonesses of S. Maria Annunciata (for musical houses in the urban topography, see Map 1).[46]

But the geographical boundaries of the diocese also included about half the State of Milan, ranging from the Swiss cantons in the north-west, down the eastern shore of Lago Maggiore, past the southern outskirts of Como, and then south into the Po plain; the eastern and western boundaries were, roughly, the Adda and Ticino rivers (cf. Map 2; Treviglio, however, with its two important houses, was still inside both the State and the diocese).[47] Conflicts between ecclesiastical and secular power—which arose over numerous issues, not limited to nuns' music—arrayed a given prelate against both the informal networks of the patriciate and the formal authority of the State: the Senate and the governor. This split also had musical repercussions. Composers working for the ducal chapel at S. Maria della Scala or employed by the patriciate in the parishes, shrines, or male monasteries of the city (S. Maria presso S. Celso, S. Maria della Passione) were not subject to episcopal mandates or pressure, as were musicians at the Duomo.[48] We shall have occasion to see how both the musical reflections of patrician devotional trends and the public association of polyphony with nuns would be far more typical of figures not connected with the cathedral.

The women in this study lived under the tenures of eight archbishops, whose varying policies were often central to their exercise of music and liturgical life: Carlo Borromeo (in office 1560–84); Gaspare Visconti (1585–94); Federigo Borromeo (1595–1631); Cesare Monti (1632–50); Alfonso Litta (1652–79); Federico Visconti (1681–93); Federico Caccia (1693–9); and Giuseppe Archinto (1699–1712). Milan was vital because of its location (closer to Protestant Switzerland and Germany than to Rome) and size (around

---

[46] I have eschewed using the word 'convent' for most female foundations. The central point of post-Tridentine policy was to force monastic enclosure on every order; in order to underline this (and also to be more faithful to the documents), I have employed the term 'female monastery' (It. *monastero*) for the houses of most orders. For male Benedictine houses, I have used 'male monastery', and for male mendicant and female Ursuline foundations with free access and egress (the Ursulines, uniquely, were not subject to formal enclosure, at least until 1612), the term 'convent' (It. *convento*). I retain the 16th-c. local orthography of S. Margarita (modern form 'Margherita').

[47] On the city, and the miraculous Virgin at the monastery of S. Agostino, see T. and I. Santagiuliana, *Storia di Treviglio* (Bergamo, 1965).

[48] Formally, cathedral musicians were subject to the chapter, not the archbishop; but the prelate could normally wield influence, as Federigo Borromeo most notably did in his forcible selection of Vincenzo Pellegrini as *maestro* in 1612.

MAP 1. Leading female monasteries in Milan, *c.*1600
[Legend:] 1, Duomo; 2, S. Radegonda; 3, S. Apollinare; 4, S. Paolo;
5, S. Agostino Bianco; 6, S. Maria Maddalena al Cerchio; 7, S. Marta;
8, S. Agnese; 9, S. Maurizio; 10, Castello Sforzesco; 11, S. Vincenzo;
12, S. Margarita; 13, S. Caterina in Brera; 14, S. Maria Annunciata
15, S. Erasmo

1600 it was the most populous diocese of the Catholic world); its
synodal legislation and institutions were promoted throughout
Europe as exemplary, partially due to the construction of Carlo
Borromeo's cult.[49] All eight prelates, however, along with most of

---

[49] But an attentive reading of the entries for the Borromeos in the *DBI*, written by
Certeau and Prodi, respectively (*DBI* xx (Rome, 1977), 260–9; *DBI* xiii (1971), 30–9), is
enough to demonstrate the gap in personal approach and pastoral philosophy between the
two central figures. In conformity with the younger Borromeo's own orthography, I have
used the spelling 'Federigo' for his Christian name.

MAP 2. The archdiocese of Milan, *c.*1600

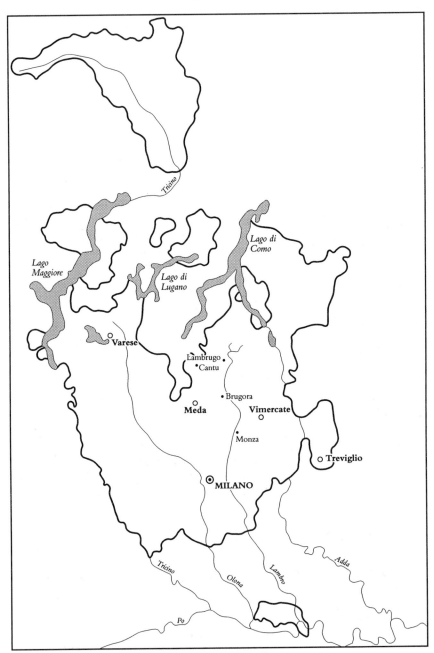

the curial officials (the *vicario delle monache* (vicar of nuns) or the vicar-general) in charge of regulating the female houses, were themselves drawn from the ranks of the local patriciate. Thus Church–State conflicts in the city also represented a primary locus for internecine political battles among the urban aristocracy, notably during Litta's years, when much of the battle would revolve around sisters' polyphony.[50]

To undertake a musical ethnography of this female monastic subculture also implies the critical understanding of its sources—essentially the testimony of witnesses and participants, each with her or his own stake in the description. Among the secular documents figure legal agreements signed by monasteries, wills and other bequests, travellers' and other outsiders' reports on music at Milanese female houses, letters from personages secular and religious (including a few from nuns themselves), and the occasional mention of ecclesiastical disputes in gubernatorial or other court documents. The church records comprise the written reports of superiors' annual visitations to houses, memoranda from the diocesan curia (or, in exceptional cases, from the archbishop himself) concerning nuns' music and daily life, and Roman correspondence, largely between the Milanese curia and the post-Tridentine institutions (the Sacra Congregazione del Concilio to 1586, followed by the Sacra Congregazione de' Vescovi e Regolari) with nominally ultimate jurisdiction over all religious.[51]

An especially important part is formed by the voluminous correspondence of nuns with Archbishop Federigo Borromeo, preserved in Milan's Biblioteca Ambrosiana.[52] Invaluable are the writings of sisters themselves, which provide evidence for both their worldview and the renown of their musical colleagues. These include two necrologies, one from S. Marta and one from S. Caterina in Brera, with short biographies, spanning the period between the late

---

[50] On the patrician composition of the curia, see Zardin, *Donna e religiosa*, 39 and id., 'Tra continuità delle strutture e nuove aspirazioni di "riforma": La riorganizzazione borromaica della curia arcivescovile', in G. Signorotto (ed.), *Lombardia borromaica, Lombardia spagnola (1554–1659)* (Rome, 1995).

[51] The Milanese curial documents are preserved largely in the Archivio Storico Diocesano Milanese, especially in sezione XII, *Ordini religiosi e congregazioni* (henceforth ASDM XII), with some materials in sezione X, *Carteggio ufficiale*. Roman sources are in the Archivio Segreto Vaticano, Congregazione dei Vescovi e Regolari.

[52] On the centrality of epistolary writing to female self-expression in this and other contexts, see A. Prosperi, 'Lettere spirituali', in Scaraffia and Zarri (eds.), *Donne e fede*, 227–52.

Cinquecento upsurge in monastic population and the early Settecento decline of houses.[53] Two other chronicles were kept by sisters in extra-urban houses (S. Maria in Lambrugo and S. Vittore in Meda) during the Seicento.[54]

There are two problems with the disciplinary records: first, they record only that activity (musical and other) deemed 'irregular' at a given point by a given bishop or the curia, and therefore do not provide a well-rounded view of daily musical life inside *clausura*.[55] More crucially, it is far easier to ascertain a prelate's views of nuns' music than it is to find the attitudes of women musicians themselves in these documents. The visitations were newly instituted proceedings that led to punishment and discipline, and nuns usually proffered only the most defensive formulations about the musical (and other) aspects of their life.[56] Thus the letters of Borromeo's cloistered correspondents, written to a generally supportive prelate, help elicit these women's views of themselves and their repertory. Other writings from musical houses are few and far between, and it is precisely the surviving music written by and for nuns which—if studied in the context of local musical styles—provides invaluable, almost unique, insight into the spiritual and aural world of these nominally cloistered performers. From the perspective of cultural history, it is remarkable—but entirely in line with Cinquecento and Seicento thought—that, of all the arts, music should provide us with the best guide to the symbolic and mental world of these women, an idea suggested by the epigraph to this chapter.

Obviously, the conditions of female monastic performance (nuns' enclosure, restricted access by outsiders, exclusively female singers)

---

[53] S. Marta's untitled profession book (BA, G. 150 *suss.*) begins in 1558 and includes successive entries for the sisters, tailing off around 1720; the 'Biografia delle monache umiliate di S. Caterina di Brera' (BA, Trotti 453) was compiled at one stroke by an anonymous monastic chronicler at the house in 1684.

[54] For the *Annales sacrae* of the former, ASDM XII, vol. 180; the *Liber cronaca* from S. Vittore, which includes brief remarks from 1619 and 1626 but really begins in 1640, is in a private collection. I thank Conte Luigi Antona-Traversi for access to this manuscript.

[55] The differences between a prelate and the diocesan officials concerning nuns' music were important, primarily in the tenure of Federigo Borromeo, since the archbishop held more liberal views than did some curial officials.

[56] One technical point largely missed in the literature based on such records is that the testimony is essentially oral; hence the written text—as we shall see below—is full of the minor contradictions and logical leaps characteristic of everyday speech and thought. For the methodological use and problems of ecclesiastical questioning, see P. Burke, *The Historical Anthropology of Early Modern Italy: Essays in Perception and Communication* (Cambridge, 1985), 40–7.

raise problems concerning the transmission and performance practice of music inside *clausura*. In Chapter 7 I explore some of the evidence on these issues, especially the vexed question of how mixed-voice polyphony might actually have been performed by all-female ensembles. I have relied on local evidence for questions of pitch-levels, vocal scoring, and the participation of instruments; but, uniquely here, I have also drawn on other contemporary Italian sources for claustral performance practice.

The relation of such performance to broader musical genres and styles is also central; in the light of all the reports on nuns' singing, it should be possible to associate preserved pieces with their activity. At first glance, the sources are disappointing: except for the fragments confiscated during a visitation, there are no surviving polyphonic manuscripts from Milanese female houses. Yet the lack is not unusual.[57] The changing tastes of the Settecento may have ensured that earlier repertory did not survive in monastic libraries even at the time of the Josephine and Napoleonic suppressions (1778–1810).[58] These closings marked a drastic break with the past: every female house in the diocese was suppressed (S. Maria Maddalena al Cerchio held on until the final Napoleonic decree in 1810) and its property dispersed.[59] The era had drastic results for urban musical sources in general; today in Milan, only the Duomo preserves an archive of pre-1800 polyphony.

[57] Little handwritten music that can be traced to female monasteries in any Italian city survives, with scattered exceptions from Bologna, Florence, Vicenza, and Naples; cf. Monson, 'Elena Malvezzi's Manuscript'. For the mid-16th-c. repertory in B-Bc, MS 27766 (written by a male scribe for two Florentine Clarissans), see P. Martell's forthcoming dissertation (University of Chicago). For the musical archive of S. Gregorio Armeno in Naples, including some seventy *buste* of polyphony (written largely by outside *maestri*), see D. Fabris, 'Generi e fonti della musica sacra a Napoli nel Seicento', in D. D'Alessandro and A. Ziino (eds.), *La musica a Napoli durante il Seicento: Atti del Convegno Internazionale di Studi, Napoli, 11–14 aprile 1985* (Rome, 1987), 421–42.

[58] On the suppressions, P. Vismara Chiappa, 'La soppressione dei conventi e dei monasteri in Lombardia nell'età teresina', in A. de Maddalena et al. (eds.), *Economia, istituzioni, cultura in Lombardia nell'età teresina* (Bologna, 1982), iii. 481–500. Further afield, the musical archives of Austrian, Bavarian, and Spanish female monasteries contain largely 18th- and 19th-c. works; see the catalogue of the Nonnberg's archive at A-Sn; R. Münster et al., *Thematisches Katalog der Musikhandschriften der Benediktinerinnenabtei Frauenwörth und der Pfarrkirchen Indersdorf, Wasserburg am Inn, und Bad Tölz* (Munich, 1975); and A. de Vicente Delgado, *La Música en el Monasterio de Santa Ana de Ávila (siglos XVI–XVIII): Catalogo* (Madrid, 1989).

[59] The one partially surviving archive from a female house, that of S. Vittore in Meda, lost much of its holdings during its suppression; L. Zoppé, *Per una storia di Meda dalle origini alla fine del secolo XVIII* (Meda, 1971), 239.

Thus, in order to approach nuns' music, I have first considered (Ch. 8) some pieces from a possible monastic repertory, based largely but not exclusively on the numerous dedications of printed music to nuns in the diocese, most markedly in the years of Federigo Borromeo's tenure, a fruitful and diverse period (1592–1632). The public association of music with famous performers might also reflect the polyphonic practice at a given house. This sample also affords some context for Claudia Rusca's recently reconstructed motets of 1630. The following chapters turn to the two completely surviving motet books (the 1642 *Concerti sacri à 2–4* and the 1650 *Salmi à otto*) of Cozzolani. And the penultimate chapter examines Cozzolani's solo *Scherzi di sacra melodia* of 1648 and the 1684 *Motetti a voce sola* written by Badalla, in the context of similar pieces inscribed to nuns.

The technical analysis of these repertories is a far from settled issue. In approaching the *stile antico* works, I have relied on the guidelines for modal procedures and dissonance treatment supplied by theorists with close connections to Milan: Pietro Pontio (*Ragionamento* (Parma, 1588) and *Dialogo* (Parma, 1595)) and Camillo Angleria (*La regola del contraponto, e della musical compositione* (Milan, 1622)), both supporters of the eight-mode system. Most helpful for these works (psalm settings, *stile antico* motets) is the synthesis of modal theory formulated by Bernhard Meier.[60] For much of the liturgical music associated with nuns, mode seems to have had several different roles. Besides the standardized affects, and the traditional modal choices for given texts, it also provided a source of melodic gestures and a series of differentiated internal cadence-points, features typical of such styles well into the Seicento.

For the early *uso moderno* works, the systems of Adriano Banchieri (1605 and 1614) provide testimony from a monastic composer who dedicated at least one print to nuns and who had warm relations with Milanese musical life; I have drawn extensively on his system of *toni*.[61] Certainly the modal systems broke down even in Milan, and, for the mid-Seicento repertory, I have employed the analytical approach of the Bolognese Franciscan

---

[60] Meier, *Die Tonarten der klassischen Vokalpolyphonie* (Utrecht, 1974).

[61] I have used the systems of Banchieri, *L'organo suonarino* (Venice, 1605) and *Cartella musicale* (Venice, 1614).

Lorenzo Penna, another admirer of nun musicians, to be found in his *Li primi albori musicali*.[62]

Yet modal and dissonance analysis does not always explain small-scale or large-scale features. There are few guidelines on two crucial points: how *soggetti* are built up into phrases and periods, and how the overall delivery of a text is constructed musically—essentially, rhetoric on small and large levels. I have both used some terms found in contemporary Italianate *Figurenlehre* and attempted to deduce evidence for recurrent musical figures associated with certain textual phrases or poetic ideas.[63] But the doctrine of figures does not explain all detail; indeed, generic and stylistic traditions often overrode rhetorical or prosodic considerations. Several of the motets analysed below seem to employ specific musical gestures, together with internal semiotic markers, in their composers' efforts to achieve the special effects (and affects) of which music alone is capable. Music and rhetoric were not considered as exactly equivalent in contemporary aesthetics, and it is thus important to highlight the differences between the traditional exegesis of a text or its projection on one hand, and the salient features of the performance indications (pitch and rhythm) for musical delivery contained in the score on the other. On a larger scale, certain formal aspects of pieces underline the verbal features of texts or (in the case of the 'static' items like psalms), actually create a structure for their delivery, characteristics shared with epideictic oratory in its most common form, sermons.[64]

Milanese musical traditions after 1580, normally considered stylistically reactionary, aesthetically dull, and ecclesiastically censured, have also only recently become the objects of serious inquiry.[65] This

---

[62] One book in the 1672 Bologna edition of the work is dedicated to nuns in Parma. Most of Penna's motet collections also contain dedications to nuns living or canonized (including Teresa de Ávila and Maria Maddalena de' Pazzi).

[63] The basic texts (*inter alia* C. Bernhard, *Tractatus compositionis augmentatus*; J. Burmeister, *Musica poetica* (Rostock, 1606); A. Kircher, *Musurgia universalis* (Rome, 1650)) are indexed in D. Bartel, *Handbuch der musikalischen Figurenlehre* (Laaber, 1985).

[64] Cf. the phenomenological approaches of F. Noske, *Forma formans* (Amsterdam, 1969), and M. Padoan, 'Sulla struttura degli ultimi mottetti vocali-strumentali di Alessandro Grandi', *Rivista internazionale di musica sacra*, 6 (1985), 7–66.

[65] Lockwood's perceptive analysis of Ruffo's masses (*The Counter-Reformation*) ends with the composer's departure from Milan in 1570–1. The view dates back at least as far as Charles Burney's 1770 visit to the Duomo in search of Ambrosian chant and *stile antico* double-choir polyphony; Burney also commented favourably on nuns' music in the city. Any examination of the repertory would be impossible, of course, without M. Donà's standard bibliography, *La stampa musicale a Milano fino all'anno 1700* (Florence, 1961), to whose author I am deeply indebted.

view is probably also overdue for re-examination.[66] Indeed, the essentially local nature of musical genres and even techniques underpins this repertory to some degree; as a first measure of comparison, and for an idea of their impact on the aural world of Milan, I have sought to place sisters' polyphonic works within the framework of Lombard styles. Still, music and musicians circulated widely in the Seicento, and I have attempted to retain the secular and sacred repertories of Venice and Bologna as a background to both the works that nuns might have sung and those that they certainly did compose. The understanding of their music begins, however, with its institutional framework and early history.

[66] For a consideration of the Milanese repertory as a whole and its place in the city, see my forthcoming *Music in Federigo Borromeo's Lombardy, 1580–1650*.

2

Patrician Institutions and their Medieval Heritage

◇

Il Monastero Maggiore di Milano, nel quale vivono al servizio di Dio gran numero di Monache delle più nobili, et principali famiglie di questa Città . . .

(its nuns to Philip IV, 1626)

The young Milanese musicians of this study entered institutions of varying character, thereby to some degree conditioning their musical life. From the Middle Ages through the Settecento, the sheer number of monasteries and their weight in urban prestige were impressive, although hardly atypical.[1] Of the forty-one female houses in the Milan of 1600, polyphony would be recorded at some two-thirds.[2] The art also became widespread in the extra-urban foundations of the diocese.[3]

The premier houses, musically and socially, belonged to the Benedictines. These had been founded by early medieval nobility,

[1] For an overview of houses, see E. Cattaneo, 'Istituzioni ecclesiastiche milanesi', *Storia di Milano,* ix (Milan, 1961), 507–721; Bologna, a smaller but equally monastic city, had some twenty-eight houses in 1588 (Zarri, 'Monasteri femminili', 410).

[2] For the urban monasteries, I have collated the 1575–6 notes of the apostolic visitor Gerolamo Ragazzoni (ASDM XII, vol. 49, fo. 84; Ragazzoni also listed twenty-four extra-urban houses in the diocese) with the entries of M. Pogliani, 'Contributo per una bibliografia delle fondazioni religiose di Milano', *RSCA* 14 (1985), 157–281. For musical life, I have used the ASDM, ASM, and ASV records; the dedications found in a census of some five hundred musical editions (largely Milanese); and the Seicento accounts.

[3] For urban houses existing in 1600, musical evidence survives for twenty-seven (66%). If dowry reduction requests stemming from novices' musical talents are added, the total is twenty-nine (71%). The number of extramural houses rose to roughly forty by 1700 (from twenty-four in 1575), for which there is clear evidence for nine (23%) and dowry requests for a further ten (total 48%). The difference reflects both the urban character of documented musical life and less rigorous episcopal control outside the city.

male and female, and retained their patrician character over the centuries.[4] Chiara Margarita Cozzolani's and Rosa Giacinta Badalla's S. Radegonda dated to before 870.[5] Public devotion to its matron saint, a Frankish queen and model of female sanctity, was continued and revived in patrician circles in the Seicento, most notably in a long *vita* of Radegund (dedicated to the homonymous institution) by the Benedictine poet and dramatist Agostino Lampugnani.[6] Other foundations famous for music boasted similar antiquity: S. Margarita from before 912; S. Vittore, named for the most important local martyr, and located 20 km. north of Milan in Meda; and, perhaps earliest of all, the Monastero Maggiore, founded around 800 (thus contemporary with the major male foundation, S. Ambrogio), whose church was dedicated to the patron of Lombards in the Carolingian era, S. Maurizio (St Maurice).[7]

A second tier of Benedictine houses, including extra-urban cloisters, was founded in the eleventh century. Even in the Borromean era, the two kinds together comprised a plurality of diocesan monasteries, and, through the Settecento, retained the independent, non-episcopal character of their origin.[8] The high dowry required for the profession of full vows as a choir nun (the *dote spirituale*) restricted

---

[4] On the order in Milan, see *RSCA* 9 (1980), especially Cattaneo, 'Il monachesimo a Milano dalle origini all'età postcarolingia', 7–29, and V. Cattana, 'Il monachesimo benedettino nella diocesi di Milano dalla fine del Medioevo all'età dei Borromei', 82–137. For a comparison of early monasteries, see A. Veronese, 'Monasteri femminili in Italia settentrionale nell'alto medioevo: Confronto con i monasteri maschili attraverso un tentativo di analisi "statistica"', *Benedictina*, 34 (1987), 355–416; Milan's institutions were founded later than the earliest north Italian cloisters (which were in Pavia, as might be expected).

[5] First named after St Wigilind, at some later point (reflecting Imperial influence) it was renamed after St Radegund (*c.*520–87). This seems to be the only foundation in Italy so dedicated. For early artistic reflections of her cult, see M. E. Carrasco, 'Spirituality in Context: The Romanesque Illustrated Life of St. Radegund of Poitiers (Poitiers, Bibl. Mun., MS 250)', *Art Bulletin*, 72 (1990), 214–35. The saint's dual status as aristocrat and nun made her an ideal patron for the Milanese foundation; her elaborate medieval iconography found a late echo in the music of the monastery.

[6] Lampugnani, *Della vita di S. Radegonda, che di gran regina di Francia si fece monaca* (Milan, 1649), noted the community's prestige in its account. Radegund still figures today in the Milanese sanctoral calendar, in contrast to her exclusion from the post-Tridentine Roman lists.

[7] For the dates, see Pogliani, 'Contributo', *ad voces*; for the remarkable history of S. Vittore, see Zoppé, *Per una storia*. The abbess of this house had seigneurial powers over the entire region until the Duecento, and retained the right to name the parish priest into the Seicento.

[8] Veronese, 'Monasteri', 381, underlines the far greater dependence on urban élites characteristic of the female houses (compared with male monasteries) in northern Italy.

entry to the select.[9] Over the centuries, these institutions accumulated financial privileges, tax exemptions, and properties in and out of the city.[10]

After the era of the commune, the order witnessed both relative stasis in the number of institutions and a period of freedom from the troubled male branch. While not changing the houses' essential character, late medieval reforms had important results, notably the adoption of the ancient plan of the double church in order to insure greater insulation of the women's community. At female houses a public church (*chiesa esteriore*) for the laity was coupled to a claustral church (*chiesa interiore*) for nuns.[11]

By the Quattrocento, female Benedictine houses easily outnumbered those of their male counterparts; around 1500, the advent of the reformed male congregation of S. Giustina of Padua (housed in Milan at S. Pietro in Gessate and later S. Simpliciano) provided new intellectual life for the order, while tying several female houses more closely to the male Cassinese (as the congregation was called after the union with Montecassino in 1506); this branch, not the other Benedictine congregations, was central to Milanese monasticism.[12] Socially, these houses were open to daughters of the urban patriciate's higher ranks, of wealthy families from other cities, and later of Milan's Spanish rulers.[13] A similar demography was typical of another patrician and contemplative order from the High Middle

[9] Even the Monastero Maggiore, in our period to host over one hundred nuns, was inhabited by only twelve sisters in 1444 (Cattaneo, 'Istituzioni ecclesiastiche', 603). Choir sisters had the right to vote for monastic office and the obligation to recite the Daily Office together (hence the name).

[10] For S. Radegonda, see the Sforza privileges preserved in ASM, Religione, p.a., 2213. The records of its lands in Bagnolo near Lodi fill several *buste* of the ASM, Religione files. For patrician bequests and legacies to the Monastero Maggiore, see ASM, Religione, p.a., 1926; this house owned property just outside the city walls, as well. Tax exemptions from the increasingly onerous fiscal burdens can be found in the ASM records for almost every monastery, Benedictine and mendicant; see ASM, Religione, p.a., 2221 for Sforza era salt-tax exemptions for S. Radegonda, for example.

[11] For this scheme, L. Patetta, 'La tipologia della chiesa "doppia" (dal Medioevo alla Controriforma)', in id., *Storia e tipologia: Cinque saggi sull'architettura del passato* (Milan, 1989), 11–71, esp. 22–8.

[12] Among other Benedictine congregations, only the Cistercians and Cluniacs had female houses in the diocese (S. Michele sul Dosso, and the extra-urban S. Maria in Cantù, respectively).

[13] Prominent nuns from Spanish or court families included Alessandra Sforza Bentivoglia at the Monastero Maggiore; Virginia Maria de' Leyva in Monza (the model for Manzoni's Gertrude in *I promessi sposi*); and Maria Faustina Palomera at S. Radegonda.

Ages, the Lateran Canonesses, in Milan found only at S. Maria Annunciata.

A second group was formed by the monasteries of a local Lombard order, the Humiliate, at first suspect for its origin in semi-heretical twelfth-century popular movements, but later incorporated into the Church structure of the later Middle Ages along with its better-known and wealthier male counterparts; the process entailed the separation of the women from the original 'double' houses.[14] Still, the Humiliate retained something of the middle-class, non-cloistered tertiary (*pinzochere*) tradition and the order shared some characteristics with the more plebeian mendicants.[15] Houses with later musical traditions highlight such trends: S. Maria Maddalena al Cerchio, S. Caterina in Brera, and S. Erasmo partook in their male counterparts' (the Humiliati's) rise to wealth and status in the Quattrocento, developing a reputation for ornate liturgy along the way.[16] After one monk attempted to assassinate Carlo Borromeo, the male congregation was suppressed in 1571, leaving the Humiliate in the five remaining houses under the archbishop's authority; the sisters followed the Benedictine Rule (but not liturgy), and at least one house made a later attempt to add the black habits of Benedict's daughters to their traditional white veils.[17]

The third stream of monastic tradition in Borromean Milan was represented by the mendicants, at first socially humbler and non-contemplative: Franciscans, Servites, and Dominicans. The female

[14] On the myths of the order's origins, and its original liturgy, see J. Wickstrom, 'The Humiliati: Liturgy and Identity', *Archivum Fratrum Praedicatorum*, 62 (1992), 195–225.

[15] Among the few studies of the order are G. A. Tiraboschi, *Vetera Humiliatorum Monumenta*, 3 vols. (Milan, 1766), and for some modern remarks, Zardin, *Donna e religiosa*, 29–57 and 137–72.

[16] The demographic profile increasingly resembled the Benedictine houses; S. Caterina in Brera had eighteen noblewomen at its Trecento separation (G. P. Puricelli, 'Cronica delle venerande memorie della Congregazione Umiliata', a Seicento miscellany, BA, H. 205 *inf.*, fo. 111ᵛ). For the order's history, Puricelli's manuscripts ('Historia Ordinis Humiliatorum', BA, C. 74 *inf.*, along with the collections C. 103 *inf.*, D. 99 *inf.*, D. 113 *inf.*, and S. 89 *inf.*) provide partially reliable materials.

[17] For the undated petition from S. Martino in Varese, ASDM XII, vol. 188: 'Le Monache del Monastero di S.to Martino in Varese . . . benchè il principio del loro instituto habbia preso il titolo de gli Humiliati; sono però effettivamente sotto l'osservanza della Regola di san Benedetto . . . già che hora portano un solo velo di tela bianca in capo, desiderebbero per maggior decoro hauer gratia un'altro velo nero, al modo che lo portano tutte le altre monache benedettine'. For early Settecento illustrations of the Humiliate's clothing (including the variant dress at S. Martino in Varese), see P. Helyot (actually M. Bullot), *Histoire des ordres religieux et militaires* (Paris, 1714–19); I cite from the revised edn. (Paris, 1792), vi. 164–9.

houses were founded later than the settlement of their male counterparts in Milan, largely in the later Duecento and the Trecento. If
the initial impetus to these congregations was non-aristocratic, later
developments linked them to the patriciate and to the dynastic rulers
of the city. A special connection to the Visconti and Sforza, responsible for the founding or refounding of several Quattrocento
Franciscan houses, characterized the mendicants.[18] Several monasteries passed from their Humiliate origins to the Dominicans
(S. Agnese) or the Franciscans (S. Orsola, S. Chiara). A fourth group,
contemplative but less patrician in origin, comprised the Augustinian
houses, which began in the Trecento. For reasons related to the mission of the order, they retained a relatively austere, more penitential
life than the Franciscans, with the single but central exception of
S. Marta; this foundation boasted a mystical tradition in the early
Cinquecento. Later, uniquely among houses, it would remain free
from the post-Tridentine imposition of *clausura*. Finally, there were
the reforming congregations of sixteenth-century origin, the
Capuchins and the Angeliche, the latter again essentially local.[19]

The monastic Rules followed by these foundations also varied; if
Benedictine and Humiliate houses employed Benedict's *regula*, the
Franciscan foundations used Clare's Rule in either the strict version
of the foundress (the First Rule) or the looser formulation due to
Pope Urban IV. The medieval synthesis of Augustine's advice governed women at Augustinian and Lateran Canoness institutions. But
since none of these Rules mentioned or regulated music, the development of chant and polyphony was specific to individual orders and
institutions.

All the houses were linked to the local economy. Mendicant nuns
supported themselves by women's handicrafts (weaving, spinning,
cooking); Carlo Borromeo's radical reform would target nuns' participation in the traditionally female control of food resources by
outlawing the feeding of men inside *clausura*. The Humiliate maintained their long-standing ties to the silk industry and to cloth-
processing.[20] Yet another source of income for the major houses,

---

[18] Female Visconti and Sforza served as patronesses of these houses; Bianca Maria Sforza
maintained close relations with S. Chiara, for instance. Zarri, 'Pietà e profezia', traces the
ties of the Clarissans to dynastic city-states.

[19] On the latter, see Baernstein, 'The Counter-Reformation Convent', 35–74.

[20] On the outlawing of feeding men, the S. Apollinare case noted below and various
orders from the 1580s for S. Vittore in Meda, ASDM XII, vol. 174, fasc. 1. For nuns' handi-
work at S. Maria Maddalena al Cerchio, see Zardin, *Donna e religiosa*, 34; for Benedictine,

Benedictine and mendicant—and another link to the patriciate—was provided by the tuition (*dozzine*) paid by the families of the young girls in residence for education (the *educande*).

Thus these monasteries were organically bound to urban society; even the reform efforts of the 1520s were initiated by Milan's Senate, not the bishop.[21] The methods of families' control over the monasteries were multifarious; *doti spirituali* provided much income, and were often needed even for everyday expenses.[22] Patrician wills often left property or Mass bequests to female houses.[23] Monasteries also carried out business transactions with families—including loans which functioned, despite episcopal disapproval, as pre-payments for daughters' *doti*.[24] From the Quattrocento, the institution of the *livello* (or annual fixed sum for expenses over and above a dowry, given by her family) both stratified class status inside the cloister and ratified professed daughters' ties to their kin. The aristocratic protectors of an institution, sometimes even the Spanish monarch or the entire Milanese Senate, provided legal and social bulwarks against later episcopal infringement.[25]

Humiliate, and Franciscan houses' work in the silk and cloth trade, see D'Amico, *Le contrade*, 133.

[21] The discussion of the laxity of religious orders and patrician reform efforts in F. Chabod, *Lo Stato e la vita religiosa a Milano nell'epoca di Carlo V* (Turin, 1971; orig. edn. 1933), 236–53, also includes (pp. 377–9) the 1521 'Istruzione del vicario e dodici di provvisione' (i.e. civic officials) for the reform of female houses.

[22] Typical is the request of 21 Aug. 1608 from the nuns of S. Marta to Federigo, asking to take money from Suor Bianca Lodovica Taverna's (1592–1680) *dote* for the purchase of yeasts (App. A, Doc. 24).

[23] For Quattrocento Requiem Mass bequests to S. Margarita, see ASM, Religione, p.a., 1899. Later wills often mentioned 'messe cantate' as well as 'messe basse' for the souls of benefactors, although the singers are not specified; for instance, the 1612 legacy of Laura Canova for 'nove messe basse et una cantata' yearly, or the will dated 19 Dec. 1687 of Carlo Francesco Rusca (probably a relative of Claudia Rusca), both left to S. Caterina in Brera (ASM, Religione, p.a., 1815). Despite all the bequests and landed property, the increase in monastic population and the difficulties involved for cloistered nuns in collecting rent (monasteries were dependent on often unscrupulous agents) meant that foundations were often in financial straits, thus necessitating the withdrawals from *doti spirituali*. Most volumes in ASDM XII contain at least one annual list of income and expenses, often showing net deficits.

[24] For a contract of 21 Aug. 1649 between S. Radegonda and the four Cozzolani brothers, the siblings of Chiara Margarita and her sister Candida Arsilia, see ASM, Religione, p.a., 2223, fo. 156; this was probably as a dowry pre-payment for the sisters' niece Anna Margarita. For Carlo's 1583 ban of the practice, *AEM* iii. 331, also in E. Cattaneo, 'Le monacazioni forzate tra Cinque e Seicento', in U. Colombo (ed.), *Vita e processo di Suor Virginia Maria de Leyva monaca di Monza* (Milan, 1985), 145–95 at 165.

[25] For the appeal of 15 July 1628 directed to the Milanese Senate from the nuns of the Monastero Maggiore, faced with transfer to archiepiscopal jurisdiction by a bull of Urban VIII, see ASM, Fondo Culto, p.a., 1926. The patrician character of the institution was

Specific families were so closely associated with houses old and new that they could exert control over these foundations; the Sforza continued their close relations with the Monastero Maggiore and S. Chiara, as did the Arconati at S. Agostino in Porta Nuova, the Serbelloni at S. Vincenzo, and the Taverna at S. Marta. Newer families also participated; even the reforming congregation of the Angeliche at S. Paolo (dating from 1535), closely linked to the Barnabite regulars, came into the sphere of the Sfondrati.[26] Patricians could directly endow places for their future female descendants, as one family did at S. Apollinare: Maria Vittoria Resta (*c.*1635–1705), the dedicatee of Caifabri's *Scelta de' motetti a due, e tre*, a Roman anthology (RISM 1665[1]), gained her place (and a large personal cell, useful for musical practising) at the house under such a bequest in 1650.[27] The high cost of the *dote spirituale* rendered the extra income from wills necessary.[28]

The Milanese patriciate itself was no monolithic formation. Its rigid structure included the sixty senatorial families; relatively newer clans, sometimes merchants or bankers, who were not allowed into the Senate but who had as much or more wealth than the traditional aristocracy; and those families associated with the Spanish governor, officials, and the rather meagre trappings of court.[29] All three would send their daughters into monasteries, but the most famous nun musicians of the Seicento did not often come from the sixty families. The Cozzolani seem to have been land-owning urban merchants or

proudly noted by the nuns themselves in an earlier attempt to remain under the administration of the Cassinese, the epigraph to this chapter (petition to Philip IV of Spain as Duke of Milan, 6 June 1626, ASM, Culto, ibid.)

[26] Baernstein, 'The Counter-Reformation Convent', 176–82.

[27] The will of 27 Apr. 1511 drawn up by Gallo Resta is in ASM, Religione, p.a., 1772; although Resta had wanted to found a new house, later documents in the file redirected the bequest to reserve two places *in perpetuum* for family members at S. Apollinare. A 1626 addendum noted the gradual rise in the cost of the *dote spirituale* from 1,000 lire in 1511 to 4,000 lire, the standard Seicento sum for the most aristocratic foundations (S. Margarita, Monastero Maggiore). For Maria Vittoria, see the list of family nuns, ibid.: 'Fù vestita sotto nominata suor Maria Vitoria Resta; li suoi parenti anno datto il vestito, e fabricato una camera che è il Camerone di Sopra. La retroscrita è morta à dì 30 gennaio de 1705.'

[28] For matrilineal dowry and *livello* legacies in the Cozzolani family, see below, Ch. 3. At S. Radegonda, the dowry in the Seicento was the unusual sum of 2,709 lire, a figure derived from an exchange rate for a foreign or previous currency.

[29] For nuns' music, Madrid came up only in appeals to the king as the secular authority of last resort in conflicts with the archbishop (as in the 1661 controversy at S. Paolo discussed in Ch. 4). On urban class structure, see D'Amico, *Le contrade*, 61–8.

craftspeople, probably in the cloth or silk industry;[30] the Clerici, who provided S. Radegonda with two renowned singers in the Seicento, achieved senatorial status only late in the century; and other musical nuns, such as Sessa and Rusca, belonged to prominent but not pre-eminent families.[31] Some novices came from other cities because of the musical renown of Milanese houses or for profession at a reduced dowry.[32]

These patrician monastic institutions shared in, and often helped create, the waves of urban devotional reform and fervour from the Trecento to the Council of Trent. Zarri's female 'living saints', court prophetesses, and pious urban women were also found in the Lombard capital; the fame of Arcangela Panigarola, a prophetess at S. Marta associated with the French rulers of the city in the years 1515–30, would continue even after Trent. Another Quattrocento visionary at S. Marta, Veronica Negroni (or da Binasco; 1445–97), was the subject of a 288-page *vita* by the urban panegyrist Carlo Torre two centuries later in 1652, one apparently financed by the sisters themselves.[33] The mystic Paola Antonia de' Negri, who resided among the Angeliche of S. Paolo, achieved fame (and later censure) throughout northern Italy in the 1550s. At S. Margarita, the venerable Maria Caterina Brugora died 'in odour of sanctity' in 1529; her death inspired the citizens to anti-French action, her body was preserved in the nuns' church for more than 200 years, and her life adduced as a model for nuns a century later by the Cassinese

[30] In 1609 Chiara Margarita's mother would ask to be buried in the Duomo. But the family name appears in no list of Milanese senators in the 16th–18th cc.

[31] None of the families of famous musical nuns seems to have held titles of nobility ('Conte'). None of the eleven patrician families analysed by one demographer (cf. below) seems to have produced nun musicians. *Pace* Bowers, 'The Emergence', 175, the encomium of Sessa in Borsieri's 1619 *Soplemento* to Morigia's *La nobilità di Milano* (Milan, 1595) did not necessarily imply that she was a member of the nobility (the book's title simply means 'renown'). The admission of poor but musically gifted girls as *professe* to monasteries above their class status was another result of the dowry-reduction process, one more characteristic of the less wealthy or extra-urban houses.

[32] At least three Milanese monastic musicians came from other cities: Corona Somenza (*c.*1530–1609) at the Monastero Maggiore, from Cremona (A. Campi, *Cremona fedelissima città* (Cremona, 1585; repr. Bologna, 1990), 191–2); Maria Catterina (Cornelia) Calegari of Bergamo; and Badalla, also possibly Bergamasque in origin.

[33] *Specchio per l'anime religiose, cioè vita della beata Veronica, monaca del venerabile monasterio di S. Marta di Milano* (Milan, 1652); the dedication to Geronima Doria Spinola is signed by the house collectively.

Lampugnani.[34] The memory of these women would hardly be absent from urban devotion and prestige in the Seicento.

The medieval heritage of these sacred virgins with a public role would provide both a locus for ecclesiastical regulation and a component of urban spiritual prestige, sometimes expressed through music. A late echo of this intercessory role of sisters, and of the 'spiritual capital' of their foundations, is found in the early musical dedications of polyphonic Office settings to female houses, in which composers (among them Costanzo Antegnati, Orfeo Vecchi, and Banchieri) asked for nuns' prayers and mediation, recalling the traditions of 'oratrici perpetue'.[35] These striking requests are not typical of inscriptions to male monks; in the later Cinquecento, the invocation of nuns connected female monastic performances of the music with its composer's wishes for its friendly reception by earthly and celestial audiences.[36]

The rising social prestige of monasteries was embodied in the Quattrocento (re)construction of many monastic churches and cloisters: S. Radegonda, S. Margarita, S. Maria Maddalena al Cerchio, and S. Bernardino alle Monache. The architecture of these churches would remain intact through the Settecento, although internal decoration would be added. The design of urban cloisters followed a standard plan, with individual variants based on the amount of land available; in the construction of monasteries and their churches, nuns' patronage and aesthetic influence were crucial.[37] But this

[34] Her *vita*, by Francesco Ruggieri, is preserved in BA, A. 257 *inf*. On her tomb, see S. Latuada, *Descrizione di Milano* (Milan, 1738), v. 204; her place in the tradition of female Benedictine sanctity in Milan was noted by Lampugnani, *Della vita*, 149.

[35] Orfeo Vecchi's inscription of his 1600 *Falsibordoni* to three sisters implored his addressees' prayers (see App. C). Further afield, Antegnati's *Sacrae cantiones* (Brescia: Sabbio, 1581) invoked the orations of Abbess Serena de' Boni at the ancient Benedictine house of S. Giulia in Brescia, while Alessandro Savioli's *Salmi intieri à cinque* (Venice: Amadino, 1597) requested the intercession of Abbess Flavia Gromella Benaglia and the other Benedictines of S. Grata in Bergamo. The now-lost Milanese reprint of Banchieri's *Vezzo di perle*, op. 23 (Tini, 1610), offered to the sisters of S. Maria della Neve in Piacenza, also remarked on the efficacy of nuns' prayers (see O. Mischiati, *Adriano Banchieri 1568–1634: Profilo biografico e bibliografico delle opere* (Bologna, 1971), 66–7).

[36] Among male Cassinese composers, dedications did not invoke monks' intercessions; cf. Serafino Cantone's inscription of his *Officium hebdomadae sacrae* settings *a 5* (Milan: Tradate, 1603) to David Cataneo at S. Nicolò del Lido (Venice); Serafino Patta's *Sacra cantica concinenda a 1–3* (Venice: Vincenti, 1609) addressed to Valeriano Degno, procurator-general of the congregation; or Gregorio Zucchini's *Motecta et missae a 4–5* (of the same year and printer) to Cyrillo Gasparino at S. Maria delle Grazie.

[37] For 15th-c. monastic churches, see L. Patetta, *L'architettura del Quattrocento a Milano* (Milan, 1987), *ad voces*, with a discussion of the claustral model, 136–9. For nuns' influence

pre-existing architectural fabric would also complicate Carlo Borromeo's exacting and detailed plans for the walling-up of female monastic life in the later Cinquecento.

Cloistered nuns' presence in early modern Milan was quite palpable from the sheer number and physical proximity of their houses in the city.[38] The plentitude led both to the physical abutment of houses in the cramped urban space and to disputes between houses over property rights. But it also moved one patrician clerical observer to remark that 'Milano sembrava tutta convertita a una clausura', a further testimony for monasteries' contribution of sacred space to the city's symbolic geography.[39]

By 1550 social diversification had led to a two-tier system: the rich (and liturgically ornate) Benedictine, Clarissan, and Humiliate houses boasted class superiority over the more humble Dominican, Capuchin, and other monasteries. The spiritual dowries required served to separate the membership of one type from the other. In the following century, this division would have important ramifications for the maintenance of musical life, via the dowry reduction requests to Rome. Patrician control ensured that any reform attempt different from their wishes would meet with strong resistance. And part of the conflict took place precisely over polyphony.

This distinction was roughly paralleled by the kind of ecclesiasti-

---

on the models of Cassinese architecture across northern Italy, and the characteristics of S. Maurizio's plan, see M. A. Winkelmes, 'Form and Reform: The Casssinese Congregation and Benedictine Reform Architecture' (Ph.D. diss., Harvard University, 1995). For the earliest (1671) description of the paintings and other decoration of urban churches, see A. Santagostino, *L'immortalità e gloria del pennello*, ed. M. Bona Castellotti (Milan, 1980).

[38] For a schematic plan of the early modern city which shows the clear distribution of female houses in the areas of medieval urban growth and along the walls, see L. Gambi and M. C. Gozzoli, *Le città nella storia d'Italia: Milano* (Rome, 1982), 99.

[39] For property litigation between two leading houses, see the documents of the 1515 dispute between the Monastero Maggiore and S. Marta in ASDM XII, vol. 101, fasc. 1. Three houses in the Brera district—S. Caterina in Brera, S. Agostino in Porta Nuova, and S. Maria della Aurora—physically bordered each other in the early Cinquecento. The quote is found in P. Morigia, *Il santuario della città di Milano* (Milan, 1641; not present in the first edn. of 1603, 129, describing the area against the western city walls, where the Monastero Maggiore, S. Orsola, S. Maria Maddalena al Cerchio, S. Maria del Cappuccio, and S. Marta (all with musical traditions) stood in close proximity (cited by G. B. Sannazzaro, *San Maurizio al Monastero Maggiore* (Milan, 1992), 158); the thought accords well with Federigo Borromeo's ideas on urban sanctoral space. On nuns' houses as female Earthly Jerusalems in the symbolic topography of early modern Bologna, see Zarri, 'Recinti sacri: Sito e forma dei monasteri femminili a Bologna tra '500 e '600', in S. Boesch Gajano and L. Scaraffia (eds.), *Luoghi sacri e spazi della santità* (Turin, 1990), 381–96.

cal jurisdiction to which nuns were subject. At the behest of urban aristocrats or sisters themselves, and in the wake of the Councils of Basle and Constance, female monasteries in northern Italy were increasingly placed under some kind of external authority.[40] Houses were administered either by the male monks, canons, or friars of their order ('regulars') or by the archbishop; the distinction was to prove fundamental and far-reaching, not least for music. By the Cinquecento, most Benedictine and Humiliate (along with some mendicant) foundations in the city were normally subject to the male branches, and this leading role of the regulars seems to have been as pronounced in Milan as in other northern Italian centres.[41] Among Benedictines, the abbot of a given male monastery was bound to visit, regulate, and (if need be) discipline a given female house, in line with Cassinese reforms; these included measures for the safeguarding of nuns' enclosure.[42] Thus, S. Radegonda was subject after 1506 to S. Pietro in Gessate and thus indirectly to the entire Italian congregation; later this jurisdiction would pass to S. Simpliciano.[43] Similar hierarchy affected S. Margarita, while the Monastero Maggiore and S. Vincenzo were actual members of the Cassinese congregation under S. Pietro in Gessate.[44] Among mendicant orders, the female monasteries were subject to a male prior; a Clarissan house such as S. Apollinare was normally visited by the Friars Minor Observant.[45]

---

[40] On the mid-Quattrocento, and not Trent, as the decisive moment of Church reform in Europe, see Wright, *The Counter-Reformation*, 264.

[41] Zarri, 'Monasteri femminili', 377. The original impulse for the subordination of female houses was a reforming one, often at the behest of nuns themselves or the patriciate, by which sisters could share in the observant movements of the Quattrocento; this was reversed after Trent, which assigned the responsibility for reform to the local bishop.

[42] The 1478 Cassinese general chapter's rules for *clausura* at the Monastero Maggiore are in T. Leccisotti, *Congregationis S. Iustinae de Padua O.S.B. Ordinationes Capitulorum Generalium*, pt. 2 (Montecassino, 1970), 16; my thanks to Mary-Ann Winkelmes and Herbert Bloch for these references.

[43] For the 1506 bull of Julius II subordinating S. Radegonda to S. Pietro in Gessate, see ASM, Religione, p.a., 2213. This kind of order was necessary because male regulars were not always willing to take over the jurisdiction of female houses. The transfer of authority to S. Simpliciano (which had joined the congregation in 1517), with aid from the abbot of S. Pietro in times of crisis (cf. below, Ch. 4) is attested by the visitation reports in ASM, Religione, p.a., 2213, 2214, and 2217.

[44] A curial note of 24 Mar. 1623 listed S. Pietro in Gessate as having jurisdiction over the Monastero Maggiore and S. Margarita, while S. Radegonda and S. Vincenzo were assigned to S. Simpliciano (ASDM XII, vol. 57, fasc. 2).

[45] P. Sevesi, 'Rievocazione dei monasteri delle Clarisse nell'Archidiocesi di Milano', *MSDM* 4 (1957), 212–26. The Lateran Canonesses of S. Maria Annunciata were subject to the male canons of the order at S. Maria della Passione.

But everyday life—including liturgy and music—was largely under the control of the nuns and their families.

On the other hand—and with later consequences for polyphony—Augustinian, Servite, and Dominican foundations generally reported to archiepiscopal authority, a situation that an intrusive prelate such as Carlo Borromeo could exploit to the full. Most extra-urban houses were also subject to the diocese.[46] But the distinction was not fixed: upon Roman intervention, female monasteries could pass from the administration of regulars to that of the archbishop or (less frequently) vice versa, and the struggle over jurisdiction would prove to be both crucial and intimately bound to music in the two centuries after Trent.

In the mid-sixteenth century, several changes began to unfold. Most obvious were Carlo's efforts, themselves simply the last—if the most radical—in a long history of reforms. But the demographic revolution was equally central. Although the number of new houses, especially Clarissan institutions, in the later Quattrocento correlates with Zarri's findings for other northern Italian cities, the most salient feature is the enormous rise in the number of young women admitted as choir nuns (*professe*) from about 1550 onwards.[47] The total number of sisters in the diocese, probably no more than 500 in the era of the Sforza, surpassed 2,000 in 1575 and reached some 6,000 by the mid-seventeenth century.[48] This trend held for both sorts of

---

[46] The visits *ad limina* in 1639 and 1657 listed three non-urban houses as subject to regulars, while twenty-five reported to the bishop; Zardin, *Donna e religiosa*, 47.

[47] Houses hosted a larger number of *professe* as well as some *converse*; these latter, from a lower social class, functioned as servants inside the cloister. *Professe* were sometimes called 'monache da offizio', or 'coriste', or 'velate'. Different orders conferred different titles upon their members: Benedictines and Lateran Canonesses were called 'Donna'; Franciscans, Augustinians, and Humiliate 'Suor'; and the Angelicans 'Angelica'; *converse* were universally called 'Suor'. For a woman servant in the Cozzolani family who became a *conversa* upon her master's death, possibly in order to serve his daughters, see below, Ch. 3. A 1578 case of a novice at S. Maria Maddalena al Cerchio, who sought to use her limited musical abilities to escape her fate as a *conversa*, is in ASDM XII, vol. 48, fo. 63ʳ: 'e di presente un'altra simile destinata per conversa la quale per saper un poco di sonar d'organi intende dimandar gratia d'esser dispensata per monaca da offitio'.

[48] For the 1575 figure, I have taken the *numeri prefissi*, the number of slots financially possible for a house (in Ragazzoni's opinion, ASDM XII, vol. 48, fos. 84ʳ–85ᵛ) as a rough guide, although this figure often bore little reality to real monastic population, often higher; see Baernstein, 'The Counter-Reformation Convent', 152–4. The possible total for all houses was 2,648. The figure of 6,000 occurs several times in Litta's writings: the letter of 26 May 1659 (ASDM XII, vol. 128, fos. 265ʳ–266ᵛ) as well as an unsigned curial note of 1663 in connection with the bishop's efforts to ban music entirely at S. Margarita (ASDM XII, vol. 83, fasc. 2). The urban population as a whole was buffeted by war and plague: D'Amico (*Le*

houses; S. Caterina in Brera was capable of housing nineteen *professe*
in 1575 but had forty-nine inhabitants in 1617, while the population
of *velate* at the Monastero Maggiore rose from ninety-one in 1554 to
133 in 1571.[49] Although the numerical growth might seem to have
enhanced the wealth of these foundations, the costs of feeding and
housing more sisters could markedly increase a house's expenses,
requiring new construction or additions.[50] A typical case is that of
the singer Paola Ortensia Serbellona, later to receive two musical
dedications, who took her final vows at S. Vincenzo on 3 October
1581 along with two other novices.[51] The only Milanese statistics on
the number of patrician girls who took the veil in the Cinquecento
and Seicento might at first be viewed with some caution; the figures
from eleven families indicate a cloistered fate for 48 per cent of
daughters of fathers born in the first half of the seventeenth century.[52] For an earlier generation, the proportion rises to some 75 per
cent.

The numbers may seem unbelievably high. Yet the archival evidence reveals that families—the Cozzolani, the Serbelloni, the
Archinti—did indeed send many or most of their daughters, generation after generation, into monastic life. Another guide to the mas-
sive claustration of young Milanese women is the body of requests to

contrade, 48–57) revised Sella's estimates ('Premesse demografiche ai censamenti austriaci',
Storia di Milano, xii. 458–78) to roughly 106,000 in 1574, with a drop after the plague, rising again in 1610 to 114,000. The 1630 plague lowered the figure to 70,000, with another
rise to 100,000 by 1655.

[49] The figures for S. Caterina have been taken from the 1575 ASDM count and the 1617
list preserved in ASDM XII, vol. 68, fasc. 1. For the Monastero Maggiore, the numbers are
derived from the 1554 Antegnati organ contract discussed below, and the former list. The
expansion of individual houses was aided by Carlo Borromeo's merger of smaller institutions (often against their will) with larger ones, as in the case of the combination of S. Pietro
Martire with S. Agostino Bianco.

[50] In 1590 S. Marta expanded the size of its church, 'dovendo ogni giorno il detto
numero [esser superato] per la quantità di molte gentildonne che desiderano di entrare in
detto Monastero' (ASM, Religione, p.a., 2135). Due to the lack of living space,
S. Radegonda bought two adjacent houses in the 1620s (documents in ASM, Religione, p.a.,
2214), justifying the purchase by the previous example of S. Caterina in Brera.

[51] A letter of 9 Sept. 1582 from the abbess Ippolita Lareana to Vincenzo [Antonino], vicar
of nuns, noted their profession (ASDM XII, vol. 140bis, fasc. 2).

[52] D. E. Zanetti, *La demografia del patriziato milanese nei secoli XVII, XVIII, XIX* (Pavia,
1972), 52, 59–60, 81–6, whose Table IV-2 analyses the marital status of women dying after
age 50 over various generations. For 1600–50, Zanetti arrived at a figure of 75 per cent
celibacy. One immediate statistical problem with this approach is that (married) women
who died in childbirth do not appear in the sample; thus the proportion of laywomen relative to the female population as a whole is likely to have been higher than 25 per cent.

the Sacra Congregazione dei Vescovi e Regolari pleading for exemptions from Carlo's stipulation that no more than two sisters could profess their vows in institutions of less than fifty; this rule was apparently another episcopal attack on family influence.[53] Most of the musicians in this study—Bascapè, Cozzolani, Rusca, Taverna, the two Clerici—entered houses in which their aunts, sisters, nieces, or cousins had taken or would take vows. The statistics do indeed point in the correct direction: the cloister was by far the most likely future for patrician girls. The numbers reinforce the evidence: being a nun was no marginal status in early modern Milan. It was far more typical than atypical.

In part, the reasons include forced monachization, best known through the true story of Virginia Maria de Leyva of S. Margarita in Monza and its treatment in Manzoni's *I promessi sposi*.[54] Despite the formal requirement that novices be questioned as to whether they wished of their own accord to take vows, patrician control and familial strategies destined large numbers of girls to the cloister from the cradle onwards.[55] This was so familiar that it made its way into verse in Milan.[56] Elsewhere, the phenomenon even received musical treatment.[57]

---

[53] For two cases at S. Maria delle Veteri, see the request approved on 30 May 1664 by the SCVR for permission to have Chiara Gioseffa Dondei enter after her two sisters, and the similar petition of 1 Nov. 1672 for Rosa Margarita Schiaffinati (ASDM XII, vol. 93, fasc. 2); also ASDM XII, vol. 86, fasc. 5 for Alessandra Giuseppina Visconti at S. Maria del Cappuccio in the 1670s. For Carlo's regulation, see *AEM*, iii. 329, also in Cattaneo, 'Le monacazioni forzate', 164.

[54] Cattaneo, 'Le monacazioni forzate', noted that involuntary religious life only created later problems for ecclesiastical authority, and was therefore strongly opposed by prelates as diverse as Carlo and Federigo Borromeo. Its ubiquity is thus a measure of familial control; the classic denunciation of the practice, by one of its victims, is in Medioli, *L''Inferno monachale'*. The canonical status of Manzoni's novel has fundamentally affected (not always for the better) modern perceptions of Milanese nuns in the Seicento.

[55] The traditional—and reductionist—explanation is economic: spiritual dowries at even the most aristocratic monasteries were only a fraction of the cost for a daughter's marriage (which latter could amount to 20,000 lire; this sum is given as her own marriage portion in a post-1581 petition by Luciana Magiola, the wife of Alessandro Sessa (possibly a relative of the composer) as her marriage dowry (ASM, Famiglie, 174)).

[56] BA, I. 60 *sussidio*, an anonymous Seicento Milanese poetic miscellany, contains the lament of a nun forced to take vows ('Monaca che si querela d'esser entrata nel Monasterio', fo. 57ᵛ; see also the following sonnet, 'Monaca che uuole insieme amar il Cielo e il Mondo', fo. 58ʳ).

[57] The long cantata entitled *La Monaca. Musica* in the miscellany I-MOe, Mus G. 239 is the lament of a nun forced to take vows and, once inside the cloister, coerced into renouncing music because of internal intrigues (the parallels with the Palomera case discussed below are striking). The large percentage of pieces by Bellerofone Castaldi in the volume suggests

But archival evidence reveals more positive motivations. For some widows, monastic life was clearly preferable to unwanted marriages; they therefore asked to become nuns.[58] Other married women petitioned the archdiocesan curia throughout the century for spiritual retreats in Milanese monasteries, providing another link between nuns and their world of origin.[59] But sincere vocations, and the rise in personal devotion throughout the period, should not be underestimated. A number of Federigo Borromeo's correspondents show self-understanding as members of a special state—sacred virgins consecrated to God. This sentiment is also evident in the collegial and sororial tone evident in women's descriptions of life in their monasteries (most notably in the necrologies from S. Marta and S. Caterina in Brera), a counterbalance to the scandals and conflicts that sometimes convulsed houses.[60]

This demographic explosion—and its linkage of nuns to their families, despite all the post-Tridentine efforts—figure strongly in female monastic music. The combination of Carlo Borromeo's restrictions with the marked growth in the population of monasteries produced a large group of patrician women whose earlier public presence in the city was at best contested and at worst eliminated. Hence the seemingly internal activities of nuns—hospital care at S. Radegonda, liturgy at the Humiliate houses, and music at many institutions—would flourish in Borromean Milan.

Early testimonies to music must be sought among the surviving liturgical books and secular documents. The manuscript production and book holdings of the most likely candidates, the Benedictine houses,

a Modenese origin, possibly around 1640. *La Monaca* is given anonymously in G. 239, and there appears to be no concordance. The cantata's unusual approach to dissonance treatment suggests the work of an amateur composer.

[58] For the 1618 request of Dorotea Rainaldi, who wanted to leave her husband to enter a monastery, ASDM XII, vol. 49, fo. 82^r; for the 1654 request of the widow Cecilia Visconti, ibid., fo. 86^r.

[59] See the requests from married women for several weeks' stay at S. Orsola (ASDM XII, vol. 103, fasc. 3), and the efforts of Giuseppa Maria di Guevara, a princess of the Trivulzio family, to visit S. Maria del Cappuccio, in ASDM XII, vol. 86, fasc. 5. For some later *licenze* at S. Radegonda (a 1717 Roman permit for M. A. G. Trotti to come to the monastery for 'esserciti spirituali' for eight days) and for other requests for the noblewoman Clara Brebbia Panigarola, who was to figure in the connections between S. Radegonda and Mathias de' Medici, see ASDM XII, vol. 129, fasc. 4. For petitions from the Archinti, Sfondrati, and Visconti to visit S. Maria Annunciata, see ASDM XII, vol. 57, fasc. 3.

[60] Another case is Angela Confaloniera's descriptions of the common joy at S. Caterina in Brera over Federigo Borromeo's gift of a *liuto atiorbato* (Ch. 3).

are shrouded in loss.[61] Few items of any sort have been preserved, and there is little evidence for scriptoria in these houses, at least through the Trecento.[62] Nor have many library inventories from any house survived. But a few medieval liturgical books, four with musical notation, can be documented as having been produced for these foundations; all raise problems of liturgy, devotion, and order-specific tradition, factors that would affect the musical repertory up to Cozzolani's 1650 Vespers and beyond.

These codices, all from Benedictine houses, have traditionally been considered as evidence for the 'monastic Ambrosian rite'.[63] If the structure and chant assignments of important Hours (Matins, Vespers) in these sources are characteristic of north Italian monastic use, still other features—Compline, Mass Proper chants, psalter texts—are taken from the Ambrosian liturgy. The books also reflect the sex of their users.[64] And the individual variations in chant assignments and Office structure among such books underline the vagaries of Benedictine liturgy and chant in Milan; indeed, it is perhaps better to consider each codex as an institution-specific Office, with differing combinations in each house of the two liturgical sources.

The winter (*pars hiemalis*) antiphoner for the Monastero Nuovo, dated 1360, was commissioned by its abbess Andriola de' Medici.[65]

---

[61] M. Ferrari, 'Biblioteche e scritto benedettini nella storia culturale della diocesi ambrosiana: Appunti ed episodi', *RSCA* 9 (1980), 230–90, whose doubts (p. 233) about books associated with female houses are gainsaid by the four musical codices below, and most of the breviaries and psalters that can be linked to nuns' foundations.

[62] For a Quattrocento breviary-psalter and a similar Office for S. Sigismondo (the legendary founder of the house) and S. Maurizio from the Monastero Maggiore, see BT, Nuov. Acq. 2 and BA, C. 2 *inf.*, respectively. The musical production of nuns' scriptoria is better documented for northern Europe; cf. R. Strohm, *Music in Late Medieval Bruges* (Oxford, 1990), 62.

[63] The scant literature includes the basic article, O. Heimling, 'Der ambrosiano-benediktinische Psalter vom 14.–17. Jh.', *Jahrbuch für Liturgiewissenschaft*, 11 (1931), 144–56, which makes the case for monastic use at male and female Milanese houses, based partially on a printed ordinal and psalter (BA, Inc. 180) produced for the Monastero Maggiore. For the 'Ambrosian' side against Heimling, see P. Borella, 'I religiosi e il rito ambrosiano', *Ambrosius*, 22 (1946), 131–7 and 'I codici ambrosiani–monastici', ibid. 23 (1947), 25–9, and C. Marcora, 'Due importanti codici della Biblioteca del Capitolo di Gallarate', *Rassegna gallaratese di storia e d'arte*, 17 (1958), 142–53.

[64] As in the Compline blessings of BA, Inc. 180: 'Jube domna [for 'domne'] benedicere' and 'Sorores, sobriae [for 'Fratres, sobrii'] estote'; cf. Heimling, 'Der ambrosiano-benediktinische Psalter', 146, or the antiphon for the Office of the Dead in the Trecento summer antiphoner, Gallarate, ssp. B: 'Extera facta sum sororibus meis' [for 'fratribus meis'], fo. 317[r].

[65] App. A, Doc. 1; for colophons, bibliographic descriptions, and the literature of all four codices, see Kendrick, 'Genres', 85–90. Two houses were known as the 'Monastero Nuovo': S. Erasmo (Humiliate) and S. Vincenzo (Benedictine). Given Medici's title and the

This manuscript shows the characteristic, sometimes unique, mixture of the two liturgies, with at least one idiosyncratic antiphon assignment.[66] The summer antiphoner now at the Archivio Capitolare of Gallarate (ssp. B [or M]), written for an urban Benedictine house (possibly the Monastero Maggiore) between 1317 and 1389, also features unique antiphon assignments for St Radegund's feast.[67] A more specialized case is the Office for Corpus Christi and its octave from 1485, preserved as part of an anonymously written calendar and martyrology from the Benedictines of S. Pietro in Brugora, north of Monza, in the Brianza region.[68] It was commissioned by the abbess Stefanina Giussani despite the house's troubled finances.[69] This single Office (Vespers, Matins, Lauds, and Mass) was clearly an object of special ceremony; its inclusion in the codex together with the central documents of nuns' individual and communal identity suggests that the musical expression of Eucharistic devotion was vital to their self-understanding.

But the most remarkable source is the earliest, the Office of St Victor written for S. Vittore in Meda in 1327, and preserved at the Trivulziana.[70] The feast itself (8 May) boasted the largest and most musically elaborate sanctoral Office in the Milanese rite as a whole, appropriate to a local martyr.[71] The manuscript provides even more

liturgical content of the manuscript, it seems more likely to have been intended for the latter.

[66] The conflation of rite is evident even in the Mass and Office for Christmas Day: if the Matins *responsorium cum infantibus*, *Congratulamini mihi omnes* (fo. 62ʳ), is Ambrosian, then monastic influence is evident in the Ingressa (fo. 68ᵛ) for the commemorative Mass of St Anastasia, *Vere gloriosa es*. The (non-monastic) antiphon for Nones on Epiphany, *Oriens exultans* (fo. 115ᵛ), replaces the Ambrosian *Omnes prophetia*.

[67] For its provenance from the Monastero Maggiore, see Marcora, 'Due importanti codici', 143; on fo. 160ᵛ, Radegund's Office features the unique antiphon text *Haec est femina beata Radegunda*.

[68] Milan, Biblioteca Capitolare della Metropolitana (Duomo), E 2 9; my thanks to Fausto Ruggieri for his help with this codex.

[69] On the monastery, see R. Beretta, *Appunti storici su alcuni monasteri e località della Brianza* (Monza, 1966), 238–9.

[70] This manuscript now forms part of a rebound codex (along with a later, illuminated *legenda* of the monastery's founders, Aymo and Vermondo, on fos. 29ʳ–39ᵛ), no. 509 in G. Porro Lambertenghi, *Trivulziana: Catalogo dei codici manoscritti* (Turin, 1884); its destination and dating are given by the colophon, fo. 26ᵛ: 'Istud offitium factum fuit ad expensas florine de sorbiate monialis monasterij de meda. Millesimo trecentesimo vigesimo septimo de mense aprilis. Magister antonius de vimercato fecit et scripsit.' A nun named Fiorina de Solbiate commissioned the *legenda* (P. Orsini, 'Il monastero di San Vittore a Meda nell'alto Medioevo', in F. Cajani, *Le vicende del monastero di San Vittore a Meda* (n.p., 1988), 135).

[71] The late 13th-c. summer antiphoner BA, M.99 *sup.* provides twenty-nine Psallendae for the Ambrosian Office of Mane for this feast.

music than is found in other local antiphoners, beginning with a pre-Vespers office and employing variant Lucernaria for Vespers.[72] Matins continued with prayers, the saint's *passio* as lessons, and a group of psalmelli with antiphons (fo. 5ᵛ: antiphon *Misericors et miseraros*; psalmellus *Beatus vir*; antiphon *Fiat pax domine*; psalmellus *Laetatus sum*; antiphon *Domine, quis habitabit?*; psalmellus *Memento Domine David*). None of this music is contained in other standard Ambrosian antiphoners of the early Trecento.[73] The codex also includes directions for S. Vittore's sisters to process into town (a settlement that they had ruled until communal independence in 1252) and back while singing, before High Mass.[74] The processional rubrics point up the leading public role of the monastery and the far from cloistered existence of its inhabitants. Whether the nuns borrowed other chants or composed their own, they clearly added music to an important martyr's Office in the Milanese liturgy. Most striking is the house's role as the custodian of the cult of St Victor and the expansiveness of its musical expression.

Although all four codices were intended for female monasteries, their music is notated at 'normal' pitch, largely within the compass *c–f'* (depending on mode).[75] This is the first, but hardly the last, instance of the difference between notated and sung pitches in the repertory. The lack of other early testimonies to notated polyphony in female houses is not surprising. Most evidence until the Cinquecento for polyphony in Milan stems from the major institutions of the city-state: the Duomo and the ducal chapel.[76] Sisters' use

[72] The service began, uniquely among Ambrosian Office books, with a highly formulaic *Te Deum laudamus* (fo. 3ʳ), whose melody is otherwise unrecorded, published by E. T. Moneta Caglio, 'Un *Te Deum* ambrosiano inedito', in C. Alzati and A. Majo (eds.), *Studi ambrosiani in onore di mons. Pietro Borella* (Milan, 1982), 167–72. The Lucernarium for First Vespers in BT, 509, *Signatum est super nos*, replaces the more usual *Lux orta est*.

[73] Bedero di Val Travaglia B (the earliest witness for the *pars æstiva* of the Milanese rite), and the later BA, M. 99 *sup*.

[74] Marginal notes on fos. 9ʳ–10ᵛ, including a note 'usque ad portam ecclesiae Sancti Johannis et deinde antifona'.

[75] For instance, the Psalmellus for the Mass of St Victor in BT, 509, *Posuisti super caput*, is notated at the same pitch-level, starting on *d*, as it is in BA, M. 99 *sup*. The few modal transpositions in the manuscripts of the *Cantus Sororum* chant repertory, the monophony for the north European Brigettines, seem unrelated to performance considerations; V. Servatius, *Cantus Sororum: Musik- und liturgiegeschichtliche Studien zu den Antiphonen des birgittinischen Eigenrepertoires* (Uppsala, 1990), 65 ff.

[76] W. F. Prizer, 'Music at the Court of the Sforza: The Birth and Death of a Musical Center', *Musica disciplina*, 43 (1989), 141–93. For a 1512 list of liturgical books in the sacristy of S. Simpliciano, not including any polyphony, U. Monneret de Villard, 'Contributo alla storia delle biblioteche milanesi', *ASL* 45 (1918), 298–9.

of improvised discant emphasizing seconds, fourths, and sevenths, characteristic of late Quattrocento Ambrosian song for vigils of martyrs (St Victor) and the Office of the Dead, might also have been heard.[77]

These chant-books also address the question of sisters' literacy. If the three Trecento codices were executed by male scribes on commission, later books may well have been written by nuns.[78] Along with a rise in monastic foundations, the early Cinquecento saw new kinds of cultural expression; the *Officium hebdomadae sanctae cura sororis Perpetuae de Birago* (Milan: Gotardo Pontano [Ponzio], 18 Mar. 1522), compiled by a member of the Monastero Maggiore, provided a Holy Week Office plus other free texts as a public presentation of important devotional themes, marking an early link between Benedictine ritual and Passiontide liturgy as mediated by nuns.

In the next generation, part of these new means of expression seems to have been organs. The agreement of 4 September 1554 between the Brescian Gian Giacomo Antegnati and the Monastero Maggiore (App. A, Doc. 2) provided for an instrument comparable to that of the church of the male superiors, the basilica of S. Simpliciano.[79] It was to have the registers and ranks of the organ at Vigevano cathedral, neither extant today. But the keyboard at the house has indeed survived, with only partial nineteenth-century rebuilding.[80] The contract itself points up the desire for a lavish organ: the nuns paid three hundred scudi (1650 lire).[81] The instrument also represented a further stage in the elaboration of their

[77] The practice is singled out for criticism in F. Gaffurius, *Theorica musicae* (Milan, 1492), i. 1 and id., *Practica musicae* (Milan, 1496), iii. 14.

[78] F. Argelati's compilation, *Biblioteca scriptorum Mediolanensium* (Milan, 1745), vi, cols. 1660–1, noted of Suor Benedetta da Vimercate (1425–1515) at S. Marta that 'artem scribendi tam optime callebat, ut ingentia volumina etiam cum musicalibus notis ad usum Chori exaraverit, aliaque scripsit'.

[79] ASM, Religione, p.a., 2147, with another record in ASM, Notarile, 1026.

[80] S. Boccardi (in Sannazzaro, *San Maurizio*, 205–6) lists the reconstructed disposition: Principale 8′ (12′ real); Ottava; Decimaquinta; Decimanona; Vigesimaseconda; Vigesimasesta; Vigesimanona; Trigesimaterza a trigesimasesta; Flauto in ottava; Flauto in duodecima; Fiffaro; Keyboard: *FF-c″*, Pedal: *FF-c*; pitch: *g′* [*sic*] = 440 Hz. This adds the Trigesimaterza and Fiffaro stops to those of the 1536 Antegnati organ for the Duomo Vecchio of Brescia.

[81] The list of family organs given in C. Antegnati, *L'arte organica* (Brescia, 1608), 5 ff. includes instruments for female houses (mainly Benedictine) in Milan, Meda, Treviglio, Varese, Bergamo, Crema, Pavia, Lodi, Cremona, Vicenza, and Padua (of which the first four cities were in the diocese of Milan).

church, whose ambitious building plans testify to its leading role among Milanese religious institutions.[82]

The remarkable decoration of S. Maurizio, including the well-known fresco cycles executed by various artists (*inter alia* Bernardo Luini) between 1510 and 1525 and the twenty-six lunette portraits of female saints, furnished an iconographic series reflecting the values of religious life in the mid-Cinquecento and a pictorial expression of the house's patrician ties.[83] Indeed, all that nuns could have seen from their *chiesa interiore* looking towards their presbytery and beyond the dividing wall to the altar in the *chiesa esteriore* would have been the frescoes depicting Christ's physical suffering, framed by images of female martyrs, while the side chapels featured land-scapes and lunette portraits of martyrs or Benedictine saints. The entire decoration stemmed from an iconographic programme incor-porating the values of female monastic life. Indeed, the symbolic ref-erences to martyrdom in S. Maurizio's plan held deeper implications. Just as early Christian women had given up their physical being for Christ and had thus achieved an intercessory status in heaven, so too nuns' sacrifice of their social being in the lineage of the Milanese patriciate provided them a place as liminal beings in the terrestrial prefiguring of the Celestial Jerusalem represented by their monaster-ies. This martyrological and angelic identification—and self-identification of female religious—would continue to resonate, above all in the sanctoral motets of the Seicento.

However, the organ's completion actually blocked the frescoes of St Cecilia and (possibly) St Juliana in the fourth side chapel on the left, a testimony to the growing importance of music over decora-tion.[84] Its most remarkable feature is its sheer size and placement,

---

[82] By comparison, the major Marian sanctuary of S. Maria dei Miracoli at Saronno would only contract for its Antegnati organ in 1578–9, well after its frescoes by Gaudenzio Ferrari; cf. Kendrick, 'La musica nel Santuario di Saronno fra Cinque e Seicento', in M. L. Gatti Perer (ed.), *Il Santuario della Beata Vergine a Saronno* (Milan, 1996).

[83] Bernardo Luini, in the fresco above and to the right of the nuns' altar grate, depicted Alessandra Sforza Bentivoglia, the governor's daughter, in the act of interceding for her par-ents; twenty years later, her name appeared in the list of nuns who signed the organ con-tract as 'reverenda madre'. ASM, Religione, p.a., 2147 also contains the nuns' contract with Francisco di Medici da Seregno for the painting of the organ case (whose wings depict St Catherine of Alexandria and St Cecilia, models for cloistered musical women). On the church's sanctoral iconography, see Sannazzaro, *San Maurizio*, esp. 43 ff. on the frescos as embodiments of Bentivoglia prestige.

[84] Sannazzaro, *San Maurizio*, 55; for the dating of the shutters, id., 'Nuovi documenti per San Maurizio al Monastero Maggiore', *Civiltà ambrosiana*, 6 (1989), 58–62 at 60.

comprehensible only if the instrument was intended to be heard over the three-quarters high wall that even today separates the *chiesa esteriore* from the *chiesa interiore*. Its location near the nuns' presbytery also permitted a partial view for outsiders in the *chiesa esteriore* of singers or instrumentalists on the organ loft, visible through the cut-out above the altar in the dividing wall, one which had been placed so that the Benedictines might see the consecration of the Host in the external church.

Today, S. Maurizio remains the most accessible example of a female monastic church—one with a long musical tradition—in Milan (Fig. 1). Its architectural plan served later as a model for Carlo Borromeo's reform architecture, later furnishing a major point of contention for disputes regarding music.[85] Quattrocento female

FIG. 1. The *chiesa interiore* at S. Maurizio; the Antegnati organ is on the left. (Photo courtesy of Mary-Ann Winkelmes.)

[85] Patetta, 'La tipologia', 32, and Sannazzaro, *San Maurizio*, 17; the 1582 plan of the city would note some twenty-seven double female monastic churches. For summary descriptions of these buildings, see the entries *ad voces* of Sannazzaro and others in the *DCA*. The sense of liturgy in a double church is difficult to obtain today; the city's current early music concert series in the *chiesa interiore* at S. Maurizio gives a partial impression. A similar architectural and iconographic plan, not as well preserved, characterizes S. Vittore in Meda.

monastic churches received later additions in accordance with this plan; the external churches provided some, often not enough, space for the audiences of nuns' liturgical polyphony. Though the main altar remained in the *chiesa esteriore*, nuns received Communion—the central event of their lives—by means of a small pass-through in the wall (the *comunichino*; at S. Maurizio, the surviving example is to the left in the *chiesa interiore*). Tellingly again, male monastic churches were never thus divided; in theory the two-church set-up rendered the inhabitants (and performers) of the *chiesa interiore* invisible if not inaudible. For Carlo's imposition of *clausura* would mean that the wall would also form a partition in this primary space for musical performance. Nuns therefore had to sing outwards from the ostensible anonymity of the *chiesa interiore* towards the *chiesa esteriore*.

The other, even more controversial, public locus in which sisters would perform was the *parlatorio*, the space to which the personal contact between nuns and the urban patrician world of their origin was ostensibly confined.[86] After Carlo's reforms, this room was divided by an iron mesh grill (the *grate* or *ferrata*) into an exterior (*forastiero*) section for families and an interior space for nuns.[87] But the grates ended neither polyphony nor talks, nor even entertainment, in the *parlatori*.

A sense of the spatial organization and sheer size of an important house is apparent from a Cinquecento plan of S. Radegonda (Fig. 2).[88] The monastery was located just north of the north transept of the Duomo. Although a nineteenth-century Via S. Radegonda still runs in this direction, the monastic edifice itself, including its Quattrocento church housing important paintings by Simone Peterzano and C. F. Nuvolone, was demolished in the early nineteenth century, a fate that also befell most other cloisters (S. Marta, S. Margarita, S. Caterina in Brera).[89] The exterior church for the

---

[86] Some houses, like S. Radegonda, had two parlours, one larger than the other, with the smaller possibly reserved for leading families.

[87] No monastic *parlatorio* has survived in its original state in Milan; estimates of size must be deduced from the surviving floor-plans. After the Tridentine decrees, conversations between nuns and outsiders were supposed to be supervised by the *ascoltatrice*, the nun in charge of monitoring the parlour.

[88] V. Seregni, 'Disegni degli Edifizij Piu Celebri di Milan', Milan, Archivio Storico Civico, Raccolta Bianconi, Tomo VIII, p. 27; cf. Patetta, *L'architettura*, 380–3.

[89] Of all female monastic churches in the city, only S. Maurizio, S. Bernardino alle Monache, S. Michele sul Dosso, S. Paolo, and S. Maria della Vittoria survive somewhat intact. S. Radegonda is replaced by a ten-screen cinema almost as popular among today's Milanesi as was the cloister's polyphonic liturgy for their Seicento predecessors. It and

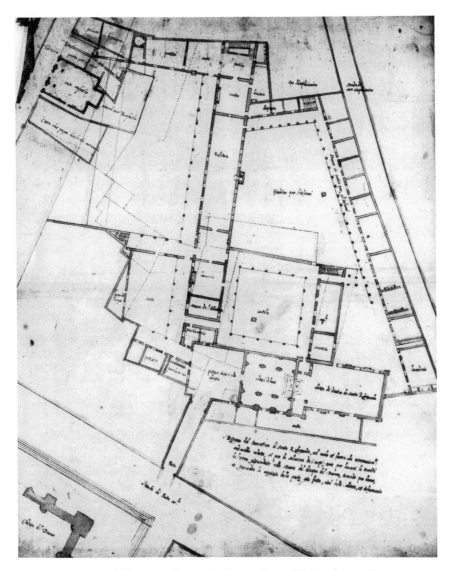

FIG. 2. Vincenzo Seregni, floor-plan of S. Radegonda

other famous houses survive only as street names: Via S. Radegonda, Via S. Margarita, Via Cerchio.

public seems to have been larger than the interior church for the nuns, even though there were up to 150 of the latter; a double *parlatorio*, extensive cells, kitchen, and hospital facilities are also clear.[90] The cells, gardens, cloisters with Cinquecento frescoes and wide gateways, and 'heavenly' singers continued to impress urban panegyrists in the later Seicento.[91]

The next record of polyphony stems from S. Apollinare. According to the episcopal visitation of 12 February 1571, at least one Clarissan had sought a permit for the pedagogical visits of an organist, a Messer Giovanni Antonio.[92] The testimony of Suor Buona, the new abbess, recounted his comings and his instruction of two musical sisters, Suor Clementina Cattanea and Suor Angela Serafina (App. A, Doc. 7a–b).[93] The visitation revealed that the *licenza* had been granted in March 1568. A Giovanni Antonio Brena, an organ-builder, had petitioned the Milanese Senate in that same year for a patent on a keyboard that could be retuned by various intervals up and down; this individual is the most likely candidate for

---

[90] Patetta's estimate for the size of the *chiesa interiore* is 160 sq. m. (*L'architettura*, 381). For photos of the last remnants, see F. Reggiori, 'Il monastero di S. Radegonda', *Città di Milano*, 41 (1925), 6–8. The extensive housing evident in the plan would not necessarily guarantee individual cells for nuns; see Cozzolani's petition of 1666 for the fact that her family also had had a cell built for her upon her profession (Ch. 3), a common practice among wealthy patricians. On the suspect nature of family cells at S. Maria Maddalena al Cerchio in the eyes of Carlo's curia, see Zardin, *Donna e religiosa*, 34–5.

[91] 'Benche situata resti quasi nel centro di Milano tal Clausura, nulladimeno vedesi ornata di Cortili, di vaghi Appartamenti con ampiezza de Giardini, e la loro Chiesa ritrouasi in Nobile Architettura antica con trè Naui . . . Può dirsi, essersi ne' nostri tempi transportato in questo Monistero il Monte Elicona all'eccellenza delle sue Velate Cantatrici; ouuero che in questa Chiesa volino eleuati spiriti, poiche sentonsi melodie da rapine': C. Torre, *Il ritratto di Milano* (Milan, 1714 (1st edn. 1674)), 338. For a comparison of the cloisters at S. Cristina in Bologna, see Monson, *Disembodied Voices*, ch. 1. For contemporary views of the pre-Seicento Monastero Maggiore, see Sannazzaro, *San Maurizio*, 174.

[92] These records are in ASDM XII, vol. 64, fasc. 2, first published by P. Sevesi, 'Il monastero delle Clarisse in S. Apollinare di Milano (documenti, secoli XIII–XVIII)', *Archivium Franciscanum Historicum*, 19 (1926), 76–99. My citations are from the ASDM manuscripts; see Kendrick, 'Four Views of Milanese Nuns' Music', in Matter and Coakley, *Creative Religious Women*, 324–42.

[93] 'When I was to be confirmed as abbess of this convent, the *padre commissario* came here for that purpose, and told me that Suor Clementina had asked him for a permit to allow Messer Giovanni Antonio the organist to enter the convent; it was he who taught Suor Clementina to sing and Suor Angela Serafina to play [keyboard]. This was so he could tune Suor Angela Serafina's keyboard, and the organ, and the *commissario* asked me if this Giovanni Antonio was a trustworthy man, and whether the keyboard could be taken out [of the cloister] for tuning.'

S. Apollinare's visitor.[94] The venue of his request, along with his lack of affiliation to the Duomo, underscores his place in Milanese patrician circles, precisely the social milieu from which S. Apollinare's nuns were drawn, one actively resisting Carlo's reform plans in female monasteries. That Cattanea was the one named sister taking singing lessons, and that Angela Serafina was similarly studying organ, suggests a repertory like that of Elena Malvezzi's contemporary Bolognese book: solo song and intabulations of motets and madrigals. But Giovanni Antonio's connection with harpsichord innovations indicates some regular use of that instrument as well.[95]

By good fortune (although not for the nuns involved), more detailed information about music-making survives from another conflict: the disputes over music, part of a larger confrontation between the curia and the Humiliate of S. Maria Maddalena al Cerchio in 1575.[96] The visitations, in late February and March, carried out by Carlo's vicar of nuns, Cesare Arese, discovered two 'canti poco honesti' (in the cleric's view, at least) in the cell of Suor Paola Giustina Carpani, one of three young musical nuns bound by ties of friendship to Suor Prospera Corona Bascapè (1550–1624), 'organista di rara et esquisita eccellenza', and Suor Prospera Vittoria Cavenaghi. Bascapè had been born into an important Milanese family; her eclectic notes on cosmology, urban history, and Humiliate tradition, preserved in her copy of a 1589 Plantin catechism, testify to her relatively advanced literacy, her knowledge of classical and Christian culture, and not least to her supernatural world-view.[97]

---

[94] The petition of 29 Nov. is in ASM, Autografi, cartella 94, n. 45bis, reproduced and transcribed in F. Mompellio, 'La musica alla corte', *Storia di Milano*, ix. 888. Retunable keyboards recur in other contexts related to nuns (Ch. 7).

[95] Part of the vicar's concern with avoiding the entrance of men into *clausura* (also evident in his desire to transport the harpsichord outside) might have been motivated by the fact that S. Apollinare had no church at this time (the old one having burnt in 1512 and the new one not being completed until 1589; Patetta, *L'architettura*, 386); hence contacts would take place in the far more suspicious space of the *parlatorio*.

[96] The records of the visitation, including the *bergamasca* fragments to be discussed presently, are found in ASDM XII, vols. 97 and 98. For a study of family ties and spiritual life at the house, and a treatment of the case as a guide to female monastic culture, see Zardin, *Donna e religiosa*, ch. 2, who notes the house's somewhat poor but still patrician status.

[97] *Esamina* (the record of the curial visitation) dated Feb.–March 1575, ASDM XII, vol. 97, fasc. 2. The epithet is taken from Puricelli's 1634 manuscript remarks on Bascapè's life (in her printed catechism, which also contains her *postille* on cosmology, history, and prayer: BA, S.P.H. IV.160) transcribed in Zardin, *Donna e religiosa*, 249 ff. (the title of which is a

Texted parts for both songs, in Bergamasque dialect, were confiscated by Arese and are preserved in the ASDM files.[98] When asked
about their origin, Suor Paola Giustina's defence was that she had
come upon them unexpectedly in a musical gift from her family, and
had then forgotten the suspicious text (App. A, Doc. 8a):

And those things that Your Reverence found in my cell—I found them in a
motet book by Orlando Lasso [added: sent me by my brother Messer Giovan
Battista] and I read them—at least the first one, and I left it on the table,
meaning to send it away . . . In the first line I read, I remember there were
the words *Vum disi madona ogn'hor*, and I don't know what came after that.
There were also some other Bergamasque songs but I didn't read them . . .
I didn't show them to any nun, except I told Suor Livia Sodania that my
brother had sent me *canzone alla bergamasca*, but I didn't want to look at them.

Suor Clemenza della Croce had given a similar if not entirely consistent explanation, saying that Suor Paola Giustina had been sent the
motet book by her cousin and tutor Giovanni Paolo Turni (App. A,
Doc. 8b).

The language of the first piece, *Vum disi, madona*, is also found in
a number of contemporary *greghesche*, a form apparently invented in
the 1560s by Antonio Molino.[99] Literary features—the bizarre language and comic stuttering repetitions—link it to a related genre, the
giustiniana.[100] This Milanese *Vum disi* appears in no printed or manuscript collection of the 1560s or 1570s.[101] But its structure (ABA')
parallels that of the three-voice *napolitane* that enjoyed popularity in
Milan from 1560 on.[102] The second piece (Ex. 2.1) is even more

slightly misleading ellipsis of Puricelli's original encomium of Bascapè, which reads 'et a suo
tempo fatta professa, donna e religiosa virtuosissima, ed *organista* di rara et esquisita eccellenza' [my emphasis]).

[98] The timing of the visitation—Carnival would have ended on 15 Feb. of that year—
points up the nature of the songs. The multiple names of literary forms—*bergamascha, giustiniana*—testify to a level of generic confusion present already in the 16th c.

[99] Molino published an anthology of musical settings of the form (including three settings by the Milanese Pietro Taglia), *Il primo libro delle Greghesche* (Venice: Gardano, RISM
1564[16]); similar incipits include Bell'Haver's *Vu la vedev madonna* and Grisonio's *Vu ha ben
casun*. I have emended Zardin's textual transcriptions in light of *Vum disi*'s polyphonic
nature.

[100] Found in *Il primo libro delle justiniane a tre voci* (Venice: Scotto, RISM 1570[17]), and A.
Gabrieli, *Greghesche et Iustiniane a tre voci, libro primo* (Venice: Gardano, 1571). In the former
collection, a similar piece is Vinciguerra's *Vu se la vita mia*.

[101] The text reads: 'Vum disi madona ogn'hora / ca vegnen nu a trovà / ch'am voli un
po' adrovà / coghe sem ne cazze fuura. / Vum disi . . .'.

[102] For Massimo Troiano's 1559 petition to the Senate for a licence to print *villanelle*, see
Donà, *La stampa musicale*, 127. Other local *villanella* or *napolitana* collections include: *De*

Ex. 2.1. Anonymous, *De tel traga*

diversi autori canzoni alla napolitana (Moscheni, RISM 1562[10]); Ghinolfo Dattari, *Canzoni vil-laneschi* (Moscheni, 1564) and Gioseppe Caimo, *Canzone napolitane a 3* (Moscheni, 1566).

mysterious; like *Vum disi*, *De tel traga* is found in no contemporary collection.[103] If the music in the curial files represents the lines in the two pieces to be intabulated, with the other parts sung or memorized by the Humiliate, Bascapè's keyboard reduction might have been an ornamented version of the simple framework represented by such parts, one of which the curial officials thought that she was capable.[104] The Lassus—clearly regarded by Suor Paola Giustina as safer music to possess—was another matter. The pan-European popularity of the composer extended also to Milan.[105] If Carpani's brother had bought her one of the Venetian editions, there would have been a large selection from which to pick.[106]

But the exhaustive questioning of the nuns elicited more information about musical life. According to Suor Vittoria Savini, fifteen nuns were capable of singing polyphony, including the three young 'compagne' mentioned and an older *maestra di cappella*.[107] Most, but not all, of these singers were associated with the group of nuns to which Bascapè belonged; the combination of polyphony and factionalism would have a long tradition. Besides their interest in the

---

[103] *Faute de mieux*, I have used the incipit 'De tel traga'. The text is fragmentary: '[an ?eight-syllable line] / De tel traga ogni di / [4 or 5 syllables] ch'ie costor / [?4 or 5 syllables] a de' fradei / ade dal salzizzon. / Quest'è ben una gran ventura / de si bona scontradura.' Its homophonic and direct style, with dialogic exchanges between the voices, places it between madrigal and villanella, typical again of local styles around 1570, such as Caimo's contributions to the *Fiamma ardente* (RISM 1586[19]).

[104] 'Et io *canto* solamente motetti spiri*tuali*, et so anche mettergli in intauolatura': testimony of Bascapè, *Esamina*, fo. 11[v]. On *intavolatura* as ornamentation, see the suggestive 'de-intabulations' offered by A. Silbiger, 'Is the Italian Keyboard *Intavolatura* a Tablature?', *Recercare*, 3 (1991), 81–101.

[105] H. Simonsfeld, 'Mailändische Briefe zur bayerischen und allgemeinen Geschichte des 16. Jahrhunderts', *Abhandlungen der historischen Classe der Königlich Bayerischen Akademie der Wissenschaften*, 22/ii (1902), 481–575, nos. 325 and 334. I have argued ('Music and Spirituality in Federigo Borromeo's Milan', paper read at the 1991 Annual Meeting, American Musicological Society, Chicago) that the early editions produced from 1584 on by the Tini family's music press suggest that Lassus was more popular in the city than even Palestrina.

[106] Venetian editions from 1568 (with RISM numbers): 1568: *Quintus liber concentuum sacrorum a 6–8* (Claudio da Coreggio = Merulo; L818); 1569: *Sacrae cantiones a 5–6* (Gardano; L823); *Sacrae cantiones a 5* (Gardano; L822); *Sacrae cantiones a 5–6* (Gardano; L824); *Sacrae cantiones a 6–8* (Gardano; L825); *Sacrae cantiones a 6–8* (Gardano; L826); *Liber sextus a 5* (Merulo; L827); 1572: *Sacrae cantiones, liber secundus a 5–6* (Gardano; L853); 1574: *Sacrae cantiones a 5* (Gardano; L875). Given the size of S. Maria Maddalena's choir (see below), even the largest-scale of these would not have presented performance problems.

[107] '*Quelle che* sano *canto* figurato sono S. Pro*spera* Corona, S. Paola Vittoria, S. Claudia, S. Sulpitia, S. Calidora, S. Bianca Isab*ella*, S. Paola Giustina, S. Bianca Gier*onima*, S. Laura Bezona maestra de capella, S. Clementia Croce hora ministra, S. Cassandra, S. Laura Cornelia, S. Madalena, S. Tranira, S. Barbara': *Esamina*, fo. 3[v].

Lassus motets, and their possible singing of the unauthorized *bergamasche*, the nuns also sang at Vespers (App. A, Doc. 8c):

And the organist is Prospera Corona and the *maestra di capella* is Suor Laura Benzona; and every feast-day they sing the Magnificat, and various antiphons. The former plays organ, and the organist accompanies their singing.

The Humiliate seem to have sung, not the psalms of Vespers (probably performed *alternatim*, as implied by 'essa sona l'organo'), but its canticle and Proper antiphons in polyphony.[108] For the latter, the *coro* might have turned to substitute texts; for Marian feasts, pieces like the five settings in Nicola Vicentino's *Moteta cum quinque vocibus* (Milan: Ponzio, 1571).[109] Curial interrogation revealed that the three young nuns often sang together, either in the cloister or in Bascapè's cell; the vicar was clearly concerned by the latter practice. They also sang in the refectory, possibly as part of after-meals recreation, although most of their colleagues showed solidarity by absolving them of any direct suspicion of having sung the *bergamasche* in public.[110] The musicians themselves were extremely defensive in their accounts:[111]

Asked, she responded: I have the organist's duty of singing and playing . . . in my cell I sing sometimes with keyboard accompaniment . . . and I sing only sacred motets, and I know how to intabulate them, and sometimes I sing with the nuns in my cell to rehearse what is to be sung.

In polyphony I sing only sacred pieces; I never sang with Suor Paola Giustina except in church, and in the refectory or the washing-room, and outside church sometimes with Suor Laura Bezona, Suor Prospera Corona, and Suor Claudia Sulpitia . . . I heard that some *canti alla bergamasca* were

[108] Despite their taste for Lassus, the Humiliate would have had to wait for an Italian edition of his early and popular *alternatim* Magnificats *a 4*; the *Magnificat octo tonorum a 4* (Nuremberg, 1565; nos. 17–24 in the modern edition, ed. J. Erb, *Magnificat 1–24* (Kassel, 1980), 245–87) were published in Venice by Vincenti in 1588; Tini's Milanese reprint followed in 1590. Collections such as Boyleau's *Modulationes in Magnificat a 4–6* (Milan: Pozzo, 1566) provided imitative *alternatim* settings in all eight tones.

[109] There seems to be no polyphonic setting of a Mary Magdalene motet in the admittedly sparse printed Milanese repertory from 1550 to 1575.

[110] 'Ho sentito alle volte sotto i claustri Prospera Vittoria et Prospera Corona et Paula Giustina et cantarono varie canzoni . . .' (testimony of Suor Constanzia de Biumi, *Esamina*, fo. 5ᵛ); 'Io non ho sentito alle sudette cantar il canto alla bergamasca i scontradura, potrebbero hauer cantato [underlined by the curial scribe:] nella camera dell'organista per imparare' (Suor Paola Ginepra, ibid., fo.11ʳ).

[111] The quotes are those of Bascapè, Cavenaghi, and Carpani, respectively: ibid, fos. 11ᵛ, 10ᵛ, and 14ʳ (Docs. 8f, 8g, and 8i).

found in Suor Paola Giustina['s cell], but I don't know how to speak Bergamasque.

I know a little polyphony . . . sometimes I help sing in church, and sometimes they rehearse in the room of Suor Laura, the *maestra di capella*—and I never sang in the garden . . . Sometimes they sang the sacred poems from the *Tesauro della Sapientia* that Messer Father Paolo gave me, and those pieces were sung by the above-mentioned Suor Prospera Corona the organist, and Suor Laura, and Suor Prospera Vittoria and other musicians.[112]

The music received or performed by the Humiliate straddles several categories: well-known *laude* (the *Tesauro della Sapientia*) written by a Bolognese nun, which saw the soul as Christ's bride; non-liturgical and liturgical polyphony; and fashionable secular genres.[113] The gift of the Lassus motets implies that the fifteen singers of polyphony would have been able to perform sophisticated music. Similarly, Bascapè's keyboard skills were apparent to contemporaries (not least the curial officials to whom they were a matter of concern). At S. Maria Maddalena, nuns employed precisely those styles and genres popular in the city as a whole.

A further point is the centrality of family ties. Suor Paola Giustina's brother was responsible (or at least was invoked as being responsible) for the shipment of the Lassus books to the cloister. Nuns' music would continue to represent an individual and individualizing link in the chain of prestige that connected cloistered women back to the patrician world whence they had come.

The differences between the two kinds of houses—richer and poorer, regular-subject versus episcopal-subject—are present in these first testimonies. Even among musical houses, other distinctions are apparent. If polyphony at S. Apollinare was dependent on one singer and one keyboard-player, then the more impressive forces—a sizeable choir (one of the largest in the city), *maestra di cappella*, organist, and *viole da gamba*—in residence at S. Maria Maddalena testify to better-developed skills and a wide repertory.[114]

---

[112] In the light of other nuns' references to her singing in the cloister, in the refectory, and in church, Paola Giustina's claims to know 'a little' polyphony were understated, to say the least.

[113] For the *Tesauro*'s editions and wide circulation in female houses, see Zardin, *Donna e religiosa*, 71 ff. The majority of the book was written by an anonymous Clarissan at Corpus Domini in Bologna; Zardin underlines the affective spirituality of the collection, with its references to the soul as the spouse of the suffering Christ.

[114] Carlo's 1575 order to 'vendere le Viole da Gamba' (ASDM XII, vol. 50, fo. 107ʳ) applied to S. Maria Maddalena and other unnamed houses. By comparison, during

The reasons for this sudden burst of musical life around 1570, especially among younger nuns like Suor Clementia and Angela Serafina at S. Apollinare and the three 'compagne' of S. Maria Maddalena, are clear from the contemporary evidence: the explosion in the houses' population, the upsurge in polyphony among monastic institutions male and female in northern Italy, the general democratization of musical literacy in Europe as a whole at this time, and a wave of popular religious devotion. But if this chapter has concentrated on the patrician background, then the curial visits point to the other central factor: the reforms and discipline which Carlo Borromeo, acting on his own changing interpretation of the Tridentine decrees, attempted to apply to nuns. The future saint's efforts would also establish the leading role of the archbishop in the regulation or promotion of claustral polyphony, and it is to the distinctly different policies and philosophies of Carlo and of Federigo Borromeo that we turn.

Boyleau's last tenure as *maestro* at the Duomo (1573–5), the *cappella* consisted of thirteen adult singers and six boys (G. de Florentiis and G. N. Vessia, *Sei secoli di musica nel Duomo di Milano* (Milan, 1986), 277 ff.).

3

From Social Disciplining to Spiritual Recreation

◇

Però mi è piaciuto estremamente, che vedo in una vostra [let-
tera], che il giorno della Pentecoste doppo cena andaste a
cantare, et a sonare. Quanto faceste bene . . .

(Federigo Borromeo to Angela Confaloniera, c.1628)

To understand the evolution of Carlo Borromeo's actual policies and
their effects on music, it is almost misleading to begin with the decisions at Trent. The discussion of male and female monastic life was
hurried through during Session XXV, almost at the end of the proceedings in 1563. But Giovanni Morone's ambitious plans for the
reform of the religious orders provoked passionate opposition, and
the vagueness of the final conciliar rules, including the prescriptions
for nuns, marked the sharp differences that continued even after the
Council's end.[1] The disagreement over sisters' liturgy was occasioned by a set of radical proposals, drafted by Gabriele Paleotti,
which would have excluded all music but chant.[2] This plan, often

---

[1] H. Jedin, *Der Abschluß des Trienter Konzils 1562/63: Ein Rückblick nach vier Jahrhunderten*
(Münster, 1963), 63–4.

[2] 'Divina autem officia ab eis [nuns] alta voce peragantur, non a mercenariis ad id con-
ductis, et in missae sacrificio ubi chorus quidem respondere solet, respondeant; partes vero
diaconi vel hypodiaconi in sacri Evangelii vel canonicae Epistolae aut alterius sacrae lectionis recitatione non usurpent. Vocis modulatione atque inflexione aliove cantus artificio,
quod figuratum vel organicum appellatur, tam in choro quam alibi abstineant'; from the
'Decretum de reformatione monialium, exhibitum examinandum patribus die 20. novem-
bris 1563', in S. Ehses (ed.), *Concilii Tridentini Actorum, Pars Sexta (17. Sept. 1562–4.Dec. 1563)*
(Freiburg im Breisgau, 1924), no. 357, 1040–4. The key word here is 'exhibitum', not
'approbatum'. The last sentence is remarkably imprecise: the 'modulation or inflection of
the voice' could also have excluded plainchant. More likely it simply referred to ornamentation or chromatic alteration of chant.

considered as the conciliar banning of female monastic polyphony, was strongly opposed and eventually deferred in the discussions; the final decree approved at the last minute (3–4 December 1563) avoided any mention of the issue, leaving it to local diocesan bodies.[3] Thus there was no Tridentine policy on nuns' music-making; this, like other points of liturgy (and music), was up to local decisions. It is telling, however, that Carlo Borromeo had copies of his friend Paleotti's proposals prepared for Milanese use, even though they had been dropped from the final decisions.[4]

The attempted reorganization of claustral life in Milan thus depended on the bishop.[5] The Milanese Provincial Council I of 1565, for whose convocation Carlo barely managed to arrive, outlined an initial programme of reform, prepared largely by his vicar Nicolò Ormaneto. Pre-Tridentine efforts, partially stemming from Matteo Giberti (the erstwhile bishop of Verona), formed the background for Ormaneto's decrees.[6] Another Veronese cleric, Alberto Lino, had been entrusted with the initial visitations and reforms in female houses, documented in a series of Lino's letters to Carlo from the summer of 1565, in which music was touched on only once.[7] The uncertainty with which Lino approached the two central questions—the importation of male music teachers into female houses, and the broader issue of whether nuns should be permitted organ-playing on principle—was evident in his letter of 1 August 1565 to Borromeo (App. A, Doc. 3):

---

[3] The idea that the Council banned nuns' polyphony stems from mistaking the presentation of Paleotti's proposals as their actual adoption (they do not figure among the items voted on 3–4 Dec.).

[4] ASDM XII, vol. 51, fasc. 1 includes local copies of this and other sections of Paleotti's proposals.

[5] *Mutatis mutandis*, this idea applies in a more general sense to the broad Tridentine decrees on music in general; local implementation—or ignoring—of the Council's precepts would be more important than a conscious effort on the part of composers to adopt a 'post-conciliar' style.

[6] E. Cattaneo, 'Influenze veronesi sulla legislazione di San Carlo Borromeo', in *Problemi di vita religiosa nel Cinquecento* (Padua, 1960), 123–66; Baernstein, 'The Counter-Reformation Convent', 122–8.

[7] BA, F. 36 *inf.*, largely transcribed in Cattaneo, 'Influenze'; my citations are from the manuscript. Although later opinion credited Carlo with the reform of egregiously dissolute female monasteries, Lino actually found few disorders among nuns; ibid. 134. The apostolic administrator Ferragata had considered only four monasteries to need reform during his 1562 visitations (C. Marcora, 'La chiesa milanese nel decennio 1550–1560', *MSDM* 7 (1961), 254–501 at 372).

I believe Your Excellency knows that almost all the nuns' monasteries have organs inside their church, which are played by one or more of them. Now the nuns educate some girls [the *educande*] to continue this task, and teach them what they know, but cannot provide them the needed perfection. So seeking for this purpose a [male] organist of greater skill and experience than their own, they have asked us to grant them this right, provided however that the organist remain in the exterior parlour, and the [student] nun in the interior one with trustworthy companions; each would have a personal clavichord, with which the organist will teach and the student learn. This right has not yet been granted them, since I first wanted to know Your Excellency's opinion. But to us it seems necessary either to prohibit completely their use of organs (Your Excellency can imagine for yourself how much tumult would result) or to permit nuns a means to use them. But certainly one could choose three or four organists, among the most esteemed and elderly in the city; such a permit could be given to these men only, if Your Lordship were so inclined.[8]

Lino's primary concern was to regulate the access of male music teachers to the monasteries, while avoiding the 'strepito' that an outright ban would cause. Carlo's response of 11 August 1565 (App. A, Doc. 4) gave testimony to his relatively open policy on nuns' music-making, at least at this stage, and to his awareness of polyphony's support among the patriciate:

Any attempt to take organs away from nuns would certainly occasion much tumult, and, even if it could be done easily, I do not know if it would be very expedient; since some good result could also be obtained from this [Lino's proposal], such as [nuns'] avoiding boredom, and also promoting devotion in their souls. Since the nuns cannot teach each other with the requisite skill, and if more able teachers are necessary, I consider the expedient that you propose to be quite good: that three or four organists of mature age and blameless life be selected, and to them alone there be given this right to teach nuns. And as to how this is to be carried out so as to be done with the necessary probity [*onestà*], and with as little danger as possible—that I leave to your judgement.[9]

The archbishop had essentially practical concerns at this stage; at stake were measures to ensure that morally reliable teachers would be provided. Polyphonic singing, liturgical or recreational, was not at issue, since Carlo wished to take advantage of the devotional stim-

----

[8] BA, F. 36 *inf.*, fo. 339^r, also Cattaneo, 'Influenze', 152–3.

[9] BA, F. 36 *inf.*, fo. 354^v–355^r. My thanks to Renée Baernstein for pointing out the existence of this letter.

ulus to the urban population provided by nuns' singing.[10] Any attempt to rescind even organ-playing would result in major turmoil in the monasteries, in which sisters would rely upon their families' backing against episcopal authority; and the use of keyboards, at least, was widespread in the female houses of the city. The centrality of organ-playing in the discussion reflected the need to intabulate lower voices of polyphonic pieces, as at S. Apollinare and S. Maria Maddalena. Possibly the requests for visiting teachers were meant simply to codify a long-standing practice in view of an arriving reformer, or perhaps sisters were actively seeking to improve the level of playing in their institutions.[11] Carlo's acceptance of the *licenza* was confirmed by the orders of Provincial Council I for nuns, written by Lino (App. A, Doc. 5). These treated the questions of male music teachers and music in the *parlatori*. Organ-playing, or sisters' right to sing polyphony in the interior churches or in their cloisters, did not appear further in these decrees.

A document that did not mention music was more vital to polyphonic practice than any conciliar decree. This was Pius V's apostolic constitution *Circa pastoralis* of 29 May 1566, which imposed (or reimposed) *clausura* on all female monasteries in the Catholic world, regardless of both their adherence to a given Rule and their previous status. Numerous religious orders throughout Italy again protested bitterly, and in Milan, Borromeo's campaign for strict claustration would lead him into a head-on clash with the urban patriciate. The physical enclosure of nuns inside *clausura* would occupy Milanese prelates for the next two centuries. And an increasingly important part of the conflict would take place precisely over the music of nuns within those walls.

The passage by a council, Tridentine or provincial, of decrees hardly ensured that such general rules would be implemented, or even known in the diocese's monasteries.[12] Borromeo's first steps

---

[10] The reference seems to be to liturgical song, in the light of the phrase 'di qui cavar qualche buon frutto, come di fuggir talvolta l'otio, et ancho di eccitar divotione', which seems more applicable to singing than to organ-playing (cf. also the Roman constitution cited below).

[11] Lino's letter was apparently the first mention of visiting organ teachers in monasteries. Other musical reasons include the growth of an independent organ repertory in northern Italy around 1550, and the upsurge in musical literacy among the urban patrician and merchant classes, the presumptive audience of the Venetian musical presses, and a group whose daughters were beginning to fill the north Italian houses.

[12] Thus the broad conclusions of Bowers ('The Emergence') and Stefani ('Sirene'), both of whom generalize to rather different ends on the basis of the printed synodal decrees, are

were literary: he had the conciliar decisions (as noted, with the addition of Paleotti's proposals) for nuns translated into Italian in 1565–6.[13] He also had a copy made of the 1534 rules of the Roman *convertite* of S. Maria Maddalena, which actually prescribed the singing of Matins, Terce, Sext, and Compline on Sundays and feasts 'so that the laity may be moved to devotion'.[14] Music, public or private, was hardly noticed in the first visitations (1566–70), such as the 1569 instructions for S. Maria in Valle.[15]

The implementation of the archbishop's overall plans, however, would entail revolutionary intervention over almost every aspect of nuns' daily life.[16] The Milanese curial records from the late 1560s on contain orders for the walling up of gates, parlours, and double churches; restricting the access of laity, even nuns' families, and clergy to monasteries; specifying the conditions for providing food and other supplies through the *ruota*, a revolving wheel at the monastery's gate; regulating confessors' visits (and providing elderly priests for this function); and forbidding nuns from leaving the institution except under conditions of fire or war—in a word, the imposition of unprecedentedly strict *clausura* on institutions which had not observed such drastic enclosure, in some cases for centuries.[17]

open to question. On Borromeo's policy shifts in 1565–6, see Baernstein, 'The Counter-Reformation Convent', 122–8.

[13] On the translations, see Zardin, *Donna e religiosa*, 50.

[14] 'acciò li secolari si movino a divotione'; the Roman rules are in ASDM XII, vol. 50, fos. 19 ff. A 1536 addendum restricted the sung daily Office to duplex feasts, while only Terce and Vespers had to be sung on Sundays and semiduplex feasts, the others left to the judgement of the abbess (ibid., fo. 26ʳ).

[15] 'In prima vi comandiamo che la chiesa sia bene offitiata et che ogni festa si canti le solite hore et il vespro et le altre hore in dispositione della madre abadessa', [Vicar-General's] 'Istruzioni', ASDM XII, vol. 93, fasc. 1. The similarity to the Roman constitution, notably the decision of the abbess about singing the minor Hours, is striking. Most visitations from this decade eschewed any mention of music (ASDM XII, vol. 62, fasc. 1: S. Agostino, undated; vol. 70, fasc. 1: S. Caterina in Chiusa, 1576; and vol. 83, fasc. 1: S. Margarita, 1567).

[16] In this period, the prelate would also seek to divide the laity in the Duomo by gender through the erection of separate entranceways for men and women, along with walls inside the nave; Wright, *The Counter-Reformation*, 231–2. On the danger that the sight of women presented for males according to Carlo, and its theological basis, see W. de Boer, 'Sinews of Discipline: The Uses of Confession in Counter-Reformation Milan' (Ph.D. diss., Erasmus Universiteit Rotterdam, 1994), ch. 4.

[17] For the sections of Carlo's 1577 *Instructiones ad fabricandas ecclesias* devoted to the proper architectural construction of female houses (including the allowable limits of windows and grates as measured in ecclesiastical cubits) so as to assure *clausura*, see E. C. Voelker, 'Charles Borromeo's *Instructiones fabricae et supellectilis ecclesiasticae*, 1577: A Translation with Commentary and Analysis' (Ph.D. diss., Syracuse University, 1977), 389–449. The problem

Internally, the orders mandated the annual election of abbesses (an attempt to limit family control over houses); limited nuns' personal property (including their affective and economic ownership of chickens and dogs); and attempted to find protectors loyal to the archbishop, not to the families accustomed to having influence over houses.[18]

Carlo's initial idea had been the regulation of the outside world's intrusion in the person of music teachers; this further and unforeseen stage of attempted control would entail both episcopal prohibition of external visitors and curial discouragement of internal musical activities whether or not they were directed to an outside audience. The next step was the visitations to extra-urban houses in the diocese.[19] Borromeo took a number of steps in order to systematize his regulation, including instituting the post of *vicario delle monache*, a curial official whose duty was to maintain discipline among nuns. Provincial Council II of 1569, which bore more of Borromeo's personal stamp, revoked the *licenza* provision, adding Carlo's concern to regulate male clerics' educational visits to female monasteries (App. A, Doc. 6).

The first recorded inspection in which music played an important role, one that marked the sea change that had occurred in Borromeo's policy, was that of 1571 to S. Apollinare, where 'Messer Giovanni Antonio' had overstayed the one-year limit of his *licenza*.[20] Carlo's discipline of an institution normally subject to regulars was a clear test of strength between archbishop and urban patriciate. The visitation followed Carlo's normal procedure, to become standard for his successors over the next two centuries. The curial officials asked questions and took depositions from individual nuns, seeking infractions of the new regulations; they later issued orders for the

with the plans for monastic architecture was that most Milanese monasteries had already been built, and it was more difficult to wall up existing structures. The two nexus of interaction with the outside world—the double church and the parlours—would be subjected to especially strict regulation; they were also the major spaces for nuns' music-making. By 1570 Carlo's friend Gabriele Paleotti had also become rigid in his opposition to female monastic polyphony.

[18] Such instructions are in ASDM, Carteggio Ufficiale, vol. 125, no. 16.

[19] Papal edicts giving Carlo the right to visit monasteries, regardless of jurisdiction, are preserved in ASDM XII, vol. 48.

[20] If the organist were indeed Brena (see Ch. 2 n. 94), it would be striking that such a figure, with far more ties to the patriciate than to Carlo's reform, would have been able to obtain a *licenza*, which Lino and Carlo had envisioned in 1565 as being restricted to the three or four 'più approbati' organists in the city.

house. The exhaustive questioning of the Clarissans, besides investigating overly familiar relations with friars and other *carissimi*, focused on the *licenza* for Giovanni Antonio, whether the nuns had physically seen or possessed it, and even whether it had been forged. A key issue was Suor Angela Serafina's giving meals to the organist, a practice linked to women's control over food resources, and one that Carlo had outlawed. The sharp interrogation also featured questions put to the organist himself, who testified that he had taught Suor Clementina to sing 'alla ferrada', at the grate of the parlour, in line with what was newly permissible, and that his lessons included some kind of written instructions or examples (App. A, Doc. 7a–d).

Borromeo's twenty-nine punitive orders, issued in March, immediately raised the level of punishment.[21] Access by anyone, male or female, without a *licenza*, was forbidden; visits in the parlours were restricted; walls at the gate and in the church were ordered raised and sealed, and duties inside the walls toughened. Carlo's reactions to the musical irregularities are contained among the penances ordered (in a separate document) for some eighteen sisters, more than a quarter of the nuns (App. A, Doc. 7d):

Suor Angela Serafina is to be without her veil [i.e. with a bare shaven head] for three months. She is relieved of the organist's duties, nor may she return to this position for six years. The large harpsichord is not to be kept in her room, but somewhere else in the house; nor can she play it or any other keyboard, nor sing polyphony for three years. And every Wednesday for six months she is to eat on the floor of the refectory, and ask forgiveness for the disturbance she caused, and for the scandal of having fed the organist inside the monastery. Nor may she go to the parlour for three months. . . . For her frequent perjury during this visitation, Suor Clementia is to perform the same penance as Suor Bianca Veronica and Suor Laura Benedetta.[22]

The Clarissans were chastised on several points, not simply infractions of the rules on music. The sheer social humiliation of the punishments, by no means the worst that Carlo would impose for other, more serious 'offences', was designed to instil fear and the loss of personal dignity among the young inhabitants of S. Apollinare. This visit

[21] ASDM XII, vol. 64; also in Sevesi, 'Il monastero', 81–5.

[22] ASDM XII, vol. 64, fo. 210ʳ; first published in Sevesi, 'Il monastero', 85 ff. Suor Clementia was punished not for her singing lessons, but for having lied to the curial officials ('Suor Clementia, per molti giuramenti falsi, fatti nella occasione della presente visita . . . faccia la medesima penitenza, che si è ordinata a Suor Bianca Veronica et Suor Laura Benedetta', ibid.)

clearly signalled Carlo's intent to answer any violation of the new orders, even the overstaying of a *licenza*, by penance that targeted the most fundamental symbols of sisters' identity. In the face of his authority, the Clarissans were apparently not able to rely on their families' support to contest the discipline.

But Borromeo's strictures at one house did not change matters elsewhere; S. Maria Maddalena al Cerchio represented the clearest case. Previous curial visits in 1568 and 1572 had not succeeded in imposing the new ideas of discipline, and Arese's February–March 1575 interrogations proved to be only the first of three that year.[23] The hardening of Borromeo's policy is evident from the severe punishment meted out to Prospera Bascapè and her companions for possessing secular music. In this case, the vicar determined, rightly or wrongly, that the two 'canti alla bergamasca' could only have been sent, not in a book of Lassus motets presented by Paola Giustina's brother, but by the nearby male Cistercians of S. Ambrogio, a clear proof of illicit relations between nuns and monks: 'some songs were found that they had intabulated, [with] apparently the most shameful words, and the nuns sang these among themselves; one assumes they were sent by friars'.[24] Bascapè and her two friends were deprived of the normal privileges of *professe*; furthermore, they were not to sing *canto figurato* for a period of six years (App. A, Doc. 8k):

Suor Prospera Vittoria Cavenaghi, and Suor Prospera Corona Bascapè, and Suor Paola Giustina Campana are to be deprived of active and passive voice, of [the right to go to] the gate, the pass-through, and the parlour, [the right] to sing polyphony for six years. Every Friday for a year, they are to voice their guilt in the refectory, and say the psalm *Miserere mei Deus* on their knees in the middle of the refectory.[25]

The sheer shame to which the nuns would have been subjected by such measures was clearly intended to deter others. But the punishments, however much they might have been intended to humiliate the *compagne*, had little effect; in Arese's words several months later,

---

[23] The earlier visits are recorded in ASDM XII, vol. 97, fasc. 1; the visit of 26 Apr. is in fasc. 6 and the August materials are in fasc. 3; the case is summarized in Zardin, *Donna e religiosa*.

[24] 'Furono trovati certi *canti che* haueuano in intauolatura, le più dishoneste parole si dicono, et le monache cantauano cioe le stesse canzone tra loro, et si tiene fosser mandate da frati', ASDM XII, vol. 97, fasc. 1.

[25] Ibid., fasc. 2, fos. 16 ff.; this represents a doubling of the penance given Suor Angela Serafina at S. Apollinare.

'various orders for obedience were given, but no one knows how to make them obey; some were given penance . . . but little did it help'.[26] Although the vicar had sought to ban singing, the house's name-day four months after the February visit (22 July), celebrated at S. Maria Maddalena as a duplex sanctoral feast (like that of an apostle, as which the penitent saint was treated in Christian legend), occasioned yet another suspect remedy for the lack of polyphony:[27]

Indeed, after last Easter a young girl called Bradamante who knows how to play the organ was in the monastery; as far as I knew, she was taken inside the house secretly and went up on the organ [loft] to play.[28]

On St Mary Magdalene's feast-day, Bradamante was in my cell to play [keyboard], and she also went up to the organ, but I didn't want to let her play because she did it so badly.[29]

Bradamante's poor performances evoked criticism and further internal dissension from the nuns, expressed to Arese during his later visits. In addition, the funeral Office of summer 1575 for Suor Clementia occasioned the Humiliate to call on external musicians, possibly the ducal chapel, to perform in the *chiesa esteriore*.[30]

Arese's reaction—his attempt of 12 August literally to shut the door of the monastery under pain of excommunication—resulted in a physical counter-attack, with 'parole insolite', on the part of some two-thirds of S. Maria Maddalena's inhabitants, in the face of which the vicar was forced to flee.[31] The resulting criminal trial which Arese opened on 26 August led to graver punishments: the keys to

---

[26] 'Si sono fatti diuersi ordini per obedire, ma non si sanno far obedire, se ne sono penitentiate alcune . . . ma poco si è giovato', ibid, fasc. 2.

[27] The 1621 *Breviarium Romanum Humiliatorum* (Pavia: G. B. Robleo) listed this feast as 'duplex' in its calendar and at p. 355; by 1751, the revised Humiliate breviary would add the dedication of the church at S. Maria Maddalena the next day and its Octave (*Breviarium ad usum monialium ordinis Humiliatorum* (Milan: G. Marelli, 1751)).

[28] 'è vero che dopo pasqua passata è stata nel monastero una giovane appellata Bradamante che sa sonar l'organo et fu condotta per quanto intesi dentro il monastero secretamente et andò su l'organo a sonare': testimony of 26 Aug. of Anna Maria Bascapè, ASDM XII, vol. 97, fasc. 3, fo. 3ʳ.

[29] 'Che la festa della madalena la Bradamante stesse in mia cella a sonare, et vene anche su l'organo ma non la volsi lasciar sonare perche sonava male': testimony of Prospera Bascapè, ibid., fo. 2ᵛ.

[30] 'Per S. Clementia si sono fatti tre ofitij da morti et vi era musica alle messe et il conuento sin qui è solito far far musica': testimony of Suor Cassandra, ibid., fo. 13ʳ.

[31] The vicar's anger at and attempted subjugation of the nuns are in his letters to Carlo, BA F. 133 *inf.*, fos. 393 (13 Aug.), 423 (18 Aug.), and 468 (27 Aug.). For a similar battle, including nuns' physical counter-attacks, at S. Cristina in Bologna in the 1620s, see Monson, *Disembodied Voices*, chs. 7–9.

the *chiesa esteriore* and to the parlours were taken away, thus effectively isolating nuns from the outside world, at least until the plague of the next year sapped the curial efforts. In his efforts, Arese was helped by the seemingly endless willingness of some of the Humiliate, such as Suor Flaminia de Tolentino, to inform on their colleagues.[32] But since music had not figured directly in the August events, no further musical restrictions seem to have been placed on the Humiliate.

Incidents like these could only have stiffened Carlo's resolve to crack down on polyphony. The association of music with illicit relations at S. Maria Maddalena testified to a broader pattern among the writings of diocesan officials that linked secular music to the corruption of morals in female houses. The documents from the 1576 inspection by Ragazzoni detailed irregular feasts and song at several houses, such as S. Agnese (App. A, Docs. 9–10). Carlo sought to implement and broaden his reforms at all the diocesan monasteries, with varying degrees of success. Provincial Council IV of 1576 formally revoked the *licenza* privilege for music teachers. Further testimony to Borromeo's stiffening attitude can be gleaned from curial notes of the late 1570s, such as instructions to eliminate polyphony from the external churches of monasteries subject to regulars (App. A, Doc. 12, referring to the Lateran Canonesses at S. Maria Annunciata).

The final push was the apocalyptic experience of the plague year 1576, which sent Carlo on a public crusade against 'frivolity', including music, theatre, and dance in all Milan; this campaign led the prelate into even sharper conflict with the city. One such case, discussed by Carlo in a letter to his vicar general Cesare Speciano, concerned the governor's musicians and their performance in the exterior church of S. Margarita (App. A, Doc. 11). The tradition of bringing the ducal chapel to the *chiese esteriori* for funerals of nuns or other patricians, or in some cases for titular sanctoral feasts, had begun at S. Maria Maddalena al Cerchio. It would last into the Settecento.

This letter marks Carlo's attempt to keep the outside musical world from any contact with nuns, and also testifies to his concern with illicit relations between musicians and nuns. It further highlights music's role as a ducal privilege and symbol of patrician

---

[32] She was the first called in the trial (ASDM XII, vol. 97, fos. 1^r–2^r), and her testimony incriminated several of her colleagues, among them Bascapè.

authority—in this case, that of the governor—in opposition to episcopal power; Carlo was clearly worried about the precedent set by
the projection of non-episcopal order into the city's churches. By the
end of the 1570s Carlo's curia returned to Lino's first choice of 1565
(App. A, Doc. 13):

And we object to the vanity which the *velate* sometimes have in playing
[keyboard] . . . Organ-playing at the houses of more reformed nuns is not
considered so necessary, so that up till now they [the nuns] have not wanted
to build organs in their churches; and the organists and singers of
polyphony are often the least disciplined and least spiritual.[33]

Certainly the strictest of Carlo's female monastic foundations, the
Capuchins at S. Prassede, organized under his patronage in 1578,
eschewed polyphony altogether.[34] And the problems of having
musically talented nuns at Borromeo's model project of S. Paolo, in
the light of the absence of an organ, were scrupulously noted by the
curia in a 1578 visitation.[35]

   To the end of his life, Borromeo targeted the houses subject to
regulars, both Benedictine and mendicant. A twelve-point memorandum written to Pope Gregory XIII in 1582 listed music among
items of 'secular' behaviour that, for Carlo, justified the subjection of
all female houses to episcopal authority:

The differences seen in the monasteries [subject] to regulars and the others, with regard to music-making, lavish festival decor, presents, receiving,
and many other licentious practices, which deeply offend the laity; all this

---

[33] Letter signed 'vicario delle monache', ASDM XII, vol. 48, fo. 65ʳ, in a discussion of
Borromeo's 1578 refusal of a dowry dispensation for Ippolita Calvi, to be admitted to S.
Maria Maddalena as organist. The vicar (probably still Arese) noted the fact that there were
already two organists in the house, one of whom was presumably Bascapè. The reference
to the more reformed nuns who did not wish to have an organ is a clear allusion to the
Angeliche of S. Paolo; around this time, Arese wanted organists to be *converse*, not *professe*
(Baernstein, 'The Counter-Reformation Convent', 164 ff.).

[34] 'Somario ò vero Relatione di quanto Giornalmente si fà, et s'osserva nel Monastero
delle R. R. Madri, & suore Capuccine di S.ta Prassede in Porta orientale di Milano 1660',
ASDM XII, vol. 125, fo. 3ᵛ, all the more remarkable in an era when polyphony was practised at a wide range of Milanese houses.

[35] 'Sono delle novitie che hanno un clavichordio nella sua cella da sonare per passatempo
specialmente per le puttine secolari, non facendo bisogno per non haver noi organo' (ASDM
XII, vol. 108, fasc. 9). The curial official had used this visit to complain about musical nuns
in general: 'quelle della musica sono più desinate et sarebbe meglio attender più al spirito'
(ibid.).

will be ended by introducing uniform discipline in those matters not covered by the [monastic] Rule.[36]

The pope was unconvinced of the need for what would have been an all-out battle with the patriciate, and Carlo's memorandum went unheeded. Such efforts, initiated by curial officials, did not stop with Borromeo's death.[37] But in the light of strong urban support for nuns' music, one must wonder which 'popolo' was being gravely offended by polyphony in the cloisters.

Although not without parallel in the strictures of other Italian prelates (for example, the Paleotti in Bologna), the unique trait of Carlo's policy was the consistency and intensity with which he pursued this goal and the explicit categorization of unapproved female (and only female) monastic music-making as sin, even as mortal sin. A study of Borromeo's music policy as a whole reveals that, at least until 1576, he was far from anti-musical; he was involved in the Tridentine discussions on propriety in sacred music, received several musical dedications himself, and in the 1570s actively recruited singers and *maestri di cappella* who fitted his rules of moral conduct.[38] But the special—and specially restricted—status of nuns called forth an individual policy on their music, especially after 1576.

How should we understand this pattern? The most striking aspect is its discipline of previously unregulated behaviour, and its

[36] 'La difformità che si uede nelli luoghi, tra i monasterii de frati e gl'altri, quanto alle musiche, adobbi, presenti, dar audientia, et molte altre cose licentiose, ch'offendono grandemente il popolo, il che si leverà introducendosi disciplina uniforme nelle cose che non repugnano alla regola': from 'Alcune ragioni per le quali si deve a gl'ordinarij la sopra intelligentia a tutti li monasterii di monache', dated 25 Nov. 1582, BA, F. 63 *inf.*, fo. 307ʳ, cited first in V. Cattana, 'San Carlo Borromeo e i monaci benedettini: Prime ricerche sull'epistolario carolino', *RSCA* 14 (1985), 111–46, which also notes (p. 114) Carlo's mistrust of the Cassinese superiors beginning with the 1568 visitation of the Monastero Maggiore (whose records in ASDM XII, vol. 101, do not, however, mention music). Cf. the 'Ricordi per il buon governo de Monasterii de Monache sottoposti ai Regolari nella Diocesi': 'Non si canti canto figurato ne si faccia musica nella chiesa esteriore delli Monasterij de Monache per qualsi voglia Caso . . .' (ASDM XII, vol. 50, fos. 66 ff.).

[37] For efforts in 1588–9 to detach S. Radegonda from the Cassinese, and the tumult thereby occasioned, see ASDM, Carteggio Ufficiale, vol. 70. These attempts were successfully resisted by the nuns' families ('si movessero a infiammare li loro [the nuns'] parenti', unsigned letter to Milan, ibid.).

[38] In 1566 Carlo had received Boyleau's dedication (which mentioned no reform plans, but rather ancient Greek theory of the modes' moral influence) of the Magnificats cited above; he had also been in touch with Munich concerning the recruitment of singers. For Pontio's encounters as *maestro* with Borromeo's puritanical phases, see R. E. Murray, 'The Voice of the Composer: Theory and Practice in the Works of Pietro Pontio' (Ph.D. diss., University of North Texas, 1989).

redefinition of formerly private realms as social. In light of the pan-European nature of such phenomena, Prodi suggested the concept of *disciplinamento sociale (Sozialdisziplinierung)* as the intellectual basis of Carlo's reform efforts, in the context of early modern expansion of the realm of the social.[39] The idea of social disciplining has not hitherto been extended to the regulation of musical behaviour in any context. But Borromeo's later policy, with its striving for public 'disciplina uniforme' and its explicit (and theologically dubious) linkage of specific forms of nuns' music to sin, is well illuminated by this concept.[40] Carlo was concerned to restrict and even, in the course of the 1570s, to outlaw the social aspects of nuns' polyphony: intercourse (in every sense) with male teachers; the public character of nuns' musical services; the singing of secular (i.e. patrician) music in the parlours; and the playing of instruments.

Borromeo's efforts were, perhaps unwittingly, hampered by the fact that his enforced isolation of nuns was not matched by replacement duties inside the cloister; the prelate had only large quantities of 'orazione mentale' to recommend to *professe* (who, after all, had the *converse* to perform menial tasks) in place of their previous public role. Carlo's efforts to banish music, one of the few remaining activities left to sisters, did not help. In the light of previous reform efforts by the patriciate and regulars, and the relatively disciplined state of Milanese female houses even before 1565, the programme of enclosure is best seen as political and cultural, not pastorally necessary, in its motivation.

[39] P. Prodi, 'Riforma interiore e disciplinamento sociale in San Carlo Borromeo', *Intersezioni*, 5 (1985), 273–85. As he noted ('Controriforma e/o riforma cattolica', 235), this concept was taken from Gerhard Oestreich (cf. W. Schulze, 'Gerhard Oestreichs Begriff 'Sozialdisziplinierung' in der frühen Neuzeit', *Zeitschrift für historische Forschung*, 14 (1987), 265–302). Although the English translation has been 'social discipline', both the German and Italian terms emphasize the processual nature of the phenomenon, and I have therefore used the more accurate 'social disciplining'.

[40] Although Carlo was generally against the participation of any religious, male or female, in secular music or theatre, the categorization of mortal sin is limited to the strictures on nuns' consorting with musicians and possible dangers to chastity resulting therefrom. In general, the restrictions on male religious would be neither as far-reaching nor as grave as those applied to nuns in Carlo's tenure. In theological terms, there is no basis in the Tridentine decrees (or in the writings of any contemporary theologians) for the designation of the singing of secular music by nuns as a mortal sin, the gravest possible offence that any Catholic could commit; Borromeo seems to have raised a disciplinary measure to a commandment. Even the visitations of his former vicar Speciano to the female houses of Cremona between 1599 and 1606 would largely refrain from regulating nuns' music (cf. Marcocchi, *La riforma dei monasteri femminili, passim*).

The resistance met by Borromeo's plans should recall the often forgotten fact that he was not always popular, either in Milan or at the Roman Curia, on account of his single-minded (more accurately, monomaniacal) dedication to his own strict interpretation of Trent.[41] It is not surprising that the tenure of his immediate (and chosen) successor, Gaspare Visconti, should have been marked by a drastic relaxation of the post-1576 norms. Nowhere is this clearer than in the case of nuns' music. Most striking are the reports at the institutions that Carlo had envisaged as models.

In 1587 the Roman Congregatio super Regulares rejected a request from S. Paolo for a funeral in the exterior church with male musicians, possibly the ducal ensemble.[42] By 1589 this house had also contracted for an organ to be built, despite the Angeliche's declaration to Carlo a decade earlier that there was no keyboard in the church.[43] Even more telling was a 1593 letter from the vicar-general prohibiting the access of male music teachers to the newly founded model Ursuline house, S. Cristina—precisely the offence chastised so severely at S. Apollinare (App. A, Doc. 14), and one which must have been so common as to provoke the order.[44] Musical life also revived at another 'problem' foundation, S. Agnese.[45] Even at S. Maria Maddalena al Cerchio, the visitations of the 1580s eschewed

---

[41] Certeau, 'Carlo Borromeo', *DBI* and J. B. Tomaro, 'San Carlo Borromeo and the Implementation of the Council of Trent', in J. Headley and Tomaro (eds.), *San Carlo Borromeo: Catholic Reform and Ecclesiastical Politics in the Second Half of the Sixteenth Century* (Washington, DC, 1988), 67–84.

[42] Letter of 31 Apr. 1587 from Ludovico Audoeno to Bernardino Morra, the Milanese vicar-general, ASDM, CU, vol. 126, no. 14.

[43] See above, n. 35. The contract of 1 June 1589 with G. B. Suardo for an organ in the *chiesa interiore* is in ASM, Notarile 19131, Ippolito Gambara. My thanks to Renée Baernstein for this document.

[44] The rather more fraternal tone of this note, compared with Carlo's orders, should also be noted. The Ursulines were the only order in Milan not subject to *clausura* (and hence to the restrictions on music), and this note extended the provisions of Provincial Council IV to them. Yet they were specially close to Carlo: he promoted their pedagogical mission vigorously, and took special interest in their conventual life. S. Cristina had been founded in 1584 at the end of his tenure.

[45] A 1580 report noted that 'Sono tre le quali sonano l'organo, et sono distribuite a sonar una volta *per* una conforme ad una lista che si fa ogni anno con la superiora' (ASDM XII, vol. 59, fasc. 4); a 1596 list gave Suor Vittoria Febronia Figina as 'organista' (ibid., fasc. 4). A century and a half later, the visitation of 20 Nov. 1710 complained that 'Alle messe si cantano canzonette volgari, e di quelle moderne, *paucis mutatis*, che udonsi ne' Teatri; usando il Cembalo, e violoncello' (ibid.).

any mention of music; at some point, Bascapè also received a new Antegnati organ on which to play.[46]

The first musical dedication to Milanese nuns dates from this decade as well. Costanzo Antegnati's *Salmi à otto voci* (1592) was proffered to the composer's aunt and her companions at S. Vittore in Meda. Again, S. Vittore had been the target of a drastic but ultimately unsuccessful curial programme in the 1580s; the visitation orders for the decade contained long directions for the rewalling of all three monastic churches, the banishing of both instruments and books of polyphony brought by visitors, and the limitation on keyboard instruments, along with the standard formulas prohibiting male access to the parlours.[47] The curial records also document the existence of several other organists besides Claudia Antegnati inside claustral walls.[48] But Antegnati's public presentation of his Vespers flouted, in the most dramatic way possible, the rules against outside shipments of polyphony.

The post-Carlo years also saw the first referrals of requests to Rome for reductions in the *dote spirituale* of musically promising novices. From the outset, the less patrician and less famous Dominican and Franciscan institutions would submit the bulk of these, as a way of attracting poor girls capable of organ-playing or other skills. Approval of the petitions was by no means guaranteed: Rome was primarily concerned with the economic viability of monasteries as a means to limit their dependence on the patriciate. The dowries represented important income, and too many exemptions were undesirable; *dote* reductions were therefore permitted only when the monastery had enough financial resources to support its population, a factor that again tended to favour musical life in the more patrician institutions.

---

[46] This instrument figured in Costanzo's list of family organs (*L'arte Organica*, 5 ff.).

[47] Repeated orders from the 1570s, 1583, and 1585 are in ASDM XII, vol. 174, fasc. 1.

[48] '1583. Ordinationes Monasterii S. Victoris, Medae . . . Li Vanatini [violini?], che sono nel monasteri, si vendino, et si comprino delle Arpicorde sende per uso di quelle che sonano l'organo'. The orders of 13 Dec. 1585 mandated 'Che non si trovino libri di canto figurato ne istromenti di sonar siano come si uogliano' (both from ASDM XII, vol. 174, fasc. 1). The 1583 order seems to testify to the presence of multiple organists at the monastery, a point confirmed by Antegnati's dedication. The family would keep its ties to the house well into the Seicento; S. Vittore's chronicler noted a ten-day visit of 22–31 Aug. 1640 by Faustino and Girolamo Antegnati to tune all the many keyboard instruments: '[1640]: Il 22 Agosto entrarono nel Monastero li Signori Faustino e Girolamo Antegnati virtuosi bresciani, che accomodarono l'organo grande, siccome pure gli organi piccioli, con il regale, e con tutti li clavezini, terminarono la loro opera il giorno 31 del mese sudetto' (*Liber cronaca*, fo. 17ʳ).

Finally, Visconti's tenure witnessed the beginnings of two related phenomena to prove crucial later: the public renown of liturgical music in the *chiese interiori* of urban foundations, and the prominence of individual nun singers. Paolo Morigia's well-known description of music at 'quasi tutti i Monasteri di Monache' in an urban panegyric of 1595 (App. A, Doc. 16) considered polyphony as a well-established feature of these houses. Similarly, the fame of such individual virtuosas as Sessa began around this time.[49] Thus, the net result of this decade can only be seen as a marked return to pre-1576 disciplinary standards, with the added fillip of public fame for female monastic musicians. The dedications of music to nuns, the growing renown of their houses, and the evident laxness at even such model foundations as S. Paolo and S. Cristina all suggest that Carlo's drastic measures—in music and in daily life—did not long survive their author.

The spread of polyphony in the last decades of the Cinquecento seems parallel, if slightly posterior, to a wave of urban devotion channelled through female monasteries. This was most evident in the redecoration of monastic churches, including nuns' commissioning of such altar-pieces as Simone Peterzano's *Madonna and Child with Sts Justina of Padua, Catherine and Radegund* (*c*.1585), which would grace the *chiesa esteriore* at S. Radegonda (Fig. 3).[50] The emphasis on the patron(ess) saint or Marian iconography found in such paintings would echo in the themes of the early motet dedications to nuns; ultimately it reflected the devotional life of patrician families. Sanctoral cults mirrored and provided a public locus for the civic religion of aristocratic clans in early modern Italy. And the simultaneous appearance of new pictorial and musical expressions of sisters' piety testifies to the increasing 'spiritual capital', population, and general cultural level to be found around 1590 in the female houses.

If Carlo's project had become one of *disciplinamento sociale*, Federigo Borromeo's tenure was marked by the opposite: the awakening of individual expression in spirituality and in music.[51] On no group would this shift have more effect than on the two generations of nuns who witnessed his term of office. The practical

---

[49] The first printed tribute to her dates from 1599 (Erycius Puteanus, *Modulata Pallas*; cf. below, Ch. 5).

[50] Also published in E. Baccheschi, *I pittori bergamaschi: Il Cinquecento* (Bergamo, 1978), iv. 556.

[51] Prodi, *DBI*, and Jones, *Federico Borromeo*.

Fɪɢ. 3. Simone Peterzano, *Madonna and Child with Sts Justina of Padua, Catherine of Alexandria, and Radegund* (Milan, S. Maria della Passione; photo courtesy of Mary-Ann Winkelmes).

records—curial documents and episcopal visitations—testify to intermittent efforts in the pastoral care of nuns, although the chronology of the memoranda is uncertain, since Federigo's tenure was long and orders were not always dated. Most of the numerous *ragionamenti* (sermons) delivered to sisters at S. Marta, S. Maria del Lentasio, or S. Caterina in Brera are undated, as is much of the cardinal's voluminous correspondence with female religious. A number of the visitations and curial orders date from quite early on in his tenure, while his frequent letters to the Humiliate, in which music plays an important role, stem from the last decade of his life. Although Federigo seems to have supported nuns' music throughout, the more relaxed atmosphere after the 1619 concordat with the Spanish allowed for greater commitment to individuals.

The first evidence for the junior Borromeo's approach to female monastic music is negative: there is no record of the kind of punitive visitation, directed at musical life, that Carlo had carried out at S. Apollinare and S. Maria Maddalena al Cerchio. The major scandal of Federigo's era, the Leyva case at S. Margarita in Monza in 1608, did not result in the prohibition of polyphony at the house even though the house's organist, Candida Colomba Trotta, was centrally involved in the crimes.[52] Federigo preferred to exhort rather than to punish.[53]

But other curial documents testify to the high esteem in which the archbishop held nuns ('the most select portion of Christ's flock'), and to the fraternal spirit in which they were treated.[54] Some orders harked back to the special public and intercessory roles that sisters had played in the Quattrocento.[55] This revival of medieval forms of devotion would be typical of Seicento Milan, notable not least in the texts of its motet repertory. Federigo lavished great care on the spiritual life and physical well-being of nuns in the diocese; in addition, he had to provide for the growing influx of women entering monastic life.[56] Sometimes the documents testify to Federigo's actual encouragement of polyphony, even against his curia, as noted by an early biographer (App. A, Doc. 44):

---

[52] For the case, famous in a fictionalized version from Manzoni's *The Betrothed*, see Colombo, *Vita e processo* 410.

[53] The *Prattica Religiosa* written for nuns by Federigo's associate Aluigi Basso listed reasons to avoid the parlours, and contained chapters on spiritual progress (6) and on self-esteem (20) in religious life (ASDM XII, vol. 51). Nothing in the treatise mentions music.

[54] 'Essendo le Vergini a Dio consecrate la più illustre portione della greggia di Christo . . .' (from an undated curial decree on *clausura*, ASDM XII, vol. 49, fo. 19ʳ).

[55] A request from the archbishop for special prayers in all the female houses of the city, in order to assure the success of the first synod of his tenure, is preserved in ASDM XII, vol. 52, fasc. 3; no such order exists for the male houses. The sense of the female monasteries as part of the diocese's extraordinary spiritual capital grew noticeably during Federigo's tenure.

[56] Large sections of ASDM XII, vols. 48–52 are filled with orders on nuns; the printing of decrees for general distribution testifies to the numbers of houses and sisters involved.

In addition, [Federigo] wanted nuns to be of good cheer, and he permitted them to perform psalmody with musical ensembles, using both organs and even other musical instruments, as long as the limits of decorum were not transgressed. He said that, through these sacred arts, nuns could be kept far from the doors [of the monasteries] and from conversations with laity; he got annoyed when anyone tried to convince him that music should be prohibited to all nuns.[57]

Compared with Carlo's visitations, Federigo's 1606 orders for the observant Augustinians of S. Caterina in Chiusa exemplified the junior Borromeo's radically different approach to music in monastic life, one unique in post-Tridentine Italy (App. A, Doc. 23):

All the nuns, mindful of their duty to praise Divine Majesty in choir, are in the future to participate in the Divine Office according to the [monastic] Rule and the decrees on this matter made in previous visitations . . . Since the necessary diligence in teaching novices song [canto] has not been employed in the past, so as to perform the liturgy with the appropriate decorum, henceforth the abbess will ensure that the necessary diligence is used by the *maestra delle novitie* . . . and, should any negligence in this task become evident, she will not permit the [novices] to leave their novitiate until they are sufficiently instructed in singing. Effort is also to be made so that the already professed nuns are to be instructed [in music] with special care.[58]

Borromeo's insistence on basic musical competence, at least in chant, as a prerequisite for the final profession of monastic vows is remarkable. The remedial music instruction for nuns who had already professed also stands out, especially in comparison with Alfonso Paleotti's strictures around the same time in Bologna.

[57] G. B. Mongilardi, 'Vita Cardinalis Federici Borromaei', BA, Y. 114 *sup.*, in C. Marcora, 'La biografia del Cardinale Federico Borromeo scritta dal suo medico personale Giovanni Battista Mongilardi', *MSDM* 15 (1968), 125–232 at 165; cf. B. Guenzati, 'Vita di Federigo Borromeo', BA, G. 137 *inf.*, fo. 366^r, also in Marcora, 'Lettere del Cardinale Federico alle claustrali', *MSDM* 11 (1964), 177–432, at 206: '[Borromeo] permise pure loro [nuns] contro il consiglio de' più austeri i canti Musicali, li suoni di varii stromenti, perchè con essi e sollevvavano lo spirito all'armonia del Cielo, ed obbliavano insieme le lusinghe del Mondo'.

[58] ASDM XII, vol. 70, fasc. 1. S. Caterina was not a completely unmusical house; the 1581 list of books owned by the nuns (in ASDM, ibid.) included one unidentifiable collection of *laude*, owned by the abbess. This is no. 122, 'Canzon spiritualle di tutte le feste del anno ad instanza di monsignor illustrissimo e reverendissimo [*sic*]', possibly one of the Turinese *Lodi e canzoni spirituali* editions from around 1580 used in the *Scuole della dottrina cristiana*. The list is analysed in D. Zardin, 'Mercato librario e letture devote nella svolta del Cinquecento tridentino: Note in margine ad un inventario milanese di libri di monache', in *Stampa, libri e letture a Milano nell'età di Carlo Borromeo* (Milan, 1992), 135–246.

Borromeo thus sought to shape nuns' music-making in accordance with his own ideas of spirituality, which emphasized humility and penitence as well as individual development. The orders are noteworthy for their implied acceptance of polyphony in church, even in penitential seasons, and of non-keyboard instruments when used outside such seasons. The point of the decrees was that music should be employed in conformity with the interior qualities of humility and penitence. Federigo's discipline functioned, not as an external body of restrictions, but rather as guidelines for the appropriate use of music by the kind of model nun that he wanted to develop in the diocese.

But the junior Borromeo was also personally interested in the spiritual and musical life of his numerous female monastic correspondents. The best witness is a long exchange of letters dating from the late 1620s between the archbishop and a nun who can be identified (on the basis of musical and other references) as Suor Angela Flaminia Confaloniera at S. Caterina in Brera.[59] This woman, remembered by her colleagues as an 'anima particolare' in the house's necrology, was born around 1599; her experiences of divine tenderness in the 1620s led her confessor to recommend her to Borromeo, to whom she wrote dozens of missives.[60] Besides her spiritual gifts, she 'sapeua di musica et cantaua il soprano', presumably until her death on 16 August 1665.[61]

The letters deal with an ongoing series of Confaloniera's spiritual crises and ecstasies; Borromeo's advice includes his prescriptions for spiritual aridity and his use of Mary Magdalene as a model for nuns. The first mention of music is found in the second volume, at a point

[59] Confaloniera as the recipient of Federigo's letters is discussed by U. Saba, *Federico Borromeo ed i mistici del suo tempo* (Florence, 1931), ch. 15. The archbishop's missives, largely concerned with spiritual direction, are in BA, G. 26 *inf.*; an extensive selection is in Marcora, 'Lettere'. Four volumes of letters from an unnamed 'Religiosa di Santa Vita' to Federigo are in BA, G. 7, 8, 11, and 12 (all *inf.*). Although Saba (p. 84) does not identify this 'Religiosa di Santa Vita', common references (in both the G. 26 and G. 7 ff. sets of letters) to the *liuto attiorbato* that Borromeo had made for his correspondent, to the drawing of an apple, and to musical life at S. Caterina argue for an ascription of the letters written by the 'Religiosa' to her.

[60] The anonymous account of her education at S. Caterina and her vocation is in BA, Trotti 453, fos. 6^r–7^v, which noted her remarkable devotional life and frequent communications with Federigo.

[61] 'et quest'Eminentis*simo* [Federigo] uolse parlarli, et se la piglio sotto la sua diretione . . . sapeua di musica et cantaua il soprano, haueua una gran carità uerso il prossimo et facceua seruitio uolontieri': ibid., fos. 6^v–7^r.

in the correspondence when Confaloniera drew a picture of a lute, with a note reminding Federigo of his promise to have one sent to her (Fig. 4).[62] The instrument might have been a *liuto attiorbato*, useful for accompanying the soprano voice.[63] After its dispatch, Confaloniera expressed her gratitude and mentioned its use in a paraliturgical Christmas celebration (App. A, Doc. 35):[64]

Dearest Father, I cannot stop thanking Your Excellency for the gift you made me, especially since it was in time to use it the first time for such a

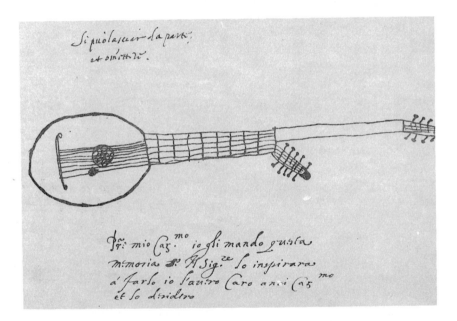

FIG. 4. Angela Confaloniera's drawing of a theorbo

[62] BA, G. 8 *inf.*, fo. 21ʳ: '*Padre* mio Car*issimo io* gli mando quessta memoria se Il Sig*nore* lo inspirara à farlo io l'asitro Caro anzi Car*issimo* et lo desidero.' Federigo's promise is preserved in his side of the exchange, BA, G. 26 *inf.*, no. 156: 'Del liuto ho caro l'avviso, fra tanto ho fatto apparecchiare un'altro ordigno faciullesco, il quale penso di mandarvelo' (also in Marcora, 'Lettere', 389). The letters are not dated but, on the basis of scattered references, probably stem from the later 1620s.

[63] On the various kinds of theorbos and chitarroni, and their voice-specific use, see D. Nutter, 'Changing the Instrument for the Music (and Vice-versa): Salomone Rossi's Chitarrone', in C. Gallico (ed.), *Claudio Monteverdi: Studi e prospettive* (Florence, 1996).

[64] 'Torno a ringratiarlo del Liuto il quale a fatto ralegrar tutte le monache con me dicendo che sentirano tanta consolatione come se fose stato suo' (BA, G. 8 *inf.*, fo. 41ᵛ). Confaloniera was at pains to avoid the vanity of individual possession of the instrument and to stress the common joy of her colleagues.

beautiful mystery; since the happiness [from the gift] I saw all the nuns had made me resolve to let everyone hear its sound. So secretly I asked a nun who plays violone and another who plays violin, and so Christmas Eve we went to perform the *matinati* for all the nuns, singing *Gloria in excelsis* and other similar verses, such as these: 'Your sweet spouse, my dear sisters, has been born today of the Virgin Mary. Good Jesus has been born as our Saviour. Come, sisters, give Him your hearts.'[65]

That such music-making would please the prelate is a mark of the intellectual and pastoral distance between the two Borromeos. Confaloniera's descriptions provide unique and valuable testimony to the role of music in the spiritual life of one nun; they also bear witness to the sheer youthful exuberance of piety among her companions, and their public celebrations (not without distant echoes today) of the Incarnation. For his part, Federigo was concerned to guide her spiritual progress; but his regard for music as an integral part of female monastic life was also evident:

But I was very pleased to see in your letter that, on Pentecost after supper, you went to sing and play [instruments]. How well you did, and how pleasing to God was that modest and holy recreation. Make sure that I hear that you do it often, especially when you find yourselves fatigued. This effort is sometimes better than conversation, and your singing holy and totally spiritual pieces, as you always do, is divine praise. When that holy distraction after supper has passed, you can return to your contemplation, sparing neither effort nor diligence.[66]

Federigo wanted to hear that nuns made music often, especially when worn-out or spiritually exhausted ('affaticato'). In this sense, music in its frequent practice was quite literally a 'ricreazione' of the spirit, a renewal of spiritual life.[67] Music thus prepared the soul for contemplation ('potete tornare alle vostre contemplationi'), and this

---

[65] Ibid., fo. 42ʳ. Confaloniera went on to note that 'il dono che ha fato a la pouera genocha ha tirato li lacrimi de gli ochi *per* diuotione a molte persone *per* sentir a sonar a si bel misterio: poi si ricordauano *poi* [underlining in original] della melodia deli Angeli' (fo. 42ᵛ). The topos of earthly music recalling heavenly music would recur in Borromeo's own writings.

[66] App. A, Doc. 36, also in Marcora, 'Lettere', 255.

[67] Lampugnani also mentioned the restorative power of music in his account of Radegund's life: 'Poiche, quando stanca era necessitata a coricarsi per ristoro delle infievolate membra, faticaua dormendo la mente, e pareua, che hor salmeggiasse con qualche canto, e non dormisse' (*Della vita*, 122).

transcendent and thaumaturgic function of the art would recur time and again.[68]

At S. Caterina, Confaloniera's music-making would have been aided by the presence of her teacher, the singer, composer, and organist Claudia Rusca, whose *Sacri concerti a 1–5* (containing small-scale sacred concertos, Vesper Psalms, eight-voice motets, and two *canzoni francesi*, the first preserved instrumental music by a woman) would soon be published by Giorgio Rolla in 1630; some of this music, thought lost since the 1943 bombing of the Ambrosiana, has been preserved in modern orchestral transcriptions and will be discussed below.[69]

Federigo's shipments to Confaloniera, and through her to S. Caterina in Brera as a whole, did not stop at *liuti attiorbati*:

I send paper to you, as a disciple, so that you may do the right things in writing, those that correspond to your true name, that of disciple. I am sending you this because the nuns cannot presume that you write, ordering paper yourself. And since this letter is the one with presents, I am also sending you a setting of the psalm *Super flumina Babilonis*, one most lovely. If you should know how to play and sing it, you will find it beautiful, and the words are appropriate for anyone who wants to fly to Heaven, as I believe you would wish, as soon as possible.[70]

Borromeo clearly felt that certain music was an aid to the preparation of a happy Christian death ('volare in alto') for nuns. It was for

---

[68] The archbishop's association of music with spiritual renewal was also shared by a musical contemporary, the veteran Cassinese composer Serafino Cantone, who justified writing a spiritual madrigal comedy: 'I knew that nothing, especially spiritual matters, was bearable if not alternated with some rest; the soul's rest is called recreation, and for this reason I thought how I might induce recreation worthy of every *virtuoso*': *Accademia festevole concertata* (Milan: Rolla, 1627), 'Ai Lettori', p. [2].

[69] For a detailed discussion of Walter Jesinghaus's and Giorgio Federico Ghedini's transcriptions (*c.*1935) of Rusca's music, along with the liturgical and musical context at S. Caterina in the 1620s, see the forthcoming edition by M.-J. Wasmer and the present writer, C. Rusca, *Sacri concerti*.

[70] App. A, Doc. 37. The penitential nature of the text should be noted. It is difficult to find a printed setting of Ps. 136 in the Milanese repertory of this decade. Several contemporary settings are small-scale concerti, including a version for alto by Pellegrini in his *Sacer Concentus a 1–6* (Venice: Vincenti, 1619). The references to 'sonarlo', however, may mean that a larger-scale piece was involved, one that involved obbligato instruments. Other versions by Mortaro, Orfeo Vecchi, Lucino, or Gabussi were earlier. But the music could also have come from outside Milan; Federigo patronized composers throughout the peninsula. Nuns at S. Caterina might not always have had access to paper; Federigo was again concerned with the self-expression of his monastic charges.

this reason that he actually sent pieces into *clausura*.[71] The letters leave no doubt: Federigo was willing to place extensive musical resources at nuns' disposition (at least in model houses subject to his authority, like S. Caterina) for their spiritual recreation and growth. This is perhaps only the most obvious example of the prelate's aesthetic tolerance and liberalism in the service of individual spiritual devotion in the diocese as a whole.

Still, Federigo's encouragement should not hide the other, restrictive side of his policy: the continuation of measures for *clausura* and their implications for music. His emphasis on personal humility ('*Humilitas*' is still the family motto) accounts for the occasional curial *memoriali* aimed at banishing ostentation from nuns' music, an especially key point given the rise of both solo singing and the small-scale sacred concerto in the first years of his tenure. Most of the documentation also dates from the early years, thus suggesting the degree to which Carlo's standards had slipped (or perhaps had never been implemented at all).

The most consistent measures were aimed at the original 'problem', that of the importation of male music teachers into *clausura*. These strictures were repeated throughout his tenure.[72] But new restrictions testify to the rise (or perhaps the resurrection) of other kinds of performance, especially over the last two decades of Borromeo's reign. Many of the curial orders have to do with music and theatre in the parlours, both strictly forbidden. Of special concern were the *mascherate* plays performed by nuns at Carnival season, with their invariable connotation of female transvestism. A series of printed orders from the vicars outlawing such theatre were predictable in their regularity as well as in their apparent ineffectiveness.[73]

[71] The archbishop sent *laude* also: 'Le laude spirituali io non mancherò di inviarle: et altre ancora, che io non vi lessi, che nel vero sono bellissime' (Marcora, 'Lettere', 385).

[72] One order noted: 'Si prohibisce ogni sorte di persone d'andare alli Monasterij delle Monache per insegnare il Canto fermo o figurato, ò per insegnare l'arte del suonare, et si la Superiora, o altra farà contro per quest'ordine sia priuata del velo, et de requisito *presente* con altre pene all'arbitrio del Superiore' (ASDM XII, vol. 49, fo. 22ᵛ, undated). Even the Lateran Canons attempted to regulate matters at S. Maria Annunciata after Sessa's death; the orders of 30 Nov. 1622 permitting polyphony only at Mass and Vespers on major feasts, 'leuata ogni vanità', along with the prohibition of music in the parlours, are in ASM, Religione, p.a., 1955.

[73] Printed orders from the *vicario delle monache* Mazenta are found in ASDM XII, vol. 50 (fo. 115ʳ [1625]; fo. 157ʳ [1618]; fo. 178ʳ [1618 again]). These would be repeated by Antonio Rusca, *vicario* in 1634–8 (ASDM XII, vol. 52, fasc. 5). The reports of *mascherate* and secular *commedie* at female monasteries began with the 1577 complaints at S. Agnese and continued well into the Settecento.

The concern with limiting ostentation also emerges from the rules prohibiting polyphony with more than two choirs, or with instruments besides organ and regal. Three of the volumes of the largest-scale music with dedications to nuns of this period, the Vespers settings of Antegnati (1592) and Mangoni (1623) and the Office settings of Federigo's protégé Orfeo Vecchi (1600) fall within the permitted categories of Federigo's term, being scored for eight voices in two choirs, with organ in Mangoni's book (possibly in the Vecchi collection as well). This provision might have been an administrative, not musical, category designed to limit dissension among musicians and to organize performances equitably.[74]

In an order more severe than the prelate's own (another mark of ecclesiastical dissension), Federigo's curia also targeted the 'ostentation' of solo singing in liturgy, especially as a distraction from the reception of the Eucharist (App. A, Doc. 32):

No [nun] is to sing solo. And at Communion at Mass, no motet should be sung or [instrumental piece] played after the Agnus Dei, so that nuns may prepare themselves for Holy Communion and show more devotion and attention in receiving it . . . Nor is it permitted, as has been ordered several times, that any nun sing solo, and music (established for the glory of God and the comforting of the faithful) should be made with gravity and devotion, without any use of secular tunes adapted to sacred words.[75]

Still the restrictions, hortatory or administrative, rarely worked. The motets dedicated to sisters in two separate collections of 1598 by Giuseppe Gallo and Agostino Soderini (composers working in patrician circles) are pieces for eight or nine voices in two choirs; Gallo's include one choir of instruments, which were to perform canzona phrases between the vocal sections of motets. Whether these pieces were performed by their addressees at S. Radegonda, S. Agnese, or S. Paolo, or executed by the ducal band in the *chiese esteriori*, the scorings and the techniques directly transgressed the curial rules. Nor did matters change later in Federigo's tenure: in 1622 the parish priest of Legnano wrote the *vicario delle monache* Mazenta, complaining of

---

[74] One wonders which polychoral repertory was being banned; there is almost no Milanese music for more than two choirs extant from Federigo's time, excepting the Duomo-specific Vespers and masses for sixteen to twenty-one voices (in four choirs) written by Donati in the 1630s. Antegnati's three-choir masses of 1603 are actually dedicated to Borromeo; hence, the prelate probably had no objections to large-scale polychorality in and of itself.

[75] Unsigned orders, 10 July 1624, ASDM XII, vol. 46, fos. 288 ff.

singing, instrument-playing, and dancing at S. Chiara during Carnival.[76] In nuns' churches, over-elaborate celebrations were forbidden around this time; the practices seemed especially prevalent on the name-day feasts (App. A, Doc. 28):

Most Reverend Mother: . . . Setting fires, shooting mortars and archebusses, playing trumpets, and similar things, are actions totally foreign to nuns' tradition and piety, and thus are expressly forbidden . . . Music is to be made only by nuns, with no instruments other than organ and regal, and for two choirs only; nor should any nun sing solo, and the pieces should be sacred and serious, far from any worldliness.[77]

A clear distinction lies between the two generations who professed vows under Federigo: the first around 1600, represented by such singers as Sessa, and the second, women like Confaloniera. They—and the music written for and by them—represent two rather different cultural moments in Federigo's Milan: the first came to maturity during the polystilistic ferment of the new century's first decade, with the public projects of the Ambrosiana, rhetoric, art, and music that eddied around Borromeo, while the growing monastic population began to display a higher and more public level of prominence in art, music, and liturgy. The second generation reflected a move away from public activity towards concern with internal spiritual states on the part of sisters, the prelate, and indeed the city as a whole.

For this younger group, the career of Chiara Margarita Cozzolani provides a typical example: wealthy-class origin, high monachization rate, family ties to monasteries, later service as abbess or prioress, and musical ability.[78] She had been born on 27 November 1602 to Giovanni Battista Cozzolani and his wife Valeria, in the parish of S. Tecla, the former summer cathedral co-extensive with the Duomo; her baptismal name was Margarita.[79] Two of the family

---

[76] Copy in ASDM XII, vol. 46, fo. 241[r].

[77] A printed order on the same points, especially music for more than two choirs and solo singing, was issued on 10 Oct. 1603 by the vicar-general Antonio Albergati; this remarked on the connection with the name-day celebrations (App. A, Doc. 22).

[78] Cozzolani's family ties to S. Radegonda and the relatively plentiful documentation of her life can be contrasted with Badalla's more obscure career.

[79] Milan Cathedral, Metropolitana, Battesimi 1598–1608, fo. 86[r]: [Nov. 1602] '16. Ad 28 suddette. Fù battizzata una figlia del Sr. Gio. Battista Cozzolani et della sua moglie nata alli 27 del presente et gli fu datto lo nome Margarita. Il compadre fù il Sig. Gio. Battista Gussano di questa parocchia.' S. Tecla had been razed in 1542, but still exists as the Duomo's administrative parish. There are no surviving records earlier than mid-1598; thus there is no

workshops were in the parish, and S. Radegonda was simply on the other side of the cathedral, another link between monasteries and neighbourhoods.[80] S. Tecla's population was comprised largely of artisans and traders, representing some of the wealthiest members of these productive strata.[81]

There is almost no documentation of the family before the late Cinquecento.[82] But several notarial acts record Cozzolani's two aunts, who seem to represent the first generation to have been nuns at the foundation that would house three generations of daughters from the family.[83] Indeed, the slightly lower dowry at S. Radegonda, and the 'upper middle-class' origin of the Cozzolani correspond to the slightly lower social status of the house, compared to S. Margarita or S. Vincenzo, and its musical renown might have represented a way to compete in urban prestige.

The first secular document that mentions Margarita and her older sister Clara is her grandmother's will, dated 8 March 1608. Anastasia Botizzi, the widow of Giovanni Antonio Cozzolani, left two hundred lire to each of her daughters, Virginia and Anna Margarita, *professe* at S. Radegonda.[84] She also bequeathed her granddaughters Clara and Margarita 1,000 lire each for their temporal or spiritual dowry, designating her two sons, Bartolomeo and Giovanni Battista, as the executors.[85]

baptismal certificate for Margarita's sister Clara (religious name Candida Arsilia). My thanks to Fausto Ruggieri for access to this document. The conjectural birth date of *c.*1620 found in some reference books is based on a misreading of her profession date (see below). Although the modern form of Cozzolani's baptismal name is 'Margherita', her surviving autograph letter is signed 'Margarita'.

[80] A request of 6 May 1650 from the male members of the family to unite the two *botteghe* is in ASC, Famiglie, busta 526/10.

[81] On the parish, see D'Amico, *Le contrade*, 63–4 and 174; in 1610 there were 3,318 inhabitants of S. Tecla.

[82] A 16th-c. petition concerning land near Bagnolo from a Domenico Cozzolani of Lodi is preserved in ASM, Fondo Famiglie, busta 'Cozzolani', while 335 *pertiche* of lands in Lesmo (in the Brianza region) belonged to a Giovanni Antonio Cozolano, according to an undated contract in ASC, ibid. On merchants' land ownership north of the city, see D'Amico, *Le contrade*, 81–2.

[83] The records of the notary G. B. Cornara of family documents for 1608–15 are preserved in ASM, Notarile, 24767–75.

[84] 'Item lego et indico et iure legati relinquo Done Virginiae, et Done Annae Margaritae sororibus de Cozzolanis filiabus meis dilectissimis monialibus professis in Monasterio San*ct*e Redigondae Mediolani libras ducentas Imper*ia*les pro singula earundem dandas semel tantum statim post meum decessum per infrascriptos heredes meos', ASM, Notarile, busta 23717, notary Dionisio Capra.

[85] 'Item lego et ut supra Clare et Margarite de Cozzolanis neptibus meis ex infrascripto Jo. Baptista filio meo libras mille Imperiales pro singula earundem dandas tempore quo

Margarita's immediate family was listed in a *status animarum* (parish report on households) dated 1609, but reflective of 1607;[86] this gave Anastasia, Giovanni Battista and Valeria, Bartolomeo, the two girls, and their four brothers.[87] At some point in the next three years, Giovanni Battista seems to have died, leaving 600 lire for the family servant Angela de Famagallo to become a *conversa* at S. Radegonda and designating his brother Bartolomeo as his executor.[88] Although Margarita and her sister thus experienced the marginalizing effect of semi-orphanage, the family's tradition of sending all or most of its daughters to S. Radegonda would have provided a secure future for the two girls. Shortly thereafter, Bartolomeo Cozzolani also was involved in the dowry negotiations with S. Radegonda for Clara Cozzolani.[89]

maritabuntur temporaliter vel spiritualiter, ita si una ex eis decederet antequam matrimonio temporali vel spirituali collocaretur librae mille dicti legati eius portio quae dande fuissent tali decedenti in totum acrescant alteri superstiti si in ipsa suscepta tempore nondum matrimonio temporali, vel spirituali atque copulata fuerint, et eueniat casus quo maritetur temporaliter, vel spiritualiter dotis . . .' (ibid.). The receipt is also acknowledged in a *confessio* notarized that day by Cornara, ASM, Notarile, 24767. Anastasia's bequest was clearly her own decision (the 200 lire to her daughters were not strictly necessary) and represents an interesting case of female-controlled inheritance. Still, the 1,000 lire represented only a part of the necessary dowry for either a monastery or for marriage; presumably the girls' father was to make up the rest.

[86] ASDM, Status animarum, S. Tecla, 1609. The report lists Anastasia Cozzolani (no age); Bartolomeo (age 42; unmarried); Giovanni Battista (age 40; his name is crossed out); Valeria, Giovanni's wife (age 31); Giovanni Giacomo (age 10); Clara (age 9); Gioseffo (age 7); Geronimo (age 6); Margarita (age 4); and Giovanni Domenico (age 2), along with five servants (two of whom are crossed out). The 1609 date, according to which Margarita would have been born *c.*1605, does not square with the S. Tecla baptismal record. If we assume that the '9' is a slip of the pen for '7' (or perhaps a date of final compilation of facts gathered in the previous two years) and that the report was finished before Margarita's birthday on 27 Nov., then the dates fall into place: Clara would have been born around 1597–8. She then professed vows before turning 18 (1614). Margarita, born in 1602, would have taken vows around her eighteenth birthday, and is to be identified with the 'Donna Chiara Margarita Cozzolana' whose profession at S. Radegonda is recorded in 1620.

[87] The report also lists, under the next entry [hence next door?], 'nella casa di Sr. Alessandro Turà, Riccardo Rognoni, Musico'. Rognoni was a viola bastarda virtuoso, composer, author of a treatise on ornamentation, and the father of the composers and instrumentalists F. and G. D. Rognoni Taeggio. On household density and fraternal cohabitation in the city, see D'Amico, *Le contrade*, 57–9 and 93–4.

[88] Giovanni Battista's will has not yet come to light. The information is deduced from a receipt to Bartolomeo from the nuns of S. Radegonda, dated 25 Oct. 1611, for the 600 lire 'pro completa solutione dotis spiritualis seu limosinae soluere promisse per quondam Cozolani Angele de Famagallo monialis nunc converse in eo monasterio', which came from the legacy of his brother, ASM, Notarile 24771, G. B. Cornara. This is presumably the same servant mentioned in the ASDM *Status animarum* report as 'Angela, serva' (age 16).

[89] The three *obligationes* for the sum of 2,709 lire date from 1615, ibid., busta 24775.

The scope of the legal alienation of professing novices is evident in the formal renunciation signed by Margarita's sister after she took vows. Candida Arsilia (formerly Clara) Cozzolani gave up all claim to her share of her father's estate, and any inheritance rights—essentially, her legal and social being—in favour of her brothers.[90] Formal approval for this step from the diocesan curia and the Senate was also necessary.[91] No such renunciation has yet come to light for Margarita, although it is likely that one existed.[92] The initial deposit of her spiritual dowry is dated 1619 in S. Radegonda's records, and the full payment was received by the monastery in 1620, thus implying that she had finished her year of novitiate by that point.[93] Rather than taking an entirely new religious name like her sister, she seems simply to have added 'Chiara' to her given name when she was vested in the black habit of the Cassinese.

The two Cozzolanis thus came to the house as the second generation, following their aunts, who were still alive.[94] Unlike Claudia

[90] 'Cum sit quod infra Clara Cozzolana ita in seculo nominata et nunc Donna Candida Arsilia diebus superioribus habitum monasticum in religione S. Benedicti de observantia alias sancte Justine de Padua congregationis cassinensis et in monasterio sanctae Radegondae huius civitatis susceperat eo quo in monasterio de preterito sit professionem emissura, sed antequam illam emittet dixerit omnem eius hereditatem tam paternam, quam maternam renunciare Jo. Jacobo, Josepho, Hieronymo et Johanni Domenico fratribus Cozolanis et eius Candidae Arsiliae fratribus et eam liberare ab omni et toto eo quod peterebit et peterit futuro tempore' (ibid., busta 24775, document dated 22 Apr. 1615). Clara had professed in 1614, according to S. Radegonda's records in ASDM XII, vol. 128, fo. 1ʳ.

[91] Both forms are dated 25 Feb. 1615; ibid.

[92] This may be due to the fact that the records of the notary Cesare della Porta were destroyed in World War II. Porta handled a number of other transactions for S. Radegonda in the 1610s (preserved in ASDM), and could have notarized Margarita's renunciation in 1620, since Cornara had stopped working in 1617.

[93] '1619 no. 42. Aliud [depositum dotis] Margᵗᵉ Cozzolani 7 Maij in Cameras Arti', ASDM XII, vol. 128, fo. 5ʳ. The 'depositum dotis' was the dowry deposit in an unnamed bank, probably the Banco di Sant'Ambrogio. The *confessio dotis*, or the receipt, is dated 29 May 1620 (ibid., fos. 1ʳ and 5ʳ); the *extractio dotis* (or actual withdrawal of the dowry payment by the monastery) is dated (in a later hand) 14 Aug. of the same year (ibid.). Thus this date of Cozzolani's profession, given by F. Picinelli, *Ateneo dei letterati milanesi* (Milan, 1670), 147, is correct. Picinelli's account was written while Cozzolani was still alive and must be considered reliable.

[94] It is unclear whether Margarita was an *educanda* at the monastery, since the girls in education were normally not listed by name. Her niece probably received her education at S. Radegonda, even though her admission broke the numerical limits allowed. A petition dated 21 Aug. 1648 and marked 'concedatur' in the SCVR files reads: 'Eminentissimi e Reverendissimi Sig.ri: Anna Maria Cozzolani Zitella Milanese desidera entrare in educatione nel Monastero di S. Radegonda di Milano; ma essendo in quello compito il numero prefisso delle educande, supplica humilmente le EE.VV. concedergli licenza di poter entrare in detto monastero per educanda sopranumeraria. Che &c.' (ASV, VR, sez. monache, 1648, lug–dic).

Rusca, who had received music instruction at home before her profession, Chiara Margarita's later compositional talents must have been in part encouraged inside cloistered walls, given her profession at age 17 or 18. Cozzolani's contemporary Picinelli reported her renown as a singer. But the scarcity of early documentation is puzzling; the lack of dedications and the absence of outsiders' reports on her singing may indicate that she was not among the most famous performers of the monastery. She appeared in the lists of nuns from the house throughout the 1620s and 1630s, but otherwise no evidence has come to light of her activities in these decades.

Cozzolani's now-lost op. 1, *Primavera di fiori musicali*, appeared in Milan in 1640, when she was about 37.[95] The book was dedicated to Archbishop Monti and was then followed by her three publications of 1642, 1648, and 1650. If Cozzolani wrote any music thereafter, it has not survived.[96] For the rest of her life, she instead filled a variety of high offices inside the house, including abbess in 1658–60 and 1672–3, as well as prioress in 1664 and 1671.[97] As a senior nun, she answered the largely *pro forma* questions about music-making in the *chiesa interiore* and the parlour put by the Cassinese superiors in the 1660s.[98] Despite later factional strife, her high status in the house is underscored by this service. Around 1665, Candida Arsilia disappeared from the lists of nuns, a death confirmed by an anonymous

---

[95] The contemporary citation for this print is given by Picinelli, *Ateneo*; a later mention is found in M. Armellini, *Biblioteca Benedicto-Casinensis* (Assisi, 1731–2). The 1856 overview of the music collection of the Berlin Gymnasium zum grauen Kloster mentions the ownership of the Tenor part-book only (cf. App. D, no. 3). If the edition appeared in Milan, it would have had to be printed by Rolla, who owned the only stock of musical type in the city.

[96] The other two works listed by R. Eitner, *Biographisch-bibliographisches Quellenlexikon der Musik* (Leipzig, 1900), iii, cols. 91–2, are an aria, *No, no, no che mare*, and the continuo part to a solo motet, *Venite gentes*, this latter (unnoted by Eitner) a setting in Cozzolani's 1648 volume. Both were in the former Königsberg University Library; according to the directors of the two Lithuanian institutions that now hold the remains of this collection (see App. D), these manuscripts are not extant.

[97] The documents of the Palomera case (see below, 96 ff.) show that Cozzolani was abbess when the scandal erupted (term of office 1658–9). The 1672 visitation records in ASM, Religione, busta 2213, noted that the Cassinese superiors 'singulares moniales post Prandium seorsum accedere iussimus ad electionem novae Abbatisse. . . . Ad M*atrem* D*ominam* Clare Margarite Cozzolane concessisse cognovimus, et hoc in primo scrutinio.' The 1673 visitation (ibid.) recorded her re-election. Terms of monastic office were normally for one year, with the elections held in conjunction with the annual visitation of the house by the superiors.

[98] Her 1670 response to the standard question whether nuns had refrained from music in the parlours was: 'Non so che dire in questo proposito' (ibid.).

letter to the Sacra Congregazione concerning the bequest of the family's personal cell inside the house (App. A, Doc. 65).[99] At the end of her life, Picinelli included a brief encomium of her and her musical companions in his urban panegyric (App. A, Doc. 67). Cozzolani's name vanished from the lists of nuns who signed *dote* contracts after the contract of 4 May 1676.[100] Since the next preserved contract was signed on 20 April 1678, she probably died sometime between these two dates.[101] Her nieces Anna Margarita and Giovanna Francesca, both musicians, would inhabit the house, later serving in similarly high office, until the eighteenth century.[102]

Another representative of this generation was Cozzolani's slightly older contemporary, the first Milanese nun to publish an entire collection of her compositions. Claudia Rusca's life and outside training were recorded in S. Caterina's necrology.[103] She had been born probably in Milan around 1593, was the sister of Antonio Rusca (later a *vicario delle monache* in the 1630s and 1640s), and had apparently professed her vows in the 1610s, possibly with a dowry dispensation.[104] Her sister Antonia Lucia, evidently not as musical, had also taken the white Humiliate habit at the house.[105] Having received Communion on 1 October 1676, Rusca fell ill that day and died on 6 October, after lifelong infirmities.[106]

---

[99] Disputes over possession and construction of cells were a recurrent feature of monastic life. Margarita, not her older sister, was the recipient of the cell (one wonders if she was sickly and not expected to survive Candida Arsilia, or perhaps her talents qualified her for special privilege), and the cell was built two years before her profession, thus testifying to her preordained vocation. The strength of family ties is witnessed by this request to pass the cell on to nieces; Giovanna Francesca (a singer) would survive past 1722.

[100] ASM, Religione, p.a., 2221, the *dote* contract of Marta Maddalena Confaloniera.

[101] Ibid. The death date of *c*.1653 given hitherto seems to be a guess based on the cessation of her editions after 1650.

[102] Giovanna Francesca as abbess signed the 1714 bequest of Antonia Francesca Clerici's harpsichord to the monastery's choir (App. A, Doc. 73). No further members of the family are recorded in the Settecento lists.

[103] 'Biografia', BA, Trotti 453, fos. 13ᵛ–14ʳ; for a complete transcription, see Wasmer and Kendrick (eds.), Rusca, *Sacri concerti*.

[104] 'fù alleuata da suoi et la feccero imparar di Musica con buon fondamento perche sapeua componere, cantaua il Soprano, et in sua giouentù era molto lodata si che fù accetata et le feccero cortesia perche esercitasse questa virtù', 'Biografia', fo. 13ᵛ. Despite Jesinghaus's historically inaccurate but ultimately provident guess (see n. 69) that she came from the Ticino, Argelati, *Biblioteca*, vi, col. 1263, recorded her brother Antonio (d. 1655) as 'Mediolanensis'.

[105] 'Biografia', fo. 14ʳ.

[106] 'et il primo giorno di 8bre faceua la Santa Comunione, et essendo alla mensa fù soprapresa dalla sgoccia, si che si portò à letto, se li diede l'olio santo et doppo sei giorni morì adi 6 8bre la Domenica del Rosario l'anno 1676 d'anni 83': ibid. There was a minor confusion of dates; Rosary Sunday actually fell on 4 Oct. in 1676.

For Cozzolani and Rusca, along with other musicians who came to maturity in Federigo's tenure, the central result of episcopal policy was to open up possibilities for musical experience unmatched in any other diocese of post–Tridentine Italy. But Federigo's policy evinced a basic dilemma. Given the patrician prestige represented by the monasteries, unleashing (or not restricting) the possibilities for polyphony inside *clausura* meant also encouraging the public attractiveness, urban prestige, and family ties of such music-making, including the inevitable internal conflicts over music. These battles over public renown, precedence in performance, and occasions for female monastic polyphony would become increasingly characteristic of the situation after Federigo's tenure; they reflected and encapsulated fissures within the families of the patriciate. And with the new emphasis on individual performance and solo singing typical of the whole Seicento (and present in the scoring and style of newer musical genres) it was impossible to avoid vanity, individual fame, and public competition among singers. Federigo never really solved the paradox, leaving it instead for future prelates to confront, each in his different way; the writings of his follower Girolamo Borsieri are deeply ambivalent on the attractiveness and danger of female monastic polyphony.[107] Meanwhile, two generations of women had been able to enjoy a marked degree of episcopal tolerance and support for the musical expression of their liturgical and spiritual lives.

---

[107] F. Pavan, 'La necessità dell'*exemplum*: Gerolamo Borsieri e la musica delle monache milanesi', paper given at the Nov. 1993 Tours Colloquium, 'Les femmes et la musique à la Renaissance'.

4

Conflict and Renown

◇

È un canto di sirena
che, per non darvi orecchio,
d'uopo saria la santità più salda,
che in sacri chiostri ancor costa gran pena.

(C. M. Maggi, *I consigli di Meneghino*
(Milan, 1697), III, iii)

The 1630–1 plague shattered the harmony and optimism of Federigo's years, despite the ritual invocations of the memories of Carlo's battles against the 1576 epidemic; due to *clausura* (ironically), it had less effect on nuns.[1] In its wake, female monastic ensembles must have figured, if they had not already, among the largest and best-organized *cappelle* of Milan.[2]

As Federigo's successor, Cesare Monti had to contend immediately with the effects of war and plague on houses in the mid-1630s.[3] The crisis of intellectual order after the pestilence affected both devotional literature and the musical repertory. Meanwhile another

[1] For Lampugnani's interpretation of the survival of all 140 of S. Radegonda's inhabitants in 1630–1 as a miracle due to their sanctity and to the holy water from their house, *Della vita*, 142–9. The only nun in this study who died in the epidemic was Agata Sfondrati. On the musical reflections of the plague in Grancini's *Sacri fiori concertati* and other editions, see Kendrick, *Music in Federigo Borromeo's Lombardy*.

[2] The 1632 listing of the Duomo's ensemble at the beginning of Donati's term as *maestro* included fourteen singers (de Florentiis and Vessia, *Sei secoli*, 279).

[3] Monti was the Vatican's second choice, due to Spanish resistance, and did not arrive in the city until 1635; A. Borromeo, 'La Chiesa milanese del Seicento e la Corte di Madrid', in de Maddalena (ed.), *Millain the Great*, 98–104. On his tenure and tastes, see the exhibit catalogue *Le stanze del cardinale Monti, 1635–1650* (Milan, 1994), especially the essays by Borromeo and Zardin. The first two hundred folios of ASDM XII, vol. 46 are filled with letters from extra-urban abbesses testifying to nuns' flight in the face of the invading foreign troops.

problem, the lack of episcopal jurisdiction during the interregnum after Federigo's death in September 1631, occasioned the first major scandal in two generations.[4] Monti's first and only pronouncement concerned the ongoing problems between the two choirs (one senior, one junior) at S. Marta, one of Federigo's favourite institutions. The division of monastic populations into two contending factions went back at least as far as the demographic upturn of the Cinquecento.[5]

The internal disputes revolved around musical precedence and performance, and dated from the Borromean years. The vicar Mazenta had already attempted to mediate between the two groups in 1620 (App. A, Doc. 30), specifying that the most senior organist or singer was to have overall charge of music-making at Mass or Solemn Vespers; she was to distribute the (?written) parts ('ella ordini quello si dovrà cantare distribuendo le parti e regolando il concerto'); in case of her infirmity, the next most senior should have charge. At Low Masses, each organist (note the implied plural) was to alternate playing and selecting (polyphonic) pieces, presumably as Proper substitutes ('Delle misse basse . . . ogni organista ne suoni e canti una per cadauna, et quei canti le parerà mà graui et ecc*ellen*ti'), with second sopranos chosen again in order of seniority.[6] All the organists in the house would be permitted to have a muted keyboard in their cells for purposes of study, another concern from the days of Carlo; if a nun did not have her own cell, she could use a 'sordino' located only in the cell of a *professa* who was a close relative.[7] Outside (male) teachers in the parlours were again barred. The order's relation to nuns' repertories is evident in the mention of the two soprano parts,

---

[4] On diocesan history in these decades, C. Castiglione, *La chiesa milanese durante il Seicento* (Milan, 1948), 13–94 and Zardin, 'L'ultimo periodo spagnolo', esp. 'Ordini religiosi e monasteri femminili', 587–92.

[5] At S. Maria Maddalena al Cerchio in the early Seicento, Suor Ippolita Besozzi (possibly the same woman to whom as a girl Prospera Bascapè had taught music) was the head of one 'fattione' striving for the election of its candidate as mother superior; see ASDM XII, vol. 97, fasc. 2, and Zardin, *Donna e religiosa*, 61.

[6] Apparently the sister in charge was to pick a polyphonic setting of a Proper item or a motet of her choice. Low Masses did not involve the entire ensemble of either choir, but only an organist who also sang at least one piece as well, presumably with organ substitutes for other Proper items.

[7] The 'Sordino' was probably a clavichord; given the normal volume of Italian instruments, this might have meant a keyboard with a buff stop, rarely found in Italy. The restriction probably was meant to limit affective relationships of any kind, another sign of the curial obsession with the purported connection of music and sexuality.

just as the Milanese sacred concerto *a 2* had turned around 1620 from a CB to a CC scoring.

The differences between the choirs are summed up in their most renowned representatives, on one hand Bianca Lodovica Taverna (the addressee of Coppini's second book of madrigal contrafacta in 1608), and on the other the Fissiraghi sisters, Aurelia Maria and Paola Benedetta, themselves recipients of a dedication by Grancini in 1631, as the strife simmered. S. Marta's chronicler noted the monastic professions, deaths, and musical careers of all three; the actual generational separation between the two sides was slight.[8] Taverna's *dote* deposit was recorded on 2 February 1606, her entry into the novitiate on 6 February 1607 (she had been born Antonia), and her profession on 16 February 1608. Her death at age 92 on 21 December 1680 occasioned the chronicler's remark that she was 'very skilled, especially in music, which she practised with great diligence to the end of her life'. Aurelia Maria (born Anna) Fissiraghi professed on 9 January 1618; her death at age 82 on 26 November 1681, along with Paola Benedetta's 1623 profession and death on 20 October 1682 at age 77 (she was 'exemplary in the observance of orders and fervent in choir night and day'), also figured in the necrology.[9]

According to the senior nuns, the junior generation at S. Marta, an institution generally seen as a model, had taken over performances to whose direction they felt entitled, usurping the rights of their elders. The disputes continued through the 1620s; after Federigo's death, another *vicario*, Federico Fedeli, had to clarify precedence in musical performance on 2 December 1631 (App. A, Doc. 40). Fedeli ordered that the older nuns were to run double-choir music when visiting prelates said Mass. At other services, 'high, or low, or private', or at single-choir Vespers, the ensembles were to take turns. The vicar also stipulated (uniquely) that that the Fissiraghi sisters were to perform. The term 'concerti' seems to refer to the performance by both S. Marta's choirs at special Masses or Vespers. The competition between the choirs (and their factions), and the weekly alternation between ensembles for ordinary services ('quando si canta

---

[8] BA, G. 150 *sussidio*; Taverna's dates are on fos. 42ᵛ–43ʳ. In view of the generational proximity, the references to 'senior' and 'junior' ensembles and sides were probably euphemisms for the sides in patrician family battles.

[9] Taverna was 'molto virtuosa massime nella Musica, quale esercitò con molto Fattica sin al fine di sua vita', fo. 42ᵛ; for Aurelia Maria's records, ibid., fos. 52ᵛ–53ʳ, and those of Paola Benedetta, fos. 54ᵛ–55ʳ ('essemplare nella osservanza delli ordini et fervente al coro notte e giorno').

solo ad un coro'), would also be found at other houses, while the use of multiple instruments and the apparent approval of private (i.e. patrician familial) musical liturgy are also noteworthy.

More fatefully, the matter came to the attention of the Sacra Congregazione dei Vescovi e Regolari, owing to petitions from the factions. On 28 May 1632 the senior nuns claimed that the juniors had annulled Borromeo's orders after his death.[10] By July 1632, however, the Augustinians had ostensibly resolved their differences; in a pattern to become familiar, the entire house sent another *memoriale* to Rome, minimizing the conflict (and reversing the story), after the failure of intervention on the part of the Marquis of Caravaggio (App. A, Doc. 41). But the nuns were not able to hide at least one famous source of turmoil:

Your Eminence should know that a few years ago a little disturbance in our monastery came about for this reason: the older [nuns] wanted to rule the younger, with such a bad result that the monastic order was ill-pleased and . . . it was resolved to have recourse to the Most Eminent Cardinal Borromeo, our archbishop, so that someone who loved our order dearly would provide a remedy . . . but on account of the death of this holy archbishop the older nuns tried almost immediately to get the orders annulled, mocking the younger ones . . . the external superiors here in Milan have tried various ways to resolve this matter . . . but one of the older nuns, Taverna, never resigned herself to reason, saying that she had such influence in Rome that she could accomplish her ends through her connections . . . the younger nuns, namely the Fissiraghi, who are of outstanding morals, and very skilled, have conducted themselves well in all the nuns' eyes, so that finally they were all content to return to the orders of our most holy archbishop.[11]

Thus all seemed in order. But according to a letter of 10 March 1634, again from S. Marta, the split had led to public scandal and in the absence of a resident prelate in the city (the house was subject to episcopal jurisdiction, and Monti was still in Spain) the dispute had been sent for adjudication to the Sacra Congregazione.[12] Furthermore, the self-regulation of the nuns was no longer acceptable to Rome, as a remarkable order of 17 February 1634 from

[10] ASV, VR, sez. monache, 1632 (gen–lug), lettere A–V.

[11] Letter of 20 July 1632, ASV, VR, monache, 1632 (set–dic). Considering that the two sides seemed to have been at each other's throats, 'un poco di disturbo' was an understatement.

[12] The letter to the SCVR reported a vote in the chapter of the monastery in favour of Federigo's old orders, ASV, VR, sez. monache, 1634 (gen–apr).

Cardinal Ginetti, the secretary of the congregation, testified: it prohibited polyphony entirely until further orders had been drafted, a command unthinkable during Federigo's years.[13] As might have been expected from an institution that had enjoyed Borromeo's active support for music-making, the nuns responded with a petition to Monti promising to regulate matters of precedence themselves and invoking Federigo's policy.[14]

Monti's own orders of 9 July 1635, drafted soon after his arrival in the city (App. A, Doc. 43), were more cautious: the archbishop cited Federigo's preceding orders, with language again in a Borromean fraternal tone ('Reverenda come Sorella'). In order to satisfy the junior musicians, Monti made an important switch: music was to be administered alternately by two older and two younger nuns, who were to make sure that every musician should have her part according to ability ('in modo che ciascuna habbi la sua parte conforme alla sofficienza'). The archbishop also ordered that replacements for these four should be elected by the whole chapter after nominations by the abbess and prioress. Monti's efforts might have been an attempt to provide for musical experience on the part of the junior singers and organists, who perhaps were simply not getting enough opportunities to perform.

The seriousness of the dissension in an episcopally administered model house was underscored by the fact that the prelate himself signed the orders. The directive also took pains to prescribe the precise (and thus presumably most musically elaborate) feasts on which the senior nuns would have responsibility: Christmas, Epiphany, Easter, Pentecost, and the name-day of the monastery (29 July), or when the archbishop or visiting cardinals would celebrate Mass at S. Marta. A further sign of Monti's newness to the situation, and of the growing involvement of Rome in musical matters, was the letter from the Sacra Congregazione to the archbishop dated 20 July 1635 (apparently in time for that year's name-day polyphony), which repeated the rules.[15]

No more memoranda to Rome or to the archdiocesan curia on this matter have survived, and music at S. Marta seems to have continued under the arrangement.[16] As a whole, the curial orders from

---

[13] App. A, Doc. 42.   [14] ASDM XII, vol. 100, fasc. 3, undated folio.
[15] ASDM, ibid., unnumbered folio.
[16] Carlo Francesco Nuvolone's first dated painting, the group portrait of the house's titular saint (with her legendary victory over the dragon Tarascus), along with the Magdalen

Monti's later years were slightly more restrictive of music in monasteries than previously. Yet Federigo's successor was no enemy of
nuns' music, at least at first: Cozzolani's op. 1 was dedicated to him
in 1640, and her four books were all published during his term. It
would be hard to imagine that the ongoing stream of dedications to
nuns and the reports of musical Vespers could have existed in the face
of episcopal opposition.[17] Less clear is the relationship of the prelate's
policy to his ostensible reform of sacred music mentioned in the dedication of Grancini's *Musica ecclesiastica da capella* (Milan: Rolla, 1645):

> Most Eminent and Reverend Prince: . . . I shall at least rejoice in having
> encountered Your Excellency's brilliance, You who (having banished from
> Your diocese that effeminate music which previously disrupted the atmos-
> phere of Your churches with profane airs) now are pleased to admit that
> other [music] which, having learnt song from the celestial sirens in Heaven,
> whence it came, revives our souls.[18]

This might be read as a unveiled criticism either of the polystilism
characteristic of Federigo's later years, or of certain styles achieving
popularity around 1640.[19] This slightly puritanical turn was matched
by Antonio Rusca's 1647 orders restricting music in the diocesan

and the two other saints venerated in the house's church, S. Lazzaro and S. Marcella, was
finished shortly thereafter, perhaps as a gesture of reconciliation; for the date of 1636, see
the reproduction and discussion by S. Coppa, *Pinacoteca di Brera: Scuole lombarde, ligure e
piemontesi, 1535–1706* (Milan, 1989), 317–19.

[17] If there was a drop-off in musical dedications to nuns over the 1630s and 1640s, as witnessed in App. C, it may be due to the numerical if not qualitative decline in Milanese music
printing. The aftermath of the plague and the ongoing wars in the hinterlands seem to have
slowed down Giorgio Rolla's output during these decades, especially of sacred concerto
prints, in which dedications are often found.

[18] 'Em.mo & Reu.mo Principe . . . mi goderò almeno d'hauer incontrato il genio di V.E.
la quale hauendo essigliata dalla Sua Diocesi quella Musica effeminata, che prima con arie
profane turbaua l'aria delle Sue Chiese, gusta altretanto di ammettere quell'altra, che
hauendo imparato il canto dalle Celesti Sirene, al Cielo, d'onde trasse l'origine, gli animi
nostri risueglia': dedication dated 23 Dec. 1644, p. [2].

[19] Besides the implied criticism of Borromeo and the gendered disdain in the reference
to 'musica effeminata', the precise target of Grancini's barb is unclear. Certainly the composer's own works of the 1640s are simpler, more penitential, and sombre than his concertos of the 1620s (*Musica ecclesiastica da capella* features woodcuts of skulls, scattered
throughout the parts of its two syllabic and homophonic Requiems, one Roman, one
Ambrosian). One likely candidate for 'effeminate music' is the textually emotive and musically extended new style of the 1640s, represented in Lombardy by the motets of Gasparo
Casati, Cozzolani, and Francesco della Porta. But given the other evidence for Monti's policy, it seems clear that the slur did not refer to nuns' music *per se*.

houses.[20] But in any case, polyphony in the most important foundations—S. Radegonda, S. Marta, S. Margarita—seems to have continued under Monti.

The next archbishop's policy was to be determined largely by
extra-musical factors. Alfonso Litta, after service in Spain, had spent
years at the Roman Sacra Congregazione dei Vescovi e Regolari, an
experience that would provide him important aid in his attempts to
discipline female monasteries and their music. Yet he began his
tenure as archbishop in 1652 in close collaboration with the Spanish
and the patriciate. Indeed, no documents concerning nuns' music
survive from the first two years of Litta's tenure, except for the
prelate's approvals of dowry-reduction requests in monasteries subject to his authority. But around 1654 his relations with the governor and the city as a whole began to degenerate, partially due to his
own ambitions for his family's advancement, and he turned to the
Vatican for support in an ongoing crisis that would evoke memories
of Carlo's conflict with secular authority over jurisdiction.[21] In the
strife, Litta regarded the Milanese Senate as his particular nemesis.
The prelate's battles with the patriciate would find one of their
fiercest expressions in his attempted return to the most restrictive of
Carlo Borromeo's policies, at least at the patrician monasteries.

Litta's targets were precisely the two most musical Benedictine
houses subject not to him, but to the Cassinese—S. Radegonda and
S. Margarita.[22] The immediate occasion for episcopal restrictions at
S. Radegonda had little to do with music in itself. And, as at S. Marta,
nuns' own strife allowed the archbishop a freer hand in discipline.
The day after Ash Wednesday, 27 February 1659, Donna Maria

---

[20] The orders included some new restrictions: no outside teachers for *canto figurato*, no
instruments other than organ and harpsichord, no cross-dressing or *mascherate* in the *parlatori* at Carnival (ASDM XII, vol. 50, fo. 158ʳ; essentially the same are found in *AEM*, iv.
986); ironically, Antonio Rusca's rules would have prohibited at least one motet (*Gaudete
gaudio magno*, with an instrumental part) in his sister's collection of seventeen years earlier.
Federigo had actually encouraged the use of melodic instruments inside monasteries,
although not in the liturgy at all times.

[21] For Litta's battles with the city, see G. Signorotto, *Inquisitori e mistici nel Seicento italiano: L'eresia di Santa Pelagia* (Bologna, 1989), 201–7; this study of local mystical heterodoxy
and ecclesiastical reaction (in both senses of the term) in mid-century Lombardy considers
popular devotional movements in the Valcamonica, and is aided by its critical distance from
episcopal hagiography.

[22] As noted, the Monastero Maggiore had passed to episcopal jurisdiction in 1626,
although not without a struggle on the part of its residents. S. Vincenzo, the other musical
Benedictine house subject to regulars, does not seem to have figured in this controversy.

Faustina Palomera, a young daughter of a noble Spanish family, reportedly broke *clausura* by leaving S. Radegonda in the company of two noble male admirers ('i suoi carissimi') and not returning until the next day.[23] She was promptly denounced to the abbess, none other than Chiara Margarita Cozzolani, and the information seems to have come from one of the most famous musicians, Angela Maria Clerici, along with two sisters from the Vimercati family.[24] Cozzolani reported the infraction to the abbot of S. Simpliciano, her Benedictine superior, and word of the violation quickly spread throughout the city. The denunciation reflected Palomera's lack of popularity among some of the other nuns, possibly based on her social origin. In her defence, Palomera was to claim alternately that she had been a victim of forced monachization, and had simply accepted the nobles' help in order to escape vows which were not legally binding, or that she had never escaped in the first place. Whether Palomera actually did leave, and under which circumstances, was almost irrelevant in the light of the timing: to have fled the Earthly Jerusalem in the company of men precisely at the beginning of the most penitential season of the year was an infraction, real or imaginary, of the most basic symbolic norms of the Milanese world, one opposed by patriciate and prelate alike, and the case could only have exploded. Indeed, it became so famous that a lament for forced monachization, apparently written by G. F. Busenello several decades earlier, was attributed apocryphally (by a Milanese Calvinist exile) to Palomera, a generation later; entitled 'De profundis: querelo d'una monaca chi si era fatta religiosa per forza', it is in *terza rima*, interspersed with Psalm 130 and the Introit of the Requiem Mass, beginning: 'Dunque a far questo passo io son costretta / In questi chiostri, in cui devo morire; / Morirò, si, ma chiamerò vendetta / *De profundis* . . .'.[25]

---

[23] The documentation of the Palomera case is voluminous; it fills much of ASDM XII, vol. 128 and is well represented in the SCVR files from 1659 through 1665 as the largest set of documents from Milan for the whole century. The actual circumstances of the *clausura* violation are taken from the minutes of the *processo* session of 29 Sept. 1659, ASDM XII, vol. 128, fasc. 6, fos. 233–44. For an overview of the case, see P. Vismara Chiappa, *Per vim et metum: Il caso di Paola Teresa Pietra* (Pavia, 1991), 20–2. Palomera's dowry had been deposited on 8 June 1650 (ASDM XII, vol. 128, fo. 7^r) and so she might have been about 25 at the time.

[24] Angela Clerici had received a motet dedication in Andrea Cima's *Secondo Libro* (1627), around the time of her profession.

[25] The text figures in a manuscript collection of Busenello's verse, probably from the 1630s or 1640s, I-Vnm, It. IX Cod. 453 (7032), fo. 177^v ff.; my thanks to Wendy Heller and

The news provided Litta with proof positive that the houses subject to the Cassinese were hotbeds of immorality, even before the trial began.[26] The convoluted *processo*, involving the triangle of episcopal authority, the Milanese Benedictines (male and female), and the Sacra Congregazione unfolded from July 1659 and continued until autumn 1660.[27] A 'Relatione' written by an unnamed male Cassinese to Rome summarized the initial unfolding of the case, at least from the Benedictines' point of view, including the reversal and closing ranks on the part of S. Radegonda's nuns once they realized the archbishop's intentions to use the incident in stiffening policy (App. A, Doc. 46):

Palomera was charged with having broken *clausura*; the abbess [Cozzolani] told her superior, the Cassinese abbot Melzi. He decided that such a crime, if it were true, should not remain unpunished and considered informing Monsignor Archbishop of what had happened. But in the light of his [Litta's] character, and the irreconcilable hatred he had shown the Cassinese (especially the abbot himself) on all occasions, he [Melzi] (agitated by many thoughts) decided to consult the President of the Senate, his relative, who . . . advised that the nuns be examined . . . which he did, discovering only the words of the two Vimercati sisters, ill disposed towards the accused.[28]

According to the anonymous Cassinese account, it was Litta who stirred up the ostensible scandal in the city. His punishments, includ-

---

Irene Alm for this information. It reappeared in the 1682 *Vita di Bartolomeo Arese* attributed by its modern editor (M. Fabi, *Biblioteca storica italiana* (Milan, 1854), 172–8) to the Milanese apostate polemicist Gregorio Leti. This was written not by Leti, but by another Milanese Calvinist convert in Geneva, G. G. Arconati Lamberti (F. Barcia, *Bibliografia delle opere di Gregorio Leti* (Milan, 1981), 569). The book was written as an anti-Catholic polemic and its information is suspect; Arconati Lamberti apparently 'borrowed' Busenello's poem for his own ends. According to the biography, Palomera had been another victim of forced monachization.

[26] Litta's letter of 21 May 1659 (before the trial began) to the SCVR complained: 'e dico che li tre Monasteri [di] Monache Benedettine sono tre ridotti di li Diavoli incarnati particularmente li due Monasterij di S. Redegonda e S. Margherita . . . oscenità, carnalità, [crossed out: non di prima classe] amicitie, participatione [in] homicidie, vitupe, rationi di famiglia, sfreggi, bastonate, carcerationi, piaghe, inimicitie, scandoli cagionati dalle Monache delli tre Monasterij me ne sono noti a centenaia' (ASDM XII, vol. 128, fasc. 6, fos. 264–5).

[27] The ordering of the records, curial notes, episcopal letters, and other materials of the Palomera case in ASDM, vol. 128 is anything but (chrono)logical.

[28] 'Relatione di quello è successo sin hora in ordine all'imputatione della Monaca Palomera di S.ta Redegonda in Milano', undated and unsigned account in ASV, VR, sez. monache, 1660, feb–mar, in packet dated 5 Mar. 1660.

ing denying the nuns the sacraments, had only caused the sisters to withhold testimony for the trial.[29] For his part, Litta regarded the whole incident as a personal affront to his dignity; his letters were filled with fury at the Senate for its ostensible insults to episcopal rank, with special offence taken at the administration of the male Cassinese.[30] As for the nuns, Litta claimed: 'they leave no corner [in the city] where they do not display [printed] victories, triumphs, mockeries of the archbishop, all of them wretched'.[31]

While the *processo*, including the questioning of all the nuns at S. Radegonda, dragged along, Litta asked the Sacra Congregazionie to issue a series of temporary punishments, not however at this point including the suspension of polyphony. Both sides lobbied Rome in the dispute, another measure of the extent to which power over female monasteries had shifted southward in the course of the century. Indeed, we owe our only autograph letter of Cozzolani, still abbess, to the dispute (App. A, Doc. 45); writing to an unnamed Roman protector of the monastery, she wearily placed the culpability for the scandal on four or five nuns, who had thrown the whole house into turmoil.[32] Although the sisters might not have anticipated the ferocity of the archbishop's response, they had no one but themselves to blame for the blow-up, which afforded Litta a pretext for the eventual restrictions on polyphony.

Internal disputes over music came up only at the end of the 1659–60 *processo*, and even then only at the prompting of the *vicario*. Maria Gusca Porra on 9 March 1660 was recorded:

She replied that one could say . . . that among Donna Chiara Margarita [Cozzolani], Donna Maria Gratia, and Donna Chiara Benedetta [the two Vimercati sisters], and Donna Maria Faustina [on the other hand], there had

---

[29] 'mentre restano prive delli Sacramenti per non pregiudicare le loro ragioni per sconsolare tanti Nobili congionti di Sangue con dette Monache, e per causare in fine qualche disordine irremediabile', 'Relatione', ibid.

[30] 'Due Monasterij di Monaci Cassinensi si trovano in Milano, Uno con la chiesa di S. Simpliciano, e l'altro con quello di S. Pietro in Gessate; l'Abbate del primo governa S. Radegonda, et essendo egli huomo novitio, è reginato da questi Monaci veterani, consultori delle Monache dissobedienti': Litta to the SCVR, 25 June 1659, ASV, VR, sez. monache, 1660, feb–mar.

[31] 'non lasciano angolo dove non pubblichino Vittorie, Trionfi, Recreationi, vili sendi, dell'Arcivescovo'; ASDM XII, vol. 128, fasc. 6, fo. 262[r]; for an earlier (1654) case of Litta's affronted self-esteem, see Signorotto, *Inquisitori*, 197.

[32] ASV, VR, sez. monache, 1660, feb–mar. My thanks to Craig Monson for pointing out the existence of this document.

always been some displeasure and dispute on account of music, but these are minor matters as far as she knows.[33]

But Regina de' Lorenzi tried to inculpate the musicians:

She says that between the abbess Donna Chiara Margarita and Donna Maria Faustina there was always a point of dissension because of music; it could be that there was some other cause, but it seemed to be this.[34]

The anti-Palomera faction also tried to blame Palomera and her faction for the battles among male clerical visitors who fought among themselves for the favour of their 'carissime'.[35] But nothing further emerged about the role of music. Hence, the various punishments meted out in 1660—privation of the veil and of active and passive voice for Palomera, and imprisonment in her cell for Angela Maria Clerici (for perjury, since she had reversed herself on her original testimony)—did not include restrictions on S. Radegonda's music, except that both Palomera and Clerici were deprived of the right to sing along with the other nuns. But the Palomera scandal marked the definitive passing of final authority to Rome. It also provided Litta with cause, although he seems to have needed no prompting, to monitor activities at S. Radegonda and S. Margarita closely.

In the wake of Palomera's trial, Litta obtained an order from the Sacra Congregazione banning polyphony at S. Radegonda at some point between 1660 and 1662.[36] This was then lifted in June 1663, the document incidentally providing a list of choir size for one of the house's two ensembles, one led by Maria Domitilla Ceva and one by Bianca Maria Ripa (later by Angela Maria's niece, Antonia Francesca Clerici).[37] And indeed, the next series of scandals in 1664–5 did

---

[33] 'Ha risposto che può dire . . . che tra D. Chiara Margarita Abbadessa, D. Maria Gratia, e D. Chiara Benedetta et detta D. Maria Faustina vi è stato quasi sempre qualche disgusto, e competenza, per causa della Musica ma sono bagatelle per quanto essa sa': ASDM XII, vol. 128, fasc. 6, fo. 238ᵛ.

[34] 'Dice che tra D. Chiara Margarita Cozzolana Abbadessa e detta D. Maria Faustina per causa della Musica vi è sempre stato un punto di discenscione, et può essere, che vi fosse qualche altra causa ma in apparenza vi era questa': ibid., fo. 241ʳ.

[35] ASDM XII, vol. 128, fo. 176ʳ.

[36] This is mentioned some ten years later, in the notarial record of Giacinto Graziani's visit of 11 Mar. 1673 (ASDM XII, vol. 128, fo. 143ʳ⁻ᵛ). The visitation refers to a restoration of polyphony by the Roman congregation on 22 May 1663, so presumably there must have been an interdict before this date, although no trace of such orders is to be found in the Roman or Milanese files. Possibly the documentation was destroyed at the time of the final lifting of the interdict in 1690 (see below).

[37] The curial files (vol. 128, fo. 144) include an order of 13 Mar. 1663 from the SCVR for the partial restoration of music, with Vespers to end before sundown; this document also

involve music directly. In the light of the ten-year history of Litta's battles with the Senate and monastic patricians male and female, the consequences were severe and would be felt for a generation. At S. Radegonda, the dispute revolved around the old favourites—music-making in the *parlatorio* on one hand, and the public, patrician nature of musical Vespers and Mass on the other. But the immediate occasion was provoked by Palomera, who had not been changed by her punishment.

In 1663 Litta had rehabilitated her to the choir and refectory, with the provision that she not come to the grates or doors.[38] As the archbishop's letter of 9 July 1664 noted, she then petitioned for the right to sing in the ostensibly anonymous context of S. Radegonda's *coro pieno*, and did so, having received permission from the abbot of S. Simpliciano, her Cassinese superior, but not from the bishop.[39] The nuns of S. Radegonda—or, more precisely, the anti-Palomera faction—sent three *memoriali* protesting her behaviour. Palomera's public singing seems to have been a major scandal, performed (according to her enemies) in order to attract her admirers, and the nuns of both factions probably—and correctly—feared the punishments that would ensue.

Matters worsened quickly. The next set of documents reveals the membership and sizes of the warring factions, each associated with one of the two musical choirs.[40] The anti-Palomera group, Ripa's

names eleven nuns as 'perite nel Canto': Angiola Maria Clerici, Antonia Francesca Clerici, Justina Suarez, Antonia Felice Lomalla, Giulia Antonia Lomata, Beatrice Suarez, Anna Margarita Cozzolani, Constanza Teresa Pallavicina, Ippolita Francesca Confaloniera, Maria Francesca Chiocca, and Giovanna Maddalena Via. Since Maria Domitilla Ceva and other known singers are not listed, this is probably the roster of one of the house's two choirs, the 'Clerici–Cozzolani' ensemble; possibly Ceva's choir, to which Palomera belonged, was being punished by continued exclusion from polyphony.

[38] ASDM XII, vol. 128, fo. 190ʳ.

[39] 'Costei [Palomera] . . . mi fece passar uffitio di permettergli, che potesse ne i concerti di Musica suonare colle altre Monache, mentre non sarebbe stata conosciuta in Chiesa . . . Arrivatimi à notitia i disordini, gli scandali, e le mormorationi . . . gli hò fatto intendere . . . che onninamente si astenghi dal Canto; mà tutte le mie operationi sono riuscite infruttuose: . . . l'Abbadessa esclama fortemente di questa petulanza della Palomera': Litta to the SCVR, ASV, VR, 1664, giu-ago. The abbess was Clara Lavinia Varese, who was obviously angry at the pretexts afforded Litta by Palomera's behaviour, even though she belonged to the Spaniard's faction (see below).

[40] Unlike the case of S. Marta, this split does not seem to have pitted senior against junior nuns. Most of the nuns involved were younger singers: both Antonia Francesca Clerici and Anna Teresa Clerici signed the anti-Palomera petition, but their older aunt Angela Maria, possibly because of her previous punishment, did not. Again, the split seems to reflect divisions among clans, since all the members of one family were lined up on one side or the

choir including the Clerici and Cozzolani, claimed that she had sown discord and acted out of vanity (App. A, Doc. 59) while the pro-Palomera choir (App. A, Doc. 62) invoked the permission granted by Don Clavarino (the monastic superior), and responded that she was being punished for her unwillingness to leave the choir in which she sang and join the other; they also protested her innocence of having offended Chiara Margarita Cozzolani. Had the two factions not sought to blame the other, however, the issue might have fallen by the wayside.

But by this time Litta had had enough, or perhaps had realized that he could take advantage of the internal split in order to strike at what he perceived to be the root of the problem, dating back to the 1659 *clausura* violation (App. A, Doc. 61):

Palomera's disobedience has gone so far that the monastery has been in turmoil, and the enclosed letter written to me; having been advised by another side that major scandals will erupt every so often, *unless polyphony is forbidden to all the nuns of this monastery*; precisely this was the origin of Palomera's crime, and will always cause disorders, perhaps even worse ones, since the entire youth [insert: 'Spaniards, Germans, Neapolitans, fops, soldiers, and whoever else arrives'] of Milan is continually going to the church of these nuns, under the pretext of entering to hear the music.[41]

The archbishop took special offence at the crowds of *cavalieri* who (he claimed) stayed at the monastery to socialize—and form close relationships—with musical nuns until all hours of the night.[42] Litta followed up by prevailing on the Sacra Congregazione to suspend polyphony again at S. Radegonda; this set of orders dropped the pretence of delegating the male Cassinese to carry out the punishments.[43]

other (Cozzolanis, Clericis, and Ripas against Palomera; the abbess Varese, the Lonatis, and Ceva for her).

[41] Litta to the SCVR, 6 Aug. 1664, ASV, VR, sez. monache, 1664, giu–ago; underlining in original.　　　　　　　　　　　　　[42] Undated report, ASDM XII, vol. 129, fasc. 4.

[43] The complete banning of polyphony by the Cassinese was endorsed by the SCVR on 16 Jan. 1665; the Roman letter is in ASDM XII, vol. 128, fo. 159. Litta's local letter, dated 11 Feb. 1665 (ASDM XII, vol. 128, fo. 160) again refers to an earlier interdict handed down by the Cassinese. The prelate's reliance on Rome is evident from the ban: 'Mon*signor* Ill.mo e R.mo Alfonso Litta Arciuescovo di Milano, come Delegato Apostolico in uirtù d'una lettera della Sacra Congre*gatione* datta in Roma alli 16 Genaro 1665 . . . ordina e commanda, e ha ordinato, e commandato sotto pena della scomunica ipso facto . . . che non permetta si canti da alcuna Monaca di Canto figurato, ne in Chiesa, ne in Parlatorio . . . & ha ordinato e comandato a tutte e ciascuna Monaca perita nell'arte del Canto figurato, che s'astegono dal d*etto* Canto in tutto e p*er* tutto tanto in Chiesa, quanto in Parlatorio.'

To make matters worse (from the archbishop's point of view), the nuns simply ignored the Roman orders. Most galling were the poly-phonic Mass and Vespers put on for the Protestant Duke and Duchess of Brunswick (Ernst August and Sophie), probably on 23 or 24 February 1665.[44] Litta wasted no time in notifying Rome:

Not only did the Benedictine nuns of S. Radegonda . . . disobey repeat-edly, but they entertained the heretic Prince and Princess of Brunswick, singing in various ways for hours on end, especially in church, where the Princess stayed.[45]

Why did the sisters do this? It is clear from these accounts, and from the travel reports to be discussed presently, that music in the female monasteries fulfilled an important civic role as a symbol of Milanese prestige. It was normative, even under extreme crisis, for visiting dignitaries to go to S. Radegonda, S. Margarita, or S. Marta for musical Mass and Vespers. Urban pride demanded—and three generations of relatively lax episcopal regulation permitted—that the sisters of S. Radegonda perform for the Guelphs. And this interna-tional and political role of nuns' music was without parallel in any other Italian city.

But this time the Benedictines and the patriciate had miscalcu-lated. Litta, armed with an order from the Sacra Congregazione to remove the abbess (Clara Varese), swept down in full force upon S. Radegonda on 23 March 1665 to enforce penance. The punishments also included the formal prohibition of polyphony in S. Radegonda's church and parlours, which Litta forced the Cassinese to execute.[46]

---

[44] Barbara Strozzi had dedicated her op. 8 cantatas to Sophie during a previous stop in Venice; the duchess also travelled with a French violin band in her train.

[45] 'Le Monache di S. Redegonda Benedettine . . . non solo hanno disubedito più volte . . . [ma] si posero à dar trattenimento al Prencipe e Prencipessa di Bransvich Heretici, can-tando in più guise hore intiere, particolarmente in Chiesa, dove la med*esima* Principessa si trasgrese', Litta to the SCVR, 25 Feb. 1665, ASV, VR, sez. monache, 1665, gen–apr. A let-ter from Litta included in the same sheaf complained about the 'Heretici, ch'erano moltissimi' at the services; the archbishop threatened to resign if polyphonic liturgy contin-ued. Litta's attitude towards public music for reasons of state is best judged from another scandal in 1661: the archbishop refused to permit the singing of the *Te Deum* at the Duomo in order to celebrate the peace between England and Spain, because he found nothing to celebrate in the fact that heretics (the English) were no longer to be killed; see S. Grassi and A. Grohmann, 'La Segreteria di Stato di Sua Santità e la Milano nell'età del barocco', in de Maddalena (ed.), *Millain the Great*, 267–83 at 276.

[46] 'Chiamai il P. Abbate Cassinense di S. Simpliciano, e le dissi, che havevo ordine da cotesta Sacra Congreg*atione* di privare l'Abbadessa di S. Radegonda per le sue trasgressioni, e per haverle permesse in altre Monache; parimente mi si comandava di far eleggere un' altra

The order banning *canto figurato* was lifted only partially in 1673, allowing musical Vespers only if finished before sundown and strictly forbidding music in the *parlatorio*.

Upon Litta's illness and move to Rome (1675), however, dissension old and new erupted again at S. Radegonda. Palomera asked the now bishop-less curia for rehabilitation to active and passive voice and to music-making in the *chiesa interiore*.[47] Furthermore, another long-standing dispute between the house's two choirs flared up: this concerned the right of singers to transfer from one ensemble to the other.[48] In the 1660s (when the numbers of the two choirs were apparently larger), several singers, including Giovanna Francesca Cozzolani (an alto) and Giulia Antonia Lonati (a former student of Ceva), passed from Ceva's choir to that of Antonia Francesca Clerici. The quarrel that ensued moved the Cassinese superiors in 1669 to a formal prohibition of the practice of switching choirs; this clearly had little impact, since in 1676 Giovanna Maddalena Via asked to be transferred from Clerici's choir to Ceva's. In line with the 1669 policy, the Cassinese refused permission for the switch, and Ceva's ensemble sent a petition with six reasons to permit Via's passage (App. A, Doc. 69).

The protest was bitter, claiming that the lack of singers had forced Ceva's choir to restrict its repertory (despite the fact that a contemporary curial note (App. A, Doc. 70) listed two more singers in her choir than in Clerici's) and asking the *vicario delle monache* to inter-

---

Abbadessa, rinuovando la prohibitione del Canto figurato, perciò havevo caro, ch'egli pure assistesse all'atto: Mostrò l'Abbate di gradire la cortesia, et unitamente alli 23. del corrente si portò al Mona*ste*ro di S. Radegonda con li miei Ministri': Litta to the SCVR, 28 Mar. 1665, ASV, VR, sez. monache, 1665, mag.

[47] 'D*onn*a Maria Faustina Palomera Monaca nel Mona*ste*ro di S. Redegonda di Milano hauendo sofferto con la douuta rassignat*io*ne, et patienza una lunga penitenza di molti anni, portandosi con intiera modestia, desidera in questi Suoi Ultimi la consolatione di essere rihabilitata a la Voce actiua, e passiua, et a la musica, che si fà in Chiesa' (*memoriale* in ASDM, Carteggio Ufficiale, vol. 92, 1675, feb–mar). The fate of these requests is unknown.

[48] The sources are contained in some ten documents in ASDM, Carteggio Ufficiale, vol. 92 (1676, apr), including a cover letter from the SCVR (to whom the matter was referred for adjudication); a copy of the Cassinese superiors' orders on passage from 1669; several Milanese curial notes; two letters from Donna Paola Francesca Mercantoli requesting passage to Antonia Francesca Clerici's choir; a letter objecting to this, from Maria Domitilla Ceva (22 Apr. 1676); and a petition signed by Ceva's choir. The curial officials had problems in reconstructing the history, as noted in the *memoriale* of 29 Apr. 1676 (ibid.), which could stand as an epigraph for all the scandals at the house: 'Doppo molte uarietà, che renduuano la uerità confusa, con esatta diligenza finalmente si è rilevato nel seguente stato: [there follows a description].'

vene (hence using the curia *against* the regular superiors) in order to renew the previous prohibitions and even to return Anna Margarita Cozzolani and Lonati to Ceva's choir.[49] Most striking was the nuns' clear linkage between suitable resources for female monastic polyphony on one hand and urban prestige on the other:

Since our choir has been notably depleted by the departure of the five above-named and of others who stopped singing unexpectedly, it cannot fulfil its duty; thus it will be necessary either to fall under this burden, or to abandon singing, [resulting] in the lessened fame and esteem of both this monastery and the city.[50]

The entire matter was once again referred to Rome, with an uncertain ending.[51]

Possibly to reconfirm the authority of Litta's successor, Federico Visconti, yet another interdict was placed by Rome on S. Radegonda in April 1681, apparently by Innocent XI, himself no friend of nuns' music.[52] The invocation of the stain to patrician honour by the prohibition of polyphony, contained in a letter of the abbess (Chiara Benedetta Secca Bozella) to an unnamed Benedictine protector, proved of no avail.[53] A 1682 attempt to rescind the strictures on

---

[49] Ceva's demand would have deprived Clerici's choir of its only member listed as 'Basso' (Lonati); it was therefore a direct attack on the opposing ensemble's ability to sing larger-scale polyphony.

[50] 'Che il nostro Coro sminuito notabilmente per l'abandonamento delle 5 prenominate e per altre che per inaspetati accidenti lasciano di cantare non può reggere alla fatica, e però conuerrà, ò cadere sotto il peso, ò tralasciare il Canto, con poca riputatione, e stima di questo monastero, quando per la Città': petition of 14 Nov. 1675, ASDM, Carteggio Ufficiale, vol. 92, 1675 (App. A, Doc. 69).

[51] There is no further record in the SCVR files from 1676–7.

[52] Two letters of 5 and 12 Apr. 1681 (ASDM XII, vol. 128, fos. 161 and 162) from the Roman prelate G. B. di Luca to the Milanese vicar-general mention this interdict, without a direct reference to music. The second recorded Innocent's delight at the governor's [G. T. Henriquez de Cabrera] betrayal of the nuns: 'Nostro Signore . . . ha sentito con molto gusto l'apposizione dell'Interdetto alla Chiesa del Monisterio di Santa Radegonda, e si è nuouamente in estremo edificato della pietà, con la quale il Signor Conte Gouernatore concorre.'

[53] Her letter of 14 Apr. 1681 reported: 'Sento dal Sig. Senatore Conte di Vimercato mio fratello hauer in risposto lei medesimo appresso VS. Ill.ma le sue intercessioni ottener qualche accaloramento di VS. Ill.ma de' Signori di Patrimonio per il riccorso da noi fatto . . . sopra l'interdetto fatto intimare da questo monsignore vicario fete alla nostra Chiesa, ben è uero che il sudetto interdetto ferisce noi, ma machia anche la riputatione in qualche parte della nobilità' (ASC, Località Milanesi, busta 399). The anonymous response of 16 Apr. (ibid.) noted the failure of efforts to lift the interdict. Again, nuns' polyphony was directly linked to patrician *onore*.

music was vetoed even though the interdict was lifted.[54] Still, Badalla managed to publish her solo motets in 1684 (in Venice), despite the formal ban.

Finally, thirty-one years after Palomera's original violation, the change in popes and the Roman connection proved decisive. Possibly approached by a Benedictine protector, the rising ecclesiastical star and convinced melomane Cardinal Pietro Ottoboni exerted his not inconsiderable influence on the now-ailing Visconti to have music restored, for all practical purposes, to its previous place at S. Radegonda (App. A, Docs. 71–2).[55] The Benedictines' ultimate victory, one that would last for another forty years, reinforces the idea of the sisters' power and allies against even the most rigid episcopal authority.

Meanwhile, also in the 1660s, Litta had gone on another reform campaign at the other 'offender', S. Margarita. In the prelate's view, this house was even more 'outstanding' than S. Radegonda for the 'secular' nature of its music-making. The tone of the curia, although shared by no one else in the city, was unmistakable in its anxiety (App. A, Doc. 48):

Music, vocal and instrumental, established for the greater glory of God and His Church, is abused by the nuns of S. Margarita, and serves to foment vice, the corruption of virtue, and irreparable ruin to proper discipline. Not a single prelate, prince, celebrity, or other well-known person arrives in this city who does not immediately arrange for entrance [there], by means of nobles or other highly placed persons, and attempts by all means to be called to the monastery, where in church or in the parlours they are entertained with [added: 'lovesick'] Italian canzonettas, sonnets, lascivious madrigals, [illegible] speeches, indecent acts, and even laments far from monastic modesty.

---

[54] A letter of 24 Oct. 1682 from Cardinal Giovanni Carsegna to Visconti declared that 'La Santità di Nostro Signore è benignamente condescessa a dar facolta, e rimettere all'arbitrio di V.E. il rimovere l'interdetto già apposto alla Chiesa delle Monache di Santa Radegonda dell'ordine di S. Benedetto di cotesta città per le cause a Lei note. Non intende però S. Beatitudine che si levi la prohibitione della Musica, machè questa resti nel suo vigore' (ASDM XII, vol. 45, fo. 95ʳ).

[55] Ottoboni's letters to Visconti are in ASDM XII, vol. 128; the request dated 28 Oct. 1690 is on fo. 164ʳ; a second letter of the same date is on fo. 165ʳ; Visconti's orders (App. A, Doc. 72) are in ASDM XII, vol. 45, fo. 188ʳ, with essentially the same information in two notes in vol. 128, fos. 166–7. For Ottoboni as music patron, see H.-J. Marx, 'Die Musik am Hofe Pietro Kardinal Ottobonis unter Arcangelo Corelli', *Analecta Musicologica*, 5 (1968), 104–77, which does not mention the cardinal's intervention on behalf of S. Radegonda.

This monastery is more like a seraglio of singers than a cloister of virgins consecrated to God.[56]

The music and *sinfonie* which they sing these days in church are more like ditties and dances that entice the senses far more than they elevate the spirits of the faithful to the contemplation of heavenly matters, the purpose for which they were established.[57]

At Carnival they dress like men, sumptuously with ornaments, lavish costumes, swords at their sides, unveiled faces, their own hair-styles or wigs . . . others dress in [added: 'laywomen's'] clothes . . . they perform very worldly plays.[58]

Litta minced no words in his remedies:

It will be most necessary to ban music entirely, the cause of all the scandals and corruption of morals, at least for three years, because otherwise it will be impossible to check the abuses, even if I were given all the authority of popes, archbishops, the king, the governor, and the Senate.[59]

A curial memorandum even compared the two houses under the Cassinese, noting that the crowds were greater at S. Radegonda 'per esser la Musica e Cantatrici molto più eccellenti' and that the actual behaviour of nuns was less scandalous there.[60]

---

[56] 'Questo monastero è più tosto saraglio de cantatrici, che claustro de' Vergini à Dio consacrate': 'Abusi', ibid., fo. 1ᵛ.

[57] 'Le Musiche e Sinfonie che stillano di cantare hoggi di in Chiesa, sono più tosto Canzoni, e Balli, che alletanno il Senso piu tosto, che solleuano la Mente de Fideli alla Consideratione delle cose celesti, fini per il quale furono Instituite':, ibid., fo. 3ʳ.

[58] 'Nel Carnouale si vistono da huomo pomposamente con Pennnachiore, habite sontu-ossisime, spade à lato, faccia scoperta, Capigliatura propria, ò posticcia . . . altri si vestano [crossed out: 'da Donne'] con habiti [added: 'di Donne'] secolari . . . Recitano comedie molto profani': ibid. abuse no. 13. Antonio Rusca's 1647 regulations had noted nuns' predilection for appearing in public with guns and swords, possibly in theatrical contexts.

[59] 'Sarà necessarissimo il leuare omniamente la musica causa di tutti li scandali, e corru-tione di costumi, almeno per tre anni, perche altrimenti sarà impossibile di moderar li abusi, et inconuenienti, benche mi concoressero tutta l'autorità de Papi, et Arciuescoui, la potenza del Re, Gouernatore, e Senato', 'Remedi', ibid. Litta moderated his stance slightly towards the end of the decade; a note of 16 July 1669 reads: 'Con sua Costitutione delli 24. Decembris che comincia *Pro comisso* [illegible] comanda che si celebrino solenemente le feste di SS. [illegible], Priori e fondatoria, senza Musica essecuire, mà nel Choro inferiore in canto fermo, ò auerle figurate all'Antiphone, Magnificat a choro pieno': ASDM XII, vol. 83, fasc. 2. Litta viewed *coro pieno* settings of antiphons and the Magnificat as a safe genre; possibly the arch-conservative, *stile antico* works that Grancini would dedicate to the prelate in his *Sacri concerti* of 1669. 'Modern' solo motets, coming into fashion with such patrician composers as San Romano (who would dedicate pieces to nuns in 1670) would thus be associated by Litta with scandals.

[60] 'Mentre gli abusi sono comuni, anzi quanto alla frequenza [of nobles at services] è più notabile a S. Radegonda, che a S. Margarita, per esser la Musica e Cantatrici molto più

S. Margarita suffered from a further problem that increased the archbishop's power: it was close to financial ruin in the 1660s.[61] The difficulties were not helped by musicians' irregularities:

Maria Calegari from Bergamo, a keyboard virtuosa, was accepted into the monastery for the usual dowry of 4,000 lire. However, the treasurer received only L. 1,500, and no one knows if the remainder was waived *motu proprio* by the abbess, or if she [Calegari] embezzled it or spent it at will.[62]

Calegari (baptized Cornelia) was a singer and composer who had professed final vows at S. Margarita on 19 April 1661.[63] Her finances could not have endeared her to the troubled house, which had only been her parents' second choice. The reported loss of her compositions, first recounted by a Settecento Benedictine, if indeed it occurred, might have stemmed from her problems and from Litta's disciplinary measures.[64] But, contrary to pious legend, she did not die soon thereafter around 1662, and her musical abilities would be available to the house until at least 1680.[65]

eccellenti, benche men scandalosi, e più moderati nella musica.' ASDM XII, vol. 129, fasc. 4, undated report.

[61] ASDM XII, vol. 83, fasc. 2 is filled with financial records documenting the monastery's problems.

[62] App. A, Doc. 47. The curial 'rimedio' was to have her pay the remainder.

[63] A contemporary account of her early career is furnished by D. Calvi, *Scena letteraria de gli scrittori bergamaschi* (Bergamo, 1664), after p. 61, who noted her origin, profession, and fame. Calvi listed a *Motetti a voce sola* as having been published in 1659, along with a series of other secular and sacred works in press, none of which seem to survive.

[64] The account of her renown, early death, and lost compositions given by Armellini, *Biblioteca Benedictino-Casinensis*, ii. 93, and repeated in all subsequent literature, is fiction, based on a letter of 17 Jan. 1713 from G. M. Giorgi, abbot of S. Simpliciano, who reported that she had died shortly after profession and that her younger sister (ostensibly the oldest, semi-senile nun at the house in 1713, but cf. below) had witnessed the dispersal of her compositions. But a series of records in the SCVR files (ASV, VR, sez. monache, 1660, gen–mar) show that her parents had first tried to place her at a reduced dowry at S. Benedetto in Bergamo in 1659–60. Despite several pleas from the nuns and a letter from the bishop testifying that Calegari 'nel suonar d'Organo, et comporre di Musica, è molto avanzata', the SCVR turned down the request. The Congregation's notes of 23 Jan. 1660 (ibid.) record Roman concern over the number of nuns in S. Benedetto, and three months later Calegari took her provisional vows at S. Margarita, where the *dote* problem may have contributed to her financial difficulties.

[65] One result of Litta's attack on the house in the 1660s was a temporary ban on new professions; hence a receipt from Francesco Fasolo of 14 Aug. 1679 (ASM, Culto, p.a., 1912) that lists her as forty-seventh (i.e. the fourteenth youngest) of sixty-one nuns is not surprising. She is missing from a further contract with Fasolo and its 1689 list of inhabitants (ibid.). Furthermore, her sister Rosa Gieronima could hardly have been decrepit in 1713; a contract of 8 Mar. 1727 (ibid.) lists her as still alive.

Eventually, after some unrecorded form of discipline had been imposed, and in line with his policy at S. Radegonda, Litta lifted the restrictions at S. Margarita in 1673–4; this may have occasioned Isabella Leonarda's dedication of a psalm setting to Gioconda Bossi at the house in the latter year.[66] This coincided with the restitution of the house's right to clothe new novices, which had been suspended in the 1660s.[67]

In the same years of Litta's clash with the Benedictines, another scandal, involving the Spanish governor, came to a head. This conflict revolved around the question that had so exercised Carlo in the 1570s: the use of ducal musicians in services at the exterior churches of monasteries. And, ironically, this case involved the saint's model project, S. Paolo. Despite Borromeo's protracted struggle for control over the Angeliche, the early Seicento evidence—the dedications around 1600 to Agata Sfondrati and the 1624 reports by the retinue of the Polish prince Władysław Wasa—point up the spread of music to this institution as well. In addition, one of the Gonzaga princesses at the monastery, Luigia Marianna, had received the dedication of Sisto Reina's *Armonia ecclesiastica* in 1653; the inscription referred to her vocal and instrumental abilities, a sign of real musical forces among the Angeliche.[68]

The case that would pit Litta against the crown arose in February 1661.[69] Francesco Caetani, Duke of Sermoneta and interim governor of the State of Milan, decided to honour the feast of Our Lady of Copacabana (2 Feb.) with a large-scale musical service in the *chiesa esteriore*, for which he obtained the nuns' consent. This feast was

---

[66] The orders from the archbishop of Ceva lifting the restrictions at the house and allowing the clothing of novices are dated Christmas 1673, confirmed by a local unsigned curial note of 2 May 1674 (ASDM XII, vol. 83, fasc. 2). For Leonarda's *Laetatus sum* from her op. 4 (an appropriate text for a house that had just been restored to polyphony and been allowed to survive, and one used in the Benedictine clothing ceremony), see App. C.

[67] Again, the long-term effect of episcopal discipline is open to question; the visitation of 17 Nov. 1731 (ASM, Religione, p.a., 1900) ordered: 'si proibisce pure il cantare, e suonare ne' Parlatori, o Foresterie, e molto meno ne' giorni di festa'; this was repeated in 1772 (ibid.).

[68] She had been born in Rome as Polissena Eusebia on 2 Jan. 1606 to Francesco of the Castiglione delle Stiviere branch of the family and took vows at S. Paolo in July 1625 (Archivio Gonzaga Castiglione delle Stiviere, b. 165, notarial act of 21 July 1625, cited in M. Marcocchi, *I Gonzaga di Castiglione delle Stiviere: Vicende pubbliche e private del casato di San Luigi* (n.p., 1990), 431 and 436).

[69] Litta's letter of 9 Feb. 1661 giving his side of the story, along with an unsigned and undated missive from the governor's side, as well as the supporting documentation for both parties, are all preserved in ASV, VR, sez. monache, 1661, feb–apr.

clearly a part of Spanish Habsburg devotion, since it had originated in Bolivia in the previous century. It did not figure in the Ambrosian calendar, and Caetani must have meant to provoke the prelate by 'out-ritualizing' him through a feast inextricably linked to royal, not episcopal, prestige.[70] Litta responded through his *vicari* by invoking Carlo's prohibition of music in the exterior churches (dating from 1576), and added that under Monti similar transgressions had resulted in punishment for the sisters and the incarceration of the musicians; he tried to dissuade the governor and warned the nuns.[71] Caetani's officials replied by citing numerous exceptions to the prohibition permitted throughout the century, and by claiming that the strictures of the Provincial Councils had never applied to the king or his representatives.[72]

The services (probably Mass and/or Vespers) were celebrated on 5 February with double-choir performances, including instruments, provided by the ducal band and singers.[73] Some of the music might have been composed by Francesco Bagatti, organist of the governor's chapel.[74] Litta, again personally aggrieved by the nuns' ostensible

[70] I collate the accounts of the two sides, ibid. The feast fell on the same day as the Purification of the Virgin Mary, and so the governor postponed the scheduled service until 5 Feb. To judge from other references to this feast's celebration in Milan (in ASM, Culto, p.a., 2084), the commemoration functioned locally as part of Habsburg devotion to the Immaculate Conception, a devotional current partially resisted by Rome, but one with important musical reflections in Austria and Spain.

[71] App. A, Doc. 51; 'Che in tempo del S. Card*inale* Monti per due contraven*tioni* furono mortificate le Monache, carcerati li Musici e fatte altre dimostra*tioni*': in Litta's, letter of 9 Feb. 1661 to the SCVR, ASV, VR, sez. monache, 1661, feb–apr. There is no record of such a case under Monti in either the Milanese or Roman files; perhaps the prelate was inventing tradition.

[72] 'da molti SS.ri particolari, i quali in occasioni di feste in Chiese di Monache havevano fatto cantare da Musici forastieri; . . . poiche la clausola generale . . . non s'intende mai per la persona del Rè': anonymous letter, ibid.

[73] 'Sabbato mattina 5. del cor*rente* nella Chiesa sodetta si fece una solenissima, e strepitosissi*ma* musica à due gran Chori, con diversi istrom*enti* di Violini, Violoni, fagotto, leuto, et altro (questi pure proibiti nelle no*stre* musiche), assistendo sempre il S.r Duca sotto Baldachino, ò sia Cortina *a cornu Evangelij nel Presbiterio*' (Litta, ibid.). The string instruments mentioned are required in several local editions, including G. A. Grossi's *Orfeo Pellegrino* (Camagno, 1659); Reina's *Fiorita corona* (Camagno, 1660); and G. Pestalozzi's *Suonate à 2–4*, op. 1 (Vigone, 1679). Litta's snipe at the participation of instruments was an attempt to expand the Duomo's restricted tradition of voices and organ only to the city as a whole, another unsuccessful episcopal campaign.

[74] In 1661 Teodoro Casati was *maestro di cappella* for the ducal chapel; he was also first organist at the Duomo, a possible conflict of interest. His two surviving books of *Concerti ecclesiastici*, op. 2 and 3 (Camagno, 1651 and 1668) contain no eight-voice music. On the other hand, Bagatti's *Motetti, messa e salmi brevi e pieni*, op. 5 (Camagno, 1672) is composed entirely of such works (in double-choir disposition, without instruments; this edition is

ridicule of the *vicario* who had served the prohibition on them, wasted no time in bringing the matter before the Sacra Congregazione, citing the various precedents of Carlo Borromeo and Monti.[75] Meanwhile, the governor notified the court in Madrid, which backed him fully. All the parties to the dispute—the prelate, the governor, and the nuns of S. Paolo—sent documentation to the Sacra Congregazione. One *memoriale*, from the side of the governor and the Angeliche, included a list of the occasions on which outside musicians had performed in the *chiesa esteriore* of S. Paolo, and another that detailed the visits of the ducal band to the exterior churches of other houses over the course of the century (App. A, Doc. 52). Despite the precedents, Litta apparently did persuade the Sacra Congregazione to punish the Angeliche, although it is unclear if the punishments were actually carried out.[76]

Yet the events at S. Paolo shed light on the relative frequency of performances by the ducal musicians in the exterior churches. The sisters were clearly concerned to establish as many precedents for the practice as possible, and hence the list taken from the ducal accounts should be presumed to be a fairly complete record. The striking point of the list is the kind of monasteries to which the governor's band came: largely the 'second-tier' musical houses of the city in the Seicento, such as S. Paolo or S. Barbara, along with the Monastero Maggiore. Foundations with more autochthonous musical traditions—S. Radegonda, S. Marta, S. Margarita—figure sparsely, if at all. For his part, Litta had to reach back almost a century to Carlo's half-forgotten rules in order to find written episcopal restrictions on

dedicated to Regina Melzi at S. Bernardino). Bagatti also dedicated his *Concerti ecclesiastici*, bk. 3, op. 4 (Camagno, 1667) to Giovanna Maria Visconti at S. Maria in Valle (this last edition also includes a *Messa concertata a 4* and two solo motets with violins).

[75] The archbishop's missive was accompanied by no less than five inserts (some sort of record for the SCVR files): extracts from Provincial Councils I and IV; sections from Pius V's *Circa pastoralis*; a formal prohibition from Litta; a list of occasions when Duomo or ducal musicians performed in the *chiesa esteriore* of S. Paolo; and a list of female monasteries in whose external churches the ducal chapel had sung since 1618.

[76] The letter to the governor of 12 Oct 1661, signed by Philip IV in Madrid, noted: 'Itase reciuido una Carta de 26. de Abril deste ano, en que referis lo que os paso usear en la celebridad de la fiesta que haceis de Nuestra Senora de Copacauana el [día] que se cantase musica secular en un Conuento de Monjas, . . . Todavia después de hauerse celebrado la fiesta con Musica [Litta] dió cuenta después a la Congregacion de Obispos en Roma, La qual ordenó mortificarse a las Monjas, y otras resoluciones que no se ha atreuido a executar . . . solo se ofrese deciros que hé estranado mucho el intento y pretension del Arcobispo, pues a los que estan representando mi Beata persona en ese Gouierno, siempre les es licito yr con la Musica a las yglesias': ASM, Culto, p.a., 2084, fasc. 7.

the practice, another sign of its secondary place in the disputes over music. Although the visits were not unknown, they were restricted to certain houses, and this point should be kept in mind in evaluating the dedications of pieces to nuns and the broader question of which repertory might have been performed by sisters and which by visiting musicians in the *chiese esteriori*.

But even Litta, unlike his model Carlo Borromeo, did not oppose polyphony *per se* in female monasteries, but only its public manifestations in those patrician institutions over which he had less control. After the prelate's 1675 departure for Rome, his curial officials issued orders in this spirit.[77] Litta himself recommended *dote* reductions for musically promising novices throughout his tenure, at least in the cases of smaller, poorer monasteries subject to his authority.[78] He was also not averse to musical celebrations at consecrations of new female monastic churches.[79] Also during his tenure, music began to appear in the visitation records for other, previously 'unmusical' extra-urban houses.[80] One typical case is that of the small Augustinian house of

[77] A letter of 30 Oct. 1675 from A. A. de Pilastri forbade music in the parlours, 'concendendo la Musica solamente nell'hore delle Messe, & Vesperi dentro le Chiese Interiori delle Monache, stando esse nelle Cantorie à tal effetto destinate, & non in altro modo, forma e tempo' (ASDM XII, vol. 52, fasc. 7). *Pace* Bowers, 'The Emergence', 143, this actually represents a more liberal policy than that of Litta's efforts *c.*1660.

[78] See Litta's letters of the following dates: 23 Apr. and 26 Sept. 1653, for Anna Lampugnana at S. Maria Maddalena in Busto [Arsizio] (ASV, VR, mon. 1652, gen–giu and 1653, ag–set, respectively; 3 Oct. 1657, for Cecilia Trabattona (possibly a relative of the composers Egidio and Bartolomeo Trabattone from Varese) at S. Maria in Cantù (ibid., 1657, mag–lug); 28 Nov. 1657 and 27 Feb. 1658, for Maria Virginia Pistagalla at S. Agostino di Porta Nuova (both ibid., 1658, gen–mar). The series slowed during the 1660s, but in 1673 Litta recommended another reduction for Bianca Maria Sant'Agostino at S. Caterina in Brera, noting that '*Questo Monastero per* l'essemplarità della Vita delle Monache è contato frà li più virtuosi di *tutta* la Diocesi' (ibid., 1673, giu–lug).

[79] An undated account of the consecration of S. Maria degli Angeli's church, at which Litta presided, recorded that 'Fatta la beneditione . . . ma avanti cominciare la Confessione [Litta] intonò l'himno *Veni creator spiritus* in ginocchio, e detto il primo verso si fermerò in piedi, sino al fine del Hinno, che si canterà dalla musica del Duomo . . . Per la strada andando dal Corpossanto a S*anta* Maria degli Angioli dal Choro alternate et dalla Musica s'anderà cantando l'hinno *Te Deum*, et il Salmo *Laudate dominum* . . .' (ASDM XII, vol. 45, fos. 65–6). Originally Ursuline, the foundation passed to the Capuchins in 1655.

[80] The orders of 2 Dec. 1651 for S. Maria in Cantù from Antonio Mattei are reminiscent of matters at S. Marta a generation earlier: 'La musica si faccia solo in Chiesa à suoi tempi, per honorar Dio, e suoi Santi, e non per piacer alle Creature, et s'introduca qualche buona Regola, che un Choro, overo una Parte suoni, e canti una settimana, et l'altro Choro l'altra settimana, e quando si fann' maggior solennità, potranno fare à due, ò tre Chori insieme, conforme al numero delle Perite nella Musica' (ASDM XII, vol. 162, fasc. 4). This Cistercian house evinced no mention of music in the extensive visitation that accompanied

S. Ambrogio in Cantù, where a curial visit of 25 April 1583 had revealed no musical duties among the sisters. But the peripatetic Reina would inscribe two motets to nuns there in a motet book of 1653, and three residents would have musical duties by 1707.[81]

What does this review of episcopal policy over a century tell us about the effective possibilities for nuns to make music? Perhaps the most striking point, one not at all expected, is that, from the time of Carlo's visitation of S. Maria Maddalena until Litta's crackdown at S. Radegonda around 1660, there is no surviving documentation to indicate that any Milanese nun was ever actually punished by a local cleric for singing under any circumstances.[82] Indeed, female monastic music in its broadest sense was admonished but never chastised in this period. Litta's offensive must have come as an absolute shock to the fourth generation of musical nuns, whose two predecessors had enjoyed either active episcopal encouragement in Federigo's time, or at least general tolerance under Monti. By mid-century, nuns at the majority of urban houses and a significant number of extra-urban foundations practised polyphony on some occasions.[83] The changing course of musical dedications to nuns highlights the public and political role of such polyphony. If the aftermath of the plague years had slowed both music publishing in general and the inscriptions to female monastic singers (from 1632 until 1655, the only dedications stem from Reina, addressed to singers and organists in both extra-urban and Milanese houses), then the prominence of nun musicians in the 1660s occasioned another wave of dedications, one which clearly flew in the face of Litta's strictures. Maurizio Cazzati's

---

its 1581 subjection to episcopal authority; S. Maria also witnessed a Palomera-like dispute over the solo singing of Giulia Colomba Romania around 1669 (ibid., fasc. 1).

[81] A 1600 visitation revealed only fourteen *professe*, which by 1707 had grown to forty-one. The visitation of this latter year noted Maria Serafina Quadri as 'maestra del canto fermo', Antonia Isabella Rota as 'organista', and Antonia Margarita Rota as 'maestra del canto figurato', another case of musical family relations (all in ASDM XII, vol. 161). For Reina's inscriptions to Candida Aurelia Archinta and Candida Maria Campi in his *Marsyae et Apollini de musices principatu* [op. 4] (Milan: Camagno, 1653), see below.

[82] The exception to this is the Roman suspension of polyphony at S. Marta in 1634. The records of hortatory decrees from Federigo's and Monti's tenures are reasonably complete. If there had been a major disciplinary case involving music, one would expect to find some trace of it. There was no mention of nuns' music in the printed decrees of the *AEM* from Provincial Council IV (1576) to Rusca's orders of 1647, whereas theatre in the parlours (especially the transvestite *commedie*) was repeatedly prohibited.

[83] This is corroborated by the dedications to nuns in such volumes as RISM 1679[1], which include singers at previously unrecorded foundations (the episcopally subject Benedictines at the Monastero del Bocchetto, S. Ulderico).

relations with the Ceva family are obvious from his three dedications to Maria Domitilla, while her rival, Antonia Clerici, would receive Giovanni Legrenzi's *Acclamationi devote* (1670) and a motet by Paolo Magni, *Ad pugnas, o furie* (RISM 1679¹). Legrenzi's inscription also reveals his debt to the Clerici family, while the public association of music with one of Litta's leading targets served as neat revenge for the composer's loss in the 1669–70 competition to replace Grancini as *maestro* at the Duomo.

The generic diversity of the inscriptions also hints at the breadth of the female monastic repertory. For the dedications from 1648 to 1679 include some eight editions of (or publications containing) solo motets or vernacular *cantate spirituali* (Reina (twice), Cazzati (twice), Casola, Legrenzi, San Romano, and the anthology RISM 1679¹); five concertos or concerto collections scored for two to four voices (Reina, Caifabri, Bagatti, San Romano, Cossoni); and five Mass or Vespers editions or items for two to eight voices (Reina (twice), Cesati, Cazzati, Bagatti, Leonarda). We shall return to the musical style of these works; but the corpus as a whole comprises a surprisingly generous share of the entire Milanese repertory, small- and large-scale, of the 1660s. In this conspectus of nuns' music, a perspective diametrically opposed to Litta's is provided by outsiders' depictions: travellers' reports, urban panegyric literature, and iconography.

If the local accounts from Federigo's years emphasize the humility and devotion of musical nuns, most of the outsiders' writings stress their technical prowess and their place in urban prestige. The travel diaries start around 1600, the beginning of the Grand Tour and its attendant reports; Jean-Antoine Rigaud's remarks on S. Radegonda and S. Maria Annunciata at Easter 1600 note the centrality of the monasteries' music to patrician social life.[84] Other accounts followed rapidly.[85] Milan's female houses were also a favourite spot for Polish

---

[84] 'Le jour de Pasques ouismes la grand Messe & vespres au dit Domou [i.e. the Duomo] . . . Nous auons ouy la musique és Nonnains de S. Radegonde, & de la Nunciade, qui ne ce peut ouyr de mieux chanter, & c'est la [S. Maria Annunciata?] ou est la presse des Seigneurs & Dames de la ville, & s'y voit arriuer force gentils hommes en housse & carroce': J. A. Rigaud, *Bref recueil des choses rares, notables . . . de l'Italie* (Aix, 1601), fo. 8ᵛ. Rigaud's trip took place during the Holy Year of 1600; his account does not mention nuns' music in any other city. The leading attraction at S. Maria Annunciata would have been Sessa.

[85] An anonymous traveller: 'Des particularités de Milan seroit chose infinie à dire: . . . la musique excellente de voix et d'instruments que font les nonnains où nous oysmes (car il estoit dimanche) partie des vespres': *Voyage de Italie* (1606), ed. M. Bideaux (Geneva,

princes.[86] Jakob Sobieski noted during his visit of September 1612, probably to S. Maria del Cappuccio or S. Maria Annunciata, that so many people crowded into the *chiesa esteriore* in order to hear a Donna Grazia that they nearly suffocated.[87] A decade later, the musical crown prince Władysław Wasa made the rounds of the most famous monasteries, stopping to hear Mass with a famous but unnamed singer at S. Bernardo (or possibly S. Bernardino alle Monache) on 18 November 1624 and then proceeding to musical Vespers at S. Paolo, where his two chroniclers recorded the 'miraculous voice' of another nun.[88] The diarist's reference to the 'vesperis a monachibus [?monialibus] . . . cantatis' implies polyphonic practice among the Angeliche by the early Seicento.

The accounts also reflect the ties between nuns' music and the social life of the aristocracy. The 1642–3 letters of the society lady Clara Brebbia Panigarola, written to Mathias de' Medici, recount the balls and other social events which the prince had frequented during his stay in Milan; part of Mathias' visit must have been a stop at S. Radegonda for music.[89] Panigarola's letters also show that nuns at the patrician monasteries kept in touch with noblewomen, yet another link to the world of the urban patriciate highlighting the porous nature of *clausura* a century after Carlo. Major political ceremonials,

1982), 49; it is noteworthy that female monastic music was considered a Milanese speciality. Friedrich Gerschow's account of the journeys of a German prince compared the singing of London boy actors to that of Milanese nuns: G. von Bülow (ed.), 'Diary of the Journey of Philip Julius, Duke of Stettin-Pomerania, through England in the Year 1602', *Transactions of the Royal Historical Society*, NS 6 (1892), 28.

[86] The Polish accounts are summarized in A. Przybos, 'Polacchi e lituani di passaggio a Milano nel Seicento', in de Maddalena (ed.), *Millain the Great*, 311–22.

[87] J. Sobieski, *Peregrynacja po Europie, 1607–1613* (Wrocław, 1991), 173–4, which mentions a church dedicated to the Virgin belonging to nuns 'ordinis Sanctae Monicae Augustiniae'. The choices would have been S. Maria del Cappuccio or S. Maria Annunciata, which latter followed the Augustinian rule even though it was a Lateran Canoness house.

[88] Stefan Pac's travel diary for 18 Nov.: 'Rano był Królewic J. M. u Św. Bernarda, gdzie mniszkę cudownie śpiewając słyszał; a że na nieszporze miał być u mniszek Św. Pawla, które gwoli Królewicowi zacną bardzo muzykę sporządziły były, i żeby ślad stracił temu gminowi ludzi, którzy nań chcąc widzieć . . .'. The Latin version of J. Hagenow summarizes: 'Religiosam apud Dominum Bernardum cantantem (Ladislav) audit, . . . Peracto prandio vesperis a monachibus [*sic*] ad Sanctum Paulum in eius gratiam cantatis interest, ubi mirifica virginis cuiuspiam vox notata' (both in A. Przyboś, *Podróż królewicza Władysława Wazy do krajów Europy Zachodniej w latach 1624–1625 w świetle ówczesnych relacji* (Cracow, 1977), 240–1). The musical ties between Seicento Lombardy and Poland were quite close.

[89] These are preserved in ASF, MP, and summarized in G. Calvi, 'I Toscani e la Milano barocca', in de Maddalena (ed.), *Millain the Great*, 169–90.

such as the 1598 entry of Margaret of Austria, or the 1649 visit of Philip IV's bride, Maria Anna of Austria, also occasioned visits to female monasteries.[90]

Who was the public who flocked to S. Radegonda, S. Maria Annunciata, and other houses in order to hear nun singers? Both the travel accounts and the disciplinary records agree on the largely aristocratic composition of the audience in the *chiese esteriori*. From Litta's complaints of the 1660s, it seems that entrance to the external churches often depended, at least for foreign visitors, on the intercession of local patricians. But there is no record of direct payments to the nuns (nor admission charged) for such services, and indeed the connotations of professionalism inherent in such payments probably would have been considered an insult to the Benedictines' social status.

Secular music in the parlours, along with the Carnival *mascherate*, was another matter, due among other things to the restricted size of the *foristerie*; these performances seem to have been by invitation only, for family and important guests, although sometimes musical or otherwise interested visitors of lower rank seemed to have wangled admission. Thus the major economic function of female monastic music seems to have been as part of the city's prestige, an aspect vital to the production and preservation of the embattled capital's renown in the troubled Seicento, and one in which monetary considerations were *a priori* excluded.

Several accounts give evidence for the crucial years 1664–5 at S. Radegonda. First are the dual versions of the 1664 travels of Cosimo III de' Medici 'in Lombardia'. The Grand Duke was a fancier of nuns: the diaries record stops at female monasteries in almost every city on the trip, including Venice (with no mention of music) and in Brescia (again with singers).[91] Cosimo, whose duchy was at least temporarily in alliance with Spain, arrived in Milan on 23 June 1664

---

[90] The custom continued into the Settecento: Emperor Charles VI's consort Elizabeth Christina visited S. Radegonda on 28 Apr. 1713, where she 'si fermò sin ad un'hora di notte [i.e. roughly 8.00] divertendosi con sentir a cantare' (from Massimo Cesati's diary, quoted in A. Giulini, 'I genitori di Maria Teresa a Milano nel 1711 e 1713', *ASL* 60 (1933), 134–49 at 146).

[91] In Brescia, 'Dopo [Cosimo] visitò le Monache degl'Angeli Agostiniane, fermandosi su la Porta del Monastero a parlar colle Madri . . . fu in Chiesa loro, dove scoperta la Madonna, una delle Monache cantò un Motetto': 'Relazione del Viaggio fatto dal Ser^mo Prn^pe Cosimo di Toscana in Lombardia . . .' (ASF, MP, filza 6382, fo. 50^v), whose dedication was signed by Filippo Pizzichi.

after hearing Mass at a female monastery in Crema.[92] Both accounts, by Filippo Pizzichi and Cosimo Pria (App. A, Docs. 57–8), of Cosimo's stay at S. Radegonda on Wednesday, 25 June (the prince's visit occurred immediately after his arrival) remark on the large number of musicians among the nuns ('e vi sono 50 Monache fra cantatrici, e Sonatrici'), the noble backing of the monastery, and the division of the ensemble into the two choirs that proved so fateful for the Palomera case ('E regna fra di loro una piccha in questa virtù della Musica, che si sono divise in due parti, non cedendo la prima alla seconda'). Cosimo's visit coincided with a period of relative peace between the nuns and Litta, after the punishments for Palomera's singing and before the Brunswick visit. Furthermore, Medici prestige was such that Litta would probably not have been able to block his visits to S. Radegonda, even if the prelate had wanted to do so.

Indeed, the nuns' dispute with Litta was not entirely absent from these accounts, despite the lack of overt reference. For the only deletion of Pizzichi's entire 144-page narrative eliminated the original mention of Litta, probably so as not to offend the powerful prelate.[93] Cosimo's visit also revealed the division of singing between the two choirs and the fact that they did not usually perform together due to the rivalries adduced. The Florentine accounts provide further, apparently customary, details of musical visits to the house: the secular (*Ariette*) music-making in the *parlatorio* afterwards with a solo singer and 'fundamente' from each ensemble, and the performance of Ceva, who accompanied herself on theorbo.

Pizzichi's travelogue also remarked on the musical activities of nuns themselves at S. Paolo: '[Cosimo went] to the nuns of S. Paolo, [the church was] very beautiful, in which he remained to hear a motet sung by the mothers, with a musical ensemble of more than women, accompanied by the *sinfonia* of various instruments.'[94] The

---

[92] 'Relazione del Viaggio fatto dal Ser^mo Sig^re Principe Cosimo Terzo di Toscana L'Anno 1664 . . . Di Cosimo Pria, di Camera di S.A.S' (ASF, MP, filza 6383); for Milan, fos. 49^v–55^r. This account was first quoted in Calvi, 'I Toscani e la Milano barocca'.

[93] 'E la pieca, e puntualità loro [of the two choirs] è di tal sorte, che separatamente stanno trà di loro, senza trouarsi mai insieme, e ciascuna parte tiene li suoi strumenti: [long deletion, under which the only legible words are: 'dall'Arcivesc^vo'] ne mai si fanno servizio in questo interesse': Pizzichi, ibid., fo. 50^v. The last words make no sense without some sort of antecedent clause, i.e. the deletion.

[94] 'Uscito alle 21 fu [a S. Celso] . . . et alle Monache di S. Paolo molto più bella, tutta ben dipinta, nella quale stette a sentire un motetto cantato dalle Madri, con un coro di musica più che da Donne, accompagnato da Sinfonia di vari strumentij': Pizzichi, ibid., fo. 53^r. Whether 'più che da Donne' refers to a collaboration between the Angeliche and male

other noteworthy aspect of the Florentine accounts is their lack of mention of other musical venues. Cosimo was by no means unmusical; and the praise he lavished on S. Radegonda, while perhaps formulaic, represents a recognition of its leading place in urban culture.

Several months before, the travelling Bolognese priest Sebastiano Locatelli had marvelled at the 'angelic' singing of the Dominicans at S. Agostino Bianco on the titular feast (29 April) of S. Pietro Martire, a house that had been forcibly united to S. Agostino by Carlo (App. A, Doc. 56). Locatelli returned on 2 May, and then again to say Mass on 3 May, during which he 'was then in Paradise during the time that they sang a *concertato* motet with violins and violone'.[95] Again, this kind of *motetto con stromenti* was being produced by those figures who would also dedicate works to nuns.[96]

At a more famous house on 1 May Locatelli heard some sort of Office, again not prescribed in any of the liturgical calendars, celebrating the beginning of the Marian month:

The beginning [of the month] was our highest consolation, because at S. Radegonda, a monastery of nuns, we could not distinguish if the singing voices were from here on earth or celestial. They sang a *Regina caeli* which showed well that they had learnt from the angels how to salute their Queen. The one who sang best of all was called Donna Angiola; she had a nightingale's throat, and executed trills that lasted so long that it seemed that her soul wanted to deprive itself of breath in order to receive the prize for its labours from Mother Mary who was honoured.[97]

Locatelli then returned for Vespers, to a church again so full of nobles that one could hardly breath; he noted other visitors' opinion that the Benedictines' music-making surpassed not only that of the Imperial Court in Vienna, but also of any other Italian centre.

We owe the last account of the mid-1660s to another court: the

---

musicians in the *chiesa esteriore* must remain open to question. Interestingly, the important musical traditions of the Marian shrine at S. Celso are not mentioned, but the less famous musical life of S. Paolo does come up.

[95] Locatelli's account is in Bologna, Biblioteca dell'Archiginnasio, B 1691, with passages first transcribed in L. Monga, 'Pagine di vita milanese nel diario di un prete bolognese del Seicento', *Libri & Documenti*, 14 (1988), 88–95. My citations are from the manuscript.

[96] Besides the two motets for canto solo with two violins in Bagatti's 1667 op. 4, Cazzati's op. 37 Mass and Vespers (1666, dedicated to Ceva) are scored largely for CATB (solo and ripieno), two obbligato violins, and 'Violone o Tiorba'.

[97] Locatelli, ibid., fo. 43ᵛ. 'Don'Angiola' must refer to the 55-year-old Angela (Angiola) Maria Clerici; although Cozzolani's *Concerti sacri* of 1642 does contain a *Regina caeli*, the scoring (AA) and age of this piece seem to disqualify it from consideration.

Estense dynasty in Modena employed the chatty Cassinese abbot of
S. Pietro in Gessate, Cesario Vernici, as its Milanese resident from
1664 to 1669.[98] His 1664–5 letters concerning the conflict between
Litta and S. Radegonda reveal him to be caught between his disciplinary duties and his social base in the patriciate.[99] As a monastic
superior, Vernici was at the centre of the battle.[100] His descriptions
of the 1664 visit of Cardinal Girolamo Colonna, Vatican envoy to
Spain, point up that Litta could be moved to grant the necessary
licenza for nuns to make music, even at a time of increased restrictions.[101] Vernici also noted that the prelate did not always win out:
'He [Litta] also embarrassed himself with judicial acts outside his
authority against the many nuns of S. Radegonda, in whose defence
the flower of the local nobility bestirred itself.'[102]

Vernici also used the Guelph visit of spring 1665 to reveal Litta's
plans for crackdowns on music at the monastery, including the episcopal trump card of invoking the visitors' Protestantism (App. A,
Doc. 64), and the abbot's own resistance:

Yesterday, [the Guelphs] went to the nuns' monastery of S. Radegonda, to
the church, with a great band of nobles, where both musical choirs [of the
house] sang together (an unusual event), among them both Ceva and
Clerici, the two famous ones, much to the pleasure of Their Highnesses.
Monsignor Archbishop, confident of his influence, raised with the abbot of
S. Simpliciano and myself the idea that we should stop the project, forbidding both music to the nuns and entrance to the said princes, since they are
heretics; this would apply to the said monastery as well as to S. Margarita,

---

[98] The Modenese–Milanese relations, including Vernici's accounts, are well summa-
rized in M. Fortini, '"Alla Altezza Serenissima di Modena dal Residente in Milano":
Ambasciatori, agenti e corrispondenti modenesi nel XVII secolo', in de Maddalena (ed.),
Millain the Great, 223–41.

[99] 'Il Breue ultimamente uscito sopra Regolari, che gouerano Monache mi da assai di
molestia con questa Curia Archiepiscopale seuera, et Arpocratica in tutte le cose, ne sarà
poco, ch'io conservi buona corispondenza', letter of 3 Feb. 1665, in ASMod, Carteggio
ufficiale, Ambasciatori, b. 114. The references to nuns in Vernici's letters end after the
Brunswick affair; apparently the Estensi had other matters for the abbot to pursue. Vernici
had also intervened on behalf of S. Margarita, asking that the house be allowed to vest three
novices for financial reasons (letter to Rome of 4 Mar. 1665, ASDM XII, vol. 83, fasc. 2).

[100] The first mention of S. Radegonda notes: 'Deuo essere un di questi giorni dal Sig^r
Don Luigi [Luis de Guzmán, the Spanish governor 1662–8] per interesso del monastero di S.
Radegonda" (letter of 31 Oct. 1664, ASMod, Ambasciatori, b. 113).

[101] App. A, Docs. 63–4; 'accidenti' can only refer to Palomera's unauthorized singing.
Again, Vernici's references to 'angelic' singing and demonic behaviour are telling.

[102] 'Si è pur anco imbarazzato con atti giuridiconali incompetenti alla sua autorità, sopra
le molte Monache di S. Radegonda, à favor delle quali s'è mosso il fior di questa Nobilta,
non hauendo esse voluto riconoscerla', letter of 18 Feb. 1665, ibid.

which we govern. But having weighed the punishment and the disadvantages, and given the weighty advantages, we firmly decided (even if [the results should be] bitter for us) not to employ tactlessness and scandalous incivility, especially since these princes were supposed to go to other monasteries, ones subject to the archbishop.[103]

The ensembles at S. Radegonda must have been truly remarkable; they were the only Milanese group of international fame in the early 1660s. Indeed, despite the renown of female monastic music in other Italian cities, no other case displays such political and musical weight in the entire Seicento. Vernici's letters leave no doubt as to music's patrician prestige and ritual nature at the Benedictine houses. Despite Litta's best efforts, polyphony in the female monasteries had become firmly institutionalized by the end of his tenure, as seen in the musical prestige of S. Radegonda and S. Margarita, the regular dowry-reduction requests for organists at smaller monasteries in the city, and the spread of music to the extra-urban foundations in the diocese. In a larger sense, however, the prelate's attempts to restrict music at the patrician houses should be seen as part of a broader episcopal move in the 1660s to discipline and to control the 'irregular' ritual behaviour and devotional life that had flourished in the city and diocese ever since Visconti's tenure, a campaign not without parallel in the various Roman condemnations of Quietism in the later Seicento and an effort not without results in the Duomo's musical repertory.[104]

The outsiders' accounts reinforce the lines of demarcation among the urban monasteries. On one hand, there were the larger foundations: patrician, often Benedictine, subject to regulars, sometimes with more than one choir, and possessing a clear role in the city's renown.[105] On the other, there were the smaller houses, for which the dowry-reduction requests were vital in attracting one or two

---

[103] Raising the spectre of heresy was a favourite recourse of Litta's; the curial denunciations of S. Radegonda and S. Margarita include deleted references to heresy arising from musical services, rather as if Litta (or someone) knew that he could not make the charges stick. Joint performances of the two choirs ('cosa insolita') could not have been completely uncommon, since the nuns had done so for Cosimo de' Medici eight months earlier.

[104] For the restrictive policies of mid-century, part of the hierarchy's turn against 'undisciplined' piety, see Zardin, 'L'ultimo periodo spagnolo', 599–600, whose description could sum up entire musical repertories, such as the works that Grancini composed for the cathedral in the 1650s and 1660s.

[105] The survival of such monastic musicians into the new century and their superiority to theatrical singers were witnessed by J. J. Quantz during a Milanese visit of May 1726 described in his autobiography: 'Unter den Nonnen traf man verschiedene mit schönen Stimmen begabte Sängerinnen an, welchen es an der guten Art zu singen nicht fehlte. Wie

skilled novices who could be counted upon to keep polyphony going; the reports from these foundations usually mention only one singer. If the larger houses were internationally renowned, still polyphonic practice at the smaller houses could sometimes be difficult and modest.

Finally, nuns and their musical culture left their mark in contemporary iconography. The mid-Seicento portraits of four daughters of Giuseppe Arconati, all future nuns, feature musical instruments—violins, cellos, and a spinet—as the most prominent objects in the compositions, functioning as symbols of the girls' characters.[106] Unlike the other attributes of secular life portrayed (their costumes), the instruments shown would not have to be surrendered by the girls upon profession—rather, the monastery would have been the best, perhaps the only, musical venue for their talents as grown women. The portraits were thus not a memory of their pre-profession talents but rather a pictorial embodiment of the skills for which they were most renowned in patrician heritage.[107]

But the most revealing, even if satirical, depiction is a drawing by Alessandro Magnasco, now in the Ambrosiana (Fig. 5), dating possibly from the Settecento.[108] Magnasco's outline depicts a group

ich denn überhaupt, in Italien, vom weiblichen Geschlechte, schönere Stimmen, und bessere Sängerinnen in den Klöstern, als auf den Theatern gefunden habe', *Lebensläuffe*, printed in F. W. Marpurg, *Historisch-kritische Beyträge zur Aufnahme der Musik* (Berlin, 1754), i. 236.

[106] The anonymous paintings, in a private collection, are reproduced in *Storia di Milano*, xi. 555 ff. and are discussed by D. O. Hughes, 'Representing the Family: Portraits and Purposes in Early Modern Italy', *Journal of Interdisciplinary History*, 17 (1986), 7–38 at 29. Of the daughters, Livia (to become Suor Anna Gioseffa at S. Agostino in Porta Nuova) is shown with a tenor violin and cello; Rosa (the future Suor Gioseffa Marianna at S. Maria Maddalena in Porta Lodovico) with her hands on a spinet; and Maria (later Suor Luisa Marianna at the same S. Agostino) with a violin. (The fourth daughter, Paola, who also entered S. Agostino, is shown with a painting; presumably she was interested in the visual arts.) The musical patronage and talents of this family (including Suor Paola Maria Arconati at S. Maria delle Veteri) had been mentioned prominently in Andrea Cima's *Secondo libro*.

[107] The musical evidence thus undercuts the conclusions of Hughes's study, which regards the objects in the portraits as symbols of missed domestic happiness, rendered unattainable by the girls' professions of vows; Hughes considers the portraits themselves as memorials of the girls' secular presence in the family. But the evidence in this chapter has underlined that the most likely way for patrician women to achieve public (and posthumous) renown was precisely as nun musicians. In light of the practical problems involved in nuns' sitting for portraits, the depictions of the girls can be seen as the only possible solution to recording them as musical members of a famous family.

[108] Magnasco, *Concerto di monache*, BA, F. 234 *inf.*, no. 800, red chalk on paper, published by F. Franchini, 'Un "concerto di monache" e altri dipinti di Alessandro Magnasco', *Arte Antica e Moderna*, 34–6 (1966), 232–5, who illustrates and discusses the finished painting. For

Fig. 5. Alessandro Magnasco, *The Nuns' Concert*

of nuns singing and playing instruments (harpsichord, violin, and cello) for a reclining bishop, who stretches out his ring to be kissed, possibly a consciously ironic juxtaposition in the light of the ongoing episcopal strictures against instruments and music in informal contexts. Other works in the artist's 'monastic cycle' depict nuns making music (one playing cello, with the instrument supported by a footstool) in parlours. Even if the intent was satirical, there could be no better indication of the fact that, a century after Carlo Borromeo's death, the content if not the form of the saint's disciplinary activity had been overturned for nuns' polyphony. The ability of female religious to achieve this was partly based on their patrician backing. But the reversal had additional roots: the history of order-specific traditions and the changing patterns of Seicento spirituality.

the initial publication, see B. Geiger, *Magnasco* (Bergamo, 1949), no. 427; cf. R. Roli and G. Sestieri, *I disegni italiani del Settecento: Scuole piemontese, lombarda, genovese, bolognese, toscana, romana, e napolitana* (n.p., 1981), no. 58. For other depictions of nuns, see Magnasco's *Concerto e laboratorio di monache* (Geiger no. 425), and another painting of nuns socializing in a musical *parlatorio* (no. 426). For a discussion (omitting nuns' music-making), see G. G. Syamken, 'Die Bildinhalte des Alessandro Magnasco, 1667–1749' (Ph.D. diss., Hamburg, 1963), 133–44.

5

Monastic Musical Traditions

◇

Der einzigartige Wert des 'echten' Kunstwerks hat seine
Fundierung im Ritual, in dem es seinen originären und ersten
Gebrauchswert hatte.

> (Walter Benjamin, 'Das Kunstwerk im Zeitalter seiner
> technischen Reproduzierbarkeit', IV)

For that plurality of Milanese patrician women in cloisters, the cultural markers of the orders—patron(ess) saints, monastic Rules, liturgical uses—provided self-identification, social grounding, occasions
for devotion, and possibilities for musical development. The preceding three chapters have highlighted the differing traditions of the various *religioni*, and thus suggest that to speak of 'nuns' *en bloc* is an
over-generalization.

The most obvious way in which orders influenced music was
monastic liturgical use, specific to each congregation even after
Trent. Although the various monastic breviaries and calendars were
rewritten in the Cinquecento, still these books, not Roman or
Ambrosian secular use, determined sisters' liturgical practice. Indeed,
the Office texts must have been completely familiar, possibly by
memory, since their recitation day in and day out was the major task
of monastic life; in the letters of Angela Confaloniera and others,
these texts took on an almost magical value for their users.

In the archdiocese of Milan and its institutions, the liturgical pic-
ture was complicated by the presence of two different uses in two
different rites: Roman rite, secular use (often at the ducal church of
S. Maria della Scala); Roman rite, monastic use (in a number of
Humiliate and Benedictine houses); Ambrosian rite, secular use (the
Duomo and many urban parishes); and Ambrosian rite, monastic use

(some Benedictine houses), each with their own liturgical books. As noted above, this last local combination varied according to house, and indeed no post-conciliar book reflecting such liturgy was ever printed.[1]

The diocese witnessed a series of battles over the employment of Ambrosian versus Roman rite, not only in monasteries but even in entire non-Ambrosian cities.[2] Far from being purely liturgical, these struggles often mirrored the contest for control over houses—and urban devotional life—between the prelate and the patriciate. In the course of the Seicento, as a mark of independence, many foundations attempted, with greater or lesser success, to switch from Ambrosian rite to Roman liturgy.[3] Even the Humiliate at S. Maria Maddalena al Cerchio made an unsuccessful attempt to jettison their order's breviary in 1630–1 in favour of the Roman books, much to Federigo's displeasure.[4] Given the paucity of *canto figurato* for Ambrosian rite (and, to a lesser degree, for items from the monastic breviaries), these moves may have been motivated also by the desire to have a liturgy with a large polyphonic repertory.[5]

Which monasteries employed which rite and use? In some cases, the practice in effect at a given visitation can sometimes be ascer-

---

[1] Under the heading of 'monastic' use I subsume those orders (Humiliate, Cistercian) whose breviaries were substantially different from the Roman, even if the form (but not the textual assignments) of their Hours (e.g. Humiliate Vespers) was essentially the same as secular use. Only among the Cassinese and Cistercians were there musically important differences in Office structure (the four, not five, Vesper psalms). Other houses employed either Roman (S. Domenico e S. Lazaro) or Ambrosian (S. Marta) liturgies; cf. Cattaneo, 'Istituzioni ecclesiastiche', 555–60.

[2] Carlo Borromeo had tried to force Ambrosian liturgy on a number of less than willing institutions, most notably in the case of the prelate's spectacularly unsuccessful attempt in the 1570s to introduce Milanese rite in Monza, with its ancient tradition of Roman liturgy, and in Treviglio; cf. Santagiuliana, *Storia di Treviglio*, 354, for the latter.

[3] Castiglione, *La chiesa milanese*, 140–1, notes such efforts, strongly resisted by Litta, after whose death, however, most of the remaining houses seem to have made the change. The dedication by Reina of a Roman-rite Vespers collection (the 1653 *Armonia ecclesiastica*) to Luigia Gonzaga at S. Paolo provides musical evidence for that house's switch away from Ambrosian rite by the mid-Seicento.

[4] The controversy was recorded by Puricelli, BA, C. 74 *inf.*, fo. 374; a copy of Federigo's order of 10 Apr. 1631 mandating the retention of their breviary is preserved on fos. 349–50; cf. J. W. Legg, 'The Divine Service in the Sixteenth Century, Illustrated by the Reform of the Breviary of the Humiliati in 1548', *Transactions of the St. Paul's Ecclesiological Society*, 2 (1890), 273–95, and Zardin, *Donna e religiosa*, 123 (which underplays the nuns' efforts to escape).

[5] It is noteworthy that the attempted switches were roughly simultaneous with the spread of polyphony in female houses. On the problems and production of Ambrosian *canto figurato*, see Kendrick, *Music in Federigo Borromeo's Lombardy*.

tained, and the results where known are included in Appendix B. S. Radegonda and S. Ulderico employed Ambrosian rite (monastic use) in 1575; similarly, S. Marta retained the Milanese liturgy well into the Seicento.[6] The non-Ambrosian but still essentially local liturgy of S. Caterina in Brera and S. Maria Maddalena was to be found in the *Breviarium . . . Romanum . . . Humiliatorum* (Milan, 1620, with a corrected reprint issued in Pavia the following year); this book was an almost unchanged edition of the 1548 Humiliati breviary, financed by the sisters (despite their later efforts at escape). The lack of manuscript sources is also an obstacle; rituals and ceremonials were largely destroyed at the suppressions, after their usefulness had come to an end.

The most musically active and liturgically distinct tradition was the Benedictine.[7] In post-Tridentine Italy, the male and female Cassinese did not boast the wide-ranging musical activity of the Franciscans. But among the congregation's seventeen composers of polyphony from 1500 to 1800, four were nuns, all in Milan or Pavia (Assandra, Cozzolani, Badalla, and Calegari), and three others had local connections.[8] The order's ritual sumptuousness and accoutrements, along with its partiality for obscure sanctoral feasts, appeared to at least one archbishop as overly secular and luxuriant.[9]

---

[6] 'L'Offizio si dice Monastico Ambrosiano come è quella di Santa Radegonda', visitation of 26 Dec. 1575 to S. Ulderico, ASDM XII, vol. 134, fasc. 1. The possession of the Novara antiphoner by S. Radegonda also indicates the use of the monastic Ambrosian rite, at least in the later Middle Ages. On S. Marta and S. Caterina, see Castiglione, *La chiesa*, 141.

[7] For Benedictine contributions to chant and polyphony, see G. Cattin, 'I benedettini e la musica', *Schede medievali*, 5 (1983), 393–418; more specialized on male Cassinese practice in the early reforming period is id., 'Tradizione e tendenze innovatrici nella normativa e nella pratica liturgico-musicale della Congregazione di S. Giustina', *Benedictina*, 17 (1970), 254–98.

[8] Cattin, 'I benedettini', lists fifteen Benedictine composers in the period but omits Badalla and Assandra (probably because they did not figure in Armellini, *Biblioteca*). If the same proportion (four of seventeen, or 24%) were applicable to the 200-odd Franciscan composers in Italy in the same period, there would have been some fifty Clarissan composers who published music (there was actually one). The local male Cassinese had problems maintaining their traditions; Carlo Cozzi, Cozzolani's contemporary and *maestro* at S. Simpliciano, was a layman. The further (Milan, Venice) from the intellectual centres of the male order (Montecassino, Naples), the stronger seems the evidence for polyphony.

[9] A post-1628 curial order on liturgy and music at Benedictine houses male and female rebuked the ornate liturgy, especially the number of clergy and vestments. The male Benedictines were reproached for their unauthorized use of mitres and their overlong processions (ASDM XII, vol. 18, fasc. 3, fo. 124ʳ). The passage on female houses attacked the multiplicity of sanctoral feasts: 'Quod multae aliae festivitates celebrantur in ecclesiis Monialium quam pro sanctis titularibus ipsarum ecclesiarum sive monasteriorum huius Patronis et Ordinis fundatoribus, atque aliqua musica exteriore, adhibito in Choro interiori

From sisters' perspectives, however, this was simply a different kind of ritual expression, incorporating the values of those patrician circles from which the order drew its members.

If all the liturgical details seem confusing to modern sensibilities, they were apparently no less puzzling to the growing number of Benedict's daughters in the early Seicento. One printed manual in the vernacular, dedicated to S. Radegonda's abbess, was produced to guide daily practice in Cassinese houses. The *Rubriche generali del breviario monastico* of 1614 was a literal translation of the Latin rules for ceremony and calendar observance found at the beginning of the post-Tridentine Benedictine breviary, for instance the 1613 Venetian edition.[10] There were two points to these instructions: the correct observance of Matins (omitted here) and the complicated question of conflicts among sanctoral and Proper (of the Time) feasts; the book also provided rules for the celebration of other Hours.

The monastic breviary divided feast-days into the usual categories: duplex (with two classes), semiduplex (also two classes), and simple feasts.[11] The distinguishing features of the *Rubriche* were apparent in the conflicts between duplex (or duplex and semiduplex, or semiduplex and simple) feasts. For these, elaborate provision was made that the Office (especially Vespers and Matins) of both days be celebrated, with the lesser or later feast simply moved to a proximate weekday.[12]

tantum Gregoriano Cantu numq*uam* sive etiam figurato, quo ad Antiphonas Vesperium pro currenti festo aut Canticum Magnificat [added: *pro* completu choro] sub poenis Abbatisse seu Prioresse Privationis officiis, Monialibus autem canentibus vocis abstineunt, et passim eo ipso incurrendis' (ibid., fo. 125ʳ); the order is likely to have been issued by Litta's curia.

[10] *Rubriche generali del breviario monastico, tradotte dal latino in volgare, da vn deuoto Religioso, a beneficio delle Monache dell'Ordine Monastico* (Milan: Heirs of Ponzio and G. B. Piccaglia, 1614), dedicated by the printer to Maria Elisabetta Trezza, abbess of S. Radegonda. For a post-Tridentine breviary, probably owned by a house in or around Milan (in the light of its current location), see the *Breviarium monasticum Pauli V. Pont. Max. auctoritate recognitum pro omnibus sub Regula Sanctissimi Patris Benedicti militantibus* (Venice: Giunta, [1613]), at I-Mb. For an earlier edition, one with notable sanctoral variants, see *Breviarium monasticum secundum ritum & morem congregationis Cassinensis* (Venice: Giunta, 1600); copy at Houghton Library, Harvard University.

[11] For instance, the 'Officio duplice' (*Rubriche generali*, pp. [5]–6) lists as duplex feasts: days from Good Friday to Easter Tuesday, Low Sunday, Ascension, Pentecost until Pentecost Tuesday, Trinity, Corpus Christi, Dedication of the titular church, duplex sanctoral feasts from the Benedictine calendar, all Octaves, St Benedict, and all patrons of the titular church, as well as any 'festa de Santi, li quali appresso qualche Chiesa ouero Congregatione sono soliti da esser solennemente celebrati', an open invitation to liturgical 'extravagance'.

[12] This is explained along with three tables for all the combinatorial possibilities of different classes of feasts in ch. 11, 'Della Concorrenza dell'Officio', pp. 29–31. For instance,

The effect of the rules was to expand the number and importance of sanctoral feasts—and hence the possible occasions for polyphony—drastically, compared with the non-monastic calendar.[13] Although the manual was intended for use at S. Radegonda and other Benedictine houses in the diocese, one other category of feasts not listed in its calendar became increasingly important in the Milanese Seicento: local saints such as Maurice or Victor.[14] Along with this specifically Benedictine liturgical 'extravagance', the increasing number and importance of sanctoral feasts were characteristic of the whole diocese in the Seicento, as in the case of S. Paolo in 1661. Musical services also occurred on non-sanctoral occasions, notably for the visits of personages such as Maria Anna of Austria in 1649 and Cosimo de' Medici in 1664.[15] A number of the early Seicento accounts by far less important travellers give the impression that polyphony was the norm every Sunday at certain houses, Benedictine and mendicant; the total number of days with *canto figurato* might well have reached eighty or ninety in the course of a year at the major foundations.[16]

For non-Ambrosian houses, Mass was said according to the post-Tridentine Benedictine missal. Those foundations (Benedictine and other) with Milanese liturgy (S. Maria del Lentasio, S. Maria Maddalena in Porta Romana) would have employed Carlo's revision of the Milanese missal, of which a sumptuous Venetian edition was

if the Vigil of a duplex feast fell on a Sunday, the Office was to be moved back a day to the Saturday before (p. 14).

[13] The calendar in the 1613 *Breviarium monasticum* lists some ninety-three duplex feasts, along with thirty-nine semiduplex and eighty-seven simple days (including the fifty-two Sundays and seven non-Sunday Common of the Time duplex feasts, the total came to 276 days a year). The 1635 Ambrosian breviary (*Breviarium Ambrosianum S. Carli Cardinalis archiepiscopi jussu editum* [Milan: Ponzio], a reprint of the 1625 edn.) listed 115 days as 'solenne' (a combination of duplex and semiduplex), and 102 simple feasts in its calendar. In 1672, the Roman protector of the Cassinese obtained a papal breve mandating the duplex celebrations of the Octaves of both Benedict and Scholastica (a copy is preserved among S. Radegonda's files in ASM, Religione, p.a., 2214).

[14] The 1613 *Breviarium monasticum* mentions neither in its calendar; although this edition only lists St Maurice with no special Matins readings or other liturgical assignments, the 1600 Cassinese breviary (fos. 389–90) gives eight Matins lessons for the feast.

[15] The 1664 petition of the anti-Palomera faction at S. Radegonda attacked her singing in polyphonic Vespers on the feast of St Barnabas and on Corpus Christi; in that year, this would suggest that at least Ceva's choir sang on 10 June (First Vespers of St Barnabas), 11 June (First Vespers of Corpus Christi), and possibly 12 June (Second Vespers of the latter).

[16] The anonymous 1606 French account refers to musical Vespers on a Sunday not further identified. A conspectus of the early travellers' reports suggests that polyphonic Vespers took place almost every Sunday, at least at the major houses.

issued in 1609.[17] Cozzolani's *Concerti sacri* contains a setting of the Mass Ordinary, an indication that this was sometimes sung in polyphony, at least at S. Radegonda. Like most local settings of mid-century, Cozzolani's omits the Benedictus, while her Sanctus and Agnus Dei are extremely short, in line with the practice mentioned in Ignazio Donati's preface to his *Salmi boscarecci* (1623). With sparse contemporary evidence, the normal items singled out for highlighting by means of vocal or instrumental polyphony—the Gradual, Offertory, and the Elevation in particular—must also have served this purpose in Milanese nuns' churches; the striking representation of Eucharistic motets in Cozzolani's books and later ('per il Santissimo') underlines the centrality of the Elevation. And several insider witnesses, among them Locatelli (who himself celebrated Mass, which he extended in order to hear more singing, much to the displeasure of his travelling companions), indicate the solo motet as the preferred genre for this liturgical moment. Other, less intimate liturgical items would seem to have been marked by large-scale polyphony as well; a nine-voice motet (for two choirs, one of voices and the other of instruments, probably members of the violin family) by Soderini in 1598 set the Ambrosian *antiphona post Evangelium* for the Common of Virgin Martyrs when celebrated as a duplex feast:

Ipsi sum desponsata, cui Angeli serviunt, cuius pulchritudinem Sol et Luna mirantur; ipsi soli servo fidem, ipsi me tota devotione committo, alleluia.[18]

The piece, rubricated 'in solemnitatis virginum' in the edition, was dedicated to Angela Caterina Brivia, 'virgini lectissimae' at S. Radegonda, and the 'sum desponsata' idea links nuns' own vocation as brides of Christ to the status of sanctified virgin martyrs.[19] This was not the last time that cloistered musicians would literally represent the symbolic speakers of a motet text.

---

[17] *Missale Ambrosianum illustriss.mi et reverendiss.mi D.D. Federici Card.lis Borromaei . . . iussu recognitum, & editum* (Venice: G. G. Como, 1609).

[18] 'To Him am I betrothed Whom the angels serve, Whose beauty the sun and moon admire; to Him alone I give my faith, to Him I commit myself with full devotion, alleluia'; Soderini, *Sacrae cantiones a 8–9*, 1598 (App. C).

[19] The text is found in *Missale Ambrosianum*, fo. 180ᵛ, with the more usual 'sponsata'. Brivia also received the inscription of *Vidi Dominum sedentem* (rubricated 'In solennitate omnium Sanctorum') in the same book. G. S. Fontana Morello's version of *Ipsi sum desponsata* (for CC) was the first piece in his *Primo libro de sacri concerti* (Milan, 1614), and was dedicated to the sisters of S. Caterina in Biella. The text also figured in the Roman Pontifical as part of the Consecration of Virgins, adding to its appropriateness.

The picture of Mass polyphony is augmented by the evidence from the other orders. The Seicento references to 'messe cantate' at S. Orsola, S. Chiara, and S. Marta did not specify individual places in polyphony, besides the Augustinians' references to 'canti gravi' in the conflicts of the 1620s and 1630s. But the irrepressible Angela Confaloniera provided evidence for one Humiliate house's practice at Mass, along with striking confirmation of how nuns could push their connections in order to obtain music:

Dearest Father: . . . You say you will not forget [to send] the musical pieces, but I am afraid that I did not express myself so that you could understand; namely, to send some toccatas for organ solo and, even better, some ricercars like those that are played at the first Secret of Mass.[20]

Whether the instrumental pieces were to sound at the Ambrosian *Oratio super oblata* (after the Credo), or (more likely) at the prayer 'Omnipotens sempiterne Deus' (before the Offertory and the Credo), is uncertain.[21]

Musical settings of the Office were another matter. Clearly the most important Hour was Vespers, and the tradition of *alternatim* performance, at least for the Magnificat, continued into the new century; Sobieski reported that Donna Grazia sang the entire canticle solo, with instrumental interludes, at one of the S. Marias in 1612.[22] The turn towards *intieri* (i.e. all verses set in vocal polyphony) psalms and canticles marked a notable extension of this Hour's importance in the Seicento.

The problems of Benedictine use were presented by the selection of psalms in Cozzolani's 1650 Vespers. Its six eight-voice *concertato* settings (Ps. 109: *Dixit Dominus*; 110: *Confitebor tibi domine*; 111: *Beatus vir*; 112: *Laudate pueri*; 121: *Laetatus sum*; 126: *Nisi dominus*)

---

[20] 'Padre mio Carissimo: . . . Mi dice che non si smentica di canti per la musica ma ò paura che io non abbi detto in maniera che mi abbi inteso, cioè di mandar qualche tocata de sonar cosi sole con l'organo e per dar meglio qualche ricercata di quelli [che] si sonano à primi secreti delle messe': undated letter to Federigo, BA, G. 7 *inf.*, fo. 321ʳ. Rusca's two *canzoni francesi* in her motet book were perhaps not enough to satisfy the nuns' needs, an understandable point in the light of the growing number of occasions for polyphony in the Seicento. Another problem was that there had not been a Milanese edition of keyboard music since G. P. Cima's 1606 *Partito* and Frescobaldi's 1608 *Fantasie*.

[21] The 1609 *Missale Ambrosianum* gives the former (the equivalent of the Roman Secret) as a short Proper prayer, while the latter, a long Ordinary oration, would have taken some three to four minutes to recite along with its attendant actions. Since there had been no Humiliate missal published since 1504, *faute de mieux* I have used the Ambrosian book.

[22] Sobieski, *Peregrynacja*, 174.

offer a seeming puzzle, for they cover a complete (five-psalm) Vespers for only one possible set of feasts in non-monastic Roman rite, the 'male cursus', or the majority of feasts from the Common of male Saints, while they are even less applicable to Ambrosian Vespers.[23] The psalms of normal Sunday Vespers in either Roman or Milanese liturgies are not completely included in Cozzolani's collection; nor are feasts of the Virgin and female saints (the 'female cursus'). Again, the *Rubriche* provided the necessary information, including the traditional Benedictine employment of only four, not five, psalms at Vespers (App. A, Doc. 27); the monastic breviary supplied the very limited psalm assignments for normal Sundays, duplex seasonal feasts, duplex and other sanctoral commemorations (male and female), and Marian feasts. Sundays and male sanctoral feasts used one set of four psalms at Vespers, while Marian and female sanctoral days employed another:[24]

Sundays/male sanctoral	BVM/female sanctoral
Dixit Dominus (109)	*Dixit Dominus*
Confitebor tibi Domine (110)	*Laudate pueri* (112)
Beatus vir (111)	*Laetatus sum* (121)
Laudate pueri (112)	*Nisi Dominus* (126)

Cozzolani's collection was indeed a complete set of Vespers Psalms for the major feasts of the year in Benedictine use only.[25] Appendix E gives the items in chant and possible polyphonic settings, along with prayers and readings, for Vespers on several different occasions.[26] On one hand, this restricted set links the *Salmi a otto* to the actual liturgy used at S. Radegonda, the only system Cozzolani would have known since her profession at age 17; on the other, it reinforces the edition's status as an internal Benedictine print and as

---

[23] The term is owed to J. Kurtzman, *Essays on the Monteverdi Mass and Vespers of 1610* (Houston, Tex., 1978), 125. This cycle includes Pss. 109, 110, 111, 112, and 121; for the Ambrosian rite, see Kendrick, *Music in Federigo Borromeo's Lombardy*.

[24] For Vespers, see *Rubriche*, 42–3.

[25] Other psalms, normally used for major feasts in secular use and hence included in 17th-c. polyphonic Vespers collections, occupy far less prominent positions in the Cassinese liturgy; *Lauda Jerusalem* was used in Friday Vespers only.

[26] The two other psalms in the *Salmi à otto* can be explained as a duplicate setting (the *Laudate pueri a 6*) and as a non-liturgical setting of a popular text (*Laudate dominum omnes gentes*). This function undercuts the double infringement of the latter's scoring (for soprano and two violins) against Antonio Rusca's 1647 rules prohibiting both solo singing and non-keyboard instruments in female monastic liturgy.

a monument of the house's music.[27] Its attractiveness on the music-publishing market might well have been limited.

Other orders' Vespers again depended on their breviaries. Although the Humiliate at S. Caterina and S. Maria Maddalena took on aspects of the Benedictine tradition, their Office structure was non-monastic: five Vesper Psalms (and four at Compline).[28] They used several different sets of psalms: for Sundays, *Dixit, Confitebor, Beatus vir, Laudate pueri,* and *In exitu* (Ps 113); for Christmas and most Marian feasts, the first three plus *De profundis* (Ps 130) and *Memento Domine David* (Ps 131); for male saints, *Dixit, Laudate pueri, Dum converteret* (Ps 125), *Credidi* (Ps 115), and *Domine probasti me* (Ps 128); for female saints, *Dixit, Beatus vir, Laudate pueri, Credidi,* and *Dum converteret;* for Corpus Christi and saints of the order, the five *Laudate* psalms. The 'salmi' mentioned in Rusca's *Sacri concerti* must have included some of these.[29] Mendicant and Augustinian sisters would have used the Roman (secular) breviary, in the case of the Clarissans and the Dominicans their order-specific book, with a five-psalm Vespers.

Of other Hours, the best documentation for female monastic polyphony survives for Compline.[30] Two editions dedicated to Lombard nuns (the second in all, Asola's 1583/7 *Duplex completorium Romanum,* and Vecchi's 1600 Office collection) contained the psalms, hymns, and responses for this Hour (in secular use); the numerous curial complaints about the length of Vespers might in part

---

[27] The provision of two Magnificats in the 1650 book is also common; if the distinction between the two is stylistic (the first setting is considerably longer, with major refrains), then the duplication may reflect the difference in musical practice between duplex (Christmas, Easter, Corpus Christi, sanctoral) and semiduplex (normal Sundays) feasts. Cozzolani's counterparts at S. Simpliciano did not restrict themselves to the Cassinese psalm cycles; both Cantone's (*alternatim*) *Vespri à versetti* (Milan: Tradate, 1602) and Cozzi's *Messa, e salmi correnti* (Milan: Rolla and Camagno, 1649); included the full Roman male and female cursus along with the Sunday psalms (both set a total of sixteen psalms). S. Simpliciano, much to the archbishop's displeasure, had obtained the right to Roman rite in the Cinquecento (Cattaneo, 'Istituzioni ecclesiastiche', 558). Male composers, not subject to *clausura,* had more motivation or opportunity to produce a complete (and more immediately saleable) Vespers collection suitable for almost any feast; the net effect is to make S. Radegonda's liturgy and its printed reflection in Cozzolani's books stand even more apart.

[28] For the psalm assignments and structure of the Hour, see the 1621 *Breviarium Romanum Humiliatorum;* Sunday Vespers are on fo. 58ᵛ, with other feasts scattered throughout the Proper and Common sections; for Compline, fo. 68ʳ. For a complete discussion of the Humiliate breviary, see Wasmer and Kendrick (eds.), Rusca, *Sacri concerti.*

[29] For a longer account, see Wasmer and Kendrick, ibid.

[30] For Benedictine use, cf. *Rubriche,* ch. 18, 'De Compietà'.

be due to the combined celebration of the two Hours.[31] Both these
prints are inscribed to mendicant sisters: the Augustinians of
S. Daniele in Verona (Asola) and three women who seem to have
been Clarissans (Vecchi); hence their employment of the secular
form of the Hour.[32]

The daily life of female monastic performers was thus punctuated
and marked by the Office. Besides their time in the choral recitation
of non-musical Hours, the women of this study must have spent
their days in the duties of nuns' lives: internal assignments (cellarer,
gate-keeper), prayer, reading, and the practice and teaching of
polyphony. Claudia Rusca's duties won her release from some (perhaps menial) tasks. Her infirmities actually granted her exemption
from the obligatory rising in the middle of the night in order to say
Matins, also providing her personal experience of bodily suffering;
the privilege may have been a further recompense for her contributions to S. Caterina's polyphony.[33]

Beyond Mass and Office, however, the ritual in which nuns established their social and spiritual identity was essential, and again the
Benedictines provided the most 'luxuriant' example.[34] The number
of new *professe* occasioned another printed manual, a 1607 guide, the
Ordo admittendi virgines ad monasterii ingressum, which regulated two
separate ceremonies: the reception of novices and their profession of
final vows.[35] This twenty-eight-page *libretto* provides detailed
instructions for both the admission and the clothing rituals.

In the admission ceremony, at the beginning of the novitiate year,
the girl was to be led from the *chiesa esteriore* to the door of the
monastery by the officiating priest, while Ps. 121 (*Laetatus sum*) was
said by the accompanying clergy. The nuns were to meet the procession at the door; the *Te Deum* was sung, and both processions

---

[31] For the other Hours, see Kendrick, 'Genres', 247.

[32] On the Goselini sisters, ibid. 405.

[33] 'facceua li suoi officij con gran diligenza, per la uirtù del cantare non li facceua tutti
. . . non poteua leuar a matutino ma era diligentissima al oratione': *Biografia*, fo. 14ʳ. For
Vizzana's similar lifelong infirmity, see Monson, *Disembodied Voices*.

[34] For the battles over ritual and polyphony in a somewhat different ceremony (one
without Milanese parallel), the Camaldolese 'Sacra', see ibid., ch. 10.

[35] *Ordo admittendi virgines ad monasterii ingressum, habitumque; regularem suscipiendi* . . .
Secundum morem Congregationis Cassinensis (Milan: Pontio & Piccaaglia, 1607). For the reception ceremonies for the Humiliate, modelled on those of the male branch, see *Breviarium
Romanum Humiliatorum* (1621), fos. 453ᵛ ff. A similar guide in manuscript for the Angeliche
at S. Paolo is in ASDM XII, vol. 96; this latter omits music altogether.

returned to the church, where Mass was said. The priest blessed the clothing, veil (*velamen*), and head-dress (*corona*) of the novice. The *Veni Creator Spiritus* was sung after the girl's tonsure, and after further responses and prayers, the novice took on her provisional black habit, carrying a lighted taper into the monastery; at the end, she formally changed her name if need be.[36] In this manual, the priest called the novice specifically the bride (*sponsa*) of Christ, as opposed to other orders' clothing rituals, which had dropped the term by 1600.[37]

Yet greater pomp was reserved for the profession of final vows. During Mass, the novice (together with the abbess) was to approach the altar in the *chiesa esteriore*, after the Offertory, the last time in her life that she would act in public space.[38] She promised her obedience to the Rule of St Benedict, and after the abbess prayed over her, she was to extend her hands 'in modum crucis' and chant (*psallendi*) 'Receive me, Lord, according to Your word, and I shall live, and do not disappoint me from my desire' thrice with three genuflexions.[39] The chaplain was then to sing the *Kyrie* and the *Pater noster*. After a series of other prayers, the novice was sprinkled with holy water and incense, while the priest intoned the *Veni Creator Spiritus*, with the nuns' chorus completing the hymn. The priest then blessed her new clothing, and the abbess, followed by all the nuns, was to give her the kiss of peace. She was then to lie (decently, the manual noted) under a pall of black cloth (symbolizing her death to the world).[40] After the Postcommunion, the priest turned to the novice and said: 'Rise, you who sleep, and leave the dead, and Christ will shine on you.' The novice was to sing or say (*cantet vel dicet*) in reply: 'I have received honey and milk from His mouth, and His blood has adorned my cheeks.'[41]

But the greatest amount of chant was associated with the actual

---

[36] *Ordo*, 'De accessu et ingressu puellarum ad monasterium', 3–12, with chant incipits for the two hymns.

[37] Ibid. 23; this was done in conformity with the 1595 Roman Pontifical. See Zarri, 'Ursula and Catharine: The Marriage of Virgins in the Sixteenth Century', in Matter and Coakley, *Creative Women*, 237–78, for sanctoral imagery in Ursuline clothing.

[38] *Ordo*, 'Ordo ad recipiendam Novitiam ad professionem', 14–19.

[39] 'Suscipe me Domine secundum eloquium tuum, et vivam, et non confundas me ab expectatione mea.'

[40] 'iacet super latus ante Altare honeste sub palio nigro ad hoc praeparato': ibid. 19.

[41] 'Surge quae dormis, et exurge a mortuis, et illuminabit te Christus'; 'Mel, et lac ex eius ore suscepi, et sanguis eius oravit genas meas.'

clothing ceremony (*velatio*) for the novice, after Mass.[42] The priests began by singing the antiphon: 'Prudent virgins, prepare your lamps, behold your Spouse is coming, leave [the world] to follow His way.' The novice then left the altar and proceeded among the nuns (still apparently in the *chiesa esteriore*), who responded by singing the same antiphon in chorus up to the word 'exite', at which point the nuns were to leave the choir with their candles lit. Then the novice was to perform (*cantare vel dicere*) the antiphon: 'And now I shall follow You with my whole heart, and I fear You, and I wish to see Your face; Lord do not put me to shame but remake me according to Your gentleness, and according to the multitude of Your mercy.'[43] After another prayer the professing nun was to sing (required; 'cantet') the great responsory *Regnum mundi*, for which the print provided the full plainchant.[44]

This was followed by the blessing of the veil, after which the new sister was to sing the antiphon 'He has placed a sign [the veil] on my face, that I may admit no other lover but Him.' After this the priest turned to the nun and said ('dicit') the antiphon, while placing the veil and head-dress on her, 'Come, bride of Christ, take the crown that the Lord has prepared for you for all eternity.' She was to respond with the antiphon 'The Lord has clothed me with a vestment of woven gold, and has ornamented me with immense jewels.' Finally, after three more prayers, the entire group of nuns was to rise, singing 'Behold, now I see what I wished, now I have what I hoped for, to Him I am joined in heaven, Him Whom I haved loved on earth with utter devotion.'[45]

The symbolism of this classically liminal ritual is striking. Offered up (the novice first approached the cloister after the Offertory) as a

[42] 'Velatio, aut benedictio monialium', 20–7.

[43] 'Prudentes Virgines, aptate vestras lampades, ecce sponsus venit, exite obviam ei'; 'Et nunc sequor te in toto corde, et timeo te, et quaero faciem tuam videre, Domine ne confundas me, sed fac mihi juxta mansuetudinem tuam, et secundum multitudinem misericordiae tuae.'

[44] Antegnati included a setting of this text for high *voci pari* of the respond (without the verse) in his 1581 *Sacrae cantiones* (dedicated to nuns in Brescia). The Bassus, the only surviving part-book, for this motet is set out in C3 clef and ranges *g–a′*. For an eight-voice local setting, see Grancini, *Messe, motetti et canzoni a 8* (Milan: Lomazzo, 1627).

[45] 'Posuit signum [i.e. the veil] in faciem meam, ut nullum praeter eum amatorem admittam'; 'Veni sponsa Christi, accipe coronam, quam tibi Dominus praeparavit in aeternum'; 'Induit me Dominus ciclade auro texta, et immensis monilibus ornavit me'; 'Ecce quod concupivi iam video, quod speravi iam teneo, illi sum juncta in coelis, quem in terris posita tota devotione dilexi.'

virgin bride of Christ, and passed over the dividing wall between the *chiesa esteriore* and the *chiesa interiore*, the girl took on a new status (a new women, as several antiphons underline) as a figure partaking both of Heaven and earth. Indeed, most of the clothing ceremony's texts were borrowed from (or shared with) items from the feasts of virgin martyrs, most notably the first such duplex feast to occur in the church year, St Agnes (21 January).[46] Each stage of the process, marked by a series of physical adornments (habit, veil, head-dress), was underlined by a sung or spoken antiphon which made reference to the sartorial symbol. The enormous length and quantity of music found in this ceremony (eight pieces in the clothing ceremony alone) is matched by no other order's ritual. The service was normally followed by festivities in the monastery, during which gifts were presented to the newly professed nun.[47] The entire procedure was a classic cultural inversion: a ceremony meant to mark the novice's death to the world instead became an occasion to show liturgical pomp, family ties, wealth, and, not least, musical ability.

The connection between profession and polyphony was present from the earliest decrees onwards: one of the first references to music in female houses attempted to regulate such ceremonies even before Carlo's advent:

Neither when nuns are clothed nor on other feasts are men to enter inside the monastery, nor may instruments be played, except the organ and the ones usually played in church.[48]

[46] In the 1600 *Breviarium monasticum*, fos. 284^r ff., the following items figured in Agnes's feast: *Posuit signum* (Matins, antiphon 3, nocturne 1); *Induit me Domine* (antiphon 4, nocturne 1); *Mel et lac* (antiphon 5, nocturne 1); *Ecce quod concupivi* (Lauds, Antiphon ad Benedictum). *Prudentes virgines* was the Magnificat antiphon for First Vespers of the Common of Virgin Martyrs (fo. 447^r), while *Regnum mundi* was the responsory for Matins, lesson 8, of the same Common (fo. 452^v).

[47] One of Federigo's printed memoranda, in ASDM XII, vol. 52, fasc. 1, lists the presents that could be given on this occasion. For Carlo's more restrictive orders on these ceremonies (which still seem to assume the presence of music), see ASDM XII, vol. 57, fasc. 2 (at the entrance of the novice, 'stando le monache retirate, in modo che non siano visti da secolari, ne si faccia musica, ma subito entrata [the novice], si serri la porta, lasciando de parte si faccia la provisione et musica').

[48] 'Quando se vestiranno monache ne in altra solenita non entrano in monasteri homini ne si sonano istrumenti excepto organo & li soliti che si soli sonare in le Giese' (order from Ragazzoni, 6 Oct. 1562, ASDM XII, vol. 52, fasc. 2), preserved along with Paolo Arezzio's 1573 restrictive orders from Piacenza on clothing ceremonies: 'Che quel di, che la putta andarà ad entrare nel Monastero, sia la matina, e non il dopo desinare, e vada accompagnata modestamente da matrone e donne gravi senza pompa, e per conto nessuno non vi siano suoni, ne instrumenti musici, sotto pena alli sonatori di scudi doi per ciascuno, e di perdere tutti gli instrumenti musici.'

The immediate points of departure for polyphony associated with clothing festivities are several: there are a few settings by Benedictine (and other) composers of the antiphons listed above, usually of *Veni sponsa Christi*, sometimes in scorings or contexts that suggest monastic performance.[49] Yet perhaps it is not surprising that most of these texts have not been preserved in polyphony; not every novice was capable of singing (hence the 'vel dicit' rubrics) and some antiphons have obscure liturgical assignments; hence their attractiveness in printed collections would be limited. Still, clothing ceremonies were an important occasion for polyphony—performed by both nuns and outside musicians—in the most Italianate of transalpine prince-bishoprics.[50]

The second connection consisted of those motet dedications temporally close to the date of final profession for their addressees. Andrea Cima's *In te Domine speravi* (*Secondo libro*, 1627) was dedicated to Angela Clerici, who appeared in the lists of professed nuns from 1628 onwards. Egidio Trabattone's dedication to a nun of a four-soprano setting of this text (1632) may well mark this common passage ('In You, o Lord, have I hoped; let me not be put to shame') as an epigraph for female monastic vocation. Similarly, Cazzati's 1659 *Cantate morali e spirituali* were inscribed to Ceva, whose first appearance in S. Radegonda's lists dates from 1659.[51] If such pieces were

[49] The setting for canto and alto by Patta, in his 1609 *Sacra cantica concinenda a 1–3*, or Donati's version for two cantos and alto, from his *Li vecchiarelli et perregrini concerti*, op. 13 (Venice: Vincenti, 1636), presumably dating from the post-plague years of crisis for the Duomo (Donati's employer) and its choirboys. *Veni sponsa* was also an antiphon for the Common of Virgin Martyrs in all rites and uses (hence its reworking to honour Catherine in Rusca's book). But Lampugnani would highlight precisely the musical nature of this antiphon in his description of profession ceremonies at S. Radegonda, included in his *vita* of the house's patroness: 'Quando giouinette vi monacate, se vi ricorda, nel far la professione del voto solenne, si canta in persona di Dio l'antifona *Vieni sponsa di Christo a riceuere la corona, che Iddio t'ha preparato in eterno*' (*Della vita*, 110).

[50] For the Benedictines of the Nonnberg in Salzburg, see E. T. Chafe, *The Church Music of Heinrich Biber* (Ann Arbor, 1987), 22–4 and 67–9, with evidence reminiscent of Milanese practice. The use of *Regnum mundi* in the clothing ceremonies explains Biber's lost setting of this text, mentioned in the Nonnberg records (ibid. 250, app. 19). Other pieces for clothing include the *laude* in Serafino Razzi's *Santuario di laude* (Florence: Sermartelli, 1609); Stradella's *Pugna certamen*; and a motet in Bonifazio Graziani's op. 20, along with pieces by Vizzana linked to the 'Sacra'.

[51] The *assignatio* of her dowry, probably at the beginning of her novitiate year, occurred on 18 Nov. 1658 in the house's records (ASDM XII, vol. 128, fo. 7ᵛ); Cazzati's dedication was dated 31 Oct. 1659, around the time of her profession of final vows. Hence, she was probably born shortly after 1640 (and would be listed still in the 1720s, according to the ASM records).

profession presents, they might have been performed at the Mass of the clothing ceremony, the ceremony itself, or afterwards during the festivities.[52]

If the annual or biannual profession ceremony would evoke the identification between nuns and virgin martyrs, a more universal ritual re-enactment was the liturgy of Holy Week. Again, the Milanese Benedictines offered the most prominent traditions. Perpetua de Birago's 1522 Office reflected not strictly monastic Ambrosian use, but rather a compilation for public consumption.[53] After the Passions, readings, and responses for the week, the book contains several important non-liturgical items: a series of prayers for every day in the week, together with woodcuts of female models of devotion (Mary Magdalene, the Virgin); an *Officium Sponsi Jesu*, a Daily Office (Lauds to Vespers) with texts featuring Christ as the Spouse of the soul; and a series of *orationes ante communione* [*sic*].[54] By the Seicento, the musical expression of Holy Week devotion would become a Benedictine speciality.[55] If Cantone offered late *stile antico* in his complex and liturgically idiosyncratic five-voice *Officium hebdomadae sanctae* of 1603, then Holy Week performances at S. Radegonda might be reflected in at least one solo motet from Cozzolani's 1648 *Scherzi: Venite ad me omnes* (which begins as a lament of the suffering Christ).[56] This sense of nuns as the guardians of Holy Week rites had been physically embodied in the iconography at S. Maurizio.

Still, a good deal of music by or for Milanese nuns did not set formalized liturgical items. Rather, the changing pattern of motet texts throughout our period highlights the order-specific traditions of

---

[52] In the Settecento, the musical tradition would become a poetic one, with verse instead of motets offered to the novice; cf. Masetti Zannini, 'Composizioni poetiche e trattamenti spirituali per monacazioni benedettine del Settecento', in G. Farnedi and G. Spinelli (eds.), *Settecento monastico italiano* (Cesena, 1990), 581–98. Goldoni would write poems for the professions of Venetian nuns in the 1750s.

[53] The colophon noted: 'Soror Perpetua de birago . . . pleraque cultui monastico necessaria edidit'; Vespers for Holy Thursday consisted of five, not four, psalms (fos. 68–70).

[54] Respectively, fos. 137–8; fos. 139–43; and fo. 145[v].

[55] The other Passiontide polyphony printed in Milan included the very simple Lamentations of Alcarotto (1570) and Dentice (1593), along with Ruffo's 1586 Holy Week responsories.

[56] In pan-European perspective, the musical setting of Holy Week liturgy seems to become increasingly feminized in the course of the century: Alessandro Della Ciaja's 1650 Lamentations were written for a female house in Siena, while a large part of the French Tenebrae repertory was first performed by Parisian nuns.

spirituality and devotion.[57] Again, the Benedictines eschewed the poverty-embracing and preaching traditions of the mendicants.[58] Most of Cozzolani's and Badalla's motets are Eucharistic or Marian, not penitential.[59] Along with the general devotional climate in Milan, Italian Benedictine spirituality itself underwent a profound change, one with remarkable parallels to the kind of affective themes and language found in Birago's Holy Week compilation, suggesting that some of the shift actually originated in female houses.[60] The turning-point for the congregation came in the mid-Cinquecento, in the later works of the abbot Denis Faucher and in the important miscellany Codex 584 at Montecassino. The intellectual tradition of the late Quattrocento Cassinese had emphasized sin, the incapacity of the will to attain salvation, and Divine benignity, all supported by Pauline epistles and patristic writings. The ultimate goal was, as it would remain later, perfection and union with God. But the new Benedictine thought abandoned these Pauline themes in favour of a heavily affective piety, based on the mystical loss of self and rapture into God on one hand, and on the obedience to superiors on the other.[61] The shift later received musical expression in Patta's motet books, characterized by their use of Song of Songs texts and other affective literary styles.[62]

[57] For the relation between the themes of nuns' piety and the liturgical books, Zardin, *Donna e religiosa*, 137-55.

[58] The possibility of preaching was excluded, given the post–Tridentine restrictions on nuns' public roles, although the emphasis on Cecilia's doctrinal role found in Lampugnani's 1619 play *Cecilia predicante* (dedicated to the Monastero Maggiore), gives occasion to the possibility of yet another case of Cassinese exceptionalism. It is precisely for this reason that the public projection of nuns' voices was limited essentially to singing; it also represented the one public occasion in early modern Milan to hear women singing polyphony on a regular basis.

[59] The only penitential motet in Cozzolani's *Concerti sacri* is the dialogue between a sinner and a guardian angel, *O mi Domine*.

[60] Birago's *Officium Sponsi Jesu* and its *orationes ante communionem* highlight this affective language: 'Veni charissime Iesu, incende me charitatis igne; vt ardeam desiderio indeficienti te desiderans; vulnera me charitatis vulnere. Incende me tui amoris igne vt te sciam amare digne veniens mane in corde meo' (*oratio*, fo. 145ᵛ).

[61] B. Collett, *Italian Benedictine Scholars and the Reformation: The Congregation of Santa Giustina of Padua* (Oxford, 1985), 247-50, describing the mid-century Cassinese miscellany, Montecassino, Codex 584. For a typical expression, see Lampugnani's preface to *Della vita*, fo. 2ᵛ: 'Tutto più, che abbiamo un Dio, che è tutta bontà.'

[62] For instance, seven of the nine solo motets in the *Sacra cantica concinenda* feature canticle texts, as do eight of the sixteen duets. In his 1613 *Sacri cantici à 1-5* (Venice: Vincenti), the pieces dedicated to the Cassinese poet Angelo Grillo are noteworthy for their highly affective character: *Amor meus crucifixus*, *Convertisti planctum meum*.

But even among the Benedictines there were differences. In the houses subject to the bishop, the evidence for musical life is more limited and temporally later, as in the 1679 dedication of a motet to Daria Piola at S. Ulderico.[63] Given the similarly patrician character of the male houses' music, one might expect dedications to nuns or other evidence of musical contact in the works of male Cassinese. Yet the episcopally encouraged split between the male and female branches of orders deepened from Trent onwards, leaving female monasteries dependent on either the patriciate or the bishop, as opposed to the closer ties between male and female regulars of the later Middle Ages.[64] Thus there are no dedications to nuns in the editions of Cantone or Ludovico Busca; nor is there any mention of the female monasteries in the records concerning music at S. Simpliciano. The split did not work in reverse; Cozzolani's 1648 solo motets were dedicated to the president of the Cassinese, Claudio Benedetti.

Rather different traditions marked the other congregations. For the Humiliate, the question of division from a male branch was irrelevant. But this order's monasteries boasted a musical life out of all proportion to their ecclesiastical importance. In part, this was due to their close ties to the archbishop, ever since Carlo himself had made the decision not to dissolve the nuns in 1571; Federigo's support of music at S. Caterina in Brera has already been discussed, and the relatively less public nature of its polyphony had been noted even by Litta. Humiliate spirituality in the Seicento was largely a creation of the sisters themselves: the surviving motets in Rusca's *Sacri concerti* are important testimony. Of the eight pieces, two are for St Catherine, one each for Christmas and Easter, one Christological, one for feasts of several martyrs, one general, and one Marian with a personal and metamusical slant. None of the texts was to be found in the 1621 Humiliate breviary or the 1609 Ambrosian missal.

The first prominent musical nun in Federigo's Milan was from another patrician order, one more independent of episcopal control;

[63] The case of S. Vincenzo, subject to regulars, is more puzzling. One of its inhabitants, Serbellona, was twice a dedicatee, yet there is little evidence for music at this house in the ASDM, ASM, or SCVR files.

[64] Zarri, 'Monasteri femminili', *passim*.

[65] Her life must be deduced from the documents in ASM, Religione, p.a., 1949; she was not listed in a contract of 9 Jan. 1588 (with Baldassare Biglia) but did figure as the thirteenth most junior nun on an agreement of 23 Aug. 1596. She must have professed around 1589, and have been born just after 1570; a contract of 26 Nov. 1616 (with Matteo de Rubeo) still

Sessa was a Lateran Canoness at S. Maria Annunciata.[65] Given the high renown in which she was held in Borromean circles, her two surviving monodies are probably more reflective of Federigo's taste than of any Augustinian tradition at the house. But she was the outstanding singer of Borromean Milan; another of Federigo's friends, the South Netherlands rhetorician (working in Milan) and occasional music theorist Erycius Puteanus used her skills as an *exemplum* of the superiority of vocal over instrumental music (App. A, Doc. 21):

In one body of music, two parts are found, the *harmonica* [vocal] and the *organica* [instrumental]. But just as the branches of the same tree or the clods from the same field are often very different, so the former is superior in age, dignity, and power. I shall try to make plain this fact in few words; being written in praise of the voice, let them be dedicated to you, Claudia Sessa. Shall I call you virgin, or Muse, you who surpass all mortal voices to universal amazement? By the vote of the present age Antiquity yields to you, and Posterity will retain your renown. What further room is left for fables? Let daughters of Jupiter hold their tongues, lest in future they seem to heckle while you sing; let Sirens be off, whose harmonies you surpass; let Echo hide her jealousy in silence, in vain she strives to repeat you.[66]

The timing and placement of the encomium were remarkable: an individual nun, whose performances would have been highly suspect and probably forbidden fifteen years earlier under Carlo, served as the public *exemplum* for the honoured position of vocal music (an art which Puteanus's treatise was designed to 'improve'), in a transalpine edition dedicated to Carlo's cousin. Sessa seems to have been the model musical nun for Federigo's early years; certainly Girolamo Borsieri's quasi-hagiography of her life and talents stressed the exemplary (and Borromean) qualities of her humility, abhorrence of public musical renown, and use of natural talent in the service of divine praise (App. A, Doc. 29).[67] If her writing was 'anzi virile' in Borsieri's

---

listed her, but Borsieri's 1619 panegyric noted that she had recently died young (i.e. in her mid-forties, in 1617 or 1618).

[66] Puteanus, *Musathena, sive notarum heptas* (Hanover, 1602), ch. v (pp. 22–3). This edition is dedicated to Federigo; the passage is largely unchanged from the 1599 Milanese edition of the treatise (*Modulata Pallas, sive septem discrimina vocum ad harmonicae lectionis*). The major difference occurs in the sentence beginning 'Hoc ipsum' (1599: 'Hoc ipsum binis hisce capitibus conabor comprobare, quae in laudem vocis scripta, sacra tibi sunto CLAVDIA SESSA virgo Deo dicata castissima, quae vocis mortales . . .': pp. 29 ff.). The standard classical associations with singing nuns—Muses, Echo, Sirens—in a work reflective of Federigo's intellectual milieu is noteworthy. Sessa achieved this renown before turning 30.

[67] Borsieri, *Soplemento* to P. Morigia, *La nobiltà di Milano* (Milan, 1619), 51–4.

eyes, still the Comascan cleric did not apply the characterization to her music, and the cross-gender epithet is not to be found in any other description of musical nuns. The idea seems to bear more on Borsieri's divided view of female monastic musicians than on any contemporary 'de-gendering' of exemplary monastic women.[68]

The split between male and female branches was also at work in the order with the leading male musicians, the Franciscans. Another printed manual, written by a friar in the later Seicento, explained the growth of music in the order (App. A, Doc. 66).[69] In this commentary (ch. 17, 'Del Canto, e Cantatrici') on Clare's Rule, music—monophonic or polyphonic—was a 'modern' custom in the female Franciscan tradition, and the parallel between nun singers and the angelic choirs is at work here as well:

Even though in the order's origins nuns practised neither chant nor polyphony, still in the course of time the male and female superiors came to introduce both in order to move the laity to devotion, thus imitating the celestial hierarchies who praise the Divine Majesty with musical choirs.[70]

Passages in Federigo's style ('la Maestra del Choro . . . procurando sopra tutto la concordia delli animi non meno che delle voci'), alternate with phrases echoing Monti's instructions to avoid internal dissension. Parts were to be distributed and instruments to be included 'vsando della musica più per mouere à diuotione, che per eccitare la curiosità'. The manual repeats the usual restrictions on male music teachers; instead, those nuns who know *canto fermo* or *canto figurato* are to teach the others. Overlong motets are not to be sung during Mass so as not to bore the officiating priest and distract the laity from devotion.[71] The rules clearly reflect an effort on the part of the regular superiors to regulate the growth of music in mid-century Franciscan institutions, one evident in the various testimonies to music at Clarissan houses: S. Chiara, S. Orsola, and S. Apollinare

[68] On the problems of Borsieri's hagiography, and the possible implications for Sessa's own style of singing, see Pavan, 'La necessità'; it is noteworthy that Puteanus's far more literary descriptions, for example, do not consider Sessa to have 'transcended' her biological sex. Borsieri's description referred only to her writing habits, not to her singing.

[69] *Regole delle Monache di S. Chiara . . . Compilate da un Religioso dello stesso ordine* (Milan: Filippo Ghisolfi, 1670).

[70] Ibid., 119. 'Religione' here means, as usual, 'monastic tradition'.

[71] 'Fugiranno le Cantilene, ò motetti troppo longhi specialmente nelle Messe per non causare tedio al Sacerdote, e far perder la diuotione, e patienza à quelli che ascoltano le Messe', possibly a reference to long solo motets at the Elevation. The chapter concludes with an anti–Semitic slur.

(including the dedications by Casola and Caifabri to the latter's inhabitants around 1660).

The mention in the *Regole* of music's purpose—to arouse devotion—seems related to the mission of the whole order.[72] In Milan, male Franciscans figured among the leading composers of the diocese.[73] Several (Cossandi, Egidio Trabattone, and especially Reina) dedicated music to nuns, or were requested as outside teachers. The penitential, predicatory, and Marian-intercessory themes of Franciscan spirituality are apparent in their motet books.[74] But curial efforts to split the male from the female branches of orders were directed primarily against the friars. The 1621 orders for the Clarissans of S. Orsola mandated a limit on name-day liturgy (a mere seven hours of Masses) and male mendicants' access (App. A, Doc. 31):

> In order to end the large turn-out of friars at this church and monastery on the occasion of the titular feast of St Ursula, we order that on the said feast no more than eight Low Masses are to be celebrated, along with the sung Mass; as for the nuns, they are to celebrate it in the usual fashion, singing and responding as the choir . . . Vespers is to be sung by the nuns only, with no priest brought into the exterior church for the prayers.[75]

Among the Augustinians the picture was more varied: some monasteries (S. Marta, S. Agnese) had an active musical life, while others had problems (S. Caterina in Chiusa, with Federigo's 1606 orders). Early testimonies to polyphony include Morigia's praise of S. Maria Maddalena in Porta Romana (1595), and Gallo's dedication of a canzona to the Mantegazza sisters at S. Agnese in 1598, while S. Marta's traditions were clear. Several of Federigo's sermons (*ragionamenti*) that mention music might have been given at this latter house. Certainly Grancini's 1631 inscription to the Fissiraghi sisters, along with the documents, implies the performance of remarkably large-scale *concertato* by the end of the archbishop's tenure. Later evidence is found at S. Ambrogio in Cantù, while Carlo Cossoni's inscription

---

[72] See 'Musica' in the *Dizionario degli istituti di perfettione*, vi (1980); B. Baroffio on the Benedictines (cols. 209–10); S. Pallini on the Observant Franciscans (219–26); and S. Zaccaria on the Conventuals (226–30).

[73] Of the roughly 450 extant single-composer editions of musicians working in the diocese between 1585 and 1700, something like eighty were by Franciscans.

[74] Kendrick, 'Genres', 265–6.

[75] In Seicento Milan, Ursula's feast-day was 21 Oct. (not marked 'solemne' in the *Missale Ambrosianum*). Despite the restrictions, Grancini would dedicate a Marian motet, *O anima sanctissima*, in 1628 to Clara Virginia Preda, the organist at the house.

of his op. I reprint to Maria Vittoria Terzaga at S. Maria del Cappuccio testifies to polyphony at another house.

Other orders were less present. Several Dominican houses occur; Morigia mentions S. Maria della Vittoria, and one of Andrea Cima's 1627 concertos was dedicated to Paola Maria Arconati at S. Maria delle Veteri, while Locatelli notes the singing at S. Agostino Bianco in 1664. Although Carlo Borromeo had personally encouraged the growth of the only congregation not bound to *clausura*, the Ursulines, this latter was relatively undistinguished musically in Milan, unlike Novara, where composers, organists, and singers flourished.[76] Capuchins show even less evidence for music-making, except for the visits from the ducal musicians to the *chiesa esteriore* of S. Barbara.

Yet despite the differences, certain occasions for polyphony were indeed common to most or all of the *religioni*. Certainly one little-studied but increasingly important ceremony was the Saturday (Commemorative) Office of the Virgin, which included the Marian litany that often concluded printed polyphonic editions. Torre's anachronistic hagiography of Veronica Negroni's life at S. Marta noted the custom; while Veronica had a dialogue with the Virgin,

The litany of the Mother of God was being sung by the nuns, since it was Saturday, and this devotion was carried out all year long . . . and while they sang, the Blessed Virgin said to her [Veronica] the *Salve regina*, the antiphon recited by the nuns after the litany.[77]

This is one likely context for the Marian motets dedicated to or composed by nuns. Cozzolani's *Concerti sacri* and *Scherzi* both have three 'general' Marian intercessory motets not linked to any specific feast, while the former book includes settings of all four Marian antiphons, sung seasonally at the end of the Saturday Office.[78] *O Maria, tu dulcis*, a 1642 solo motet for alto, repeats the invocation and the ritual

---

[76] The curial files do not mention music; a dedication to Constanza Francesca Brasca (S. Marcellina) is in RISM 1679[1] (Angelo Zanetti, *Si Virgo pro nobis*).

[77] 'dalle Monache veniuano le Littanie d'essa Madre di Dio Cantate, essendo giorno di Sabbato, vseà questa diuozione tutto l'anno . . . e mentre cantauano la B.V. le andò dichiarando tutta la Salve Regina Antifona recitata dopo le Littanie da loro stesse': Torre, *Specchio per l'anime*, 203–4.

[78] Another puzzling text is *Venimus in altitudinem maris* (1650), which uses the language of Matt. 8: 23 ff. (Jesus and the storm at sea) in a Marian intercessory context.

catalogue of praise characteristic of litany texts, while echoing the *Salve regina*:

> O Maria, tu dulcis, tu pia
> tu clemens, tu dulcis, tu pia mater Dei, o Maria.
> Tu vera infirmorum salus,
> tu vera peccatorum refugium, o Maria
> tu vera afflictorum consolatrix, o Maria
> tu vera spes omnium fidelium, o Maria
> tu sponsa, tu virgo, tu mater,
> tu Spiritus Sancti sacrarium, o Maria
> o advocata nostra,
> respice in nos oculis misericordiae tuae,
> o clementissima Regina.
> Respice in nos in hac lachrymarum valle
> gementes et flentes
> respice in nos qui suspiramus
> ad te clamantes,
> clamamus ad te suspirantes.
> O Maria, tu via, tu stella,
> tu lumen, tu mater Dei, o Maria.[79]

Cozzolani's setting, fifty-seven of whose 128 measures are occupied by the words 'O Maria', reinforces the litany-like character of the text, more publicly intercessory than Rusca's Marian motets. More puzzling is the lack of other documentation for polyphonic litany settings in Milanese female houses besides the five editions dedicated to nuns that include such pieces; given its apparent antiquity, litany singing may also have been something of an oral tradition.[80]

But the documents pinpoint an even more central occasion, one which houses from S. Maria Maddalena al Cerchio in the 1570s to S. Maurizio in the 1740s would exert their utmost to celebrate poly-

---

[79] 'O Mary, you who are sweet and merciful, you holy mother of God; you are the true health of the sick, the true refuge of sinners, o Mary, you the true consoler of the afflicted, o Mary, you the hope of all the faithful, o Mary, you spouse, virgin, mother, temple of the Holy Spirit; o Mary, o our advocate, look down on us with the eyes of your mercy, o most kind Queen. Look at us, sighing and mourning in this valley of tears, look at us who sigh to you while crying out, we cry to you while sighing. O Mary, you path, star, and light, you mother of God, o Mary.' The echoes of the Roman antiphon used from Trinity to Advent ('O clemens, o pia', 'gementes et flentes in hac lachrymarum valle') may mark this piece as originating in the litany of a summer Marian feast.

[80] Among editions dedicated to nuns, Mangoni's 1623 Vespers, Reina's 1653 *Armonia ecclesiastica*, Cesati's 1655 *Sacra melodia*, Bagatti's 1672 motets, Mass, and Vespers, and the 1678 reprint of Cossoni's *Primo libro de motetti* all contain Marian litany settings.

phonically, even if it meant a direct challenge to episcopal authority: the titular feast of the monastery.[81] Among the Humiliate in the Seicento, for instance, the saint's day itself was augmented by the duplex feast of the dedication of the church on the following day; to this were added the Octaves of both feasts.[82]

The very first dedication of polyphonic pieces to nuns (Antegnati in 1592) remarked the connection with name-day celebrations at S. Vittore in Meda. A 1598 double-choir motet by Soderini, *Saule, Saule, quid me persecutis?*, was rubricated 'In die conv[ersionis] S. Pauli' and inscribed to Agata Sfondrati at the eponymous house; the text seems well suited to the Angeliche's titular festivities.[83] Although not explictedly entitled 'dialogue', the motet sets the words of the exchange on the road to Damascus, the Risen Christ being given to choir I and Saul to choir II. The piece is a slightly later musical pendant to the elaborate Pauline iconography of the church created from 1564 to 1588, including Antonio Campi's fresco of the *Conversion of St Paul* in the *chiesa esteriore*.[84]

In a later generation, the continuation of the name-day tradition is evident in Rusca's two motets for St Catherine, possibly intended for 25 and 26 November, the feasts of the patroness and of the Dedication of the monastic church. *Veni sponsa Christi*, a solo motet for soprano, reworked the standard antiphon text for the Common of Virgin Martyrs in the Humiliate breviary:

Veni sponsa Christi, veni dilecta Deo Catharina, amata Deo Catharina, accipe coronam quam preparavit tibi Rex tuus et Deus tuus. Circumdabit

---

[81] A later invitation from the abbess of the Monastero Maggiore to the Austrian governor and his wife to attend the feast-day (1 May) of St Sigismund, the legendary founder of the house, requested 'accio venghini avvisati li musici di codesta corte Reale, affinché assistino si alla Messa cantata, che al Vespero di detto giorno, conforme al solito, et antiquato costume' (ASC, *Località milanesi*, 230, letter of 20 Apr. 1748).

[82] According to the 1751 breviary (but not that of 1621; cf. above, Ch. 3) at S. Caterina in Brera, 25 Nov. was celebrated as a duplex, while the dedication of the church on 26 Nov. was a 'principale', with Octaves for both. At S. Maria Maddalena al Cerchio, 22 July (St Mary Magdalene) was followed by 23 July (dedication of the church). The institution-specific nature of the calendar is obvious.

[83] 'Saule, Saule, quid me persecutis?' | 'Quis es, Domine?' | 'Ego sum Jesus, quem tu persequeris; durum est tibi contra stimulum calcitrare . . .', with the added words: 'Quoniam vas electionis es mihi, ut portes nomen meum coram gentibus et regibus et filiis Israel.' There is no other setting in the Milanese repertory. The text figures as the first lesson of Matins for the Conversion of St Paul, 25 Jan., in the post-Tridentine Roman breviary.

[84] On the decoration, see L. Carubelli, *DCA* iv (1990), 2653–6.

vernantibus rosis et coruscantibus gemmis caput tuum in aeternum, alleluia.[85]

If music had followed painting in the later Cinquecento, the pattern would be reversed at S. Caterina; a decade after Rusca's volume inscribed to Federigo, Francesco del Cairo would paint the altar-piece for the house's *chiesa esteriore* of the Alexandrine saint's Mystic Marriage, in which the hitherto unidentified kneeling male patron in the foreground can only be the beloved and deceased prelate to whom the motet book had been dedicated.[86]

But name-day polyphony would continue even later; Badalla's *O quam laeta* is one of two pieces in the entire Italian repertory to cel-ebrate Radegund:

> O quam laeta, o quam jocunda
> lucet dies illustrata
> quam Beata Redegunda
> est ad caelos exaltata.

O vere felicissima sorte, quam candida columba, cum suo divinissimo sponso sedet in gloria. Haec est illa virgo sapiens quae Jesu amando castis-simo sanguet amore. Nec est cuius ardentissimam charitatem aquae multae extinguere non potuerunt . . .[87]

The textually free but metrically standardized aria verse ('O quam laeta'), together with the use of other saints' symbols (Scholastica's dove) and the reworking of biblical tags (notably an important verse from the Song of Songs), highlight the ways in which the expres-sion—but not the content—of monastic sanctoral devotion in music changed over the century.[88]

---

[85] 'Come, bride of Christ, come Catherine beloved by God, take the crown which your King and God has prepared for you. Your head will be crowned with flowering roses and shining gems for all eternity, alleluia.'

[86] Cf. L. Basso's entry in *Francesco Cairo 1607–1665* ([Varese], 1984), no. 26 and p. 132, which does not identify the male figure. The painting is preserved in the Musée des Augustins, Toulouse.

[87] 'O how happy, o how joyous shines that light-filled day when blessed Radegund has been raised to Heaven. O most happy fate, that the spotless dove sits with her divine Spouse in glory. This is that wise virgin who, loving Jesus, bled with chastest love; nor could many waters drown her most ardent devotion . . .'. The other motet in her honour, Cazzati's *Sonet caelo vox jucunda*, had appeared eight years earlier (*Il sesto libro delli motetti à voce sola in Soprano*, op. 63 (Mantua: Osanna, 1676)).

[88] 'Haec est virgo sapiens' was a common tag from Proverbs, used in Benedictine use, Antiphon 1 for Lauds and the daily Hours (in Ambrosian rite, the verse for the Vespers *responsorium cum infantibus*) for the Common of Virgin Martyrs. The citation of Cant. 8: 7 ('Many waters cannot extinguish love, nor rivers drown it') was used as an emblem of

Yet the talents of female monastic musicians might also have occasioned other sanctoral pieces, not explicitly connected with nuns. Name-day settings for houses dedicated to the Virgin are often lost in the flood of general Marian motets. But other titular saints, chosen only as patrons of female monasteries (not other institutions) in Milan, are honoured in motets found in some unexpected sources. First is Vicentino's setting of *Ave virginum gemma Catherina*, in his 1571 book. Far from a Roman Mass Communion (an unlikely textual choice for a composer assigned to an Ambrosian-rite church), this item figures in the 1548 Humiliati breviary—and not in the contemporary Ambrosian books—as the Magnificat antiphon for Catherine of Alexandria's feast-day:[89]

> Ave virginum gemma Catherina,
> ave sponsa regis regum gloriosa,
> ave viva Christi ostia
> tua venerantibus patrocinia
> impetrata non deneges suffragia.[90]

This, the only sanctoral motet in the collection, could well have been set by the theorist for a performance—by nuns or others—in the institution using such a breviary, distant only 300 metres from his parish of S. Tommaso in Terra Amara: S. Caterina in Brera, whose name-day would have been celebrated as a duplex sanctoral feast.[91]

A generation later, the wave of sacred concerto collections in Milan occasioned other pieces linked to monasteries. Indeed, the role of female houses in the new styles is highlighted by two motets (among a total of three sanctoral texts) in the second concerto collection by a composer working in the city, Giovanni Battista Stefanini's *Motetti a 2–3* (Milan: Tini, 1606). The book by the new

female love for Christ, whether on the part of the Virgin, Mary Magdalene, or female saints. The freedom of late Seicento motet texts is evident; despite the references, Radegund was neither a virgin nor a martyr.

[89] *Pace* H. Kaufmann, *Nicola Vicentino: Life and Works* (n.p., 1966), 88–9, the use of this text in a 1474 Roman missal did not accord it a place in Vicentino's Ambrosian-rite collegiate church of S. Tommaso. Nor is it likely that the motet dates from the theorist's Ferrarese years: there was no church in that city dedicated to the Alexandrine saint.

[90] 'Hail Catherine, gem of virgins, hail glorious spouse of the King of Kings, hail living sacrifice of Christ; to those who honour you, you do not deny your intercession nor approval.'

[91] The latest setting of this text in Lombardy is unequivocally a name-day piece for nuns: Fontana Morello's 1614 version (CC), which immediately followed the *Ipsi sum desponsata* dedicated to the sisters of S. Caterina in Biella.

maestro at the ducal stronghold of S. Maria della Scala includes a three-voice concerto for St Margaret, *Ave sancta virgo Margarita*, on a text that does not figure in the Ambrosian (or Benedictine) liturgical books and was thus probably written for a special occasion in imitation of a canonical antiphon, perhaps that of Catherine of Alexandria:

Ave sancta virgo Margarita, virginum gemma, quae Christum amasti in vita tua, ne dedigneris commorari nobiscum in terris, quae nunc inter Angelos gloriosa coruscas in caelis.[92]

Its scoring and destination, along with Margaret's less than prominent place in the diocesan or monastic calendar, point to nuns' performance at the eponymous house; the motet is written for two canti and tenor, the latter in C3 clef with the range g–g'.[93]

Stefanini's collection includes another piece for martyrs commemorated in Milan only by a female monastic church: St Maurice and his companions. *Triumphant sancti* is scored for CT, using the Psalmellus from Ambrosian Lauds (a slight variant from the Magnificat antiphon for Benedictine Vespers) for 22 September:

Triumphant sancti martyres Christi, qui sub Maximiano mortem decreverunt suscipere: et cum sancto Mauritio regna caelestia sumpserunt.[94]

---

[92] 'Hail, holy virgin Margaret, gem of virgins, you who loved Christ in your life. Do not disdain to abide with us on earth, you who now shine gloriously among the angels in heaven.' The working of standard phrases ('gemma virginum') points to a newly composed text. The Modenese Stefanini had begun his itinerant career in Turin, but there was no foundation of this name in that city; cf. L. Tamburini, *Le chiese di Torino dal Rinascimento al Barocco* (Turin, 1957), 485 ff. In the composer's home town, the church of S. Margherita was a male Franciscan house without a musical tradition until the later Seicento (G. Soli, *Chiese di Modena* (Modena, 1974), ii. 376). Nor was there another S. Margarita in Milan. The saint's feast (5 July) was not marked 'solemne' in the Ambrosian sanctoral calendar (cf. the 1609 *Missale Ambrosianum*); her monastic commemoration (20 July) was 'simplex' in the 1600 Cassinese breviary, fo. 350[r].

[93] For the print's non-monastic buyers, transposition was in order; the organ part is a *basso seguente* pitched down a fourth. Again, the iconography seems to date earlier (or later) than the musical celebration: the contemporary accounts of Santagostino and Torre mention only mid-Seicento paintings of the saint in the *chiesa esteriore*.

[94] 'The holy martyrs of Christ triumph, they who chose to suffer death under Maximian, and with St Maurice they have received the kingdom of heaven.' The text (including 'sumpserunt' in the first sentence) is the Psalmellus for Ambrosian Lauds; the 1600 *Breviarium monasticum* (fo. 390[r]) gives the same text with the reading 'assumpserunt' as the Vespers Magnificat antiphon. Two centuries earlier, Stefanini's version was the antiphon for Lauds in the Office of St Sigismund and St Maurice contained in the Quattrocento codex belonging to the Monastero Maggiore, BA, C. 2 *inf.*, fo. 10[r].

Stefanini's version can be dated to 1605 or 1606.[95] This same text (in its Cassinese version, reading 'assumpserunt') was set by another musician at S. Maria della Scala, the prematurely deceased Gerolamo Baglioni; the duet in his posthumous *Sacrae cantiones a 1–6* (Milan: Tini, 1608) is again scored for high voices (CT, the latter in the range *e–f'*). Yet another piece, this time for CATB, in Baglioni's collection reworks a standard introit text in order to honour the Benedictines' patron alone:

Gaudeamus omnes in Domino, diem festum celebrantes sub honore Beati Mauritii martiris, de cuius solemnitate gaudent Angeli, laetantur Arcangeli, laudantes benedicunt Dominum.[96]

The identification between nuns and singing angels is again present, with the addition of 'laetantur arcangeli' to the textual model. When the Monastero Maggiore's inhabitants performed this work in the *chiesa interiore* of S. Maurizio, they again literally enacted the formal message of the text.

Perhaps the most striking sanctoral motet not explicitly inscribed to nuns honoured a saint whose cult was represented in the city only by the one Humiliate house not mentioned hereto, a martyr so obscure as not even to figure in the diocesan calendar:

Tortus certamina martir Erasmus suscepit et superavit; coronam auream dedit illi Deus textam lapidibus praetiosis. Celebrate triumphos, carminibus jubiliationis nobiscum canite; benedictus Deus qui dedit illi victoriam gloriosam. Alleluia.[97]

---

[95] The feast-days for these two pieces provide evidence: Stefanini had still been in Turin as of Christmas 1604 (G. Roncaglia, *La cappella musicale del Duomo di Modena* (Florence, 1957), 88). But the dedication of his 1606 book was dated 23 Oct. Hence, *Triumphant sancti* might have been first heard on 22 Sept. 1605 (less likely 1606) and *Ave virgo* on 5 July 1605 or 1606. Stefanini's next publication, the 1608 book of five- and eight-voice motets, included a piece, *Sancte Paule apostole*, possibly meant for name-day celebrations at S. Paolo.

[96] 'Let us all rejoice in the Lord, celebrating a feast-day in honour of the blessed martyr Maurice, on whose festival the angels rejoice and the archangels are glad; let all those giving praise bless the Lord.' Since performances in the first decade of the century by the ducal band in the *chiesa esteriore* at S. Maurizio were not recorded in the account-books dredged up for the 1661 S. Paolo controversy, the Benedictines are likely to have sung this piece as well.

[97] 'The martyr Elmo received and overcame his trials of torture; God gave him a golden crown made with precious jewels. Celebrate his triumphs, sing with us in songs of jubilation; blessed be God who gave him this glorious victory, alleluia.' No other church in the city besides S. Erasmo was dedicated to Elmo, nor was he listed in the 1609 *Missale Ambrosianum*'s calendar; his feast was 2 June in the 1621 Humiliate breviary (fo. 340).

The 1619 setting for canto solo by Gabussi's successor as *maestro* at
the Duomo, Vincenzo Pellegrini, is markedly virtuosic, ranging up
to *g″* in its beginning melisma (for the 'tortuous' nature of 'tortus'),
and emphasizing the high register of the part in a way unthinkable
for the cathedral's boy choristers, with whom Pellegrini would have
problems throughout his tenure.[98] At least by the second decade of
the new century, S. Erasmo would share the musical life of its sister
houses.

Later in the Seicento, the sharp rise in the number of sanctoral
feasts and their polyphonic celebrations in the diocese paradoxically
renders such identifications more difficult, as motets were designated
as being 'per un santo' or 'per una santa', or supplied with the generic
'N.' in place of a specific name.[99] This practice had begun in the first
decade of the century (another kind of 'luxuriant' ritual practice) and
is evident even in Cozzolani's *Scherzi*. Certainly the spread of
polyphony to the smaller female houses, and other institutions, contributed to this 'universalizing' treatment for motets found in printed
collections. As late as 1658, Bagatti's *Ornate thalamum* (for CA; *Sacri
concerti a 2–5*, bk. 1) would explicitly honour the patroness of one of
Litta's targets, S. Margarita (even if the edition's index rubricated the
motet as being only 'per una Vergine'), using a mixture of verse and
prose (a *prosimetrum*) that again resonated with biblical, liturgical, and
bridal imagery for both its subject and its singers:

Ornate thalamum, o Sion filiae,
ad sponsum properat virgo Margarita
triumphans.
Hanc sponsus vocitat nocte concubia,
haec surgens properat sacra connubia
suspirans.
O beatissima Margarita, tu es virgo sapiens, et una de numero prudentium
quas Dominus vigilantes invenit, vade ergo laeta ad sponsum, vade, coronaberis.

---

[98] The motet is found in Pellegrini's *Sacer concentus*; on his problems at the Duomo, see
Mompellio, *Storia di Milano*, xvi. 524 ff.

[99] But Grancini, in his new position at the Duomo under Monti, seems to have destined
at least one more musically referential motet for Paola Serbellona's successors at S.
Vincenzo: the text of *Hodie cantent angeli* (from his *Quinto libro de' concerti* (Milan: Rolla,
1636)) reads, 'Hodie cantant angeli, laetantur archangeli; cives sanctorum, et domestici Dei
exultant in solemnitate sancti martyris Vincentii . . . [text missing] in organis, cytharis, in
voce tubae, alleluia.' The piece is scored for CCB, or TTB, or B with two violins; possibly
a reflection of an original CCA scoring.

Vade, diva, virgo prudens
vade gemma caeli splendens
ad aeternas nuptias;
Jesus sponsus en invitat,
te dilectam en expectat
inter Sion filias.[100]

With the rise of centonized motet texts, it is often only the musical highlighting (by sudden homophony or polyphony, or a striking modulation) of a key liturgical quotation (Magnificat antiphon or Matins responsory) from the Office of a given feast or Common embedded in the text that underscores the link between a motet and a specific feast, and we shall see some such examples in Cozzolani's works. These sanctoral motets, clearly written for female monastic performance, along with the dedications of the early Seicento, underline the proportion of the Milanese repertory composed originally for nuns.[101] And the specifically musical embellishment of houses' liturgy in the Seicento was unmatched by contemporary literature, church decoration, or architecture.

Thus all the devotional exuberance reflected in the monastic customs, beginning (or re-emerging) in Federigo's tenure—the projection of sanctoral cults into urban life by means of polyphony, the clothing ceremonies, Holy Week meditations, Marian services—highlight the continuation, with a more formalized content, of medieval traditions in early modern Milan. But this increasingly

---

[100] 'Prepare the bedchamber, o daughters of Sion, the virgin Margaret triumphant hastens to her Spouse. Her Spouse calls her at bedtime; rising, she hastens to her holy marriage with sighs. O blessed Margaret, you are the wise virgin and one among the prudent whom the Lord found awake, so proceed gladly to your Spouse, go, you will be crowned. Go, holy, prudent virgin, go, resplendent gem of heaven, to your eternal wedding; Jesus, your Spouse, invites you, His love awaits you among the daughters of Sion.' Italian poetic metre frames the biblical and liturgical tags in prose in the middle section ('Haec est virgo sapiens, et una ex numero prudentium', from the Common of Virgins, and 'Veni, coronaberis' from the Song of Songs). Despite the accentual differences, Camagno printed 'muglier' [*sic*] above 'virgo' and 'N.' above 'Margarita' so as to render the piece suitable for any female saint.

[101] For the period of App. C (1592–1679), there survive roughly 325 editions of polyphony printed in Milan (or elsewhere, by composers working in the city); of these, about forty-five (14%) have dedications to nuns in the diocese, with another seven (2%) composed by sisters and another ten or so with sanctoral motets that can be linked to female monastic churches only. If we add dedications to or compositions by nuns in neighbouring dioceses (Pavia, Novara, Como) to be found in this census, the totals rise to about fifty-five, ten, and fifteen respectively. Despite Litta, in the period 1650–79, of fifty-five urban editions, fourteen (25%) contained dedications to nuns.

musical ritual growth also raises the overall context: the ideological and symbolic world within which nuns' polyphony functioned and flourished.

6

Nuns' Music in the Milanese World-view

◇

Così con varie tempre, e frà cotante
Dolcezze scopre in Musica gentile
Del' Paradiso un picciolo sembiante.

(Anon., sonnet 'In lode della compositrice', Cozzolani, *Scherzi*)

Two printed objects, spanning the period, highlight the profoundly supernatural and transcendent ideology of urban society, including its musical nuns: the 1578 city map in which the Trinity (having ended the plague) hovers over the Lombard capital; and Filippo Picinelli's encyclopaedic compendium of the metaphoric and emblematic content of the natural world, his *Mondo simbolico*.[1] For women like Angela Flaminia Confaloniera, music had meaning as part of a larger, divinely ordained world order: it was a vehicle to communicate eternal truths of spirituality and cosmic harmony. But given the polyvalence of symbols and texts in early modern Milan, it is important to delineate the transcendent content of nuns' music, both for performers themselves and for their urban audiences, with the maximum specificity possible, and with attention to the actual music linked to such symbolism.

Polyphonic liturgy came to prominence in the context of the centrality of religious—and political—ritual in the city, a point of consensus despite the controversy over the possible novelty (and hence, modernity) of such centrality.[2] Whatever their origin, a constant

---

[1] Nunzio Galiti's map is reproduced in Gambi and Gozzoli, *Le città . . . Milano* 73. Picinelli, *Mondo simbolico* (Milan, 1653), had numerous reprints (and a remarkable reception history in Germany), and furnished 'un infinito numero di concetti' to preachers, poets, and others.

[2] The debate (obvious in the disagreements between A. Buratti *et al.*, *La città rituale: La città e lo Stato di Milano nell'età dei Borromeo* (Milan, 1982), on one side and Zardin, *Riforma cattolica*, on the other) over whether the Borromean era represented a different and consciously modern 'ritualization' of urban life is not crucial here.

stream of cultic events marked public time and provided occasions for social display in the city: devotional processions (especially during the crucial plague years 1576 and 1630), pilgrimages to shrines on sacred mountains, festive ecclesiastical or royal entrances, funeral pomp, Marian invocation, sanctoral feasts, and open-air spectacles ranging from heretics' confessions to inaugurations of monasteries.[3] As can be seen especially from the musical evidence, this ritualization of social life grew by leaps and bounds up until the later Seicento, despite episcopal efforts such as Litta's to rein it in.[4] But this was not simply an ecclesiastical phenomenon; political and religious ritual were essentially fused, and all urban social layers participated in public ceremonial life, each with its own forms and institutions.[5]

Patrician families and the female inhabitants of 'their' monasteries saw sanctoral or Marian devotion as representative of their local prestige and honour; in the words of a Marian motet by Cozzolani, 'te corde et cantu, te ore ac votis hodie honoramus, cuius memoria terra nostra triumphat'.[6] The altar-pieces, additional feasts, biographies, and relics devoted to Mary or the saints all provided a locus for the expression of leading families' wealth and spiritual values. The growth of sanctoral devotion in the early seventeenth century, represented as well in the late *stile antico* and early concerto repertory, parallels the influence of such families.

One aspect of urban piety is also relevant to this musical repertory: the promotion of female saints, often linked to specific houses, as models for nuns and laywomen and as public objects of devotion.[7]

---

[3] On this, *La città rituale*, *passim*, and the illustrations in de Maddalena (ed.), *Millain the Great*, 154 ff. For some musical examples composed on the occasion of Maria Anna's 1649 visit, see the ceremonial eight-voice motets written for the entrance of the princess and of the papal legate by Grancini: *Ista est speciosa* (using the language of the Song of Songs) and *Sacerdos et pontifex* (both in I-Md, Maestri di cappella, busta 21), respectively.

[4] Zardin, 'L'ultimo periodo spagnolo', 592–7.

[5] Hence, public ritual was not an activity forced on an essentially secular patriciate by a series of theocratic archbishops; rather, it was an open form which different social strata (patricians, artisans, ecclesiastics) filled with their own content.

[6] The quote is from the 'general' Marian duet *Surgamus omnes* (1642). The text of this motet quotes part of Giuseppe Rovetta's general sanctoral piece, *Surgamus ergo, cantemus ergo* (*Motetti concertati a 2–5*, op. 3 (Venice: Vincenti, 1635, with a 1640 reprint), which reads: '. . . in solennitate S. N. . . . quem votis honoramus hodie, cuius memoria terra nostra triumphat', one of several indications that Cozzolani was familiar with the Venetian motet repertory of the 1630s.

[7] On the usefulness of sanctoral cults for the understanding of social ideology in early modern Italy, see Burke, *The Historical Anthropology*, 59; for devotion to the two Sts Gertrude around 1650, see the appendix to Lampugnani, *Della vita*.

Whether these women were the patroness saints of a foundation, or local figures from the Milanese past whose canonization the urban patriciate was eager to support, the century witnessed a notable upsurge in the breadth of female sanctity. Both S. Margarita and S. Marta pushed their own inhabitants' causes for sainthood.[8] The Augustinians even attempted to obtain a place for Veronica Negroni in the diocesan sanctoral calendar on 15 January, before any official permission from Rome. This growth in local veneration is especially noteworthy given the rise of the 'generic' sanctoral motet ('Sanctus [or Sancta] N.'), in which local or institution-specific saints could be musically honoured.[9]

One such case was that of S. Radegonda's patroness. Lampugnani's *vita* of Radegund provided an elaborate account of the Frankish queen as an ideal nun.[10] The hagiography, aimed at the saint's 'divoti', linked her life to the spiritual and patrician prestige of the Milanese foundation, including several miracles attributed by Lampugnani to the monastery's sanctity. The Cassinese abbot also included numerous references to Radegund's love for sacred song, and to the imperfections of modern *salmeggiare* (this latter, presumably, to underscore by contrast the musical traditions of the house).[11] The *vita* ended with a great responsory and a prayer to be used in the saint's Office, not found in the Cassinese breviary or the *Rubriche*.

The philosophical point of departure for such public piety and the concomitant flowering of ritual polyphony in Federigo's Milan lay in the prelate's adherence to one strain of Christian optimism, that

---

[8] On 9 Sept. 1637 S. Margarita commissioned Diomede Croce to construct the case for the canonization of Brugora (ASM, Religione, p.a., 1915); the whole *busta* is filled with popular (often semi-literate) testimonies to her miracles; it also includes her portrait and two more copies of Ruggieri's *vita*.

[9] For the letter of 27 Dec. 1627 from the prioress Giulia Vittoria Cremona to Canon Gerolamo Settala, asking for advice on fixing the date so as not to conflict with the Octave of the Epiphany or the feast of the Name of Jesus, and suggesting 15 Jan. as the first possible occasion, see ASDM XII, vol. 100, fasc. 5; S. Marta was still using the Ambrosian breviary.

[10] For a 1566 *vita* of the saint, dedicated to Maria Felice Maggiolini at the house, see Zardin, *Donna e religiosa*, 221. A pre-1612 list of the fifty-six books owned by the Ambrosian Hermitesses of S. Maria sopra Monte in Varese included an anonymous *Vita de santa Redegonda con la vita di S. Marta e S. Maria Maddalena* (L. Zanzi, *Sacri monti e dintorni: Studi sulla cultura religiosa ed artistica della Controriforma* (Milan, 1990), 210–11); the three provided models for active, contemplative, and 'combined' female Christian life.

[11] Lampugnani, *Della vita*, 5, 41, 47, and 122, with another story (not present in the original hagiographic tradition) of her disdain for a sister who had heard secular musicians sing known melodies, a thinly veiled reference to outside musicians (ibid. 80–1).

which saw creation as a manifestation of divine goodness.[12] Drawing eclectically upon a long, largely Pythagorean, tradition, Borromeo considered the ordered harmony of music to reflect that of creation, and music-making to allow performers (and listeners who grasped the *affetto* of the music) to tune their souls to the accords of the natural world. The prelate's thought reflected more widely held cultural attitudes, not least those of this study's subjects.

The connection between such musical symbolism and female religious was exemplified by one strand in Borromeo's own fascination with and support of ecstatic nuns.[13] The most prominent recipient of Federigo's efforts was Caterina Vannini of Siena (1562–1606), a young girl forced into courtesan status, who then repented and led an exemplary—and mystical—life. Her musical abilities were praised by Borromeo in his biography of the visionary.[14] The nexus of polyphony and transcendence became increasingly central for both the prelate and his monastic charges.

One musical path to ecstatic behaviour raised the question of female spirituality and female epistemology as related to music. It surfaced most prominently in the chapter 'De Canto, et de Sono' in book iv of Federigo's treatise on female mysticism and its pastoral care, *De ecstaticis mulieribus et illusis* (published 1616; excerpts from the Italian draft are given as Doc. 26).[15] In this work (itself a reflection of the century's feminization of piety), Federigo postulated that the natural constitutions of men and women were different; the sexes received Divine illumination and perceived the phenomenal world

[12] The essential link between Borromeo's optimism and his aesthetics was pointed out first by P. M. Jones, 'Federico Borromeo as a Patron of Landscapes and Still Lifes: Christian Optimism in Italy, c. 1600', *Art Bulletin*, 70 (1988), 261–72, followed by her 'Bernardo Luini's *Magdalene* from the Collection of Federico Borromeo: Religious Contemplation and Iconographic Sources', *Studies in the History of Art* (Washington, DC), 24 (1990), 67–74; for further elaboration, see ead., *Federico Borromeo*.

[13] This concern found its expression in the prelate's obsession with female mystics: he visited and wrote to them from the beginning of his adulthood onward; he recorded their visions, and even travelled in order to examine new reports of ecstatic women. The defence of Federigo for this behaviour forms a large part of Saba, *Federico Borromeo ed i mistici*; its almost frantic quality, and apportioning of mystical experience to women exclusively, are reminiscent of the alienation that Coakley has found among the Quattrocento male Dominicans in charge of Catherine of Siena's cult (Introduction to Matter and Coakley (eds.), *Creative Women*). This would not be the only 'medieval' trait in Federigo's character.

[14] Cf. Saba, *Federico Borromeo*, *passim*.

[15] Since the prelate only began his literary career in 1609, the actual date of writing falls between these two years; I quote from what appears to be an Italian draft (given the marginalia later worked into the printed Latin edition) preserved in BA, G. 26 *inf.*; the chapter on music occupies fos. 247^r-250^r. The chapter numbers differ between manuscript and print.

differently. The treatise considered that women were more prone to both true and false (even diabolical) ecstasy than were men, and enumerated the pastoral lessons to be drawn from this fact; in this sense, it marked a change from the long tradition of Christian possession literature largely undifferentiated by gender.[16]

Music's role arose from Borromeo's observation that female ecstatics sang the Office unconsciously while in ecstasy.[17] Turning to the playing of instruments, Borromeo gave a practical example, perhaps that of Vannini:

An ecstatic woman of holy life, who later died reputed of great holiness, once was forced by the pleas of her companions . . . to give them some sign and example of Paradise's harmony. So she most humbly . . . took a lute in her hands . . . and touching some courses played a song so delicate, but so removed from the melody (*aria*) and form of those we are accustomed to hear on earth . . . that such melodic turns and harmonic progressions had not been heard. Now this woman continued to play and sing only a short time before becoming enraptured (*rapita*).[18]

The lessons were clear: although both singing and playing may have aided in achieving rapture, the actual experience of ecstasy served to impede performance, and music was therefore a preparation to trance. Physical perception (the woman's arm hurt after she played the lute) was suspended, not heightened, during ecstasy. Finally, this case was of an *ecstatica* whose mysticism had been 'certified' by ecclesiastical authority (a rather post-Tridentine touch), and so its lessons were generally applicable to others.[19] Although the prelate did not

---

[16] Borromeo was less than precise in his use of the terms 'ecstasy' (Lat. *ecstasis*), 'rapture' (*raptus*), and 'trance'; in received usage, 'ecstasy' means a loss of sensory and all external phenomena owning to the essence of God experienced internally (this is further subdivided according to the intellectual or spiritual origin of ecstasy); while *raptus* (Eng. 'abduction') refers to the highest possible perception of the internal effects of God's sweetness. These definitions are found in the widely circulated (even in Milanese female houses; see Zardin, *Donna e religiosa*, 225) works of Bonaventure.

[17] BA, G. 26 *inf.*, fos. 247ʳ–248ʳ, in bk. iv.

[18] 'Vna estatica di santa vita, la quale poi è morta con fama di gran santità, tal uolta era costretta dalle preghiere delle sue compagne . . . a dare ad esse alcun segnale, et alcun esempio, come fosse l'harmonia del Paradiso: Ella siccome humilissima . . . prendeua nelle mani un liuto . . . e toccando alcune corde di esso insuonaua un canto cosi delicato, mà insieme cosi lontana dall'aria, e dalla forma di quelli che sono consueti à sentirsi in terra . . . che già già maniere somigliansi di canto, et andamenti simili di consonanze, non si sentiuano. Hor questa donna non procedeua innanzi un piccolo spatio di tempo cantando, e suonando ch'essa restaua rapita': G. 26 *inf.*, fos. 248ᵛ–249ʳ.

[19] For approaches to the essential questions (music as preparation for trance, suspension of normal mental functions in musical trance), see G. Rouget, *Music and Trance* (Chicago, 1988).

state so explicitly, the mystic was probably improvising before ecstasy.

Women of Vannini's sanctity were not present among the Milanese nuns to whom Federigo wrote and preached, especially in the last decade of his tenure. But their rich description of their internal states evoked the prelate's concern with his charges' spiritual lives, evident in his correspondence and the many *ragionamenti* given at S. Marta, S. Caterina in Brera, and S. Maria del Lambrugo.[20] If Federigo was concerned to tailor his pastoral advice to the vocation of his flock, his view of music's role was also shaped by the objects of his address. An important text for musical aesthetics was Borromeo's twenty-four-page Assumption Day sermon on music given to nuns at an unnamed monastery, probably in the later 1620s, which detailed his views of music's role in female monastic life (App. A, Doc. 34).[21]

Borromeo began the homily by invoking a poetic conceit that tied the Assumption to music: the topos of angels' song, surely no accident considering that the prelate's audience was probably composed of musical nuns. The prelate followed earlier Florentine aesthetics in his three requisites for good music: a good voice, technically competent composition, but most importantly, the *affetto*.[22] This last had two aspects: the musical setting should fit the words, but even more crucially, the manner of singing and the *affetto* of the singer should move the audience.[23] For this, *devotione* and *pio affetto* were essential; Federigo's example was that of an unnamed Ferrarese musician (probably Luzzaschi, whom the archbishop had aided after 1597), who sang a 'sol verso' of a setting of Petrarch's *Hor che'l ciel, e la terra* for the Pope.[24] The musician did so without *passaggi*, or artifice, but with such *affetto* as to move the hearers immeasurably.

---

[20] These are preserved largely in the Ambrosiana manuscripts, although at least one printed collection of *Ragionamenti* was produced in 1632.

[21] 'Dell'Assontione della B.V.', BA, F. 4 *inf.*, fos. 357^r–368^v. The volume contains other *ragionamenti* given at S. Marta and S. Caterina in Brera, and these two houses seem the most likely candidates for the locus of the sermon.

[22] 'la buona voce . . . la compositione . . . giuditiosa . . . la 3.a et quella che più importa è l'affetto': ibid., fo. 357^v. For the broader Seicento context of the relationship between competent music-making and divine praise, see A. Luppi, 'Immagine e funzione della musica sacra nella trattatistica di area lombardo-padana nel medio Barocco', in A. Colzani *et al.* (eds.), *Tradizione e stile* (Como, 1989), 29–72.

[23] As in ancient music, Borromeo noted (fo. 358^v); the Florentine influence is evident.

[24] This might have been the famous version of Luzzaschi's teacher Rore, first published in the Flemish master's *Primo libro à 5* (1545); on Federigo's patronage of Luzzaschi, see J. A.

The prelate mentioned the mysterious 'Cavagliere del Leuto' as a further example of music's power before returning to his principal theme, the idea of unfeigned spiritual devotion as a prerequisite for *buon affetto* in singing.[25] Again, the condemnation of vanity in music probably reflected the growing fame of individual nun singers and the cult of the individual musician evident in the travel reports. According to the *ragionamento*, too many *passaggi* precluded the possibility of devotion.[26] But contrary to the usual interpretation of post-Tridentine or Milanese aesthetic severity, the prelate did allow for expressive and rhetorically clear ornamentation in melodic lines.[27]

Singing only to please others, or straining to make the nun's voice audible from afar, also rendered true *divotione* impossible. In the middle of the sermon, Borromeo recalled the angels of the initial conceit as models for musical nuns to imitate. He then passed to an example of an unnamed 'santa anima', who unconsciously sang 'Sanctus, Sanctus, Sanctus' while sleeping, underscoring his interest in automatic behaviour, ecstasy, and music. Two other cases followed, one of a nun who was enraptured while singing and playing, and whose instrument continued to play of itself; the other was Vannini, of whom he repeated the same story that had figured in the printed treatise.[28]

The 1598 memorandum to abbesses written by Federigo's vicar Giorgi highlighted another association of nuns' music (App. A, Doc. 18):

Owens, 'The Milan Part-Books: Evidence for Cipriano de Rore's Compositional Practice', *JAMS* 37 (1984), 270–98, and Kendrick, *Music in Federigo Borromeo's Lombardy*.

[25] This figure has traditionally been identified with the Roman Lorenzini (H. Sybrandy, *NG* xi. 234–5).

[26] fo. 363ᵛ; Federigo was not the only local figure to inveigh against over-elaborate *passaggi* as a distraction from devotion: the performance instructions provided by the composer for the very first small-scale concerto edition published in Milan, Scaletta's *Cetra spirituale a 2–4* (1605), included (after long directions for the organist) the remarks: 'Gli cantori poi se consideranno quale & quanto sij il torto che si fà alle compositioni, & al compositor di quelle, quando ò non fanno sentir le parole spiccate, ò le confondono con un torrente di gorgia, ouero non attendono al significato di quelle . . . Et prima io in particolare desidero, che queste mie fatiche siino cantate, con quella maggior gratia, che dal Signore gli sarà concessa, facendo in ogni modo sentir le parole chiave' ('A gli honorati Organisti, e Cantori', p. [2]).

[27] 'Io non nego che qualche passaggio non si habbi à fare nel canto': *ragionamento*, fo. 363ᵛ. This distinction is analogous to that in Borromeo's visual aesthetics between 'substantive' and 'superficial' ornament; cf. Jones, *Federico Borromeo*, 112.

[28] For Vizzana's similar idea ('et erit vox mea quasi cithare citharizantium'), cf. Monson, *Disembodied Voices*, 105–10.

And on the same occasion [of Advent] we shall also tell you that, just as certain devout persons abstain from certain foods and train themselves in fasting and other penances, it would conform to ancient monastic custom to refrain from polyphony in these days; nor at other times to use instruments other than the organ and regal. And therefore you should have care not to permit lutes to be played in church, nor any nun to sing solo in a vain and worldly manner; nor is music to be made in the parlours, exterior or interior, nor in any adjacent room, under any pretext.[29]

The most striking feature of this note, besides its apparent ineffectiveness, is Giorgi's equation of polyphony with food and chant with fasting. In the light of the symbolic associations outlined by Caroline Walker Bynum, the analogy runs deeper: female control over food (including fasting and other 'abnormal' eating practices) as a way in which, besides expressing their spirituality, women exercised a degree of individual power and leverage in society. The music of Milanese nuns brought them individual and international renown; it played a central role in the ongoing urban conflicts of the Seicento, and the equation of food and polyphony seems pointedly appropriate.

Hence, Federigo's thought reflected broader cultural associations among nuns' music, ritual, and transcendence. For better (from the perspective of the patriciate, the travellers, and so on) or for worse (from the point of view of Carlo Borromeo and Litta), female monastic polyphony and its practitioners exercised a special attraction and enjoyed a ritual status unlike that of male musicians, monastic or secular. The first element of otherworldliness was the physical location. For the walls of the monastery demarcated an earthly Jerusalem, a sacred space and *locus amoenus* partaking of both Heaven and earth.[30] Nuns were even admonished to consider the exegetical meanings of Jerusalem as a guide to their common life.[31] Again, Federigo's letters to Confaloniera drew the explicit link to music:

---

[29] ASDM XII, vol. 50, fo. 162ʳ.

[30] Guenzati began the chapter of his biography devoted to Federigo's policy on nuns with the remark: 'Sì come li sagri chiostri sono tanti Paradisi terrestri, in cui l'innocenza verginale pasce co' purissimi suoi gigli lo Sposo Celeste, così egli è d'uopo, che li Vescovi sieno tanti Serafini alla custodia di quelli . . . Questa massima già scritta nel Cuore a' Federigo, pria anche che venisse al governo della Chiesa di Milano, tosto arrivato già lo stimolava ad isfogare il suo gran spirito nelle visite de Monisteri' (Marcora, 'Lettere', 204).

[31] Mazenta's reflections for Advent (ASDM XII, vol. 48, fos. 112 ff.), addressed to the 'Molto R.R. sorelle nel Signore' on 12 Nov. 1621 (two days before the beginning of Ambrosian Advent), was a lengthy exegesis of Isa. 60: 1, 'Surge, illuminare Jerusalem', which drew explicit parallels between the glory of the New Jerusalem and female houses.

Thinking of our spiritual garden, and of that garden that could be called the *hortus deliciarum*, it appeared to me as a solitary place, in which . . . there dwelled only some virgins . . . and sometimes a distinct voice was articulated in some parts. Even if it was not completely recognizable what it sang, still it was clear that it was a sung psalm or hymn, recited with devotion . . . If, by chance and good luck, you were one of these hermitesses, you would examine what your life ought to be, and which Rule should be observed in this new *collegio*.[32]

Nuns' (and only nuns') cloisters provided a foretaste of Paradise on earth, for both their inhabitants and the diocese as a whole. Federigo's insistence on the anonymity of the singing voice in the ideal monastery combined well with his prohibitions of vanity in real-life singing. But monasteries also functioned as a liminal space in which the distance between sinful human condition and eternal bliss was overcome, another medieval tradition in support of which Federigo was almost alone among post-Tridentine prelates. This can only have been reinforced by the spatial divisions characteristic of female monastic performance alone: the *chiesa interiore* and the *parlatorio di dentro* on one hand, and the *chiesa esteriore* and *parlatorio di fuori* on the other.

But if the monasteries were a stepping-stone to Heaven, their inhabitants were an earthly prefiguration of the angelic choirs, and their audible music a pale reflection of the celestial harmonies awaiting the saved individual soul:

Now the Spouse, all celestial, delights in the voice, and in hearing the sound of a poor shepherdess' [i.e., a nun's] words. What should the shepherdess do for that Spouse, what should she discuss with the angels? . . . Indeed, if ever you are made worthy of angelic song (that is, hearing it), those of you who know how to sing and play will find such disproportion and almost (I daresay) ugliness in your own song, that hearing it [earthly music] will seem strange, and in singing you would displease yourselves, and be ashamed to have such little skill and knowledge in the song with which you celebrate the greatness of God.[33]

---

[32] 'Pensando al nostro spirituale Giardino, et a quell'Horto che propriamente si può chiamare Hortus deliciarum, esso mi si è rappresentato come un luogo solitario nel quale . . . habitassero solinghe alcune Vergini [NB: feminine plural] . . . E talvolta ancora alcuna voce articolata si sentiva in alcune parti, la quale quantunque a pieno non si facesse conoscere che cosa ella intonasse, tuttavia pur si scorgeva che era Canto di Salmo o d'Hinno, che divotamente si recitava . . . Se voi hora foste per caso, et per buona vostra ventura una di queste Romite, voi hora rivedrete qual vita esser dee la vostra, et qual regola si osservi in questo novello Collegio': BA, G. 26 *inf.*, letter no. 135.

[33] 'Hora lo Sposo [Christ], che era tutto celeste si diletta della voce, e di sentire il suono delle parole di una povera pastora, che deve fare la pastora verso quello sposo, che ragiona

Borromeo's description of female monastic singers anticipated
Angelo Berardi's justification at century's end of nuns' polyphony as
a sonic representation of the divinely instituted essence of music
itself.[34] Time and again, the angelic topos underlay accounts and
dedications from Antegnati onwards, who stressed the incorporeal
nature of nuns' music;[35] it is no surprise that the best-known description of nuns' music in Federigo's era (App. A, Doc. 16), written by
a Gesuato, employed not only celestial similes, but rather actual
heavenly attributes of the singers at S. Maria Maddalena in Porta
Romana and S. Maria della Vittoria.[36] This chapter's epigraph, from
the first encomium in Cozzolani's 1648 *Scherzi*, underlines the ways
in which one 'Musica' (the composer) functioned as a small simu-
lacrum (a word with a long Platonic tradition, also used in connection with music by Federigo) of Paradise.

It is to this universal mental category of the monastery as earthly
Jerusalem and its singers as terrestrial angels that we owe the remarkable uniformity of outsiders' reports on nuns' polyphony.[37] For
observers musical and unmusical over the two centuries from
Morigia to Burney employed the same semantic field—'ravishing',

con gli Angeli[?] . . . Anzi se mai sarete fatta degne del canto Angelico, ciò di sentirlo, voi
che sapete cantare, e suonare, troverete tanta sproportione, et quasi, che io non dissi brut-
tezza, nel vostro canto, che a voi parerà cosa strana l'udirlo; e cantando voi voi dispiacerete
a voi stessa, e ve ne vergognarete di havere cosi poca habilità, e scienza in esso canto, con
cui celebrate le grandezze di Dio': Federigo to Confaloniera, BA, G. 26 *inf.*, no. 30.

[34] 'Felice [a character]: La Musica . . . è necessaria alle Monache, rappresentandosi in quel
Sacro Choro di Verginelle la Musica istessa, si può dire di loro ciò, che disse S. Paolo della
Chiesa Eph. I . . . E queste sempre stanno unite con Giesù Christo loro caro Sposo: Virgines
enim sunt, & sequuntur Agnum quocum ierit': Berardi, *Ragionamenti musicali* (Bologna,
1681), 'Dialogo Secondo', 109–10. The theorist's last quotation (from Rev. 14: 4) actually
inverted the gender of the biblical citation, which had referred to virgin men who had not
'defiled' themselves, not unsullied women; the passage was also used in the Consecration of
(female) Virgins.

[35] 'Quali Salmi come tutte le altre mie compositioni date alla stampa, all'hora io reputo
c'habbiano conseguito il fin loro, quando sono cantate, & vdite da persone, che dal gusto
di questo strepitoso rimbombono d'aria fra vilissimi corpi ristretta e percossa ergono il
desiderio à gl'eterni e perfettissimi concerti de chori Angelici nel Paradiso, come sò che voi
fate, che perciò vi prego siate contente farmi parte de frutti delle vostre feruenti orationi':
Antegnati, dedication, p. [2].

[36] Morigia, *La nobilità di Milano*, 306–7. Besides the prefiguring of Federican themes
('Chori Angelici'), and the explicit citation of the houses, the passage presaged the spread of
nuns' musical renown during the Seicento.

[37] Even the very first sonnet (coyly marked 'd'Incerto') in praise of Cozzolani prefixed
to the *Scherzi* noted the resemblance: 'Dal casto petto d'amor' sacro piena / Scioglie questa
si dolce i' dotti accenti, / Che qual del Tempio armonica Sirena, / Fà, che dormano al
Mondo i' cori intenti.'

'heavenly', 'angelic'—to describe sisters' music: not fanciful descriptions, but rather a realized set of expectations embedded deeply in one city's culture.[38]

One case of this repertory's role in ritual life was provided by Emanuele Lodi's description of the musical liturgy performed at S. Vittore in Meda on the occasions of the finding (in 1619) and solemn translation (1626) of the bodies of the house's legendary founders, Aymo and Vermondis (App. A, Doc. 33).[39] The background had been provided by yet another case of sisters' attempts to add sanctoral devotion, this time the Benedictines' successful prodding of Federigo to celebrate these saints, who had not previously figured in the diocesan calendar and whom the archdiocese had not recognized.[40] The Mass and Vespers celebrated with polyphony performed by the nuns were among the most impressive public functions of Borromeo's tenure. On the rediscovery of the saints' bodies on 24 April 1619, Federigo

entered the monastery, where he was received in procession with much jubilation by the nuns under the baldacchino, as they sang the psalm [actually the canticle for Lauds] *Benedictus Dominus Deus Israel* and accompanied him to the interior church.[41]

For the translation of the saints' bodies and the consecration of the new shrine on 13 June 1626, the procession

entered the church . . . with bells, the organs, trumpets, drums sounding . . . arriving at the main altar, the relics were deposited . . . as the nuns sang the litanies with organ accompaniment.[42]

---

[38] As in Locatelli's travelogue: 'In order to hear divine singing we betook ourselves to the nuns of S. Pietro Martire, who sing like angels in accordance with the customs of this blessed region': 'Viaggio in Francia' (App. A, Doc. 56).

[39] E. Lodi, *Breve historia di Meda e traslazione de' santi Aimo e Vermondo* (Milan, 1629; repr. Milan, 1741, a testimony to the continuing prestige of the house). The two locally venerated saints were considered to have established the monastery after a vision of the late imperial martyr St Victor.

[40] Cf. the calendar in the 1609 *Missale Ambrosianum*; for the efforts of S. Vittore's inhabitants, see Zoppé, *Per una storia*, 189 ff.

[41] Lodi, *Breve historia*, 13. Because of the liturgical placement of the canticle, few polyphonic settings survive. The only local version published between 1600 and 1630 was the five-voice motet by G. A. Cangiasi, in his *Melodia sacra* (Milan: Tradate, 1612). The solemnity of the occasion, with the references to multiple choirs and organs at S. Vittore, renders this setting unlikely to have been heard on this occasion; it is not impossible that one of S. Vittore's organists might have set the canticle.

[42] App. A, Doc. 33.

The published eyewitness account reflected the activities appropriate to each participant: Federigo blessing the relics, and the nuns (as an earthly prefiguration of the angelic choirs) singing canticles, hymns, and litanies in polyphony in a sort of liturgical dialogue. The writer of the house's *Liber cronaca* described both occasions, probably from memory, noting that Federigo cut Vespers short on the 1626 feast because of the press of the crowd in the *chiesa esteriore*.[43] For this feast, the major public celebration of important local saints (and hence an occasion for urban patriotism), the nuns of S. Vittore used all the musical means at their disposal.[44]

But if on one hand female monasteries were earthly Paradises, on the other some less sympathetic observers considered them as equivalent to theatres, with all the dangers to *clausura* and chastity that the status implied. The ritual space of female monastic music was by no means uncontested. A late visitation order gave instructions for the physical distancing of singers and instruments at the Monastero Maggiore:

We order the aforesaid Reverend Mother Abbess to lower the organ with its choir-loft within three months; some time ago it was erected too close to the surface of the wall that divides the interior from the external church. This [is to be done] as necessary to take away any sight-line into the said external church, [and is to take place] under pain of suspension from monastic office and the deprivation of active and passive voice.[45]

How this could have been carried out in practice at S. Maurizio is by no means clear; the Antegnati organ and its loft show no signs today

[43] Except for the descriptions of the 1619 and 1626 festivities, the book's entries begin in the late 1630s. For the accounts of the 1626 events, *Liber cronaca*, fo. 13^{r-v}.

[44] Lodi's description of the titular church of S. Vittore (there were others, dedicated to different saints, in the monastic complex) noted: 'Vedonsi anche tre Organi: il maggiore nel frontispicio della Chiesa sopra la porta, per dove s'entra, e gli altri due, uno per parte, i quali ora ad uno, ora a due, e molte volte anche tutti tre, conforme che sono più, e meno i Cori di musica, sono da diverse eccellentissime Organiste con soave armonia sonati, tanto più quando si sentono insieme con la musica' (*Breve historia*, 23). This seems to indicate that there were three ensembles at the house by the 1620s; Antegnati's 1592 dedication and scoring had implied only two (see Ch. 8). Presumably all performed together at the ceremonies on 13–14 June. All three instruments were dismantled in the early Ottocento.

[45] 'Ordiniamo a *detta* Reverenda Madre Abadessa di far abbassare in termine di tre mesi l'organo con la Sua Cantoria, quali tempo fa si fecero alzare troppo vicino alla superficie del muro, che divide la Chiesa interiore dall'esteriore: e ciò, quanto bisogni, *per* togliere ogni veduta in *detta* Chiesa esteriore; sotto pena di sospentione dall'uffizio et priuatione di voce attiva & passiva': orders from the 1705–6 visit of Giovanni Archinto, ASDM XII, vol. 101, fasc. 2.

of having originally been placed higher on the west wall of the *chiesa interiore*, and the enormity of the task was probably impossible in the space of three months. Furthermore, the sight-lines from the *chiesa interiore* through the grate above the altar barely permit a view of singers in the organ-loft.[46] Similar, earlier orders survive for S. Agostino in Porta Nuova.[47] They testify to the very public and visible place of female monastic singers at the heart of patrician liturgical and para-liturgical devotion.

Indeed, the tension between anonymity and renown for individual singers was implicit in all the external testimony. If prelates and curias were concerned to make monastic musicians as anonymous as possible (whether by discipline or by persuasion), still the musical dedications and the travellers' reports underline the fact that famous singers were well known by name in the city. This was possible because, as Locatelli noted at S. Agostino Bianco, the large grates over the altar were kept open, not only during Mass but thereafter as well (unlike the case in his native Bologna).[48] Jakob Sobieski in 1612 was able to see the age and physical repulsiveness of Donna Grazia.[49]

The prominence of individuals was no surprise. Litta's complaints about certain female monasteries as seraglios of singers rather than terrestrial Paradises came to the fore during the crisis of the 1660s precipitated by the prelate's attempts to eliminate or restrict patrician devotion. The tension between these two views of monastic music—nuns as members of angelic choirs and nuns as ill-concealed opera singers, with all that the latter status implied—would remain

[46] There exist further, rather vague references to a second organ with a *cantoria* on the opposite wall of the *chiesa interiore* in the Settecento (Sannazzaro, *San Maurizio*, 61, citing I. Rossi, *La chiesa di San Maurizio in Milano* (Milan, 1914), 116). If this second keyboard were some sort of positive organ or regal set on a wooden platform, it would have been much more feasible to lower; Archinto's orders may well have referred to this (now lost) other instrument. Certainly the preceding, similar orders of 1609 (while the house was still subject to the Cassinese) reported two organs, one smaller: 'Quando la Colerina dell'Altare è aperta stiano calate quelle dell'organo, et organetto, acciò non siano uiste le cantatrici da quelli che sono in Chiesa' (ASM, Religione, p.a., 2172).

[47] 'Ordini, e Decreti de' Superiori: . . . Si levino ad ogni modo tutti gli instrumenti dal piano della chiesa, come troppo vicino e familiari alla crate dell'altare, e di molto disturbo a celebranti e l'asconcino soppra il palio dell'organo assai capace, e bisognando allargarsi alquanto verso la strada con star' lontano alla finestra della chiesa almeno due bracchia' (ASDM XII, vol. 62).

[48] 'The large grate [*ferrata*] over the main altar was open from the beginning of Mass; nor do they open it only at the Elevation and then close it immediately (as they do in Bologna), but it stayed [open] the whole morning': 'Viaggio', fo. 51[r] (App. A, Doc. 56).

[49] Sobieski, *Peregrynacja*, 173–4. See above, Ch. 4.

invariant over the entire period of this study. In the city's eyes and
ears, musical female religious were a vital part of the symbolic economy of Milan. As permanent virgins, they had been removed from
the normal channels of the familial exchange of women. Their sanctified status was underlined by the spatial function of their monasteries as a new kind of urban shrine.[50] And the sheer number of women
'sacrificed' in this way represented another example of conspicuous
consumption in early modern Italy: in this case, the ritual redirection
of what would have been the city's stock of nubile brides, offered up
in the clothing ceremonies by patrician fathers, for the purposes of
local spiritual prestige.[51] Their singing—besides being the only activity connected to liturgy and prepared by their domestic education—
served to mark their status as earthly angels, whose music sonically
and symbolically represented the celestial choirs, not least by the
extraordinarily high timbres of their vocal ensembles.[52] This phenomenon of nuns as musical mediators to heavenly realms, besides its
inherent association with trance and ecstacy, both replaced the public and political role enjoyed by sisters before Trent, and provided a
new kind of symbolic invocation by which the city could overcome
the ideological and economic problems of the Seicento.

But the perspective of its external function in the prestige economy
tells only one side of the story. That sisters themselves had somewhat
different ideas of the nature of musical devotion—as well as the fact
that practice had loosened by the 1620s—is underlined by the five
(or more) solo motets that opened Rusca's *Sacri concerti*, dedicated to
Federigo. These include the one piece, *Salve, regina caelorum*, that
seems to incorporate some of Rusca's own ideas on music's meaning
(cf. below, Ch. 8). Thus, the symbolic function of nuns' polyphony
in the urban world has to be balanced against sisters' own ideas of
devotion and its musical expression.

The proof text that they used for their spiritual lives was the cen-

---

[50] On relics and their monastic custodians in Milan, see Morigia's exhaustive catalogue,
Santuario della città e diocesi di Milano (Milan, 1603).

[51] On conspicuous consumption, see Burke, *The Historical Anthropology*, 132–49; for nuns
as symbolic sacrifices of urban pride in some Quattrocento cities, see Zarri, 'Monasteri femminili'.

[52] Given the large proportion of early Seicento sacred music that would have been transposed down in the daily practice of other ecclesiastical institutions, the registral contrast to
other cities must have been all the more striking.

tral book of Seicento devotion, the Song of Songs.[53] For women and men in and out of the Catholic world, this short Old Testament canticle provided a wide array of allegorical tropes for earthly phenomena, ranging from the entirety of soteriological history, to the provision of models for daily Christian life, to comfort in the often difficult personal search for Christ.[54] It would be difficult to overestimate the meaning of this stunningly beautiful text, with its exotic poetic language and mysteriously discontinuous narrative, for the self-understanding and mystical world-view of everyday women and men in the seventeenth century. Tags, paraphrases, and extended quotes from the canticle run throughout Angela Confaloniera's, Flaminia Annoni's, and others' letters; they constantly recur in Federigo's writings, and above all in his missives to cloistered correspondents.[55] Certainly the centrality of the canticle to spiritual life in Federigo's time is manifest not least in the extraordinary number of Song of Songs settings—some two hundred—in the Milanese musical repertoire from his tenure.

One point of approach for sisters' understanding is provided by Borromeo's own interpretation.[56] Federigo's three commentaries on the book are largely philological, explaining only the literal sense of the canticle.[57] At first reading, they fall into neither of the major

[53] The essential trends in medieval exegesis are outlined in E. A. Matter, *The Voice of My Beloved: The Song of Songs in Medieval Western Christianity* (Philadelphia, 1990), which expands the classical work of Friedrich Ohly in ways to which I am deeply indebted.

[54] On the remarkable exegeses generated in the Seicento by this shortest biblical text, and their musical reflections, see Kendrick, '*Sonet vox tua in auribus meis*: Song of Songs Exegesis and the Seventeenth-Century Motet', *Schütz-Jahrbuch*, 16 (1994), 99–118.

[55] Imagining a dialogue among nuns, Borromeo wrote to Confaloniera: 'Una direbbe tal volta: Qualis est dilectus tuus ex dilecto: qualis est dilectus tuus, et dilecto quia sic adiurasti? [taken from Cant. 5: 9] Et un'altra direbbe, quo declinavit dilectus tuus, et querimus eum tecum? [5: 17] . . . overo parlando ancora più apertamente constretta direste, dall'amore: Adiuro vos filiae hierusalem, si inveneritis dilectum meum, ut nuncietis ei quia amore langueo' [5: 8], BA, G. 26 *inf.*, no. 119. I shall have occasion to return to the centrality of the dialogue, and of this last citation in particular, for the musical expression of female monastic spirituality.

[56] Borromeo's *ragionamento* at S. Caterina in Brera, dated 12 Oct. 1628 in the Ambrosiana manuscript (F. 4 *inf.*, fo. 427)—and therefore one which Confaloniera and Rusca must have heard—began with a triple explication of the passage 'Nigra sum, sed formosa' (Cant. 1: 4 ff.): 'nigra' referred to the work of the active life, 'formosa' to the contemplative life, both necessary for the model nun; 'nigra' also symbolized bodily pain that nuns endured, 'formosa' their spiritual happiness; the 'blackness' of the canticle's spouse also reflected the fact that God's gifts are often unprepossessing in appearance. Possibly some of the missing two- to four-voice concertos in Rusca's book set canticle passages.

[57] 'Notae in librum Canticum Canticorum Salomonis', BA, F. 26 *inf.*; 'Interpretatio Cantici Canticorum secundum editionem Caldeam', R. 180 *inf.*; and 'Observationes in Job et Isaiam et Cantica Canticorum', G. 309 *inf.*

traditions of Song of Songs exegesis characteristic of the West: the allegorical view, which interpreted the male and female lovers of the book as symbolizing Christ and the Church, respectively, and the tropological view, which explained the characters as representing Christ and the individual soul.[58] But perhaps this is a result of the polyvalence of the text in Federigo's use, and of the common trend towards the provision of a literal interpretation of the book's perplexing narrative.[59] Some passages in his letters to nuns reveal— unsurprisingly, given the prelate's emphasis on the individual—an adherence to the tropological interpretation.

But Borromeo also availed himself in his writings for nuns of another, secondary exegetical tradition, that which identified the woman lover of the canticle with Mary Magdalene.[60] Given Federigo's use of the Magdalen as a model for nuns (by virtue of her penitence and contemplation), it is no surprise that his monastic correspondents developed this interpretation, explicitly invoking her mourning at Christ's Tomb as a metaphor for their own spiritual states:

Bitterly I prayed my Lord, with humility, that He would reveal to me what He wanted of me . . . and I seemed to hear an inner voice which said, 'Why are you crying, my daughter?' and this made me break out in greater tears than before; and I saw St Mary Magdalene, when she mourned at the Tomb, and the Lord asked her, 'Woman, why are you mourning?' and she responded, 'They have taken away my Lord and I don't know where they put him; if you took Him, tell me and I will take Him.' And that is how my soul could respond, and it did; namely, I find myself without, deprived of my Lord's presence, and I don't know why.[61]

---

[58] On the distinction, see Matter, *The Voice*.

[59] One of Federigo's commentaries reflects the second interpretation: 'Quanto alla natura et alla qualità di questo componimento egli è Carmen pastorale; ouero Egloga ouero Idylium come chiamare lo vogliamo . . . quanto al soggetto sicuramente è l'amore diuino; et si finge l'anima auesa da un celeste ardore, et infiammata di somma carità uerso di Dio' (BA, F. 26 *inf.*, fo. 272ʳ).

[60] This interpretation dates back at least as far as Alan of Lille's *In cantica canticorum . . . elucidatio* (Matter, *The Voice*, 167), and was expressed to some degree in the Magdalen hymn tradition. Until the Seicento, it was very much a minority exegesis, behind both the major currents.

[61] Suor Aurelia Maria at S. Caterina in Brera to Federigo, BA, G. 265 *inf.* n. 4,: 'Amaramente pregaua il mio Signor con humilta che mi volesse scoprire quel che uoleua da me . . . et mi pareua sentir vna voce interna che mi disse che piangi figliola, e che me fecce prorompere in maggior pianto di prima et se me presentò Santa Maria Magdalena quando piangeua al monumento et che il Signor le disse mulier quid ploras et che essa rispose Tulerunt Dominum meum et nescio vbi posuerunt eum si tu sustulisti eum dicite michi et

Time and again, the sisters who wrote to Federigo constantly framed their behaviour in the language and actions of the canticle's female Spouse, following a long (only seemingly paradoxical) tradition of the identification of the book's passionate eroticism with female monastic chastity.[62] This monastic interpretation of the Song's spousal desire and love had been present since Bernard of Clairvaux, and this trend in the book's tropological exegesis, in which the nun figured as Christ's bride—literally as the canticle's female Spouse—seems actually to have gained ground in the seventeenth century, in line with the increasing monastic population. We shall have occasion to see the ways in which the Song of Songs and its imagery underlie a wide range of motet texts in those repertories associated with Milanese nuns.

That Federigo's interpretation(s) of the Song of Songs were also shared by a broader public than simply the audiences of his *ragionamenti* is underlined by a published treatise, apparently originally intended for nuns: *I tre piaceri della mente cristiana* (Milan, 1625); in Latin translation as *De christianae mentis jocunditate* (Milan, 1632). This essay underlines the tropological exegesis of the canticle;[63] it also quotes important tag lines (often set in music), in the context of the visions of late medieval female saints, as the cure-all for earthly despair, the thaumaturgic text *par excellence*.[64] The Song of Songs was the essential book in the prelate's vision of the 'joyous' Christian soul, one which his charges shared, and I shall have occasion to return to its musical avatars below.

Sisters also could have elaborated their own spirituality on the

ego eum tol*l*o. E cosi poteua rispondere l'Anima mia, e cosi rispose, cioè, mi trouo senza, et priua della presenza del mio Sig*n*ore e non so la causa.'

[62] For the long exegetical history of the book's spousal love as specifically female monastic marriage to Christ, see J. Bugge, *Virginitas: An Essay in the History of a Medieval Ideal* (The Hague, 1975), esp. 59–67.

[63] The citations begin in bk. I, ch. vii (henceforth I. vii), 'De Divinis Jocis', with references to Cant. 2: 9; 3: 2; and 5: 4. For the tropological interpretation, II. xi: 'Certissime tenendum est hoc, sponsus esse Christi animas eas, quibus Gratiae diuinae pars affulsit, proprie, inquam, et germane sponsus . . . Ideo Sponsa [NB: the *female* spouse] illa Canticorum designat animas omnes addictas, charasque Deo, etiamsi fortasse deesset illis aliquid ex ea flamma, et ardore, quem nunnullae sanctiores animae habuerunt.' A. Martini, *I 'Tre Libri delle Laudi Divine' di Federico Borromeo: Ricerca storico-stilistica* (Padua, 1975), 192, notes that the treatise was originally written for the diocese's nuns; but its publication in Latin testifies to its wider destination. Along with the *Tre Libri delle Laudi Divine*, this text was central to Borromeo's optimistic spirituality.

[64] As in I. vii (p. 20): 'Nunc Canticorum colloquia audite, quae medicinam afferre possint huiusmodi plagis: *Vulnerasti cor meum, soror mea sponsa, vulnerasti cor meum*' (Cant. 4: 9).

basis of the recommended devotional literature, at some houses probably the only non-scriptural material in their libraries or personal collections. The prelate's letters to nuns counsel the identification with biblical figures; curial documents for more general use emphasize the reading of standard Italian versions of medieval manuals of piety, sometimes the works of Jean Gerson.[65] This kind of reading matter explains the refashioning of pre-Tridentine themes in those works that express female monastic spirituality. Such local works as Basso's *Ritratto della perfetta monaca* preached the standard Borromean virtues of humility and simplicity.

But the prelate's or curial ideas for nuns' spirituality were not the only currents circulating in the monasteries, and the Seicento witnessed an explosion of sometimes suspicious charismatic movements and affective devotion aimed at women in and out of cloisters.[66] In their emphasis on individual illumination and eschewal of the need for good works or ecclesiastical authority, these popular movements in Lombardy approached Quietism and soon ran afoul of Rome, although not without leaving traces in the motet repertory of the 1630s and 1640s.[67] In a wider context, Bynum's outline of feminized piety in the late Middle Ages is again suggestive, at least for the origins: devotion to the suffering body of Christ as the principal point of piety, in this case with the added (and barely secondary) theme of Marian intercession.

This revolution in devotion, starting around 1630, had specific themes and objects. First is the emphasis on the individual's relation to Christ, one which presupposes the soul's internal illumination and purification, but which also stresses the physical body as the locus for Jesus' redemptive action. The two ideas combine in the ritual means for Christ's intervention, the Eucharist, now accorded a reworking of symbolic proof texts (notably the Song of Songs) like that found in G. B. Novati's (*c*.1590–1648) *Eucharistici amores ex canticis canticorum*

---

[65] The curial 'Modo di esaminare le Citelle desiderose di Monarcarsi', probably from the 1620s (ASDM XII, vol. 50, fo. 131), includes recommendations for the novices to read Basso's catechism and his *Ritratto della monaca perfetta*, among other books, including Italian versions of Gerson.

[66] Zardin, 'L'ultimo periodo', 590 ff.; for the female following of the 'Pelagian' movement, organized around the ideas of G. P. Casolo, see Signorotto, *Inquisitori e mistici*. For the links between S. Caterina in Brera and female lay penitents or tertiaries, see Zardin, *Donna e religiosa*, 215.

[67] For Litta's predictable reaction to heterodoxy in the Valcamonica, see Signorotto, *Inquisitori e mistici*.

(1645).[68] Second (again unsurprisingly in light of Federigo's thought) is the exaltation of Mary as intercessor for the faithful, and her removal from humanity.[69] Both turns implied a remarkable lability of traditional symbols, attributes, and even narratives: the mixture of the two Spouses' words in the canticle, the redirection of Christ's features to Mary (and vice versa), and the possibility for individuals to create their own images of Christ and the saints given such flexibility. From his own narrow point of view, it was no wonder that Litta intervened drastically to halt such symbolic confusion.

Female monastic spirituality fed both from and into these new topics and language of devotion.[70] The most famous female Benedictine mystic of the new century, Bl. Giovanna Maria Bonomo (1606–70), gave expression to the classical stages of mystical annihilation with a new kind of vocabulary.[71] Bonomo's emphasis on the individual's dialogue with the suffering Christ as a means to union with the divine was evident in her treatises, her letters, and her lost poetry.[72] The letters written by Federigo's cloistered correspondents stress the key personalized themes: the centrality of the Eucharist, the meditations on the physical Passion of Christ, the sacrifice of the nun's own suffering as part of her identification with her Spouse, the intercessory role of Mary and the saints. For the women of this study, this symbolic system provided the structure of their self-understanding and mission in life. But it also was shared by men and women outside the cloister.

The first musical reflections of this new spirituality are to be found around 1625, in the books of Gerolamo Casati and Alessandro Grandi, or in such anthologies as those of Lorenzo Calvi in Pavia. In the wake of the plague, however, this new literary language would dominate the work of the new, post-1630 generation, in Venice the

---

[68] This book is a 396-page exegesis based on the idea of the love of the individual soul (*Sponsa*) for the Eucharistic Christ (*Sponsus*). It thus relates the rapturous language of the canticle to the individual's reception of the Host.

[69] Again, Novati provided the standard local text: *De eminentia Deiparae Virginis Mariae* (Bologna, 1639 and 1650), a 430-page Mariology with many Song of Songs citations.

[70] For the overall outlines of female monastic spirituality in the Seicento, see M. Caffiero, 'Dall'esplosione mistica', in Scaraffia and Zarri (eds.), *Donne e fede*, 327–74, esp. 329–33.

[71] On her, see the outline and bibliography in F. G. B. Trolese's entry to the catalogue *Santità e religiosità nella diocesi di Vicenza*, ed. R. Zironda (Vicenza, 1991), 145–51.

[72] The devotional works include: *Confusione del christiano in non corrispondere all'amore mostrato da N.S. Gesù Christo . . .* (Bassano, 1659), her meditation on the Passion; *Tesoro dell' anima christiana* (Bassano, 1661); and *Meditazioni sulla Passione di Gesù Christo* (Bassano, 1752).

early works of Rigatti and on the *terraferma* the extraordinarily popular collections of the Novarese *maestro* Gasparo Casati.

The most notable aspect of the 'non-liturgical' texts set by composers of the new Lombard style around 1640 was the turn away
from scriptural (Song of Songs or Psalm) settings or language,
towards affective, literary, and highly individual Eucharistic devotion, followed closely by a new emphasis on the mediatory role of
Mary. Cozzolani's motet books highlight this new trend far more
than they reflect Borromean spirituality; wonder at Jesus' *benignitas*
(also shifted from the traditional Cassinese emphasis on the benignity
of God the Father), lengthy Marian acclamations, and Eucharistic
rapture underlie almost every non-liturgical text.[73] Some examples
demonstrate the highly affective piety, references to standard liturgical items, and reworkings of late medieval devotional language:

> O dulcis Jesu, tu es fons bonitatis
> fonsque amoris
> et apud te est fons vitae
> o dulcis Jesu.
> Bibat ergo in te solum anima mea
> ad te solum confugiat
> ad te die nocteque clamet . . .[74]
> (*O dulcis Jesu à 2*, 1642)

> Bone Jesu fons amoris
> Jesu, vita cordium,
> bone Jesu, purioris
> animae solatium;
> Nos aeternae fac bonitati
> in hoc mundo subiicio;
> O beata mellitudo,
> Jesu cor amantium
> increata pulchritudo
> dulcis esca mentium,

---

[73] These themes and their poetic language spread quickly throughout the Lombard concerto repertory; they are represented even in the works of the increasingly conservative
Grancini (*Sesto libro de' sacri concerti* (Milan: Rolla, 1646)). Their durability in the sacred
repertory is highlighted by even such late works as Mozart's Offertory for Corpus Christi,
Venite gentes (K. 260/248a; 1776), whose text still employs such poetic conceits and language.

[74] 'O sweet Jesus, You are the source of goodness and of love, and in You is the source
of life, o sweet Jesus. So let my soul drink only from You, let it flee to You, let it cry to
You day and night.'

da dulcedinem beatorum
da pulchritudinem Archangelorum . . .[75]
   (*Bone Jesu, fons amoris à 2*, 1642)

O quam bonus es, o quam suavis
o quam jocundus, mi Jesu;
O quam benigna es, o quam dulcis
quam delitiosa, o Maria.
Diligenti, suspiranti,
possidenti, degustanti te.
O me felicem, o me beatum.
Hinc pascor a vulnere,
hinc lactor ab ubere,
quo me vertam nescio.
In vulnere vita,
in ubere salus
in vulnere quies,
in ubere pax,
in vulnere nectar
in ubere favum
in vulnere jubilus
in ubere gaudium
in vulnere, Jesus,
in ubere, Virgo . . .[76]

(*O quam bonus es*, 1650; also set by Porta, 1648 and Grossi, 1659)

Not all Cozzolani's motets employ this highly personalized literary approach, although they are quite characteristic of the solo motets and the duets, while her 1650 collection uses them exclusively for the concertos and dialogues *à 2–5*. But the presence of such texts sets the mid-century Lombard concerto off from earlier Milanese motet books, which largely eschew the emphasis on individual devotion, favouring instead texts centonized from the Song of Songs or

---

[75] 'Good Jesus, source of love; Jesus, life of hearts, good Jesus, solace of the most pure soul; give us perpetual good in this world. O blessed honeyedness, Jesus, the lovers' heart, uncreated beauty, the sweet food of minds; grant us the sweetness of the saved, the beauty of the archangels . . .'.

[76] 'O how good You are, o how soft, o how joyous, my Jesus; o how kind you are, how sweet, how delightful, o Mary, in seeking, sighing for, having, tasting you. O blessed, happy me! Here I feed from His wound, there I suck from her breast; I do not know where to turn next. In Your wound is life, in your breast, salvation; in Your wound, rest, in your breast, peace; in Your wound, nectar, in your breast, honey; in Your wound, rejoicing, in your breast, joy; in Your wound, Jesus, in your breast, o Virgin . . .'. Cf. App. F, no. 1.

liturgical items. Rather than dismissing the remarkable language, and the equally novel musical means it inspired, as simply overly emotive, erotic, or exaggerated, we would do well to remember the revolution in spirituality of which they are markers, a sea change that determined the intellectual and symbolic formulation of the world shared by both nuns and the urban audiences who heard their music in the *chiese esteriori*.

There is one final notable feature of these new motet texts: their marked emphasis on the individual body as a locus for the redemptive action of Christ, and a new stress on the physical wounds of his Passion. It becomes impossible to separate Christological from Eucharistic devotion, the wounds of Christ from His redemptive action on the individual soul, as in the words of the opening solo motet from Cozzolani's 1642 *Concerti sacri* make evident:

> O quam bonum, o quam jocundum,
> quam suave, quam delectabile
> habitare in corde tuo, o bone Jesu.
> Venite, omnes animae sanctae,
> intrate per regiam portam,
> intrate per latus Salvatoris,
> ad gaudia caelestia venite, intrate;
> venite ad consolationem Angelorum,
> venite, intrate et videte
> quam benignus sit Dominus
> diligentibus se . . .[77]

The references to the believer's physical and spiritual being ('infunde animam meam, o dulcis Jesus') was linked directly to his or her reception of the Real Presence of Christ's body in the Eucharist. The 1648 *Scherzi* made the references even more explicit and graphic, as in *Venite gentes*:

Venite gentes, properate populi, currite ad agni nuptias. Ecce sacrum convivium in quo Salvator sumitur; aeterni patris filius vinum hic bibitur germinans Virginis. Esurientes edite Panem Angelicum, nihil est dulcius, nihil suavius, nihil jocundius; sitientes bibite calicem Domini, divinum sanguinem bibite.[78]

---

[77] 'O how good, o how joyous, how sweet, how delightful it is to live in Your heart, good Jesus. Come, all you holy souls, enter the royal gate, enter the Saviour's side [wound], come to celestial joys, enter; come to the angels' solace; come, enter, and see how good the Lord is to those who seek Him.'

[78] 'Come, you nations; hasten, peoples; run to the Lamb's wedding. Behold the holy

As a musical representation of a tradition dating to Birago's *orationes ante communionem*, these motets seemed to have been used to prepare the spirit for the reception of Communion (despite the curial warnings against singing, especially solo, at this moment in Mass). Eucharistic piety in the Milanese Seicento is still unexplored, but the general point of these motets—both Cozzolani's and those of her Lombard contemporaries—and their literary style is clear: the emphasis on and the adumbration of the mystery of the Incarnation (the Nativity, Eucharist, and Passion), recreated in ritual and personalized for the individual believer.[79] The opening of Cozzolani's *Quis audivit unquam tale?* (1650), a Nativity piece ending with a processional crowning of the Christ Child, summarizes the latter idea:

Quis audivit unquam tale, quis vidit huic simile? Obstupesce caelum, admirare terra, suscipe orbis universae; Deus usque ad carnem descendit, caro usque ad Deûm ascendit; Verbum caro factum est. Virgo quem genuit adoravit. O descensum profundissimum, o ascensum sublimissimum . . .[80]

Added to these traditional objects of female devotion, however, was a new layer, one without parallel in the late medieval evidence: the role of Mary as intercessor. In part, this was a pan-Catholic phenomenon, which Federigo's extreme devotion to the Virgin had advanced even further in Milan. But the omnipresence of Marian invocation in Rusca's and Cozzolani's books, and the evident feeling with which these pieces were composed, suggest that this was not an extraneous (male-imposed) feature in sisters' spiritual life, but rather an enrichment of the symbolic hierarchy of their world.[81] If one counts the four Marian antiphons set in the *Concerti sacri*, over half the book is devoted to motets exclusively or centrally featuring the Virgin, while the bloc of four solo pieces in the 1648 *Scherzi* forms another testimony to such veneration. And the Double

---

meal in which the Saviour is ingested; wine, the Son of the Eternal Father born of a virgin, is drunk. You hungry ones, eat the angels' bread, for nothing is sweeter, nothing softer, nothing more joyful; you thirsty ones, drink the Lord's chalice, drink the divine blood.' Cf. Novati, *Eucharistii amores*, 112: 'Christus in Eucharistica mensa est praecipua voluptas animae divino amore efferuescenti.'

[79] This emphasis neatly combines anti-Protestant theology (the Real Presence of Christ) with Federigo's stress on the individual Christian's path to devotion.

[80] 'Who ever heard such a thing, who ever saw something like this? Be amazed, o Heaven; be astounded, o earth; absorb this, o universe: God has descended to flesh, and flesh has ascended to God; the Word has become flesh. The Virgin adores Him Whom she bore. O deepest descent, o most sublime ascent . . .'.

[81] *Pace* the insights of Bynum, *Holy Feast*, 269.

Intercession—salvation from Christ's blood and Mary's milk—underlies two important concertos in the 1650 *Salmi a otto*. This Marian cult represents one of the most characteristically seventeenth-century features of nuns' devotion, expressed precisely through music, as motet texts underline:

Amate, o populi, Mariam, Matrem pietatis, sponsam charitatis, mare gratiarum, populi amate. Haec est mare quod vos ducit, haec est gratia quae vos ditat, haec est sponsa quae vos vocat, haec est Mater quae vos alit. O Mater, o Sponsa, o Mare, o Maria gratia plena, tu tota pulchritudo, tu tota gratiosa, tu tota speciosa . . . (*Amate, o populi, Mariam*, 1648)[82]

Still, the most passionate textual language in Cozzolani's motet books, as we shall see below, is reserved largely, but not exclusively, for the traditional emphasis on the Passion of Christ, and the new kind of individual self-identification with Christian martyrdom. In order to gauge the depth of Marian invocation, and the larger shifts in symbolic meaning evident in the repertory, we need to turn to the musical evidence. But to understand the actual conditions and effect of such ritual music the problems of its transmission and performance must be addressed.

---

[82] 'O peoples, love Mary, the mother of piety, the spouse of charity, the sea of grace, love her, o peoples. She is the sea who leads you, she is the grace who enriches you, she is the spouse who calls you, she is the Mother who nourishes you. O mother, o spouse, o sea, o Mary full of grace, you are all beauty, all grace, all lovely . . .'.

7

Ad usum Sanctimonialium

◇

Quod si ternis vocibus accomodentur, suauior modulatio ori-
etur, si Bassus & duo Cantus simul iungantur, vel Bassus & duo
Tenores, aut Bassus Cantus & Tenor, vel tandem Altus & duo
Cantus, ad vsum Sanctimonialium.

(*Psalmi ad officium vesperarum . . . Romano Michaele . . . Auctore*
(Rome, 1610), 'Ad Lectorem')

All the evidence raises one central question, a prolegomenon to any
analysis of the repertory: given both the episcopal efforts to isolate
these women from the musical life of their class origins, and the practical problems attendant upon the availability of solely female voices,
how did monastic musicians transmit and perform polyphony? The
first problem was education. The 1565 Lino– Borromeo correspondence had already addressed this issue, and the problem seemed
insoluble for both sides: prelates who could not politically afford to
ban music but who wanted to regulate female houses, and nuns concerned to have training. *Professe* normally took final vows by age 18
(it was in families' interest to have them do so earlier), while Carlo
wanted contact with the outside world to be kept to a minimum.
How could girls whose secular instruction ended in early adoles-
cence be trained to any professional level?

The efforts of nuns and their families to circumvent the restrictions of *clausura* would exercise two centuries' worth of archbishops.
First, there was the simple ignoring of the rules banning music teachers; for this there is negative evidence—the continual repetition of
the prohibitions, visitation after visitation, year after year.
Sometimes, however, families did procure valid *licenze*.[1] Although

---

[1] Presumably outside male teachers would have been paid, not by the nuns themselves
(who had at best limited *livelli* at their disposal), but by families; in Bologna, Ottavio
Vernizzi was paid a regular stipend at S. Cristina in 1623 (Monson, *Disembodied Voices*, 61).

the documentation is intermittent, several cases highlight the practice: S. Apollinare's Clarissans demonstrated its early use in 1568. Prospera Bascapè and her *compagne* at S. Maria Maddalena employed various means for both the novices and the *professe*: outside male teachers with a permit (which provoked the usual curial anxiety), domestic education provided by families before profession, and the teaching of *canto figurato* by skilled nuns inside the cloister:

These nuns [the fifteen who sang polyphony] have taught others; namely, Suor Cassandra and Suor Laura learned from Mother Maria. Others learned at home, one teaching the other, except that [vicar's underlining of the next clause] Messer Alessandro Calegari came sometimes to teach polyphony; he was sent with a *licenza* by Messer Padre Paolo from the monastery of S. Ambrogio, who (they say) sent him to S. Maddalena [al Cerchio], and it was he who taught Paola Giustina.[2]

Licenze for outside male teachers ceased after Carlo's puritanical turn of 1576, and apparently Visconti continued the policy. But nuns and their families could pressure the regular superiors to act differently. A letter to the *vicario delle monache* showed the Congregation on Regulars' position in one striking case at the beginning of Federigo's years, in which the Roman secretary feared that local implementation would be lacking (App. A, Doc. 15):

Most Reverend Lord: It has come to our attention that Giulio Cesare Gabussi received a permit from the superior of Observant Franciscans to teach music at the grates of the monastery of S. Bernardino to Suor Alma Ginevra, much to the astonishment of Their Most Illustrious Excellencies, since it is a highly inappropriate action. Thus the order's [cardinal] protector has been asked to discipline the superior, and Their Most Serene Lords have decided that you should revoke the said permit on the basis of this letter, not permitting that nuns be allowed to learn music from outside persons under any conditions, either in the aforesaid monastery or any other. Please do not hesitate to execute this order diligently, and may the Lord preserve you. From Rome, 31 October 1594. Cardinal Alessandrino.[3]

Suor Alma Ginevra received instruction from the *maestro* at the Duomo, the city's leading musician. The Franciscan connection is

---

[2] 'Queste hanno imparato alcune, cioè S. Cassandra, et S. Laura l'ano imparato da Madre Maria. Le altre hanno imparati in casa, l'una ad altra, senon che [underlined] alle volte è venuto M. Alessandro Caligare à insegnar canto figurato mandato da M. P. Paolo de licentia del monastero [di] S. Ambrogio, qual dicono lo manda anche alla madalena et lui ha insegnato a Paola Giustina': testimony of Suor Vittoria Savina, *Esamina*, (see Ch. 3), fo. 3ᵛ; Calegari is unrecorded among Milanese musicians.

[3] ASDM, Carteggio Ufficiale, cartella 32, vol. 70, unpaginated sheet.

clear: the Observant *ministro* set up the *licenza* (to which he was not legally entitled, since it was an episcopal prerogative). It is a measure of the power of the regulars, and of the Clarissans, that Gabussi, Carlo's own second choice as *maestro* (and a pupil of the Franciscan Costanzo Porta), should within a decade of the saint's death be caught with a formally invalid *licenza* to teach a nun.

Although this order seemingly ended requests for the *licenza*, another petition six years later, this time for a novice's violin teacher, underscored the contrary.[4] The practice would continue throughout the century, as several *memoriali* from the most musically famous house in the city testify. In 1661 Carlo Francesco Ceva, a Milanese business agent (representing Genoa) and veteran patron of music secular and sacred, requested the Sacra Congregazione dei Vescovi e Regolari that Fra Antonio Cossandi, an experienced (and sexagenarian, so as to avoid any hint of scandal) Franciscan composer and quondam *maestro* at S. Francesco, be permitted to teach his daughter Maria Domitilla in the church of S. Radegonda (see App. A, Doc. 50).[5] The future head of the monastery's other choir, Antonia Francesca Clerici, had her father request the same privilege, this time asking for the castrato Domenico Broglio (possibly another non-threat to chastity) in 1662 (see App. A, Doc. 53). After service in Venice and Vienna, Broglio had come to Milan early in the 1660s.[6] The wording of both petitions indicates that these were not

---

[4] App. A, Doc. 19; the request was denied.

[5] For Carlo Ceva, see B. E. and J. L. Glixon, *Marco Faustini and Operatic Production in Seventeenth-Century Venice* (forthcoming); my thanks to Beth Glixon for this information. Nor was Ceva a stranger to sacred music: Grancini had dedicated his *Concerti ecclesiastici*, book 7, to him in 1650. Cossandi had worked earlier in Crema, and had published a collection (*Motetti a 2–5*, (Milan: Rolla, 1640)) not unlike the new Lombard style of the 1640s. The reference to the 'piccio foro del Torno' may indicate some way of keeping Cossandi at a spot at the gate (the 'torno' was the rotating wheel through which supplies were passed into the monastery). That such a request could have been made, however, indicates that the Palomera scandal had not yet spread to music education in 1661.

[6] Broglio started his career in S. Marco in 1649; see Glixon and Glixon, *Marco Faustini*. The records of the Viennese court chapel in L. Ritter von Köchel, *Die kaiserliche Hof-Musikkapelle in Wien von 1543–1867* (Vienna, 1869), 58 and 63, list him as a soprano employed 1650–62, while an undated list of Duomo singers under G. A. Grossi (in office 1669–84) records him again (de Florentiis and Vessia, *Sei secoli di musica*, 279). As 'Musico di Sua Caesarea Maiestà', he was also the dedicatee of a motet in Cazzati's *Quinto libro de motetti a voce sola*, op. 39 (Bologna: Silvani, 1666; Maria Domitilla Ceva also received a dedication in the volume). He might have provided Clerici and her choir newer styles than those taught by Cossandi.

extraordinary actions, even at a time of increased episcopal restriction.[7] Even after Litta's efforts, the practice continued at S. Radegonda; a later, undated note listed 'Bartolomeo Castello, musico' among other authorized visitors to the monastery.[8]

Often sisters (especially those, like Ceva and Clerici, in charge of the ensembles) needed to continue their musical education past profession. The content was vague; 'cantare' could mean anything from sight-singing to composition. But the contact—intermittent, quasi-legal, and fraught with possibilities for scandal—between outside teachers and nuns would have allowed for female monastic musicians to stay current with the trends in the city and indeed in Lombardy as a whole, a result reflected in the repertory.[9] In a broader sense, the whole concept of the *licenza* represents a regulation and restriction— but not a complete abolition—of the previous ties between monasteries and urban life (*Sozialdisziplinierung* again).

The *licenze* also bore on the *educande* at female monasteries. As Lino's letter had noted, the training of these girl pupils in music dated to the mid-Cinquecento; a decade later, Bascapè taught the 11-year-old Cecilia Besozza.[10] Curial memoranda mentioning music instruction survive from the well-documented era of Federigo.[11] But this expedient was not a vehicle for the large-scale musical education of young women.[12] Indeed, a 1663 request from an *educanda* at

---

[7] One possibility why the requests might have gone to Rome would be that, in the light of the disciplinary measures taken against S. Radegonda, 'irregular' matters were being referred to the SCVR.

[8] ASDM XII, vol. 128, fo. 175ʳ; Castello was presumably the same figure who published a motet (*Venite angeli*) in RISM 1679¹.

[9] The question of precisely which male musicians were able to obtain *licenze* also affected nuns' contact with urban music. The case of Gabussi, *maestro di cappella* at the Duomo, teaching at S. Bernardino seems to be rather an exception due to the Franciscan connection. More typical are musicians working in the ducal chapel, the parishes, or for private noblemen—Cossandi, Broglio, Castello; these figures from the musical world of the patriciate are precisely the composers who would dedicate motets to nuns.

[10] 'Et ammaestro una putta secolare appellata Cecilia Besozzo d'anni undici, et gli insegno anche a cantar nel loco del lauoro delle putte secolari, et de rari viene nella mia cella et nella [underlined by the vicar:] cella stano molte monache a lauorare', testimony of Bascapè, *Esamina*, fo. 11ᵛ.

[11] A list of teaching duties for *figliole* specified that 'Le insegni ancor à leggere bene, servire, cantare, et à quelle che saranno abili, a suonare et l'Abaca' (ASDM XII, vol. 46, fo. 286ᵛ); these rules appear between directives dated 1607 and 1624.

[12] Unlike the Venetian *ospedali*, Milanese monasteries did not educate and endow large numbers of poor girls in preparation for marriage. In Milan, secular institutions such as the Collegio della Guastalla served this purpose, also providing musical instruction; Soderini's 1598 motets featured a piece (*O stupor, o gaudium*) inscribed to Marta Ferreria, 'Moderatrici, & Musices perfectae in Collegio Guastalla'.

S. Marta, Margherita Zapatta, to the Sacra Congregazione for an outside *maestro* (App. A, Doc. 54) suggests the problems in some houses' teaching.[13] Predictably, Litta's response cited the policy of Provincial Council IV (misattributed, perhaps deliberately, to Council I) and noted that any permission would damage discipline, especially at S. Marta, exempt from the grates and gates of *clausura* (App. A, Doc. 55).[14]

The need for special instruction in training nuns and the *educande* to sing is also evident from the one local musical edition that does mention the subject: the often-cited preface to Donati's second book of solo motets (1636). The composer noted that he had written out the *passaggi* and provided information on vocal technique (*gorghe*, articulation) 'for the education of boy and girl pupils, or nuns, and for those who have no natural inclination'.[15] His two pedagogical solo motet collections are more than written-out passage-work; they are well-planned rhetorical demonstrations of how to set a text, especially texts for personal or domestic devotional use (*Salve regina*, *Voce mea ad Dominum clamavi*). Their interior cadences explore standard modal degrees, and they usually end with a vocal peroration as climax. Possibly the veteran composer had been moved by Milan, with its female monastic ensembles as the largest musical survivors of the plague, to mention 'monache' in the 1636 volume, his new collection of solo pieces.[16]

But a darker side of musical education was sketched by Sessa's panegyrist, the Borromean follower Borsieri. In his attacks on forced monachization, the Comascan cleric noted that parents eager to send their daughters into *clausura* would often provide music instruction for the young girl, thus making her more attractive to a monastery

---

[13] The request might reflect a fall in the musical standards of S. Marta, the ageing of Bianca Taverna and the Fissiraghi sisters, or simply a matter of prestige.

[14] Typically, Litta also resurrected an ancient decree from the Sacra Congregazione dated 13 Sept. 1583 outlawing access to the grates on the pretext of teaching music. The prelate could not restrain himself from yet another self-reference as overworked supervisor of 6,000 musically competitive nuns: 'Non meritano dunque di essere essaudite le accluse preghiere, massime, che trovandomi nella Citta e Diocesi sei milla e più Monache, con molte centinaia d'Educande, al momento dilusciarebbero l'instanze e le gare' (letter to the SCVR, 14 Feb. 1663, ASV, VR, monache, 1663 (gen–apr).

[15] 'per Educatione de figlioli, & figliole, ouer Monache, & per quelli che non hanno dispositione Naturale': 'Avvertimenti per potere insegnare', p. [3].

[16] The 1634 *Primo libro* was evidently a reprint of an earlier, now lost, edition. Printed didactic editions would have been necessary both because of the restrictions on contact with sisters and because of the large numbers of women within *clausura* requiring training.

(and more eligible for dowry reductions) and alluring her with a possible future musical career inside cloistered walls.[17] Borsieri's own encomium of Sessa took pains to stress her unforced and warmly desired monastic vocation, almost as an antidote to this further—and musical—abuse of the religious life.

Another puzzling point of education and culture is the sometimes problematic relationship between musical and written literacy. In many Milanese houses there seems to have been a high correlation between musical ability (or duties inside a house) and Italian, even Latin, literacy.[18] Apart from the question of the literary authorship of the motet texts set by Rusca, Cozzolani, and Badalla, their compositions evince understanding of the poetic metre, literary conceits, and textual imagery of this Latin poetry and prose. Yet a number of visitations in neighbouring dioceses point up that (at least in some of the provincial or less patrician houses) nuns were capable of singing *canto figurato* and even of composing without necessarily possessing high literacy; in some cases, singers seem to have been illiterate in both Latin and Italian.[19] The cohabitation of literacy and illiteracy, to modern thinking unusual, underlines both the spread and democratization of music among female religious in the poorer and less patrician houses, along with the vital function of public polyphony in the external prestige of a house.

Yet, after all, nuns did train their colleagues to sing and play. The evidence spans a century and a half, from the round-robin teaching of Bascapè and Carpani at S. Maria Maddalena, to the early Settecento travellers' accounts of music at S. Radegonda.[20] Specific mention of duties appears sporadically; according to the accounts of the 1660s, Ceva and Antonia Clerici had responsibility for the preparation of their respective choirs at S. Radegonda.[21] Several visitations

---

[17] Borsieri's epistolary comments on the matter are preserved in the Biblioteca Communale of Como, and are tellingly discussed by Pavan, 'La necessità'.

[18] Zardin, *Donna e religiosa*, 58–60, 127 ff.

[19] Marcocchi, 'La riforma', pp. xli–xlii, gives reports noting thirty-five nuns of forty-eight capable of singing chant and polyphony at S. Benedetto of Cremona, while at S. Monica thirty-four of ninety-three *professe* did not know how to write but knew how to sing chant. In some Cremonese houses, up to half the nuns were semi-literate. G. Sanvito, 'Organi, organisti, organari nella diocesi di Novara nel secolo xvii', *Novarien*, 12 (1982), 105–47, quotes a visitation report to the Ursuline *collegio* in Galliate, which considered the composer Maria Xaveria Peruchona to be only moderately literate.

[20] At S. Agnese, a 1596 list gave Suor Angela Felice Chura as 'violino, e *maestra* delle scolare' (ASDM XII, vol. 59).

[21] For Ceva's chagrin at losing a singer whom she had trained to the 'Clerici–Cozzolani'

noted women as 'maestra del canto figurato', and the number of references to 'madri concertatrici' seems to define the duties and prestige of this post. Again, the best witness to training inside *clausura* was a nun who does not seem to have been musical before her profession, Angela Confaloniera, who wrote the archbishop in the final halcyon days of Federigo's tenure (App. A, Doc. 39):

Dearest Father: I write to greet you humbly and to let you know something which, if it does not please you, it would be important to know so that it not be done. The situation is this: there is a nun here, the one who taught me how to sing and play [keyboard]; she is the sister of Signor Antonio Rusca.[22]

Claudia Rusca, who had enjoyed the benefits of musical education in her family house before her profession, was also evidently in charge of the musical training of nuns at S. Caterina. Some of her *educande* also became sisters, continuing the traditions into the late Seicento by teaching their juniors.[23] Ironically, the hierarchy's attempts at enclosing nuns must have provided monastic musicians (freed from the menial tasks filled by the *converse*) with a large amount of free time outside the hours in choir to study and to practise. But clearly the question of musical continuity based on a single musician in a foundation could also be tenuous. And for all the renown of a S. Radegonda or a S. Margarita, polyphonic practice at some smaller, poorer houses must have been quite simple, subject to interruption by death or ageing.

This latter problem was addressed by the dowry-reduction requests to Rome.[24] The petitions, characteristic of less populous,

choir of S. Radegonda, see the letter of 14 Nov. 1675 from her choir to the Cassinese superiors (App. A, Doc. 69), point 2: 'è saputa di D. M. Domitilla Ceua le fù tolta la Sig.ra Lonati alla quale essa haueua con grandissimo stento insegnato'. A list of duties at S. Apollinare dated 25 Sept. 1728 noted 'Reverenda Madre Maura' and 'Sor Antonia Cattarina' as 'maestre del Canto Figurato'; this is possibly another two-choir division of a house's forces (ASDM XII, vol. 64, fasc. 2).

[22] Confaloniera to Federigo, undated letter, BA, G. 8 *inf.*, fo. 469ʳ.

[23] 'Suor Ottauia Fulgenza Bonfanti fu messa nel Monastero in Educatione . . . imparò a cantare et facceua il Contr'Alto, sonaua l'Organo benissimo et essercitò quest' uirtu tanto volontieri che era di gran Gusto, si fece poi Monaca al suo tempo . . . finì li suoi Giorni alli 13. Febraro 1687' (*Biografia delle monache umiliate*, fo. 19ʳ); 'S. Hieronima Cattarina Casati è stata in educatione in cotesto monastero . . . imparò à sonare d'organo, et à cantare il contr'alto, e cantaua benissimo, a su tempo venne Monaca . . . et nel cantare non mancaua di far tutto il possibile et anche insegnaua con ogni aplicatione' (ibid., fos. 19ᵛ–20ʳ).

[24] I thank Craig Monson for pointing out the existence of most of these documents to me.

episcopally subject monasteries, suggest that (as Borsieri had inti-
mated) musically talented novices were valued precisely for their
abilities in coaching their companions, to the point that the gain in
prestige represented by public polyphony outweighed the loss of a
dote spirituale.[25] Yet the requests are not completely representative,
since they include only those houses in which musical traditions
were dependent on the induction of a single musically talented girl;
they came primarily from mendicant foundations, and increased dra-
matically from 1637 on.[26]

A later document, the 1714 bequest of the harpsichord belonging
(jointly via family ties) to the recently deceased Antonia Francesca
Clerici and Giovanna Gioseffa Caccia at S. Radegonda, testifies to
one house's internal continuity.[27] Their relative Anna Teresa Clerici
destined the instrument for the use of the house's *cantoria*. It was a fitting testimony—underlined by the endowment of three sung
Requiems—to the patrician traditions of music at S. Radegonda that
nuns from the major musical families (Cozzolani, Clerici, Caccia)
would sign off on this will.

But if a good deal of effort and politics supported musical training,

[25] 'Le Monache di S. Clara di Legnano Diocesi di Milano humilissime serve dell'EE.VV.
trovandosi bisognose d'Organista sia per il servitio della loro Chiesa, come per insegnare à
cantare all'altre, et essendole presentata occassione della signora Anna Colombana' (petition
of 3 Sept. 1655, ASV, VR, monache, 1655 (set–dic)); 'Nel Monasterio di Santo Agostino
in Porta Nova di Milano fà bisogno una Organista . . . Di presente è capitata occasione di
Maria Virginia Pistagalla Giovane di molta modestia e bontà, virtuosa non solo per l'Organo
mà anco per la musica, et altri Instrumenti, anche buona per insegnare ad altre' (petition of
28 Sept. 1657, ASV, VR, monache, 1658, gen–mar)). In the light of the two musicians from
the Arconati family (Ch. 4 above) who took vows at this latter house, it is questionable if
music's survival depended on Pistagalla's admission; on the other hand, the keyboard-play-
ing Arconati had professed elsewhere (S. Maria Maddalena al Cerchio).

[26] The first recorded request was from S. Erasmo; on 1 Aug. 1585 the abbess, Paola
Camilla Robbia, wrote the Roman congregation for a reduced dowry for Lucrezia Trida on
the basis of her musical abilities (ASV, VR, posizioni 1585, Milano; first cited in Masetti
Zannini, *Motivi storici*, 154). There was another case in 1591, for Clemenza de' Grassi at [S.
Domenico e] S. Lazaro (ASV, VR, Reg. Episcoporum 22 (1591–2), fo. 23ᵛ, 10 Oct. 1591
and fo. 69ʳ, 20 Apr. 1592). Although the requests stem largely from the less musical houses,
even foundations previously noted for polyphony would submit such petitions; Paola Maria
Anna Isella asked Rome for a remission at the Monastero Maggiore in 1666. The curia
would recommend its denial on the grounds that 'fù questa Novitia doppo l'ingresso data
in custodia ad una Monaca, con titole di Regolatrice, che governandola à capriccio, e facen-
dola cantare sola à sua dispositione, anche à secolari ne Parlatorij, diede alle monache occasione di doglianze' (both documents in ASV, VR, sez. monache, 1666, giu–ago).

[27] App. A, Doc. 73; ASM, Religione p.a., busta 2221, bequest dated 31 Jan. 1714. Three-
register Italian harpsichords were not altogether common instruments.

what was it that they were being trained to sing and how good were their performances? One answer might be inferred from the 1664 Medici reports, which remarked on the skills of S. Radegonda's two choirs 'come qualsivoglia buon professore', on a professional level, thereby implying that the monastery was more the exception than the rule.[28] All the outsiders' accounts from Morigia onwards, however, singled out different individual houses in the city. Although the Benedictine foundations may have held leading places, especially in the later Seicento, it seems that at any given time five or six institutions were capable of professional performances in the ears of visitors; for some listeners, like Locatelli, they were simply the best ensembles in Catholic Europe. These reports made no mention of any particular style associated with female monastic music.[29]

Which specific pieces were performed by these women? Because of the dispersal of monastic libraries at the suppressions, there are few indications of the music that female houses actually possessed.[30] But several mid-Seicento copies of local Lombard repertory have inscriptions with hints of monastic ownership, including a copy of G. B. Mazzaferrata's *Sacri concerti a voce sola* (Milan: Camagno, 1661), formerly held at S. Maria del Lentasio; Gerolamo Casati's motets *a 1–3*, book 5 (Milan: C. F. Rolla, 1657) and Orazio Tarditi's *Sacer concentus a 2–3*, op. 35 (Venice: Vincenti, 1655), both the erstwhile property of a Donna Angela Giustina Mugiasca (i.e. a Benedictine); and the *Motetti ecclesiastici . . . a voce sola* (Milan: Camagno, 1659) by Federico Pedroni, once belonging to an Angelica Maria (a member of the Angeliche).[31] Again, the editions represent small-scale music popular

---

[28] The question of whether musical nuns should be considered professional musicians is somewhat misleading. On one hand, those novices who received dowry exemptions had to be good enough to justify the financial burdens; on the other, the social status of musicians in Seicento Milan was so low that, even if questions of gender had not been present, patrician nuns could never have considered the option.

[29] Musicians' reports date only from Alensoon and Burney in the Settecento, neither of which mention any sort of amateur technical levels at S. Radegonda or S. Maria Maddalena al Cerchio.

[30] The 1581 list from S. Caterina in Chiusa and a slightly later one from S. Maria sopra Monte in Varese include only *laude* editions; Zardin, 'Mercato librario', 202, and Zarzi, *Sacri monti*, 210.

[31] The Mazzaferrata (in I-Mb) is inscribed 'Ex libris Monasterij B[eata]e M[aria]e Lauretani Mediolani'; the copies of the Casati and the Tarditi are at I-COd, as is the Pedroni (A. Picchi, *Archivio musicale del Duomo di Como: Catalogo delle opere a stampa e manoscritte dei secoli XVI–XVII* (Como, 1990)). The last book also features a handwritten change from 'Bartholomei' to 'Agustini' in a sanctoral motet, suggesting that Augustine's feast-day was important at Angelica Maria's foundation.

in the parishes, not associated with the Duomo, and usable either in liturgy or in recreational singing.[32] In an earlier generation, Agata Sfondrati asked a monastic friend to procure copies of Banchieri's sacred concertos.[33] Nuns also owned and used printed liturgical books that included chant, Ambrosian or monastic.[34]

There are two other striking features in the evidence for nuns' polyphony: the role of orality, and the marked disjunction between the reports of weekly liturgy and parlour concerts on one hand, and the size of the preserved possible repertory on the other. There are few mentions of written or printed parts used by monastic singers and players, but Confaloniera, for one, noted that she sang a motet from memory (see below, Ch. 12). Likewise, the requests for outside *maestri* testify to the need for non-written musical education. The possibility remains that some polyphony was performed from memory, and that the methods applicable to orally transmitted traditions might also be useful for the Seicento.

Similarly, the sheer size of nuns' liturgical and non-liturgical repertory must have been remarkable, and by no means reflected in the preserved editions. To take one important decade, there survives no Vespers polyphony printed in the city during the 1660s. Even if the output of the Venetian and Bolognese presses of the decade are included in a possible repertory, there is still no match between the weekly Vespers at S. Radegonda recorded in 1664–5 and the surviv-

---

[32] The increasing popularity of the solo motet is witnessed by editions issued by the tireless if inaccurate Camagno around 1660 (Pedroni, 1658; F. Casola, 1660; G. B. Mazzaferrata, 1661; both these latter feature dedications to nuns). Casati's book includes highly affective texts set to the quick declamation, long melismas, and ostinato sections characteristic of the new style Lombard motet.

[33] As noted proudly by the composer himself, who may have had ties with S. Cristina in Bologna: 'Intorno al libro de' miei concerti ecclesiastici, ch'ella mi chiede ad instanza della Madre Angelica Agata Sfondrati Monaca in S. Paolo costì di Milano, io resterò fauorito in seruirne l'vno, e l'altra, sì come pure l'vno, e l'altra ringratio di tanto onore, onde essaltano le mie fatiche': *Lettere armoniche* (Venice, 1628), 79, undated letter to the Olivetan Michele Misseroni, Milan. The two editions to which Banchieri referred are unclear; perhaps the eight-voice *Concerti ecclesiastici* of 1595, and/or the now lost *Concerti moderni* [*a 2*] (Milan: Lomazzo, ?1617), or possibly one of the three volumes of the *Nuovi pensieri ecclesiastici* series; for these, see O. Mischiati, 'Adriano Banchieri (1568–1634): Profilo biografico e bibliografia delle opere', in *Conservatorio di Musica 'G. B. Martini' Bologna: Annuario 1965–1970* (Bologna, 1971), 53 and 174.

[34] The copy of the *Psalterium, cantica et hymni, aliaque divinis officiis ritu Ambrosiano psallendis . . .* (Milan: Pontio & Piccaglia, 1618) in I-Bc has a flyleaf inscription 'Questo libero è di D. Paola Felice Curiona'; she was probably a Benedictine or Lateran Canoness at a house using the Milanese rite (S. Ulderico, S. Maria del Lentasio, or S. Maria Annunciata), in a final flowering of monastic Ambrosian liturgy.

ing music possibly performed by the house.[35] We are accustomed to begin with musical sources, and then to extrapolate to musical life; but in this case, only a fraction of the repertory has been preserved, and it is helpful to invert the methods of traditional historiography.

With so few editions known to have been owned by houses, what might be some other indications for a female monastic repertory? That one volume composed by a nun was—and was meant to be— performed inside monasteries is suggested by the continuation of Confaloniera's letter to Federigo (App. A, Doc. 39):

This nun [Rusca] knows how to compose, and she has composed a good number of motets, and her brothers are having them printed, and they want to dedicate them to Your Most Illustrious Lordship as a sign of the gratitude owed to you for the benevolence you show our monastery. These pieces have been much praised, and I think they will be liked in monasteries; and this young woman is very spiritual, and I think they [the motets] have been composed with much devotion, and so she would like to dedicate them to you, since there is no one else whom our monastery loves more. But it would please me to know your wishes.[36]

Rusca's motet book originated at S. Caterina, and Confaloniera, at least, thought the contents suitable for other houses. Yet the problems remain; the reports of frequent and extensive liturgical polyphony cannot be explained only by the surviving music written by nuns. The logical place to look for female monastic repertory is among the genres and styles publicly associated with sisters, both the formal dedications and the kinds of sanctoral motets discussed above.[37] Distinctions can be made among the monastic addressees: those women clearly responsible for polyphony in their houses were in a different category from those nuns for whom there survives rather less evidence of personal musical ability or communal musical life.[38] Still, even these latter printed inscriptions suggest that such

[35] Only Porta (1656/7) and Bagatti (*Messa e salmi*, op. 2 (1659)) had produced local large-scale collections in the decade before the reports from the Benedictine houses.

[36] BA, G. 8 *inf.*, fos. 469ᵛ–470ʳ; in reality, Rusca was around 37, six years older than Confaloniera.

[37] The very first dedication, Antegnati's 1592 Vespers, stated explictly that the Benedictines' performance had moved their author (known better as an organ-builder) to publication. App. C lists the dedications; all pieces after 1608 include a continuo or organ part.

[38] Several of the larger-scale dedications of the 1650s (Corona Madruzzi by Cesati in 1655) seem to bear more on their addressees' dynastic status and reputations for holiness than on their musical abilities.

repertory could have been performed in female houses with capable singers.

A different kind of dedication was that of individual motets contained in a larger collection.[39] Male dedicatees of such motets, more typically found in Seicento concerto or solo collections, were often singers at the Duomo or in the parishes; by analogy, the inscriptions of single pieces to cloistered women probably mark repertory that well-known monastic performers did sing or might have sung.[40] It was not unusual to associate diverse music with nuns, unsurprisingly given the musical polystilism of Federigo's Milan. But the trajectory of the dedications—starting with the psalm settings of Antegnati and the Office polyphony or domestic genres (contrafacta or Penitential Psalms) of Vecchi, then continuing through the ever-increasing *stile moderno* concerto settings from 1610 on—parallels Federigo's growing concern with the vanity of solo singing and 'ostentatious' musical styles. It also corresponds to the changes in the Lombard repertory as a whole. In conjunction with the travel reports on individual singers, they indicate that the genres of music universally associated with nuns metamorphosed, even during Borromeo's tenure, from *stile antico* liturgical settings and spiritual contrafacta to a more virtuosic style in the 1620s and beyond. Confaloniera's letter testifies that the music nuns wrote was indeed used in their monasteries; the music of the urban patriciate—like so many other elements—likewise found a home inside *clausura*.

Yet the practical question remains: how did they do it? A good deal of the pieces written by nuns, including about half the music in Cozzolani's 1642 motet book as well as the overwhelming majority of her 1650 volume, includes scoring for tenor or bass voices.[41]

---

[39] Personal inscriptions of single motets occurred more often in Milanese than in Venetian prints (possibly because of local pride), and should be considered with the more numerous dedications to male religious. Few Venetian editions include a personal dedication of a single motet. But some Milanese prints—from Mortaro's 1602 collection through RISM 1679[1]—contain many; one such edition, Andrea Cima's 1614 *Primo libro delli Concerti*, contains inscriptions to numerous male singers as well as to Giovanna Canevesa at S. Chiara.

[40] Otherwise it would be difficult to understand the reason for such inscriptions, often found in collections dedicated as a whole to male patrons. Single-piece dedications to men who were not musicians were usually to religious superiors or minor nobility. Yet nun singers by virtue of their status were incapable of such authority: they had renounced their inheritances, and were considered legally dead to the world (to use the standard anthropological distinction; however, this should not be construed to mean that they lacked power, merely authority).

[41] Of the twenty-one pieces in the 1642 *Concerti sacri*, some ten call for tenor and/or bass in combination with higher voices (twelve if we count the two pieces marked as 'due canti,

Similarly, many dedications (including the first seven prints with female monastic addressees) involve lower voices.[42] In some of these works, liturgically or syntactically necessary text is stated only by tenors or basses. Ex. 7.1, a solo setting of a half-verse from Cozzolani's 1650 *Dixit Dominus*, is simply unperformable at written pitch by any female voice, and its effect (especially the cadential *D*) depends on the specific sonority of the bass voice. Cozzolani requires a wider tessitura from the bass part than from any other vocal type; the 1642 *Obstupescite gentes* (AB), for instance, ranges from C

Ex. 7.1. Cozzolani, *Dixit Dominus* (1650), bars 20–34

ò tenori'; in the 1650 *Salmi à otto*, the respond *Domine ad adiuvandum*, six psalm settings (*Dixit Dominus*, *Confitebor tibi Domine*, *Beatus vir*, *Laudate pueri*, *Laetatus sum*, and *Nisi Dominus*), as well as the two *Magnificat* settings, are all scored for eight *concertato* (i.e. not always set up as two antiphonal choirs) voices: CCAATTBB. The six motets scored variously for three, four, and five voices all require at least one tenor or bass.

[42] Antegnati's *Salmi à otto* is scored for two choirs of CATB; Cortellini's 1595 Vespers and Vecchi's 1601 Penitential Psalms for six mixed voices; Gallo's and Soderini's double-choir motets of 1598, overwhelmingly for two CATB (sometimes SAAT) ensembles; Vecchi's *falsibordoni* (1600) for four to eight mixed voices.

('gustatur') to *e'* ('in hymnis ac canticis'); these are the outside limits of the part in the *Concerti sacri* as a whole. By contrast, the ranges of the tenor, alto, and canto parts are all less than two octaves in both the 1642 and 1650 books (see Ex. 7.2). Given the public nature of female monastic music, and the absence of any records concerning a major scandal of importing men inside enclosure, it must be assumed that performances took place in the *chiesa interiore* or in the *parlatorio*, and that only nuns were involved.[43]

Ex. 7.2. Voice-ranges in Cozzolani's motet books

A chronological approach first considers the problems in the performance of *stile antico* polyphony; it is also essential to distinguish between notated compositional pitch and performance pitch. If Lombard pitch, like that of the 1533 Antegnati organ in Brescia, was somewhat higher (perhaps by a semitone) than modern standards, then the Monastero Maggiore's 1554 instrument (g'= 440 Hz or a'= 490 Hz) was slightly higher even than the local norm, perhaps another testimony to high pitch at least in the early days.

The repertory suited to single-sex choirs is of course equal-voice pieces, and the later Cinquecento witnessed a minor boom in such *voci pari* repertory, both Mass and Office settings and motets, with notable examples written by Asola, Merulo, the Cassinese Placido Falconio, and others in Lombardy and the Veneto. Indeed, the first two printed editions dedicated to Italian nuns consist of works *a vocibus paribus*: Antegnati's 1581 *Sacrae cantiones a 4*, inscribed to the ancient Benedictine house of S. Giulia in Brescia, and Asola's double Compline settings (1583/7), addressed to S. Daniele in Verona. Whether written in high clefs (Antegnati), or in a somewhat lower restricted-range clef combination (Asola), these pieces observe the norms of the equal-voice setting: the duplication of one compositional voice (and the omission of another) in the reworking of an

---

[43] The travel accounts, which mention hearing nuns sing in church, and then performances in the parlours, seem to bear this out. The one exception might have been S. Paolo in 1661, at which there was possible collaboration between a band in the *chiesa esteriore* and nuns on the inside.

essentially CATB scoring, and the restriction of the overall range to two octaves. Performance by all-female choirs of these pieces might well have required intonation at various pitch-levels. From the perspective of the *voci pari* repertory, the overall range—not the notated pitch—of a Cinquecento piece or collection might have determined its performability.[44]

Yet the changing demography of Milanese houses also interacted with performance practice. Some later evidence suggests that a large group of potential singers, like the flood of novices entering the monasteries in the later Cinquecento, might have extended the vocal ranges of an all-women's choir; Alexander Ellis's late Victorian survey of English women choristers found the composite range of a large group of sopranos to be from *f♯* up to *f‴* and even *a‴*.[45] For Ellis's altos, the bottom register extended down as far as *c* or *b*, and up to *d♯″* or *g″*. More realistic might be the mean limits: sopranos *f–b″*; altos, *d♯–g♯″*. The overall range of a female choir able to select unusually low and high voices might have been *d♯–b″*—two octaves and a minor sixth.

At S. Agostino Bianco, Locatelli marvelled on 3 May 1664 at a singer so low that only the sight of her habit revealed her sex.[46] Foreign but contemporary evidence seems to bear out the lower end of nuns' tessituras.[47] At the other end of the vocal spectrum, some internal evidence from the music dedicated to or written by Milanese nuns suggests that notated high *c‴* was by no means impossible, at least for some singers in the later Seicento.[48] Perhaps the

---

[44] The dedication of Tommaso Baldoni's *Vespri per tutte le solennità dell'anno . . . a sei voci pari* (Venice, 1601), a Paduan collection, seems to assume either all-male or all-female performance of its contents.

[45] A. J. Ellis, 'On the History of Musical Pitch', *Journal of the Society of Arts*, 5 March 1880, 293–336, cited from the modern reprint: Ellis and A. Mendel, *Studies in the History of Musical Pitch* (Amsterdam, 1968). I have calibrated Ellis's various tunings so that all pitch-levels are expressed in terms of *a′* = 440 Hz in equal temperament; the differences between equal and mean-tone tuning are not significant for the present discussion.

[46] 'ue n'era una, ch'hauea un basso si profondo, che se non l'hauesse veduta con gli occhi miei, haurei dubitato ui fosse un'huomo tra di loro' (App. A, Doc. 56).

[47] The motets and Mass written for Parisian nuns at the houses of Port-Royal and the Abbaye-aux-Bois by Charpentier range down to notated *f* in the lowest voice (a female 'haute-contre'). When the difference between 17th-c. Parisian pitch (*a′* = roughly 392 Hz) and Lombard pitch (*a′* = anywhere from 465 to 492 Hz) is calibrated, the French nuns' *f* represented an absolute pitch (hence a bottom limit for vocal tessitura) that would have been notated as *d* or even *c♯* in Milan.

[48] Both the 1620 ornamentation model (*Quanti mercenarii*) dedicated to Ginepra Crivelli at S. Margarita by Francesco Rognoni Taeggio, and at least one piece in Badalla's 1684 *Motetti a voce sola* call specifically—and unavoidably, as a goal of scalar runs—for this pitch.

exceptional local monachization rate was indeed the precondition for the remarkable growth in nuns' polyphony.

There is one later piece of evidence for vocal possibilities. The Grand Tour of the Dutch amateur musician Jan Alensoon brought him to S. Radegonda on 16 January 1724, when he noted in his travel diary:

Shortly after dinner I went . . . to listen to the famous Signora Quinzana sing; she sang three or four cantatas, and accompanied herself at the harp-sichord . . . I was amazed when I heard that her voice could reach the high-est *a″* of the harpsichord, and descend to the second *d* below, two and a half octaves altogether; she sang a nice canto, alto, and tenor.[49]

At least one nun could sing almost the entire range considered pos-sible here for sisters' choirs as a whole. Obviously Rosalba Quinzana, the *maestra di canto figurato* in the early Settecento, was an exception, but the case points up the actual capabilities of S. Radegonda's inhab-itants.[50] As Alensoon noted, her low range was not infrequent in female houses.[51]

The growing practice of polyphony among Italian female religious occasioned a number of Seicento documents, editions, or prefaces which mention performance adaptations for nuns. The evidence is

---

[49] 'Kort na den eeten ben ik gegaan . . . om de vermaarde Signora Quinzana te hooren singen, sij song wel drie of vier Cantaten, en sij accompagneerde sig selfs met de clavercim-bel . . . ik stont verstelt, wanneer ik hoorde, dat sij met haar stem kon klimmen tot de hoog-ste A van de clavercimbel, en daalen tot de tweede D van onderen, zijnde twee en een half octaaf; sij song een schoone Cant, Alt en Tenor . . . ': 'Dag-register van een korte Reijs . . . door mij M.r Jan Alensson gedaan in de jaaren 1723 en 1724', Amsterdam University Library, XV-E-25, p. 102; first cited and discussed in K. Vlaardingerbroek, 'Faustina Bordoni Applauds Jan Alensoon: A Dutch Music-Lover in Italy and France in 1723–4', *Music and Letters*, 72 (1991), 536–51. I thank Dr Vlaardingerbroek for pointing out this and other passages.

[50] On her status, at S. Radegonda, see the records in ASM, Religione, p.a., busta 1935, concerning Paola de' Pietra, her musical pupil who fled the monastery (with an English Protestant) and was eventually exonerated on the grounds of forced profession (in the more liberal climate of Austrian Lombardy), recounted by C. A. Vianello, 'Il dramma e il romanzo di Suor Paolina dei Conti Pietra', *ASL* 60 (1933), 150–74, and, in a broader con-text, by Vismara Chiappa, *Per vim et metum*. For an account of her singing and of Carnival theatre (including the much-forbidden cross-dressing of nuns), see the former, 153–5. Quinzana figures in a number of other Settecento travellers' accounts of music at S. Radegonda; the deposit of her dowry took place on 1 Feb. 1682 and she took vows in Feb. 1683 (ASDM XII, vol. 128, fo. 8ᵛ); her birth date was thus *c*.1665–70. In 1727 she was still the *maestra* at the house, according to the ASM documents; when Alensoon heard her sing, she must have been in her fifties.

[51] 'alwaar ik in de kerk seer fraaij hoorde singen . . . verscheijde vrouwen heb ik in Italie een Tenor hooren singen': Alensoon, 'Dag-register', 71, on a performance at S. Radegonda.

not completely Milanese, ranging from Lombardy to Rome. But *in toto* the suggestions help us approach the performance options for several different repertories in the new century: the continuing *stile antico*, small-scale concertos, and even *concertato* liturgical works for four to eight voices.[52]

The first specific directions stemmed from Romano Micheli's 1610 three-voice Vespers, scored for two high voices and vocal bass with continuo, a Borromean edition if ever there was one (it is dedicated to Federigo and bears the archbishop's coat of arms prominently on its title-page). This Roman product noted:

Thus if [the contents] are to be sung *a 3*, a sweeter harmony will result, if two cantus parts and a bass are combined, or two tenors and bass, or cantus, tenor, and bass, or else two cantus and alto, for the use of nuns.[53]

Thus the printed bass voice could be used as an alto.[54] This has two implications: the explicit invocation of the octave transposition upwards of bass lines for nuns, and the octave parallel between bass and alto voices suggesting the lower range of the latter.[55] A good part of this print is in high clefs (G2/G2/C4) in any case (which suggests that nuns might not always have been able to sing C4 lines at pitch), but of the normally cleffed (C1/C1/F4) psalms, *Laudate Dominum* requires an *E* and a *D* (each once). Apparently female monastic choirs with enough singers could be expected to sing down at least to *e*. The listing of singers at S. Radegonda in the 1670s (App. A, Doc. 70) noted women as sopranos, contraltos, and 'bassi'; this last term is probably a catch-all for those who could handle the lower parts as sung, in modern tenor range.[56]

[52] Local pitch seems to have stayed high; in mid-century, Doni recorded a suspiciously regular rise ascending the Italian peninsula, with 'quel [tuono] di Lombardia' a half-step lower than the highest (Venetian), and a minor third higher than Neapolitan, cited in Mendel, *Studies in the History*, 236.

[53] The original is the epigraph to this chapter.

[54] Micheli's print is a relatively simple, reduced-scoring print quite common early in the century (his *Laudate Dominum*, for instance, sets only the second half-verse and the doxology polyphonically).

[55] Presumably the organ was to play at notated pitch, thus functioning as a *basso seguente* at the lower octave.

[56] Perhaps the most difficult dedication is Cazzati's 1666 *Messa e salmi*, op. 37; the mass is scored in Bolognese style, with CATB solo and ripieno (overall range: *F-e″*), 2 violins (range: *c′-a″*), and two continuo parts; the collection also includes pieces for ATB. Transposition up a fifth of all parts puts the voices uncomfortably low (for women) and the strings wildly high. Possibly only the vocal bass parts were transposed up an octave, with low female voices on the tenor parts (the 1676 list of Ceva's ensemble noted Donna Bianca Maria and Donna Maria Vittoria as 'Basso') and all other parts at pitch.

This octave displacement of a bass part was also in more general use in the new Milanese concerto repertory of the early Seicento.[57] Equally important, in small-scale two- or three-voice works employing some sort of CB, AB, CCB, or CAB scoring, octave transposition upwards of the lowest voice in nuns' performances would seem to be sanctioned by composers and theorists alike.[58] Typically, the first printed mention of such adjustments is found in an edition dedicated precisely to the most fervent supporter of nuns' polyphony in Italy, Federigo.

The other clue to such octave transposition of bass lines lies not in scorings, but rather in the high range of the tenor part in both Rusca's and Cozzolani's printed editions. The compass of both tenor lines in Rusca's reconstructed Magnificat is *f–a'* (a *quinto tono* piece), while several of Cozzolani's concertos call repeatedly for the high *a'*. If the 'bassi' nuns were put on this line, and any lower parts taken up an octave, the result (even in later repertories) would have again been plausible for female monastic ensembles. Similarly, Cozzolani's *Ave regina caelorum* (1642; Ex. 7.3) calls for at least one exposed tenor entrance on *g'*, while the 1650 psalms and concertos similarly rely on high tenors; perhaps this is more explicable given S. Radegonda's low altos.[59]

The transposition seems to have been in use over several generations; if applied to Cozzolani's *Regna terrae* (1642; CCAB), it results in a CCAA texture, like *Psallite superes* from the same book. Similarly, the CCB *Quis audivit unquam tale?* from the 1650 book would then become a CCA piece. Furthermore, the big dialogues from this edition (the Christmas, Easter, and St Catherine works) all eschew the bass voice; between the use of 'bassi' singers on the tenor

---

[57] G. P. Cima's *Hodie Christus natus est*, published in Scaletta's 1605 *Cetra spirituale*, is scored for CB (clefs C1 and F5), with the rubric: 'Alzando il Basso per ottaua seruirà per Alto & Canto.' This procedure explains not only the Micheli book, but also Pompeo Signorucci's *Salmi, falsobordoni e motetti a tre voci* (Venice: Amadino, 1602), largely cleffed G2/G2/F3, written for Venetian nuns.

[58] The classic statement was Donati's in the *Salmi boscarecci*: 'Prima dunque si potrà cantare a sei voce sole con li primi sei libri [part-books]; ne si può tralasciare alcuna di queste sei parti, ma per penuria di Soprani si può cantare il primo Soprano in Tenore, discosto però alquanto dal Tenor principale. Et volendo servirsene le Monache potranno cantare il Basso all'Ottava alto, che riuscirà un Contralto', which assumes female performance of tenor lines at pitch.

[59] There is another unavoidable tenor *a'* in the solo opening of *Venite sodales*. Comparison with contemporary editions is difficult; Rovetta's *Salmi a 3–4*, op. 7 (Venice, 1642), asks for a *d–g'* range in its tenor part.

Ex. 7.3. Cozzolani, *Ave regina caelorum* (1642), bars 20–6

lines, and the octave transposition of bass lines, some items in the
1642 and 1650 editions become relatively easy to perform. Thus the
evidence provides guidance for an important slice of the local repertory around 1600: *voci pari* works at a suitable pitch-level; at least in
larger houses, unaccompanied *stile antico* pieces (with the two-
octave-and-a-sixth compass) intoned near notated pitch; later,
octave transposition for one or more voices in the most favoured
scorings of the early concerto *a 2* or *a 3* in the city (CB or CTB).[60]
In retrospect, this last expedient applied to bass lines might also
explain the double-choir dedications of the 1590s.

---

[60] Here, the differences in the development of the Milanese concerto are crucial; the preferred scoring in the early collections (Scaletta, *Cetra spirituale*, 1605; Lucino (ed.), *Concerti*,
1608 (RISM 1608[13]); Assandra, *Sacri concerti*, 1609; and G. P. Cima, *Concerti ecclesiastici*, 1610)
was CB, not CC. Only after 1620 did the high-voice duet become the usual ensemble.

Yet not all houses could draw upon the resources of S. Radegonda. One guide came from an extra-urban monastery whose inhabitants filed a petition with the Sacra Congregazione in 1600:

Recently the vicar-general of Milan issued an order that some nuns of this diocese could no longer use musical instruments except the organ and the regal. Now, since the nuns of S. Maria Maddalena of Monza in the said diocese find themselves completely without voices that function as basses for their polyphony, they use a violone da gamba for this purpose, having no other choice unless they desist from polyphony altogether. They would like to continue this in order not to deprive themselves of polyphony, and so they have recourse to Your Illustrious Lordships, asking humbly that they deign to concede them this favour, and order the said vicar that, in the light of this need, he allow them to use this instrument.[61]

Certainly some smaller houses in the later Cinquecento might have simply employed a bass violin or gamba to cover low vocal lines. There exists a surprisingly large amount of evidence for melody instruments inside *clausura*, doubly so in view of Carlo Borromeo's strict opposition to the practice;[62] this began with Carlo's 1575 order to sell the viole da gamba at S. Maria Maddalena al Cerchio and other houses in the aftermath of his visitations.[63] Further references include the orders of the 1580s to sell the violins at S. Vittore in Meda;[64] the request for an outside teacher of string instruments for a novice at S. Apollinare;[65] and the presence (and complicity) of a nun violone-player during the Leyva case at S. Margarita in Monza.[66]

Despite all the episcopal efforts to ban non-keyboard instruments, these Cinquecento practices would continue in the new century, with important evidence for nuns' abilities to play the obbligato instrumental parts (largely strings) that figured in both sacred and secular music after 1620. At S. Caterina in Brera, Confaloniera's para-

---

[61] App. A, Doc. 20, first cited in Masetti Zannini, *Motivi storici*, 151–2; the edict was probably one of Giorgi's occasional bannings of non-keyboard instruments, such as his 1598 rules on Advent (see above, Ch. 3). The request was denied in Rome. No other musical evidence survives from this house; a visitation record of 8 May 1585 listed nineteen nuns and four *educande* in residence, without any mention of music (ASDM XII, vol. 180).

[62] Almost every curial instruction concerning music contains some such formulation as Ferragata's 1562 prohibition of instruments besides the organ at clothing ceremonies (ASDM XII, vol. 52, fasc. 2).

[63] 'Vendere le Viole da Gamba', ASDM XII, vol. 50, fo. 107ʳ.

[64] ASDM XII, vol. 174, unnumbered folio.   [65] Assandri's request cited above.

[66] Suor Eliodora had a violone case in which the body of Caterina da Meda (the nun killed by Leyva's lover) was smuggled out of the monastery (records in Colombo, *Vita e processo*, 410).

liturgical celebrations included players of 'violino, e violone';[67] while Rusca's motet book included two *canzoni francesi*, along with an apparent violin part in a sanctoral motet. The mid-century documentation of nuns who played violin, violone, and theorbo is extensive: Grancini's dedication of a canzona to a lutenist and organist at S. Bernardino alle Monache;[68] Cozzolani's scoring for violins in two of her psalm settings;[69] the travel reports of *motetti con stromenti* at S. Agostino Bianco, or the 'cantatrici, e sonatrici' at S. Radegonda, in the 1660s; the listing of two or three sisters as violin-players, a violone-player, and a chitarrone-player associated with each of that house's two choirs in the mid-1670s;[70] the slightly later bequest of a violetta to a *conversa* at S. Apollinare;[71] and Bagatti's mention of Giovanna Visconti's (at S. Maria in Valle) violin skills.[72]

Stringed and plucked instruments were in use over a geographically and temporally wide range of female houses. Because of the plebeian and secular associations of the violin (and because of the contact with secular music teachers), Carlo's curia was firmly opposed to its use by nuns; Federigo raised no such objections, at least in non-liturgical contexts, while his curia, as noted, on occasion banned melody instruments in nuns' churches. Like so many other decrees, these restrictions were ignored in practice by the later Seicento.

[67] The Christmas 'matinata'; these are the same two instruments needed in Assandra's 1609 *O salutaris hostia*.

[68] *La Bariola*, in the 1631 *Sacri fiori concertati*, dedicated to Antonia Maria Gallina.

[69] *Laudate pueri* (2C, 2T, 2Vl); *Laudate Dominum omnes gentes* (C, 2 Vl). Unlike the case of Sulpitia Cesis's 1619 motet book from Modena (which includes scoring for trombones, and whose local copy (in I–MOe) bears personal initials [of nun performers?]), or of the reports from S. Vito in Ferrara of nuns playing cornets and trombones, there is little evidence for nuns employing wind instruments in Milan; in general, there is little specific scoring for winds or brass in Milan after 1600. But the instrumental demands of Badalla's cantata *O fronde care* for two trumpets or violins, with two 'flauti' in an internal section, suggest that these instruments were not unknown in the later Seicento at the monastery.

[70] ASDM, Carteggio Ufficiale, vol. 92 (App. A, Doc. 70); the presence of a string band for each choir brings the performance of mid-century concerted music well within the realm of possibility.

[71] The list of 27 Feb. 1702 detailing items sent by Alfonso Brezzi to Suor Teresa Brezzi included 'Un Cembalo di Annibale . . . Una Violetta di sei Corde del S. Grancino et . . . due sacche da Violino' (ASM, Religione, p.a., busta 1772). This is almost the only evidence for a *conversa*'s musical activity. No harpsichord-maker by this name is recorded in Milan at this time; neither are there any records in Giovanni Battista Grancino's output of a six-stringed viola. The instrument was likely to have been a treble viola da gamba, of which only a few from the workshop survive (C. Beane, 'Grancino', NG vii. 630).

[72] Cf. the dedication of the *Concerti ecclesiastici*, bk. 3 (Milan: Camagno, 1667) in App. C.

Keyboard instruments were less of an issue. Even before Lino's compromise of 1565, houses had contracted for organs, beginning with S. Vincenzo's 1536–9 commissioning of an organ from Gian Giacomo Antegnati.[73] This was the first contract for an Antegnati instrument in the entire city in the Cinquecento, followed by S. Eustorgio and the Duomo.[74] Organ restorations could be funded from the *doti*; a 1596 petition (denied) from S. Bernardino alle Monache to the Sacra Congregazione (App. A, Doc. 17) asked for 1,000 lire from Suor Alma Ginevra's dowry for repair.[75] Besides the organ's role in *basso seguente* or basso continuo parts, the numerous Cinquecento references to *intavolatura*, notably to Prospera Bascapè's abilities at S. Maria Maddalena al Cerchio,[76] show up the importance of keyboard intabulation skills, appropriate for simpler repertories featuring a greater degree of homophony or at least declamation of the complete text in the upper voices.

Yet the repertory after 1620 continues to present problems, evident in the large-scale psalms of Cozzolani. In these latter, and even in some of the four-voice CATB concertos of both 1642 and 1650, the only voice singing at certain moments, or bearing phrases necessary for a complete declamation of the text, is the bass.[77] Some smaller-scale scorings (notably the very popular ATB ensemble) of mid-century are also troublesome. For *stile antico* and even *concertato*

---

[73] The agreement for 1,120 lire is noted in ASM, Religione, p.a., 2298, with a copy in ASM, Notarile 8656, notary Bernardo da Lesmo; organ-case expenses from August 1537 and March 1538 are in ASM, Religione, ibid.

[74] H. Klotz, 'Antegnati', *NG* i. 451.

[75] The denial must have been reversed (or ignored) by the next decade, since a curial memorandum of 6 Aug. 1602 noted that the Clarissans had overstayed the *licenza* of the visiting organ-builder; ASDM, Carteggio Ufficiale, vol. 70. A similar request (of unknown fate) for organ repair, dated 15 Feb. 1595, for S. Maria Maddalena in Busto [Arsizio] is in ASDM, ibid.

[76] See above, Ch. 2 at n. 104.

[77] There are a number of bass solos in Cozzolani's concertos and psalm settings: 'Quis loquetur potentias' and 'Quid hoc convivio' in *Obstupescite gentes* (1642); 'Dabit ei Dominus' in the trio *O gloriosa Domina* (1642); the section 'Quare apenditis' in *O quam suavis est, Domine* (1642); the solo 'Cantate Deo' in *Regna terrae* (1642); the section 'Deus usque ad carnem descendit' in *Quis audivit?* (1650); the half-verse 'Exortum est' in *Beatus vir* (1650); and a duet for two basses at 'Quia respexit' of the 1650 Magnificat I. There are also passages in Cortellini's 1595 Vespers and in Vecchi's 1601 Penitential Psalms in which a vocal bass is necessary for a statement of the complete text. In the light of Vecchi's concern with text-setting and rhetoric, it would seem unlikely that omission of phrases would have been acceptable. By way of comparison, Donati's *Salmi boscarecci* collection is careful to mark the tacet sections for those psalms requiring instrumental doubling, when performed by female choirs.

mixed-voice pieces that do not exceed the overall compass of two octaves and a sixth, one possibility is that of *upward* transposition (of all parts) by 'standard' intervals (fourths and fifths, inversions of the normal downward transpositions).[78] A number of references from Lombardy require its consideration; concertos spanning the century (again by composers working in the parishes: G. P. Cima, Grancini, and San Romano) mention upward transposition of all parts by a fourth or fifth.[79]

Again, some Roman evidence directly invoking sisters is helpful; Pompeo Natali's 1662 *Madrigali, e canzoni spirituali e morali* included (as the composer remarked in his preface) a continuo line transposed up a fifth or down a fourth for ten pieces so as to make these low *voci pari* works accessible to nuns.[80] Natali's adjustment took ATB pieces originally cleffed in the combination C3 (range g–a'), C4 (e–g'), and F4 (F–d) upward by a fifth, into a scoring of C1/C1/C3; thus the new alto ranges down to c.[81] This procedure would not only render low-voice concertos (AT, TB, or ATB) possible but would also make normal (CATB) four-voice works available to sisters.[82] A late echo may be heard in Alensoon's 1724 description of ensembles at S. Radegonda: 'these ladies sing four-voice pieces; the cantus is very high, the alto like a canto II, the tenor like an alto, and the bass like a tenor'.[83]

But even the standard (and, for mean-tone keyboard tuning after 1600, easy) transpositions might not always have worked, especially

[78] Taking pieces up a fourth or fifth around 1600 also concurs with the higher pitch-levels 'per voci' found in several concertos of Banchieri's *Ecclesiastiche sinfonie*, op. 16 (Venice: Amadino, 1607).

[79] Grancini's *Exsurge, Domine* (from the 1628 *Concerti à 1–4*) is scored for AA with possible transposition up a fifth for CC.

[80] 'Si è posto nel fine del Basso Continuo, vn'altro Basso trasportato per commodità dell'Organista, acciò quelli Madrigali, ò canzoni, che sono à voci pari, si possino cantare à due Soprano, e Contralto: cioè, il Contralto seruirà per Primo Soprano, il Tenore per Secondo Soprano, & il Basso per Contralto; E così saranno anco à proposito per Monasteri di Monache': 'Al Lettore', p. [3]. The connection of vernacular religious pieces and nuns is again noteworthy.

[81] One piece (*Stolt'è l'alma*) originally employs F3 for its bass part. Natali provided no transposition for the CCB pieces; presumably their lowest vocal part would have been taken up an octave by nuns. The transposed continuo line is either down a fourth (five pieces) or up a fifth (five pieces), with octave displacements so as to keep the part within the compass of the bass clef.

[82] Without the specific reference to nuns, Tommaso Cecchino's *Messe a due* (Venice: Vincenti, 1628) had included provisions for transpositions up a fourth (three masses) or a fifth (two Masses).

[83] 'deese dames singen stukken met vier stemmen, de Cantus is seer hoog, de Alt als een

for pieces with a larger overall range or for monastic choirs without good low voices.[84] Other Milanese evidence suggests less 'normal' transpositions;[85] the testimony associated with monasteries derives from the problems inherent in retuning mean-tone keyboards to the pitch-levels that would have required sharps and flats outside the system.[86]

Chronologically first is the case of Giovanni Antonio at S. Apollinare. The surviving repertory of the 1560s and 1570s in Milan is largely for CATB; a keyboard that transposed upwards might well have helped the Clarissans to perform such works.[87] Second are the instructions for retuning harpsichords by all possible intervals (including augmented fourths and major sevenths); these are found in the supplementary material to G. P. Cima's 1606 *Partito de ricercari, e canzone francesi*, dedicated to Caterina Assandra before her profession of vows. Cima's instructions were new, and unparalleled in the Italian repertory; they were also the only advice on transpositions that considered *upward* displacement to be the norm. Despite the evident problems in their implementation (not least in the difficulties of retuning organs by nuns who were presumably not trained as organ-

Canto secondo, de Tenor als een Alt, en de Bas als een Tenor': 'Dag-register', 71. In the light of Alensoon's description of 'various women in Italy who sang tenor', this arrangement would have allowed the singers at S. Radegonda to handle most CATB pieces. The passage is also noteworthy in view of the paucity of four-voice sacred music in early Settecento Milan; it suggests that S. Radegonda's repertory in the 1720s also included relatively older works.

[84] For instance, a four-voice piece ranging from *F* to *e″* (the outside limits, without ledger lines, of the F4 and C1 clefs), transposed up a fifth results in a total compass of *c–b″*, possibly too low for nuns. The *F–e″* range is the normal tessitura of *stile antico* music in the C1/C3/C4/F4 clef arrangement.

[85] This was done across the street from S. Radegonda at the Duomo; a handwritten note in the organ part-book of Donati's *Secondo libro delle Messe a 4–5* (Venice: Vincenti, 1633) preserved at I–Md remarks over the *Missa brevis a 5* (which is already set out in high clefs): 'un tuono più alto', making it perhaps a piece to train the choirboys in *stile antico*. Further afield, Benedetto Magni's *Concerti a 1–4* (Venice: Amadino, 1612; Magni was working in Ravenna) contains four (two of two-tenor duets and two of low-voice trios) rubrics 'Alla Quinta alta' (thus rendering them suitable for sopranos) and two duets (*Salvum me fac* and *Quemadmodum desiderat*) with the note 'alla 6. alta'.

[86] Essentially the same procedure as the variable intonation outlined above, applied here to the Seicento repertory, which after 1598 (the *basso generale* part for Vecchi's *Salmi intieri*) in Milan was printed with an organ part and hence implied the participation of a keyboard. This underscores the ways in which Milanese editions were hardly behind the times in their adoption of the *basso generale*.

[87] If the keyboard transposed down, and nuns transposed up (by the equivalent inversion), the accompaniment would have been in a lower tessitura while eliminating any possible problems with unusual chord inversions.

builders), they might well have been intended to help guide Assandra in her musical duties, and at the least testify to interest in the problems of unusual upward transpositions in the early Seicento repertory.

The instructions in Penna's *Li primi albori*, another theoretical treatise dedicated to nuns three generations later, also highlighted the issue.[88] Chapter 19 of Book III, 'On playing a second, third, fourth, or fifth lower or higher', provides for clef transposition of continuo lines to any diatonic scale degree up or down, without concern for mean-tone retuning.[89] The point would then be to attain a suitably (high) pitch in those situations where there was no one to sing the low parts, or to transpose normally cleffed pieces into a suitable range for nuns.[90]

The practical problems of the diatonic transpositions were real but limited.[91] Depending upon mode and accidentals present in a given piece, certain 'non-standard' transpositions required chromatic inflections already present in the tonal vocabulary and mean-tone tuning of the Cinquecento. A piece in fifth mode, for instance, with no chromatic inflection beyond B natural and F♯, would employ only C♯ and G♯ if taken up a whole tone. But if the bass part of such a fifth-mode piece obeyed the normal modal limit (in which the subsidiary

[88] Penna was interested in nuns' music; besides the treatise, two of his motet collections are dedicated to (sanctified) nuns, and his first print contains a dedication to a nun in Casale Monferrato, where he was then working.

[89] 'Del suonare vna, ò due, ò tre, ò quattro, &c. Voci più basse, ouero vna, ò due, ò tre ò quattro &c. Voci più alte'; that Penna eschewed Cima's wilder transpositions (augmented fourths, major sevenths) makes this procedure somewhat more credible.

[90] This again raises the question of how *high* nuns could sing, since that marks the upper limit of upwards transposition. Top parts cleffed G2 in pieces dedicated to nuns tend to reach *g″* or *a″*; a transposition up a tone for most high-clef works, and up a fourth, fifth, or sixth for normally cleffed pieces, would bring them into a total notated ambitus of *D/E-a″*, which might have been possible for larger female choirs. The entire timbre would have been utterly different for Seicento ears, and contributed to the 'ethereal' effect of nuns' music, in combination with the official (but practically non-existent) invisibility of the musicians behind the wall between the *chiesa esteriore* and the *chiesa interiore*.

[91] For Cima's system, see C. G. Rayner, 'The Enigmatic Cima: Meantone Tuning and Transpositions', *Galpin Society Journal*, 22 (1969), 23–34, hampered by its use of the major–minor key system. Transposition up a perfect fourth or fifth requires only one pitch to be retuned; up a major second or minor seventh requires two; and up a minor third or major sixth requires three. Other transpositions require more retunings and were presumably less common. One problem with performances using this procedure is that it is much easier to retune a harpsichord than an organ. Cima's system considers all transpositions as being upwards; this flies in the face of the overwhelming evidence for *downward* transposition in most repertories outside nuns' music.

alto and bass parts lie within the ambitus of the relative plagal cofinalis), its notated range would go down to *c*; transposed, this would require the lowest female voices to sing *d*, a plausible expedient.[92]

These scattered instructions and evidence for the transposition of entire pieces upwards by various intervals are unsystematic and *ad hoc*; yet that might be an argument for their use. For different monasteries would have had variable needs, depending upon the piece and the nuns available to sing, and guides to performance would have had to embrace a range of possibilities. In the light of the two or more choirs in the same foundation (S. Marta, S. Radegonda), and the fights over singers, the same piece might have had different transposition needs from week to week. Some of the standard marvelling by outsiders, like Locatelli's, may simply have been in appreciation of nuns' success at performing polyphony normally sung by male voices.

These ideas have allowed us to close in on the performance practice of various parts of the Milanese repertory. The possibility of low alto ranges in larger houses expands the *voci pari* repertory to the larger *stile antico* genres; alternatively, the use of solo voices with keyboard intabulation would render this latter possible without transposition; and the transpositions (octave and non-octave) would allow nuns to perform all voices of pieces (even those exceeding the two-and-a-half-octave range) in both older and modern styles.

In this light, such apparent anomalies as the scoring of Cozzolani's Vespers can be explained as the result of the real disjunction between the actual performance conditions of a given institution and its repertory, on one hand, and, on the other, the far more standardized public presentation of music, especially in printed editions designed, after all, for the market.[93] To summarize the performance possibilities by musical style and institutional size (with contemporary sources in parentheses):

[92] For an example of such a piece dedicated to nuns, see Antegnati's 1592 *Laudate pueri*; Cortellini's setting of the same text ranges slightly lower, to B♭ in the Bassus part.

[93] These kinds of discrepancies, and the range of performance options they occasioned (octave transposition of lines, pieces to be performed either *a 4* or *a 5*, optional ripieni) seem to increase in the early Seicento repertory. The printed presentation of music did not keep pace with the widely varying musical resources of ecclesiastical institutions. For one Roman edition designed for nuns, see Massenzio's 1631 motets *a 2–6*, op. 10 (*Sacri motetti a due, et a piu voci da potersi cantare si da voci ordinarie come ancora da Monache*), whose bass part (used only in the larger-scale pieces) is written in C4 clef; the contents consist of high-voice duets and trios along with four- to six-voice concertos scored variously for CCAB, CCCAB, and even CCCCCB.

Stile antico polyphony
   1. High-clef pieces *a 4* or more
Larger houses: all parts at notated (Lombard) pitch or up a tone, with
   or without keyboard (transposition: Duomo notes on Donati
   Masses of 1633); or as below
Smaller houses: voices on top, keyboard reduction or melodic bass
   instruments for lower parts (Bascapè at S. Maria Maddalena al
   Cerchio; S. Maria Maddalena in Monza 1600)
   2. Normally cleffed works *a 4–6*
Larger houses: all parts up a fourth, fifth, or larger interval, with or
   without organ (Brena, Cima 1606; possibly Alensoon 1724);
   melodic bass instruments for lowest voice, or keyboard reduction
   of lower voices (as above under 1); possibly bass lines up an octave
   with all other parts at pitch (Donati 1623)
Smaller houses: as above under 1, or with bass lines transposed up an
   octave
   3. Double-choir works *a 8*
Both: duplication of the procedures under 1 and 2 above; probably
   less likely in smaller houses (but see Vecchi 1600)

Stile moderno works
   1. High-voice *concertato* pieces
Larger houses: no problems
Smaller houses: no problems if enough singers available
   2. Works for a single low voice with high voices (CB, CCB)
Both: lower (lowest) voice up an octave (Cima 1605, Micheli 1610)
   3. Small-scale lower-voice pieces (e.g. the ATB motets in
Cozzolani's op. 2)
Both: transposition of all parts up a suitable interval, possibly a fifth
   or an octave (Natali 1662, Penna 1672)
   4. Large-scale *concertato* (4–8 voices, including Cozzolani's 1650
Vespers)
Larger houses: octave transposition of bass lines (Donati), with organ;
   all other parts at pitch
Smaller houses: less likely

   What might have been the size and configuration of nuns' ensembles? The infighting at S. Marta and S. Radegonda has shown that
these were not strictly musically organized groups (reflecting social
tension, seniority, and class origin); likewise, they seem to have
performed together only on major occasions. Yet the episcopal

restrictions ('a due Chori soli') seem to indicate that more than two were in place at certain institutions; furthermore, many of the early Office settings and motets dedicated to nuns in Milan require two (not necessarily strictly antiphonal) choirs.[94] Certainly the three organs used during the 1619/26 translation festivities at S. Vittore in Meda had ensembles attached to each. There is a certain tradition of Milanese two-choir music from Visconti's tenure onwards, some of it associated with the Duomo. These large-scale resources were less characteristic of the parishes and male monasteries. Thus it is hard to escape the conclusion that it was sometimes female monastic choirs in Milan that cultivated polychoral styles, at least on major feasts, especially in the wake of the plague years.[95]

How many nuns might have been involved in music-making, and how many singers might have been on a part? Here, there is more evidence from the mid-seventeenth century than earlier, although the 1575 accounts of music at S. Maria Maddalena al Cerchio mention fifteen sisters capable of *canto figurato*. The next set of musical rosters dates from the 1660s: Litta's order of 1664 for S. Radegonda mentions sixteen names (probably singers from one choir), while the Medici travel accounts refer generally to a total of about fifty, or more vaguely to 'la gran parte' of the house's population. More telling of size are the petitions to the Sacra Congregazione over the Palomera case, signed by the competing choirs in 1664–5; Maria Domitilla Ceva's ensemble had twenty-seven members, while Antonia Francesca Clerici's had seventeen.[96] In the more troubled times of the mid-1670s, each choir had been reduced to three sopranos, two or three contraltos, one or two 'bassi', and six or seven

---

[94] Cozzolani's Vespers (unlike Cozzi's 1649 eight-voice settings from S. Simpliciano) requires eight *concertato* voices, arranged in a mixture of two-choir and duet (e.g. CI/CII) configurations. Unlike the characteristic Venetian mixture of a cappella (of soloists) and a ripieno ensemble, the Milanese houses seem to have employed roughly equal-size choirs, another Roman characteristic.

[95] Of all Vecchi's works, representing a cross-section of the repertory at S. Maria della Scala, only the 1590 *Missa, psalmi ad vesperas domenicales* and the 1600 falsobordone collection (the latter dedicated to nuns) employ double-choir scoring. Cantone's 1599 motets (S. Simpliciano) are also *a 8*, while his 1603 Holy Week settings are for five voices. None of G. P. Cima's (at S. Maria presso S. Celso) music requires more than six voices. Again, in a later generation, it was the two composers in Benedictine houses (Cozzi and Cozzolani) and the Duomo figures (Turati, Grancini) who provided eight-voice music for the festivities associated with the 1649 entry of Maria Anna of Austria.

[96] As noted, these were also social, not only musical, lines of demarcation; it would seem unwarranted to deduce that twenty-odd nuns routinely sang in Ceva's choir.

instrumentalists; for the first and only time, these documents named specific singers and instrumentalists by voice-range and instrument.[97]

But by Milanese standards of mid-century, these were sizeable ensembles. The Duomo seems to have employed between fifteen and twenty-five musicians; the ducal court a similar number, with rather more instrumentalists represented.[98] Even if not all S. Radegonda's singers were of professional quality, the group as a whole (counting the unnamed *sonatrici*) was, at least at some points in the century, the largest musical chapel in the city. If, during good times at S. Radegonda, there were some thirty to forty musicians (including six or seven string-players, three or four keyboard-players, and two chitarrone-players, as detailed above), divided into two choirs which did not perform together every week (as stated in Vernici's letters), then a four-voice piece performed *a coro pieno* by one choir might have had two to four singers on a part; an eight-voice motet, one to two (plus string- and continuo-players in both cases). The numbers at other houses would differ according to the resources of the monastery in question; Locatelli mentioned five singers at S. Pietro Martire (S. Agostino Bianco) in 1665, with frequent references to solo performance. Solo singers were also mentioned by the Polish princes earlier in the century.

The Milanese evidence is somewhat less conclusive regarding the exact place in the *chiesa interiore* from which nuns would have sung. The ninety-four surviving choir-stalls at S. Maurizio are set facing each other in the nave of the nuns' church; the Antegnati organ is several metres above the choir, on the north wall (to the left in the interior church). There is room for perhaps six to eight singers on the surviving organ-loft; to this must be added the accounts of a second organ and its platform. None of the curial documents mentions any further location for nuns' choirs; and thus joint performances with musicians in the *chiesa esteriore* were probably unlikely. A further

---

[97] App. A, Doc. 70; Ceva's choir, even in its reduced state, would have been just large enough to perform Bolognese-style liturgical music, although such performances would have been one on a part. Clerici's ensemble, with its six singers, could not have done so, and the dispute over passage from one choir to another may well have revolved around this point.

[98] The personnel lists given in de Florentiis and Vessia, *Sei secoli*, 278–80, range from fifteen singers in 1612 to eighteen in 1638 and twenty-one in the 1670s, often four singers in each of five voice-ranges (with two sets of sopranos: boys and *castrati*); Donati's four-choir Ambrosian ceremonial settings of the 1630s would thus have been performed one on a part.

problem, not mentioned in the records, is posed by the difficulties in co-ordination with invisible ensembles.

How frequent might polyphony have been? The early Seicento evidence, as noted above, argues for major feasts (Christmas, Easter, Assumption) and name-day celebrations at houses like S. Marta, while the travellers' reports indicate polyphonic Vespers almost every Sunday at S. Radegonda. Later, in 1690, the decree that S. Radegonda wrenched from Visconti restored *canto figurato* for Mass and Office (presumably Vespers) on major feasts: Christmas, Circumcision, Epiphany, Easter, Ascension, Pentecost, Corpus Christi, St John the Baptist, SS Peter and Paul, All Saints', Marian feasts (probably Nativity BVM, Annunciation, and Assumption at the very least), and commemorations of Benedictine saints, some fifteen days.[99]

The discussion until now has focused exclusively on sacred music, obviously the majority of the preserved repertory associated with nuns. Despite the curia's best efforts, however, it is clear that nuns practised secular genres and styles within *clausura*. From the *greghesche* fragments at S. Maria Maddalena through the 1664 Medici visit accounts to the early Settecento travellers' reports, madrigals along with arias and *canzoni* are all mentioned in connection with nuns' music-making. Cozzolani and Badalla both wrote secular pieces, which, despite the official restrictions, survived into our century. Indeed, considering nuns' ties to the life of the urban patriciate, including its festivities and music, it is no surprise that so many references to *ariette* and cantatas exist.

The question of secular music is inseparable from that of its primary locus, the *parlatorio*, and from diocesan efforts to establish—and nuns' efforts to resist—control over this other nexus between sisters and their world of origin. Almost every curial decree on nuns' behaviour prohibited music in the parlours, often with the explicit mention of secular music, and clearly the custom persisted for some two centuries. Sixty years after the Medici travel reports of *ariette* in the *parlatorio* in the 1660s, Alensoon not only heard Quinzana and other nuns in the parlour (accompanied by themselves and by the

---

[99] The ailing Visconti issued the order on 8 Nov. 1690 (ASDM XII, vol. 128, fos. 166–7). Several duplex feasts of Benedictine saints were celebrated in Seicento Milan: the 1604 *Breviarium Ambrosianum* lists St Nicholas of Tolentino, St Remigius, and St Gall in this category. The feast of all Benedictine saints (celebrated on 13 Nov. according to the 1613 breviary) was also presumably included in this edict.

male Benedictine Vignati); the Dutchman also performed for them, apparently from a keyboard in the *parlatorio forastiero*.[100] Tied to this were the frequent prohibitions of parlour theatre, including *mascherate* that involved nuns' shedding their habits for secular or even male costume. This took on special urgency at Carnival, and, as noted, Federigo's vicars simply printed decrees (largely invariant in content if not in wording) for distribution to all the female monasteries of the diocese.

One clearly impossible act, even in Federigo's Milan, was the public association of secular music with nuns. Thus, there are no dedications of such pieces, even individual canzonettas or arias. But sisters are recorded as having sung (and composed) secular music.[101] The Milanese vernacular repertory of the Seicento has been even less studied than has sacred music, but some local music survives, along with some documented operatic productions from mid-century on. Certainly Badalla's two cantatas are not atypical of late seventeenth-century style.

But there is another way in which the coexistence of secular and sacred made its presence known: the irruption of 'worldly' styles into liturgical music. Already under Federigo there had been episcopal concern over this issue, but, as might be expected, it reached new heights (or depths) under Litta. The prelate complained constantly in the 1660s about the singing of psalms to 'canzonetta' melodies at S. Margarita, S. Radegonda, and even S. Paolo (in the 1661 dispute). At least one psalm setting written by a nun in Lombardy, Leonarda's 1674 *Beatus vir in Arietta*, made the explicit connection with such forms. Yet an overview of the Milanese Vespers repertory after 1650

---

[100] 'Naademiddags ging ik de vermaarde nonne en sangster in het Klooster van S.ta Radegonda, Quinzana genaamt, besoeken, mij wierd buijten de tralie in de spreekplaatse (of parlatorio) een Clavercimbel gebragt, werdende versogt voor haar te singen, de meermaalen hier booven gemelde Cantaat met twee stemmen [a solo work composed by Alensoon that employed both low and high vocal tessitura], t'welk ik deed, waar oover sij seer verwondert was, waar op sij een groote quantiteijt nonnen haalde, voor welke ik, op haar versoek, de selve Cantaat nog wel vier of vijfmaalen song, ondertussen kwam l'Abbate Don Giuseppe Vignati, zijnde een groot componist en eerste Bascontinuist in de Opera' (Alensoon, 'Dag-register', 7 Jan. 1724, p. 75); 'Naa den eeten heb ik . . . weeder de Quinzana weesen besoeken, die voor mij weeder seer aangenaam en kunstig song, verders hoorde ik een seer mooij nonnetje twee Cantaten singen, werdende geaccompagneert met de Clavercimbel door l'Abbate Giuseppe Vignati' (ibid., 19 Jan., p. 104). None of Vignati's few surviving works is explicitly connected with S. Radegonda.

[101] A generation after Litta's complaints, Alensoon noted cantatas composed and sung by a nun: 'sij [Quinzana] song wel drie of vier Cantaten . . . twee van de Cantaten die sij song waaren van haare Compositie' (16 Jan. 1724, 'Dag-register', 102).

reveals no marked turn towards secular or strophic styles.[102] The constant references to singing psalms to secular tunes leave no alternative to the conclusion that the female monastic choirs did precisely that on occasion, simply adopting verses to suitable (?triple-time) melodies. In so doing, they would have carried Federigo's taste for contrafacta one step further, although hardly to the archbishop's liking.

The links to the outside musical world, and the various possibilities for nuns to adapt its music to their own performing forces, help to place the numerous Office and motet dedications in the context of Milanese traditions. These begin with works for and by nuns during the relatively peaceful—and musically fecund—years of Federigo's tenure.

---

[102] This is certainly true for such editions as Bagatti's 1659 *Messa e salmi brevi* and his 1672 *Motetti, messa e salmi.*

8

Continuity and Innovation from Antegnati to Rusca

◇

Sonet vox tua in auribus meis; vox enim tua dulcis.

(Cant. 2: 14)

The first traceable corpus of pieces associated with sisters comprises *stile antico* Office settings, followed by the early concertos in *stile moderno*. The new century's contributions to genres whose origins dated to the Cinquecento overlap both these repertories: Gallo's and Soderini's 1598 double-choir motets, Vecchi's 1601 Penitential Psalms, the contrafacta by Cavalieri and Coppini, Sessa's monodies, and Rognoni's 1620 pedagogical divisions. This patrician repertory—the kinds of works that Claudia Rusca would have heard and performed as a young Milanese musician—allows us to place the remnants from her *Sacri concerti* in context.

The first dedication, Costanzo Antegnati's Vespers, falls within the surprisingly limited Lombard tradition of eight-voice antiphonal settings. Although the composer had claimed that his impulse to publish had stemmed from the Benedictines' performance on their name-day, still the entire volume included more psalms than the selection for 7 or 8 May 1590 or 1591, and, again perhaps due to publishing considerations, was more typical of secular than monastic use (or Ambrosian rite; cf. App. C. 1).[1] There is no overriding organization; Antegnati

---

[1] The inclusion of *In exitu* and *Lauda Jerusalem* and the setting of *Memento Domine David* (in Roman usage, assigned to the Common of a Confessor Pope, but in Milan used only as the fourth psalm for Thursday) both indicate Roman rite. The normal placement of *In exitu* runs counter to Benedictine use (in which it was sung on Monday), again perhaps a publishing convention.

seems to have followed standard modal choices for specific psalms.[2]

The first characteristic of the book is the number of its psalms set out in an unusual clef configuration (C1/C2/C3/C4 or F3) in both choirs. This system accounts for eleven of the fifteen items (in both authentic and plagal modes), plus the Magnificat. Three others, plus the respond, are set out in high clefs (G2/C1/C3/C4).[3] The point of the unusual cleffing is not to indicate a very high absolute pitch, but to restrict the total overall range of most psalms, with a smaller gradation between successively lower voices. The ambitus is either two octaves and a second (bass = C4; two psalms and the Magnificat) or two octaves and a fourth (nine psalms). The solution seems like a compromise between *voce piena* and *voci pari* ensembles, one due perhaps to the conflicting demands of the collection's origins and the standardization of printed collections. Despite the expansiveness of the scoring, the Brescian organist's settings traverse a wide range of styles, from short imitative passages and florid doxologies to homophonic declamation for each choir, with occasional recourse to falsobordone, notably in the longer psalms.[4]

The settings that would have been sung by the Benedictines for their name-day Vespers, the first four psalms in the collection (*Dixit, Confitebor, Beatus vir, Laudate pueri*), represent the more elaborate side of the book: largely syllabic settings, with combinations of choirs for final verses and melismatic doxologies. *Laudate pueri* (the only one in high clefs, according to its mode, 5) illustrates Antegnati's methods.[5] Here the half-lines are again apportioned largely between the two choirs, with a single tutti cadence on the *finalis* a quarter of the way through (v. 4) at 'laudabile nomen eius' (bars 21–3; see Ex. 8.1). Since the single affect of this psalm text is praise, in rhetorical terms

[2] On modal organization, the classic article is H. S. Powers, 'Modal Types and Tonal Categories in Renaissance Polyphony', *JAMS* 34 (1981), 428–70. The standard patterns depended on psalm text: in Vecchi's 1590 print, for instance, *Dixit* and *Confitebor* are in first and second mode, respectively (as in Antegnati); Vecchi's *Beatus vir* and *Laudate pueri* are in the plagal cofinalis relative to Antegnati. These associations would persist into the Seicento.

[3] The exception is *Beati omnes*, an anomaly in other regards. This setting pits a low *voci pari* ensemble against a normally cleffed choir, the only use of different scorings, and a counter-example to the Venetian practice of setting a slightly higher choir I against choir II. In assignment, *Beati omnes* is not prominent (the fourth psalm for First Vespers of Corpus Christi in both the Roman and Ambrosian breviaries).

[4] At 'et posuisti super me manum tuam', *a 4* and *a 8*, in *Domine probasti me*; 'speravit anima mea in Domino' in *De profundis*; and 'tabernaculum Deo Jacob' in *Memento Domine David*.

[5] Modern edn. in Kendrick, 'Genres', 915–42.

Ex. 8.1. Antegnati, *Laudate pueri* (1592), bars 18–24

this cadence marks the end of the exordium. Some of the half-line settings seem to be simple harmonizations of an embellished reciting-tone (bars 33–40, 47–51 and 51–6, 65–70). But the psalm tone had additional implications: Antegnati repeated a rising F–A–C bass line (on the *finalis*, mediant, and *repercussio* of the mode) in linear fashion at bars 33–4 and in contrapuntal elaboration at bars 57–60. The fifth-mode character of the piece is underlined by a larger-scale projection of the same idea: half-verses cadencing on any of these three pitches.[6] The cadential goals derived from the psalm tone are clear (see Table 8.1). The plan holds strictly to Pontio's outline of structural pitches for this tone: the 'cadenze proprie' on F and C outline the piece, while the 'cadenza altera' on A is reserved for verse 7 ('Suscitans a terra inopem', the verse furthest from the predominant affect).[7]

TABLE 8.1. Structure of Antegnati, *Laudate pueri*

Verse	Choir/Cadence	Verse	Choir/Cadence
1a	[chant: C]	1b	I: A
2a	II: C	2b	I: C
3a	II: C	3b	I and II: F
4a	II: C	4b	I and II: C
5	I: C (overlapped with v. 6)		
6	II→I: C		
7a	II: A ('mi' clausula)	7b	I: A
8a	II→I: F	8b	II: F
9a	I: F	9b	III→I: C
Dox a[a]	II: F	Dox b	I and II: F

[a] A caesura divides the doxology at 'Sicut erat in principio'.

But within this modest style there were clear methods for rhetorical emphasis. The first tutti ('laudabile nomen Domini', bars 21–4) is framed by the long pedal-points in the outer voices on the reciting-tone of the mode, and the sudden sound of the tutti (Ex. 8.1). At

[6] The F–A–C progression generates larger phrases, for example, bars 65 (2nd semibreve) to 70 and bars 79 (2nd semibreve) to 87. The parallel nature of the construction is characteristic of the whole piece, and represents the composer's response to the parallel structure of the psalm.

[7] For the classifications of modal cadences in psalm tones, see Pontio, *Ragionamento di musica*, 99–120, with a summary in Meier, *Die Tonarten*, 91–2.

bar 57, homophony suddenly gives way to short imitation, and from here on the timbre of the piece is marked by each of the two cantus parts exploring the range around the top f''. A brief tutti at '[matrem] filiorum laetantem' demarcates the end of the psalm, and the doxology is characterized by the shortest interchanges between the choirs to be found in the piece, a final F–A–C motif in the bass (bars 90–4), and the cadence, this time with pedal-points in the outer voices on the *finalis*, not on the *repercussio* as was the case at the end of the exordium (in Burmeister's terms, a *supplementum* to demarcate the conclusion).[8] A larger-scale reinforcement of this parallelism is provided by the cadential plan of verses 8 through the doxology, which reverse the pitch goals of verses 2–4 so as to end on the *finalis* instead of the *repercussio*. The doxology also receives the greatest amount of antiphonal phrasing between the two choirs; Antegnati saves the brief imitative entry within a choir for the spatial reference of 'ut collocet eum'.

This *Laudate pueri* can thus be viewed as a polyphonic projection of the psalm tone along two separate axes. The paraphrase of the reciting-tone in the top parts, the repeated use of the F–A–C motif, and the embellishment of the *terminatio* all represent an extension of the psalm-tone formula into *Laudate pueri*'s melodic vocabulary. But the *supplementum* C at the end of the exordium, and the cadences on the reciting-tone in verses 4 through 6 (both paralleled by analogous passages on the *finalis* at the end of the psalm) point to Antegnati's setting of the entire text in a large-scale harmonic design that parallels the structural pitches of the tone, with the cadence of verse 1 on the mediant followed by a major internal cadence on the reciting-tone (corresponding to the interior caesura of the psalm tone); this is then balanced by the repeated cadences on the *finalis* towards the end and in the doxology (corresponding to the tone's *terminatio*).

Another fifth-mode *Laudate pueri*, from the second collection dedicated to a Milanese nun, Camillo Cortellini's 1595 six-voice Vespers inscribed to Paola Serbellona at S. Vincenzo, provides interesting points of comparison. Around 1590, the *chiesa esteriore* at the house had received its frescos by Aurelio Luini; they depicted the martyrs St Vincent and St Lawrence, along with the Passion; Cortellini's inscription followed closely on the painting cycle.[9] Perhaps in

---

[8] *Musica poetica* (Rostock, 1606), 53.

[9] On the preparatory drawings and the cycle, see N. W. Neilson, 'A Drawing by Aurelio Luini', *Master Drawings*, 25 (1987), 151–2. On the pictures, Santagostino, *L'immortalità*, 49–50.

keeping with the less prominent place of S. Vincenzo in urban musical life, the collection is simpler than Antegnati's; Cortellini's limited selection of nine psalms in this first edition (the Benedictine male/female cursus plus Pss. 113, 116, and 147) reflected the need for only six items to cover major feasts at S. Vincenzo. The collection would prove quite popular in the following century, with three reprints (minus the dedication and with further settings added).

Certainly Cortellini's *Laudate pueri* moves within a narrower range of contrast and emphasis, as the structural outline of the verses manifests greater restraint among the internal cadences (see Table 8.2). This scheme renounces cadences on the mediant (the 'cadenza altera') or on any other modal degree (D or G, the 'cadenze per transito'). The large-scale symmetrical structure of the Antegnati setting (with the major internal cadence on the reciting-tone) is lacking here, as well. Rather, Cortellini uses a sort of textural refrain: a tutti (outlining either the reciting-tone or the modal species of fourth in the cantus: 'a solis ortu'; 'Quis sicut Dominus'; 'Matrem filiorum laetantem'; 'Sicut erat') that provides internal punctuation. Elided cadences feature more prominently, especially at the end of verse 5 ('qui in altis habitat'; Ex. 8.2), and in the second half of the setting, providing a sense of irresistible speed-up towards the doxology. Again, the constantly changing combinations of voices colour the various paraphrases of the psalm tone in the two top voices, Cantus (bars 3–5, 17–20, 28–31, 36–9) or Sextus (bars 8–13, 20–8). The textural climax is afforded by the quick homophonic tutti declamation

TABLE 8.2. Structure of Cortellini, *Laudate pueri*

Verse	Cadence	Verse	Cadence
1a	chant: C	1b	F
2a	C	2b	F
3a	C	3b	C
4a	F	4b	F
5	F (before verse ending)		
6	F		
7a	F	7b	C
8a	F elided to 8b	8b	F
9a	C elided to 9b	9b	F
Dox a	C	Dox b	F

Ex. 8.2. Cortellini, *Laudate pueri* (1595), bars 16–24

Ex. 8.2. *cont.*

with a slower harmonic rhythm in the doxology. The almost exclusively syllabic settings, and limited tessitura of the parts, must have made this edition attractive to a wide range of institutions.[10] Cortellini's *Laudate pueri* represents a different approach to psalm composition, one oriented more to the vertical harmonization of a top line, and more flexible in its approach to the declamation of specific verses. Antegnati's dual melodic and harmonic projection of the reciting-tone is here replaced by melodic paraphrase.

Even simpler is the first entire inscription of liturgical polyphony by a Milanese figure, Orfeo Vecchi's *Falsi bordoni figurati sopra gli otto toni ecclesiastici . . . Magnificat, & Te Deum laudamus* (1600), addressed to three women, at least one of whom was a nun in an unnamed, probably Clarissan, house.[11] The unpretentiousness of the collec-

---

[10] Modern edn. in Kendrick, 'Genres', 943–56. The overall range of the setting is two octaves and a sixth (B♭–g″). None of the individual parts exceeds a ninth, and the largely conjunct motion of the part-writing renders the music accessible. All-female ensembles could perform *Laudate pueri* with five sung voices and organ at modern written pitch, without any loss of text; alternatively, with high sopranos and low altos, the piece could be intoned up a fourth and all parts vocalized.

[11] The dedication is inscribed 'Alle molto illustre et reverendissime Signore, Suor Clara Francesca, et Clara Gieronima Goseline, et Clara Pompilia Adda, nel Signore

tion's contents was offset by the luxuriousness of its presentation; it was one of four Milanese prints of the new century to feature two-colour printing on its title-page. It was also the only local edition besides the monumental Duomo publications to be issued in choir-book format.[12] The dedication does not mention the practical use of the volume, concentrating instead on the spiritual prestige of its addressees. The book contains simple chant embellishments: fal-sobordoni *a 4, a 5,* and *a 8* in all the tones; Magnificats in *alternatim* and full settings in the same scoring; doxologies *a 8* in all tones; and a two-choir Te Deum *a 9,* with only three verses sung by the tutti. An eight-voice *Gloria Patri,* an inserted doxology for a psalm which had been sung in falsobordone *a 4* or *a 8,* shows Vecchi's sonorous yet restrained writing (Ex. 8.3).

But if the music is simple, easy enough to be sung by even untrained musicians and suitable for foundations with either many or few singers, the scoring and vocal ranges are more puzzling. The print includes duplicate four-voice falsobordoni in the third and eighth tones, one cleffed high (G2/C2/C3/F3) and marked 'alla 4 & 5 bassa', one cleffed normally (C1/C3/C4/F4) with the rubric 'all'alta'; both were to be intoned at (or transposed to) other pitch-levels. Still, the overall range in both sets is at least two octaves and a fifth (for example, in the eighth-mode *alla bassa* set, *c–g″*; in the *all'alta* group, *G–e″*). If the lower-pitched set marked 'all'alta' were transposed up a fourth or fifth, there remains a slightly wide total ambitus for a nuns' choir, perhaps *c–a″*. But this is an eminently prac-tical collection and Vecchi was no stranger to a choir's possibilities. With the growth in female monastic population, it was possible to assume wider ranges for polyphonic pieces.[13] Ecclesiastical demog-raphy held other implications; the edition also had to be useful in the smaller institutions—male and female—of the diocese, hence the more generic scoring and modest musical demands. The sim-plicity and standardization of the book, combined with its elegant

osservandissime'. Clara Goselina's title, plus the professed name of all three ('Clara'), render a Clarissan house likely.

[12] The Lüneburg copy of the edition was brought from Vienna (another testimony to Vecchi's transalpine influence) by J. J. Löwe von Eisenach; see H. Walter, *Musikgeschichte der Stadt Lüneburg* (Tutzing, 1967), 132.

[13] The 1604 Giunta catalogue (transcribed in O. Mischiati, *Indici, cataloghi e avvisi degli editori e librai musicali italiani dal 1591 al 1798* (Florence, 1984), 18–19 and 110–34) mentions a 'Basso per l'Organo dei Falsi Bordoni figurati' by Vecchi, presumably the organ part for this collection.

Ex. 8.3. Orfeo Vecchi, *Gloria Patri octavo tono all'alto* (1600), bars 1–7

presentation, recall the flood of printed orders and rubrics for liturgy in the diocese as a whole and for female monastic life in particular, dating from Federigo's tenure.[14]

Only three of eight part-books survive from Giovanni Antonio Mangoni's *Messa, e salmi* (1623), dedicated to the Clarissans of S. Pietro in Treviglio. The overall style seems closer to Antegnati than to the Vecchi falsobordone collection. Here again, vocal scoring is an issue: the title-page describes the collection as being for two choirs, one of 'voci puerili', one of 'voci pari'. Frustratingly, the only extant part-books are from choir II (A: C4; B: F4). If the first choir were scored for something like CCAT, and the second for an ATTB *voci pari* ensemble (a unique combination of high and low equal-voice groups in the Milanese, and perhaps any other, repertory), then the Clarissans might have been able to perform the collection by transposing the whole second choir an octave up, avoiding inversions by using an organ. Although this would have entailed the loss of the registral contrast, still, in an echo of the *voci pari* tradition, another collection associated with nuns required restricted-range ensembles.

Yet composers working for the patriciate continued to develop other forms rooted in the late Cinquecento. The cross-section of such music afforded by associations with nuns highlights a number of new formal innovations, some with lasting effects; unlike the Office settings, these pieces might have been performed in the interior or exterior churches, or (in the case of the madrigal contrafacta and monodies) inside cloisters for spiritual recreation. The largest-scale pieces, and the ones most closely related to *stile antico*, are the double-choir settings in two publications of 1598: Gallo's *Sacer opus musici . . . liber primus* and Soderini's *Sacrae cantiones a 8–9*. These books were the first large-scale collections by composers working in the parishes and contained some of the first dedications of individual pieces to singers and religious male and female. These inscriptions (both feature four motets addressed to Milanese nuns) tie the social and devotional ambitus of the editions firmly to patrician families.[15]

Giuseppe Gallo's collection, edited and perhaps compiled by Aurelio Ribrochi, is divided into four sections: six double-choir motets *a 9*, most with four instruments and five voices; a mass; eight

---

[14] Its printing in the Holy Year of 1600 may also bear on its 'monumental' presentation as a standard reference book for religious institutions in the diocese.

[15] Gallo was a Somascan priest, a member of a pedagogical order; Soderini was the organist at S. Maria della Passione, although there is no dedication to Sessa in his book.

(typically antiphonal) eight-voice (purely vocal) motets; and two canzonas. The dedications to nuns include three from the first group (*Veni electa mea*, *Ecce angelus de caelo*, and a Magnificat), the mass, and a canzona.[16] Along with the other five motets in the first section, *Veni electa mea* (addressed to Archilea and Angelica Archinti at S. Radegonda, the first public tribute to the house's music) displays a formal novelty with important descendants in the Milanese repertory:[17] a motet which appears at first glance to be the combination of a new vocal setting of the text (in choir II) along with a pre-existing canzona in the instrumental parts (choir I), in this case Claudio Merulo's 1592 *La Benvenuta* (in a simplified version without the virtuoso figuration of the printed keyboard edition).[18]

Yet the reworking is more complex than immediately apparent. For the tuttis, Gallo wrote new instrumental parts (not found in the original canzona) that meshed with the vocal lines, then dovetailed with Merulo's canzona phrases (marked off by dotted lines in the example); these latter formed instrumental interludes between the declamation of the motet text (Ex. 8.4). Furthermore, the original canzona was approached with some freedom; only two periods were reused in the new motet.[19] The vocal sections, which stray little from the modal *finalis*, begin with brief imitation and cadence in homophony. The result is more like a vocal gloss on *La Benvenuta* than a simple dissection and reworking.

The next piece in the book, *Ecce angelus de caelo*, introduces a genre

---

[16] The *Missa sine nomine* is inscribed 'Ad modum reverendis matribus S. Ioannis Baptistae Civitatis Laudensis'; S. Giovanni Battista was a female Benedictine house in Lodi. Ribrochi signed the dedication on 1 Jan. 1598. A manuscript note (over the Magnificat) in the D-Mbs copy of the *partitura* reads 'Viola brazo'.

[17] The piece is rubricated 'In festivitatibus B.M.V., virginum ac mulierum sanctarum'; the generality of the destination implies that it is a cento. The surviving part-book (A1) is not texted, and the *partitura* gives only cues, from which, however, the entire text can be reconstructed: 'Veni electa mea, [et ponam in te thronum meum]; quia [concupivit Rex] speciem tuam; Specie [tua, et pulchritudine tua] intende, [propere, et regna], quia [concupivit Rex speciem tuam]', a responsory.

[18] The original had appeared in the *Canzoni d'intavolatura* . . . *libro primo* (Venice: Gardano, 1592; mod. edn. by P. Pidoux (Kassel, 1941)); other pieces in Merulo's book also circulated in MS without the ornamentation; cf. the edition by B. Thomas (*Fourteen Canzonas for Four Instruments* (London, 1982)), based on a source now in Verona.

[19] The pattern of reworking is as follows: Gallo's bars 1–8 are taken from Merulo's bars 1–8; 37–44 = 9–16; 62–73 = 17–27 (including the corrupt readings of the 1592 print, e.g. c' against $c'\sharp$ on the downbeat of b. 62); 83–93 = 17–27 (displaced by a semibreve). Gallo's remaining material is new.

Ex. 8.4. Gallo, *Veni, electa mea* (1598), bars 31–42

Ex. 8.4. *cont.*

of greater importance: the dialogue.[20] This motet, rubricated as
'Dialogismum Angeli cum mulieribus', is inscribed to Maximilla
Biumia at S. Radegonda, and includes one ensemble of voice (the
angel at the Tomb) plus four instruments and another of four voices
(the two Marys).[21] Its melodic material in both choirs, however, is
canzona-like, called *La Galla* in the instrumental ensemble but based
on no known surviving piece (hence probably newly composed,
possibly a self-identifying reference by Gallo).[22] Easter dialogues of
angels and the women at the Tomb, both favourite models among

---

[20] The text is taken from Matt. 28: 2 ff.; more cogently, it is a synopsis of the five
antiphons for Easter Vespers in the Roman rite (*Angelus autem* to *Respondens autem*), with
which it shares its eighth (or seventh) mode.

[21] Given the normal clef combination for instrumental choirs in this book
(G2/C1/C3/C4 or F3), probably the third line down in choir I (C2) was texted.

[22] *La Mantegazza*, dedicated to three eponymous sisters at S. Agnese, is a typical eight-
voice canzona; *Quis es tu?*, a vocal eight-part motet addressed to the 'pudicissimae' Zanobia
Visconti and rubricated for St Agatha, may also have been a clothing piece for a novice,
given the conflation of liturgical texts noted above. That Gallo could include canzona material (a genre that Carlo would have banned in 1576) in such motets is yet another testimony
to the interplay of sacred and secular in Federigo's Milan.

Federigo's similes for sisters, would have a long tradition in nuns' polyphony. Ribrochi's preface makes much of this new mixture of styles, and it continued in use as late as Rusca's motets. The remarkable feature is that motivic ideas and melodic phrases from two seemingly diverse genres could be singled out and recombined in a new sort of piece, a concept that would recur in the early sacred concerto, and a formal experimentation not unknown in the other arts of Federigo's Milan. And the employment of popular patrician music in combination with religious texts would last well into the new century.

Agostino Soderini's book published later the same year contains a wide range of pieces, large-scale works destined for major and sanctoral feasts. Again, several motets are dedicated to nuns at S. Radegonda, with the name-day dialogue for Agata Sfondrati at S. Paolo. Soderini's volume opens with two double-choir dialogues, and the genre (not always explicitly named) is central to the collection as a whole, including: *Saule, Saule, quid me persecutis?*; *Ave Virgo, decus*; *Dic nobis, Maria*; *O rex gloriae*; *Angelus autem Domini*; *Quae est ista?*; and *Interrogavi Angelum*, the last a nine-voice piece with unspecified instruments.[23] The dialogue motets in both books extended the traditions of the genre to settings of scriptural texts, another formal idea that would have a long heritage in the new century.

For *Dic nobis, Maria*, inscribed to Francesca Stampa at S. Radegonda, Soderini selected the exchange section of *Victimae paschali laudes*, another Easter piece featuring the topos of women at the Tomb. The centrality of Mary Magdalene makes this a fitting dedication to nuns. The sequence melody is not directly quoted or paraphrased in this setting, but it may well have determined modal choice (1). Here, as in other dialogues, there is a tutti refrain ('Dic nobis'; Ex. 8.5), with the Magdalen's statements given to a series of smaller voice-groupings, rising in tessitura from Tenor and Bass II and increasing in texture from two to four voices as bicinia and tricinia. A large-scale tutti takes up almost the last half of the piece, with a remarkable *supplementum* on the *finalis* enlivened by cross-rhythms. Given the traditions of music at S. Radegonda, and the absolute lack of any evidence for performances in the *chiesa esteriore*, the Benedictines were presumably the intended performers of this

---

[23] The surviving copy of Soderini's book lacks both a *nona vox* and a *partitura*; although no pre-existing canzona melodies are used in the three nine-voice pieces with instruments, these are a clear imitation of (or parallel to) Gallo's.

Ex. 8.5. Soderini, *Dic nobis, Maria* (1598), bars 1–12

piece. *Dic nobis, Maria* is set out for two high-clef (G2/C2/C3/C4) choirs, and the nuns would have had to execute the piece at something like written pitch (the top part ranges up to g'' and the lowest to c), another argument for the use of an organ to help out on the bottom line. In its topic and dedication, *Dic nobis* was Soderini's counterpart to Gallo's *Ecce angelus de caelo*.[24]

If his 1600 falsobordoni collection had exemplified simplicity, Vecchi's 1601 Penitential Psalms, his second collection dedicated to a nun (again Agata Sfondrati at S. Paolo), represents the other extreme—a highly personal and technically artistic cycle, the first dedication of music in thoroughly imitative polyphony. Certainly Agata herself was among the most literary and cultured members of the family at S. Paolo, and an important figure in the public renown of the Sfondrati; as noted, she later requested copies of Banchieri's motets.[25] Vecchi's inscription notes her culture ('humanitas') and her pleasure in the composer's earlier works.[26] Like the 1600 falsobordoni, this edition employs normal, sometimes low, scoring and cleffing.[27] Late Cinquecento use of the seven-psalm series tended towards private, non-liturgical contexts.[28] Vecchi's collection was the only setting of the cycle in Lombardy; unlike Andrea Gabrieli's 1583 version, it was not a direct imitation of Lassus's Penitential Psalms, although several passages recall the Munich Kapellmeister. In contrast to the systematic modal plan of Lassus, and his imitators, this cycle remains in the penitential third mode until the last psalm.[29]

[24] Soderini's piece was followed by Gabussi in text and mode: the latter's *Dic nobis, Maria a 4* appeared in the large-scale anthology *Concerti de' diversi* (RISM 1608[13]).

[25] She wrote a history of the Angeliche and other works; see Baernstein, 'The Counter-Reformation Convent', 180–1 and 213–15. The niece of Niccolò Sfondrati (Pope Gregory XV, 1590–1), she was born (as Barbara) in 1565, taking her vows in 1582, and serving as prioress for several terms in the first decade of the 17th c., falling victim to the plague in 1631; her elaborate *vita* was written by another nun at S. Paolo in 1635.

[26] 'Et quoniam meis praesertim musicis lucubrationibus, quales quales sint, delectari te scio.'

[27] Pss. 1–4 are set out in the clefs C1/C1/C3/C4/C4/F4 (Cantus, Sextus, Altus, Tenor, Quintus, Bassus); *Domine exaudi . . . et clamor* and *De profundis* in the lower C1/C4/C3/C4/C4(F4)/F4 system; and *Domine exaudi . . . auribus* in high clefs, G2/G2/C2/C3/C4/F3. Total overall range in any given psalm is three octaves.

[28] For a complete list and an application of Meier's ideas, see S. Schulze, *Die Tonarten in Lassos 'Bußpsalmen' mit einem Vergleich von Alexander Utendals und Jacob Reiners 'Bußpsalmen'* (Neuhausen-Stuttgart, 1984). Vecchi's cycle was the last in Italy and one of the last anywhere. On the use of the cycle, see P. Bergquist's introduction to his edition of Lassus, *Seven Penitential Psalms and Laudate Dominum de Coelis* (Madison, 1990).

[29] Lassus's cyclical approach to modal choice contrasts with Vecchi's preference for unified modal affect; the former's chromatic experiments are also absent from the 1601 psalms.

The *prima pars* of the seventh psalm, *Domine exaudi orationem meam*, exemplifies the translucent style that brought Vecchi contemporary fame. It also offers the greatest number of common features with Lassus and Gabrieli; like their settings, this final piece begins—and stays—in the brighter seventh mode. The four verses of Ps. 142 are set out in clear fashion, and the exordium of the piece ('Domine . . . deprecationem meam'; Ex. 8.6) presents the means of rhetorical support: cadences, vocal texture, and the tension between *cantus durus* and *cantus mollis*.

After the opening acclamation pitting the outer voices against the middle, Vecchi sets the first plea twice ('exaudi orationem meam' for C6A; bars 3–8 and 8–14), with the repeat rescored (T5B) and punctuated by the added cadential formula in Altus on g' (bars 11–14). While 'auribus percipe deprecationem meam' features the first tutti scoring, the noun 'deprecationem' evokes sudden B♭s and a move towards flat hexachords for the next plea, with an elided cadence on the surprise B flat at bar 17.[30] But the tutti flowers into a full cadence on the *finalis* two bars later, marking the end of the exordium with the Sextus's ascent to the high g''.

Vecchi then provides a parallel musical setting for a parallel textual construction 'in veritate tua | exaudi me in tua justitia' (eliding the received literary break between verses 1b and 1c), closing the first verse with a weak and overlapped cadence on the *finalis* (b. 25). The rest of the *prima pars* then elaborates the ideas of the exordium: internal cadences 'per transito' (vv. 2a and 3b) answered by 'cadenze principali' ending verses (D: 2b; G: 3c, 4b); symmetrical and changing vocal scorings to set off the beginnings of verses (v. 2a: C6AT; v. 2b: A5TB); a *cadenza in mi* on a to set off the humility of 'cum servo tuo';[31] and brief visits to *cantus mollis* to underline 'affective' words: 'inimicus', 'sicut mortuos', 'et anxiatus est'.[32] The ending, 'in me turbatum est cor meum', is marked again by texture: smaller vocal combinations that slowly expand into a tutti in order to set the idea of the 'troubled heart', unlike the syncopations of Lassus and Gabrieli. Although the initial musical idea 'Domine exaudi' resembles Gabrieli's, and certain traits (the turn to *cantus mollis* for 'sicut

---

[30] This case of *commixtio tonorum* (the combination of modes with different finals) could be added to those cited by Meier, *Die Tonarten*, 338–57, to highlight the affect of a textual phrase.

[31] For similar cases in mode 7 to express servitude, see ibid. 257.

[32] For similar *commixtiones tonorum*, see ibid. 297–9.

Ex. 8.6. Vecchi, *Salmo settimo* (1601), bars 1–19

Ex. 8.6. *cont.*

mortuos seculi') were pioneered by Lassus, still Vecchi's piece artic-
ulates its musical ideas on a larger span, and his melodic lines tend
towards long conjunct arcs rising to a specific modal goal. The wide
overall range of the cycle (*F–g″*) would have required the kinds of
adaptations described above for monastic performance. Still, this
cycle was at the heart of music in Federigo's early years; written by
a composer patronized by both Borromeos, the best-known
Milanese figure around 1600, it features penitential but finally optimistic modal choice. It would be difficult to conclude that these *stile
antico* pieces were in any way marginal in the Lombard capital.

The first flowering of madrigal contrafacta in the early years of
Federigo's tenure has been apparent for some time.[33] The editions
began in 1600, with Geronimo Cavaglieri's first *Nova metamorfosi*
volume, again dedicated to a nun (Suor Ottavia Cattanea at S.
Orsola).[34] Several editions with texts by Cavaglieri and Vecchi provide substitute devotional words for a wide variety of madrigal composers, Roman and northern, including Marenzio, Orazio Vecchi,
and Andrea Gabrieli.[35] The early reworkings are unspecific, employing Song of Songs or other scriptural texts, and taking few pains to
match even the affect of the new Latin text, let alone its syntax or
phonetic content, to that of the original.[36] But in light of Federigo's
emphasis on 'ricreazione spirituale', the need for such pieces in Milan
was obvious.

A far more artistic and altogether remarkable effort was the three-
volume series, issued in 1607, 1608, and 1609, featuring some of
Monteverdi's best-known—and most controversial—works from
Books III, IV, and V, along with madrigals by others. The new texts
were written by Aquilino Coppini, a rhetorician and follower of
Federigo's in the circle that had also included Puteanus. Typically,
the first volume in the set was dedicated to Federigo, with the

---

[33] The initial helpful introduction is that of M. A. Rorke, 'Sacred Contrafacta of
Monteverdi Madrigals and Cardinal Borromeo's Milan', *Music and Letters*, 65 (1984),
168–75.

[34] Although most literature cites a 1599 Milanese *editio princeps* for Simone Molinaro's
Fatiche spirituali books (which survive only in a Venetian reprint of 1610), I have found no
trace of such an edition. But the practice had commenced with pieces in Vecchi's thrice-
printed 1597 five-voice motets. There is no other record of Cattanea's musical activities.

[35] The editions appeared only after Federigo's appointment as archbishop.

[36] Cf. also the illuminating comparisons in A. Delfino, 'Geronimo Cavaglieri e alcuni
contrafacta di madrigali marenziani', in M. T. Rosa Barezzani and M. Sala (eds.), *Luca
Marenzio musicista europeo* (Brescia, 1990), 165–216.

explicit connection to the prelate's large-scale and long-awaited Ambrosiana project.[37]

Even before beginning the series, Coppini had devoted considerable thought to the rhetorical use of vocalic sounds, poetic metre, and verbal accent; his undated *Tractatus de elocutione* discusses these matters at some length. Nor is it surprising that the second volume in the series (now lost) was dedicated to Bianca Taverna at S. Marta.[38] Besides eight contrafacta (which do survive in manuscript) in this volume of the Monteverdi works, the other originals included two madrigals by G. P. Cima (source unknown), one by Giovanni Croce (unknown), two by G. P. Flaccomio (unknown), one by Marenzio (from Book I *a* 5), one by Merulo (from RISM 1583[12]), one by Flaminio Tresti (unknown), and four (including a two-part setting) by Giovanelli (Book I *a* 5).[39] The inclusion of Cima, Merulo, and Tresti suggests that local pride was at work in both the dedication and the selections, more so than had been the case in Book I.

Coppini seems to have fashioned some reworkings in the 1608 volume for the dedicatee and her institution. The new text for Giovanelli's *Ardo sì/Ardi e gela*, for instance, begins as *Ardeo in hac flamma/Marta soror*, incipits that suggest the female vocation of following Christ together with the Johannine account of the resurrection of Lazarus (in which his sister Martha figures prominently), thereby neatly referring to all three saints (Martha, the Magdalen, and Lazarus) specially venerated at S. Marta. All these figures would later be commemorated in C. F. Nuvolone's altar-piece for the *chiesa*

---

[37] On the aesthetics of the series, see Kendrick, 'Genres', 423–5 and the forthcoming edition of the Monteverdi contrafacta ed. by A. Blachly and id.

[38] The only surviving printed copy was lost in the 1943 fire at the Ambrosiana. *Pace* Rorke, the early Cinquecento mystical and political tradition at S. Marta was not continuous throughout the century that separates Negri from this print. Likewise, the interpretation of Federigo's *ragionamenti* as ecstasy-inducing speeches at joint 'mystical sessions' between the prelate and the nuns is somewhat off the mark. As noted above (Ch. 3), the *ragionamenti* were sermons at Mass, and their intellectual purpose is to show the reasons (*ragioni*) behind a point of exegesis or doctrine, not to induce ecstasy on the part of their audience.

[39] The dedication is lost, except for the passages transcribed in E. Vogel, *Bibliothek der gedruckten weltlichen Vokalmusik Italiens* (Leipzig, 1892), i. 520. The Monteverdi contrafacta are preserved in the four part-books (the Altus is missing) D-Rp, A.R. 964–84; G. Haberkamp, *Bischöfliche Zentralbibliothek Regensburg: Thematischer Katalog der Musikhandschriften* (Munich, 1989), i. 148. Despite this catalogue, the source of the manuscript, which includes numerous Catholic pieces, was unlikely to have been the Protestant Gymnasium Poeticum, and some of the other contents suggest a date around 1640; my thanks to Steven Saunders for his ideas on this codex.

esteriore noted above.[40] Other pieces also bear monastic stamp; the metamorphosis of Monteverdi's *Ch'io t'ami* recalls Federigo's philosophy of the monastic life and the prelate's predilection for hermits:

> Te sequar Jesu, mea vita,
> per ardua virtutum,
> sic te secuti sunt
> in eremo multi;
> nec timuerunt ire
> inter feras, per duros vepres,
> saxa, et per alpestres montes
> sine lamentis, et pro amore tuo
> tulere omnia sine lamentis.[41]

Coppini's preface to the 1608 volume lauded Monteverdi's Book V highly for its *rappresentativo* settings:

The representational music of Signor Claudio Monteverdi's Fifth Book of madrigals, ruled by the voice's natural expression in moving the *affetti*, influencing our ears with sweetest *maniera*, and making a most pleasant tyranny over our souls, is well worthy of being sung and heard not only (as others have said out of spite) in the meadows and among cattle, but rather in the haunts of the most noble souls, and in royal courts; and it can also serve many as an infallible norm and plan for the harmonious composition of madrigals and canzoni according to the best teaching . . . [42]

The passage is a clear reply to the various criticisms of the Cremonese composer launched by Giovanni Maria Artusi from 1600 to 1608; Coppini backed up his words by including a contrafactum of every single madrigal mentioned (and attacked) by Artusi, spread out over

---

[40] Cf. Santagostino's description in *L'immortalità*, 40–1.

[41] 'Jesus, my life, I shall follow You through the difficulties of virtue, just as so many have followed You in hermitage; nor did they fear to go among beasts, through thorns, rocks, and alpine mountains without complaint, and to suffer everything without complaint for the sake of Your love'; text from the part-books in D-Rp. Cf. Jones, *Federico Borromeo*, 130–5, on Borromeo's fondness for and patronage of pictorial depictions of hermits in rocky landscapes.

[42] 'La Musica rappresentativa del quinto libro de' Madrigali del Sig. Claudio Monteverde regolata dalla naturale espressione della voce humana nel movere gli affetti, influendo con soavissima maniera ne gli orecchi, e per quelli facendosi de gli animi piacevolissima tiranna, è ben degna d'esser cantata, & udita, non già (com' altri per livore disse) ne i pascoli, e trà le mandre; ma ne' ricetti de' più nobili spirti, e nelle regie corti; e può anco servire à molti per infallibile norma, & idea di comporre armonicamente conforme alla legge migliore Madrigali, e Canzoni . . .': 'A benigni Lettori, & intendenti della Musica', cited in Vogel. The references to 'pascoli' and 'mandre' are not to be found in Artusi; they must refer to other criticisms of Monteverdi's 'rustic' style.

the three volumes of the Milanese series. In the controversy, the 1608 foreword was the strongest statement of support for the madrigals in all Italy.[43] Despite the preface, only three of the eight reworkings in this second volume actually came from Book V, and only the second one of these (*O Mirtillo*) had actually been targeted by the Bolognese theorist:

Coppini	Original	Book
Animas eruit	*M'è dolce il penar* (Guarini)	V
Florea serta	*La giovanetta pianta*	III
O dies infelices	*O com'è gran martire* (Guarini)	III
O infelix recessus	*Ah dolente partita* (Guarini)	IV
O mi fili	*O Mirtillo* (Guarini)	V
Praecipitantur	*O primavera* (Guarini)	III
Qui regnas	*Che dar più vi poss'io*	III
Te sequar	*Ch'io t'ami* (Guarini)	V

But *O infelix recessus* gives an idea of Coppini's skills in creating words to match Monteverdi's setting:[44]

Guarini: Ah dolente partita!
Coppini: *O infelix   recessus!*
          ah, fin de la mia vita!
          O deplorande   finis!
          da te parto e non moro? E pur i' provo
          Ergo sumus damnati?   et perferemus
          la pena   de la morte
          poenam aeternae mortis?
          e sento nel partire
          Abite   maledicti
          un vivace morire,
          properate nocentes
          che dá vita al dolore
          ad aeterna   tormenta
          per far che moia immortalmente il core.
          ibi vos rodet   immortalis   vermis.

---

[43] By now it is almost superfluous to point out the combination of religious intent and aesthetic radicalism evident in Coppini's manifesto.

[44] Noteworthy is also the predilection for Guarini among the originals, one shared by Federigo's disciple Borsieri; cf. Pavan, 'La necessità'. Translation: 'O unhappy departure, | o deplorable end! | Thus are we damned? and we bear | the pain of eternal death? | Depart, o cursed, | hasten, you evil ones, | to eternal torments; | there the immortal worm [Satan] will gnaw you.'

The line-up of verbal assonance, syntactical similarity, and parallel meaning is obvious at first glance, and Coppini's skill in imitating not only the meaning but the phonetic content of the poem is remarkable. The most interesting feature of this recasting is that Coppini took his cue for the shift of tone and mood in line 5, not from Guarini's text ('E sento nel partire'), but from Monteverdi's music. For the rhetorical *homoioteleuton* in bar 56, after the *cadenza in mi* on the reciting-tone, is the only complete silence in the madrigal. Coppini seized on Monteverdi's moment of canzonetta-like rhythm and turn towards the pitch centre D ('E sento nel partire') to create a dramatic change in the text. In characteristically optimistic style, the fear of damnation is replaced by the forceful banishment of evil from the world to Hell ('Abite maledicti').[45]

At the same time, the transmutation does not entirely work. 'Ibi vos rodet immortalis vermis', for instance, while conveying the sense of perpetual agony, misses out on Guarini's elegiac tone, a sentiment underlined by Monteverdi's dual motifs of descending perfect versus diminished fourths and agonizingly drawn-out descents from the upper *finalis* in all voices, which never quite adumbrate the entire modal octave ($a'-a$) until the last two statements (Tenor and Alto, bars 90–5). Still, Coppini's achievement should not be underestimated; the contrafacta, consciously designed to mirror both poetic procedures and their musical interpretation, should be considered not as a 'chastened' version of salacious madrigals, but rather as a re-reading, a dramatic reinterpretation in sacred terms of an entire work of art, words and music together. Since Taverna took her vows in February 1608, this collection may have functioned as a belated profession present.[46]

The high-voice monodies written by a famous singer, Claudia Sessa, raise no problems of performance. Her two contributions to the 1613 *Canoro pianto di Maria Vergine sopra la faccia di Christo estinto*

---

[45] Coppini's 'congregational' shift from singular ('Da te parto e non moro', 'Et pur i' provo') to plural number ('Ergo sumus damnati?', 'Et perferemus') should be noted as well. Similarly 'optimistic' themes characterize other reworkings in this volume; *O com'è gran martire* is transformed by Coppini into a consideration of the vanity of human action ('O dies infelices | Sine fructu transactus') and confidence in divine benignity ('Nunc te Deum amabo . . . Qui solus es felicitas aeterna').

[46] All the aesthetic evidence associated with the contrafacta series undercuts the traditional interpretation, in which these pieces served as a 'safe' way to perform great music otherwise censored by an omnipotent Church. Monteverdi's and others' madrigals included in the collection usually call for the standard tessitura of three octaves (*O infelix* spans the range $A–g''$).

(RISM 1613[3]) were settings of texts on the various parts of the Dead Christ's face, written by the prolific Cassinese poet Angelo Grillo (whose secular pseudonym was Livio Celiano).[47] Grillo's Marian meditations employ Marinist methods: word repetitions with transformed meanings, extravagant similes, and unexpected line-lengths. The inclusion of a relatively novice composer, the most famous female monastic singer in northern Italy, in this anthology of musical devotion to the Passion is reminiscent of the long association between female monastic piety and reflection on Christ's suffering.

The longer setting, *Vattene pur, lasciva orrechia humana* (Ex. 8.7), explores a sort of harmonic parallel to Grillo's oxymoronic conceit. For the first two stanzas of this piece on F in *cantus mollis* (Banchieri's tone 11), which consider first vainly ornamented human ears, and then Christ's bleeding ears, cadence on the wrong pitch (B♭) and make prominent use of E♭ as a melodic goal setting the vanity of human adornment ('pomposa', 'sorda'), a note foreign to the mode and one that seems to imply a pitch-centre of B flat.[48] The third section of Sessa's song sets Grillo's ending couplet and the surprise conceit of the poem that Christ's bloody ears are actually 'due vermiglie rose' ('Anzi l'horecchie sue si sanguinose / altro non son che due vermiglie rose'). It employs another prominent E♭ ('si sanguinose') in the couplet's first line; then it switches, with a flurry of *crome* in both bass and voice ('altro non son che due'; a *climax* in Nucius' sense), to the real final of the piece, F.[49] The revelation of the poetic conceit is highlighted by the surprise shift to the real modal centre after the B flat cadences, which had been used for 'pomposa e sorda'; the whole procedure shows a degree of sophistication on the part of a novice composer.

If *Vattene pur* had reflected north Italian song, the ornamentation in *Occhi, io vissi di voi*, the piece on Christ's eyes, seems to reflect

---

[47] On Grillo, see E. Durante and A. Martellotti, *Don Angelo Grillo O.S.B. alias Livio Celiano: Poeta per musica del decimosettimo secolo* (Florence, 1989). Cecchino's *Canti spirituali*, op. 3 (Venice: Vincenti, 1613) also opens with five strophic meditations on various parts of the Dead Christ's body.

[48] At least one cadence seems to bespeak inexperience on Sessa's part. The half-close on 'vermiglie brine' would appear to be some sort of *cadenza sfuggita* on F, in line with the avoidance of F until the last couplet (sect. 3). But on the other hand Sessa seems to have been concerned with finding a melodic rhyme for 'brine' that matched the cadence at 'crine'. The compromise solution is the $g'-f'-g'$ over a static bass c at 'brine', a solution that sounds unusual even by early Seicento standards. For internal pitch goals of the *undecimo tono*, Banchieri, *Cartella musicale*, 134–5.

[49] J. Nucius, *Musices poeticae* (Neisse, 1613).

Ex. 8.7. Sessa, *Vattene pur* (1613)

Florentine styles; Sessa emphasizes phrase endings (not necessarily words; the first melisma is on 'vostra') through passage-work over static basses. Here the central poetic conceit, the oxymoron of 'per far vivace morte al mio martire', is set to a long and dissonant *catabasis* (in Kircher's terms) of the *trilli* that descend from *c″* to *d* over a *supplementum* (Ex. 8.8).[50] Sessa's use of ornamentation for expressive ends recalls Borsieri's posthumous encomium of her vocal technique. She was famous for her *trilli* and *accenti*, and the style of these pieces reflects his comments: 'She died young, at the time when she began to compose those same musical pieces which she then sang on feast-days, which would have increased the perfection of her singing, although she was already a most exceptional singer.'[51]

Ex. 8.8. Sessa, *Occhi, io vissi* (1613), bars 23–31

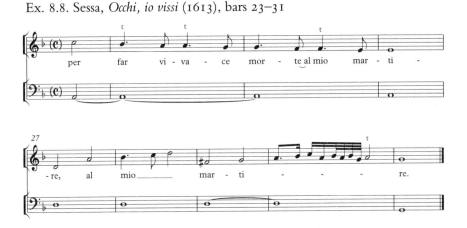

Another example of virtuoso singing, Francesco Rognoni Taeggio's ornamentation examples (from his *Selva di varii passaggi*), are wildly difficult pieces dedicated to two otherwise unknown nuns. *Quanti mercenarii*, divisions for the top line of a contrafactum that had first appeared in Vecchi's popular 1597 first book of motets, was inscribed to Ginepra Crivelli at S. Margarita (its penitential text, exemplifying the Federican theme of personal humility, stems from

---

[50] *Musurgia universalis* (Rome, 1650), bk. VIII, 145.

[51] App. A, Doc. 29: '[Sessa was] pronta, e veloce ne' trilli, affetuosa, e padrona negli accenti, e sopra il tutto così prattica delle altrue compositioni, che poteua chiamarsi in vn tempo stesso musica, e recitatrice . . . È morta giouana, e nel tempo, ch'ella cominciaua a comporre quelle stesse opere musicali, che poi cantaua nelle feste, ciò che hauerebbe accresciuta in lei la perfettione del cantare, benche già fosse cantatrice singolarissima.'

the story of the Prodigal Son, Luke 15: 17–19).[52] In the nature of its graces, Rognoni's treatment of Palestrina's *Io son ferito* mixes late Cinquecento styles of conjunct semi- and demisemiquaver ornamentation ('surgam, et ibo ad patrem meum'; Ex. 8.9) with more modern dotted and leaping figures ('Pater, peccavi').[53] They therefore mark a new kind of improvisatory style, one far less bound to the previous century's conjunct divisions. Rognoni's pedagogical goal is underlined by the notated rubato at several points, one of two kinds in early Seicento theory and practice.[54] This rubato includes a series of unmeasured *semicrome*, probably indicating some sort of *accelerando*, and the anticipation of a structural pitch, found also in Caccini.

But the striking feature of the piece is its outspoken virtuosity: a two-octave tessitura, large leaps, and brilliant cadential formulae, often on exposed high notes ('et ibo'). More subtle goals are also present: breath control ('et dicam ei') and the ability to sustain long, unornamented notes after passage-work ('fac me sicut unum'). The overall range of the piece is remarkable; Rognoni's version displaces the tessitura of the original's cantus part (a tessitura retained in the original Latin contrafactum), which normally cadences on *a′*, up an octave, thus enhancing the virtuoso effect of the piece, for whose audience the original low-lying top part must have been fixed in memory.[55] The extreme difficulty of the example is daunting. But in connection with the other mention of nuns in a pedagogical context, Donati's solo motets, the inscription suggests that Rognoni's versions

[52] Modern edn. in Kendrick, 'Genres', 1034–42. Rognoni's other example is an embellished top line for Mortaro's canzona *La portia* (from the *Primo libro de canzoni* (Venice: Amadino, 1600); modern edn. of the original canzona by J. Ladewig, *Italian Instrumental Music of the Sixteenth and Early Seventeenth Centuries*, xiii (New York, 1988)), dedicated to Gracia Crivelli at the same house. Rognoni's setting of the latter features the rubric 'Modo di Pasegiar con regola naturale al Canto', so apparently both were meant to be sung, one with text, one without.

[53] In order to fit the extra syllables of the biblical text as given by the original contrafactum, Rognoni included several unornamented notes from the altus part ('Et non sum dignus'); this has the rhetorical effect of underlining the *humilitas* of the passage by a sudden turn away from ornamentation. For a modern edition of the ornamented line, see R. Erig and V. Gutmann (eds.), *Italienische Diminutionen: Die zwischen 1553 und 1638 mehrmals bearbeiteten Sätze* (Zürich, 1979), 252–68.

[54] R. Greenlee, 'Singing *dopo il tatto*: Zacconi's Tempo Rubato and *Sprezzatura*', in *Abstracts of Papers Read at the 58th Annual Meeting of the American Musicological Society, 4–8 November 1992*, 12–13, which notes Zacconi's distinction between tempo rubato (singing before or after the beat in an unchanging *tactus*) and actually changing tempo.

[55] Ironically (perhaps intentionally so), the Prodigal Son's humble plea for forgiveness is set to one of the most elaborate and outlandish examples of ornamentation in any of the didactic literature.

Ex. 8.9. F. Rognoni/Palestrina, *Quanti mercenarii* (1620), bars 39–56

were meant to serve, not as discrete compositions in their own right, but as models whose decoration could be applied to other pieces in the kinds of solo singing expected in the most famous and patrician institutions, such as S. Margarita.[56]

If the Cinquecento-style polyphony dedicated to nuns had ranged from highly functional to highly artistic, the Milanese concerto repertory beginning in 1605 would focus attention on solo singing and technical abilities.[57] But G. B. Stefanini's St Margaret motet half a generation before Rognoni, *Ave sancta virgo Margarita*, shows in its opening imitative period the real links between tricinium style and the new concerto (Ex. 8.10). Though the text is that of an antiphon, the music is set out in a form familiar from the late Cinquecento: ABB, with a short coda and with the upper two voices reversed in the repeat.[58] The possibilities for a new approach to texts are evident in this piece; as his motets of 1604 show, Stefanini was perfectly capable of large-scale imitative polyphony. The advantages of the new style lay in the heightened contrast between motifs setting short syntactical units ('Ave sancta virgo' versus the homophony of 'ne dedigneris'), the full cadences and rhythmic halts designed to set off new ideas ('gloriosa coruscas in caelis'), and even the subtle references to the opening point of imitation in the coda (a case of rhetorical *epanadiplosis*).[59] One final point is a new delight in sheer texture and timbre: the upper lines that weave in and out around the top of the modal range (g''; Banchieri's mode 1 transposed up a fourth for high instruments) and the ethereal sonorities of the opening.[60] When three Benedictines sang this piece, the result must have been enrapturing and the sonic effect, with all the cadences on the high g'', 'angelic'.

[56] Donati's pieces are not technically on the level of Rognoni's examples, although they by no means eschew difficulty. The difference may be that the solo motets were meant for the instruction of relative beginners, while the *Selva de varii passaggi* pieces were meant for advanced singers.

[57] On the problems of the traditional Viadana-centred historiography of the genre, and for a consideration of the early Milanese background, see Kendrick, 'Genres', 435–9.

[58] The form would have been familiar from such six-voice pieces as Merulo's *O Rex gentium* (from *Il primo libro de motetti a sei voci* (Venice: Gardano, 1583; repr. Milan: Tini, 1586; mod. edn. by J. Bastian in Merulo, *Musica sacra*, iv (Neuhausen, 1977), 58–62), or Lassus's apparently late *Fratres nescitis* (*Cantiones sacrae a 6* (Graz, 1594); ed. F. X. Haberl, *Sämmtliche Werke* xv, (Lepizig, 1903), 95–7). Noteworthy is Stefanini's expansion of both the B section ('ne dedigneris') and the coda relative to the Cinquecento models.

[59] M. Vogt, *Conclave thesauri magnae artis musicae* (Prague, 1719), 150.

[60] As with most of the high-clef pieces discussed henceforth in this chapter, the organ part is printed a fourth lower, at Banchieri's 'tuono per voci'; *Cartella musicale*, 113.

Ex. 8.10. Stefanini, *Ave sancta virgo Margarita* (1606), bars 1–10

Stefanini's and Girolamo Baglioni's settings of *Triumphant sancti* afford interesting points of comparison in the light of their composers' common employer and the temporal proximity of their origin: the pieces share a common *tono* (Banchieri's second) and scoring (CT). Stefanini's approach took the mode and incipit of the Ambrosian chant antiphon as the basis for its initial idea (Ex. 8.11), while Baglioni's melodic motifs were freer, more soloistic, and more aimed at the expression of a single word (*hypallage*, or free inversion for the two settings of 'mortem'; Ex. 8.12).[61] Structurally, Stefanini placed the major internal cadence at 'decreverunt suscipere | et cum sancto Mauritio' on D, while Baglioni's is on G. The approach to this caesura and to the final cadence highlights another point of divergence: Stefanini's preference for gradually increasing contra-

---

[61] Burmeister, *Musica poetica*, 58.

Ex. 8.11. *Triumphant sancti*: (a) Ambrosian chant incipit; (b) Stefanini (1606), bars 1–16

puntal texture contrasts markedly with Baglioni's use of solos rounded off by homophonic declamation in both voices.

The latter procedures—simpler textures, exact repetition—also characterize Baglioni's four-voice (CATB) motet for St Maurice, *Gaudeamus omnes . . . beati Mauritii*, which repeats the motifs for each syntactical unit of text, first in CA, then in TB, the most florid being

Ex. 8.12. Baglioni, *Triumphant sancti* (1608), bars 33–61

reserved for 'gaudent Angeli' (Ex. 8.13), another reference to the motet's singers. Here again, emphasis comes by homophony: the tuttis for the opening triple-time 'Gaudeamus', the demarcation of the second section ('de cuius solemnitate'), the contrast of 'laetantur

Ex. 8.13. Baglioni, *Gaudeamus omnes* (1608), bars 81–94

Archangeli', and the closing *supplementum* on the *finalis* in the canto.

Two concertos explicitly inscribed to a nun (Paola Serbellona) feature in the next major single-composer concerto collection, G. P. Cima's 1610 *Concerti ecclesiastici.*[62] Both show the earmarks of the early style: slow declamation, well-defined phrases that cadence on important modal degrees, and modest overall length. Both are echo motets, of a kind best known from Monteverdi's *Audi coelum* (1610). In light of the canticle's centrality to Federigo's thought, it is no surprise that the first of these pieces is a Song of Songs setting, *Surge propera* (text from 2: 10 and 14). Cima picked a passage that played off both the singer (dedicatee) and the genre of the piece, and the text uses two discontinuous canticle verses, not the normal selection of 2: 10–12 or 10–13. In these verses, the speaker is the male spouse of the canticle, inviting his beloved (in Federigo's exegesis this meant polyvalently the individual soul and the individual nun) to come, for her voice is sweet and she is fair ('vox enim tua dulcis, et facies tua decora'). This had a dual contemporary interpretation: the invitation directed the Christian to imitate the suffering Christ, and the nun in particular to accept her (in daily reality, not necessarily desired) vocation.[63]

At least one Benedictine, in a letter to the archbishop, quoted this passage as a mark of her desire to follow Christ (while reversing the canticle's speakers): 'On St Catherine of Siena's feast-day, after Communion, I prayed Him [Christ] to do His will in me, saying that canzonetta of the female spouse, *Sonet vox tua in auribus meis, vox enim tua dulcis.*'[64] In Borromeo's 'optimistic' view of the individual, the beauty of the canticle's beloved was interpreted as the intrinsic attractiveness of the soul (this latter symbolized by the canticle's

---

[62] This is probably the best-known Milanese print of the whole century, on the basis (ironically) of its sonatas.

[63] The 12th-c. canticle interpretation of Bernard of Clairvaux (Sermo LXI) refers to the image of the dove in the cleft rock as a symbol for the soul seeking refuge in the gaping wounds of Christ; see Matter, *The Voice*, 137. Cima's piece uses only the biblical text with its implied references; later repertory would make the description of Christ's wounds as a source of rest and nourishment far more graphic and explicit.

[64] Laura Maria Cotta at S. Maria del Lentasio to Federigo, undated, BA, G. 265 *inf.*, no. 47, fo. 129ʳ: 'il giorno di S. Caterina di Siena dopo la *Santissi*ma Comunione pregandolo [Christ] che si degnesse di fare sua voluntà in me, et dicendo quela Canzonetta della Sposa cioè *sonet vox tua in auribus meis, vox enim tua dulcis*'. Again, the Eucharistic association of Cotta's thoughts should be noted.

spouse). In the case of female religious, this 'spiritual beauty' was underscored by the special value he placed on the status of nuns.

So this was a highly appropriate piece to dedicate to a nun. But another conceit points up why the piece should have been inscribed to a monastic singer. For this is almost the only passage referring to auditory perception ('sonet vox tua in auribus meis │ vox enim tua dulcis') in the canticle, which is otherwise filled with references to sight and touch. In this sense, the passage becomes an epitome of nuns' singing ('sonet vox tua', i.e. let Serbellona's voice resound).[65] The text thus has a musically referential meaning: nuns' singing as a metaphor for the intrinsic and divinely created goodness of the world.[66]

But the conceits work on the level of genre, as well. For the echo features of the motet (possibly chosen for more prosaic reasons; cf. below) derive from the physical setting of the verses among rocks and caverns ('in foraminibus petrae, in caverna maceriae'). The classical legend of Echo had referred to the lonely caves in which she went to dwell after her rejection by Narcissus.[67] The entire semantic field of association—rocks, Christ's Passion, song, and the canticle passage—would recur within three years as the virtuoso peroration to Marino's *Diceria sacra seconda: La musica*, the poet's effort to prove the musicality of the Passion and Redemption.[68]

---

[65] A letter from Federigo to Confaloniera invoked precisely this passage as a cure for spiritual aridity manifested through music: 'Nell'ultima vostra mi dite, che le voci delle Monache vi paivano roche, e rozze, e dure, e ingrate all'orecchio. Solo credo, et voglio, che consideriate per confirmatione di ciò che nella Cantica è scritto, et è una bella cosa, La sposa che nella Cantica era dimostrata sotto la figura di una Pastorella ragionando col suo Sposo . . . [che] le disse . . . Sonet vox tua in auribus meis' (BA, G. 26 *inf.*, letter no. 38). Shortly after the publication of Cima's motet, Francis de Sales's report on the singing that he heard at an unnamed Milanese female monastery in April 1613 again cited this canticle verse as a prooftext for divine praise; *Traité de l'Amour de Dieu*, bk. 5, ch. 11 (mod. edn. in *Œuvres*, ed. A. Ravier (Paris, 1969), 597 and 1733).

[66] Lampugnani would also recall this passage in a musical and spiritual context in his account of Radegund as ideal bride of Christ (and thus as nun), typically reversing the literary speakers: 'Hora m'auueggo, qual si fusse il canto, del quale egli tanto spasimaua nella Cantica, fino a chiedere alla sposa, che cantasse *Fac me audire vocem suam*. Diceva egli: *Sonet vox tua in auribus meis. Vox enim tua dulcis*. Come dir volesse: Vn cuore, . . . per essere per amore mio, tutto cordato nell'altrui volere . . . fà si dolce harmonia alle mie orecchie, che, ne la più gustosa, ne la più cara, io posso hauere' (*Della vita*, 41).

[67] '[Echo] Spreta latet silvis pudibundaque frondibus ora │ protegit et solis ex illo vivit in antris': Ovid, *Metamorphoses*, iii. 393–4.

[68] 'E sicome la voce è stromento con cui si palesa e publica l'interno concetto dell'animo, così Cristo è mezo, per cui si communica a noi la paterna volontà . . . E finalmente, se Eco abita nelle concavità de' sassi e nelle profondità delle grotte, ecco la pietra incavata: *petra*

Cima's setting in the optimistic eighth mode relies largely on harmonically closed phrases (extended by the echos in Cantus II).[69] The
only use of imitation in the piece (bars 1–2) starts off the period, but
the rest of the piece works by phrases that explore hexachords over
a slower-moving bass. The first invitation ('Surge propera') is
rounded off on the *finalis* (b. 18); its adumbrations of direct address
'speciosa mea . . . colomba mea' traverse A and D (bars 22 and 31)
and are returned to G (b. 34). The setting of the new canticle verse
(2: 14) explores the reciting-tone of the mode, with conjoined
phrases for 'ostende mihi faciem tuam' (bars 44, 55). The key phrase
'sonet vox tua' is the first to explore the entire tessitura of the mode
(bars 55–65); Cima gives its complement 'vox enim dulcis' (again,
referring to the individual soul in contemporary exegesis) the standard expressive gesture of a cadential note sharpened and harmo-
nized by a descending third, a *mutatio toni* (bars 66–70; Ex. 8.14). This
raises a pitch outside the normal *musica ficta* accidentals to be found
in this mode, namely the *finalis* G. From bars 65 to 80, Cima tele-
scopes the same series of cadences (A, D, C) on successively more
important modal degrees (first found in the bars 22–34 period), allot-
ting the first two to one member of the parallelism ('vox enim dulcis') and the reciting-tone of the mode to the second ('et facies tua
decora'); this compression lends rhetorical emphasis to the key
phrase of the text, the one that combines the 'sweetness of voice'
with the 'physical beauty' of the canticle's female spouse. The extension of the final phrase (the only one set for both cantus parts) then
returns to the *finalis*, not without an unusual cadence (unresolved tri-
tone), due to the mode.

Despite the effects, to all intents and purposes these are solo
motets; the genre is less common in the early Milanese concerto
repertory than is the duet. But the occasional second voice in the
two echo motets dedicated to Serbellona formally sidestepped the
curial prohibitions against nuns' solo performance, while showing

autem erat Christus; ecco le spelonche profonde: *in foraminibus petrae et in caverna maceriae'*,
from G. B. Marino, *La musica: Diceria seconda sopra le sette parole dette da Cristo in croce*, in
Dicerie sacre e La strage de gl'innocenti, ed. G. Pozzi (Turin, 1960), 330–1. Novati's canticle
exegesis also linked the clefts of the rocks to the Passion and the Eucharist; *Eucharistici amores*,
254.
   [69] Modern edn. in Kendrick, 'Genres', 1023–30. I return to the modal descriptions of
Angleria, *La regola*, 80–5; this treatise was dedicated to Cima. On the affectual associations
of the modes, see Meier, *Die Tonarten*, 369–87. Among others, G. Zarlino, *Istitutioni har-
moniche* (Venice, 1573), bk. IV, chs. 18–29, characterized mode 8 as happy without 'lascivia'.

Ex. 8.14. G. P. Cima, *Surge propera* (1610), bars 66–75

off a singer's vocal abilities. Despite the subterfuge, in other respects these pieces conformed to Federigo's ideas: optimistic or meditative texts to relatively simple, syntactically clear music. The consolidation of the concerto in Milan would be accompanied by an increasing number of dedications to nuns, works whose aesthetics began to stretch these principles.

The initial pieces, however, reflect not a sudden flood, but a gradual increase.[70] Meanwhile, the solo motet had begun to develop its own generic traditions: freer text selection, more adventurous approaches to dissonance treatment, greater emphasis on sheer vocal display, and a propensity for abstract musical design. Vincenzo Pellegrini's *Tortus certamina* for S. Erasmo displays these characteristics: vocal writing found nowhere besides the ornamentation treatises (Ex. 8.15); quirky sequences involving unusual dissonances (bars

[70] Andrea Cima's 1614 *O domine Jesu Christi*, addressed to Giovanna Canevesa at S. Chiara, seems, on the basis of its one surviving voice, to show a slightly more florid style than his brother's 1610 print. Francesco Robbiano's *Congratulamini mihi omnes* (1616), inscribed to an Ambrosian Hermitess cousin at the Sacro Monte of Varese, is also a simple, sectionalized piece.

Ex. 8.15. Pellegrini, *Tortus certamina* (1619), bars 31–79

Ex. 8.15. *cont.*

40–3); and a final 'alleluia' section that explores the entire vocal tessitura of the piece in different rhythmic guises. If this motet is meant as a notated version of song at the Humiliate house, the technical capabilities of the sisters must have been remarkable. Still, the syntactic norms of the concerto *a 2* are at work: subtle recalls of the closing of the opening section (bars 26–9 vs. 76–9), the separation of verbal units by vocal rests and bass-line motion, and the remarkable (and rhetorically heightened upon repetition) highlighting of 'Benedictus Deus qui dedit illi victoriam gloriosam' by rhythmic augmentation and a return to the previous modal centre. Such procedures, along with the vocal writing, recall Rognoni's *Quanti mercenarii*, suggesting again that the interplay of styles was more complex than has been assumed.

Still, the early dedications are largely of a more typical genre: the concerto *a 2*. Around 1620, these pieces began to employ more marked melodic contrast; triple-time sections grew from interjections to stable areas in their own right. The almost innately sectionalized genre of the dialogue evinced a notable gain in popularity. Many of these traits are reflected in the concertos of the 1620s addressed to nuns. Indeed, the inscriptions around this time may even point to female religious' role in the increased popularity of the duet.[71]

Francesco Bellazzi's 1622 *Vox dilecti mei* (CC or TT), inscribed to

[71] Even in the hinterland, for instance, the only two high-voice duets in Fontana Morello's 1614 *Primo libro* have connections with nuns.

two Orrigoni relatives (one the organist) at S. Martino in Varese, uses the now-familiar Song of Songs tags referring to nuns' Spouse,[72] while his *Missus est Angelus* (CAT) is a straightforward Annunciation scene, again setting the words of the angel quite literally in the mouths of their terrestrial representatives, female monastic singers. The musical style of *Vox dilecti* is still very much that of the previous decade: long, well-defined melodic arches; reliance on the final of the *tono* (Banchieri's mode 2 again); and a final climax ('amica mea'), here provided by the closer imitation in the voices (Ex. 8.16; bars 59–65).[73] Michelangelo Grancini's *O anima sanctissima* (1628) shows the extension of the form.[74] Grammatical clauses are allotted melodic motifs, then worked out in sequence before cadencing in passages of

Ex. 8.16. Bellazzi, *Vox dilecti mei* (1622), bars 55–65

---

[72] 'Vox dilecti mei; ecce iste venit saliens in montibus, transiliens colles, en dilectus meus loquitur mihi: surge propera amica mea et veni.'

[73] One other trait which this kind of concerto shares with the *stile antico* repertory is the local modulation away from the *finalis* only in the last few melodic periods.

[74] This piece is scored for canto and alto, not the most common combination in the early Milanese two-voice concerto; Grancini's motet suits a monastery with only a few singers of different voice-ranges, a foundation like S. Orsola, where its dedicatee, Clara Virginia Preda, was organist.

parallel thirds; the composer's penchant for the exact (almost obsessive) sequential repetition of motifs is also much in evidence in this motet. Andrea Cima's second book of 1627 shares this extended length.[75] But the structural procedures are essentially unchanged from his brother's 1610 book.

Nuns' singing skills are on display in one concerto from Cima's book, *Vocem Mariae*, whose text is a piece for the Visitation, paraphrasing Elizabeth's salutation of Mary (Luke 1: 41–2). The inscription to Anna Tetoni and a 'Sor Giramma' at S. Bernardo would also make sense if the singers were kinswomen; the Gospel passage recounts the meeting of the two relatives Elizabeth and Mary. The feast-day was yet another aspect of late medieval female piety to re-emerge in the Seicento.[76] And Cima's motet adds introductory text to the Gospel account, so as to stress the auditory and vocal aspects of the encounter:

Vocem Mariae audivit Elisabeth et factum est ut audivit salutationem, exultavit infans in utero, et repleta est de Spiritu Sancto et voce magna exclamavit et dixit: Benedicta tu inter mulieres, et benedictus fructus ventris tui, alleluia.[77]

This CA duet is generated by its melismas, starting with a long triple-time section for 'exultavit infans in utero *e*-ius', appropriately declamatory ornaments for 'exclamavit, et dixit', and a fivefold repetition of 'benedicta tua inter mulieres' (Ex. 8.17). In this penultimate section, Cima's extension of the early concerto's procedures is clearly on display: the inversion of the scalar idea between 'benedicta tu inter mulieres' and 'et benedictus fructus ventris tui' is then capped off by the long duet melisma on 'tui', and the interplay of these sets the sweetness of 'blessed is the fruit of your womb'. The overlapping voices, sequential entrances on unexpected pitch-levels, and dissonances (seconds, ninths, sevenths) that resolve upwards had already been theoretically justified by Angleria's *La regola del contraponto* of 1622; again the effect as sung by the dedicatees, with interweaving voice-crossings, must have been 'heavenly'. The

---

[75] *Secondo libro delli concerti ecclesiastici* (Milan: Rolla, 1627).

[76] On the vicissitudes of its popularity, and its centrality in female devotion, see G. Zarri, 'Dalla profezia alla disciplina (1450–1650)', in Scaraffia and Zarri (eds.), *Donna e fede*, 177–226 at 188.

[77] '*Elizabeth heard the voice of Mary*, and when she heard her greeting, the infant in her womb rejoiced, and she was filled with the Holy Spirit, and in a loud voice she cried out and said: Blessed are you among women . . .'.

Ex. 8.17. A. Cima, *Vocem Mariae* (1627), bars 84–115

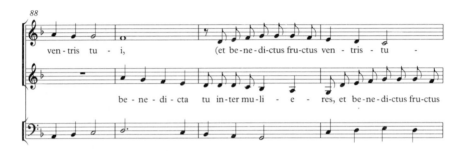

Ex. 8.17. *cont.*

concluding 'alleluia' features dotted upward scalar motion, a recurring sign of closure, and further chains of sixteenth-notes in both voices. Still, the concerto remains strongly anchored to its *tono* (Banchieri's mode 2) throughout its interior cadences. This work is one of only two double dedications in the entire Milanese concerto repertory.

Two remarkable but incomplete pieces from the very end of Federigo's tenure complete this conspectus of the early sacred concerto seen through the prism of dedications to nuns. Egidio Trabattone's *In te Domine speravi* (*Il terzo libro de concerti a 1–4*, 1632) was dedicated to Antonia Carcana at S. Antonino in Varese and is scored for four sopranos, a unique combination in any Milanese print of the time.[78] Although only three of the voice parts (and no continuo) survive, the general style is clear: four equal parts, written in imitation, with each textual phrase allotted a contrasting motif.[79] On the other hand, Grancini's *Adjuro vos, filiae Hierusalem* (1631), for the Fissiraghi sisters at S. Marta, takes its puzzling text from the Song of Songs (5: 8; 7: 1; free references to 7: 12):

Adjuro vos, filiae Hierusalem, si inveneritis dilectum meum, ut nuncietis ei quia amore langueo. | Quam pulchri sunt filii principis | Et sicut dies verni circundabant flores rosarum.[80]

The opening is a favourite tag from the canticle, used repeatedly in Federigo's letters to nuns as a key phrase for the invocation of divine love; its omnipresence in the Milanese (and other) concerto repertory seems to result from its functional reference to the individual soul's search for Christ.[81] For 'Adjuro vos' is drawn from the section

---

[78] Male (boy or castrato) sopranos were at a premium; many of the transposition adjustments, and the need for *voci pari* pieces, stem from this fact. The situation could only have been worse in Varese, where Trabattone worked. In general, small-scale concertos with more than two sopranos (except for special cases like the Duomo, evident in Grancini's *Tre pueri* for CCC, 1636 *Concerti ecclesiastici*) were either transposed down or probably performed in female monasteries.

[79] The scoring is similar to that of Massenzio's op. 10 motets, another late echo of the *voci pari* tradition. Trabattone also used a rhythmic cliché for his treatment of 'In te Domine speravi; non confundar in aeternum'; the durational values of this phrase are almost identical with, but slightly more square than, those of Schütz's setting in *Symphoniae sacrae* I (1629).

[80] 'I adjure you, daughters of Jerusalem, if you should find my beloved, tell him I droop for love. How handsome are the prince's sons. And like a spring day flowering roses surrounded [them].'

[81] To pick only a number of settings during Federigo's tenure: Baglioni, *Sacrae cantiones* (1608); G. P. Cima, *Concerti ecclesiastici* (1610); F. Beccari, *Sacrae concerti*, bk. 2 (Tradate, 1611; as a dialogue scored SSAT); Biumi, *Concentus musicales* (Rolla, 1629).

of the canticle that represents the nadir of the female spouse's (sc. the soul's or the nun's) quest for her beloved (sc. Christ), after the watchmen have found and beaten her, like the state of spiritual aridity in which nuns often found themselves.

But the other two sections of the motet text point to other canticle references: the beauty of the male Spouse, and the Garden of Earthly Delights in which the spouses' love would be consummated (sc. the union of the soul with Christ).[82] This emphasis on creation's goodness symbolized in flowers gave rise to an entire category of sanctoral, Eucharistic, or Marian motet texts that invoked such imagery ('Florete flores'). A similar final phrase had been set in Rusca's *Veni sponsa Christi* for St Catherine, published a year earlier, as the final crowning of the virgin martyr. Thus, the only way in which the entire text makes sense is as a reference to nuns' love for Christ in His beauty, a reminder of female monastic vocation, as in Federigo's letter to Confaloniera: 'or, speaking even more openly, you would say of [Christ's] love: *Adiuro vos filiae Hierusalem*'.[83] It served to remind S. Marta's warring factions of their common status, or perhaps to reward the dedicatees for their virtuous behaviour.

Grancini's set-up was unusual as well. There were almost no *concertato* seven-voice motets in the entire local repertory, and the extremely high scoring of all parts was likewise uncommon. Although there is no 'Alla Quinta bassa' rubric, still the organ part is again printed a fifth below, implying transposition down in most institutions except female monasteries.[84] The first textual fragment ('Adjuro . . . quia amore langueo') is set to two pairs of motifs, each member of which is run against the other in double counterpoint (Ex. 8.18). The pairs are separated by a firm cadence on the *finalis*

[82] 'Mane surgamus ad vineas; Videamus si floruit vinea, Si flores fructus parturiunt, Si floruerunt mala punica', Cant. 7: 12; the floral references recall Federigo's optimistic appreciation of the natural world. He catalysed the creation of the pictorial genre of the Madonna and Child inside a floral still life through his encouragement of Jan Brueghel the Elder's paintings on this theme, and floral imagery suffused his interpretations of the Song of Songs; on the former, see Jones, *Federico Borromeo*, 84–6. For the connection between the canticle (especially the garden mentioned therein) and its symbolic floral representation, Borromeo, *De christianae mentis jocunditate*, Bk. II, ch. xi, 'De Libris Canticorum', which interprets the garden as the goodness of creation; this is reflected in such paintings as Brueghel's *The Element of Earth* (Paris, Louvre; cf. Jones, *Federico Borromeo*, 79–80).

[83] 'overo parlando ancora più apertamente constretta direste, dall'amore: Adiuro vos filiae Hierusalem . . .'.

[84] 'Basso per l'Organo' with one flat, with *finalis* on C; voice-parts with no flats on G. Down a fifth, the cleffing would be suitable for institutions with male singers: C2/C2/C4/F3/F4 (surviving parts only).

Ex. 8.18. Grancini, *Adjuro vos, filiae Jerusalem* (1631), bars 34–50

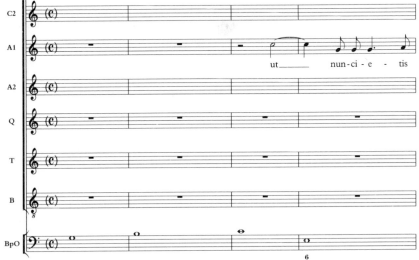

Ex. 8.18. *cont.*

('dilectum meum'). The next idea, 'Quam pulchri sunt filii Principis', is set to a quick interior triple-time section; and the three ideas in the final section ('sicut dies', 'circundabant', 'et lilia convallium') each receive separate motifs which are not run against each other. The piece closes with a long *supplementum* in Canto I. The surviving voices are also clearly differentiated in complexity; the Canto Primo and Alto Primo parts are allotted longer phrases, more dramatic entrances (the high g'' of the Canto I statements of 'Adjuro vos'), and more extended counterpoint. If this piece reflects the capabilities of S. Marta's junior choir, the ensemble would seem to have consisted of three or four polished singers, with less experienced voices on the other parts; possibly the harder (or higher) lines were intended for the two Fissiraghi sisters.[85] *Adjuro vos* forms a fitting conclusion to this repertory, typical of the entire collection in which it appears.[86]

Many of these features of the 1620s are reflected in the surviving works from Rusca's *Sacri concerti*.[87] Owing to Ghedini's taste or preferences, the vocal and instrumental orchestrations of Jesinghaus's transcriptions include probably less than half the original, fairly sizeable edition. Missing are all the four-voice psalms (probably at least five items, in the light of the breviary) and concertos, the eight-voice falsobordoni and *Gloria Patri*, and all but one each of the *a 2* and *a 3* pieces. Still, the solo motets, the two small-scale concertos, and the two eight-voice pieces afford a remarkable, if partial, view of one sister's musical world and of S. Caterina in Brera's repertory.

The larger-scale works include one generic motet, *Omnes gentes* (Ps. 46: 2–3) and the Magnificat. The former is a straightforward antiphonal piece with solos ('Jubilate Deo') and duets ('Quoniam Dominus excelsus'), and again a series of textural (tutti) refrains. The Magnificat is a more ambitious piece; still very much in *quinto tono* (F with one flat; Banchieri's mode 11, pitched at the level 'per voci puerili'), and containing some paraphrases of the psalm tone in the

[85] The missing parts—Canto II and Alto II—open the piece and provide some of the missing counterpoint and 4–3 suspensions at cadences; Grancini's formulaic style renders a reconstruction less speculative than would appear at first glance.

[86] On the *Sacri fiori concertati* as a collection that sums up the spiritual and musical trends of Federigo's last years, as well as a stylistic point to which Grancini was never to return, see Kendrick, *Music in Federigo Borromeo's Milan*.

[87] On the source problems, see above, Ch. 3; for the 'de-transcriptions' of Ghedini's manuscript scores, the reconstruction of the original edition, and other source problems, see Wasmer and Kendrick, Rusca, *Sacri concerti*.

two canto parts, it provides a changing array of scorings, with some unexpected and effective tutti entrances (paradoxically on 'dimisit inanes').[88]

The first solo (T1) provides a short example of Rusca's melodic lines; the first phrase ('Et exultavit') explores first the modal species of fifth (*f–c′*), then the fourth (*c′–f′*), then combines the two ('in Deo salutari') with the characteristic dotted rhythms of the 1620s (Ex. 8.19). Several solos ('qui potens est') begin by citing the psalm tone but then go in rather different directions. Several of the duet sections are simple but effective ('Quia fecit mihi magna', Ex. 8.20); Rusca evidently had talent in crafting her lines for relatively novice singers (like Angela Confaloniera) at S. Caterina. The rhetorical emphasis in this setting is given by the variably scored repetitions of 'omnes generationes' and 'misericordiae suae', perhaps an idea of what some Humiliate considered important in this standard text, recited every day. And here we might even approach Confaloniera's ideas of what

Ex. 8.19. Rusca, Magnificat (1630), bars 8–23

---

[88] There are several changes relative to the Vulgate text (or for that matter, that of the Humiliate breviary).

Ex. 8.20. Rusca, Magnificat (1630), bars 58–68

constituted 'musica spirituale': not simple or clear music *per se*, but settings that highlighted the values guiding their lives.

The two concertos *a 2* contrast strongly. *Gaudete gaudio magno* sets a non-breviary text for the duplex Common of Several Martyrs, scored for two canti and beginning with an instrumental part (probably violin, in the light of Confaloniera's references and some similar pieces in the local repertory); this latter is a standard seventh-mode canzona opening (Ex. 8.21).[89] The vocal lines are simple, and the instrumental opening recurs thrice, twice to mark off new textual sections, and once as a tutti da capo at the end. The structure is essentially unchanged from Gallo's 1598 motets that use a canzona as an internal marker for phrases, again similar to patrician music that Rusca might have heard in her youth.

[89] The canzona references mark it as more indebted to the styles of the 1610s than Grancini's 1631 *Quid est quod dilectus meus*, a Song of Songs dialogue scored for CB and violin. The most likely occasion for its performance was a feast of local martyrs (SS Gervasius and Protasius, or SS Naborius and Felicius).

Ex. 8.21. Rusca, *Gaudete gaudio magno* (1630), bars 1–15

Jesu, dulcis amor meus (CC) is an entirely different kind of piece. Its text, written in fluctuating line-lengths, uses late medieval language in its Christological meditation:

Jesu, dulcis amor meus, alleluia, ego amor tuus; praebe mihi ergo cor tuum. O bone Jesu, tu toto tum mihi dedisti . . .[90]

The intensity of the text moved Rusca to the employment of the solo motet's language: difficult ornamentation (another sign of the more ample space for *passaggi* in Federigo's later years), and an opening melodic phrase that changes hexachords twice in its first five bars (Ex. 8.22). This opening phrase returns (set for both voices) at 'O

Ex. 8.22. Rusca, *Jesu, dulcis amor meus* (1630), bars 1–14

[90] 'Jesus, my sweet love, alleluia, I am your love; grant me then your heart. O good Jesus, you gave [yourself] to me *in toto* . . .'. A setting of a similar text was inscribed to the two Arconati sisters (one monastic, one not [yet?]) by Andrea Cima in 1627: 'O Jesu mi

dulcissime Jesu'. Yet the essential optimism of the text is captured in the final 'alleluia', occupying the last quarter of the motet, with ever-tighter imitation between the two voices, descending, rising, then descending to the final (F) with the dotted figures as a sign of internal closure.

Most if not all the motets *a 1* have been preserved, owing to Ghedini's predilection for rescorings for solo voice with orchestra.[91] The texts of *Consolamini popule meus* and *Exultate caeli* recall the spirit—and the texts—of Confaloniera's Christmas *matinata* (see Ch. 3):

Consolamini popule meus, loquimini ad cor Jerusalem, et advocate eum, quoniam Verbum caro factum est. Annunciate ei, quoniam audita est vox angelorum dicentium: Gloria in excelsis Deo, alleluia.[92]

Exultate caeli, plaudite gentes, jubilate populi, cantate Angeli in cimbalis et organis . . .[93]

Certainly the former ends like the *versetti* sung by the Humiliate as described by Confaloniera, and this kind of motet that functions as a long *introduzione* to a hymn-like final section will recur in later repertory. Yet the symbolic resonance of the texts was greater: both the exegetical meanings of Jerusalem and the invocation of singing angels would have reminded S. Caterina's performers of their own special place in the allegorical system of Federigo's Milan. Indeed, the optimism of *Consolamini popule meus* reversed the spirit of the second Matins lesson for Christmas (from Isa. 40: 1 ff.), used in all breviaries, including the Humiliate's, replacing the liturgical call to penance with a literal musical enactment of the angels' song, performed by those singers who, in their own and others' eyes and ears, actually *were* terrestrial angels.

dulcissime, humiliter te oro, ut cor meum ures amore tuo; fac, dulcissime Jesu, ut tibi solo nunc et semper intendam, ut me ad te perducas; dissolve me, mi Jesu, et me ad te perducas, ut canticis et organis laudare te possim in regno tuo, alleluia', another motet referring to singing.

[91] Most concerto editions of the 1620s contained far more duets than solo pieces; on this point, and for the two traditional but interesting canzonas, Wasmer and Kendrick, Rusca, *Sacri concerti.*

[92] 'Comfort ye, my people; speak to Jerusalem, and tell her that the Word has become flesh. Tell her that the voice of the angels has been heard saying: Gloria in excelsis Deo, alleluia.' In her teens, Rusca could have heard Gabussi's setting of a similar text (without the singing angels, another female monastic feature) *a 2* from the 1608 *Concerti de' diversi*: 'Consolamini popule meus et exultate: Hodie Christus natus est, gaudete con laetitia.'

[93] 'Rejoice, heavens; clap, ye nations; be jubilant, ye peoples; sing, ye Angels with cymbals and organs . . .'.

The two St Catherine motets, *Veni sponsa Christi* and *Tu, filia Dei*, are both scored for canto solo, but without the virtuosity evident in some other contemporary solo motets. As noted above (Ch. 5), the former employs a cento from the Office, whose familiar sources are reflected in the musical setting.[94]

In contrast, the latter uses the style and vocabulary of a sequence:

> Decora Jesum sequeris,
> hymnosque dulces personas,
> reddis vota Altissimo,
> in saeculorum saecula
> semper cantas: Alleluia.[95]

Veni sponsa Christi is a relatively simple piece, with obvious rhetorical devices (a *corona* for 'accipe coronam'; Ex. 8.23). But in *Tu, filia Dei*, other traits of the solo motet are present: freer dissonance treatment and greater motivic interplay between voice and continuo, which generates phrases ('tu rosa martyrum' and 'in saeculorum saecula'). The closing 'alleluia' is linked to its preceding verb 'cantas'. Yet the most telling and unusual text is the motet that possibly opened the collection: one that invoked Mary not only as the inspiration for one nun's music, but even as the very instruments of sound itself:

Ex. 8.23. Rusca, *Veni sponsa Christi* (1630), bars 28–37

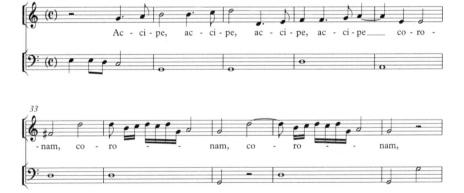

---

[94] No other text honouring the Alexandrine saint had been set in the urban repertory since Vicentino's *Ave virginum gemma Catharina* back in 1571.

[95] 'Beautiful, you follow Jesus; you make sweet hymns resound; you make your vows to the Most High; for ever you sing "alleluia".'

Salve, regina caelorum,
salve, deipara virgo,
salve, domina cordis mei;
charitas tua, dulcissima virgo,
et ardens amor tuus vocem movet
ut moduler, ut cantem in suave carmen:
Tu laetitia cantantium . . .
tu cythara et fistula,
tu chorus et organum . . .[96]

Rusca's setting relies first on the tension between the first-mode implications of the opening gesture and a repeated cadential figure in voice and continuo firmly on A (ninth *tono*; Ex. 8.24). The important syntactical divisions of the text's opening (quoted above) are marked by this latter figure, not by the fewer cadences on D. 'Ut moduler' is set off by the fastest motion heard thus far, and the catalogue of Marian praise ('tu laetitia cantantium') switches back and forth from triple to duple time. Almost imperceptibly, the vocal tessitura grows in this section (f'' for 'tu cythara'). The final peroration ('tu castissima mater Dei, vita mea, amor meus, et gaudium meum') uses all the means seen thus far plus others: dotted rhythms ('gaudium'), a leap of a minor ninth in the voice ('amor meus'), and a final reworking of the *nono tono* cadential figure that ends almost surprisingly on D (Ex. 8.25). It is almost as if Rusca used all the compositional methods at her disposal for this text; if it were a proem to the collection, *Salve, regina caelorum* would have been a compendium of the procedures to be heard in the remaining contents.

---

[96] 'Hail, Queen of the heavens; hail, God-bearing virgin; hail, lord of my heart; your burning love, sweetest virgin, moves my voice to play and sing in sweet song: you, joy of singers . . . you, lute and pipes; you, chorus and organ . . .'. There are no other settings of this text in the Milanese repertory. In the later years of Federigo's tenure, Marian solo motets often opened local concerto collections (*Flores praestantissimorum virorum*, RISM 1626[3]; Grancini, 1628 and 1631), as an invocation of the prelate's patroness (he is buried at the Marian altar of the Duomo).

Ex. 8.24. Rusca, *Salve regina caelorum* (1630), bars 1–19

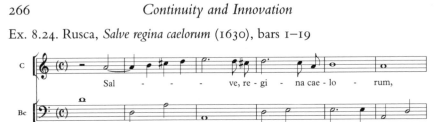

Ex. 8.25. Rusca, *Salve regina caelorum* (1630), bars 75–104

Ex. 8.25. *cont.*

9

A Nun's Music among the Genres of Mid-century Lombardy

◇

Dal casto petto d'amor' sacro piena
Scioglie questa si dolce i' dotti accenti
Che qual del Tempio armonica Sirena,
Fà, che dormano al Mondo i' cori intenti.

(Anon., Sonnet 'In lode della
Compositrice', *Scherzi*, 1648)

The works composed by Chiara Margarita Cozzolani and Rosa Giacinta Badalla represent different moments in S. Radegonda's repertory.[1] Because they spent their adult lives inside the house's porous *clausura*, their music provides testimony to their reception of genres in Lombardy. Cozzolani's production includes some of S. Radegonda's repertory at mid-century, and her output represents one of the larger surviving body of works composed by a woman before 1800.

The one part-book of her *Primavera di fiori musicali* (1640) extant in modern times did not survive World War II.[2] She produced another substantial collection within two years. *Concerti sacri*, consisting of

---

[1] Maria Calegari's editions reported by Calvi, *Scena*, must be considered lost, contrary to the catalogue of B. G. Jackson, '*Say Can You Deny Me': A Guide to Surviving Music by Women from the 16th through the 18th Centuries* (Fayetteville, Ark., 1994), 77. This gives the works reported by Calvi as being in press (madrigals *a 2*, and masses *a 6*) as located at I-Bc (which they are not), along with an entry mistaking the incipit of Gaspari's summary of Calvi in the I-Bc card catalogue ('Troviamo un magnifico elogio *di questa musicista in G. Calvi, Scena* . . .' [my emphasis]) for a separate work by Calegari for voices without continuo.

[2] The holdings of the Berlin Gymnasium zum grauen Kloster were destroyed along with the Singakademie library; see C. Wolff, 'From Berlin to Lódz: The Spitta Collection Resurfaces', *Notes*, 46 (1989), 311–27.

twenty concertos *a 1–4* and a Mass Ordinary, was inscribed to Prince Mathias de' Medici, whose military career had taken him from Florence to Milan a generation before his nephew Cosimo, in late winter 1640–1.[3] That the dedication reflected some kind of contact between Mathias and Cozzolani, and that it was something of an afterthought, was noted by a Milanese patrician, Constanza Vittoria Arcimboldi, in a letter to the cadet Medici off at war:

In addition, I will count on having met Your Highness's taste in the following matter: I trust you will not be displeased that on my advice or urging Donna Chiara Margarita Cozzolani has dedicated her books of music to Your Highness; they will be presented to you by the Marchese Guicciardini.[4]

Mathias was no stranger to music: he patronized singers and composers associated with early Venetian opera, and established a troupe in Siena in 1646.[5] In the absence of music theatre in Milan, the prince could well have visited the institutions best known for singing, the female monasteries; indeed, Cozzolani's dedication drew the explicit parallel between her works and the songs of Greek drama, a comparison that would have confirmed Litta's worst fears two decades later.[6] The simile, unusual for a motet book, may also embody something of the composer's own conception of her book; if some of the pieces represent works that Mathias could have heard in winter 1640–1 (*Ecce annuntio vobis*, for Christmas; *O gloriosa domina*, for the Annunciation; and *Ave mater dilectissima*, for Easter)

---

[3] On Mathias's stay in Milan, highlighted by numerous social occasions, see Calvi, 'I Toscani'.

[4] 'Dell'altro, se saprò d'incontrare in questo il gusto di V.A.S. alla quale confido non sarà dispiacciuto che per consiglio, ò instanza mia Donna Chiara Margarita Cozzolani habbi dedicati à *Vostra Altezza Serenissima* li libri di musica che gli saranno presentati dal Marchese Guicciardini': letter of 20 Mar. 1642, ASF, MP, filza 5423, fo. 171. Cozzolani's dedication had been dated from S. Radegonda on 25 Feb. 1642. Lorenzo Guicciardini was a noble Florentine associate of Mathias; see W. Kirkendale, *The Court Musicians in Florence during the Principate of the Medici* (Florence, 1993), 390.

[5] On Mathias as patron, the classic study is L. Bianconi and T. Walker, 'Dalla *Finta Pazza* alla *Veremonda*: Storie di Febiarmonici', *Rivista italiana di musicologia*, 10 (1975), 379–454 at 434–8.

[6] As Bianconi and Walker noted, the Mathias correspondence in ASF, MP, is both voluminous and misleadingly organized. A direct reference to S. Radegonda among the minutes of the prince's letters has yet to emerge. But given Mathias's passionate enthusiasm for singers, and the remarks in Cozzolani's dedication ('La gratia, che V.A.S. mi fece già di solleuare questi miei di Musica componimenti dal basso natiuo all'alto de' suoi encomij, quando si degnò con orecchio cortese dar à quegli ricetto fuggitiui nelle mie voci . . .'), the prince himself must have heard some of the motets in winter 1641.

others, most notably the long *O quam suavis est* for Corpus Christi, seem to encapsulate S. Radegonda's role in public urban liturgy. While the high-voice duets, the compositional generic norm of Cozzolani's generation, largely eschew standard texts, the settings of the Marian antiphons *Regina caeli* (AA) and *Salve [o] regina* (AT) cast these traditional items as new-style motets. Several pieces use stanzas of Office hymns in centonized or free contexts: *O gloriosa Domina* and *Lauda Sion salvatorem* (this latter is the last section of *Obstupescite gentes*). Besides non-liturgical occasions, these motets' use at Mass or as antiphon substitutes at Vespers, or as additions to the Saturday Marian Office, is likely as well.[7] And the wide variety of topics and texts in the collection point to no single specific occasion for the performance of its contents, other than Mathias's putative visits.

During the remainder of the 1640s, Cozzolani must have been busy producing the *Scherzi* and the large-scale Vespers and concertos contained in the *Salmi a otto concertati* of 1650.[8] As noted, the twelve solo motets of 1648 were inscribed to the Cassinese president.[9] The dedication of the 1650 book was also to an outsider, in this case the Venetian patrician Alberto Badoer (1597–1677), bishop of Crema. The most likely occasion on which Cozzolani could have met the prelate was the June–July 1649 triumphal entry of Maria Anna of Austria into Milan; Badoer was in the suite of the papal legate Nicolo Albergati Lodovisi on this occasion.[10] Ironically, Albergati, as archbishop of Bologna, was fresh from his efforts to find a middle ground between the Camaldolese nuns of S. Cristina and Roman authority.[11] The Spanish-language chronicle written by the master of ceremonies recorded a visit by the entourage to S. Radegonda on 26 June 1649.[12]

[7] The length of some of the concertos in the 1642 book, and especially of those in the 1650 *Salmi a otto*, fits with the prohibitions against overly long items at Mass noted in the later Franciscan rules.

[8] The up-to-date nature of these collections, similar to the works of Casati and Porta, precludes any dating on stylistic grounds of most concertos earlier than *c*.1635.

[9] Benedetti had also received a dedication from the Cassinese Vicenzo Tuzzi (*Missa cum psalmis à 3*) in 1628, during an earlier term as president.

[10] Badoer was also the dedicatee of G. A. Grossi's *Messa, e salmi bizarri*, op. 1 (Milan: Rolla, 1640), a 'witty' Vespers collection typical of the new Lombard school. The prelate was renowned for his patronage of female monasteries in Crema; A. Saba's entry in the *Dictionnaire d'histoire ecclésiastique* (Paris, 1931), vi, cols. 151–2, mentions his visit to Milan.

[11] On the conflict in 1647–8, see Monson, *Disembodied Voices*, 172–9.

[12] J. Cigoña, *Entrada en este Estado, y ciudad de Milan de la Reyna Nuestra Señora Doña Maria Anna de Austria* (Milan: Malatesta, 1649), 23–4; this account also mentions visits to other musical houses, including S. Marta, S. Margarita, and the Monastero Maggiore.

The most immediately impressive feature of the 1650 book is its sheer size and opulence.[13] The genre of eight-voice Vespers settings, while popular earlier in the century, had suffered a decline in the wake of the 1630 plague and its effects on church choirs; there were some nine new Italian editions (not counting reprints) outside Milan in the years 1630–50.[14] Cozzolani's collection consists of two strikingly different layers: the respond, six Vespers psalms, and two Magnificats (all *a 8, concertato*), with the subcategory of the solo *Laudate Dominum* and the four-voice *Laudate pueri* (both with two violin parts that provide *sinfonie*);[15] and the eight concertos and dialogues *a 2–5*, rather larger-scale pieces than the motets of 1642. This kind of division, in which Vespers settings occupy the majority of the publication, combined with a substantial representation of concertos, is unknown among north Italian editions of the decade.[16]

But its most immediately arresting feature is that Cozzolani signed the dedication to Badoer *from Venice*.[17] Either the composer obtained an unrecorded and apparently unprecedented *licenza* from Monti's curia to leave both the cloister and the city, or (even more astoundingly) she simply broke *clausura* in order to travel outside the diocese and indeed the State of Milan, and then emphasized the fact in the

---

[13] Why this print should bear the same designation, 'op. 3', as does the 1648 *Scherzi* is a mystery, possibly due to Vincenti's mistakes.

[14] These include P. P. Sabbatini (working in Rome), 1630; S. Bernardi (Salzburg), 1632; E. Rossi (Loreto), 1638; Merula (partially *a 8*; Bergamo), 1639; G. F. Sances (Vienna), 1643; O. Polidori (Chieti), 1646; N. Fontei (Verona; *salmi brevi*), 1647; V. Mazzocchi (Rome; *a 9*), 1648; and O. Tarditi (Faenza), 1649. Of these, the Polidori and the Fontei both feature *concertato* first choirs (with more syllabic and declamatory writing for the second).

[15] These latter pieces, with their structural ('semiotic') instrumental refrains and their largely *concertato* vocal writing, seem closer to the tradition of the *motetto con strumenti* than to any of the mid-century psalm traditions.

[16] The inclusion of two different categories of pieces in the same edition is striking. Of comparable eight-voice Vespers prints from *c.*1650, Cozzi's book contains two eight-voice motets (actually written by Grancini) and Tarditi's contains only Vespers items. In Reina's 1648 *Novelli fiori ecclesiastici*, an *opus primum*, there are two eight-voice motets (both dedicated to nuns, and both used as Mass Proper substitutes) included among the standard Vespers settings, and a Mass Ordinary. Perhaps the yoking of (formally, if not content-wise) archaic Vespers and modern concertos reflected Cozzolani's limited access to printers, compared with the unrestricted status of male monastic composers. The pieces would then have been thrown together as a one-time opportunity to publish some of S. Radegonda's larger-scale repertory of the 1640s, a possibility whose uniqueness would be underscored by Litta's future policy.

[17] The dedication reads 'D. Chiara Margarita Cozzolani. Di Venezia, a di 31 di gennaio 1650'; Venetian publishers seem to have followed mainland, not local, conventions for dating. Thus the year of publication was (new style) 1650, not 1651.

public dedication.[18] In either case, the idea—and the print, with its two-colour title-page in the Canto I part-book—are a remarkable testimony to the status of the monastery and its musical inhabitants.

The association of the volume with the pomp of the royal visit underscores the question of the liturgy that the future queen and Badoer would have heard on 26 June 1649. The normal feast celebrated that Saturday was the semiduplex commemoration of the Roman martyrs SS John and Paul.[19] But the complexities of Cassinese use provide another possibility: both 24 June, the Nativity of St John the Baptist, and 25 June, the newer and local celebration of the twelfth-century Benedictine abbot St William of Vercelli, had been listed in the most recent edition of the monastic breviary as duplex feasts.[20] The *Rubriche generali* directed that, in the case of a conflict between such feast-days, both First and Second Vespers were to be celebrated for both, with the second (or less important) feast transferred to the next day. First Vespers of St William would have been postponed to 25 June, and Second Vespers to 26 June.[21] For a royal audience, Solemn Vespers would more likely have been celebrated on the duplex feast of a local saint of S. Radegonda's order, rather than on a semiduplex of non-Benedictine and non-local martyrs, and I have provided the items for Second Vespers of St William from the Common of a Confessor not a Pope as found in the Cassinese breviary (App. E, 1A).

Textual support for this idea is provided by at least one motet: the 'generic' sanctoral *Venite sodales* includes part of the lesson (for both First and Second Vespers) from Ecclesiasticus (31: 8–9) for this

---

[18] *Concerti sacri*'s inscription to Mathias was signed by Cozzolani from S. Radegonda and the dedication to Benedetti of *Scherzi di sacra melodia* was undated and 'un-placed'. There was no reason for Vincenti to have faked Cozzolani's presence in Venice; the reasonable conclusion is that Cozzolani did indeed travel. This would be the only recorded case of such an exemption from the norms of *clausura* in the entire Milanese Seicento. Badalla's dedication of her *Motetti a voce sola*, also published in Venice, was signed from S. Radegonda on 10 July 1684.

[19] Whatever the feast, the timing of the visit on a Saturday would have allowed also for polyphony at a Saturday Office of the BVM; some of the more puzzling settings (*Venimus in altitudinem* or the two Double Intercession pieces) might have been heard in this context.

[20] See the calendar in the 1613 *Breviarium monasticum*, fo. xxvi[v]: 'Gulielmi Abbatis duplex cum commemoratione Octavae Joannis [the Baptist]', missing in the 1600 Cassinese breviary.

[21] *Rubriche generali*, 'Della traslatione delle feste', pp. 25 ff.; the tables at the end of the volume (p. 71) repeat this information, and specify that the Nativity of St John the Baptist was a duplex feast of the first class, not to be moved. The feasts of all Benedictine saints were duplex of the second class (ibid. 72).

Common. Cozzolani set the passage prominently, as the first duet section (AB) after the tenor solo opening: 'Quis est iste? et laudabimus eum, qui post aurum non abiit . . . fecit enim mirabilia in vita sua' (Ex. 9.1).[22] The setting of the sanctoral name ('beatus N.') in this piece suggests four syllables with penultimate accent (as I have added in Ex. 9.2): 'Guglielmus' could easily have been sung on 26 June 1649. In addition, structural features of one psalm setting, the *Beatus vir in forma di dialogo*, emphasize verses that concern the deeds and goodness of the just man; this may also be a sort of hidden (and even multiple) reference to an outstanding male ecclesiastic.

Despite the generalities of the texts, and the lack of Benedictine saints explicitly honoured, some other occasions for motets are indeed traceable. The 1648 *Venite populi* (for any female saint) is striking, with its four-syllable accented name and its references to the saint's flight from the world:

O beatam, o felicem N.; illam mundus peperit, mundus illam alluvit; illa mundum sprevit, mundum illa fugit . . . Dilexit illa caelum, a caelo bona expectans, bona aeternum duratura . . .[23]

Cozzolani's emphasis in the musical setting is on the saint's beatitude and her contempt for earthly matters, underlined by the musical repetition of 'fugit' (Ex. 9.3); these features are not a standard part of most female sanctoral hagiographies. The motet's references to heavenly riches and the disdain of earthly wealth find resonance in Radegund's flight from queenhood, her contempt for her noble status, and her largesse to the poor. All these traits figure in Lampugnani's *vita* of the Frankish queen.[24]

Similarly, the St Catherine dialogue (which invokes the Alexandrine, not the Sienese, saint, to judge by its references to Catherine's royal status) *O caeli cives* (1650) seems puzzling in the

---

[22] 'Who is this man? and we will praise him, for he did not pursue riches . . . he worked wonders in his lifetime'. Typically, *Venite sodales* reverses the liturgical text, which reads: 'Beatus vir, qui inventus est sine macula, et qui post aurum non abiit, nec speravit in pecunia thesauris; quis est hic? et laudabimus eum; fecit mirabilia in vita sua' (Lesson for both First and Second Vespers, *Breviarium monasticum* (1613), fo. xlvii'). The motet text seems to refer further on to a virgin male saint: 'Tu candidus, tu nives purior' (b. 44).

[23] 'O blessed, happy N.; the world bore and nourished her, but she scorned and fled the world . . . She delighted in heaven, expecting her reward from heaven, ready for eternal delights . . .'.

[24] Her refusal of earthly riches, and flight from the world, are mentioned in the preface (fo. 2') and occupy almost all of Book I of *Della vita*.

Ex. 9.1. Cozzolani, *Venite sodales* (1650), bars 35–56

Ex. 9.1. *cont.*

Ex. 9.2. Cozzolani, *Venite sodales* (1650), bars 51–9

light of the monastery's dedication.[25] But this text is vague enough that its original version may have also read 'Radegunda' (again scanning like 'Catharina'), all the more likely since queenship did not figure prominently in Catherine's hagiography. In the published version, Cozzolani or Vincenti could have substituted a more widely venerated female saint for the Frankish patroness, whose duplex feast was limited to Milanese Cassinese houses. A generation later, the rubric of Cazzati's 1676 motet for St Radegund (another piece for Maria Domitilla Ceva to sing) reads 'Trionfo di S. Radegonda, e serve per Santa Catharina'.[26]

[25] Complete text in F. Noske, *Saints and Sinners: The Latin Musical Dialogue in the Seventeenth Century* (Oxford, 1992), 14–15.

[26] Her feast is not listed in the calendar of the 1613 *Breviarium monasticum*; it does, however, appear in the 1604 *Breviarium Ambrosianum*. The linkage of the two saints in Cazzati's

Ex. 9.3. Cozzolani, *Venite populi* (1648), bars 55–71

This conflation of saints had had a long history. Local tradition had already mixed the two in medieval hymnody; a thirteenth-century Milanese Benedictine hymnal substituted 'Radegondis' for 'Katharinae' in *O rex benigne Domine.*[27] Peterzano's altar-piece for Cozzolani's house (see Fig. 3) depicted three saints: Justina of Padua (patroness of the Cassinese), and Radegund, together with Catherine's Mystic Marriage to the Infant Jesus, a theme that summarized nuns' vocations, and *O caeli cives* seems like a musical

Sonet caelo vox jucunda was their queenly status; the second aria of this piece reads 'Sumite citharas, / alati musici; / plaudite Virgini, / vivat bellatrix fortis, / indomita pugnatrix, / vivat invicta triumphatrix.'

[27] G. M. Dreves, *Analecta hymnica medii aevi*, xxii (Leipzig, 1895), no. 401, and iv (Leipzig, 1888), no. 310, respectively.

pendant to the altar-piece.[28] Given the musical fame of S. Radegonda, *O caeli cives* was the most appropriate parallel to the new altar-pieces that other monasteries' *chiese esteriori* were receiving in the 1630s and 1640s.

Whatever their origin, do the publication dates of Cozzolani's collections reflect the order of their composition? Some notational clues are found in the mensuration symbols for triple time; while the 1642 book uses both $\odot^3_1$ and the simple **3**, the 1648 and 1650 editions both employ only the latter.[29] Vincenti had both symbols in his type-founts; the simplification of triple-time notation seems to point to a later origin for the 1650 collection. The duets and the dialogues in this book, compared with those of the 1642 collection, are also longer. The best explanation is that the 1648 solo motets and 1650 concertos were indeed composed later than much of the *Concerti sacri*; the 1650 psalms, which (as we shall see) share and outdo certain structural features of the *salmo arioso*, may have been worked up over the 1640s.

But Cozzolani's compositional technique in relation to its musical environment raises another issue. She first published her music at age 37, and there is no evidence for or against *licenze* at S. Radegonda in the years after 1620. She had professed at age 17, unlike Claudia Rusca, who took vows late and had apparently had musical training in patrician circles.[30] Yet the *Concerti sacri* evince remarkable parallels to, and in some cases even developments of, the 'new Lombard style'. Even given the porous *clausura* of Federigo's and Monti's years, her apprenticeship remains puzzling.

The local changes in concertos and Vespers characteristic of the 1630s provide one point of context for Cozzolani's books. The new style achieved its widest diffusion in the collections of the Novarese Gasparo Casati, having been prefigured in some *terraferma* and Venetian repertory in the late 1620s. Shortly after Cozzolani's first

---

[28] The scarce Peterzano literature has identified the female saint on the left holding a book (the Rule) and wearing an elaborate classical belt (symbolizing chastity) as Clare, but Justina seems the far more logical iconographic choice. Ironically, Peterzano's monument to Benedictine tradition hangs today in a side chapel at S. Maria della Passione, directly facing Daniele Crespi's memorable portrait of the fasting Carlo Borromeo, the arch-enemy of monastic independence.

[29] In a similar vein, A. Curtis, 'La Poppea Impasticciata, or, Who Wrote the Music to L'Incoronazione (1643)?', *JAMS* 42 (1989), 23–54.

[30] If her family had continued to reside close to the Rognoni musical dynasty (see Ch. 3), she could have received lessons in her early teens from either Francesco or Giovanni Dominco Rognoni Taeggio, both active into the 1620s.

two books, Vincenti also began to print the concertos of Francesco della Porta, working at the patrician shrine of S. Maria presso S. Celso. There is at least one text-setting shared between Porta and Cozzolani, an unusual phenomenon in the Milanese repertory, and I have used his music as another touchstone for comparison.[31]

The texts of the new Lombard concerto are quite different from the short liturgical or scriptural passages set in the earlier concerto. Instead, the small-scale motet features long, newly written (or newly centonized), and (most vitally) highly emotive and personalized literary language. Its subject-matter often focuses on individual devotion and requests to Christ or Mary. Indeed, the topics covered by Cozzolani's works fit well into the new devotional currents of mid-century: in *Concerti sacri*, there are six Marian motets (plus all four Marian antiphons), along with three extended Eucharistic texts, two Christological pieces, one each for Christmas and Easter, one penitential dialogue, and a general (possibly sanctoral) motet (*Regna terrae*; text from Ps. 67: 33–6).[32]

Cozzolani's *Scherzi* and the concertos of 1650 evince the same mixture of traditional (Eucharistic) and new (personalized Christological and Marian) devotional topics: the *Scherzi* include four Marian pieces, three Christological motets, two Eucharistic items, and three pieces for feasts (Christmas, Easter, and general female sanctoral). The motets in the *Salmi a otto* are roughly parallel: two Double Intercession pieces, two Nativity, and one each for Mary, a male saint, Easter, and St Catherine.

Who might have written the non-scriptural, non-breviary texts set in Cozzolani's collections? There is no indication of authorship in any of the Milanese repertory. The texts did not circulate independently of their musical transmission, and these free texts after 1640 are almost never set twice in Milan. In the light of the close ties to

---

[31] Porta is the only Milanese figure after Orfeo Vecchi to have received the 'honour' of ultramontane piratings of complete books; his *œuvre* is well worth further study. He and Cozzolani were the only two Milanese composers after Donati and before Badalla to have their works printed in Venice.

[32] There is no liturgical assignment in monastic use for all three verses of *Regna terrae* set by Cozzolani. If 'Mirabilis Deus in sanctis suis' is taken (as it was commonly but incorrectly) as referring to 'saints' (not 'holy places'), then this was used as a sanctoral motet. There is no other setting of this text in the Milanese concerto repertory of the 1630s or 1640s, and it may have functioned either for feasts of multiple martyrs (the 'Mirabilis Deus' quotation, again accentuated musically by tutti homophonic declamation, was the verse and respond for First Vespers of that Common according to the 1600 Cassinese *Breviarium monasticum*, fo. 429ᵛ) or possibly for the feast of all Benedictine saints (13 Nov.).

urban life enjoyed by S. Radegonda, an outside origin is plausible. Some texts for music, and some pieces, came from outside, as Bianca Ripa's choir testified in their 1664 attempts to maintain contact with the urban world ('se [the choir] vuol continuare nel canto . . . esser li tal volta fortasse valersi di persone virtuose, ma però di boni costumi per haver parole e compositioni nuove, per messe e Vespri'; App. A, Doc. 59). But at the more patrician houses, some nuns were quite capable of writing Latin, and an internal source for some of Cozzolani's motet texts should not be ruled out *a priori*. In numerous motets, textual centonization plays an important role, most notably with regard to Song of Songs fragments.

The pattern of versification in the free texts, like that in the later Roman solo motet, is largely Italian, not classical.[33] The aria-like periods tend to set six-syllable lines, while the more declamatory sections often set a kind of prose poetry. Yet this mixture of genres was not novel; it had had a long history in the form of the *prosimetrum*.[34] The authors of the motet texts seem to have adapted this literary form precisely because of the opportunities it afforded for musical contrast.

The first noticeable musical feature of this new Lombard motet is its formal dimensions. If even the expanded concerto in the 1620s consisted of a limited number of discrete sections without refrains, the motets of the 1640s, by the internal expansion of sections through repetition of phrases and periods, the increasing use of partial or full refrains, and the turn to a schematic plan consisting of rapidly alternating and contrasting metres, lengthened motets considerably. The continuo part of a motet usually fitted on a printed page or inside an opening in the 1620s, but by the 1640s these parts spill over to two, three, and four complete pages in the part-book.

But there were more pervasive elements. One fundamental change took place in rhythmic structure. First, this was a matter of declamation: quick note-values replaced semibreves, minims, and semiminims. Second, the predictable speed-up within phrases in the earlier

---

[33] The best (and only) study of the Roman repertory is S. Shigihara, 'Bonifazio Graziani (1604/5–1664): Biographie, Werkverzeichnis, und Untersuchungen zu den Solomotetten' (diss., Bonn, 1984), who notes similar points; the repertory of the the 1640s, however, shows the formal conventions of Graziani's texts and musical procedures as rather less *ex novo* than appears at first glance.

[34] For an overview of the medieval avatars of the *prosimetrum*, see P. Dronke, *Verse with Prose from Petronius to Dante: The Art and Scope of the Mixed Form* (Cambridge, Mass., 1994).

style gave way to far less order and rhythmic hierarchy; melismas often occur early in a phrase, and climax and closure are achieved by texture and overall homorhythm. Further, a series of typical figures, later to be justified and categorized by theoreticians such as Bernhard, recurs in the setting of individual words or literary ideas. Most apparent is the use of *anaphora*, sequential repetition of a melodic idea in one or several voices, which undergirds especially the triple-time aria sections.[35] *Anaphora* leads to the organization of melodic periods by symmetrical parataxis, a rhetorical device found also in Borromean sermons, and used by Marino to demarcate sections in the prose of the *Dicerie sacre*.

One other notable aspect of the generation of the 1640s is the faster motion and structural function of the continuo part. 'Walking' bass ostinatos, descending tetrachords, and repeated patterns all help shape melodic periods and phrases. Further hallmarks of the new style include textual recitation on repeated notes against a moving bass. For singers and composers accustomed to earlier styles—concertos in two or three sections, developing a set of similar melodic ideas in steady declamation, in which each melodic idea sets a phrase or clause of text—the new Lombard style must have been a not unwelcome shock.

A setting of *Tota pulchra es* (1640) by the Novarese *maestro* Gasparo Casati highlights the difference; if earlier versions of this Song of Songs passage (the text concerns the beauty of the individual soul, in Borromean exegesis; of Mary, in more traditional commentaries) had been slow and balanced pieces, then the frenetic energy of Casati's motet seems to represent a conscious flaunting of the normal approach (Ex. 9.4). Similar infringements and inversions of tradition characterize other pieces in both Casati's 1640 *Terzo libro* and the 1643 *Primo libro*, most notably the extravagant solo setting in the latter of the most universal and objective text in Catholic culture, the *Pater noster*. In Cozzolani's motets, this freedom with generic traditions became a hallmark of the new style in Milan.

Liberty with liturgical texts also characterizes Casati's Vespers settings. His psalm collections were called by their editor (or publisher) *salmi ariosi*, 'tuneful' psalms with added reference to the formative

---

[35] That only Bernhard uses this term (cf. Bartel, *Handbuch*, 114–15) highlights his concern to legitimize the common practice of the music of his youth: namely, the new Italian styles of the 1640s (Casati, Rigatti, Tarditi) rapidly exported to Germany.

Ex. 9.4. Gasparo Casati, *Tota pulchra es* (1640), bars 1–14

principles of *arie*: internal (sometimes partial) refrains, virtuosic vocal writing, occasional ostinatos or quasi-ostinatos. Thus the conventions of these Vespers settings were again based on the flaunting of the received traditions of a genre, in this case the liturgically correct and sequential setting of Psalm texts.[36] In the light of the texts' shift of both devotional themes and literary language, these musical changes of *c.*1640 can plausibly be interpreted as the response of Casati and others to the demands of a new kind of spirituality, circulating in northern Italy in the post-plague intellectual crisis, as outlined above.

Concerti sacri was among the first editions in Milan itself to take up the new style.[37] The matter is complicated by the mysterious and sudden fall-off in Milanese concerto prints after the plague, a drop that lasted over a decade. But the role of Cozzolani's editions in the style's diffusion is evident on a number of counts. First is the sheer length of the pieces, due to the expansion of periods by parataxis and sequence; the increase in sectionalization, with sometimes rapid alternation between common- and triple-time sections; the use of scalar or repetitive bass-line phrases, which rarely approach true ostinato; the emphasis on conjunct triple-time melodies and the employment of short common-time sections, most notably as codas or introductions.[38]

[36] Perhaps Noske's idea of the 'naive formal experiments' of Cozzolani's *Beatus vir* ('Sul dialogo latino del Seicento: Osservazioni', *Rivista italiana di musicologia*, 24 (1989), 330–46 at 343) should be applied, if at all, not only to her pieces but to the entire Lombard large-scale repertory of the 1640s.

[37] Egidio Trabattone's *Quarto libro de concerti* is roughly contemporary with Cozzolani's book (the preface is dated two months later than *Concerti sacri*'s), and Trabattone's volume shows influence from the new trends, especially in its duets; certainly the texts echo the non-scriptural language of Casati. The appearance of the new style had been preceded by a hiatus in Milanese concerto editions; the books of Grancini (1636), Beria (1638), and Trabattone (1638) all still reflect the late 1620s, evidently as local composers assimilated the new developments.

[38] These traits have been explained by the putative influence of operatic styles on church music (J. Roche, 'Cross-Currents in Milanese Church Music in the 1640's: Giorgio Rolla's Anthology *Teatro musicale* [1649]', in A. Colzani *et al.* (eds.), *La musica sacra in Lombardia nella prima metà del Seicento* (Como, 1987), 13–29 at 20). Yet mid-century Milan was not a leading centre for either opera or secular cantatas (the first Venetian opera produced was probably Cicogni/Cavalli's *Giasone* in 1649). This argument falls easily into an anachronistic historiography that considers all stylistic change to have originated in the better-known genres. Nor does operatic influence explain the three- and four-part writing in the works of Casati, Porta, and Tarditi. The growth of triple-time passages and increased sectionalization in Milanese repertories developed from aspects of the sacred concerto in the late 1620s; these parallel but do not directly imitate trends in Venetian opera and Roman cantatas.

Second is the almost ubiquitous use of writing in thirds or sixths, characteristic of the duets and duet-texture sections in larger-scale pieces. Motifs introduced by a solo voice are later (as a *climax*, in rhetorical terms) set in parallel thirds or sixths underneath. Points of imitation are short and generally not developed; rather, a plethora of motifs constitute a single concerto. Similarly, strict contrapuntal technique is relatively little used. This style's aesthetics were not based on hypotaxis and organic growth; rather, a given piece applied one or more structural concepts ('conceits') to the projection of a text, standard or new. But subtle melodic recurrences were by no means excluded.

One immediately striking feature of all three books is the widespread use of refrains, even outside genres where they might be expected (such as dialogues); these occur in most Vespers settings, in certain solo motets, and in many two- to four-voice concertos (even if a distortion of the liturgical text, as in the Marian antiphons, ensues). They are used not so much to lend unity to a piece (an idea foreign to contemporary aesthetics) as to underscore rhetorical points, and the detailed analyses below will engage several such cases.[39] The source for the refrain structures is found in the repertory of Cozzolani's young adulthood, most notably the *cantilena* motets in Alessandro Grandi's popular *Celesti fiori*, book 5, of 1619, and the similar pieces in Giovanni Antonio Rigatti's first book of 1634.[40]

These trends continued in the psalms and concertos of 1650, in which refrain structures undergird almost all the psalms and most of the concertos. The other traits of the 1642 concertos also extend into the *Salmi a otto*; even the eight-voice psalms often break down into solos or duets alternating with tutti homophony. The Vespers settings are marked by *concertato* writing in all parts. But sometimes, especially for the martial conceits of *Dixit Dominus*, florid passages involve all eight voices, often in alternation or dialogue. Thus the procedures of the duet are central to both the 1642 and 1650 books, whether small- or large-scale concertos, or the psalms.

---

[39] On the semiotic use of refrains and 'quasi-refrains' in Grandi's 1629 *motetti con strumenti*, see Padoan, 'Sulla struttura'.

[40] Grandi, *Celesti fiori . . . libro quinto* (Venice: Magni, 1619, with a fourth reprint in 1638), features five cantilena motets for Marian and sanctoral feasts (as noted below, Ch. 10, this collection also included a Marian motet text later set by Cozzolani); Rigatti, *Primo parto de motetti a 2–4, con alcune cantilene con suoi ripieni a beneplacito* (Venice: Magni, 1634, with a reprint of 1640), includes an equal number. The straightforward triple-time refrains and solo/duet sections underlie such pieces as Cozzolani's *O gloriosa domina* (1642).

The other noteworthy feature of the latter book is the large number of dialogues. Yet these traits were presaged in the opening of Cozzolani's self-conscious dedication to Badoer in his capacity as shepherd (of souls):

Loving shepherds, while they feed their beloved flocks, often entertain them with the harmony of instruments and the melody of songs . . . In the same way, so as both to imitate the talents shared by the best shepherds, and to requite in part the great debts that I owe to Your Excellency's kindest courtesy towards me in having often favoured and praised my rough songs, I wanted to compose and dedicate this *armonia* to your extraordinary taste and merit . . . The melody, my creation, has not a little of the rustic and sylvatic; in this sense, it is indeed pastoral and corresponds to the metaphor.[41]

But the pastoral conceit of the dedication and canzonetta-like style of the contents reveal more, linking both the psalms and the concertos of the print to the aesthetics—and the canzonetta genre—of the favourite poet of Cozzolani's generation, Marino.[42] At the same time, the refrains and occasional *piva* sections in both layers of the edition highlight an even more directly eclogical link between the composer's reference and the musical structures of the book's contents.[43]

Overall, Cozzolani's books feature essentially three kinds of new writing beyond the homophonic declamation and the imitative motifs in the concertos of the 1620s: a strongly declamatory solo style, used to set statements written in prose (Ex. 9.1), normally in common time; a conjunct triple-time writing, used normally for verse texts (hymns and 'free' motets in regular metre), but capable

---

[41] Text in App. D, no. 7.

[42] As in Marino's own dedication, 'Lettera I', from *La Sampogna* (Paris, Venice, and Milan, 1620; mod. edn. V. De Maldé (Milan and Parma, 1994)), ll. 164–72: 'Et anchorché il dono non sia di lira ma di sampogna, non sarà, se non m'inganno, contuttociò disdicevole; ché chi è avvezzo, non dico solo ai dolci concenti delle lire, ma anche agli strepiti delle trombe, abbassi pure per qualche poco l'orecchie al rustico suono della musica selvaggia, poiché né anche Apollo, nel tempo che ne' boschi menava vita pastorale, non si sdegnava d'ascoltare le semplici canzonette de' rozi contadini.' For the continued popularity of Marino among Milanese *educande* even in the 1690s, see C. M. Maggi, *I consigli di Meneghino*, I., v, ll. 465–6: '[Donna Alba] L'ha tutt a menadid | El Marin, l'Ariost, el Pastor fid.'

[43] Cozzolani was not the only composer to write pastoral sacred music at mid-century; Agostino Vanzoglio's *Il pastor pan a 1–4* (Milan: Rolla, 1650), a fairly typical concerto collection, mentions classical antiquity in its dedication (as had *Concerti sacri*) and includes a solo *motetto con stromenti*, *Gaudeat mecum coelum*, entitled 'La Pastorale di Pan'.

also of infiltrating liturgical settings (the 1650 *Laetatus sum* is mostly in this style, as is the 1642 *Ave regina caelorum*); and the quick antiphonal interchange of a short motif among various voices, normally setting a single verbal idea, and often built over a harmonic sequence (Ex. 9.5). Cozzolani's use of counterpoint is not unlike that of her Milanese contemporaries; motifs are short and usually brought back into homophony after two or three bars. Statements can occur on any pitch, not necessarily on important modal degrees. Unsurprisingly, the 1642 mass, although a *Messa concertata*, offers some of the longer points of imitation to be found in her works (Ex. 9.6).

Yet the departures from *stile antico* practice reveal not Cozzolani's distance from her musical environment, but rather her proximity to it. The relaxation of Zarlino's rules for dissonance treatment began not in the Seicento, but rather with Artusi's writings of the 1580s.[44] These were transmitted through early seventeenth-century treatises. Some of the parallel seconds and sevenths found in Cozzolani's concertos were considered permissible as figurations of structural voice-leading. The standard local treatise, Angleria's *La regola del contraponto*, included (pp. 24–6) a number of cases of 7–8 resolutions in the bass, or parallel sevenths in the outer voice, not to be found in other late Cinquecento theorists.[45] A comparison of one passage in Cozzolani's *Obstupescite gentes* (1642) with Angleria's rules shows the similarity (Ex. 9.7).

Likewise, the occasional parallel octaves in the tutti sections of Cozzolani's 1650 Vespers had first been introduced two generations previously by the well-respected Benedetto Pallavicino.[46] By established standards, a passage from the end of the *Laudate pueri a 8* (1650) is not unusual (Ex. 9.8); the parallel voice-leading is simply a sonic reinforcement, as is the identical pitch-content (displaced by an octave in one or the other voice) of the two bass parts in tutti sections.[47]

[44] C. Palisca, 'Die Jahrzehnte um 1600 in Italien', in F. Zaminer (ed.), *Italienische Musiktheorie im 16. und 17. Jahrhundert* (Darmstadt, 1989), 265–72.

[45] This may well indicate that the traditional view of strict Seicento fidelity in contrapuntal theory to the practice of the preceding century has been overstated at least for sacred repertories; for a similar tack, see R. Groth, 'Italienische Musiktheorie im 17. Jahrhundert', ibid. 318–21.

[46] On doublings in Pallavicino's 1605 *Sacrae Dei Laudes* and their anticipations in the works of Ingegneri, see K. Fischer, 'Nuove techniche della policoralità lombarda nel primo Seicento', in Colzani *et al.*, *La musica sacra in Lombardia*, 46–50.

[47] An even more striking example can be found in the last three measures of Cozzolani's Mary Magdalene dialogue (1650), in which the four-part texture suddenly merges into three real voices by the *unisono* in the two alto parts (with somewhat heterophonic declamation).

Ex. 9.5. Cozzolani, *Surgamus omnes* (1642), bars 101–35

Ex. 9.6. Cozzolani, *Missa* (1642), bars 116–27

Ex. 9.7. (*a*) Cozzolani, *Obstupescite gentes* (1642), bars 101–4; (*b*) Angleria, *Regola del contraponto* (1622), p. 58

(*a*)

Ex. 9.7. (*b*)

Ex. 9.8. Cozzolani, *Laudate pueri a 8* (1650), bars 189–92

Cozzolani's practice, like that of her contemporaries, also underscores the rhythmic placement of dissonant contrary motion.
Relatively strong dissonance can occur on the last subdivision of a
metric unit (the third minim or semibreve in triple time, or the last

semiminim in common time), especially if the voices in question are proceeding by contrary motion to a consonance on the next *tactus* (Ex. 9.9; this includes an unresolved seventh at 'ora pro nobis'). Bernhard would legitimize the procedure as a 'quasi transitus'.

Another notable trait in Cozzolani's style, not found as regularly in Casati or Porta, is the *cadentia duriuscula* (in Bernhard's terms), an antepenultimate seventh-chord used to mark internal closure. Ex. 9.10 from *O caeli cives* may stand for many such cases in both books. Another important gesture, one unmentioned in the rhetorical treatises, is the unexpected inflection of a flat third in a melodic line just before a cadence (Ex. 9.11); this functions as an internal sign of demarcation. Two kinds of chromaticism are evident: a melodic form, used to underline phrases of sorrow or to provide another kind of syntactical marking for the closure of long melodic periods (Ex. 9.12); and a chromatic bass, used to generate sequences that often set parallel textual constructions. These parallelisms underscore the rising intensity of the literary imagery (Ex. 9.13).[48]

Cozzolani's approach to melodic dissonance is relatively restrained. Most striking is the *subsumatio* (or *cercar della nota*), for expressive effect: the melodic progression 7-#2–3 (over a static bass) occurs at several places, among them Ex. 9.14.[49] This relatively free approach to dissonance treatment is characteristic of the entire generation of the 1640s. In addition, certain verbal ideas seem to have elicited remarkably similar melodic and harmonic gestures in the Benedictine's output. One is a written-out fermata with a drop of a third or fourth in either of the outer voices, used to express a moment of sheer contemplation ('o', 'proh') and found in a number of otherwise different motets (Ex. 9.15); in rhetorical terms, an *exclamatio*. This kind of recurrent passage seems to mark a transition from rhetorical figure to semiotic marker. Overall, Cozzolani and her Lombard contemporaries took certain specific liberties with, and exaggerated several parameters of, traditional theory: the relative stability of the seventh, the rhythmic delay and metrical shortening of melodic resolutions, and the release of weak-beat simultaneities from the rules of counterpoint.

[48] In this respect, Cozzolani's practice is not different from that of Casati, Porta, or Turati. Whatever her individual traits as a composer, unusual employment of chromatic gestures was not among them.

[49] On this figure, see Bernhard, *Ausführlicher Bericht vom Gebrauche der Con- und Dissonantien*, ch. 15, summarized in Bartel, *Handbuch*, 254–6.

Ex. 9.9. Cozzolani, *Regina caeli* (1642), bars 80–94

Ex. 9.10. Cozzolani, O caeli cives (1650), bars 130–4

Ex. 9.11. Cozzolani, Venimus in altitudinem maris (1650), bars 189–93

Rhythmic structure on small and large scales also represents a point of differentiation between the concertos of 1642 and 1650. The most immediately apparent feature of the earlier books is the quick swing back and forth between triple- and duple-time sections, sometimes only three to four bars in length. Such sections are usually longer in the later book (perhaps another sign of compositional chronology).

But in both volumes, the sheer rhythmic energy requires some kind of final grounding and conclusion. This was provided by some sort of stable closing section, often in triple time, setting a hymn stanza or a new text in regular poetic metre, a kind of pseudo-sequence or pseudo-hymn. This feature, typical of Cozzolani's concertos, is especially evident in the Eucharistic or Corpus Christi pieces (O quam suavis est of 1642). The deployment of these techniques occurs in relationship to the text being set; rather than an abstract organizing principle for the entire text, such formalized

Ex. 9.12. Cozzolani, *Tu dulcis, o bone Jesu* (1650), bars 33–7

structures are saved for either the principle affect (Cozzolani's *O dulcis Jesu* or *Bone Jesu fons amoris*), or for the climactic image or intellectual transition in a given text. Many of the concertos, especially the larger-scale pieces, end with such a section; the other possibility is a well-known form such as the *ciacona*, to which the penultimate section of *O quam bonus es* (1650) is set. Indeed, one of the most remarkable and characteristic traits of Cozzolani's collections is the way in which the tension, energy, and departures from generic traditions found in the new concerto style, adumbrated at length, suddenly dissolve into such stable endings, using literary texts and musical forms popular among and well known to the large numbers

Ex. 9.13. Cozzolani, *Quid, miseri?* (1642), bars 8–16

Ex. 9.14. Cozzolani, *Quid, miseri?* (1642), bars 176–9

of patricians who flocked into S. Radegonda's *chiesa esteriore*, another musical reflection of popular devotion in early modern society.

The procedures of *Colligite, pueri, flores* give a good idea of Cozzolani's deployment of internal sections along with her means for emphasizing important textual passages. The motet sets the typical

Ex. 9.15. Cozzolani: (a) *Quis audivit?* (1650), bars 133–9; (b) *Tu dulcis* (1650), bars 133–7

(a)

(b)

floral Eucharistic conceit, this time with specific reference to Corpus Christi.[50] Indeed, its opening imperatives invoke the most public and famous activities of nuns: 'Servants [of the Lord], collect your

---

[50] 'O quam laeta dies, o quam festiva et plena gaudiis, in qua recolitur panis ille suavissimus.' In 1640 and 1641, the feast fell on 7 June and 30 May, the time at which flowers would have been budding in the Lombard landscape, given the 'Little Ice Age' that prevailed in Europe at the time. For the direct equation of flowers and the Eucharist, see Novati, *Eucharistici amores*, 243–4.

flowers, cover the ground with flowers; servants, strike up your song, sing to the citharas; virgins, strike the cymbals [*cimbala*, with a possible gloss 'harpsichords'] with your fingers.'[51]

The motet begins with a triple-time solo, firmly based on the *finalis* G, which introduces two motifs to become of great importance later on (Ex. 9.16). Cozzolani crafted her melodic periods carefully: the first sixteen bars outline the modal fifth, rounded off with an idea (bars 12-14) that recalls the earlier descents, and a bass transitional phrase. This recurs at the end of the second idea ('floribus sternite terram'), with a cadence now on the lower *d'*, providing another musical end-rhyme. The entire period is concluded by the statement of 'sternite' a second higher (bars 33–5), finally cadencing on the *g'* *finalis* after the previous breaks on the mediant (b. 14) and the *repercussio* (b. 24) of the *tono*; again a symmetry whose balance is obscured but real. Another parallel textual construction, again referring to music ('Inducite, pueri, cantus'), evoked a *metabasis*, bringing in the second voice as an unusual surprise (bars 36 ff.). What seems to begin as a repetition of material from the opening is then treated in sequence, underlined again by Canto II for the literal reference (to female virgin musicians) to 'pulsate, virgines, cimbala digitis', and broken by an *exclamatio* for 'o' that leads into the end of the exordium with a firm cadence on G.

The first citation of liturgical texts (the Magnificat antiphon for Corpus Christi, and strophe 7 of *Lauda Sion salvatorem*, the sequence for the same feast) evokes a move towards sharper hexachords to set the miraculous effects of the Eucharist ('panis ille suavissimus de caelo praestitus . . . epulemur in hac mensa novi Regis'). It is then succeeded by a long scalar *catabasis* motif, taken from the motet's opening, to express the spiritually inebriating effect of the Host ('et inebriemur a torrente voluptatis'), with a final *cercare la nota* idea for the direct congregational address ('o carissimi').[52]

---

[51] '[solo:] Colligite, pueri, flores; floribus sternite terram; [duet:] inducite, pueri, cantus; juvenes, psallite citharis; pulsate, virgines, cimbala digitis.' The other major artistic activity of Milanese nuns, as Locatelli would note in 1664, was the collection and preparation of floral garlands. Hence a visitor who heard this piece sung by S. Radegonda's inhabitants would also have perceived a direct reference to the musical and non-musical presence of sisters in the city, an enactment of female monastic life through song.

[52] Again, the language of the Song of Songs is not far distant in the adoration of the Host, as Novati's 1645 treatise would show.

Ex. 9.16. Cozzolani, *Colligite, pueri, flores* (1642), bars 1–44

Ex. 9.16. *cont.*

The second half of the piece reworks some other melodic ideas from the first half: moving towards even sharper regions (E), it recalls the descending scales ('affluentia') and at last returns to the *finalis* with the mention of song ('et parili concentu hilari cantemus'). At this point (bars 150–65) one might expect a pseudo-hymn as a stable conclusion, but its arrival is delayed by yet another recall of earlier material, in this case the 'o quam laeta dies' ideas of bars 64–84, here compressed to heighten the rhetorical effect ('o quam festiva, o quantis plena gaudiis'). Finally, Cozzolani sets the pseudo-hymn, another quotation from the Corpus Christi sequence (strophe 21, 'Salve [for 'ecce'] panis angelorum'), to one of the most attractive melodic periods in *Concerti sacri*, one that recalls the melodic trajectory of the motet's opening (Ex. 9.17), and again (as in the opening) introduces Canto II in a *metabasis* unexpectedly on a phrase ('panis vere, panis care') that will become the internal refrain of this section. Cozzolani evades textual doggerel ('panis vere, panis care, | ave mundi salutare') by a contrasting but balanced phrase (bars 183–9) set off by a *cadentia duriuscula*. She then recalls the 'o quam laeta' idea yet again, this time for the personalized affect of 'o quam dulce te laudare' (bars 194–205, similar to 150–65). The section also retraces the harmonic path to E (bars 200–5), then uses the refrain 'panis vere' to settle back on the *finalis*. Finally, the last invocation of the Host ('ave, ave, salve, salve') provides another relationship not present in the text, in this case a melodic recall of 'o carissimi' at the end of the first half, thus linking the Real Presence to Its congregational epiphany as mediated by Its musical female monastic custodians. As a whole, *Colligite*'s large- and small-scale parallelisms, along with its internal cross-references, mark it as a notably successful essay in the conventions of the new-style motet.

Finally, what might have been the reception or the popularity of Cozzolani's motet books? The 1642 book, unlike Cozzolani's op. 1, was printed by Vincenti in Venice, ensuring a wider distribution. Besides the prestige of this place of issue (most male Cassinese composers in northern Italy also were published by the same firm), Cozzolani's book seems to fit well in the series of up-to-date motet collections which the printing house had been issuing since the late 1630s.[53] Ambrosius Profe's reprinting of *O dulcis Jesu* seven years later

---

[53] The question of why, or which, Milanese composers would have their music appear in Venice when Giorgio Rolla's presses stood ready at hand is far from being answered; the major figures at the Duomo (Turati, Grancini, Grossi) had their music printed locally.

Ex. 9.17. Cozzolani, *Colligite, pueri, flores* (1642), bars 157–93

Ex. 9.17. *cont.*

indicates that one Protestant cantor thought that the piece was representative among the new Italian styles included in his anthology, the *Corollarium geistlicher Collectaneorum*.[54]

For the difficult question of contemporary reception, there are two sets of evidence, neither conclusive. First are the performance markings—clarifying accidentals, *ficta*, clefs, bar-rests, and tacet sections—handwritten in the Bologna and Wrocław copies of the prints. All three copies of the 1642 and 1650 editions include such markings, suggesting that these exemplars were used at least once.

---

[54] There is no need to postulate a special connection for the 1649 reprint; Profe seems simply to have acquired Venetian editions on a regular basis, including presumably the 1642 *Concerti sacri*. Cozzolani's piece is the only non-Venetian motet included in the *Corollaneum*. There is no textual difference between the original and the reprint, except for Profe's replacement of Vincenti's (semi)breve ligatures by a more normal symbol. The topics of the Lombard motet of the 1640s (with the marked turn towards Eucharistic texts that stressed the Real Presence of Christ in the sacrament, and the ubiquity of Marian pieces) meant that transalpine anthologizers who wanted their collections to appeal to Protestants had their choices limited to the most Quietist texts set, and this factor, along with the concision and balance of the music, may explain the choice of *O dulcis Jesu* over the other new-style duets.

Second are Vincenti's stock-lists from 1649, 1658, and 1662;[55] the first of these features the just-printed solo motet book, and the others include both the *Scherzi* and the *Salmi a otto*, both at the printer's normal prices for volumes of their size and genre.[56] The *Concerti sacri* appear in none of the catalogues. Vincenti's policy seems to have been one of relatively large print runs and infrequent reprints of a given edition.[57] Hence, the presence of a volume on a later stock-list cannot be directly interpreted as commercial success. The publisher also kept a large stock of old music, in some cases dating back to the 1620s, and the presence of the *Scherzi* or of the *Salmi* twenty years after their publication is not necessarily an argument for their commercial success.[58]

Why might *Concerti sacri* have disappeared? Again, there seem to be two possibilities. First, it may not have withstood the fairly heavy competition in the genre of the concerto. Second, although the more traditional multi-voice concertos and simpler duets of the 1620s are not the predominant element in the volume, they are present, and the collection may simply have seemed too old-fashioned for Vincenti to reprint or keep in stock. By contrast, the solo motet book was a publishing category just coming into its own in the 1640s and 1650s, obviously with a large market, and so Vincenti could have kept the 1648 book in stock. The reverse of the coin with regard to the 1650 print seems to obtain: Vincenti did not have many new eight-voice Vesper books (especially in *concertato* style) on hand, and so Cozzolani's collection was a welcome selling-point. As we shall see, it also contained some remarkable music. Taking the scanty evidence together, it seems that Cozzolani's music was sold and sung as

[55] Collected in Mischiati, *Indici*, as nos. IX, IXbis, and X.

[56] The 1648 *Scherzi* (consisting of eight quaternions) were priced at 7 lire in all three catalogues; by comparison, Tarditi's slightly larger 1648 solo motet book (eight and a half quaternions) and Laurenzi's 1644 collection (nine quaternions) both sold for 7 lire, 10 soldi. The 1650 Psalms were priced at 14 lire; Tarditi's slightly larger eight-voice Vespers of 1649 sold for the same.

[57] This makes the frequent reissues of Gasparo Casati's works all the more striking, rather as if the Venetian printers did not realize how popular the new style would turn out to be.

[58] But manuscript copies of two pieces from the *Scherzi*, along with one secular aria, circulated later in Protestant Germany. For *Venite gentes* and *No, no, che mare* see App. D; the former and *Quis mihi det [calicem bibere Domini?]* were listed in the 1686 Ansbach inventory; see R. Schaal, *Die Musikhandschriften des Ansbacher Inventars von 1686* (Wilhelmshaven, 1966), 42 (fo. 987). This collection does not seem to have survived; my thanks to Kathryn Welter for her aid on this point.

much as that of any Milanese composer of the decade. A closer examination of the three collections' procedures for the structural projection of a text, in the context of similar repertory, might indicate why.

10

Spirituality and Style in Cozzolani's Music

◇

> In queste carte armoniche loquaci
> Questa, ch'è di virtù concorde cetra,
> Spiega gl'accenti, ond'i' macigni spietra,
> E ferma à suo voler' l'aure fugaci.
>
> (Anon., Sonnet 'In lode della
> Compositrice', Cozzolani, *Scherzi*, 1648)

Cozzolani's deployment of musical structure and surface features framed the polyphonic projection of the texts' spirituality into the urban world. As noted, the duets of the *Concerti sacri* best manifest the new style's characteristics: quick declamation, long triple-time periods, ostinatos or quasi-ostinatos, and climax by texture.[1] The mercurial change of affect between sections is also a feature shared with and expanded from Casati's works. *Bone Jesu fons amoris*, *O dulcis Jesu*, *Colligite pueri*, and *Surgamus omnes* are the classical high-voice pieces of this stamp. To this group, stylistically if not textually, may be added the Marian antiphons *Regina caeli* (AA) and *Salve [o] regina* (AT).

The general Marian motet that opens the duets, *Surgamus omnes*, is a deceptively simple piece, shifting frequently into triple time, beginning with the *metapoiesis* (madrigalism) of a trumpet-like fanfare whose textual justification ('et recinente tuba') comes only towards the end (b. 153), and featuring closely spaced elided entries for 'surgamus'. Like *Colligite pueri*, the motet falls into two large parts, with a cadence on the final (G) halfway through (b. 99); the section

---

[1] Two (*Colligite, pueri* and *O dulcis Jesu*) are designated for CC or TT. There are neither compositional nor technical differences between these and those not rubricated for transposition downwards (*Colligite* is like *Surgamus* and *O dulcis* like *Bone Jesu*); possibly this was a printer's convention to enhance the collection's attractiveness.

immediately following, adumbrating Mary's virtues ('o caeli decus, o mundi splendor'), begins as if restarting another leisurely series of triple-time solos.[2] But Cozzolani quickens the phrase rhythm by a series of inflections on the *cantus durus* side of the pitch spectrum, followed by a startling (and repeated) turn towards *cantus mollis* for 'peccatorum advocata' (see Ex. 9.5). She then ends the motet by the classic methods of the new Lombard style: close imitation and long melismas in thirds ('tibi laudes ac triumphos decantent'), making *Surgamus* one of many pieces about the joys of singing.

Bone Jesu, fons amoris shows off the new features: a highly personalized text imploring Christ's presence, this time with a congregational shift that leads again to heavenly melodies ('ut cantemus, ut jubilemus . . . in aeternum'; see p. 172); an opening section (Ex. 10.1) built on a descending tetrachord ostinato; quick exchange of phrases between the voices; and, most subtly, a sort of motto formed by the bass-line motion of the opening common-time phrase (*a–f–d–e–a*), which recurs at the end of the exordium ('O beata mellitudo') and at the close of the piece ('in aeternum'), another case of rhetorical *epistrophe*. Yet here the internal logic of the piece seems to demand more; the sheer drive and tension of the opening ostinato is offset by not one but two closely imitative sections at the end ('fac habere premium' and 'ut cantemus'). The inwardness and rhythmic prose of the text moved Cozzolani to two anachronistic, almost forgotten gestures: the 1620s-like *trilli* and *accenti* on 'o [beata mellitudo]'; and a series of internal cadences on G in what is essentially a piece on A (*nono tono*).

Probably the most concise and balanced example of the 1640s duet is *O dulcis Jesu*, the piece reprinted by Profe: its exordium is formed by the praise of Jesus, set in a rounded form ('O dulcis Jesu, | Tu es fons . . . | et apud te . . . | o dulcis Jesu'). This opening is followed by two groups each consisting of a declamatory common-time section and a motivically driven triple-time section;[3] an imitative section ('cum sanctis tuis') provides climax, and a slightly extended version of both 'O dulcis Jesu' periods from the exordium round off the work, with a final common-time peroration based on the diminution of the opening motif of an upward tetrachord (Ex. 10.2;

---

[2] Again, the other internal cadences have little to do with D: they fall on A (bars 40, 80, 96, 146) or C (bars 34, 140).

[3] One other detail is the harmonic progression by fifths that eschews a 'local' leading-note (bars 56–7; the natural sign is explicit); this progression recurs in several pieces.

Ex. 10.1. Cozzolani, *Bone Jesu, fons amoris* (1642), bars 1–55

Ex. 10.1. *cont.*

Ex. 10.2. Cozzolani, *O dulcis Jesu* (1642), bars 132–66

Ex. 10.2. *cont.*

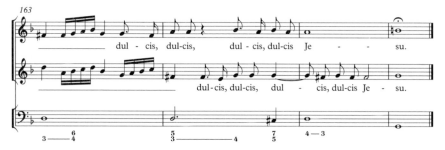

bars 162 ff.).[4] The ostinato of the opening, like that of *Bone Jesu, fons amoris*, seems to serve a structural, not primarily expressive, function.[5]

Regina caeli uses the 'alleluia' refrain already present in the antiphon text again in a surprising way. The opening of this G-final piece negates the *cantus mollis* signature with repeated B♮s in another flowing triple-time section, after introducing a simple rising motif ($d'-e'-f\#'g'$). The invocations ('Regina caeli', 'ora pro nobis, regina caeli', which take up the opening rising motif) repeat words in a liturgically incorrect fashion ('laetare, regina caeli'), and are separated by the 'alleluia' settings. These latter are given four different musical motifs (Ex. 10.3), of which the third exploits the spiky *consonantia impropria* G–B♭–F♯. Cozzolani's deployment of internal refrains is again not straightforward:

Invocation 1
Alleluia (motifs 1, 2, 3)
Invocation 2
Alleluia (2, 4)
Invocation 3
Alleluia (4)
[double bar]
Invocation 5
Alleluia (1, 2, 3, 3 transposed)

The surprise comes in bar 92 (see Ex. 9.9), with the repeat of the initial three 'alleluia' motifs; the coda takes the last melodic idea up a

---

[4] A case of the rhetorical term *complexio*, a figure from the beginning of a piece used at its end.

[5] Not a semiotic marker of lament as in Venetian opera; cf. E. Rosand, 'The Descending Tetrachord: An Emblem of Lament', *Musical Quarterly*, 65 (1979), 346–59.

Ex. 10.3. Cozzolani, *Regina caeli* (1642), bars 23–46

Ex. 10.3. *cont.*

fifth so as to emphasize the conflict between *cantus mollis* signature and *cantus durus* melody that had been present in the very opening periods; another kind of rounding-off, and another piece on a standard liturgical text that creates its own rhetoric as it goes along. The other striking sonic feature of the antiphon is the frequent cadences on the low *g*, a tribute to another talent of S. Radegonda's singers.

Finally, *Salve o regina* marks new features in the process of refrain troping; here the recurrent triple-time tag 'salve . . . spes nostra salve' (Ex. 10.4) underlies the first sixty-six bars of the piece, with three statements closing firmly on the *nono tono* A. The other petitions to Mary ('Ad te suspiramus'; 'Eia ergo'; 'Et Jesum benedictum') elaborate new motivic ideas. The return of the refrain brings back not the opening (as in *O dulcis Jesu*), but rather the final two statements of the opening section (bars 26–66 = 161–201), with a final coda that again recalls the moves towards D heard earlier in the piece.

A close analysis thus reveals these duets to be not shapeless and iterative, but rather close-knit and subtly unified. Their structural principles recur in many, larger-scored works in both the 1642 and

Ex. 10.4. Cozzolani, *Salve o regina* (1642), bars 1–66

Ex. 10.4. *cont.*

Ex. 10.4. *cont.*

1650 collections. The compositional and rhetorical techniques developed therein were decisive for the more ambitious pieces. Still, some concertos *a 2* are simpler. *Obstupescite gentes* is an introduction to a homophonic setting of *Lauda Sion salvatorem*, and thus another Corpus Christi piece that focuses on the physical presence and emotional effect of the Eucharist ('quid hoc cibo suavius? per quod dulcedo spiritualis in suo fonte gustatur'). It is planned as a series of solos that again build to textural high points, both in the free-texted section and in the hymn strophe (relatively long imitation for 'in himnis et canticis'; Ex. 10.5). Similarly plain is *Alma redemptoris mater*, a CB duet constructed again of solos, with heightening achieved by imitation ('virgo prius ac posterius'), gradually increasing chromaticism ('Gabrielis ab ore'), and finally the chromatic *anabasis* beginning on almost every modal degree, setting the intercession 'peccatorum miserere' (Ex. 10.6), but never straying far from the F final.

The trio *O gloriosa domina* is quite simple, with its three solos and four refrains all firmly based on E; the piece, less extended and complicated than the other large-scale concerti, might have been included only because Mathias had heard it in spring 1641, even

Ex. 10.5. Cozzolani, *Obstupescite gentes* (1642), bars 111–28

though Annunciation fell in Holy Week that year. Its literal returns and unelaborate solos again recall Rigatti's cantilena motets of 1634, with their tutti refrains. The quartet *Regna terrae* takes a freer approach: an opening that recurs twice literally to close the exordium and the piece (bars 38–52 and 133–47), with internal variants that begin differently but end the same (bars 82–98) or are reworked and expanded (bars 110–27), an expansion of the basic form of the cantilena motet. Again, this basically simple celebratory piece is set out on a G final, with internal cadences on A and C.

Yet some trios show other facets of mid-century style. *Ave regina*

Ex. 10.6. Cozzolani, *Alma redemptoris mater* (1642), bars 95–105

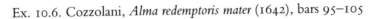

caelorum (in the popular ATB scoring) manifests a far more homogeneous, less sectionalized approach to texture, metre, and declamatory effect (Ex. 7.3). It also has a remarkably similar contemporary counterpart, Antonio Turati's setting that appeared in 1651. Cozzolani's version strays little from its final, while Turati's keeps the opening invocation on the final and then features major internal cadences on D and F. The difference in overall length is due primarily to the longer melodic periods and repetitions of material in Cozzolani's version, most notably in 'salve radix' and the long sequences on 'Gaude, virgo gloriosa'; by contrast, Turati relies more on irregular phrase-lengths and solo–tutti exchanges. There is nothing in Cozzolani's setting like the long conclusion on 'et pro nobis semper Christum exora' in Turati's setting, introduced by the 6♭–3♯ simultaneity on 'Christum'.[6] Turati creates the climax of his piece out of the repetitions of this textual phrase, whereas Cozzolani lays the stress on an earlier address, 'Gaude, virgo gloriosa', with its *alla zoppa*

---

[6] The stress on Marian intercession in Turati's version suggests that the piece might date from his years (1631–42) at S. Maria presso S. Celso, not from his tenure at the Duomo (1642 until his death in 1650), where he was occupied with rebuilding the choir and with larger-scale liturgical pieces. For transcriptions of both, Kendrick, 'Genres', 1080–99.

rhythm. If Turati's setting highlights intercession, Cozzolani's underscores rejoicing, a distinction not atypical of the two composers and their institutions.

Perhaps it is no surprise that the most extended trio is the Corpus Christi piece, *O quam suavis est, Domine*, given both nuns' personal devotion to the Body of Christ and their place in the city as custodians of the Eucharist. The text of this 223-bar motet begins with the renowned Magnificat antiphon for Corpus Christi, followed by Song of Songs tags as a first climax ('venite, gustate, bibite, comedite, et inebriamini, carissimi', with a similar exegesis to that of *Colligite, pueri*) and free material, including sequence quotations changed from plural to singular ('o panis angelorum, o esca viatorum, o fons deliciarum, ad te confugio', reminiscent of Birago's meditations a century earlier, along with 'tu *me* [for 'nos'] pasce, me tuere, tu me bona fac videre in terra viventium', taken from strophe 23 of *Lauda Sion salvatorem*).

Cozzolani begins with a long period, firmly on the final G, for alto solo, setting the antiphon text; the contrasting ideas ('o quam suavis' and 'esurientes') are set off by different metres and turns to *cantus durus* and *cantus mollis* respectively, while the whole period is unified by a series of successively lower cadential pitches (d', b, a, g) in the voice (Ex. 10.7). The triple-time tutti entrance comprises the first of several internal 'venite' refrains, which lead directly to a passage for the canticle tag ('et inebriamini') cadencing on C. The solos (T and B) are then followed by another 'venite, reficite vos', again turned towards the personal effect of the Eucharist, with a chromatic *catabasis* limning the *d–g* fifth, combined with an *extensio* (dissonance prolongation) to set 'you will not lack along [life's] way' ('et non deficietis in via'; Ex. 10.8). Each section features progressively stronger semantic markers of closing, *cadentiae duriusculae* replaced by *consonantiae impropriae*.

Given the public and popular nature of the feast, it is no surprise to find a hymn phrase at this point ('O Panis Angelorum', set in the familiar triple time), leading into a fluid section that switches back and forth between homophony ('tu me pasce, me tuere') for the personal effects of the sacrament and imitation used for its praise ('o esca, o sapor, o vita'), rounded off with the typical compression of motifs ('o esca gentium, o sapor mentium'). But this flows directly into another 'venite' that synthesizes the melodic material of the previous settings of this word; repeating the cadence on C, this prepares the

Ex. 10.7. Cozzolani, *O quam suavis est* (1642), bars 1–63

Ex. 10.7. *cont.*

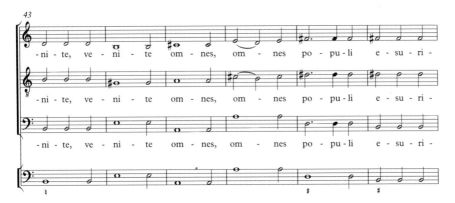

Ex. 10.7. *cont.*

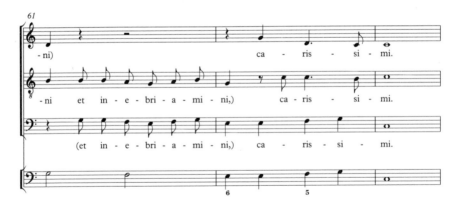

Ex. 10.8. Cozzolani, *O quam suavis est* (1642), bars 90–109

second, this time extended, hymn citation: 'Panis Angelicus' in triple
time (Ex. 10.9), taken from strophe 6 of the Matins hymn for the
feast, *Sacris solemniis*. To conclude this second section ('gaudete et
cantate et collaudate eum in aeternum'), Cozzolani provided the full

Ex. 10.9. Cozzolani, *O quam suavis est* (1642), bars 150–67

range of closing techniques: a 'presto' accelerando, quick motivic interchange among the voices, tags from the previous 'venite' refrains, and a final common-time coda, all firmly on G, the final of most chants for the feast. The length—and attractiveness—of this piece, along with its unusual double sequence interpolation, suggest that it may have accompanied a Corpus Christi procession, by nuns or others.[7]

Of all the new genres found in Seicento Milan, the dialogue was clearly the most central, a phenomenon evident in Cozzolani's motet books as well. Only recently has the prominence of the dialogic principle in early modern thought become apparent.[8] The historiography of the musical form has been clouded by teleological approaches that saw it only as a precursor of the oratorio.[9] But as Michel de Certeau has noted, the dialogue was the central method and genre of Seicento spirituality, providing a vehicle for the expression of individual affect, whether of generic figures (the soul, angels), scriptural characters (Adam, Mary, Christ), or historical saints (Ambrose); this latter could include political references.[10]

Dialogic procedures were also central to Federigo Borromeo's ideas of the communication between humans and God. In *De christianae mentis jocunditate*, the prelate devoted a section (bk. I, ch. 4) to internal colloquies of mystics, using the examples of several medieval female saints (Angela of Foligno, Gertrude of Brabant) who spoke directly with members of the Trinity; Borromeo's language is close to the texts of the Milanese musical dialogue.[11] In this treatise, Federigo also used other dialogues between female mystics and

---

[7] For a parallel among medieval English nuns, see M. Rubin, *Corpus Christi: The Eucharist in Late Medieval Culture* (Cambridge, 1991), 247.

[8] P. Burke, 'The Renaissance Dialogue', *Renaissance Studies*, 3 (1989), 2–14.

[9] The pioneering study was H. E. Smither, *A History of the Oratorio* (Chapel Hill, 1977), i. 91–117; for a fuller overview, see Noske, *Saints and Sinners*.

[10] Certeau, *La fable mystique*, 216–25. Mystics of the period pointed to the possibility of the soul's speech with God; Certeau underlines the speech-act nature of the spiritual dialogue. Even the literary traditions and the imagery associated with the motet texts underlined the dialogic associations of the *prosimetrum*; cf. Dronke, *Verse with Prose*, 2–5 (on the processual nature of the form) and 99–104 (on Song of Songs and metamusical themes in the *prosimetra* of Mechthild of Magdeburg). On anti-Arian musical dialogues in Lombardy around 1640 as a trope for the Spanish Habsburgs' opposition to Protestantism, see Kendrick, *Music in Federigo Borromeo's Lombardy*.

[11] 'De Colloquis interioribus', which began with an account of one of Angela's visions in which the Holy Spirit spoke to her: 'Sum ego Spiritus Sanctus, qui ad te descendi, ut animo tuo afferem eiusmodi solatium, quale gustasti nunquam.'

female saints as a model specifically for nuns' spiritual communication.[12]

Cozzolani's dialogues thus stand on their own terms as emblems of spirituality, without necessary relationship to the oratorio, while avoiding the received classifications of the form into 'historic', 'biblical', and 'dramatic' categories; they take up generic traditions of the *dialogo in musica* in Lombardy and above all in Milan.[13] There are eight explicitly designated dialogues in Cozzolani's books, four in each. The spread of the genre is remarkable, encompassing as it does acclamatory (*Psallite superi, O caeli cives*), biblical (the Christmas and Easter pieces), consolatory (*Ave mater dilectissima*), and liturgical (*Beatus vir*) settings, as well as the only two penitential motets in Cozzolani's entire output (*O mi domine; Quid, miseri?*).[14] Old Testament or narrative texts are in the minority here, as is true of the entire Lombard repertory, and it would be misleading to consider these pieces in the light of the Roman or Emilian oratorio. But the ubiquity of the dialogue marks it as a primary genre, a form capable even of irruption into other genres.

The very first examples in the city, dating to the second decade of the century, were not necessarily a female monastic genre like the solo *cantata morale e spirituale* discussed below. But the representation of dialogues in Cozzolani's prints, even more striking when one considers that over half the 1650 volume is devoted to the Vespers settings, marks off the genre as especially appropriate to S. Radegonda, at least, by mid-century. The various examples of the form in the two books use different means towards the end of portraying the conflict (question) and its resolution. The dialogue between a soul and its guardian angel, *O mi domine* (AT), is one of Cozzolani's more extended and chromatic works. This motet portrays the progress of a soul from the recognition of its deformation by sin, surrounded by evil, to the recognition of divine mercy and benignity through repentance to final optimistic rejoicing. Cozzolani sets the soul's initial statement of despair to a monody unlike any other solo writing in her surviving books (Ex. 10.10). The melodic line of this opening

---

[12] Book III contains one *colloquium* between Mary Magdalene and Catherine Vannini and another between the Magdalen and Mary of Oignies (pp. 110 and 125).

[13] Noske, *Saints and Sinners*, 28–9; Kendrick, 'Genres', 599.

[14] Most Milanese prints of the early and middle Seicento have one or two dialogues among their contents; the four contained in both the 1642 and the 1650 prints are somewhat exceptional.

Ex. 10.10. Cozzolani, *O mi domine* (1642), bars 1–40

Ex. 10.10. *cont.*

hovers around D over a static bass, and is filled with the rhetorical figures of doubt and sorrow. Only slowly, with the recognition of sin, does the tessitura grow outwards. As the soul's recognition of its state progresses, the tessitura gradually expands upwards and the modal centre turns towards F ('nunc deformata peccato'). The end of the plea turns back to D, employing the characteristic diminished fourth to sum up the soul's plight ('da consilium, da robur, fer auxilium'). The entire effect owes more to Donati's extension of Florentine monody than it does to Cozzolani's declamatory or arioso writing in the solo motets of *Concerti sacri*.

The angel's response retraces the same harmonic path, but moves by leaps and breaks into a short triple-time arioso ('Age, viriliter'), before turning towards sharp hexachords and cadencing on A. The entire musical process is repeated in abbreviated form for the next exchange, with the encouragement of the angel's plea being reinforced by another ascending chromatic bass line ('plora consistere'). This finally sets the stage for the soul's penitence ('Heu me peccatrix'). Cozzolani sets the actual confession first with descending lines cadencing on low *f* ('astigate maxillas'), followed by a recall of the initial recitation on *d'*, then with a final plea cadencing on the high *f'* ('Peccavi, Domine sancte'). The angel congratulates the soul in another triple-time arioso, and the soul recognizes divine mercy with another Song of Songs tag ('vocem Dei mei . . . dicentis: aperi, amica, mihi, deliciae meae esse cum filiis hominum'). The soul then passes to meditation on divine 'benignitas' and 'bonitas' with a modally closed triple-time arioso ('O magna caritas'). The angel's last solo statement before the final tutti features the first real melismas of the piece ('et verta cantus'). As we shall also see in the Easter dialogue, settings of lamentation or penitence require the balance of long, multi-sectional final tuttis. In *O mi domine*, this consists of two sets of linked triple/duple-time sections, without long solo interludes.

The characteristics of *O mi domine*—gradually increasing melodic complexity, closed triple-time sections, balancing final tuttis—are also found in the other two-voice consolatory dialogue from the 1642 book, *Ave mater dilectissima*, but with a number of new twists. This piece is an imaginary conversation between the risen Christ and Mary, the latter apportioned the larger share of the music.[15] The consolatory linkage between this piece and *O mi domine* is underscored by the double texting and rubrication of a similar work in Turati's 1651 collection.[16]

Ave mater dilectissima begins with an opening plea from Christ for His mother to cease mourning, one set to modally closed music with frequent cadences on the *finalis* (C) and limited tessitura. Mary's initial motif repeats the shape of Christ's a fourth higher. Mary's greeting to her son ('salve, fili mi') is soon followed by a canticle tag ('O quam dulcis, o quam suavis vox tua in auribus meis') in common time. Mary's recognition of Christ's triumph brings her line up to a high *g''* ('te video triumphantem') before another cadence on C. This salutation ends with a short triple-time refrain ('valete lachrymae',

---

[15] See Kendrick, 'Genres', 1067–79; Christ's part is given to an alto (it is often assigned to a bass), while Mary is a soprano. This seems to reflect performance conditions at S. Radegonda; in the light of Cozzolani's preference for alto scoring and possible personal voice-type, it may also indicate some kind of personal identification with Christ, not with the Virgin; cf. Bynum, *Holy Feast*, 268 ff. In her youth, Cozzolani might have heard G. C. Ardemanio's textually similar dialogue *a 1*, *Consolare, o Mater* (published in the 1612 *Aggiunta prima*; RISM 1612⁹).

[16] Turati's dialogue *Consolare, o Mater* (AT) is listed as 'Per la Resurrettione di N. Sig., e per vn'Anima riconsolata'; the alternative texts (a feature of this collection) assign the lower part to Jesus, while the upper voice is either Mary or the individual soul.

separated by another canticle tag 'quia quem diligit anima mea'; the high *g″* returns on the recurrence of the refrain). Christ's second salutation of His mother breaks into lyrical triple time before closing with the 'iam cessa morire' phrase. The final duet, again without a duple-time section, brings back the 'valete, lachrymae' refrain. The modal stability of this piece, uncharacteristic of Cozzolani's 1650 dialogues, points up its roots in earlier local tradition.

Similarly, the four-voice dialogue *Psallite superi* is relatively direct. Its unusual scoring (CCAA) points directly to S. Radegonda's choir. The core of its text lies in the Marian exegesis of Song of Songs 6: 9 (*Quae est ista?*), and as a motet, usually for the Feast of the Assumption, this passage had a long career in polyphonic settings.[17] Local settings alone, starting with the first concerto dialogue in Milan, Ghizzolo's *Quae est ista?* (1611), provide comparison.[18] Cozzolani's piece fits into a specific kind of setting for this text, the four-voice (or larger) concerto.[19] Most related to the traditions of female monastic music is Trabattone's five-voice dialogue setting (1625), dedicated to Paola Galla at S. Cristina and again scored for high voices (CCCAT; all three canto parts range to *f″* or *g″*).[20] The dialogic nature of the setting stems not from question/answer procedures but from the interchange among voices.

Cozzolani chose to approach the text as a sectionalized dialogue.[21] The changes from Trabattone's version must have been due to Cozzolani's reception of the cantilena refrain motet found in Rigatti's 1634 *Primo parto*; like the Venetian pieces, but on a larger scale, *Psallite superi* consists of a triple-time refrain ('Psallite superi' set for three voices, which frames the question ('Quae est ista . . .?') and

[17] 'Quae est ista quae progreditur quasi aurora consurgens, pulchra ut luna, electa ut sol, terribilis ut castrorum acies ordinata?' spoken by the chorus in reference to the female Spouse of the canticle. The substitution of 'ascendit' for 'progreditur' links the text to the Assumption and is known as a Vespers antiphon for that feast at least as early as the Antiphoner of Compiègne (*c*.880; cf. B. Stäblein, *Die Musik in Geschichte und Gegenwart* (Kassel, 1949–51), i, cols. 545–9); cf. Matter, *The Voice of My Beloved*, 153).

[18] Ghizzolo's setting appeared in *Concerti all'uso moderno* (Milan: Tini & Lomazzo, 1611).

[19] On the earlier settings, see Kendrick, 'Genres', 610–14.

[20] The continuo part is a *basso seguente*; if this piece had been performed at S. Cristina (a foundation not otherwise noted for music), the tenor part could have been sung up an octave without damage to the harmonic fabric.

[21] The exact text of *Psallite superi* is not known from any other setting and may have originated within monastic walls. Noteworthy is the lack of Marian intercessory references, different from the Franciscan treatments of the theme. Although the piece is labelled 'dialogo', it does not fall within the categories of 'dramatic dialogues' that have been the focus of generic study. Rather, it might be called an 'acclamatory' work.

Ex. 10.11. Cozzolani, *Psallite superi* (1642), bars 1–40

Ex. 10.11. *cont.*

its response ('Maria est . . .'). The entire pattern of refrain–question–answer (Ex. 10.11) is repeated thrice, each new answer representing both an increase in melodic elaboration and an added voice. The modal structure is also repetitive: refrain (D), question (F), answer (A or D). Cozzolani plays the expansion of the statements off against the patterned harmonic structure: answer 2 (C2) comes to a mid-point cadence on G ('soli Deo placeat') and then uses a simple but effective *mutatio toni*, or sharpening of the *finalis*, moving from seventh to ninth mode to underline the mystery of the Incarnation ('spiritu sancto superimpleta') before cadencing on the expected A (Ex. 10.12). The *catachresis* (falsobordone-like) texture of answer 4 ('Maria est, singularis inimicis diaboli') is then succeeded by a question that, for the first time, ends on the *finalis*, marking an end to the open-ended nature of the dialogue; the final refrain is scored for all four voices and is capped by a common-time repeated plagal cadence. Noteworthy, as well, are the small-scale incremental emphases, for example the expansion of the high point of the melodic range from d'' to f'' between answer 1 and answer 2 ('solem justitiae peperit' and 'miseris mortalibus depluat').

Indeed, the last dialogue of the 1642 book, *Quid, miseri, quid faciamus?*, marks a step away from the cantilena refrain motet, although it sets the first two-thirds of a text found in Grandi's *Celesti fiori* of 1619, one likely source of the refrain procedures to be found in the *Concerti sacri*. Its Marian intercessory text, echoing the Magnificat, sets the faithful (ATB) in dialogue with the Virgin (C):

ATB: Quid, miseri, quid faciamus in hac vita, privati vultu tuo, suavissima Virgo, clementissima Maria?
C: Invocabitis unigenitum Dei Filium quem ego genui, quem semper adoro, qui potens fecit; fecit mihi magna, et ipse erit vobiscum in tribulatione . . .[22]

[22] 'What, miserable ones, shall we do in this life, deprived of your glance, sweetest Virgin, most merciful Mary? You will invoke the only Son of God, Whom I bore, Whom I ever adore, Who has done great things for me; and He will be with you in tribulation . . .'. Cf. Novati's view that Mary's intercession was worth more than that of all the saints combined; *De eminentia deiparae Virginis Mariae*, 383. Grandi's original (which would have been accessible in the 1638 reprint of the *Celesti fiori*) also sets two tenors (the faithful) against a solo soprano (Mary); Cozzolani's version replaces Mary's final statement (containing most of the glosses on the Magnificat) and the final tutti found in the earlier piece. Yet the similar melodic profile of the openings of both the lower voices and the canto part in both settings suggests that Cozzolani almost certainly had to have known Grandi's motet, although the pieces then go different ways.

Ex. 10.12. Cozzolani, *Psallite, superi* (1642), bars 53–77

This dialogue again divides into two roughly equal parts: the troubles of the faithful on earth and the Virgin's intercession (bars 1–101), and the consolation of such mediation (bars 102–218), the latter again divided in half by the entrance of the tutti 'Alleluia' (b. 152). The piece constantly returns to internal cadences on its *tono* (1; D), with the lower voices echoing the words of Mary ('qui potens'; bars 24–32 reworked at 54–63).

If the 1642 dialogues had used conservative means for individualizing texts, the larger-scale 1650 examples would employ all the techniques of the new style for more public occasions; they seem to represent the more public and structurally incremental side of S. Radegonda's repertory. All feature multiple internal refrains. The simplest is the Christmas piece, *Gloria in altissimis Deo*, although it contains the only 'staging', with its concluding tutti repetition marked 'si vadi unitamente à poco à poco scemando la voce quasi allontanandosi'.[23] The procedures are familiar: the high-voiced angels, together with the shepherds (another pastoral conceit, scored for AT); tonally stable areas (on G, in *cantus mollis*); solos that gradually increase in complexity (angel 2: 'vobis edicitur Virginis partus', with its dissonant triple-time conclusion); and a closing tutti 'alleluia' built on a quasi-ostinato. The repetition of the angels' internal refrain 'agite [ergo] pastores' (b. 102) is slightly expanded and begins on different pitch-levels, again using the 6♭–3♯ sonority ('adorate') as a mark of closure.

Similarly, the Catherine (or Radegund) dialogue, *O caeli cives*, is essentially iterative and additive.[24] Its 231-bar length marks it for another festive occasion, possibly Radegund's feast-day in August 1649, after the pomp of the royal entrance. The poetic conceit of the dialogue, which features humans (TT) asking angels (CCC) for the saint's resting-place immediately after her death, was described in Lampugnani's *vita* of the Frankish queen.[25] The piece begins in the accustomed way: harmonically stable pairs of question and answer

---

[23] Transcription in Noske, *Saints and Sinners*, 217–26; 'soften the voice together as if little by little, going away'.

[24] Transcription in Martna Furman Schleifer and Sylvia Glickman (gen. eds.), *Women Composers: Music by Women through the Ages*, ii (New York, 1995); the text is also in Noske, *Saints and Sinners*, 15–16.

[25] His description of Radegund's 'felicissimo transito' reads: 'Ma que' angeli, che la conduceuano [into Heaven] risposero: Già il fatto è fatto, che deggiam noi di nuouo fare! Già il Paradiso l'ha riceuuta alla beata gloria. Già gli eserciti cantanti nel natale del Signore replicano i canti, e le loro melodie' (*Della vita*, 128), followed by a further account of the nuns who sang around her deathbed. Again, Cozzolani's piece literally enacts angelic and monastic themes in spirituality.

(CCC; again the 'heavenly' angels represented by the highest voices in S. Radegonda's choir, in a *catachresis* texture). The constantly varied internal refrain is formed by the tenors' questions ('dicite nobis, ubi . . .?'). After excursions to G and D, Cozzolani accelerates the dialogic interchange ('ergo casta Christi sponsa Catharina in caelo quiescit?—in aeternum'; bars 162–71). But here the concluding interchange and tutti are actually less stable in pitch-centre, with a shift towards sharper hexachords (C, G, D; bars 180–97), another iteration from *cantus mollis* to *cantus durus* for the tutti ('in aeternum, in caelo nunc regnat'; bars 197–216), which again ends on the modally furthest point of remove, a very distant D, as if to make up for the static text ('in aeternum cantabit: alleluia'). Cozzolani then runs the motif through a circle-of-fifths progression (D–G–C [*supplementum*]–F) in order to close the dialogue.

Cozzolani's dialogue on the Magdalen at the empty Tomb of Christ (1650) echoes the themes if not the methods of Soderini's *Dic nobis, Maria*. Her first point of departure from the tradition is to pick the Johannine version of the story (20: 11–18), which places Mary Magdalene alone at the Tomb. The literary text of the piece is a cento drawing on the most popular tags of the female Spouse of the Song of Songs.[26] The dialogue highlights the interweaving of the central mystery of faith with the key text for nuns in Borromean Milan. The point of the cento is to expand the brief and fairly cold interchange at the Tomb by use of canticle verses and free text into the kind of emotive, affect-laden statement of Mary's grief and questing for Jesus that was central to sisters' own consideration of themselves as female religious and as believers.[27] From the point of view of Christian optimism, the long concluding tutti that follows this scene, written in rhyming short lines like a hymn, and emphasizing first-person plural verbs ('dicamus laetantes, psallentes') is necessary to balance the mourning of Christ's death.

Cozzolani's setting underscores precisely the points of grief and optimism. Like the 1642 *Regina caeli*, its opening is modally ambiguous, with the first vocal pitch in the narrator's part contradicting the *cantus mollis* signature (in Bernhard's terms, a sort of *inchoatia imper-*

---

[26] The association of the Magdalen with the female beloved of the canticle, as noted above, dates to Alan of Lille and is present in Federigo's exegesis cited above. For a Eucharistic exegesis of the Magdalen as the *Sponsa*, see Novati, *Eucharistici amores*, 213.

[27] Suor Aurelia Maria's explicit identification of herself with the lamenting Magdalen will be recalled here. For a transcription, Kendrick, 'Genres', 1100–27.

fecta), followed by the horizontal diminished fourth and the harmonic diminished seventh ('plorans'). Here the tension is not so much harmonic (the Testo's opening statement comes to cadence on G, and the vocal statements oscillate between that pitch and an unhierarchial number of other cadential pitches), but rather related to the ever-growing length and complexity of the Magdalen's lament. Her first question is quite short, ending on the *cadenza in mi* for the interrogative ('vidistis?'). The next extended statement, the beginning of her lament, features another *antistoichon* for 'et non inveni'. Mary's third entry, the description of Jesus, is her longest solo yet; it employs two melodic ideas, one a sequenced period ('Dilectus meus'), and the other a shorter phrase for 'totus amabilis'.

But the melodic and harmonic centre-piece is provided by her last solo statement, one that makes explicit the link between the male beloved of the Song of Songs and Jesus ('Dilectus meus . . . crucifixus Jesus est'; Ex. 10.13). This again divides into two contrasting periods, one describing the crucified Christ, complete with another *consonantia impropria* (a diminished seventh), and then a striking *mutatio toni* to the sharp side (g♯) of hexachords for the direct address to the missing Christ ('O mea lux, ubi es?'). This is then balanced by a turn equally as far towards flat hexachords for the final affective canticle quotation 'Veni, dilecte mi, veni, amore tuo langueo'. The added parallelism of 'amore tuo moriar' is brought back to a cadence on the reciting-tone of the whole piece (D). The angels interrupt with the news of the Resurrection with a quick, two-period reply set in thirds; this goes from the reciting-tone back to G.

The closing section of this piece then has the task of reflecting universal Christian joy. Cozzolani divides the setting into three balanced periods: 'Dicamus ergo gaudentes . . . alleluia'; 'O dies serena . . . o dies beata'; and 'Cantemus . . . canamus, alleluia'. This tutti is characterized by quick rhythms for the verbs, capped by short imitation, and unified by a cadential figure (B♭–E♭–C–D–G) repeated in the bass in both triple- and duple-time sections of the 'alleluia' (Ex. 10.14). The second section varies the pattern by breaking down the voices ('O dies serena') and repeating the music of the first 'alleluia', complete with cadential figure, this time separated into duple- and triple-time statements.

The Easter dialogue seems to bespeak a higher level of planning than was the case in the 1642 dialogues. In its clear portrayal of central themes in female monastic spirituality, emphasis on the

Ex. 10.13. Cozzolani, *Maria Magdalene* (1650), bars 85–115

Di-le-ctus me-us, a - mor me-us, spe-ci-o-sus_ for-ma prae fi - li-is ho - mi-num;

Cru-ci - fi-xus, (cru-ci - fi-xus) Je - sus_ est, cru-ci - fi-xus Je - sus_ est.

O me-a lux, u-bi_ es? O a-mor me-us, u - bi_ es? O vi-ta me-a, u - bi_ es?

Ve - ni, ve - ni, (ve-ni, ve - ni,) ve - ni, (ve-ni) di - le - cte_

mi, di - le - cte_ mi, ve-ni, (ve-ni,) a-mo-re tu - o_

lan - gue-o, ve-ni, (ve - ni,) a-mo-re tu - o_ mo - ri-or.

Ex. 10.14. Cozzolani, *Maria Magdalene* (1650), bars 159–68

Magdalen, and overall tone of Christian optimism, it sums up the intellectual atmosphere of the post-Federican generation. And in its highly conscious use of melodic differentiation, rhetorical figures, and modal goals, it stands as a compendium of Cozzolani's work.

The liturgical pieces in her books contrast sharply: the 1642 mass is a typical mid-century *concertato* setting, which uses short points of imitation, generous amounts of homophonic declamation, and a certain amount of triple-time setting, without the expansiveness of the duets. But the Vespers are a different story. Cozzolani's eight-voice settings represent a fairly unusual and ceremonial genre, by the standards of mid-century Milan. Indeed, neither Casati nor Porta seems to have left any examples. But if the form of Cozzolani's psalms is traditional, the compositional means are not, and this feature stands in contrast to contemporary eight-voice Vespers repertory in Lombardy and Emilia: Reina (1648), Cozzi (1649), Tarditi (1649), and the works that Turati wrote across the street from S. Radegonda at the Duomo in the 1640s.

The most notable aspect of Cozzolani's Vespers is the way in which *concertato* style, employing florid solos and duets, is found in all the voices and in all the settings.[28] This is characteristic of all the eight-voice settings, and in this sense the psalms are a relatively homogeneous group of pieces. One structural difference among them is formed by those pieces that trope a refrain, often a two-part form, into various spots in the text (*Dixit Dominus, Beatus vir, Laudate pueri* (I), *Laetatus sum*) as opposed to those that do not (*Confitebor tibi Domine, Nisi Dominus*).[29] One point on which the volume does accord with local tradition is the choice of mode and affect for each psalm. Cozzolani followed some typical choices, even as late as 1650: *Dixit* in first mode; *Confitebor* in second (on G); *Beatus* in third (or fourth); *Laudate pueri* in eighth; *Laetatus* in sixth (in its Seicento position on *c*); and *Nisi* in seventh.[30]

---

[28] Several contemporary collections claim to use *concertato* style in one (less often, both) choirs of the eight-voice ensemble; Reina's 1648 *Novelli fiori*, for instance, has a double-choir *concertato Dixit* along with a *concertato* choir I in its other settings, and similar procedures obtain in Cozzi's 1649 book. However, these tend to be shorter, less florid interjections of a single word or text phrase, unlike Cozzolani's settings, which treat entire verses and half-verses in *concertato* style in all voices.

[29] The division does not correspond to possible origin; on the occasion of Badoer's visit, both kinds of psalm setting would have been heard.

[30] On similar modal associations, see Kendrick, 'Genres', 645.

The musical procedures write the language of the duets and the four-voice concertos large. The tutti sections are usually homophonic; they often recite text, sometimes over a simple *piva*-like bass. Antiphony between the choirs is simply one among a number of resources, not the structural approach to the entire psalm, with frequent recourse to a kind of *bassetto* texture *a 3* or *a 4*, scored CCA or CCAT, also found in *Psallite superi* and *O caeli cives*.[31] Within the verses, the compositional procedures are not dissimilar to Cozzolani's writing in small-scale concertos, the most evident influence of duet texture.

The respond *Domine ad adiuvandum* is still very much an eighth-mode piece, with its cadences on G and C. The textual freedom and quasi-refrains typical of the collection as a whole begin immediately: the overall form is ABA′ CDC′, where B and D are *concertato* sections and B rearranges the text 'Domine ad adiuvandum me festina' into 'festina Domine'. The most immediately striking feature of *Dixit Dominus* is not its refrain, but the apparently unique detail that the refrain is the *doxology*'s opening ('Gloria Patri . . .'), troped into the text after the very first verse and on three later occasions in the long psalm (Ex. 10.15, which follows immediately on the bass solo of Ex. 7.1). Although refrains do occur in the Vespers of Casati and Tarditi, the use of the 'Gloria Patri' displaced to various parts of the psalm is found only in Cozzolani's psalms. For a Milanese audience of the 1640s, unused to refrains in psalm settings, the effect must have been uncommon, even 'witty'.[32]

The severe and judgemental references of the text ('confregit in die irae suae reges', 'implebit ruinas') seem to have moved Cozzolani to military and fanfare-like effects in her musical setting. Certainly the declamatory refrain, over a *piva* bass, highlights this rather severe *affetto*. Also evident is another characteristic of other psalm settings in the 1650 book, the use of an internal refrain ('implevit ruinas') *within*

---

[31] The combination of two or three cantus parts with two tenors is surprisingly common in the 1650 print; it underlies the *Laudate pueri a 6* and *O caeli cives*. This ensemble might have been selected to show off the extremes in tessitura of S. Radegonda's choirs.

[32] This feature marks *Dixit* as a 'salmo bizzarro', a clever and modern piece within the traditions of the genre. In conjunction with the constructivism of *Beatus vir*, perhaps *Dixit* served as a proem to an entire collection of *salmi bizarri*, like Grossi's 1640 collection, also inscribed to Badoer. On the changing use of the term 'bizarro' to mean 'fashionable' in Rome around 1640, see also R. R. Holzer, '"Sono d'altro garbo . . . le canzonette che si cantano oggi": Pietro della Valle on Music and Modernity in the Seventeenth Century', *Studi musicali*, 21 (1992), 253–306 at 287–8.

Ex. 10.15. Cozzolani, *Dixit Dominus* (1650), bars 34–8

a verse, leading to an ABCBC' structure. *Dixit* is one of the longest setting (per number of psalm verses) in the collection, and its varying textures (solo tenor for 'Tecum principium', a kaleidoscopic *bassetto* at 'Tu es sacerdos', and eight-part *concertato* writing at the repeat of 'conquassabit capita') seem to provide a conspectus of the contents of the *Salmi a otto*.

If Ps. 109, with its unusual refrain, constantly varying textures, and martial affect represents one side of this collection, *Confitebor* displays another. The *concertato* duet and trio writing found in the first psalm are present here as well ('Confitebor', 'Confessio et magnificentia'), as are the tutti declamatory, martial, and antiphonal sections ('Memoriam fecit', 'Sanctum et terribilis'). *Confitebor* also follows the standard modal choice of *secondo tuono* (down a fifth with one flat). The difference here begins on the structural level: there are no refrains in the strict sense. Instead, the common pun of the return of the opening at 'Sicut erat' is employed; this feature seems to be normal for Milanese settings of this text in the 1640s.[33] However, one feature distinguishes *Confitebor*: the return of this opening's 'walking' bass at two points: in a triple-time form at verse 7, 'Ut det illis' (b. 104), and at the canto duet 'Redemptionem misit' (verse 9). Thus *Confitebor* represents a more subtle recurrence of the refrain idea that characterizes almost all the eight-voice settings. Second are smaller-scale features: the declamation in the tuttis is rather quicker than in *Dixit*; and there is more interest in local solo–tutti contrast ('Fidelia omnia'). Cozzolani highlights the 'fearful' affect of the half-verse 'The fear of the Lord is the beginning of wisdom' by a *syncopatio* and a turn to *cantus mollis* (Ex. 10.16; bars 179–89). The whole effect is to move *Confitebor* closer to the *salmo corrente*, without however falling into the largely antiphonal homophonic declamation characteristic of that subgenre. Only at the end of the text, with the long ('eternal') melodic periods on '(Laudatio eius) manet in saeculum seculi', does Cozzolani revert to the more expansive manner of Ps. 109.

The pervasive influence of the dialogue made itself felt in even this genre: Cozzolani's setting of *Beatus vir* is rubricated 'in forma di Dialogo', the only psalm setting in the Milanese Seicento repertory to bear such a designation. The 'dialogic' influence functions on both the small-scale level (the verses are largely multi-voice *concertato* passages), and in the overall structure. For the psalm is interspersed

---

[33] It is used in the *Confitebor* settings found in Grancini's 1643 *Novelli fiori ecclesiastici* and Cozzi's 1649 *Vespers*.

Ex. 10.16. Cozzolani, *Confitebor* (1650), bars 179–89

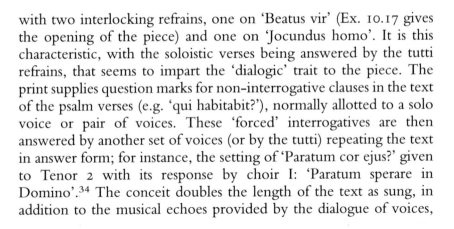

with two interlocking refrains, one on 'Beatus vir' (Ex. 10.17 gives
the opening of the piece) and one on 'Jocundus homo'. It is this
characteristic, with the soloistic verses being answered by the tutti
refrains, that seems to impart the 'dialogic' trait to the piece. The
print supplies question marks for non-interrogative clauses in the text
of the psalm verses (e.g. 'qui habitabit?'), normally allotted to a solo
voice or pair of voices. These 'forced' interrogatives are then
answered by another set of voices (or by the tutti) repeating the text
in answer form; for instance, the setting of 'Paratum cor ejus?' given
to Tenor 2 with its response by choir I: 'Paratum sperare in
Domino'.[34] The conceit doubles the length of the text as sung, in
addition to the musical echoes provided by the dialogue of voices,

---

[34] The original text is, of course, not an interrogative: 'paratum cor ejus sperare in
Domino'.

Ex. 10.17. Cozzolani, *Beatus vir* (1650), bars 1–7

and the unpredictable returns of the two refrains; *Beatus vir* is one of the more extended and individually reworked psalms in the mid-century north Italian repertory.[35]

These dialogic procedures—the question-and-answer structure of the psalm verses, interspersed with the two refrains—are brought to a climax three-quarters of the way through the piece, with the juxtaposition of both refrains' incipits as a sort of motto ('Jocundus homo'/'Beatus vir'; Ex. 10.18). The longest musical peroration is reserved for a repeat of verses 7 and 6 (in that order: 'In memoria aeterna erit justus'/'quia in aeternum non commovebitur'); these verses recall the just man, possibly deceased. This device answers another forced interrogative setting of verse 10 ('desiderium peccatorum peribit?').

The musical emphasis on 'in memoria aeterna erit justus', and on the words and deeds of the just man, along with the freedom with which Cozzolani approaches the psalm text, suggest the interpretation of this section (and of the entire psalm, given the stress on 'Beatus vir' and 'Jocundus homo') as a tribute to a virtuous, joyous, generous, and deceased man. Some possibilities include: St William of Vercelli (if the psalm had indeed been performed during his Second Vespers in 1649); a former Benedictine superior; or perhaps even Federigo Borromeo. The process for his canonization would stall in the anti-Quietist Rome of the later Seicento; certainly 'jocunditas' was one of the prelate's most heartfelt values (as in *De christianae mentis jocunditate*), and his memory would be held sacred by the Benedictines of S. Maria in Lambrugo.[36]

The most likely motivation for the procedures of colloquy in this psalm is the pastoral conceit of the collection as a whole, and its dialogic implications. For the dialogue is the pastoral genre *par excellence*,

---

[35] For instance, Cozzolani changed the declamation of verse 7, 'In memoria aeterna erit justus; ab auditione mala non timebit' into 'In memoria aeterna erit justus; justus erit in memoria aeterna; jocundo homo, ab auditione mala non timebit. Non timebit? Non timebit.'

[36] Their anonymous chronicler movingly lamented the prelate's passing, his sanctity and intercession, and his kindness towards nuns: 'A di 21 *settem*bre [1631] il sopra*detto* Ill.mo Sig.r Cardinale Boromeo . . . finalemente è morto . . . ne mi pare di douere pasar con silenzio la liberalità et grande carita uerso le sue peccorelle [nuns], masime nel tempo della grande carestia, et pestilenzza, *che* ben si puo con uerita dire ch'habbi seguito le pedatte di Carlo San*to* et in soma, à lasiatto chiaro indicio di santità di uitta si *che* si spera col fauor di Dio et sua intercesione inpetrar delle gratie, et non in particolare *per* essere da *q*uesta anima santa mo*l*to amate, et molte uolte à hautto a dire ch'erauamo la pupila de soi hocchi': *Annales sacrae*, fo. 277[v].

Ex. 10.18. Cozzolani, *Beatus vir* (1650), bars 245–52

and its invasion here of a far-removed genre seems to be a tribute to its influence in Milan, and to Cozzolani's own conception of her book. The psalm setting links Cozzolani's techniques to contemporary ideas of psalmody as a dialogue between the individual and God, associated specifically with nuns: 'E perche il salmeggiare è un colloquio che fa l'huomo con Dio', as Lampugnani had put it in his encomium of S. Radegonda a year before the publication of the *Salmi a otto*.[37]

If *Dixit* had troped the doxology into the verses, the eight-voice *Laudate pueri* reverses the process by troping the opening refrain ('Laudate') into the doxology (Ex. 10.19), another witty or 'bizarro' feature. This has the effect of making the first member of the doxology into yet another ABA′ verse: 'Laudate pueri' (tutti)–'Gloria' (CI and II)–'Laudate Dominum' (tutti); this procedure had been heard earlier at 'Quis sicut Dominus' and 'suscitans'. This setting picks a less standard but still common modal assignment (8) for the laudatory affect of the psalm, and *concertato* writing is much in evidence, notably at the CCA *bassetto* setting over a descending ostinato tetrachord at 'Sit nomen Domini'. But the other notable feature of this setting is the apportioning of solos to Alto I, a favourite voice-type for Cozzolani. This voice introduces phrases ('Quis sicut Dominus', 'suscitans', 'et de stercore') that are then taken up by the tutti.

The smaller-scale setting of *Laudate pueri* (II; CCTT2Vl) shares its G *finalis* with the larger version. Indeed, its constant return to G and similar melodic figuration give it the sound of a strophic variation. Yet, in line with the *motetto con stromenti* tradition, the structure features the interaction of the two-period refrain opening ('Laudate pueri . . . nomen Domini') with the instrumental *sinfonie* and a gradually thickening texture:

A (ab)	'Laudate . . . nomen Domini'	TT
B	'Sit nomen . . . benedictum'	CC
Sinfonia		
Aa		
C	'A solis . . . laudabile nomen Domini'	CC
Sinfonia (variation)		
D	'Excelsus . . . gloria eius'	CC (echo)
Ab (abbreviated)		
E	'Quis . . . respicit humilia'	CI

[37] *Della vita*, 47.

Ex. 10.19. Cozzolani, *Laudate pueri a 8* (1650), bars 165–73

Ab (abbreviated)		
F	'Suscitans . . . populi sui'	C2
Ab (complete)		
G	'Qui habitare . . . laetantam'	CC, 2Vl
Dox a interlaced with A (ab)		
Dox b		Tutti

If this solution is somewhat more formalized, still the parallels with the eight-voice setting in *tono* and structure suggest that these are alternative approaches in basically the same vein.

Again, *Laetatus sum* tropes the opening refrain—or more precisely, a period of the refrain—into the doxology. But the approach to refrains in this clearly *sesto tono* (on C) piece is somewhat more complex. First, the opening 'Laetatus sum' tag is divided into two melodically related but distinct periods (Ex. 10.20). It is the second of these, which moves towards A, that is recalled between verses 6 and 7 ('et abundantia diligentibus te' and 'Fiat pax'); the first returns after the opening peroration (TI and II) of the doxology. We shall see the importance of motion towards the sixth scale-degree in other pieces. The parallel textual construction ('et abundantia') in the second halves of verses 6 and 7 moved Cozzolani to a repeat of material, in effect forming a second, internal refrain; this also is used in the short solos of verses 8 and 9. Parallelism is again central, and this procedure will also be found in the concertos of the 1650 book. The structure of the psalm is as follows:

Verse		*Pitch-centre(s)*
1a	Laetatus sum (period A)	C
	Laetatus sum (period B)	C→A→C
1b	In domum	C→A→C
2a/b	Stantes erant	A→G
3a	Jerusalem	A
3b	Cuius participatio	C
4a/b	Illuc enim (TI solo)	C
Ref	Laetatus sum (period B)	
5a/b	Quia illic (TII solo)	C
6a	Rogate	C→A
6b	Et abundantia	A→C
Ref	Laetatus (period B)	
7a	Fiat pax	A
7b	Et abundantia (music of 6b)	A→C

Ex. 10.20. Cozzolani, *Laetatus sum* (1650), bars 1–38

Ex. 10.20. *cont.*

8a/b	Propter fratres (CI solo)	C
9a/b	Propter domum (CII; = music of v. 8)	C
Dox	Gloria	C
	Laetatus (period A)	G
	[repeated, the second time with Laetatus, period B on G]	
	Sicut erat	C

Finally, *Nisi Dominus*, a typically seventh-mode piece, returns to the refrain-less structure of *Confitebor*. Again, as in 'matrem filiorum laetantam' in *Laudate pueri*, a long peroration on the final half-verse ('non confundetur cum loquetur'; see Ex. 10.21) sums up the affect of the entire psalm.

The two Magnificats share the same surface features: homophonic declamatory tuttis, *concertato* solo to quartet writing for the verses, florid doxologies. They differ in *tono* (*primo* and *nono*, respectively), and structural principles. For the first setting represents one of the more outstanding cases of refrain troping to be found in the whole Lombard repertory; in this case, a verbal insertion of 'anima mea magnificat Dominum' (or 'magnificat anima mea Dominum') between half-verses or even in the middle of a sentence ('fecit mihi magna | magnificat Dominum anima mea'). Here, there is no musical refrain, simply the unpredictable repetition of the verbal phrase set to the music of the surrounding sections (Ex. 10.22). There is no precedent in any psalm setting for this, and the effect is that of a *salmo bizarro* topping off an already witty and idiosyncratic collection. By contrast, the second canticle simply proceeds in liturgically correct fashion through its text.[38]

Cozzolani's large-scale procedures are clear and recurrent: the refrain or da capo structures are achieved either by troping the opening verse into later sections (*Laudate pueri*, *Laetatus sum*; this is also found in the solo *Laudate Dominum* and the *Laudate pueri a 6*) or by troping the doxology (*Dixit Dominus*) among *earlier* verses. Only *Nisi Dominus* eschews the repetition of textual and melodic material. Thus the structure if not the forces of Cozzolani's *Salmi a otto* are paralleled in Casati. The use of refrains, *concertato* solos, and clearly differentiated melodic material, all of which are found in the 1650 volume, are also characteristic of the psalm repertory of the 1640s. Cozzolani's book is a collection of *salmi ariosi* on a large scale,

---

[38] Given the omnipresence of the refrain principle in the Vespers, this would suggest that the first, not the second, setting was the one heard on 26 June 1649.

Ex. 10.21. Cozzolani, *Nisi Dominus* (1650), bars 92–9

Ex. 10.21. *cont.*

96
Non con - fun - de - tur cum lo - que-tur i - ni - mi - cis su - is in por -
Non con - fun - de - tur cum lo - que-tur i - ni - mi - cis su - is in por -
- ta, Non con - fun - de - tur cum lo - que-tur i - ni - mi - cis su - is in por -
- ta, Non con - fun - de - tur cum lo - que-tur i - ni - mi - cis su - is in por -
Non con - fun - de - tur cum lo - que-tur i - ni - mi - cis su - is in por -
Non con - fun - de - tur cum lo - que-tur i - ni - mi - cis su - is in por -
- ta, Non con - fun - de - tur cum lo - que-tur i - ni - mi - cis su - is in por -
Non con - fun - de - tur cum lo - que-tur i - ni - mi - cis su - is in por -
5
98
- ta, i - ni - mi - cis su - is in por - ta,
- ta, i - ni - mi - cis su - is in por - ta,
- ta, i - ni - mi - cis su - is in por - ta,
- ta, i - ni - mi - cis su - is in por - ta,
- ta, i - ni - mi - cis su - is in por - ta,
- ta, i - ni - mi - cis su - is in por - ta,
- ta, i - ni - mi - cis su - is in por - ta,
- ta, i - ni - mi - cis su - is in por - ta,

Ex. 10.22. Cozzolani, Magnificat (I; 1650), bars 51–6

presumably for the two ensembles of S. Radegonda performing together. The comparison with Cozzi's and Turati's more modest efforts points up the fact that musically (apart from the qualities of sisters' singing) there was nothing quite like this to be heard anywhere in Milan during the decade: the infusion of an essentially familiar scoring with the compositional techniques of the new-style Lombard motet. If these works are any measure of S. Radegonda's ceremonial repertory in the decade, it is no wonder that the *chiesa esteriore* was crowded with visiting dignitaries: the music was either more novel and exciting (compared with the Duomo) or on a larger scale (compared with repertory at S. Maria presso S. Celso or S. Maria della Scala). Indeed, the main parallel in the northern Italian repertory is with S. Marco: the *concertato* solos, instrumental ritornelli, repeated textual declamation, and highly sectionalized approach found in some psalm settings of Cavalli's *Musiche sacre* (1656).[39]

Finally, the other concertos—from duets to quartets—of the 1650 book reveal something of Cozzolani's development. If on one hand

[39] Cf. Cavalli's *Dixit a 8* or *Lauda Jerusalem a 8* (transcribed in J. H. Moore, *Vespers at St. Mark's* (Ann Arbor, 1979), ii. 1–32 and 93–107, respectively) with the excerpts given here. That Cozzolani could not have heard this music makes the similarities all the more striking.

these pieces are marked by greater length, on the other non-parallelisms begin to affect her style, and the confined balance of the 1642 pieces is often missing. The text of *Venimus in altitudinem maris* (CC) is again unusual; to the quotation of despair used in Holy Week liturgy (Ps. 68: 3; here in a plural form) it adds a free reworking of Jesus' calming the storm at sea (Matt. 8: 24), given a Marian twist with the Virgin, not Christ, as the intercessor who saves the faithful from physical and spiritual storms on earth.[40] The motet juxtaposes strongly contrasting sections ('venimus in altitudinem' with 'et motus magnus factus est') and internal repeated phrases. By this point, however, simple refrains are no longer enough; the piece is structured by a constantly variable triple-time recurrence of 'succurre, o pia' or 'curre, Maria', usually extended so as to end on the *finalis* G (bars 95–104). The last plea of the faithful, 'fiat magna tranquillitas', ends on the sixth modal degree (E), followed by an *allegro* reworking of the 'stella maris' idea from the opening back on the *finalis*, and closing with an extended version of the refrain. *Venimus* thus marks a link between the more iterative structures of the 1650 book and the cantilena refrain motet.

Quis audivit unquam tale?, another Nativity piece (CCB), repeats its opening arioso refrain two-thirds of the way through the piece; most striking, however, is the contrast between the sections of antiphonal motifs and invertible counterpoint ('laudemus cum angelis') on one hand, and florid declamation on the other. Again clearly on G, the most surprising aspects of its solos and duets are the kaleidoscopically changing textures and unexpected extensions of melodic ideas ('o vere partum', treated first contrapuntally and then homophonically in a parallel to the dual nature of Christ). The simplicity of such Christmas pieces evoked directly representational music, for instance the *catabasis* and *anabasis* for 'o descensum profundissimum, o ascensum sublimissimum' (Ex. 10.23). The final section, swinging between homophony and polyphony, highlights the sheer adoration of the action:

---

[40] No likely feast or occasion in the 1640s, apart from general Marian intercessory devotion, suggests itself for this motet. The literary conceit of the piece may be due to a transfer of Radegund's hagiography to the Virgin; Lampugnani's *vita* had recounted how the queen's intercession (in the form of a dove) had saved Frankish ambassadors in peril of shipwreck (*Della vita*, 94–5).

Nos quoque devoti et humiles, adoremus cum pastoribus, laudemus cum angelis, laudemus Regem Salomonem, in diademate carneo quo Illum coronavit mater Sua, Virgo Maria.[41]

The *corona* figure for 'coronavit' again underscores the direct relation between text and music in this public piece.

Venite sodales, the 'generic' sanctoral piece (ATB), is longer and more ambitious, but shows a similar reiterative structure. Its middle section is formed by a three-verse strophic form ('O floscule, beate floscule', scored successively for A, T, and AT) punctuated by a continuo ritornello. Here, there are two multi-sectional tuttis (another sign of the dialogue's influence on the concerto), one marking

Ex. 10.23. Cozzolani, *Quis audivit?* (1650), bars 85–95

---

the end of the exordium ('Mirabilis Deus in sanctis suis', another sanctoral reference), and a more extended one rounding off the piece ('Ergo laetantes'), with another syncopated homorhythmic phrase ('vive in aeternum').

One concise example of Cozzolani's approach to texts as reflected in phrase and period structure is *Tu dulcis, o bone Jesu*, a setting of a free text on an important topic, the Double Intercession of Jesus and Mary; as one might expect from the subject and the scoring (AATT), parallelism is an important feature. The text alternates the praise of the two, with unison declamation, switching after a cadence on the *finalis* D to more personal sentiments, and concluding with another pseudo-sequence:

> . . . Cantabo semper de Te, Domine,
> cogitabo semper de te, domina,
> exaltabo in Te, Rex Angelorum,
> te magnificabo cum Filio, regina caelorum.
> Ave ergo, cordis mei Jesu,
> salve, salus mea Jesu.
> Tu mater sancta,
> tu mater pia,
> tu mater clemens,
> in hac mundi via,
> impetra veniam,
> obtine gratiam . . .[42]

The first triple-time section is allotted to two parallel periods (one for AA on Jesus, one for TT on Mary). Yet the correspondence breaks down on smaller levels. The text of the two parallel thoughts ('Tu dulcis, o bone Jesu' [i.e. His body is sweet to the taste], | 'Tu suavis, o alma Maria') includes two extra syllables in the second line; Cozzolani therefore had to add an extra bar (bars 23–4) in order to achieve correct declamation (see Ex. 10.24). Furthermore, the structure of the two periods does not scan evenly: seven versus nine bars (also noteworthy is the motivic interplay of the continuo in bars 10–14 with the interrupted voices, another new feature of the 1650 concertos), followed by seven plus one plus nine.

The other major piece on this subject in the 1650 book, the CC duet *O quam bonus es*, shows different procedures at work in

---

[42] 'I shall always sing of You, o Lord; I shall always think of you, o queen; I shall exalt in You, King of the Angels; I shall magnify you with your Son, queen of the heavens. Hail, Jesus of my heart; hail, Jesus, my salvation. You, holy mother, pious mother, merciful mother, our path in this world, gain us mercy, obtain us grace . . .'.

Ex. 10.24. Cozzolani, *Tu dulcis, o bone Jesu* (1650), bars 1–23

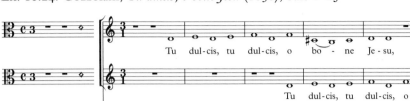

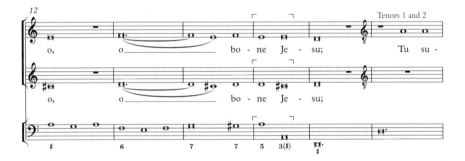

text–music relations and internal structure (see App. F). In subject it is also a key piece. For its literary text, which (unlike *Tu dulcis*) moves immediately to the personal, combines the two major topics of Cozzolani's motets, Eucharistic devotion and Marian acclamation, by the use of a topos that harks back to medieval piety and boasts an important iconographic tradition, one closely associated with specifically female piety: the double meditation on the wounds of Christ Crucified and on the Virgin's milk as bodily salvation and as nourishment for the Christian. If Christ's side saved the believer, then Mary's milk nourished the Redeemer, and the Fountain of Salvation fed by these two sources received numerous illustrations in late medieval and early modern Europe. Cozzolani's unusual inclusion of two pieces on the topic in the 1650 book reveals the importance of the combination for her own devotion. The corporal emphasis of the text of *O quam bonus*, the length of Cozzolani's setting, and the multiplicity of highly charged similes and images set it into a category apart from the 1642 motets.

Caroline Walker Bynum has outlined the ways in which the Double Intercession was associated with and given expression by female mystics of the later Middle Ages;[43] its reappearance in early Seicento Milan is another mark of the essentially medieval character of spirituality in the city. *O quam bonus es* is not alone in its musical treatment of the Double Intercession; *Tu dulcis, o bone Jesu*, however, lacks the detailed corporal and affective imagery of the duet. In the context of female monastic spirituality and reading matter, Novati's Eucharistic theology, along with the omnipresence of the Song of Songs, provides the intellectual background to Cozzolani's motet.[44]

One such pictoral representation of the topic was created by Melchiorre Gherardini in the 1640s for Porta's church of S. Maria presso S. Celso.[45] In this painting, Catherine of Siena presses her lips

---

[43] *Holy Feast*, 270–4, which also provides some iconographic examples from the 15th c. for the topic.

[44] For the idea, Novati, *Eucharistici amores*; in addition, Cant. 5: 1 reads (the male Spouse is the speaker): 'Comedi favum cum melle meo; Bibi vinum meum cum lacte meo. Comedite, amici, et bibite; Et inebriamini, carissimi.' The Eucharistic exegesis of this passage is obvious, and the transfer of 'lacte meo' to the Virgin, in light of Seicento Marian devotion, not unexpected. The musical emphasis on the word 'inebriamini' found in Cozzolani's 1642 *O quam suavis est* and 1648 *Venite, qui esauritis* underscores the centrality of this quotation from the canticle.

[45] The painting is reproduced in Kendrick, 'Feminized Devotion, Musical Nuns, and the "New-Style" Lombard Motet of the 1640's', in K. Marshall (ed.), *Rediscovering the Muses: Women's Musical Traditions* (Boston, 1993), 124–39.

for nourishment to the wounds of the Crucified Christ, with her mouth shaped to receive the Host. Uniquely among non-scriptural or non-breviary motet texts in Milan, *O quam bonus es* was set by three composers: Porta (*Motetti a 2–5* of 1648), Cozzolani, and Grossi (*Orfeo pellegrino*, 1659).[46] The text itself (which bears the unique rubric 'Si lodano le Piaghe di Christo, & le Mamelle della Madonna', again emphasizing the bodily nature of salvation) consists of a series of parallel comparisons of the two fluids, along with exclamations of their effect on the believer. The overall structure of the text marks a meditative progression from the initial wonder at the *benignitas* of Jesus and Mary, through the Christian reaction to such goodness, to a final consideration of life and death.

The meditative path of this text—from the corporeal nourishment of the Christian by blood and milk to the concluding juxtaposition of food and drink, laughter and joy, life and death ('O potus, o cibus, | O risus, o gaudium, | O felix vita, beata mors')—may seem unusual. But again, Federigo's writings highlight the associations. Several chapters in *De christianae mentis jocunditate* (I, 9 and III, 13) use precisely these ideas. The first, 'On heavenly laughter', gives as examples an unnamed female mystic and then St Catherine of Genoa, both of whom experienced the heights of divine sweetness in the form of interior laughter, granted them after they had achieved the highest state of spiritual perfection, that of perfect emptiness (*annihilatio*) wishing only for God.[47] The connection with Christian death is provided by a later chapter, 'On the most joyous death of various persons', in which Federigo again reports the happiness felt

---

[46] It seems to have been a point of pride for composers to create (or have created for them) unique motet texts. Porta's setting probably dates from the period 1642–7 and may relate to the painting. The fact that at least some of his concertos were newly composed in 1648 is evident from Vincenti's annoyed note that two of them (not including *O quam bonus*) had to be placed at the end of the edition, after the Marian litany (contrary to usual practice), because they had not arrived from Milan in time. This problem may also have occasioned Cozzolani's physical presence in Venice two years later for the production of her collection, the next Milanese work to roll off Vincenti's presses (see Ch. 9 n. 18). Grossi's setting survives without a continuo part, but seems to fit more into the *motetto con strumenti* tradition, and I have excluded it from consideration here.

[47] 'De caelesti Risu', pp. 26–7: 'Narrauit mihi ecstatica quaedam grandis natu, et spectatae eadem sanctitatis, contigisse sibi, ut inter ecstasim tali quadam iucunditate afficeretur. Dixit ipsa: Domine, nihil aliud a te expeto, quam te ipsum . . . Neque vltra responsum accepit, sed tanta suauitate risus interioris delibuta est, ut pene moreretur; ecstasisque illa longi temporis fuit', followed by a similar account of Catherine of Genoa.

by several medieval female mystics while dying.[48] The entire meditative path represents a typically 'optimistic' treatment of the standard topos of the *memento mori*; it was recalled a year before
Cozzolani's book in Lampugnani's account of Radegund's sanctity.[49]

Porta's version features careful declamation and motifs crafted to
fit each clause or phrase. Porta's setting anticipates or parallels
Cozzolani's in several regards: the use of 'O me felicem, o me
beatum' as an internal refrain; the dialogic interchange between the
voices to set the praise of Jesus' and Mary's goodness; and the stability of a final section for 'O potus, o cibus', here over a quasi-ostinato.
Cozzolani's approach to this text is somewhat different:[50]

Unit	Bar	Beginning of text	Pitch-centre(s)
A	1	'O quam bonus'	B♭→G
B	10		G→B♭
A	28	(Canto II)	B♭→G
B′	37	(2 voices, extended)	G–B♭
C	70	'diligenti'	B♭→G
Da	79	'o me felicem'	G→B♭
Db	82		B♭→G
Da	85		G
Ea	88	'Hinc pascor'	G
Eb	92	'quo me vertam'	G→B♭
F	97	'In vulnere vita'	B♭
Da	118	'o me felicem' (twice)	G
Eb	124	'quo me vertam'	G→B♭
Ga	129	'Sanguis emundat'	B♭→D
Gb	145	'O vulnera'	B♭→C
Gc	150	'Aurea vulnera'	C→G
Ha	158	'Sanguis amabilis'	B♭
Hb	162	'manna jocundior'	B♭
Hb	171	instrumental ritornello	B♭
Ha	180	'Lac exoptabile'	B♭
Unit	Bar	Beginning of text	Pitch-centre(s)

[48] 'De jucundissimo nonnullorum obitu'; a preceding chapter (III, 11), 'Quibus sit ama-
bile mori', had introduced the topic as the summation of the Christian soul's happiness.

[49] A long account of her 'felicissimo transito' is in *Della vita*, 126 ff., immediately after
the abbot's description of the contents of her visions.

[50] I have assigned upper- and lower-case letters to sections and their constituent melodic
ideas. Padoan, 'Sulla struttura', makes the point that in this kind of analysis (and repertory),
the repetition of even small blocks of material is more important than the sheer length of
sections, and so seemingly disparate chunks of music each receive separate designations.

Unit	Bar	Beginning of text	Pitch-centre(s)
Hb	184	'favo nobilius'	B♭
Hb	193	instrumental ritornello	B♭
I	202	'Te amo'	B♭→G
Da	212	'O me felicem'	F
I	213	'Te amo'	F→B♭
Da	223	'O me felicem'	G→B♭
Db	226		B♭
Da	228		B♭→G
Eb	231	'quo me vertam'	G→B♭
Ea'	236	'Hoc sanguine pascar'	G (ends on D)
J	241	'O potus' [*ciacona*]	B♭
K	262	'O felix vita'	B♭

Most immediately noteworthy is the rather complicated system of internal refrains ('o me felicem' and 'quo me vertam'). But equally audible is the constant oscillation between the modal areas of B flat and the sixth degree G, a completely different approach from that of *Tu dulcis*.[51] This tension between the two pitch-centres is seconded by the two approaches to large-scale structure: on one hand, a traditionally rhetorical approach, with the musical adumbration of Jesus' wounds and Mary's milk marked off by the end of the exordium ('in vulnere vita, in ubere salus', a reiteration of the basic conceit of the piece), underlined musically by the first large stable section on B flat, and followed by further reflections on the theme. On the other hand, a chiastic structure is also present: the repetition of the Da, Db, and Eb sections towards the end of the piece provides large-scale symmetry, with the final sections anchored securely on B♭ (especially by the ostinato for 'O potus, o cibus') as opposed to the constant tonal oscillation of the opening.

The beginning of the piece is somewhat reminiscent of two-voice dialogues, with self-contained statements of the opening idea in each voice. The duet begins with a long, melodically rounded, and harmonically closed period for first soprano (meditating on Jesus' wounds), which ends (after a surprising lowered third for purposes of closure on the last statement of 'Jesu') on the *finalis*. The basic harmonic tension of the piece, that between B flat and G, is introduced already in the extension of the first phrase ('o quam jocundus mi

[51] On such relationships in a younger contemporary with later ties to S. Radegonda, see R. Emans, 'Die einstimmigen Kantaten, Canzonette, und Serenaden Giovanni Legrenzis' (diss., Bonn, 1984), 108 *et passim*.

Jesu'), which moves from the former to the latter for the switch to triple time that balances the opening common-time period. The surprise off-beat entrance of the second voice on the same pitch seems to exploit precisely the restricted visibility characteristic of nuns' performing spaces.

The consideration of Mary's milk, given to the second soprano, is heightened by another surprise—the entrance of the first voice just after the switch to triple time (b. 38). The tessitura of both parts is extended outward (g'' on 'quam jocundus' and d' on 'degustanti te'), which sets up the *mutatio* to G. The shift from the contemplation of the external objects (wounds and breasts of Christ and Mary, respectively) to the interior state of the singer (listener?) is marked by a phrase to serve as an internal refrain, 'O me felicem, o me beatum'.

So far, we have heard the initial praise of Jesus and Mary (set firmly on B flat) and then the introduction of the key images of tasting and food ('diligenti te . . .'), which swings around to G. The next section moves to reflection on the singer's actual feeding from Jesus and Mary ('Hinc pascor a vulnere'); it concludes with the 'O me felicem' refrain, this time directed so as to end on B flat. The relatively slow bass and passing back and forth of the short melodic ideas reinforce the contemplative nature of the section. The last section of this half, a renewed contemplation of wounds/breasts in the light of their effect on the individual soul, restates the B flat/G polarity ('Sanguis me emundat').

A rest in this meditation is provided by the next period ('Sanguis amabilis'), with its stability in B flat and its solo scoring (for each voice in turn, separated by a continuo ritornello using the bass of its second phrase).[52] The next section, 'Te amo', returns to the consideration of the individual's soul, again using the B flat/G contrast and heightening the motivic density by a combination of the 'o me felicem' and 'quo me vertam' mottos. But in this section, a new tension characterizes the 'o me felicem' refrain: cadences on G with phrase-endings alternating unpredictably between *cantus mollis* (B♭ as the third) and *cantus durus* (B♮ as the third), lessening the stability of the internal refrain. The juxtaposition of blood and life, milk and (Christian) death is emphasized by the expressed desire of 'Hoc sanguine pascar', 'let me feed from His blood', which ends on a half-cadence in G.

---

[52] There is a similar framing ritornello in *Venite sodales*.

By this point in her career, however, Cozzolani had other means for imparting a sense of closure. The penultimate section moves the meditative progress of the text from Jesus and Mary as food to the consideration of eternal joy ('O potus . . . o gaudium'). Cozzolani set this to another kind of stability: the well-known *ciacona* bass, with progressively more elaborate versions of a single phrase in the top voices. The link between life and death, of divinely nourished life as the necessary precondition for a happy death, the ultimate fate of the believing soul, is set to a long closing adagio section, which again repeats the move to G (bars 262–71) and returns to the same minor-third inflected B flat cadence that had closed off the opening statement, perhaps the strongest mark of closure at Cozzolani's disposal.

At the same time, the point of this piece is the contemplative motion from the individual to Jesus and Mary as food and back to the individual soul, a move summarized by the B flat/G oscillation.[53] But just as important are Cozzolani's means for sectional contrast and climax, ones dependent on abstract and arbitrary motifs unlike the direct representation of the more public pieces in the volume. The motet provides 'rapturous' music, with its short motifs, static basses, and phrase expansion, for the meditative passage from the most basic imagery of female piety, Jesus' blood and Mary's milk, to the consideration of the believer's eternal fate. *O quam bonus* expands the medieval heritage of piety towards a musical and universal end. It serves as a summary of Cozzolani's work in the duet medium.

In several key respects or genres—the dialogues, the *salmi ariosi*—her motets either introduced new stylistic trends to Milan or took established local traditions in new and sometimes surprising directions. In the 1650 book, not all the expansions of her earlier concerto form have the same compelling logic of *O quam bonus*. But there is no evading her place among composers in the Milan of the 1640s.

---

[53] The piece marks a transition from modality not because of its key signature, but because its harmonic goals and oscillation have nothing to do with important modal degrees.

Solo Motets and their Background from Cozzolani to Badalla

◇

> Dio sà, che incontro sono per hauere, al primo suo comparire
> alla luce questi miei Componimenti? . . . chi sà, che hauendo io
> creduto d'insinuar ad altri vagezza di cantar questi miei Motetti,
> non ne tragga io medema stimolo di piangere le mie sfortune?
>
> (Badalla, 'Al benigno lettore', *Motetti a voce sola*, 1684)

The years between Cozzolani's books and Badalla's solo motets witnessed the high and low points in the urban politics of nuns' polyphony. Yet the most remarkable feature of the concertos and Vespers dedicated to sisters in this generation was precisely their normality: the inscriptions by Sisto Reina, Giovanni Battista Cesati, or Francesco Bagatti are of standard pieces in a variety of scorings, with little sign of the *voci pari* or 'motetti per monache' tradition. Even the one Roman anthology, Giovanni Battista Caifabri's 1665 book addressed to Maria Resta, consists of typical duets and trios by leading figures (Graziani, Carissimi), including CB and ATB motets.

The compositional methods of the local repertory represented yet another extension and to some degree a standardization of the techniques found at mid-century. The literary language of the small-scale concerto became more artistic and less personal, without the heightened tone of pieces like *O quam bonus es*.[1] Motets grew longer, owing to the repetition of exact sequences and the more marked division among sections. If the text of Reina's 1653 *Cara vulnera Christi* evokes the themes and vocabulary of mid-century Quietism,

---

[1] Bagatti's 1659 *Ornate thalamum* (Ch. 5) provides one example.

still the musical means (extended triple-time sections, and a complete da capo) represent different procedures from Cozzolani's.[2]

In the first major concerto collection inscribed to a nun, Bagatti's Book 3 of 1667, sequences and suspensions would generate even longer melodic periods, ones not necessarily motivated by text; the 'Eia ergo' section of *Salve regina* (ATB), for instance, is built entirely of 7–6 suspensions over a bass that descends in chromatic half-notes from *c'* down to *E* (Ex. 11.1). Carlo Giuseppe San Romano's 1668

Ex. 11.1. Bagatti, *Salve regina* (1667), bars 79–87

[2] The words, with their references to Jesus as Spouse and lover, highlight the feminization of piety and seem appropriate to their dedicatee's devotion: 'Cara vulnera Christi, amoris origines vitae, qui vos non amat amare nescit, qui vivit intra vos extra vivere nequit. [instrumental ritornello] Anima quae amas, veni, et, si non amas, veni, lava te his undis; merge te his fontibus; quam pulchra, quam amans, quam candida emerges imo nec emerges; sed pulchra, sed amans, sed candida intra divinos latices vives, quia in te non vives sed in sponso, sed in amante, sed in Jesu felicissima vives; sic edocta, sic amans, sic laetabunda

Marian motet addressed to an Archinti who maintained the traditions at S. Maria Annunciata again recalls medieval sequences in its text, matching the regularity of its music:

> Salve, sponsa Creatoris
> salve, fons veri dulcoris,
> nostri cantus non ignoris,
> salve, laeta domina . . .[3]

Finally, the last concerto edition inscribed to a sister, the local 1678 reprint of Carlo Donato Cossoni's originally Bolognese op. 1, expands and continues the central place of the dialogue; five of its thirteen pieces are in this genre.

Mass and Vespers Ordinary settings were not dissimilar; Reina's 1653 *Armonia ecclesiastica* consists of multiple psalm settings from a sequence usable only for First Vespers of the male sanctoral cursus (Pss. 109, 110, 111, 112, and 116). It is completely *concertato*; even the respond *a 2* (CA) features motion in parallel thirds and sixths, along with a triple-time doxology that would have evoked Litta's wrath for its 'mondanità', all the more so for being dedicated to Luigia Gonzaga at S. Paolo.[4] Maurizio Cazzati's op. 37 of 1666 contains standard Emilian approaches: a *concertato* mass, well-sectionalized psalms, with only a *Laetatus sum a 4* set in modified *stile antico*. Perhaps most revealing of the new formalization is Isabella Leonarda's 1674 *Laetatus sum*, set syllabically and without internal refrains.[5] Bagatti's 1672 *Motetti, Messa e salmi brevi, e pieni*, dedicated to Regina Melzi at S. Bernardino alle Monache, is an expansive collection, containing Vespers for almost all possible feasts in the Roman breviary (sixteen psalms, with two Magnificats, ignoring Ambrosian rite in yet another 'affront' to Litta), a syllabic *Messa breve*, and two ceremonial motets, both with a da capo.

Within this mid-century Milanese repertory, the solo motet represents an important and idiosyncratic subgenre. Its modest

---

cantabis. Cara vulnera [da capo] . . . nequit. Alleluia.' The emphasis on 'candida' seems yet another personalized reference to the dedicatee, Candida Archinta at S. Ambrogio. For a musical example, see Kendrick, 'La musica nel Santuario'.

[3] 'Hail, spouse of the Creator, hail, source of true sweetness, do not spurn our songs, hail happy Queen.'

[4] For a discussion and examples, see Kendrick, 'La musica nel Santuario'.

[5] Although Gioconda Bossi, to whom the work is dedicated, was an alto, the vocal parts are not differentiated in complexity.

performance requirements meant that even smaller houses could cultivate the form, while the solo singing of the 'star' nuns like Ceva, Clerici, or Palomera at S. Radegonda clearly attracted notice.[6] That sisters both owned copies of such collections as well as received numerous dedications of solo motets reinforces the idea of the genre's popularity within *clausura*. By century's end, the number of inscriptions in such collections as Carlo Federico Vigoni's *Nuova raccolta* (RISM 1679[1]), and the overwhelming scoring of the genre for canto or alto, indicate that nuns were among the primary performers of this genre in the city. The Eucharistic references of many solo motet texts point to performance as Elevation pieces, music to prepare the soul for the reception of Christ's Body, despite the repeated curial warnings against solo pieces in the context of Communion.

The association with nuns is underscored by publication history. If we exclude Carlo Landriani's book of 1652, Cozzolani was the only urban composer to publish solo motets between Donati in 1636 and Casola in 1660.[7] Her seventeen surviving examples of the form represented its principal projection into the aural world of the city for a generation. The four pieces in *Concerti sacri* embody the first Milanese appearance of several new traits in the subgenre.[8] Donati's collections had represented a fusion of late Florentine monody (*accenti*, scalar *passaggi*) with the motif-driven phrases of the 1620s, setting scriptural or breviary texts in a rhetorically clear style. Cozzolani's 1642 solo motets, on the other hand, evince the defining characteristics of the genre typical of the decade and beyond: the exclusive use of long, free (non-scriptural) texts (sometimes in a flowery poetic language), set in constant alternation between duple and triple metres, with emphasis on the sequential (but sometimes unexpected) repetition of a single melodic figure. In other words, they reflect an intensification of certain musical parameters found in the new-style duet, and indeed these pieces are more similar to Casati than to Donati. Since there is no possibility for textural

---

[6] The questions of transposition are largely absent; almost the entire Milanese solo repertory is scored for canto or (less frequently) alto.

[7] Donati's second book (along with some examples by Grancini) appeared in the former year, Casola's motet collection in the latter (both mention nuns in some context). I exclude Milanese editions by extra-urban figures (e.g. Reina, in Saronno); Picinelli, *Ateneo*, mentions no other (now lost) editions.

[8] Again, Casati had provided the first examples of the new style in Lombardy as a whole, with the *Sacri concenti a 1*, op. 2 (Venice: Magni, 1641).

climax, internal cadences are marked by melodic perorations and semiotic *cadentiae duriusculae*.

As noted above (Ch. 6), *Concerti sacri*'s first solo motet, *O quam bonum*, conflates Christological and Eucharistic vocabulary. Its musical structure also juxtaposes the quick triple-time long periods with common-time declamatory sections. The opening is formed by one of the former, again on an ostinato that quickly dissolves, setting the joys of living in Jesus' heart (Ex. 11.2).[9] The opening works as a series of long descents with unpredictable cadential points (d', e', a'). This is then rounded off with a recall of the opening ostinato in diminution (bars 36–8). The following invitation to the 'animae sanctae' (another Quietist reference) takes an unexpected inflection towards flat regions in order to underline Jesus' benignity ('et videte quam benignus sit Dominus diligentibus se'). The 'Lord's door' into which the just will enter and from which they will feed is a reference again to the wounds of Christ's side, as in *O quam bonus es*.[10] And the first half's climax, the reference to the sweetness of Paradise, evokes the gestures of the 1620s and 1630s: the twice-repeated *mutatio toni* (g'; c''; d''; Ex. 11.3) and a cadence on the reciting-tone, E.

At this point Cozzolani brings back the entire opening section at its original pitch, with its last phrase ornamented (bars 151–85 = 1–35). Then the text's speaker suddenly switches address to Jesus ('Aspice, respice, Domine, populum istum'), asking that the faithful be admitted into His heart (again a presupposition of nuns as perpetual intercessors); the rhetorical repetition one tone higher concludes on A. The final plea ('let this your people always say: "Here we live, for we have chosen Him"') is another triple-time section that balances the opening, and the apostrophic 'Alleluia' is set over a long descending bass that limns the modal octave twice. The final gesture once again recalls the closing signals of an earlier generation: the leaps to ornamental dissonances over three pedal-points, and the forte/piano repetition of motifs. The language of the text is entirely typical of the post-1630 inwardness, while the combination of small-scale gestures from the 1620s with the musical procedures of the new generation seems appropriate for an introductory (in a double sense)

---

[9] The similarity of the bass pattern (structural pitches a–f–d–e) to that of the opening of *Bone Jesu, fons amoris* is noteworthy; perhaps this was a marker of the associative field of Jesus' goodness for Cozzolani.

[10] 'quia haec porta Domini; justi tantum intrabunt in eam, et ibi pascua laeta inveniunt', set to a long move from G to E.

Ex. 11.2. Cozzolani, *O quam bonum, o quam jocundum* (1642), bars 1–40

Ex. 11.3. Cozzolani, *O quam bonum, o quam jocundum* (1642), bars 135–50

motet. *O quam bonum* presents some of the topics and musical methods of the book as a whole.

The Christmas motet *Ecce annuntio vobis* (C) is a more iterative piece with no sectional refrain. Its exordium is longer (bars 1–41), beginning on a short three-bar ostinato; then the vocal line gradually extends its range up to the high *e″* and then down to the low *d′* (for 'gaudium'). Once again (as in Rusca's *Consolamini, popule meus*), the idea of the angelic message is highlighted by an extremely high continuo line, this time repeating the *piva* bass on G and A in order to achieve rhetorical heightening (*analepsis*; Ex. 11.4):

quia facta est multitudo caelestis exercitus laudantium et dicentium: Gloriam parvulo, qui est Christus.[11]

A musical end-rhyme, a rhetorical *homoioptoton* or *epistrophe* for '. . . qui est Christus', transposed to various pitch-levels, holds the numerous musical ideas together. The heightened tone of the one

[11] 'And suddenly there was a multitude of the heavenly host, praising and saying: Glory to the infant who is Christ.'

Ex. 11.4. Cozzolani, *Ecce annuntio vobis* (1642), bars 73–129

Ex. 11.4. *cont.*

adagio section, 'venerari natum de Virgine', ends with a *cadentia duriuscula* and another version of the *epistrophe* (Ex. 11.5). Finally, the essentially additive structure of the motet finds a brake in a closing triple-time 'alleluia', a phrase repeated up a second and then up a fourth (bars 198, 207, 218), and a concluding broken enunciation; this whole section is then repeated 'presto' in a closing gesture already familiar from the multi-voice concertos (bars 232–65), followed by a final gesture that recalls the 'qui est Christus' *epistrophe*.

Ex. 11.5. Cozzolani, *Ecce annuntio vobis* (1642), bars 142–9

O Maria, tu dulcis, the litany-like alto solo mentioned above (Ch. 5), is the shortest piece in the book and Cozzolani's briefest overall. But its structure shows the principles of the refrain motet again at work, with simple emphasis on the *finalis* and the dominant:

Section	Bars	Beginning of text	Pitch-centre
A	1–20	'O Maria'	g; ostinato
Ba/Bb	21–42	'O Maria, tu dulcis'	g→D→g
C	43–55 free	'Tu vera infirmorum salus'	g

Section	Bars	Beginning of text	Pitch-centre
Ba	56–67 like 21–34;	'O Maria tu sponsa'	→g
D	68–99 free	'O advocata nostra'	→D
Bb	99–106 = 35–42	'O Maria'	g
Ba/Bb	107–128 = 21–42	'O Maria, tu via'	g

The opening period, over a three-bar descending bass ostinato, is carefully balanced: two descents from the opening leap of a fourth, and a final peroration that outlines the entire range of the *tono* (*g′*–*g*; Ex. 11.6); indeed both the A and B sections are essentially composed-out descents in the vocal line. The catalogue of Marian virtues is set to the free sections C and D, with the latter extended for the plea for intercession ('respice in nos oculis misericordiae tuae'), highlighted also by the move to the pitch-centre D. The interrupted refrain (Ba) then is given its original complement (Bb), and the whole piece rounded off by a complete statement of the refrain; the musical structure underlines the litany-like character of the text.

Concinant linguae, the Marian piece that circulated under Carissimi's name in Paris, provides some idea of more extended rhetoric in the solo motet.[12] Here, irregular parallelism determines the structure; the opening seventy bars are comprised of two large-scale periods, both of which begin similarly and end on the *finalis* D. Each period is composed of three sections: an opening triple-time invitation ('Concinant linguae' and 'frondeant arbores'); a contrasting move ('jubilent corda' and 'surgat Auster'); and a longer, vocally challenging peroration ('et gaudio cuncta' and 'resonent valles'). Yet the melodic material and the metre contrast strongly in both the latter, and the metamusical reference to 'cantibus avium' evokes some of Cozzolani's most unusual and difficult passage-work (Ex. 11.7), as a *metapoiesis* for avian song (together with an unresolved ninth to accent the *cadentia duriuscula* at bars 68–70).

This opening had started and ended on D in the most marked way possible, while the heavenly invitation ('vos principes caeli, pompa solemni ducite') rests firmly on C. But another musical allusion, this time to earthly modulation ('dum nos in terris modulantes'), provokes a move back to D. And in the light of all the stability provided

---

[12] Although the text is newly written, the Song of Songs continues to resound: 'Surgat Auster, perflent venti . . .', an invocation of the natural world to praise Mary, directly recalls the words of the Sponsa: 'Surge, aquilo; et veni, auster; Perfla hortum meum, et fluant aromata illius' (4: 16). Novati, *De eminentia*, 47, quoted precisely this verse in praise of Mary's holiness.

Ex. 11.6. Cozzolani, *O Maria, tu dulcis* (1642), bars 1–42

Ex. 11.7. Cozzolani, *Concinant linguae* (1642), bars 51–70

by hymn-like sections in the duets, it is no surprise that the final half of the piece should be a triple-time pseudo-hymn ('Te laudamus, te benedicimus'). In this half, the parallelisms work differently. The 'hymn' stanza is first set to a two-period section that repeats the C/D polarity in its cadential plan (bars 103 and 121, respectively), with the second phrase irregularly transposed up a second. This is then interrupted by a common-time apostrophe (the 'gaudia matris habens, cum virginitatis honore' quoted above, p. 11), ending firmly on D (b. 128). The stanza then seems to begin anew, but the two-part symmetry of its first statement is avoided and elided. Cozzolani gives the new phrase ('O Maria, te laudamus') an *ouvert* and a *clos* ending, and the common-time coda uses both melodic (the *trilli* and dotted figures familiar from the concertos of the 1620s) and harmonic (another 6♭–3♯ sonority, followed by a *cadentia duriuscula*) signals for closure. In that sense, *Concinant linguae* combines some of the structural features of the duets with the melodic vocabulary of the solo motet.

Given the liberties of both the psalm settings and the *motetto con stromenti*, it is surprising that Cozzolani's solo *Laudate Dominum* with two violins (1650) is not even freer than its simple structure would indicate: an opening section 'Laudate . . . omnes populi' for solo voice, long instrumental ritornello, and tutti (with recalls of the opening at the end); the remaining psalm text, which moves from B minor to D minor; the return of the opening vocal idea and the ritornello, and then another troped doxology. This begins with new material but then interlaces the setting of 'laudate' in the middle of 'et nunc et semper', then surprisingly sets this last verbal phrase to the music of 'omnes populi laudate' from the very first tutti. Again here, the surprise is not the use of the refrain but the way in which the first section is split and recalled unexpectedly—a final reflection, again, of the *salmo bizarro*.

The solo motet is thus the freest genre of the post-1630 generation, open to greater textual and formal liberty than even the new-style duet. Its development over the rest of the century, however, would witness a slowly increasing standardization and ossification, on the levels of both literary language and musical structure. The *Scherzi* represent a further stage in the advance of musical (as opposed to textual) structural principles: Cozzolani's use of vocally challenging but regular melismas, transposable phrases, and internal repetition has become far more widespread. The literary language of the Eucharistic motets, filled with second-person plural imperatives

('Venite gentes, adorate'), highlights the 'public' nature of mid-century devotion to the Host (the Elevation as the public showing of the mystery of the Real Presence).[13] The extent to which the genre played off individual virtuosity, and the degree to which it was the first form to afford musical considerations pre-eminence over textual structure, are shown by one passage from *Venite, qui esuritis* (Ex. 11.8). The long sequence, among the most 'extravagant' melismas in the entire Milanese repertory up to this point, sets the central verse from the Song of Songs (5: 1) that combines references to wine and milk (this had also been central to the 1642 *O quam suavis*). Its universal exegesis (of the 'drunkenness' implied by 'inebriamini') was as a reference to the highest effect of the Eucharist (in both species) on the individual Christian soul, an idea that seems to undergird Cozzolani's prolix setting of the passage.[14]

The first piece in the book, *Alleluia, cantemus* (for Easter), is yet another musically referential opening motet, whose opening recurs

Ex. 11.8. Cozzolani, *Venite, qui esuritis* (1648), bars 23–38

---

[13] The popularity of other Eucharistic devotion in Milan, especially the Forty Hours, should be remembered. The 1670 Franciscan *Regole* specifically warned against the habit of singing overlong motets at Mass; the Elevation, where the duties of the celebrant were short, was a prime target.

[14] Novati, *Eucharisti amores*, stops just short of this verse, as if it were the implied climax of the exegesis. For the text see Ch. 10, n. 44.

in toto twice. Of the sections that it frames, 'O lux triumphalis' is a complete ABA form, and the recurrent cadences in the *primo tono* may stem from such Paschal chants as *Victimae paschales*. By contrast, *O Jesu, meus amor* sets a prose text immediately reminiscent of Birago's meditations:

O Jesu, meus amor, mea vita, meum cor et omnia mea lux, mea sors. Amo te, bone Jesu, vel si me fugias, sequar te . . . converte faciem tuam, o mi Jesu, revertere, heu; mi Jesu, perimis me. Veni, amo te, mea felicitas . . .[15]

Cozzolani set this highly charged text on the soul's search for an often elusive Christ, full of the new bodily imagery of devotion ('mi Jesu, perimis me'), in a rather different way. The fleeing Christ is symbolized by a cadence on the distant F♯ (Ex. 11.9; the piece is on D), and the night of death stands out by its sharp recitative-like character. Again, as in *Ecce annuntio vobis*, there is a short tag-like refrain or *epistrophe* that constantly recurs at varying pitch-levels, in this case the simple upward motion of 'amo te'. And the final section of the motet is a written-out ritardando that ends *più piano* (p.p., one of the first uses of this dynamic level) with the *epistrophe*.

Ex. 11.9. Cozzolani, *O Jesu, meus amor* (1648), bars 47–53

As if in answer to all the 'veni's addressed to Jesus in this motet, the next three pieces all begin with the more public imperative 'venite', aimed at the urban audience; two Eucharistic or Elevation pieces followed by another Passion meditation. *Venite gentes, properate populi* makes the explicit link between Christ's marriage to the soul and the

---

[15] 'O Jesus, my love, my life, and all my light, my fate. I love You, sweet Jesus, and if You flee me, I shall follow You . . . Turn Your face to me, o my Jesus, return, my Jesus, annihilate me. Come, I love You, my happiness . . .'. The theme of annihilation was one of the most common ideas in early modern mysticism; for its expression in a sainted monastic contemporary, see A. Riccardi, 'The Mystic Humanism of Maria Maddalena de' Pazzi', in Matter and Coakley, *Creative Women*, 212–36.

Eucharist.[16] This text, with its personalized references ('hunc panem comede, si pauper es'), receives a balanced setting, with outer sections clearly on the final (F) that frame internal *mutationes toni* in the direction of D and G. Like several of Casati's solo motets, its final section is a stable and fairly virtuosic 'alleluia', a procedure that would become normative later in the century.

Venite ad me omnes begins with the words of the languishing Christ that end in a chromatic *catabasis* for His death (Ex. 11.10); the idea again suggests the female monastic singer as oracle of the Host. But in typically optimistic fashion, the text changes speaker, turning to the joyfulness of the Passion ('nolite ergo flere . . . sed celebrate amorem, et dicite: o verbera salutifera, o plagae plenae gaudiis . . .'). Cozzolani extends the statement of the last textual idea by repeating the entire last period largely up a fifth, and by expanding the simple 'amoris Christi monumenta' into yet another virtuosic melisma.

There follow two motets, probably for the Annunciation, that revolve around the salutation 'Ave'.[17] *O quam tristis est anima mea* sets the familiar topos of the Eva/Ave dichotomy:

Ex. 11.10. Cozzolani, *Venite ad me omnes* (1648), bars 41–51

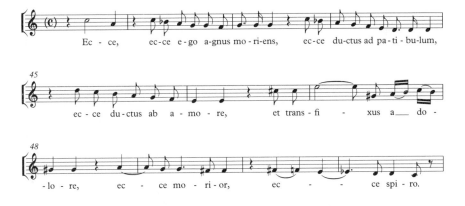

[16] 'Come, nations, hurry, peoples, to the Lamb's wedding. Behold the sacred meal in which the Saviour is contained . . .'.

[17] Ambrosian rite downplayed the liturgical importance of this feast (celebrated in the diocese on the (Ambrosian) sixth Sunday of Advent); if the destination of these motets and of the 1642 *O gloriosa domina* is any indication, the female Benedictines seem to have been important urban custodians of the Annunciation, unsurprisingly, given their symbolic place as earthly angels.

O quam tristis est anima mea, dum recordor tui, o Mater Eva . . . gustasti paululum dulcedinis, et ecce nos morimur . . . ubique dolor, ubique luctus, suspiria, languores, martiria, aerumnae, miseriae, vulnera, mors . . . Consolatur sed anima mea, cum recordor tui, o Maria . . . Eva credendo nos perdidit, tu credendo salvasti, Eva nos pauperes, Ave tuum divites fecit.[18]

The theme (and its devaluation of women) was common in Christian literature, dating to Justin Martyr. But it was rare in the Milanese Seicento, with no apparent iconographic treatment, and largely absent from Federigo's Mariology and that of Novati.[19] The only similar motet appeared later: Carlo Landriani's 1652 *Ave, o nova Eva*; it appears that Cozzolani herself must have selected this topic. She set the text to a slightly unbalanced binary structure, with both halves cadencing on G; Eve's duplicity leads into extremely flat regions of *cantus mollis* while Mary's 'Ave' immediately shifts to *cantus durus*. The motivic use of the descending fourth actually breaks up the poetic contrast of 'Eva mortem dat aeternam, | Ave vitam sempiternam'.

The vocal line of the next motet, *Ave Maria, mater Dei*, begins on the same *g'* on which the previous piece had ended. Again here there is a textual refrain, with 'Ave' set to different motifs; only the very last ritual repetition of 'Ave' echoes the end of the first triple-time section. If these two Annunciation pieces had worked around 'Ave', the next two Marian motets ring changes on 'amate' in the context of public devotion to the Virgin's intercessory role. *Amate, o populi, Mariam* separates the catalogue of praise ('haec est mare quod vos ducit, haec est gratia quae vos ditat'), set to common-time florid recitative, from the imperatives addressed to the urban audience ('properate, filii, ad matris brachia'), presented in triple-time aria style. *Succurre, o diva clemens* is a much more personalized piece, setting a sinner's plea to the Virgin. Again, Cozzolani contrasts the tonally stable invocations of Mary with the chromatic lament of the

---

[18] 'O how sad is my soul, when I remember you, Mother Eve . . . you hardly tasted sweetness, and behold we die . . . everywhere [there is] pain, mourning, sighs, weakness, sufferings, hardships, misery, wounds, death . . . but my soul is consoled, when I remember you, Mary . . . Eve by believing ruined us, you by believing saved us; Eve made us paupers, your Ave made us rich.'

[19] It is avoided in Novati's *De eminentia*, 397, which draws the parallel between the tree of Paradise and the Cross, but omits any mention of Eve; Cozzolani thus stood alone in her choice of this topos. For a contrary opinion to mine, one which places the emphasis on the centrality of female agency, see Zarri, 'Dalla profezia', 188.

Ex. 11.11. Cozzolani, *Succurre, o diva clemens* (1648), bars 83–8

Heu— iam lan-gue-o,   heu— iam do - le-o, heu___ iam pe - re-o,

sinner (Ex. 11.11, for 'heu, iam langueo, heu, iam doleo, heu, iam pereo'). The peroration, literary and vocal, is saved for the key semantic concept 'Ama, Mater, ama, Virgo, ama, Sponsa'.

The last two pieces in the collection, *Venite populi* and *O praeclara dies*, return to the world of urban public devotion. The former (for a generic female saint) repeats its triadic second section ('alleluia') at the end; its repetition of 'mundum illa fugit', noted above in reference to Radegund, is all the more striking for the amount of the motet that expresses generalized sentiments set in triple time on the *finalis* F, balanced by extended melismas ranging into *cantus durus* ('gaude, fruere sempiternis'). The longest motet in the book, *O praeclara* (for Christmas), recalls the iterative procedures of *Ecce annuntio vobis*: no internal refrains, remarkable vocal virtuosity, and large-scale tonal stability (on C; *undecimo* or *duodecimo tono*), along with yet another apparent *piva* section ('allegro') for 'gloria in excelsis Deo', the climax before the last 'alleluia'. Yet even in such an extrovert piece, the mystery of the Incarnation, expressed again in the same phrase that meant so much to Rusca, provoked a moment of chromatic heightening ('et annunciemus in universa terra: Verbum caro factum'), another late sign of the importance of Christ's Body dating from the traditions of female spirituality that Bynum outlined.

Yet the most remarkable piece in the *Scherzi*, one which belies the collection's title, is the antepenultimate, *Quis mihi det calicem bibere Domini?* It sets a meditative text on Jesus' suffering (starting with a reference to His own prayer in Gethsemane), framed in the most heightened and personal vocabulary to be found in this motet collection, as it turns to the personal imitation of Christ:

Quis mihi det calicem bibere Domini? O bone Jesu, dulcis Jesu, care Jesu, cupio dissolvi pro te. O patiar, o urar, o secer, o moriar pro te. Vincla, catenae, venite, properate, saevite, ligate clamantem vos: Bone Jesu, o patiar, o urar, o secer, o moriar pro te . . .[20]

---

[20] 'Who will give me the Lord's chalice to drink? O good Jesus, sweet Jesus, dear Jesus, I wish to be destroyed for You. O let me suffer, let me be burned, let me be cut in pieces,

The text immediately evokes the semantic field of martyrdom, with invocations interspersed among the 'Bone Jesu, o patiar' refrain, as the singer moves from the consideration of Christ's Passion to her desire for its *imitatio*. Most notable is the extremely graphic nature of the imagery:

> O aquae submergite,
> flumina obruite,
> ignes incendite,
> cruces suspendite,
> lanceae, gladii, fulmina,
> figite, fodite, sternite me.[21]

But in a typical turn, the torments end again optimistically with the happiness of a martyr's death; the vocabulary presages that of *O quam bonus es*:

O dulcis penae, tormenta mellea, felicia vulnera, beata mors.[22]

What occasioned the link among song, Christological meditation, and the scientific detailing of martyrdom? A growing corpus of popular literature, dating to the late Cinquecento, offered vernacular accounts (often in literally excruciating detail) of the torments of early Christian martyrs for Christ, systematized and organized according to the method of inflicting suffering. Best known was Antonio Gallonio's 1591 *Trattato degli instrumenti di martirio*, whose forty-six illustrations depict almost all possible physical means of torture, with long disquisitions on their precise application and lists of early Christian martyrs to whom they had been applied.[23] The highly technical vocabulary ('pectines', curry-combs, or 'ungulae', iron claws) of such literature was also to be found in motet texts for the feasts of martyrs.

But if the success of Gallonio's book reflected the fact that the

---

let me die for You. You bonds and chains, come, hasten, rage, bind me who cries to you: Good Jesus, o let me suffer, let me be burned, let me be cut in pieces, let me die for You . . .'.

[21] 'O waters, drown; rivers, submerge; flames, ignite; crosses, suspend; lances, swords, thunderbolts, pierce me, stab me, strike me down.'

[22] 'O sweet pains, honeyed torments, happy wounds, blessed death'.

[23] A. Gallonio, *Trattato de gli instrumenti di martirio, e delle varie maniere di martoriare usate da' Gentili contro Christiani* (Rome, 1591), dedicated to Olimpia Orsina Cesis, Duchess of Acquasparta, with Latin and vernacular editions throughout the new century. Cesis was one of the pious Roman matrons of the later Cinquecento; the 'scientific' interest in early Christian suffering parallels other contemporary studies of Christian antiquity.

aspiration to martyrdom was one of the most typical characteristics of popular devotion in early modern Europe, the impossibility of heroic death for everyday Catholics (not to mention cloistered nuns) became ever more apparent in the course of the Seicento, with the end of the initial missionary efforts. In the latter part of the century, the quotidian suffering of the body increasingly substituted for physical martyrdom. The expression of this transfer seems to have reached one peak in nuns' autobiographies, and the musical placement of the desire for martyrdom literally in the mouth of those figures—female religious—whose lives and vocation had been identified with their publicly sacrificed status for their Spouse, seems only appropriate.[24] Indeed, Cozzolani's motet is one of the most passionate and intense expressions of this wish to be found in the Italian Seicento.

The motet is cast in *cantus mollis* on C.[25] Besides the now-familiar internal refrain, the rhetoric of the piece seems to have worked by virtue of a series of ever more sweeping scalar runs as the emotional tone of the text rises. The first of these is found in the exordium (Ex. 11.12) to set the key idea, by now a commonplace of north Italian devotion, 'cupio dissolvi pro te', concluding with an unusual descending major ninth (one of Bernhard's *saltus duriusculi*). This exordium consists of four phrases, each but the last ending on a half-cadence (G, D, G) in order to set the interrogatory nature of the text; Cozzolani used the climactic final phrase as the internal refrain. The motet's balance is highlighted by the sequential repetitions of 'o patiar . . .' and by the recollection of the opening $c'-e_b'$ idea just before the cadence ('o moriar pro te'), ending firmly on C.

The second section of the motet consists of three petitions to the instruments of torture ('Vincla, catenae, venite'; 'O aquae, submergite'; 'Pectines, ungulae, belluae vulnerate [me]'), each rounded off by the 'o patiar' refrain.[26] The first invocation uses martial figures for

---

[24] For 17th-c. autobiographies of French nuns, in which the inachievability of martyrdom was transferred to physical mortification, surgical operations, and daily pain for love of their Spouse (including the 'absence of God' familiar from Federigo's correspondents' writings), see J. Le Brun, 'Mutations de la notion de martyre au XVIIᵉ siècle d'après les biographies spirituelles feminines', in J. Marx (ed.), *Sainteté et martyre dans les religions du livre* (Brussels, 1989), 77–90; my thanks to Brad Gregory for these references.

[25] As in its listing in the Ansbach inventory: 'ex C ♭'.

[26] Although *Quis mihi det* evinces no sequential following of Gallonio's encyclopaedic summary of torture, still all the references of the motet text were available in his book. The motet's first petition invoking chains and bonds uses instruments exhaustively described in ch. 3, while the second, the wish for drowning and burning, recalls the methods catalogued

Ex. 11.12. Cozzolani, *Quis mihi det?* (1648), bars 1–21

'properate', balanced by a long descending *trillo* figure (possibly a dissonant *multiplicatio*) for the self-description of 'clamantem, amantem vos' ('me, who cries to and loves you, the torture instruments'). If the first petition moved to B flat, the second and third then cadence on G before the next statement of the refrain, whose rests are also elided in another rhetorical heightening. And the invocations reach their climax in a series of long descents for 'trucidate haec viscera' ('cleave these my viscera'), another musical mark of the new emphasis on bodily organs as a locus for suffering.

The contemplation of martyrdom's joys, in the last section, is again threefold: a first triple-time period repeated down a fourth and extended so as to end on G, ending with a conjunct triple-time gesture for 'beata mors' that would also be employed for the same words in *O quam bonus es* of two years later; then a phrase ('sic fuso sanguine, soluto corpore'), that does the opposite (taken up a fourth), with a long ending melisma for 'volem' that returns to C. The final period 'te fruar . . . in aeternam et ultra' ('I shall enjoy You . . . in eternity and beyond') begins by recalling the *c″–g′* gestures of the motet's opening, ending with a final *più piano* adumbration of the

in chs. 11 (pp. 139–40 and 150–3) and 8 (pp. 93–105, with illustrations for both). The third petition uses the vocabulary of martyrdom: iron curry-combs (*pectines*), metal claws (*ungulae*), both in ch. 5 (pp. 62–9), and exposure to wild beasts (*belluae*), in ch. 11 (pp. 134–6 and 142–3).

other melodic idea from the first period, the *c''–e♭''* (Ex. 11.13), one that provides a musical counterpart to the setting of 'o patiar, o urar'. *Quis mihi det* is one of the more balanced and impassioned pieces in the Milanese solo repertory, one whose local compositional gestures heighten the marked intensity of the vocabulary but whose careful structural planning imparts an equilibrium entirely absent from the text.[27]

Ex. 11.13. Cozzolani, *Quis mihi det?* (1648), bars 124–40

The structure of the *Scherzi*'s devotional themes is loosely chiastic: two pieces on public (Easter) and personal (Christological) topics; three pieces that limn the 'venite' invitation to Eucharistic and Passion devotion; two 'Ave' motets followed by two 'amate' works, all Marian, again alternating the social and the personal; another Christological motet (with an interruption for the female sanctoral piece); and a final Christmas piece that balances the initial Easter setting. The musical settings traverse a wide range of styles, from the

---

[27] A less charged text from the same year, Cazzati's *Quis dabit mihi tantem charitatem?* (*Il secondo libro de motetti a voce sola*, op. 6 (Venice: Gardano, 1648)), also received a less elaborate musical setting. It is set on a *cantus mollis*-inflected B flat, with a loose musical refrain ('Quis dabit mihi') transposed to various modal degrees. But its second half is comprised of a diatonic ostinato aria ('semper clamet et dicat'), finishing with a short recitative peroration that returns to flat regions in its vocal line; a more modest effort.

refrain-driven aria-like works to looser, more improvisatory structures, all within the context of virtuosic singing and obvious hexa-
chordal moves for specific textual ideas. Sadly, the continuo part
does not survive.

A decade after the *Scherzi*, the appearance of the solo *cantata morale e
spirituale* was linked directly to nuns.[28] Cazzati's 1659 book inscribed
to Maria Domitilla Ceva set two kinds of texts: the *morale* pieces
(almost Stoic reflections on virtue) and *spirituale* cantatas on the
familiar topics (Christmas, Christ crucified, male martyrs).[29] The
opening piece, *La Verità sprezzata*, sets the lament of Truth, abandoned on the sands.[30] Comprised of several recitatives, a strophic
aria, a free aria, and a final recitative, the cantata alternates between
D and B flat to express Truth's varying hope and despair. Its indebt-
edness to the canzonetta tradition is evident in the penultimate 'aria
adagio', with its recurrent and rhyming cadential figure ('il giorno
sarà', 'la vita torrà'). The *spirituale* pieces are not different in procedure; presumably both kinds were to be 'animated by [Ceva's] harmonious voice', as the composer's dedication put it.

The next major collection, dedicated to Ceva's rival Antonia
Clerici, was Giovanni Legrenzi's op. 10. It was inscribed in 1670,
despite (perhaps literally to spite) all Litta's strictures, and shows possible links to S. Radegonda's music in at least two pieces: the opening *Angelorum ad convivia mortales surgite* (C), and *Plaudite vocibus* (T),
for St Benedict.[31] The first is an Elevation piece:

---

[28] Cazzati's was the first *cantate morali e spirituali* book; its 1679 reprint was dedicated to
Isabella Leonarda. The second such book, Carlo Grossi's *Sacre ariose cantate* of 1663, was
inscribed to Elena Cornaro Piscopia, the Venetian patrician, doctor in philosophy, musician, and Benedictine tertiary.

[29] Part of the conventions of the genre seems to have been the avoidance of any mention of God or Christian doctrine in the *morale* pieces.

[30] 'Sorgea nel Cielo à pena l'Alba nascente, e pargoletto | il Sole d'Anfitrite | nel sen
cheto dormia, | quando trà mille schiere | sù le minute arene | tutta in vista tremante |
avinta di catene, | la Verità volgea mesta le piante, | e all'aure de sospiri trofeo del suo
dolore | seco giva, così sfogando il core: | "E dunque al mio tormento | congiurarete sem-
pre, | o cieli irati? . . .".'

[31] Two sanctoral motets honour Francis and Anthony and are thus less likely to stem
from S. Radegonda's liturgy; possibly they are related to Legrenzi's still unclear whereabouts
in the years leading up to 1669. *Festivi martires, virgines hilares* (B), for St Catherine, would
also seem a likely female monastic piece except for its adherence to the conventions of the
motetto per basso solo (the vocal line is often a *diminutio*, an ornamented version, of the continuo part, a feature not typical of motets for alto).

Angelorum ad convivia mortales surgite, accurrite laetantes, ad escam aeternitatis, parate praecordia, vovete suspiria. Sub cibi specimine vos nutriet Deus, vos sanguinis munere depascet ad aethera . . .[32]

The structure is simple: two florid declamatory sections (both moving from E to G) introduce two strophic arias. The remarkable features of the motet lie in small-scale detail; the virtuosity of the solo part is used to underline the miracle of the Real Presence in the second declamation, with its florid cadence for 'adorate', its open and closed endings for the two statements of 'ad terrae salutem', and its unusual rhythmic placement of the final cadence that sums up Eucharistic theology:

Mortales, colite, adorate faelices, sub pane sub potu, en Deus descendit ad terrae salutem.[33]

This leads directly into an 'allegro' peroration built on the repetition of a single pitch in the vocal line regardless of the harmonic implication of the bass. But this is not the last unexpected cadence; the final strophic aria 'Errores fugate, mundate vos pectora' is based on the same repetition of a cadential pitch ahead of the actual resolution of the continuo line (an *abruptio*, in rhetorical terms), a rhetorical figure chosen to set the affect of fleeing sins.

Although *Plaudite vocibus* is rubricated 'per un Santo', it would be hard to apply the text of its second aria to anyone but the founder of Western monasticism, to be sung by Clerici on his feast.[34] And the salutation of Benedict is set to an 'aria largo' with recurrent melodic and bass patterns (Ex. 11.14), while the final 'Alleluia' would have provided Clerici with obvious opportunities for vocal fireworks.

This solo repertory evinces distinct parallels with the familiar distinction among recitative, arioso, and aria style found in the

---

[32] 'Rise, you mortals, to the angels' banquet, hurry gladly to the food of eternity; faithful souls, prepare your vitals, dedicate your sighs. Under the form of food God will feed you, fortify you with His blood . . .'.

[33] 'O happy mortals, worship and adore; behold, God descends to save the earth, in the form of bread and drink.'

[34] 'Ave eremi cultor inclite / Ave lumen supernae Curiae / Ave splendor Ecclesiae / Beate Benedicte' ('Hail, glorious founder of hermitage, hail, light of the heavenly Curia, hail, splendour of the Church, blessed Benedict'). The vocabulary of 'lumen supernae Curiae' might be another patrician gibe at Litta's rather unheavenly staff, again implying that monastic traditions took precedence over episcopal policy. For the 1704 claims of the Bolognese Camaldolese that Benedict, not the archbishop, was their true superior, see Monson, *Disembodied Voices*.

Ex. 11.14. Legrenzi, *Plaudite vocibus* (1670), bars 77–89

literature on the secular cantata. But it is important not to gloss over the differences. In contrast to Cozzolani's constantly changing sections, the Milanese solo motet of the Seicento's last quarter is built in longer discrete units, sometimes da capo arias. The literary language of the solo motet also became far more stylized and uniform: the second-person plural imperatives found sometimes in Cozzolani's *Scherzi* became ubiquitous, and the literary conceits formalized: 'martial' references to battle and war (often for pieces on martyrs), 'affective' treatments of the individual soul, and even the *piva* tradition for Christmas pieces. One other notable aspect of the texts is that the grammatical gender of their speaker has changed; if Cozzolani's works still use masculine first-person pronouns, by the later Seicento, in the works of Badalla but also in those of her male contemporaries found in RISM 1679[1] or 1692[1], the motets normally employ feminine forms (e.g. 'sum beata' in Badalla's *Non plangete* or 'Superno sum vulnerata amore', from A. D. Legnano's *In dolore afflicta* of 1692). The change might have been linked to the overwhelming spread of female monastic singing by century's end.[35]

Among the four dedications to nuns found in the 1679 *Nuova raccolta* (the major local anthology), the most remarkable is the young Paolo Magni's 206-bar 'breve tributo' (actually the longest motet in the collection) to the skills of Antonia Clerici, the 'most melodious swan' and the 'Siren of our times', *Ad pugnas, o Furie*.[36] The piece is rubricated 'per un Santo ed in ogni tempo', and the opening aria puts the standard martial words, again recalling Gallonio, in the mouth of a male martyr, with clear references to Christian heroic virtue:

> Ad pugnas, o Furie,
> ad arma, o Tiranni,
> ferte flammas,
> Tetri abissi date poenas,
> ferte strages,
> me cruciate, me ferite.[37]

Magni set this to virtuosic conceits, cast in an ABA aria form (Ex. 11.15). The standard melodic gestures almost mask the real brilliance of the setting: surprising leaps and syncopations for 'ad arma'; loose inversions of melodic ideas (bars 9–13 echoed in 21–5); and the final use of *antistoichon* (held notes in the vocal line over an often dissonant moving bass) to symbolize martyrological constancy. And the recurrence of the martial vocabulary ('ad arma') in the second aria (so marked; bars 69 ff.) evoked a return to the vocal figuration of the opening. The real surprise, however, in both the motet text and the musical setting, is reserved for the 'adagio e affettuoso' section (bars 93 ff.; Ex. 11.16):

> O dulce martirium,
> o cari dolores,
> vivo si pro te morior,

---

[35] Perhaps in these texts it is the soul (*Anima*, normally feminine) who speaks. On the other hand, the speaker of the text of Appiano's *Quid me tentatis?* (RISM 1679[1]; the piece was dedicated to Antonia de' Capitani at S. Vittore in Meda) makes specific reference to 'Sola desiderat Anima mea' in the third person.

[36] For this collection and the 1692 *Sacre armonie a voce sola* (RISM 1692[1]), see F. Passadore, 'Le antologie lombarde a voce sola di Carlo Federico Vigoni', in A. Colzani *et al.* (eds.), *Tradizione e stile: Atti del II convegno internazionale di studi sul tema: La musica sacra in area lombardo-padana nella seconda metà dell' '600* (Como, 1989), 221–54; on Magni, see Walker, *NG* xi. 494–5.

[37] 'To battles, o Furies; to arms, o tyrants; bring the flames; give me the foul abyss's torment; prepare destruction, torture and wound me.'

o mi suavissime Sponse,
respiro si per te spiro,
o mi dilectissime Jesu.
Jubilo in tanto incendio,
refrigeror in tanto ardore,
ergo lictores ferite inhumani.[38]

The sudden switch in affective tone is matched by Magni's move to the sharpest tonal regions in the piece and indeed in the collection as a whole (starting on B, and moving to F sharp for the sweetness of 'o mi dilectissime Jesu'; b. 110), followed by dialogic phrases that rush on to the plea for martyrdom ('ergo lictores ferite inhumani'; bars 115–21). The marked musical contrasts convey the change in affect better than does the text (Ex. 11.16): a *cadenza in mi* for 'martirium' and 'dolores'; the rewriting of the voice/bass dialogue to echo 'vivo si pro te morior' by 'jubilo in tanto incendio', along with the sharply delineated melodic motifs that set the textual oxymora ('jubilo in tanto incendio, refrigeror in tanto ardore'); the motion to the remote F sharp for 'mi dilectissime Jesu'; and a final brilliant vocal peroration that at last reaches the high *d″* for 'ferite inhumani' (bars 115–20). It is as if the motet text had been written to follow the musical form. But the devotional inversions of this section are also

Ex. 11.15. Magni, *Ad pugnas, o Furie* (1679), bars 1–32

---

[38] 'O sweet martyrdom, o beloved pains, I live so as to die for You, my sweetest [male] Spouse, I breathe so as to sigh for You, o my most beloved Jesus. I rejoice in such a fire, I freeze in such burning; therefore wound me, you inhuman lictors.' The latter were the Roman officials in charge of scourging; the text recalls the technical vocabulary of Gallonio, *Trattato*, ch. 4.

Ex 11.15. *cont.*

Ex. 11.16. Magni, *Ad pugnas, o Furie* (1679), bars 93–121

noteworthy: the ostensibly male martyr speaks in the words of female devotion to Jesus, including the address to Christ as male Spouse. And the vocabulary, along with the dual destination (martyr/nun), shows how the language of sanctoral corporeal suffering was transferred musically to the individual Christian soul.

Magni responded to all the surprise conceits by ending this section (b. 121) on the dominant, and then introducing yet another return to the martial beginning of the piece ('ad pugnas'), thus rounding off the first half of the motet in an ABACA form, not unlike the ariettas that the recently deceased Litta had struggled so fruitlessly to banish from the *chiese interiori*. The piece then proceeds to the relative stability of a strophic aria ('Mille flammae | Carae poenae'; bars 135 ff.), followed by a da capo 'Alleluia' with a curiously inconclusive final cadence. With a more extrovert, formalized literary and musical vocabulary, *Ad pugnas* repeats the same ideas found in Cozzolani's *Quis mihi det*: the meditative progression from the Passion to the individual's wish to experience the same exquisite and beloved torture, exemplified in the physical torments of suffering for Christ. Its placement literally in the mouth of the most famous female monastic singer in the city was only appropriate.

Whether or not Badalla actually heard the dedicatees of such motets sing 'their' pieces, still the generic and structural changes of her generation are evident in her own collection. She probably listened to such a motet as *Ad pugnas* only from within the *chiesa interiore* of S. Radegonda after her profession, for she was not Milanese.[39] Her relationship to the homonymous families of Bergamo (or Vigevano) is hypothetical, although her dedication of the motet book to a socially climbing Bergamasque nobleman may point to her origins in the former city.[40] The preface to her motet book notes her 'acerba mia età

[39] There is no record of such a family in Milan in the ASM, or ASC records, nor in the voluminous files of the Istituti per l'Assistenza Beneficaria, Milan.

[40] The inscription was to Carlo Vincenzo Giovanelli, a landowner who six years earlier had been raised to the status of Count of the Holy Roman Empire by Leopold I (F. Schröder, *Repertorio genealogico delle famiglie confermate nobili . . . nelle provincie venete* (Venice, 1830), 374; I thank Massimo Ossi for this reference). Whether Rosa Giacinta was a relative of the Giacomo Badalla who signed a financial note to Count Caleprio in Bergamo on 27 Apr. 1675 (Bergamo, Biblioteca 'A. Mai', Archivio Caleprio, Carteggio 1664–1705) is open to question. For prominent members of the Decembre Badalla family in Vigevano, see the Consegna populazione files in that city's Archivio Storico Civico.

(puoco fà uscita dal quarto lustro)'; she was just over 20. Thus she might have been born around 1662, and have taken her vows at an early age. Her dowry was deposited on 19 November 1677, and her final vows were professed a year later.[41] She appears on S. Radegonda's lists throughout the rest of the century, until 1703, while a dowry receipt of 8 August 1719 omits her name, which suggests that she died between those years.[42]

Her two vernacular cantatas represent the only non-printed and non-Latin-texted music clearly associated with S. Radegonda. The dedication of the large-scale cantata *O fronde care* (A, two 'violini' or 'trombe' with two 'flauti' in an internal aria) was inscribed 'Al qualificato merito dell'Ill.mo, e R.mo Sig.re Abb. Camillo Tellier di Louvois'; the bibliophile and future vicar in Rheims, Camille Le Tellier, abbé de Louvois (1675–1718), a cadet son of the statesman Michel-François Le Tellier, probably visited S. Radegonda on a Grand Tour in 1699–1700.[43] The initial 'O' in its manuscript source frames an illustration of a pensive cleric sitting in a garden, probably a portrait of Le Tellier (in the *hortus conclusus* of the cloister's musical world) drawn by one of S. Radegonda's inhabitants.[44]

The other cantata, *Vuo cercando*, is musically plain with simple recitatives, an opening arietta, and two da capo arias.[45] But its text, using floral and garden imagery as a metaphor for individual creativity, is explicitly self-referential, as in the last recitative:

> Signor, se d'un tal fiore,
> ne fai prodigo dono al mio desio
> vò presentarti anch'io
> (benche vil contracambio a tant'onore)
> un mazzetto di Rose e di Hiacinti
> colti ne' miei recinti.[46]

---

[41] The records of the first deposit 'in cancel*laria*' and of another, dated 21 Nov. 1678, are in ASDM XII, vol. 128, fo. 8ᵛ.

[42] Both these latter documents are in ASM, Religione, p.a., 2217.

[43] On him, see the entry signed 'Weiss' in L. G. Machaud's *Biographie universelle* (Paris, n.d.), xxv. 362–3; for his visit to Italy, the letter of spring 1700 from the Benedictine protector Guillaume La Porre cited in E. de Broglio, *Mabillon et la Société de l'Abbaye de Saint-Germain des Prés* (Paris, 1888), ii. 232.

[44] Reproduced in J. Ecorcheville, *Catalogue du fonds de musique ancienne de la Bibliothèque Nationale* (Paris, 1912), iii, after p. 16; the abbé presumably took the piece back with him to Rheims, whence it arrived at the Bibliothèque Nationale.

[45] Edition by Kendrick in Glickman and Schleifer (eds.), *Women Composers*, ii.

[46] 'Lord, since with such a flower You make such a prodigal gift to my wish, so I wish to present You (though slight recompense for such honour) with a garland of roses and hyacinths grown in my own cloistered keep.'

Typical, as well, is the deliberate ambiguity of the cantata's addressee: a secular patron who supported the speaker's music, or perhaps God as the giver of individual talent, or both.

The dedication of the 1684 *Motetti* is unremarkable.[47] But the first notable feature of the collection is Badalla's preface to the reader, without parallel in any other Milanese motet book:

God [alone] knows what reception these my compositions will have upon their first appearance in public . . . who knows, since I have trusted others with the fancy of singing these my motets, but that I myself may receive an occasion for lamenting my sorrows? . . . In any case, I present them to you, gentle reader, as essays (*saggi*). If I hear that they are not displeasing, I shall be emboldened to test your kindness with more numerous examples. Live well. [followed by a woodcut of a bouquet of roses and hyacinths][48]

The compositional self-awareness of a young composer, and her consciousness of the often difficult public reception of her works, are striking.[49] We shall have occasion to see the ways in which at least some of the motets were *saggi*.

But the collection, in context, was unusual and important in other regards. It was the only Milanese single-composer edition of solo motets in the twenty years between the reprint of Cossoni's op. 12 (1675) and Brevi's op. 5 (1695); again, a nun represented the major local composer of solo motets for a generation.[50] Its publication while the prohibition of polyphony at S. Radegonda was still in effect was a blatant flaunting—or perhaps simply an ignoring—of Visconti's authority. And the liturgical destination of its contents, in the light of the generic traditions of the solo motet, was singular: no Elevation or Passion texts, but three pieces 'per ogni tempo', three generic sanctoral, two Christmas, and one motet each for Easter, Corpus Christi, BVM, and St Radegund. The 'ogni tempo' texts include personal references, and the entire book seems to be yet

[47] The volume was produced by Giuseppe Sala in Venice, at the beginning of his career as a music publisher and just before the death of his sponsor Natale Monferrato; see R. A. McGowen, 'The Venetian Music Printer Giuseppe Sala: New Information Based upon Archival Documents', *Fontes artis musicae*, 36 (1989), 102–8. The motets were not listed in Sala's catalogue of 1715; cf. Mischiati, *Indici*, 339–44.

[48] Text in App. D (and the epigraph of this chapter); the floral imagery in self-referential contexts will recur frequently.

[49] For more concealed self-referential ideas in Vizzana's *Sonet vox tua*, see Monson, *Disembodied Voices*, 80–91.

[50] If we take original editions by urban composers, the gap is even wider; C. G. San Romano's collection had appeared back in 1670.

another monument to nuns' (or one nun's) devotion and to S. Radegonda's traditions.

The motets in the 1684 book are with few exceptions composed of discrete sections, with an 'Alleluia' as the last. Relatively few sections are explicitly designated as 'Recitativo' or 'Aria', but two clear kinds can be differentiated: a sort of florid declamatory recitative, always in common time, that repeats no material (textual or musical) and that includes a surprisingly large percentage of the difficult passage-work to be found in the collection; and the various aria types, cast in standardized forms, of which the following can be described in roughly decreasing order of importance: the bass ostinato aria; the 'free' aria, normally a complete ABA da capo form (of one poetic stanza); the motto or *Devisen* aria, which in Badalla's book normally states its motif in the continuo part first; and the strophic aria *stricto sensu*, recognizable by the explicit designation of 'prima' and 'seconda' strophes. Their frequency in the 1684 book favours the first two: ostinato bass (eleven); free ABA (ten); motto (five); strophic (three); other (two).[51]

In this style, the repetition of material on standard scale-degrees—first, fourth, fifth—became more prevalent. The sequences are often driven by vocally demanding motifs. One other characteristic of Badalla's book is her constant employment of *antistoichon* in the vocal part, in almost every motet; this is not unknown in the 1679 and 1692 books, although it seems more characteristic of pieces written by singers than of others. The freedom of the recitative arioso should not be underestimated. The peroration from the 'Fortunati mortales' section of Badalla's Corpus Christi motet *Pane angelico* is without parallel in the entire Milanese repertory of the later Seicento (Ex. 11.17); again, Eucharistic devotion provoked the most striking musical gestures. In this passage, Badalla seems to push the conventions of the recitative arioso, writing the passage up to high *c'''* simply because someone at S. Radegonda could sing it.[52] This conscious expansion

---

[51] I exclude the 'Alleluia' sections from this count. Examples that fit none of the outlined models are listed as 'other'. Of the motto arias, only one states the theme first in the voice.

[52] Two other textual points should be noted: the rhetorical *synaeresis* (elision) of Latin syllables, unknown in the mid-century repertory and a mark of the influence of vernacular poetic/musical forms on the late Seicento motet (along with the strong Italian overlay in texts); and the frequent musical references in the motet texts (for instance, the Easter motet *Silentio, o carae turbae* includes an aria that begins 'Cum grato concentu, cum dolci armonia, | Vos notae canorae cum me resonate'). On another such piece (Meda's 1691 *Cari musici*) as a proem to a nun's motet collection, see Kendrick, 'Four Views'.

Ex. 11.17. Badalla, *Pane angelico* (1684), bars 155–62

gu - sta-te de - li-ti-as, et an-ge-li-co pa-ne re-fe-cti can-tan-do ju-bi-la -

- te, can-tan-do ju-bi - la - - te.

of the procedure is remarkable, coming as it does from the *opus pri-mum* of a composer in her early twenties. A similar liberty towards the expected course of sequences is shown in a passage from the aria 'Solum Jesum amare' from *Animae devotae* (Ex. 11.18). The individuality of Badalla's collection lies precisely in its refusal to follow the predictability of the harmonic sequences and melodic passage-work.

The opening section of the very first motet again summarizes both the Christian soul's and nuns' specialized vocation as brides of Christ, despite the 'sfortune' Badalla had lamented in the preface, using the semantic field of heat and cold as metaphors of human passion for Christ:

> O quali incendio,
> o quanto ardore
> cor consumis,
> dulcissime Jesu,
> animae amanti;
> aut mitiga ardorem
> aut dona amor caelestis
> almae vigores.[53]

Badalla uses sharp and flat hexachords to divide the section: a peroration over a static bass (A) for 'O quali . . . ardore'; a sudden turn to *cantus mollis* for the sweetness of Jesus ('cor consumis . . . dona amor'); and a return to 'hard' (*cantus durus*) regions for 'amor caelestis

---

[53] 'Sweetest Jesus, with what fire, with what ardour You consume the heart of a loving soul; heavenly love either moderates the soul's burning or grants it strength'.

Ex. 11.18. Badalla, *Animae devotae* (1684), bars 158–75

. . . vigores', with the final section paralleling the opening pedal-point and composing out the initial vocal peroration (Ex. 11.19).[54] The text later calls on the soul to rejoice in its union with Jesus, its glory and life.

But the most explicit floral self-identification, with a specific reference to her religious name, is found in the antepenultimate recitative, with its *circulatio* for the crown of 'Corona splendet immortalis':

[54] Badalla still was thinking of *toni* transposed; although the section (and the motet) is clearly on A with a sharp third, the key signature is only two sharps, evidently a case of G mode taken up two fifths.

Ex. 11.19. Badalla, *O quali incendio* (1684), bars 1–17

Felicissima sorte, non caduchae rosae florent et Hiacinthis sempiternis Corona splendet immortalis.[55]

The musical emphasis on the setting of 'corona', along with the other references, again mark this piece as intimately linked to the Cassinese clothing ceremonies, the crowning of the novice in the Consecration of Virgins, here in a last musical avatar. This recitative is followed by a relatively simple da capo 'aria risoluto' and the final 'Alleluia'. In its surprising cadences, long vocal pedal-points, ostinato basses, and hidden parallelisms, *O quali incendio* is again a compendium of the methods on display in the rest of the volume, a proem not only to one nun's vocation, but to the compositional means at her disposal for the setting of relatively standardized texts.

This individual approach to fixed forms recurs throughout the first three motets of the volume; the opening of the second (generic sanctoral) piece, *Tacete, o languidae armoniae*, not only employs the rhetorical figure of *tmesis* for the silence of 'facete', combined with an *epizeuxis* for the word itself ('tacete, o la—[rest], o la—, tacete o languidae') but sets the literary idea ('languidae armoniae') with a repetitive and inconclusive harmonic support, culminating in a surprise cadence for 'mestae notae' (Ex. 11.20). Yet the call for languid music to be silent in honour of the saint's triumph is a purely rhetorical gesture. The turn to the martial jubilation of martyrdom, as in the earlier motets on the topic, evokes a remarkable vocal display in the remainder of the section. The free and long aria 'Victoria resonate, decantate, Chori aeterni' uses all the resources: a continuo ostinato; an *antistoichon* on the exposed high g'' for 'victoria', followed by another for the 'eternity' of 'Chori aeterni'; and the metamusical references of 'iterate in tanto die | vos terrenae melodiae'. But the references to martyrdom again recall heroic sanctoral suffering; the 'victoria' aria is followed by the long declamatory 'O, cum quanto valore' describing the saint's resistance to torturers:

O, cum quanto valore, cum quali animo invito, anima bella, resistendo, non cedendo in ostinata pugna cum tiranno inimico, te costantem demostrasti et vincendo triumphasti.[56]

[55] 'By most happy fate, imperishable roses flourish, and the immortal crown [*corona*, with a possible gloss also as a nun's head-dress as in the 1607 Cassinese clothing manual] shines with perpetual hyacinths.' Perhaps this piece was sung at Badalla's own clothing ceremony, or else it was simply an epigraph for monastic vocation in general. For *circulatio*, Kircher, *Musurgia universalis*, VIII, 145.

[56] 'Oh beautiful soul, with what valour, with what courage, resisting, not ceding, in hard battle with the enemy tyrant you showed yourself faithful, and in winning you triumphed.'

Ex. 11.20. Badalla, *Tacete, o languidae armoniae* (1684), bars 1–8

This explodes again into martial figuration over a drone bass for 'in ostinata pugna' and surprising passage-work for 'triumphasti'. 'Nunc sta in gaudio' is a strophic aria, and the final 'Alleluia', unusually, tosses its motto back and forth between bass and voice, with a peroration on the highest extended passage-work to be found so far. Its motif recalls that of 'A mundo perfido' from *O quali incendio*, the first piece about female monastic vocation. Thus *Tacete, o languidae armoniae* evolves musically into yet another motet about the Christian's (and the nun's) own identification with martyrdom, one that provokes ever more distinctive compositional gestures.

Perhaps the text of the next motet, *Animae devotae*, moved Badalla to the relatively open forms and unexpected twists of the musical setting. For its language recalls one last time, albeit in the vocabulary of the late Seicento, the public intercessory and spousal role of nuns:

> Animae devotae,
> animae piae
> unitae, venite,
> volate, gustate,
> quantae delitiae, o quantae
> in Jesu amato amante.[57]

The opening employs all the mechanisms of wonder at Jesus' love: surprising and high sequences for 'volate'; moves towards flat

---

[57] 'O devout and pious souls united, come, hurry, enjoy, o how many delights in loving beloved Jesus.'

hexachords (in the already two-flat piece on G) for the softness of 'Jesu amato amante' (b. 22), and a final 6♭–3♯ (a *consonantia impropria* of the most striking sort) sonority to mark the cadence (Ex. 11.21). 'Tantae stellae in fulgido caelo' relies on a bass ostinato stated on G and D, while the next aria, 'O animae amatae', not only drops the two-flat signature (while employing numerous notated flats) but actually (and unusually in Badalla's output) ends on the dominant D. The next recitative, 'Ah delitiae mundanae', traces an unexpected harmonic path from B flat to G (with an augmented sixth for 'spinae insidiosae' of worldly temptations), while the constantly varying bass ostinato of 'Solum Jesum amare' works in sharp contrast to the smooth and conjunct vocal line. As in other cases, the motif does not return at its original pitch after its statement on the dominant. To conclude the unexpected features of this motet, the final and free 'Alleluia' sets florid passage-work against simple scalar minims, both in the vocal line and the continuo. The liberties of *Animae devotae*, on both formal and phrase levels, find few parallels in the Milanese repertory or even in some of the other motets in Badalla's book.

If the first three items, prominently featured at the beginning of the collection to mark its origin and ambience, had used surprise and asymmetry to express essentially personalized sentiments, the next four motets, for major public feasts—Easter, Corpus Christi, and Christmas—evince greater regularities because of their ritual contexts. *Silentio, o carae turbae* features an absolutely regular bass *Devisenaria*, 'Cum grato concentu', with the motto on G, A, C, or D (occasionally metrically displaced) in every measure. In the florid connecting declamatory section, 'Osanna, surrexit Dominus', the peroration is saved for 'resurrexit in caelis, osanna in terris', but with an unexpected cadence to lead into an unmarked strophic aria, 'Dulcis amor, Jesu care surrexisti'. The final 'Alleluia' is simply a continuo/voice motto aria. Similarly, despite the vocal fireworks noted above, *Pane angelico* is quite regular.[58] Its first aria, 'De caelo rapidi', is a complete ABA with a middle section that moves to B flat; the second, 'Tanto prodigio triumpha amor', has a similar plan, with a variably natural or flat third and a long but perfectly sequential climax on 'gaudio'.

But the structure of the first Christmas piece, *Scintillate amicae stellae*, is already looser; it opens with a complete three-part aria with

[58] Transcription and commentary by Kendrick, in Schleifer and Glickman (eds.), *Women Composers*, ii.

Ex. 11.21. Badalla, *Animae devotae* (1684), bars 1–25

Ex. 11.21. *cont.*

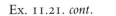

Je-su a-ma-to a - man - - - - - - te.

another unique feature, a middle section in a different (triple) metre, 'Et fugate obscura nubila'. This B section also moves away from G to E, and indeed the repeat of 'Scintillate' proceeds on this new pitch-centre until Badalla's change of the last statement of the text so as to end on G (Ex. 11.22). The adagio section 'Quando pia Maria donat misero mundo' avoids the expected musical rhyme in the two long perorations on 'fabricatorem' and 'auctorem', and the aria 'Iam venit dilectus' is a complete tonally stable ABA. Badalla reserves the unexpected peroration in the penultimate recitative, 'Amantissime Jesu', for the believer's internal bodily warming of the Christ-Child amidst the chills of the winter night: 'et ne inter frigora tremas, in meum cor descende'. The final adagio aria, 'Flammae amatae', is connected directly to the presto 'alleluia', for which reason it also moves from the C of its beginning to the G of the motet as a whole.

The cold winds and humble surroundings of Christ's birth also recur in the text of *Non plus ultra*. Here again, the forms are looser: two ostinato arias, one on a three-bar figure ('Non plus ultra') on A, and then (after a curiously inconclusive linking declamatory section that ends on F), another ('Siccae paleae') over a constantly variable bass pattern. The next aria, 'Cessate, o rigores', begins as a continuo/voice *Devisen* form, but turns out as a complete ABA with a strongly contrasting middle section that moves from D to G. The entire motet, however, is unified by a recurring motif (e''–$f[\sharp]''$–g'') in the vocal part (aria 1: 'superni throni' and 'honoris et memoria'; aria 3: 'o frigidi venti'; and several occurrences in the final 'alleluia').

The two alto motets (placed by convention at the end of the book as in RISM 1679[1] and 1692[1], and both generic male sanctoral pieces) depart from the models established in the other motets.[59] *Fugite, umbrae malignae* reserves the technical difficulties for its opening

---

[59] In the light of the scoring for alto in the two manuscript cantatas, Badalla herself may have sung this voice-type; she professed vows just after the listing of singers in the 1675–6 dispute.

Ex. 11.22. Badalla, *Scintillate, amicae stellae* (1684), bars 1–13

declamation, followed by an aria ('Sancti in mundo fortunati') without parallel elsewhere in the book: a bipartite form both of whose sections end on D, using a repetitive but not ostinato bass. The second aria, 'Angelici chori festivi, sonate' is a long strophic piece, while the concluding 'alleluia' uses a two-part continuo/voice *Devisen* form. If this motet calls on Heaven to rejoice at the saint, *Totus mundus ecce tremit* begins in Hades (complete with classical references; the first aria reads 'Flammae scintillate, furiae ululate; Pluto est vinctus et tormentis est cinctus') before passing on to jubilation. The more unusual poetic conceits seem to have evoked somewhat different procedures in the composer; the florid declamation of the opening by a surprising harmonic move, first to D and then (after an

exposed augmented sixth) to E with a natural third. The first vocal
line of the first aria works then by contrast ('Flammae' versus 'Pluto
est vinctus'), not repetition, although there is a quasi-ostinato bass.
The long peroration in the next recitative ('in tanta victoria') deliberately avoids musical rhyme with the poetic complement ('in indi-
cibili gloria'). The regularity of the next ABA aria, 'Sunt in caelis
tantae palmae', contrasts sharply with the move to flat regions and
florid passage-work of the following section (again with classicizing
text), 'Paraninphi coelestes'. The final 'alleluia', with its repeated
opening phrase, is reminiscent of several forms in other motets, with
melodic affinities to 'Non plus me tentate' in *Non plangete*, to be discussed presently.

The text of the Radegund motet, *O quam laeta*, is specific in more
ways than one. Its inclusion, not as a generic female sanctoral piece
(with 'Radegunda' substituted by 'N.'), but as a motet unusable outside the Milanese monastery, points directly to the house's prestige.[60]
And the second strophe of the last aria, 'Vos Angeli electi', is linked
directly to the final motto 'Alleluia' by means of a presto accelerando
that highlights the crowning of Radegund. Its text includes another
self-referential floral allusion, one that again connects the composer
to the crowns of female monastic vocation (Ex. 11.23):

> Vos Angeli electi
> coronas formate,
> et Jesu dilecti
> iam sponsam ornate,
> in soavi amoenitate ['presto']
> Redegonda[m] incoronate.
> Bellisimae Rosae,
> Hiacinti odorati,
> vos violae amorosae
> narcisi beati,
> in soavi amoenitate ['presto']
> Redegonda[m] incoronate.[61]

The motet might also represent Badalla's response to Cazzati's
Radegund motet, which she could have heard Maria Domitilla Ceva
sing on some 11 August between 1678 and 1683. Both begin with

---

[60] The other Radegund piece is Cazzati's 1676 *Sonet caelo vox jocunda*.

[61] 'Elect angels, make a crown and adorn the spouse of beloved Jesus; crown Radegund
in sweet delight. Most beautiful roses, fragrant hyacinths, you loving violets, blessed narcissi,
crown Radegund in sweet delight.'

Ex. 11.23. Badalla, *O quam laeta* (1684), bars 127–42

3/8 arias in tonally sharp regions (Cazzati on A, Badalla on D). Yet the two motets then take different paths. Badalla's recitatives are longer and more florid, and the aria structure more varied. As with the other public pieces, the sequences of *O quam laeta* are, at least at first, more regular than the norm. The declamatory sections are somewhat melismatic, the opening aria 'O quam laeta' is a simple ABA, and the surprises of the middle 'Nunc forte, de morte' are confined to its dotted rhythms in the vocal line over a triplet bass ostinato (Ex. 11.24), along with the rerouting of the repeat of its opening section in order to cadence firmly on A. As if to compensate, 'Vos Angeli electi' ends on F sharp, and the 'alleluia' is a two-part form in which the opening period ends on B minor, and the second section reiterates the D that had not been heard since the opening.

Perhaps the most contrast-laden item in the whole book is the

Ex. 11.24. Badalla, *O quam laeta* (1684), bars 72–92

penitential *O serenae pupillae*.[62] The opening declamation is propelled by the juxtaposition of contradictory ideas and their musical reflection (Ex. 11.25):

> O serenae pupillae, o cor jucundum,
> lacrimas praeparate,
> surgite, non tardate;
> errores multi sunt, culpae sunt tantae,
> et tu, anima ingrata,
> damna maculas tuas, fugite peccata.[63]

The section works by the dissonances over the long pedal-points, the sudden move to F for 'surgite', and the return to D for 'et tu', as the speaker admonishes her soul—a penitential *scena*. The first aria, 'Quantae stellae', is a by now familiar ostinato piece on A, in which the pattern is articulated on scale-degrees 1, 5, 7, 5, and 1; most of the text is a standard natural simile which recalls the outward happiness of the opening depiction of the soul ('quantae stellae in caelo serenae, quanti in prato varii flores') only to contrast the enormous burden of sin ('tanti mecum sunt errores'), a poetic move that Badalla set by a change in the direction and character of the vocal line, a surprise truncation of the ostinato and the move to G before a return to material that creates a musical rhyme with the opening of the aria, another rhetorical *complexio*.

The next recitative, 'Ergo surge', returns to the poetic language ('anima, non dormire/si non cupis perire') and the harmonic areas (F/D) of the opening section. Badalla then brusquely interrupted the next triple-time adagio ('quam soave Jesu care') with a presto 'Iniquae tristitiae', the most strongly contrasted B section in the book. More surprise moves to flat regions characterize the next recitative ('et omnia peccata hodie lavabo'), and only the completely stable ABA aria, 'Deh suscipe me, Redemptor amate', provides the first moment of peace in the whole motet. However, the surprises are not over: this closed form ends on the wrong pitch, A, and the final 'alleluia', the first binary form in the book, is needed to bring the contrasts to some sort of conclusion by having both its repeated sections end on D.

---

[62] Its 'per ogni tempo' rubric almost indicates the personalized and devotional affect of the text.

[63] 'O peaceful eyes, o happy heart, prepare your tears; arise, do not wait, for your errors are many and your guilt is great, and you, ungrateful soul, condemn your stains, flee your sins.'

Ex. 11.25. Badalla, *O serenae pupillae* (1684), bars 1–17

The motet for the Nativity of the Virgin, *Non plangete*, may serve as a complete example of Badalla's *saggi* (see App. F). At first glance the opening text appears difficult, until one realizes that the literary conceit, obscure even by the standards of this repertory, presupposes that the speaker (singer) addresses the souls of Old Testament prophets, languishing in Limbo until their future Harrowing by the Risen Christ:

> [Aria:] Non plangete, no,
> antiqui Patres,
> in umbra taciturna,
> in cella nocturna
> limbi obscuri;
> gaudete, non plangete.
> [Recitative arioso:] O veridici prophetae,
> vaticinia beata,
> iam ex radice Jesse
> nata est virga,
> beatissima Virgo
> quae germinabit Nazarenum florem
> et producet Salvatorem.[64]

Since the birth of Mary was the first tangible sign of the immanence of the Incarnation, the text calls on these 'antiqui Patres' to rejoice at the feast. The rest of the motet moves on to more personalized sentiments; one declamatory section begins 'In glorioso estasi, pro tanto contentu, elevatur anima mea pro Maria nascente . . .' (another reference to the soul in the third person and hence an implication that 'sum beata' indicates that the motet's speaker is female), and the penultimate aria is on the standard personalized topos of 'Non plus me tentate, mundanae Sirenae', followed by an 'alleluia'.

Unusually for the collection, this piece opens with a triple-time ostinato aria clearly in A (with a natural third). Badalla conveys the 'dark' affect of the text ('non plangete . . . in umbra taciturna, in cella nocturna') by the *antistoichons*, here used to obscure the phrase-endings and impart a sense of irregularity relative to the bass ostinato, and by the constantly changing pitch-levels of this figure, which is introduced successively on scale-degrees 1, 5, 7, 3, and 1 (A, E, G, C, A).[65] This sequence is tied to the ideas introduced in the poetic lines: 'Non plangete', scale-degree 1; 'Patres/in umbra' on 5; 'in cella nocturna', 7; the affective turn to 'gaudete', 3, with a stabilization of

---

[64] '[Aria:] Do not weep, o ancient fathers, in your silent shade, in your nocturnal cell of dark Limbo; rejoice, do not weep. [Recitative arioso:] O true prophets, blessed foretellings, now a rod is sprung from Jesse's root, the most blessed Virgin, who will sprout the Nazarene flower and produce the Saviour.'

[65] Cf. the pattern for another ostinato aria on A, 'Quantae stellae in caelo' in *O serenae pupillae*.

the pitch-centre C and another surprising vocal display for 'gaudete'; 'non plangete', 1 (with a return of only the first two phrases of the opening period).

'O veridici prophetae' is cast as standard recitative arioso, tonally stable and with the expected sequential passage-work as peroration. The next aria, 'Cara dies', is another preferred form, the continuo/voice *Devisenaria*. Here, the *antistoichon* is reserved for 'caeli aeterni', with musical rhyme on 'inferni' but also on 'beata'. In this aria, the motto is introduced on a variety of scale-degrees, forming internal cadences less stable than in the ostinato aria. 'In glorioso estasi' is another freely flowing recitative arioso, and 'Non plus me tentate', a da capo, repeats the internal cadential sequence of 'Non plangete': 'Non plus', 1; 'mundanae sirenae', 5; 'iam vestrae catenae', 7 (this last tonal area somewhat less stable without a full cadence); 'nunc sunt conquassatae', 3; and 'non plus', another abbreviated return, 1. The final 'Alleluia' is a short *Devisen* form, with the return of the opening phrase altered to a closed ending on A (as opposed to its *ouvert* half-cadence on E in b. 5). But beyond the structural planning, the most immediately striking feature of the motet is its sheer melodic inventiveness and unexpected thematic development.[66]

Compared with the licence of the mid-century solo motet, such a piece as *Non plangete* obviously represents a formalization. Standard aria forms are applied to metrically and affectively regular stanzas, with contrast provided by individual words (the arpeggiated leaps on 'conquassatae' in 'Non plus me tentate'). Yet within this style, Badalla's works represent a fresh and original approach: the melodic invention, surprising sequences, and large-scale planning (evident in the 1–5–7–3–1 internal cadence sequence noted above), all combine to set these motets somewhat apart from the pieces in the contemporary local anthologies.

Sadly, perhaps because of Visconti's policy, or for other reasons, Badalla's fears were indeed realized. Whether, in the words of her preface, she ever achieved that 'maturezza in quest'arte, che non si perfettiona se non con la longhezza de gl'anni', we shall never know; she published only the *Motetti a voce sola*.

---

[66] Cf. Emans, 'Die einstimmigen Kantaten', 376–80 on the general lack of such harmonic planning in Legrenzi's arias.

12

Conclusion

◇

'Le regole della musica sono le stesse della Perfettione'
(Bl. Isabella Tomasi (1645–97), undated essay)

On the most immediate level, female monastic music in Milan had everything to do with the city's patriciate and urban politics. Family ties organized the social and musical aspects of nuns' lives: the patrician composition of monasteries, the financial and social links, even the reciprocal influence of musical styles flourishing in the ecclesiastical institutions of the urban élite. Families also supplied musical necessities: instruments, teaching or lessons when a *licenza* could be obtained from a willing curia, and printed music (in the case of Bascapè). Their support was vital in conflicts with episcopal authority. In return, nuns' music functioned as an emblem of prestige for the city as a whole, serving, as Morigia said, to lure the important visitors, local and foreign, to the *chiese esteriori*. The frequency with which their music was mentioned underlines nun musicians' status as the most precious symbol of patrician pride and piety, a piety that did not necessarily coincide with episcopal guidelines.

But musical sisters played another role in urban life. For the women of this study, polyphony was the central method of asserting their institutions' and their own prestige and status in the symbolic world of the city. Clearly, a part of their renown was the prefiguring of angelic choirs represented by nun musicians, with all the transcendent associations that have been outlined here. No other ensembles—at the Duomo, at S. Maria della Scala or S. Maria presso S. Celso, or at the viceregal court—are mentioned in the travel accounts or in outsiders' musical dedications with anything like the same frequency. Nor did any other group of musicians evoke such fierce controversy in the political triangle of Rome, the Milanese curia, and the city's patriciate. And this seems to have been one of the 'particularités' of Milan, as the anonymous 1606 travelogue remarked (see Ch. 4). Hence, the fame of nun musicians points to their key place in the symbolic economy of prestige, attracting the attention and patronage of outsider visitors and underlining the city's claims to be a second Rome.

There is no mistaking the economic crisis that affected Lombardy in the Seicento, however it may be considered, and the production of costly and exquisite goods was key to the wealth and prestige of Milan.[1] In this sense, nuns' polyphony was another Milanese speciality, part of the network of symbolic value that the patriciate used to maintain the city's status and privilege. From Ceva's complaints in 1675 about the loss of prestige she feared were her ensemble to be decimated by futher transfers, we can sense the vital role played by music-making for the projection of nuns' voices (literally and figuratively) into the exterior world of urban society, and through that society into the consciousness of outside visitors as well. Indeed, in terms of the classical anthropological categories, the women of this study transformed themselves from an unmarked status (anonymity, death to the world) by means of their polyphony into marked beings (individual fame, supernatural mediation). They were not only the most famous musicians, but also the most famous women of the early modern city.

Nuns' ensembles in Milanese life also raise comparisons with other institutions of women musicians in north Italy: the *concerti delle donne* (*dame*) that spread outwards from Ferrara in the 1570s and, later, the Venetian *ospedali*. Certainly parallels seem apparent at first glance: the public nature of music in the Milanese *chiese interiori* like that of Venice, and several similarities with the singing ladies of the courts; and the role of female ensembles in catalysing new musical styles (for Lombardy, the association with nun singers of such genres as the high-voice duet from the 1620s on, the solo motet at mid-century, and the *cantata morale e spirituale* in the 1660s). In the absence of a real local court in Milan, the choirs of S. Radegonda or S. Marta in some ways functioned as a patrician equivalent to the ducal high-voice *concerti* in Ferrara, Mantua, and elsewhere.

---

[1] For one revision of the traditional concepts of regression and refeudalization, see Sella, *Crisis and Continuity*. Whether Sella or his opponents be right, the point remains that the production of prestige items supported the urban economy.

Yet many local details undercut such analogies. The social function of the female monasteries differed from those of the ducal households or the Venetian conservatories; this had implications for the stability of musical ensembles (once professed, musical nuns like Bascapè or Taverna normally had opportunities to perform for the rest of their lives, without the upheavals that dissolved the ducal *concerti* or the graduation of girls from the Venetian conservatories into marriage). Furthermore, such comparisons understate the degree to which nuns' music-making was a locus for conflict within cloistered walls: the apparently frequent disputes that the curia tried to hold in check, the most furious of which resulted in the suspension of music (as at S. Marta in the 1630s and S. Radegonda later in the century), reflected and focused tensions within the patriciate as a whole. In as far as they were detonated by the actions of nuns themselves, they provided the conservative elements in the ecclesiastical bureaucracy an opportunity to banish polyphony.

Also uncharacteristic of the other women's ensembles are the seemingly contradictory values placed on this music-making: on one hand the valorized elements of transcendence associated with nuns' performances in the special ritual space of the *chiese interiori*; on the other the passionate, almost obsessive concern with regulating the details of such performances on the part of prelates as diverse as Carlo and Federigo Borromeo. But perhaps the contradiction is only apparent; if nuns' musical liturgy was indeed the most important, most 'heavenly' form of organized prayer in the city (as it apparently was for Federigo, at least), then it had to be carried out correctly. In this respect (as in many others), the disputes over monastic polyphony came down to differing views between nuns (along with their families) and the hierarchy concerning what was appropriate— that is, different views of piety and its musical expression.

In this sense, as might seem obvious, the best comparisons are to be made with the cloistered musicians of Bologna whose lives and music have been outlined by Craig Monson. But even here, there are important practical and theoretical differences: the lack of Milanese evidence for nuns' collaboration with male musicians in the *chiese esteriori*, the more uniformly strict episcopal policy of the Paleotti, the somewhat different genres associated with Milanese houses, and the European fame of their performances. This further underscores the need for detailed study of individual cities and dioceses in this as in other repertories; facile assumptions about 'Italian nuns' as a whole have sometimes clouded our understanding of specific cases.

Thus, some initial points of comparison with nuns' polyphony in other cities suggest themselves: unlike Ferrara and Modena, for instance, music was not confined to one or two leading houses in the city; nor did the documentable use of large instrumental ensembles (including winds) at S. Vito in Ferrara or S. Gemigniano in Modena play a major role in the Lombard capital. Again, the Venetian case seems different: lower monachization rates, the presence of the *ospedali*, and the public role of non-cloistered women musicians all resulted in a different profile for music in the female houses of the maritime capital.[2] But one line of demarcation is common to Milan and Bologna: the chasm between the more patrician houses and the more plebeian foundations. The former normally evinced subjection to regulars (not the bishop), lack of dowry-reduction requests, Roman liturgy, double-choir (or larger) musical resources, and public renown for performances in the *chiese interiori*. The latter category tended to show the reverse: closer ties to the prelate, more numerous dowry reductions, Ambrosian rite, greater reliance on solo singing, and a less prominent place in the travel accounts or urban literature.[3]

One feature emerges strikingly from all the Italian accounts of female monastic music, whether Bottrigari's and Artusi's reports on S. Vito, the dedications to musicians in Bologna, or the Milanese evidence reviewed here: at least in certain cities at certain times, nuns were central in urban musical life, and their performing abilities ranked among the best of their cities ('come qualsivoglia buon professore'). To judge from the evidence of the sanctoral motets discussed in Chapter 5, more of the local repertory than is immediately apparent is directly related to sisters' performances. At certain times the output of female monastic composers had at least an honourable place in north Italian repertories, and the skills of nuns' ensembles helped catalyse genres and styles at frequent moments. Such points

[2] The motet books of Signorucci and Rovetta mentioned above provide some evidence, but Moore's exhaustive study of the Venetian archives (*Vespers at St. Mark's*, i. 278) turned up only one document, on outside musicians' performances in nuns' churches. Studies of female monastic music in the cities of the Venetian *terraferma* are needed, e.g. Suor Alba Trissina in Vicenza; on her, see Kendrick, 'Trissina', in Schleifer and Glickman (eds.), *Women Composers*, i.

[3] There are obvious exceptions: S. Marta, a highly patrician house, was subject to the bishop and used Ambrosian rite. But the general criteria tend to hold.

still await awakening from the documentary evidence; they have hardly influenced most of the literature.[4]

The demographic and ideological changes that began under Austrian rule after 1706 would affect nuns' music as well. Some foundations retained their musical prominence until the suppressions of the 1780s. But there were increasing limitations: the monachization rate dropped sharply, and even the most independent houses became subject to the archbishop (S. Apollinare in 1730, and S. Radegonda in 1736–7 as an aftermath of the de' Pietra scandal). Dowry-reduction requests continued on a somewhat smaller scale throughout the Settecento, but it is hard to avoid the impression that musical life focused on two rather different phenomena: the solo singing of a few *virtuose* at a house, and the visits by outside musicians for the annual name-day celebrations. Music in other religious institutions, such as the confraternities at S. Fedele, played an ever-increasing role in urban devotional life, and the special relationship between spiritual prestige and musical performance at female houses seems to have weakened. For nuns' own music-making, the Settecento was the century of decline.

Yet even the twilight evoked the same symbolic associations in outside visitors. Charles Burney's 1770 travelogue (App. A, Doc. 74) reiterates the familiar themes, this time expressed by a professional composer and Protestant critic of many other Italian customs: heavenly female monastic singing, the connection with urban patrician composers,[5] the power of the single voice (an inhabitant of S. Maria Maddalena al Cerchio or the eponymous house in Porta Romana performing a motet by Sammartini), and the equation of nuns' music

---

[4] Hence the unlikeliness of Denis Stevens's remarks on the famous Monteverdi letter of 23 Feb. 1630 (no. 121 in Stevens (ed. and trans.), *The Letters of Claudio Monteverdi* (London and Boston, 1980)), which mention the composer's work on motets for the nuns of S. Lorenzo. Monteverdi would have produced 'music . . . easily sung by a unison choir of soprano voices' (p. 398; there is no evidence that the profession of vows raised altos' tessitura), such as *Sanctorum meritis* (I) or *Jubilet tota civitas* in the *Selva morale*. The idea that these pieces' style lends itself to a kind of *unisono* performance (like the *Sonata sopra Sancta Maria* in the 1610 Vespers?) is also without foundation. One might with equal justification ask which virtuoso or large-scale pieces in the *Selva* might have been written for S. Lorenzo.

[5] Hence Burney's reference to 'B. S. Martin, who is Maestro di Capella, and teaches to sing' at the house, may not be entirely inaccurate. It is unlikely that Sammartini would have been the *maestro* (there are no records at any point of a man filling that task at any female house), but it is quite possible that he taught in the parlour, and he may well have been hired to conduct music in the *chiesa esteriore* annually, on the house's name-day, in line with the other Settecento evidence for outside musicians performing at such ceremonies.

with food.[6] And the persistence of these ideas suggests a final symbolic valence, one that would continue to the end of the *ancien régime*:[7] female monastic musicians who provided spiritual nourishment to the city, in the same way that nuns had been considered as the preferred ritual custodians of the Body of Christ from the later Middle Ages onwards, evident not least in the Elevation, Corpus Christi, and Double Intercession motets of Chiara Margarita Cozzolani.

One central recurrent question is that of the two centuries' worth of see-sawing disputes, regulations, orders, restrictions, and permissions between ecclesiastical authority on one hand and musical houses on the other. At first glance, there seems to be no rational explanation: the Tridentine decrees had empowered bishops to set binding policy for their diocese, and disputes could be referred to the Roman congregation. Yet several major points in this study suggest that printed or even written orders had little to do with daily musical practice in Milanese female monasteries: the repetition of the same decrees (against more than two choirs in nuns' liturgy, or most strikingly against music in the *parlatori*) over and over, the documentary testimony of outsiders to 'forbidden' practices (Ceva's singing of solo motets in the 1660s, or Alensoon's accounts of secular music in the *parlatorio*), and even ecclesiastical records themselves (the string-players listed in 1676 at S. Radegonda). In part, this is witness to nuns' determination to arrange their music in line with their own desires and position as patrician representatives.

Yet the insufficiency of the curial rules to describe musical practice suggests more: that nuns' (and, given the absence of these restrictions from male monastic music, *only* nuns') music and liturgy were

---

[6] On the performance at S. Maria Maddalena: 'It was by far the best singing, in every respect, that I had heard since my arrival in Italy . . . At my first coming I both hungered and thirsted after music, but I now had had almost my fill.' Burney's account suggests that the same solo motet for the titular feast would have been sung at Mass (in the morning) and repeated at some point at Vespers; implicit also is the idea that enough items in both services were performed in polyphony to motivate his visit. Sadly, no piece by Sammartini for St Mary Magdalene seems to have survived; cf. N. Jenkins and B. Churgin, *Thematic Catalogue of the Works of Giovanni Battista Sammartini: Orchestral and Vocal Music* (Cambridge, Mass., 1976).

[7] As the 1666 travelogue of Margarita Teresa, the Emperor's bride, in the city noted: 'Il rimanente di quella settimana [for six days from 26 Sept. Margarita] l'impiegò in visitar Conuenti di Monache. In ogn'vno fù riceuuta, e diuertita con musiche, rinfreschi, & altri trattenimenti': G. Gualdo Priorato, *Historia di Leopoldo Cesare*, iii (Vienna, 1674), 31.

governed by unwritten limits, including the allowance on a regular basis for cloistered musicians to practise the polyphonic styles popular in the city as a whole regardless of the conciliar or synodal decrees to the contrary. It was precisely the cases that overstepped this tacit understanding (whether on the part of episcopal authority or nuns) that revealed the underlying structures and power relationships in the city: Carlo's attempts at social disciplining at S. Apollinare and S. Maria Maddalena, or Palomera's temporary flight from *clausura* and its consequences. The repeated curial decrees, episcopal visitation orders, and nuns' formal submission (as in the punishments meted out to Bascapè and her companions, or the restrictions at S. Radegonda after the Brunswick visit in 1665, and perhaps Litta's disciplining of S. Paolo after the 1661 ducal musicians' visit) reflected not practical reality but rather the assertion and maintenance of formal status within a given social structure on the part of both prelates and nuns.

Nuns, whose public and sanctoral roles had been forced inside *clausura* by Carlo's interpretation of the Tridentine decrees, used their music in order to re-project their status into the ritual life of the city. Thus such 'disobedience' as S. Apollinare's overstaying of the *licenza* for Giovanni Antonio, S. Marta's continued squabbles in the 1630s, or S. Radegonda's music-making for the Guelphs in 1665 were not simply mistakes based on an underestimation of episcopal power. Rather, they were conflicts necessary to the continued projection of female monastic ritual and music in the public life of Milan. Sisters could count on their families' backing to combat episcopal restrictions, and the negotiated nature of the practical limits to their music-making meant that outright bans on polyphony were unlikely to endure for any length of time, even under Carlo Borromeo or Litta. None of the punishments seems to have been enforced in full or for very long: Bascapè was back as one of the organists at S. Maria Maddalena by the time of Calvi's 1578 dowry-reduction request;[8] the strictures at S. Radegonda and S. Margarita were imposed, revoked in part, renewed, and finally lifted in the course of the later Seicento. One could ask for no better tribute to the power both of

---

[8] Here also, Zardin's interpretation (*Donna e religiosa, passim*) of Bascapè's life and musical career as a conversion to Carlo Borromeo's ideas of female monastic perfection is open to discussion. The failed implementation of Carlo's strictest ideas, and the fundamental change in Federigo's policy, especially for nun musicians, seem to indicate that it was not Bascapè, but rather the conditions of female monastic life (and music) in Milan that had fundamentally changed between the late Cinquecento and the Seicento.

nuns' family backing and of the valued status of their music. If the musical evidence is any guide to daily life, then we might rethink some received wisdom; the failure of the episcopal decrees, the continuation of public roles for nuns, and the resurrection of medieval piety in both the language and the topics of the motet repertory all argue against the marginalization normally considered to have been suffered by female religious.

The formal aspects of sisters' music-making are also noteworthy. The ritualization of urban life in Milan represents a challenge to Keith Thomas's idea of the 'decline of magic' that Burke has chronicled in early modern Italy over the sixteenth and seventeenth centuries.[9] Within the Milanese system, liturgy in female monastic churches—which was essentially synonymous with music—was a prized entity. The setting of such music—a special ritual space that outsiders conceived as an incarnation of the Heavenly Jerusalem—and the 'heavenly' singing of its performers, seem to have evoked exactly those characteristics that Morigia remarked in 1595: wonder and piety in an outside audience.[10]

The circumstances of performance for this repertory were crucial to its effect. The real problems with vocal ranges in music by and for nuns, along with the evidence for nuns' performances, underscore the likelihood of at least one stage of difference between the execution of pieces and their transmission in print or manuscript, especially in the light of such practical considerations as the lack of paper and the real dangers for nuns in receiving written music from the outside, at least in the stricter houses.

The importance of the order-specific breviaries and local traditions parallels other local liturgies and their musical reflection. In a certain sense, the disputes over services in the *chiese interiori* point up the inseparability of liturgy and music, at least from an ecclesiastical point of view. Perhaps most surprising is the diversity of practice in the diocese and the political battles over Ambrosian versus Roman rites as played out in the female houses. The infractions of nuns and the admonitions of bishops revolved around not the use of 'unauthorized' texts in musical items (an issue in Venice, Rome, and else-

[9] Burke, *The Historical Anthropology*, 223–38.

[10] Again, this interpretation attempts to do justice to the mixture of piety and prestige present in such events as the 1664 visits to S. Radegonda. To consider the public nature and worldly character of nuns' music exclusively as a manifestation of the secular is an attitude shared by two unlikely companions: Litta and some modern musical historiography.

where) but rather the adaptation of secular musical styles (and perhaps actual melodies) in liturgical polyphony (the warnings against 'canzoni profani accomodate sotto parole sacre').

Yet the contradictory attitude towards contrafacta parallels the divided view of nuns' music itself. If both Federigo's support for such projects as the Coppini series and the free flow of styles and genres between sacred and secular repertories in the early Seicento represent a policy based on Christian optimism, then Litta's frantic efforts to banish 'profanità' from monastic music corresponds to the mid-century episcopal crackdown noted in several other areas.[11] The nuns of S. Radegonda, S. Margarita, and S. Paolo (whose music shared procedures with secular genres) could well have claimed, in response to Litta's strictures, that they were only following a previous philosophy. And from the point of view of consistent Christian optimism, it would be hard to imagine a response.

But if music leads us to re-examine social history, so too the archival evidence and cultural context might cause a re-evaluation of the motet and psalm repertory of nuns, who gave voice (literally) to the most important values of society, expressed in the Eucharistic, Marian, and Song of Songs texts. The motet topics and themes of Rusca's book embody sisters' own reworking of Federigo's ideas of spirituality, unlike those of the more independent Cassinese houses. The relative simplicity of the edition represents an adaptation of urban styles to the real but incipient talents of her colleagues: a selection of certain, not the most virtuosic, trends in the concerto of the 1620s in the city in the service of humility and self-expression, one that differed in its details from Federigo's liberal but controlling prescriptions for musical religious. And the musical means of Cozzolani's and Badalla's works seem to have highlighted and even inaugurated some trends in the urban patrician repertory: the turn towards refrains in the 1642 book, the formal experimentation with liturgical texts found in the 1650 Vespers, the move away from scriptural and breviary sources in the course of the century (with a major break again around mid-century), and the stylization both textual and musical of the increasingly important solo motet.

---

[11] Even such a sympathetic observer as Locatelli shared the general schizophrenia; after the long ecstatic descriptions of female monastic polyphony, the final entry for Milan in his travel account (App. A, Doc. 56, fo. 54) suddenly turned to the supposed polarity of 'le Sirene di quei Monasteri' contrasted with cloistered holy souls.

Perhaps the most notable aspect of Cozzolani's *œuvre* is the way in which a nun took up (in the *Concerti sacri*) the genres and conventions of the new Lombard style, and (in the 1650 collection) employed these procedures on a large scale, both in terms of scoring and sheer dimensions of pieces; this is most immediately apparent in her fusion of the *salmo arioso* with the conservative traditions of the eight-voice Vespers settings, and in the extended procedures of such concertos as *O quam bonus es* and *Venite sodales*. But even the 1642 pieces, in their reliance on the new form of the multi-sectional concerto and their semiotic employment of dissonance and chromaticism, reflect major changes in urban musical style. The centrality of the dialogue in female monastic music, seen in both the Benedictine's works and in the dedications to nuns, highlights the ties between the genres of spiritual literature and thought on one hand and musical forms on the other.

The expansiveness, abstract formal structure ('alleluia' sections), and sheer vocal virtuosity of the *Scherzi* also shared generic norms for the solo motet that would last into the new century. Badalla's 1684 book shows a compositional self-awareness and a willingness to exploit certain aspects of the generic traditions of the late-century solo motet in the interest of personal expression. The cross-section of local repertory provided by the music publicly associated with nuns calls into question the traditional view of the city's conservatism and resistance to stylistic diversity.

When linking specific composers or pieces to the trends in devotional life, however, the evidence is often less direct. None of the outsider accounts mentions the composers of the music performed in the *chiese interiori* (or *esteriori*, for that matter), but only the nun performers. While this is another testimony to the priority of performance over composition in Seicento musical life, it would still be helpful to know which pieces sent audiences or nuns into devotional states; in the case of Federigo's female ecstatics, a correlation between repertory and trance would help contextualize the prelate's generalizations concerning the spiritual power of music.

Yet another interpretation is possible. Perhaps the specific piece, genre, or style was completely irrelevant to the production of devotion on the audience's part.[12] Certainly Borromeo's Assumption Day

---

[12] This would underscore Rouget's cross-cultural point (*Music and Trance, passim*) on the importance of the entire venue of music, not specific compositional styles, for the induction of ecstasy.

sermon on music, with its emphasis on interior preparation and humility, and its citation of Luzzaschi's performance of a Rore madrigal as a model for *affetto*, supports this idea. On this view, the privileged space, consecrated status of performers, and prefiguring of Heaven associated with nuns' music alone (alone also in the sense that these connotations were not associated with male monastic liturgy and music) could attract the laity and stimulate piety. Whether the music was composed for performances at S. Radegonda in the 1660s by Bagatti, Cazzati, or Ceva might have been irrelevant for its effect. A more direct testimony is furnished by Confaloniera's letter to Federigo, which mentions Rusca's compositions both as having originated at S. Caterina in Brera and as being suitable for other female houses. The idea implies that there were pieces *not* suitable (on whatever grounds) for nuns, and so the question of specific repertory is not completely irrelevant.

Still, important testimony weighs in against the complete acceptance of this hypothesis. There is a good deal of evidence, at least for certain houses at certain times, of the non-devotional aspects of nuns' music: admirers thronging the *chiese esteriori*, friendships and visits in the parlours, transvestite theatre at Carnival, the rise of 'star' singing, and the inevitable jealousies, quarrels, and competition within the artificial constriction of *clausura*. For nuns and their families, this did not contradict the religious aspects of music-making; but this other side of musical life, reflected in the distorted prism of the curial and visitation records, should also be kept in mind as a corrective to the more idealized views of Borromeo and Morigia on cloistered musicians as earthly angels.

Beyond all its external function and transcendent associations, how did musical activity function to shape the lives of its female monastic practitioners? It is difficult to obtain the sense of a 'life cycle' for musical nuns; many singers rose quickly to fame at a young age (Sessa, Ceva, Antonia Clerici). Women like Rusca, Taverna, and Quinzana seem to have performed well into their later years. For some nuns, like Cozzolani, the demands of monastic office combined with external factors seem to have militated against participation in the daily musical life of the house as they grew older.

The publication of music was more difficult, and indeed there was a flavour of one-time opportunity to many editions: along with other cases (Assandra in Pavia, Vizzana in Bologna), several women (Badalla, possibly Calegari) published their only book at an early age.

But others (Sessa, Rusca, Cozzolani) did not have their music printed until later in their careers. And some nuns whom we know to have composed (Quinzana) seem not to have sent their works to the presses. This obviously depended on external factors, notably episcopal policy. What was possible under Federigo Borromeo or Monti was simply not possible under Litta.

And this phenomenon entails a further point: the remarkable growth in female creativity in early modern Italy, to be found in the visual arts (Fontana, Anguissola, Gentileschi, Sirani), literature (Colonna, Stampa), and far from least music—a counter-example to the idea of the Renaissance as a decline in women's status. In the light of the evidence, the women of this study were anything but 'spiritual eccentrics', as one critic has characterized them.[13] Although it was unusual for nuns to publish their music, and indeed something fragile and unique is associated with almost all the editions except those of Cozzolani and Leonarda, still Milanese society considered female monastic singers as a special part of the prestige economy, by no means freaks of nature; on the contrary, they best embodied (in Federigo's terms and in the encomiums of Sessa) the natural goodness of creation. None of the contemporary outside witnesses seems to have regarded the singers and composers of Milanese cloisters as bizarre or marginal phenomena. And the largely religious ideology and values of those women whose testimony has been preserved—Angela Confaloniera, Rosa Badalla, the anonymous chroniclers—were not separate from and contrary to those of the urban society whence they had come; nor did they represent an oppositional tradition of aesthetic expression. Rather, they derived from, and sometimes actually developed, ideas or styles present in urban ideology and music; their practitioners were hardly marginal figures, but rather the most prized exponents of the most popular currents of spirituality. The musical formulation of devotion in sisters' motet books was obviously individual, related to their status as brides of Christ and to their personal self-identification, but it hardly represented some sort of irreducible idiolect. Indeed, it sometimes raised the general compositional norms of urban repertories to new (and to judge by the manuscript transmission of Cozzolani's pieces, popular) artistic levels.

Similarly, there is no evidence universally linking nuns' music to sexuality, except in the minds of obsessed male prelates such as Carlo

---

[13] S. Cusick, review of *The Crannied Wall*, *JAMS* 47 (1994), 348.

and Litta. Although at certain moments there were crowds of male admirers in the *chiese esteriori* for women like Palomera, entire segments of the testimony—the early witnesses around 1600, the music at S. Caterina in Brera or S. Marta—are utterly lacking in such associations. Whatever the constant cultural associations of female monastic polyphony might have been, sexuality was not among them.

Finally, the early modern period seems to have witnessed a change in the patterns of medieval spirituality outlined by Caroline Walker Bynum. The centrality of female figures such as the Virgin, Mary Magdalene, and the patroness saints, evident in the motets of Rusca, Cozzolani, and Badalla, stands in sharp contrast to (northern European) female identification with Jesus. The intercessory role of Mary, and the model nature of the Magdalen or Radegund, find their most sincere expression precisely in the musical evidence. Although some of the medieval associations (the Eucharistic, or the provision of spiritual nourishment via musical nuns) remained constant (or even grew stronger), this new layer of female devotion seems to mark another point of contrast with earlier kinds of spirituality, one that cannot be dismissed as simply male-imposed (no one forced Rusca or Cozzolani to compose or publish their lengthy and intense Marian motets) or insincere.

Thus an even more central question arises: what might music have meant for nun musicians themselves? Again, Angela Confaloniera provides invaluable testimony to its role in one nun's spiritual life and to its place in her world-view:

Then I set myself to playing lute while singing, now one thing and now another. And so singing and playing at fancy, I sigh deeply now and again. O how I like this feeling of [divine] love, which shows it needs everything, even two signs for unburdening itself. And Your Excellency thought I would not learn to play the violin; but certainly I would, for I know all the characteristics of such instruments. O joy of love, what can it not do? . . . One recent Sunday after supper, many of my companions were walking along, and meeting me, asked me to accompany them. And as I was there, I began to sing, and sang a motet by heart, while they rested from their weariness, and, while I sang, I felt my heart catch on fire, so that it seemed to the others as if I were mad.[14]

On St Benedict's feast at three o'clock, Vespers were sung in polyphony, and at the second psalm I remembered the feast of the Blessed Virgin [the

[14] App. A, Doc. 38a.

Annunciation], and it so struck my mind that it seemed as if I were sleepy, and could not speak. It seemed that my soul had been abducted at the behest of the sweetest Virgin, and I wanted to understand how she was in the days before the Lord took on human flesh.[15]

O dearest father, when shall I go to see that which I sometimes seem to hear in my spirit, that splendid cohort of angels, so lovely, so sweet? O what joy will then be mine! Now I know how on that feast of the Blessed Virgin I felt a joy, a sweetest melody, and was not able to accompany them [the angels' song]. O God, o dearest father, even if I knew how to do what they do, I would not have been able, for at this moment I felt myself powerless. I can do this only through the sweetness of an instrument, a lute; while playing whose strings (as I said) and sounding the word 'Jesus', it seemed that I was extracting feelings from it, and so I stopped, unable to proceed, because my mind had flown to God, carried by these words.[16]

In her typically direct way, Confaloniera adumbrated the important functions of music in nuns' identity: the experience of divine love, the self-identification of nuns with the angels whom they represented in the symbolic economy, the rapture of the mind to God through music (not necessarily on the 'correct' liturgical occasion), and the sense of imitating Mary (not Jesus) by being the Lord's hand-maiden, all these sentiments provoked by polyphony. Music's role in encapsulating the highs and lows of interior spiritual life could not be more clear.[17] Whether in or out of liturgy, the motets, canzonas, and *laude* that Confaloniera sang or heard represented the central aspects of her internal spiritual state. Such personal testimony to music's power is infrequent in early modern Europe, even rarer for women musicians, let alone cloistered nuns. Polyphony was central to nuns' lives, perhaps the second most important act in their experience after the reception of Communion, with which it was closely associated by virtue of the Elevation motet and by the symbolic equivalence of music with food.

But even more in these women's lives was at stake. Federigo's active support of music as spiritual recreation and as an avenue for

[15] App. A, Doc. 38b; S. Caterina followed the Benedictine rule and so Benedict was a saint of their *religione*; hence there was another occasion for polyphonic Vespers. Confaloniera was meditating on the Annunciation because the Humiliate celebrated Benedict's feast on 21 Mar., four days earlier (*Breviarium Romanum Humiliatorum*, fo. 325ᵛ). The second psalm of First (or Second) Vespers would have been Ps. 116, *Laudate Dominum omnes gentes*, which had no Marian connotation (ibid.).

[16] App. A, Doc. 38c.

[17] The role of orality in this musical culture is also underlined by the references to singing motets from memory.

the individual soul to perceive the divinely created harmony of the universe evoked in his correspondents at S. Caterina in Brera a sense of the art as a metaphor for nuns' ascent to spiritual perfection. Confaloniera's references to the 'rough voices' of her companions were her image of spiritual aridity. In this world of intense self-examination and heightened emotional reaction, music itself became a symbol of a woman's personal path to the highest stages of the contemplative vocation. It is illuminating to compare Confaloniera's thoughts with Isabella Tomasi's own interpretation of a popular author for Seicento nuns, Jean Gerson. Tomasi's biographers have noted the increased prominence of musical metaphors in Gerson's depictions of the spiritual life, and Suor Maria Crocefissa's retelling of a central metaphor in nuns' standard reading matter laid the equivalence bare:

The rules of music are the same as those of spiritual perfection; in the latter there are suspensions, short and long rests, syncopations, triplets, and clefs . . . minims, *crome*, and *semicrome* . . . the clefs serve to change the mutations [in a double sense], which are quite frequent in the course of spiritual perfection . . . these sounds make for pleasing listening when they are well regulated by the beat of divine conducting.[18]

In Tomasi's rewriting of Gerson, the physical embodiments of music—notes, rests, syncopations, *tactus*, consonance—became a symbol for the daily practice of the ascent to perfection. Similarly, in Rusca's *Salve regina caelorum*, Mary passed from the simple inspiration of music to a metaphor for the instruments and sounds of music itself, without any apparent change in the musical setting. In this sense it seems appropriate to speak of a 'musical world-view', present not only among cloistered musicians, but in the intellectual world

---

[18] 'Le regole della musica sono le stesse della Perfettione: in essa vi sono dei sospiri, delle pause, delle sincope, le triple e le chiavi . . . bianche, neri e semicrome . . . le chiavi servono per cambiar le mutanze quali sono assai spesso nel corso della Perfettione . . . questi suoni fanno un grato sentire quando sono ben regolate dalla Battuta della divina direttione': Maria Crocefissa, undated 'relazione', Rome, Biblioteca Casanatense, MS 4920, transcribed in Cabibbo and Modica, *La santa dei Tomasi*, 117. As the authors note, the comparison between music and the spiritual life plays an important role in Gerson's later mystical writings, especially the collection of treatises known as the *Collectorium septem sportarum*. But *pace* Cabibbo and Modica, this passage seems to represent Tomasi's own formulation and development of Gerson's citation of the Magnificat tone (*Collectorium super Magnificat*, ed. in *Œuvres complètes* (Paris, 1971), viii. 169–71) as a meditative ladder, on whose pitches and syllables the Christian was encouraged to stop in order to reflect on moral and spiritual qualities associated with each pitch and syllable. There were no references in Gerson to 'sospiri', 'neri', or 'semicrome'.

exemplified by female monastic culture as a whole. Apart from the generalized Pythagorean and Platonic ideas on music as a microcosm of the universe, the distinctive feature of these women's formulations is their explicit linkage of their own contemplative vocation (and, despite all the circumvention, there was none other possible in the post-Tridentine Church) to the very essence of music.

I began this study by outlining the historiographic problems of the repertory. First is the extent of our ignorance of the context and styles of Seicento sacred music. Milanese monastic liturgy, performance practice, and local musical styles represent only the prolegomena to the detailed analysis of a specific repertory. But most strikingly, there is no contemporary evidence for its secondary status in Seicento Italy; it cannot be over-emphasized that Catholicism provided a shared set of values and beliefs for all of society, including its composers, monastic or lay. Thus the texts and their context become central to the understanding of the repertory. The traditions of Song of Songs exegesis, for example, provided a range of possibilities for its varied musical settings. The sea change in compositional approach represented by the new style of the 1640s—Casati, Porta, and not least Cozzolani—was directly tied to the changes in motet texts and the more general shift in devotional life in mid-century. The use or abuse of historiographic paradigms also exerts direct influence on our views; inaccurate generalizations about the repertory have become unavoidable and key points evident in the archival documents or musical repertory have been overlooked. In Milan, one of these was the central role of ostensibly marginalized and enclosed nuns.

The question of nuns' music returns us to the various heuristic approaches mentioned above: reverse Burckhardtianism, structuralism, and essentialism or biological reductionism. While the first two have sometimes been substantiated, the heuristic value of the last-mentioned seems rather more questionable on the basis of the Milanese sources. A strictly reductionist view would imply that, for example, the solo motets of Cozzolani would be more akin to Barbara Strozzi's op. 7 motets (to take the case of two women composers whose careers were separated by only a decade) than to the procedures found in Casati or Porta. Yet this is clearly not the case: Strozzi's motets reflect somewhat different devotional priorities, and their formal means set them apart from the Lombard traditions of the solo motet.[19] Purely on the basis of structure, it would be hard to group Badalla's 1684 collection together with Leonarda's op. 11 *Motetti a voce sola* of the same year in a category separate from the collections of RISM 1679[1] or 1692[1], or to attribute differences only to the composer's sex.[20]

Yet if biology does not explain style satisfactorily, still the social interpretation of nuns' womanhood was central to the conditions of their music. Time and again, the special status of specifically *nuns'* music has arisen in contexts negative and positive: episcopal concern (not to say paranoia) about the links between public music-making and chastity, but also Federigo Borromeo's views of sacred virgins who were musicians as providing the best earthly foretaste of Paradise; patrician support for their monasticized musical daughters; and, not least, composers' tributes to cloistered singers. These themes are far more characteristic of the female than of the male monastic musical world. And, on the broadest historiographic level, their musical elaboration shows that for all the medieval basis of devotion and literary genres, the early modern period did indeed bring new content and forms into expressive culture.

Thus, an approach to the musical world of Milanese nuns has to include the centrality of these women's status as female religious, a status in which class, gender, belief, and vocation (or lack thereof) were inextricably fused. What is to be learnt from the compositions written by and for these women—not least the motets of Rusca, Cozzolani, and Badalla—is a sense of music's provision of a public artistic projection of these nuns' most deeply held beliefs and values (not only religious ones); an understanding of its links to and differences from the genres of urban music as a whole; and an appreciation of the richness of female monastic culture whose expression (the life's work of women such as Bascapè, Sessa, Cozzolani, Ceva, or Quinzana, to name only one example from each of this study's five generations) towards both the city and the cloister was

---

[19] A strictly reductionist approach might find it difficult to explain, for instance, why only Cozzolani first among Milanese composers should have chosen to set a text on the Eva–Ave dichotomy (*O quam tristis*, 1648), a standard topos in the discourse of female inferiority.

[20] The clear playing with the extremes of vocal tessitura, and the formulaic pitch construction of aria-like sections, both of which have been noted in the discussion of Badalla's book, are entirely absent in Leonarda's collection. On the latter's large-scale borrowing (in a motet) from a Legrenzi cantata, another problem point for reductionism, cf. Emans, 'Die einstimmigen Kantaten', 109 and 134.

increasingly—and, in the light of these women's 'musical' views of spiritual perfection, fittingly—channelled through music. Despite all the restrictions and oppression, at certain times these women enjoyed the highest symbolic prestige of any social actors in the city, one due precisely to their gender and to their command of polyphony.

APPENDIX A: DOCUMENTS

◇

1. Archivio Storico Diocesano, Novara, sig. A2, fo. 204^v
Iste liber est Religiose et honeste Domine Andriole de medicis monasterii
noui professe. Hunc librum fecit fieri suis propriis expensis a presbytero antonio de vimercate benefitio ecclesiae sanctae mariae rippis porta vercellensi.

2. ASM, Religione, p.a., busta 2147
1554 Instrumento d'obbligo fra Giacomo Antegnati et le Rev^e Mri del
Mon^{astero} Magg^{iore} per la fabbrica di un Organo, che dovevasi fabbricar' da
detto Giacomo con suoi gratti come deue Essere.
In Nomine Domini anno a nativitate Eiusdem millesimo quingentesimo
quinquagesimo quarto Indictione xiij die Martis quarto mensis septembris
Convocato et congregato capitulo et conventu reuerende et venerande dom-
inarum abbatisse et monialium monasterii, maioris Mediolani ordinis sancti
Benedicti de observantia ad ferratam forestarie dicti monasterii ubi solent
pro similibus negocijs congregari de mandato reverende domine Hieronime
de Brippio Dei gratia dicti monasterii abbatisse et sono campane premisso
ut moris est et in qua quidem convocatione et congregatione aderant ipsa
domina abbatissa et cum ea et penes eam infrascripte venerande domine la
madre d. Eufrosina citadina priora, D. Maura Taverna, d. Iudith da
Fiorenza, d. Polissena Simoneta, d. Aurelia de Rocij, d. Cornelia di Capri,
d. Angela Seraphina da Terzago, d. Bona Maria de Porri, d. Faustina de
Barzizij, d. Cassandra del Conte, d. Angela Benedetta de Fideli, d. Inchina
da Corte, d. Angiola Margarita Marauiglia, la matre d. Angela Francesca da
Birago, d. Constanza Maria Pirogalla, d. Bianca Margarita Vincemala,
d. Francesca Seraphina Resta, d. Gabriella Resta, d. Justina da Birago, d.
Sigismonda Panigarola, d. Francesca da Murano, d. Isabetta da Corte, d.
Adriana Resta, d. Anastasia de Santo Zorzo, la Reverenda Madre
d. Alessandra Sforza Bentivoglia, d. Bona Hieronima da Casale, d. Prospera
da Fiorenza, d. Illuminata Taverna, d. Innocentia Caima, d. Dorothea
Thebalda, d. Antonia dalla Croce, d. Paola da Corte, d. Bartolomea di
Malete, d. Candida di Panceri, d. Matilda di Panceri, d. Livia Vincemala,
d. Isabela della Croce, d. Paola Camilla Alfera, d. Paola Francesca
d'Appiano, d. Francesca Ludovica de Pagani, d. Agnesa da Serono, d. Laura

da Fiorenza, d. Violanta da Beolco, d. Ludovica Bellabocca, d. Hieronima Torella, d. Emilia da Cusano, d. Bianca Lucretia Barbavara, d. Genevra di Ferrari, d. Giulia di Ferrari, d. Bernardina di Merli, d. Mansueta di Cernusculi, donna Ambrosia da Rivolta, d. Clara da Landriano, d. Giovanna Maria di Ghisolfi, d. Hieronima Maria da Lecco, d. Lucia da Riva, donna Maddalena da Lecco, d. Battista da Lecco, donna Daria Lucia da Fontana, d. Thadea di Zucconi, d. Angela Hieronima da Riva, d. Francisca Violanta Bentivoglia, d. Francesca Catarina di Rorij, d. Bianca Maria da Vimercato, d. Beatrice de Vecchi, d. Bianca Francesca Vesconta, d. Illaria Leona, d. Hortensia de Clari, d. Bianca Taverna, d. Gioanna Tolentina, d. Flavia Zuccara, d. Leonora Cotta, d. Cecilia de Arona, d. Daria de Arona, d. Placida Magionna, d. Felice da Homato, d. Angela Caterina Morona, d. Corona Somenza, donna Claudia da Dugnano, d. Susanna da Canobio, d. Constantia de Bussi, d. Hippolita Gallarata, d. Domicilla Purisella, d. Bianca Ludovica Moresina, d. Laura Pelegrina Landriana, d. Tarsia Gallarata, d. Vittoria Biraga, d. Theofila da Cusano, d. Angela Beatrice dalla Croce, d. Ottavia Pusterla, donna Hieronima Catarina Panigarola, d. Barbara Panigarola, d. Archilea da Brivio, donna Camilla dalla Croce, d. Terentia de la Croce, d. Laura della Tuona, d. Angela Violanta Biraga, e d. Paola Aurelia Moresina que sunt maior et sanior pars et plusquam due partes ex tribus monialium monasterii predicti ut dixerunt etc. suis nominibus proprijs et nomine et vice etc. aliarum monialium absentia dicti monasterij pro quibus promittunt de rato etc. sub reflectione etc.—

Ipse domine Abbatissa et moniales parte una, et dominus Johannes Jacobus de Antignatis filius quondam domini Bartholomei porte ticinensis parochiae sancti Alexandri in zebedia Mediolani parte altera

Voluntarie etc. ex omnibus modo etc.—

Deuenerunt ad pacta et conuentiones mutua stipulatione interveniente ut infra videlicet

Primo quod predictus dominus Johannes Jacobus teneatur et obligatus sit et ita remittet obligando etc. pignori predictis domine abbatisse et monialibus presentibus etc. eisdem construere organum unum illius altitudinis et latitudinis cuius est organum ecclesie santi simpliciani Mediolani, et cum illis registris et capitulis et aliis cum quibus factum est organum ecclesie maioris civitatis viglevani, et que registra et capitula et alia dabuntur mihi notario per reverendum magistrum presbyterum Zirium de Merlinis de leuco capellanum ducalem ecclesie sancti Ambrosij maioris Mediolani et ipse partes imponunt mihi notario ut inseram ipsa registra et capitula ut supra in presenti instrumento prout dabuntur per ipsum reverendum dominum Zirium. Et ipsum organum teneatur facere et construere hinc ad festum nativitatis domini nostri Jesu Christi anni 1555 proximi futuri et prodeant omnia suis expensis proprijs ipsius domini Jacobi excepta capsa organi et pozolo super quo firmabit*ur* organum que capsa et pozolum fiant expensis monialium et monasterij—

Idem convenerunt q*uod* p*re*dicte revere*nde* do*m*ine abbatissa et moniales teneant*ur* dare p*re*dicto domino Johanni Jacobo pro constructione dicti organi ut supra de p*re*senti scuta quinquaginta auri que faciunt libras ducentas septuaginta quinqu*e* imp*er*ial*es*, et que seu valutam confitet*ur* recepisse—Ab ipsis do*m*ina abbatissa et monialib*us* p*re*sentib*us* p*re*sentiabus, Alia scuta quinquaginta seu valutam ad computu*m* librarum quinque cu*m* dimidio pro scuto in festo paschatis resurrectionis Domini proxi*m*o futuro, Alia scuta quinquaginta seu ualutam ad computu*m* ut s*up*ra in festo Sanc*ti* Martini exinde proxi*m*o futuro, Alia scuta quinquaginta seu valutam ad computum ut s*up*ra cum perfectum fuerit instrumentum et organum que sunt scuta ducenta. Item alia scuta centum seu ualutam ad computum ut s*up*ra que sunt completa solutio p*re*tij et mercedis dicti Do*m*ini Johann*is* Jacobi pro dicto organo infra annum unum immediate sequutum, post dictum organum perfectu*m* cum expensis etc.—

R*egi*strando—

Quare etc.—

Que omnia etc.—

Insup*er* partes iuraverunt, fieri contra*hunt* et non contrauenire etc.—

Que omnia facta sunt ad presentiam reuere*ndi* do*m*ini don Ambrosij de Mediolano Dei gratia abbatis s*anc*torum Petri et Pauli de Glassiate predictis consentientis et interponentis auctoritarem suam. Actum in dicta forestaria dicti mon*aste*rij p*re*sentib*us* p*re*sentib*us* [*sic*] Joseph de Taliabolis filio do*m*ini Johannis Antonii porte ticinensis par*ochie* Sanc*te* Marie Beltradis M*edio*lani et Hieronimo Mantegatia filio s*pectabilis* do*m*ini Ambrosij por*te* cumane par*ochie* s*ancti* Carpofori intus M*edio*lani, pronotariis.

Testes sp*ectabiles* d. Georgius Balters fil*ius* quo*ndam* domini Melchioris por*te* orient*alis* par*ochie* s*ancti* Babille foris M*edio*lani, d. Alexander Rigonus filius D. Johannis Angeli por*te* vercelline par*ochie* Sanctorum Naboris et Felicis M*edio*lani notus, et R*everendus* Domin*us* presb*yter* Ambrosius di Scopertis filius quonda*m* do*m*ini Bernardini por*te* ticin*ensis* par*ochie* S. Quirici M*edio*lani omnes etc.

3. Lino to Carlo Borromeo, 1 August 1565, BA, F. 36 *inf.*, fo. 339

Credo che V.S. Ill.ma sappia che quasi tutti li Monasterii delle Monache hanno gli organi dentro la loro chiesa, li quali sono suonati da una, ò più di esse. Or perché le M*ad*ri si allevano qualche giovane che habbia a succedere in quell'officio, alle quali insegnano ciò che sanno, ma non le possono dare quella perfettione che bisognerebbe, ricercandosi a questo un'Organista di maggior scienza et esperienza di loro, ci fanno istanza di concederglielo a questo effetto, con questo però che l'organista stia nel Parlatorio di fuora, e la monacha in quello di dentro con buona compagnia, e ciascun habbia il suo Clavicordo, col quale il Maestro insegni et la discipola impari. Questo non si ha loro anchora concesso, volendo prima intendere la mente di V.S. Ill.ma sopra ciò. Ma ci pare ben necessario, ò di prohibire loro del tutto l'uso de gli organi, il che quanto strepito causaria V.S. Ill.ma lo può da se stessa consistare, ò di concedere loro il modo di poterli usare. Ma si potria ben fare scelta di tre ò quattro Organisti delli più approbati et maturi che si truovano nella città, alli quali soli si concedesse tal licenza quando V.S. Ill.ma fosse di tal parere.

4. Borromeo to Lino, 11 August 1565, BA, F. 36 *inf.*, fos. 354^v–355^r

Il cercar de leuar gli organi a le suore partorirebbe senza fa*llo* molto strepito, e quanto ben anco si potesse facilmente farlo, non so se fosse molto espedi*ente* potendosi anco di qui cauar qualche buon frutto, come di fuggir talvolta l'otiò, et ancho di eccitar diuotione, negli anime loro, poi che le monache non possono con quella pe*rf*ettione che sar*ia* bisogno insegnar l'una à l'altra, et se ha necessità di maestri più potenti, approvo per assai buono qual espediente che voi proponete, che si faccia scelta di tre ò quattro organisti di età matura, et di uita incolpata, ai q*u*ali soli si dia questa facoltà d'insegnare a' suore. Et q*u*anto al modo che si habbia a seruare in q*u*esto, acciò si faccia con la debita onestà, et con qual minor pericolo che si può, me ne rimetto alla prudenza uostra.

5. Milanese Provincial Council I (1565); *AEM* I, 145–6

Nemini omnino, neque sacro, neque profano, neque mari, neque foeminae, liceat adire Monasteria monialium docendi causa cantum, quem *figuratum* vocant. In iis tamen Monasteriis, in quibus non in exteriori ecclesia a saecularibus, sed intus a monialibus organo sonatur, permittere poterit Superior alicui viro, moribus et aetate ab Episcopo probato, ut foris ad fenestellam collocutionis monialem organistam tantum sonandi artem edoceat, si in eo studii genere plus proficere necesse habeat. Haec autem intus, ad ipsam fenestellam discens, commorabitur; cui semper adsistent duae ex iis, quae audiendis sermonibus praepositae sunt. Quae contra fecerit, sive Praefecta, sive alia, velo privetur, aliisque praeterea poenis afficiatur, arbitratu Superioris. Organum autem in posterum ne constituatur, nisi locus in quo apte locetur, Superioris iudicio ante probetur. Prohibentur etiam moniales ipsae intus, aut per alios foris sonare musicis instrumentis, praeter organum et harpichordium, quo ars organo sonandi discitur.

6. Provincial Council II (1569), *AEM* II, 76

Clerici in eo officio ne se exerceant, ut ullas mulieres, etiam quavis dignitate illustres, doceant legere, scriberere, aut canere, aliove cujusvis generis musico instrumento sonare; nisi ii sint, quibus aetate, moribus et vita probatis, Episcopi judicio, id permissum est, facultate ab eodem scriptis data.

Ne libris item de musico cantu obscoene vel parum pudice conscriptis illi utantur.

7a. Suor Buona's testimony, visitation of S. Apollinare, 12 February 1571, ASDM XII, vol. 64, fo. 204ʳ⁻ᵛ

Quando io dovevo esser confirmata madre di questo convento, come fui, uenne qua il Padre Commissario apostolico per effetto, et mi disse che suor Clementina gl'haueua dimandato licenza di poter far uenire in conuento Messer Giovanni Antonio organista che insegnava à cantare ad essa suor Clementina et a sonare a suor Angela Serafina, et questa per far acconciare l'istrumento de suor Angela Serafina, et l'organo, et il commissario domandò me se questo Giovanni Antonio era huomo dabene, et se l'istromento si potesse portar fuorij à far acconciare . . . et il Padre Commissario ne disse poi haverli dato la sudetta licenza, la quale licenza io non la viddi, se non in questo ultimo giorno [quando] è nato questo romore[;] ma suor Clementia mi disse all'hora che l'haueua hauuta, et intesi che l'haueua mostrata alla tornera suor Michela, che adesso è Vicaria, et da qui è nato che io l'ho lasciato intrare l'anno passato una volta ad acconciar quest'instromento senza però che vi mangiasse.

7b. Ibid., fo. 204ᵛ

E passato l'anno che suor Clementia mi disse haver hauuto la licenza di introdurre Messer Giovanni Antonio in convento ad acconciar l'istromento, ma io non ho già memoria di hauerla letta, et quando l'havrei ben letta, non haurei potuto conoscere la mano.

7c. Testimony of Giovanni Antonio, ibid., fos. 206ʳ and 206ᵛ

Interrogatus, a quibus monialibus sibi fuerit dictum ipsas obtinuisse dictam licentiam a dicto Commissario?, respondit: Io lo intesi da suor Clementina Cattanea, alla quale io insegnava di cantar alla ferrada, se non da altri con lei era presente sor Angela Serafina, quando lei mi disse, che haueano ottenuto questa licentia . . . Et exhibita sibi quadam scriptura incipiente: Si concede licentia etc. de anno 1568 die 17 martii, qua lecta, propius constituit, dixit: Questa è certa quella licentia che io dico . . . Interrogatus: An a praedictis monialibus unquam rogatus fuerit ad aliquid scribendum, et si quid scripserit? respondit: Io non ho mai scritto cosa alcuna per loro, se non le lettioni che io le dava.

7d. ASDM XII, vol. 64, fo. 210

Suor Angela Serafina stia per tre mesi senza il uelo. Sia priua dell'ufficio di organista, nè si possa rimettere a questo officio per sei anni. L'arpicordo grande non stia in camera sua, ma altroue in conuento, nè lei possa sonar su quello, o altro instromento, nè cantar per tre anni canto figurato. Et per sei mesi ogni Mercordì mangi in refettorio in terra, et domandi perdono del disturbo, che ha hauuto per causa sua, et del scandolo de haver dato da mangiare in conuento all'organista. Nè uada per tre mesi al parlatorio.

8a. *Esamina* of S. Maria Maddalena al Cerchio, 28 February 1575, ASDM XII, vol. 97, fasc. 2, fo. 2^r

Et quelle cose che V.R. trovò nella mia cella li trouai in vna copie de motetti de Orlando Lasso [added: mandatami da messer Giovan Battista mio fratello] et li lessi uno cioe la prima et li lasciai sopra il tauolino a intensione di mandarli via . . . In quella prima linea ch'io lessi mi ricordo che vi erano queste parole *Vum disi madona ogn'hor*, et no so che cosa seguisse [fo. 14^v] Erano anche altre canzoni bergamasche ma io non li lessi . . . Io non li mostrai ad alcuna monaca seno che dissi a Suor Liuia Sodania che mio fratello mi haueua mandato canzone alla bergamasca, ma ch'io non volevo guardarli.

8b. *Esamina*, ibid. Interrogata igitur, [dixit] quod[:] V.S. trovò nella cella di suor Paula Giustina quelli paperi, e motetti, erano una tra che gli scrisse il S. Gio: Paolo Turni suo cugino et tutore, quale io hauendo letta conteneua cose honeste et lei disse hauerla ascolta per dubitare si gridasse anche per simili lettere et io vidi et lessi di quelli motetti che mi parvenero del [crossed-out: 'libro'] orlando compositore de motetti.

8c. Testimony of Suor Giulia di Conte, *Esamina*, fo. 8^v

E l'organista si dimostra Prospera Corona et la maestra di capella suor Laura Benzona, et ogni festa si canta il magnificat, et diuerse antifone. Essa sona l'organo, et l'organista le canta nel organo.

8d. (Ibid.). Ho sentito alle volte sotto i claustri Prospera Vittoria et Prospera Corona et Paula Giustina et cantarono varie canzoni.

8e. Testimony of Suor Constanza de Biumi, *Esamina*, fo. 5^v

Io non ho sentito alle sudette [the three young nuns] cantar il canto alla bergamasca i scontradura, potrebbero hauer cantato [underlined by the vicarial scribe:] nella camera dell'organista oue cantarono alle volte et io no'l so et Paula è solita andar nella [underlined again:] camera dell'organista per imparare.

8f. Testimony of Suor Prosper Corona, *Esamina*, fo. 11^v

Interrogata respondit: Ho offizio del organista, da sonar et cantar col organo . . . Nella mia cella io canto alle volte nel Instrumento . . . et io canto solamente motetti spirituali, et so anche mettergli in intaulatura, et alle volte canto con le monache nella cella a prouar quello si ha da cantar.

8g. Testimony of Prospera Vittoria Cavenaghi, *Esamina*, fo. 10ᵛ

Io canto solamente in canto figurato cose spirituali, non ho mai cantato con S. Paula Iustina se non in capella, et in refettorio o in lavorario, et anche fuor di capella canto qualche volta con S. Laura Bezona, S. Prospera Corona e con S. Claudia Sulpitia.

8h. (Ibid.)

Ho inteso che si sono trouato alcuni canti *alla bergamasca* [underlined] a S. Paula Iustina, ma io no so parlar alla bergamasca.

8i. Testimony of Suor Paola Giustina, *Esamina*, fo. 14ʳ

Io so un poco di canto figurato . . . io aiuto in chiesa a cantar qualche volte, et alle uolte si prouiano nella camera di Suor Laura maestra di capella—et non ho mai cantato in giardino.

8j. Testimony of Suor Paola Giustina, ibid.

Alle volte si è cantato le versi spirituali del Thesauro di sapientia datome da Messer Padre Paulo, et si è cantato de queste cose predetta Suor Prospera Corona organista, et Suor Laura, et Suor Prospera Vittoria et altre della musica.

8k. Undated orders (1575) signed by Cesare Arese, ibid., with a draft version following

Suor Prospera Vittoria Cauenaga, e Suor Prospera Corona Basgapera e Suor Paula Iustina Carpana stiano priuate di voce attiua, e passiua, di porta, torno, e parlatorio, di [original draft version: poter] non cantar canto figurato per il tempo [original: sara poi arbitrario a Mess.r Ill.mo Aricuescovo] di sei anni, dicano ogni venerdi per vn'anno sua colpa in reffittorio et il salmo, Miserere mei Deus, [next 4 words not in original] in genocchi in mezzo il refittorio cominciando Suor Paola Justina subito fatta la Benedittione della Mensa detto salmo, et respondendoli le altre due a versetto per versetto alternamente con alta voce et in fine del salmo basciando caduna la terra tre volte vna doppo l'altra—vadino tutte tre a dormire nel dormitorio accomodando i suoi letti, cioe una da vn capo, l'altra in mezzo, et l'altra dall'altro capo del dormitorio. Lasciando le loro celle, nelle quali andauano a star altre come se dira alla Madre ministra.—Et di poi detta Suor Paola Iustina stia priuata di scriuer ne far sciuere lettere ne altro ad alcuna persona—et per detto tempo di sei anni tutte tre senza altre in compagnia siano tenute fare l'officio, et tutti li servitij pertinenti al Infermaria.

9. ASDM XII, S. Agnese, vol. 59, fasc. 1, unsigned letter bound with 1576 visitation records

Monsignore ne aviso deli desordini che se fanno al monasterio de Santa Agnesa con grande frequencia di gente, . . . la terza festa del Spiritu Santo passai per quela contrada . . . et senti neli suoi parlatori sonare destinti de clavichordo cantare.

10. Ibid., fasc. 5

Ogn'ano il Carnavale si fanno delle maschere assai delle monache travestite de diversi sorti de habiti de frati, et de secolari; ed ancora con pugnali espade et mangiano cosi travestite in refectorrio . . . Fanno delle comedie de amor dishonestissime tra di loro, et piu le recitano anzi [illegible] a loro frati nelle forester sendovi una ferrata tramella solamente leuata internamente . . . Le Monache stravestite de diverse sorte de habiti ballano con li frati alla fenestrina.

11. Carlo Borromeo to Cesare Speciano, 5 July [15]79, BA, F. 54 *inf.*, fo. 14^{r–v}

Il Marchese Gouernatore . . . l'altro giorno, che si fece la festa nella chiesa del Monastero di Santa Margherita, uolse andarui, et farui cantare da i suoi musici, con tutto ch'egli fosse auuisato prima da i Padri, che hanno cura di quel Monasterio, che ui era ordine espresso del Visitatore Apostolico, che non si potesse far musica nella chiesa esteriore dei monasterij de monache et sebene questa non è ordine mio, ma come ho detto del Visitatore Apostolico . . . tuttavia ho uoluto passarla cosi, non mostrando di saperlo. Ma questo cantare di musica nelle chiese delle monache è ben cosa perniciosissima, et spesso se ne sono viste disordinationi notabili delle monache stesse, massime che simile sorte di musici sogliono essere assai rilasciati. Et poiche il Marchese ha uoluto andare ad una chiesetta piccola, come è questa di Santa Margherita, è segno, che l'habbia fatto più tosto per usare di questa libertà de suoi musici, che per altro rispetto et uorrà forte andare cosi negli altri monasterij, il che potete imaginarvi di quanto danno sarebbe. Anzi io temo, che uorrà anco cominciare a pretendere, che i suoi musici cantino in duomo, ò in altra chiesa, doue sia il capitolo, et musica del duomo, il che non è usato, ne si permetterebbe senza commissione particolare di N.S. Ho uoluto dirui tutto questo, accio lo facciate sapere a S.S. se cosi vi parea bene.

12. 'Ordini stabiliti in Roma dal R. Padre Generale delli canonici Regolari per li monasterij di Monache badati dal B.P. Abbate della passione di mílano': ASDM XII, vol. 48, fo. 88; 25 February 1581

Ne mai puossano li canonici, o altri far musica nella Chiesa esteriore, ma solo cantare gl'ufficij in canto firmo, al quale non rispondino Le Monache, alle quali sia permesso pero tra di lor in chiesa far musica.

13. Letter signed 'vicario delle monache', ASDM XII, vol. 48, fo. 65 (*c.*1585)

Et si obsiesca alla vanita che alle volte hanno le velate nel sonare . . . Che il sonar' de organi presso alcuni monasterij di monache più riformate non è tenuto di tanta necessità di modo che sin qui non hanno uoluto erigere organi nelle lor chiese et le organiste et cantore di canto figurato spesse volte sogliano esser le manco disciplinati et manco spirituali.

14. ASDM XII, vol. 74, fasc. 4

Alla Rev. Madre delle Virgini di Santa Cristina di P.C. Molto Rev. Madre. Li prohibimo con la presente che per l'avenire sotto pena ad arbitrio nostro non permetti ch'alcuno Musico si accosti a cotesto suo Monastero per insegnar à cantar, ò sonar, revocando perciò ogni faccoltà comunale senza nova nostra licenza. Con che Iddio vi benedica. Dall'Arcivescovado li xxij Ottobre 1593. Come fratello Il Vicario generale.

15. ASDM, Carteggio Ufficiale, cartella 32, vol. 70

Molto Reuerendo Signore: Si è saputo, che Giulio Cesare Gabusdi habbia hauuto licenza dal ministro di minori osservati di poter insegnare musica alle grate del Monastero di s. Bernardino à suor Alma Ginevra, con gran'ammiratione delle SS. Loro Illustrissime, per esser cosa molto inconveniente, e perchè si è comisso al Protectore dell'ordine che corriga il Ministro, li Serenissimi Loro Illustrissimi han' resoluto, che doviate voi rivocare detta licenza in uirtu di questa mia, non permettendo, che ne in questo monastero ne in altri imparino le monache musica da persone di fuori in qualsivoglia modo; Onde non mancate di esseguire con diligenza: Iddio la preservi. Di Roma li ultimo di ottobre 1594. Al piacer nostro Il Cardinale Alessandrino

16. P. Morigia, *La nobilità di Milano* (Milan: Ponzio, 1595), 306–7

Dirò ancora come in questa nostra Città quasi tutti i Monasterii delle Monache fanno professione di Musica, cosi del suono di più sorte d'istromenti Musicali, come di cantare; & in alcuni Monasterii ci sono voci tanto rare, che paiono angeliche, & à sembienza di sirene allettano la nobilità di Milano d'andargli ad vdire. Ma frà gli altri ce ne sono due degni di lode, che non sono inferiore a niun'altro nell'eccellenza Musicale, che sono il Monastero di S. Maria Maddalena vicino à S. Eufemia, l'altro è quel dell'Assonta detto del Muro; queste venerabili Religiose, oltre alla santa osservanza della vita Apostolica, sono ancora virtuosissime, e nella Musica esercitate, cosi ne' suoni, come nel cantare, & si sentono voci scielte concordevoli in armonia, con vnione di concerti di voci diuine, con mescolanza de' suoni, di modo che paiono Angelici Chori, che addolciscono

l'orecchie de gli vditori, e vengono lodate da gli huomini intelligenti di tal
virtù.

17. ASV, VR, posizione 1596, lettere M–P

Illustrissimi e Reverendissimi signori: Le Monache di san Bernardino di
Milano dell'ordine dell'osservanza di san francesco hanno un organo nella
loro Chiesa, del quale per esser rotto non sene possonno servire; . . . ne
havendo il modo di poterlo fare; senon con pigliare parte della dote di
qualche monacha percio supplicano V.S. Signori Illustrissimi farle grazia di
concerderle licenza di poter levare lire mille della dote di Suora Alma
Genevra monaca in detto luogo per la restauratione di detto organo.

18. B. Giorgi to all abbesses, 20 November 1598, ASDM XII, vol. 50, fo.
162

E con la medesima occasione [of Advent] non lascieremo di dirle, che si
come molte persone Religiose s'astengano da certi cibi, e si essercitano in
digiuni, & altre opere di penitenza, sarebbe conveniente all'antica osservanza Monastica tralasciar la musica figurata in questi giorni: ne in altri usar
mai altri stromenti che l'Organo, e Regale. E perciò doverete hauerci consideratione, ne permettere che in Chiesa si suoni liuto, che alcuna Monaca
cantando sola a si modo, c'habbia del vano, ò profano; ne si faccia musica
in Parlatorij, fuori ne dentro, ne in altra stanza ivi vicino sotto qual si voglia
pretesto.

19. ASV, VR, posizione 1600, lett. H–M, Milano

Illustrissimi et Reverendissimi Signori: Hieronima Virginia de Assandri mentre era al secolo ha imparato assai à sonar de Violino, et Violone, hora è
entrata nel Monasterio di S. Appolinare dell'ordine de Santa Chiara
dell'osservanza in Milano, et già è messa in capitulo et mentre dura l'anno
della professione per poter in tal monasterio honorar il Signor Dio desiderra
finir' d'imparare di detti instrumenti: Supplica perciò VV.SS:ri Illustrissimi
à farle gratia à darle licenza che durante l'anno del novitiato il suo maestro
possa andar'al parlatorio à insegnarli con l'assistenza dell'Abbadessa, et
ascoltatrice di detto Monastero.

20. ASV, VR, posizione 1600, lett. H–M, Milano

Il vicario generale di Milano fece alli giorni passati un editto che alcune
monache della detta diocesi non potessero per avanti servirsi della musica
d'instrumento alcuno fuor che organi et regali. Hora trovandosi le
monache di santa Maria Maddalena della terra di Monza della detta diocesi
prive al tutto di voce che servi per basso per agiuto della loro musica si
servino per tale effetto di un violone da gamba non potendo far altrimente

se non si lasciara totalmente la musica, il che desiderano fare tuttavia per non privarsi di musica, et però ricorrono alle illustrissime signorie loro supplichevolmente pregandole si degnino concederli tal gratia ordinando al detto vicario che stante la detta necessità le lasci usar questo instromento.

21. E. Puteanus, *Musathena, sive Notarum heptas* . . . (Hanover, 1602; first edn. as *Modulata Pallas* (Milan, 1599)), 22–3

In vno Musicae membro duas partes repperi, HARMONICAM & ORGANICAM. Sed vti eiusdem arboris rami saepissime discrepant, eiusdem arui glebae: ita prior ista, Antiquitate, Dignitate, Potestate praestat. Hoc ipsum paucis verbis conabor, palam facere. Quae in laudem vocis scripta, sacra tibi sunto CLAVDIA SESSA virgo, an Musa dicam? quae voces mortales miraculo universo praestas. Tibi praesentis seculi suffragio cedit Antiquitas, & honorem habitura est Posteritas. Fabulis quid ultra loci? Illae Iouis filiae ora compescant, ne te canente obstrepere deinceps videantur: Sirenes facessant quarum tu concordiam superas: Echo silentio invidiam suam tegat, frustra te referre conatur.

22. A. Albergati to all female houses, 10 October 1603, ASDM XII, vol. 52, fasc. 3

Reuer*ende* Sorelle in Christo. Nelli giorni quando celebrate la festa della vostra Chiesa si sono auuertite alcune cose intorno alle Messe, alla Musica, Ministri, suppelletile, à gl'apparati & altre spese che si fanno, quali son giudicate lontante da quella pietà, modestia, è religione, che si deue mostrare in tali occasioni, è massime da Monache, c'hanno a seruir à Dio senza ombra alcuna di vana ostentatione, ma più tosto col spirito interiore che con apparenza esteriore . . . Volendo far Musica, non si passino due Chori con Organo e Regale al più; e niuna Monaca canti sola, altrimente sarà priuata del cantar anco in compagnia, e tutto questo s'osserui sempre in altri tempi ancora.

23. ASDM XII, S. Caterina in Chiusa, vol. 70, fasc. 1, visitation orders of 1606

Tutte le monache, ricordevoli d'esser tenute à lodar la D*iv*ina M*a*està nel choro, all'auenir convoglino alli divini officij secondo la regola, et decreti sopra di ciò fatte nelle visite passate . . . Puorchè per l'adietro non si è usata la debita diligenza nell'instruire le novitie nel canto, acciò il servizio divino si face con quel decoro, [che] si conviene, all'auenire la madre auerta si face la debita diligenza dalla maestra delle novitie . . . et conoscendosi qualche negligenza in questo esercizio, non le lasci uscire di nouiciato, se prima non saranno suffice*nteme*nte instrutte nel canto. Si faccia ancora qualche diligenza, acciò quelle monache, che già sono fuori della selvola [the year of novitiate] con quale particolare studio restino instrutte.

24. Nuns of S. Marta to Federigo Borromeo, 21 August 1608, ASM, Religione, p.a., 2145

Si supplica V.S. Ill.ma far gratia alle Monache di S. Marta di Milano di poter [far] disponibile lire 1058, che sono della dote spirituale di suor Bianca Lodovica Tauerna, per comprare fermente che per il bisogno del Monastero, non si puo far di meno, con questa gratia si spera di ottenere da V.S. Ill.ma per la solita sua bontà.

25. G. P. Barco, *Specchio religioso per le monache* (Milan, 1609), 123, 125

Se tra i divini ufficii [a nun] canta o in voce, o con l'organo canzoni profane, e poco honeste, et se n'accorge, pecca mortalmente, contra il decreto del sagro concilio di Trento . . . Se fuori de' divini ufficii canta madrigali, canzonette, villanelle profane, et poco honeste, pecca più, o meno secondo l'intentione, e le circostanze . . . Quelle, che praticano frequentemente con musici senza licenza, parlando alla porta, o in parlatorio, pigliando da essi canti, mottetti, e simili cose, senza licenza, peccano; et molto più, se sono canti profani, et il peccato e anco mortale, quando per la qualità de' musici, e la frequenza loro mettono probabilmente a pericolo la castità.

26. F. Borromeo, Italian draft of *De ecstaticis mulieribus et illusis*, Book IV, ch. 38; BA, F. 26 *inf.*, fos. 247–50

Ritornando poi à parlare delle ecstatiche si hauranno ad investigare due effetti ueramente merauigliosi in esse, cioè ch'esse cantano tal'uolta l'officio diuino distesamente, e per longo spatio. Di questo non accade dubitare, poiche molti esempi si ritrouono; e del suono potrò raccontarne uno, il quale ne i nostri tempi è accaducto sicurissimamente: E come queste cose non e cosi ageuole da raccontarsi. E prender si dee alcuna similitudine. Sono tal uolta alcuni huomini cosi trascurati nel recitar l'offitio diuino, che essi ueramente non solo non pensono à quello che si fa, e si dice, ma non uedono neanche cio che loro sta d'auanzi, ne ueggono chi passa uicino, ne sentono le uoci altrui, tanto stranno assenti in quei loro pensieri. Hora come posson essi recitar l'officio diuino à mente? Quella parte che essi sanno già a memoria possono recitarla in questo modo. Nella loro mente già risiedono le specie intelligibili, e di queste per uia della reminiscenza si pascuale la potentia intellettiua; . . . Parlando poi del suono io raccontarò quello che è auuenuto certissimamente ne i nostri giorni. Vna estatica di santa vita la quale poi è morta con fama di gran santità, tal uolta era costretta dalle preghiere delle sue compagne, le quali tutte erano eleuati spiriti, e celesti a dare ad esse alcun segnale, et alcun esempio, come fosse l'harmonia del Paradiso: Ella sicome humilissima, e che non istimaua di hauer gratia maggiore delle Compagne, fatta in prima alcuna resistentia, di buona uoglia poi compiaceua loro, e con lieto animo. E cosi nella presentia di esse sole, prendeua nelle mani un liuto, poiche ne i primi suoi anni haueua imparato à sonare, e toccando alcune corde di esso insuonaua un canto cosi delicato, mà insieme cosi lontana dall'aria, e dalla forma di quelli che sono consueti à sentirsi in terra, che affermato hanno persone dignissime di fede, che qua giù maniere somiglianti di canto, et andamenti simili di consonanze, non si sentiuano. Hora questa donna non procedeua innanzi un piccolo spatio di tempo cantando, e suonando ch'ella restaua rapita, e all'hora cessaua il canto, ma seguitaua à suonare, punto non errando nelle vere consonanze. Passato poi alcun altro puoco spatio di tempo, ella tornaua in se, e si arrossiua, che in presenza delle compagne hauesse perduto i sentimenti, e doleauasi alquanto del braccio e della mano destra, con cui moueua le corde. Alcune belle cose si douranno qui considerare. Ella cessaua dal canto, incominciando le Estasi, perche gli Istrumenti, e gl'organi della voce doueuano essere impediti dal rapto. Le doleua poi il braccio, e la mano, imperoche era suo proprio, quando perdeua i sentimenti, di inrigidirsi, e di essere alquanto [illegible] in tutta la persona, e percio in lei il mouimento all'hora delle mani era cosi violenta, e nociua l'operazione poi del braccio, e della mano [illegible] faceuassi quasi in quel modo, che i dormienti fanno cose somiglianti. Mà però in ciò si ha da credere che ui fosse opera diuina speciale, poiche le Estasi di lei sono state giudicate per commune con sentimento spontanario e procedenti da Dio, e lontane da Diabolici inganni.

27. *Rubriche generali del breviario monastico* (Milan, 1614), ch. 17, pp. 42–3

Del Vespero. 17. Al Vespro si dice il *Pater noster*, l'*Aue Maria, Deus in adjutorium*, &c. Di poi si dicono quattro Salmi con quattro antifone, come nel proprio, ouer commune de Santi sono segnati. Ma nelle Domeniche & ferie, l'antifone, & Salmi sempre si dicono come nel Saltario (come ancora nel tempo Pascale si dicono i Salmi sotto vna Antifona *Alleluia*) se non saranno assegnate altre antifone, & Salmi di proprio, & come nelle Domeniche dell'Aduento, & li tre giorni auanti Pasca, che si dicono antifone, & Salmi di proprio.

2. Dopò i Salmi, & antifone si dice seconda la qualità dell'officio il Capitolo, il resposorio breue, l'hinno, il versetto, l'antifona al Magnificat, con l'istesso Cantico, *Kyrie*, il *Pater* con voce chiara, *Dominus vobiscum*, & l'oratione; tutto si dice de Tempore, ouer di Santo secondo la qualità dell'offitio.

3. Dopò l'oratione si fanno le commemorationi della Croce, della Madonna, de gli Apostoli, di S. Benedetto, & della Pace, come si hà nelle proprie rubriche. Si finisce il vespro come l'altre hore.

28. ASDM XII, vol. 51, fos. 136 ff., with another copy dated 1619 in fasc. 3 of the same volume

Molto Rev. Madre . . . Il far fuochi, sparare mortaletti, et archibuggi, suonare trombe, et cose simili, è cosa totalmente aliena dalla religione e pietà Monachale, che percio espressamente si prohibiscono . . . La Musica si faccia sempre dalle Monache, ne con altri Stromenti che d'organo e regale, et a due Chori solij; ne alcuna Monacha canti sola, ed i canti siano sacri, e gravi, e lontani da ogni profanità.

29. From G. Borsieri, *Soplemento* to Morigia, *La nobilità di Milano* (Milan, 1619), 51–4

Di Donna Claudia Sessa cantatrice singolare, detta la Monaca dell'Annonciata. Cap. XIV.

E stata Claudia Sessa donna à tempi nostri singolare non solamente per la musica, ma ancora per le altre rare qualità. Hà suonato di varij stromenti, ed accompagnato il suono con vn' armonia così mirabile, che non hà hauuto cantore, che pur habbia potuto pareggiarla. Poiche cantando nella Chiesa interiore dell'Annunciata, doue haueua vestito l'habito monacale, si faceua conoscer' equale, e spiritosa nel mouimento della voce, pronta, e veloce ne' trilli, affetuosa, e padrona negli accenti, e sopra il tutto così prattica delle altrue compositioni, che poteua chiamarsi in vn tempo stesso *musica, e recitatrice,* dando loro spesso quello spirito, e quella viuacità, che forse regolarmente non haueuano. Perciò era si grande il concorso de' popoli à quella Chiesa nelle feste, che molti erano costretti à starsene fuori, quasi ciascuna festa ordinaria, per lo cantar di lei fosse anzi la principale della Chiesa. Inuitata dalla Catholica Reina Margarita d'Austria, che l'haueua vdita cantare, ad andarsene in Ispagna alla Corte, non volle acconsentire allo inuito facendo intender à S. Maestà, che si haueua preso quel monastero per vna perpetua clausura. Il Serenissimo di Savoia, e ciascuno de' figliuoli di lui l'hanno più volte vdita anco suonare. Ciò, che hanno fatto anco quei di Parma, e di Mantova, i quali soleuano dire, che non equalmente restauano sodifatti dal cantar di Claudio Monteuerde, nè di qual'altro Musico recitatiuo, che spesso vdissero nelle lor corti, benche l'vno, e l'altro professasse d'hauer' al proprio seruigio i migliori musici di questi tempi. L'Arciduca Alberto, e la Serenissima Infanta Isabella, mentre dimorarono in Milano più volte finsero d'esser costretti ad vscir di corte con determinatione di far essercitio per andarla ad vdire, e nella Chiesa, e nel Parlatorio. I Cardinali Aldobrandino, S. Giorgio e Piato per vdirla hanno più volte celebrate le lor Messe in quella Chiesa, il che hanno fatto anco diuersi Nuncij Apostolici, e Vescoui forastieri, che si son taluolta trouati in Milano di passaggio. Non è stato gouernatore dentro questa Città, mentr'ella hà cantato, che non habbia sino voluto prender con lei famigliarità. Imperòche il Conte di Fuentes per nemico, che paresse de' complementi soleua chiarmarla figliola sua, e il Contestabile di Castiglia, e la moglie l'amarono tanto, che presero licenza di entrar nel monastero stesso à visitarla, ed à gustar delle virtù, che in essa risplendeuano. Era nondimeno ella così modesta, ed humile, che talhora si faceua scrupolo di conscienza à riceuer' alcune delle lor visite scoprendo allo incontro di hauer maggiormente à core lo atte*n*der' a' diuini vfficij nella Chiesa stessa non meno di quel, che solesse farsi qualsi fosse altra semplice monaca, e spirituale, e supponendo di cantar nelle feste per la sola gloria del sommo Fattore, à cui quei giorni son consacrati, non per lo acquisto dell'honor mondano, e del concorso popolare. Pregata ad impetrar gratie da' Gouernatori per colpe di persone grandi soleua spesso modestemente iscusarsi; si compiaceua però di chiederne loro alcune per altre persone, alle quali potesse giouar l'affetuosa charità, ch'ella mostrò più volte in simili occorrenze e non indarno. S'è talhora veduto alcun forastiero dimorar' in Milano oltre il bisogno, benche negotioso per altri luoghi, solamente perche seguiua alcuna festa, onde si sarebbe potuta vdire, e più volte se ne sono anzi veduti molti venirui perciò fino da paesi lontani. Era poi appresso ingegnosa, e graue nello scriuer rispondendo alle lettere di chi la fauoriua con gratia, e con sodezza anzi virile. Amaua sommemente la modestia anco in altrui, e passaua ciascun'vfficio di charità, che passi l'vna con l'altra monaca, nel Monastero con quella prontezza, che può mostrar chi non hà contrario impedimento. Si scopriua candida di costumi, e tanto, che alcuni Principi doppo, che con essa hebbero fauellato, dissero, che quando non l'hauessero conosciuta per angiolo nella voce, hauerebbero confessata creatura angelica nel procedere. Non nutriua superbia, che la rendesse impratticabile con suora alcuna del Monastero, nè doppiezza, per cui paresse sospettosa à cui si fosse, che n'hauesse prattica. Mangiaua, e beuea modestemente, e faceua copia al Monastero tutto de' doni, che le veniuano spesso recati. È morta giouana, e nel tempo, ch'ella cominciaua comporre quelle stesse opere musicali, che poi cantaua nelle feste, ciò che hauerebbe accresciuta in lei la perfettione del cantare, benche già fosse cantatrice singolarissima.

30. ASDM XII, vol. 100, fasc. 3 [S. Marta]

Molto Reve*ren*da Madre: Acciò all'auenire l'Inimico Infernale non habbi occasione di perturbare la pace in cotesto Conuento per cause *d*ella musica, mà si lodi il Sig*n*ore in questa parte con q*u*ella mag*gio*re perfettione e carità sia possibile, scriuo all' R.V. l'inf*rascri*tti capi da osservarsi irremissibilm*ente* da tutte q*u*elle sorelle che attendono al cantare, e suonare sotto pena d*el* silentio e privatione di tal'essercitio per anni due, e in caso di transgressione, incarico all*a* R.V. l'essecutione della detta pena.

1°. Che la Monaca Maggiore di professione trà le Organiste, e Cantatrici haverà cura, e sopraintendenza della musica in maniera che, douendosi cantare qualche messa, ò Vespro solenne, ella ordini quello si dourà cantare distribuendo le parti e regolando il concerto; e quelle saranno dimandate a cantare, doueranno punt*ualmente* andarui.

Quando la mag*gio*re sarà infirma in modo che no*n* possa fare l'officio suo sottoentrarà la 2.a à regolare la musica in participatione, quando si possa, della Maestra Maggiore.

Delle misse basse, se ocorrerà, ogni organista ne suoni e canti una per cadauna, et quei canti le parerà mà graui et eccellenti. Auuertendo che douendo cantare due soprani si pighi per 2.a quella [che] segue di professione all'organista, e non quella [che] piacerà all'Organista.

Non potendo per caso una suonare per infirmità ò altro accidente, non douerà ella sostituire altra a suo arbitrio, mà subintrerà quella seguitarà in ordine.

Delli Vesperi festiui le organiste ne suoneranno una per cadauna, proponendo i canti et inuitando quell'aiuto sarà bisogno.

Sarà lecito a tutte le Organiste tenere in Camera un Sordino per studiare, evitandosi omninamente li Clauicimbali ò altri stromenti strepitosi, et caso che alcuna di quelle non hauisse Cella per suo uso potrà tenere il strumento nella Cella di una Monaca Professa sua parente più prossima e congiunta di sangue e non altremente.

Non admetterà la R.V. alcun Organista, ò Musico a trattare con le sue Monache per causa di ammaestrare, ò comporre canti. E se alcuna Monaca per tal occasione anderà à Parlatorio, Porta ferradina, ò Torno senza licenza *in scriptu* scritta dell' Illustrissimo e Cardinale Arcivescovo resti subito priua di Parlatorio et altre sudette commodità di uisite per un'anno intero. Tanto m'è parso scriuere alla R.V. in questo particolare e Nostro Signore ha [illegibile]. Di Casa à 22. Novembre 1620. VVR

Come fratello nel Signor

A. Mazenta Vicario Generale delle Monache

31. Unsigned orders, 1621, ASDM XII, vol. 103, fasc. 1

Per levare il numeroso concorso de frati a questa chiesa e Convento in occasione della festa titolare di S. Orsola, ordiniamo che nella detta festa non si celebri più di otto messe basse, et la Cantata, per il Monastero delle quali, observando le Monache secondo lo stile comune cantar e rispondere quello spetta al Choro . . . Il Vespero si cantarà solo dalle Monache senza alcun Sacerdote apportato nella Chiesa esteriore per le Orationi.

32. Unsigned orders, 10 July 1624, ASDM XII, vol. 46, fos. 288 ff.

Niuna [monaca] canti sola. E quando si deue fare la communica frà la messa non si deue cantare motetto ò suonare doppo l'Agnus Dei, acciò più prontamente le monache si possano preparare alla Santa Communione, et euincer maggior diuozione et attentione in riceuirla . . . Non permetta ancora, come altre volte è stato ordinato, che alcuna Monaca canti sola, et la musica instituta per gloria di Dio, e sollenamente di quale de' fideli, si faccia con gravità e divotione, lasciando alcuni canti di musica profana accomodati sotto parole sacre.

33. E. Lodi, *Breve istoria di Meda e traslazione de' santi Aimo e Vermondo* (Milan, 1741; first published 1629), 16–21

[On the feast of the translation of the saints' relics on 13 June 1626:] Alle hore 20 [Federigo Borromeo] entrò nel Monastero con la Stolla, ed essendo esso Illustrissimo accolto sotto il Baldachino dalle Monache, fu accompagnato alla Chiesa interiore a suono di campane, cantandosi da esse Monache, che andavano a due a due in canto figurato il Salmo *Benedictus Dominus Deus Israel* . . . [after Federigo took the relics] cantandosi dalle Monache alcuni motetti col Regale, mentre fra tanto dette Reliquie si collocavano nella Cassa.

Spedita questa fonzione . . . s'inviò la processione verso la porta grande . . . cantandosi dalle Monache in canto figurato il Salmo *Laudate Dominum de Coelis* . . . la processione entrò nella Chiesa . . . sonandosi le campane, gli organi, le trombe, tamburi . . . Gionti all'Altare maggiore, fu depositata la barra cantandosi dalle Monache con l'Organo le Letanie . . .

[The next day] Dopo pranso si sonò il Vespro alle 18 . . . [Federigo] vestito in Pontificale, dopo cantato dalle Monache un motetto con l'Organo . . . l'Illustrissimo Signor Cardinale intonò l'Inno *Te Deum* . . . Le Monache seguirono a cantarlo in canto figurato . . . [the procession went] verso la Chiesa interiore, seguendo le Monache a cantare in canto figurato l'Inno *Te Deum laudamus* . . . mentre i Maestri attendevano ad accomodare la mensa sopra dell'Altare (cantando frattanto le Monache alcuni motetti nell'Organo).

34. From Federigo Borromeo's sermon, 'Dell'Assuntione della B.V.' (*c*.1625), BA, F. 4 *inf*. fos. 357 ff.

Salendo la B.V. al Cielo non per uirtù propria come *Christo* ma partita da gl'Angeli non è da credere che quelli celesti spiriti stessero in silentio ne che le loro lingue fossero tardi a cantar' le lodi di tanto triunfo anco canta la Santa Chiesa: Assumpta est Maria in Celum gaudent Angeli; adunque per accompagnar'il canto dell'Angeli diremo qualche cosa circa la musica spirituale, cioè circa di quella musica e canto che si ordina a gloria di Dio, et diremo di quelle cose che si ricercano per far buona una musica ouero per cantar bene et con piacer de chi ode; dico adunque che la prima cosa che si ricerca per cantar bene è la buona uoce; la 2.a e la compositione che sia giuditiosa et bene compartita, ma la 3.a et quella che più importa è l'affetto il qual'anco si può intender in due modi et è che la compositione del canto sia conforme all'affetto delle parole[:] uoglio dire che se le parole sono malanconi che anco la compositione sia graue, et se le parole sono allegre, anco il concerto sia tale, ma questo affetto sia misterioso et non quello di che io intendo trattare et nel quale consista la perfettione della musica la qual non nasce dalla compositione del canto ne da alcun'arteficio, ma dal modo del cantare e dal affetto de colui che canta et di questo gl'Antichi hanno fatto tanta stima che ne dicono cose grandissime . . . Io uoglio raccontare alcuni essempij ch'io proprio ho udito in materia di Musica et *primo* sappiate che ui fù in Ferrara un Musico eccelente, il quale faceua [illegible] come attenti et fuori di se quelli che l'udiuano, et questo non era *per* la buontà della uoce, ma *per* il modo del cantare *per*che una uolta essendo alla presenza del Papa et cantando un sol uerso che dice: Hor che il Cielo, et la terra el uento tace, queste poche parole cantate da costui con quel suo *mo* tanto raro fece star sospesa l'aria del sommo Pontifice, et ancora di tutti questi che l'udeuano, et erano *presenti* come cosa dilleteuole et grata oltra modo costui non faceua passaggi, ne altro artificio di uoce, ma con un semplice *mo* ma graue, et pronuntiato con affetto faceua quella grata armonia nel orrechie delli audienti; l'istesso faceua un altro Musico eccelente nominato il Cauagliere del Liuto perche sonaua eccelenti*ssime* questo Istrom*ento*[:] egli anco cantaua di *mo* marauigliosa se ben la uoce no*n* era buona ma più tosto aliqu*anto* rauca, nondimeno egli cantaua alcuni salmi con tanto bella maniera che attraheua a se gl'animi delle *per*sone si che ueniuano anco da lontano *per* ascoltarlo, tal è qu*esto mo* di cantare che nasce dall'affetto, et no*n* dall'Arte . . . Io non nego che qualche passaggio non si habbi à fare nel canto, ma dico deue esser fatto a tempo, a misura et con gratia, et non con mo' tale che si leua la diuotione et il senso alle parole *sante* talm*ente* che paiono più tosto uanità che cose indutiue d*e*lla diuotione, et piu presto si perde il *sen*so di chi canta, et di chi ode che se ne faceua acquisto, ma non si ferma qui il diffetto che segue in questo modo di cantare *per*che ne sono accompagnati molti altri come l'affettatione del dire in modo che pare la persona ascolti se stessa . . . Questo e il mo' di ca*n*tar di qu*e*lli che cantano senza spirito di deuotione et non cercano imitar gl'Angeli, li quali in questa festa accompagnauano cantando la Regina del Cielo, [illegible] portata alla gloria celeste, il qual costume et modo di cantar desidero non sia da uoi imitati, anzi accio sia in uoi accessa il desiderio di far a Dio una uera Musica sp*irit*uale, con l'acquisto delle *sante* uirtù et anco che nella Musica [illegible] si cerchi non la uanità et gloria del mondo, ma l'acquisto del sp*irit*o di Dio, et la uera diuotione interiore . . . Io ui dirò altri due essempij di anime *sante* che con il canto si dilettauano di lodar Dio; Vna ui fù che sonando et cantando era eleuata in sp*irit*o et l'istrom*ento* seguitaua à sonare da se stesso forse *per* mano delli Angeli, et l'altra era S*ant*a Caterina Senese, la qual sonaua et cantaua beni*ssim*o, et alle uolte pigliaua l'istrom*ento per* sonare, qu*al* era un liuto, et per se poseua una coprilina di *p*aglia in capo che gli copriua gli occhi, et qu*esto* faceua *per* non esser ueduta *per*che hauendo cantato, et sonato un puco si eleuaua in sp*irit*o et nondimeno perseueraua à sonare, onde poi ne restaua molto adolerata *per* la fatica che duraua à mouer le mani mentre il corpo era abbandonato da sensi, tornata in se alle uolte cantaua tanto bene pero anco dell'ordinario et chi l'udiua si marauigliaua come di cosa non più udita, et ella diceua[:] non ui marauigliate perche questo modo di cantare l'hò imparato in Cielo, et iui li Santi cantano a tal maniera et di continuo lodano Dio à imitatione di quali diui si ordinare il nostro canto, et non per alcuna uanità, della quale Dio ui guardi.

35. Angela Confaloniera to Federigo Borromeo (*c.*1630), BA, G. 8 *inf.*, fo. 42^r

*P*adre car*issi*mo, non posso finir di ringraziar V.S. Ill.ma del dono che mi à fatto e molto più per eser stato a tempo di poterlo adoperar la prima uolta a si bel misterio poi che per l'alegrezza che io vidi che ebero tutte le monache mi risolsi di uoler far sentir à tutte il suo sono. E cosi secretamente feci inuito a una che sona il uilone e un altra il uiolino e cosi la notte del *S*anto Natale andavimo a far li matinati a tutte le moniche cantando[:] Gloria in eccelsis et altri uerseti simili a questi che io dirò cioe[:] Il dolce sposo uostro sorelle mie Hoggi è nato dall*a V*ergine *Maria*. E nato il Bon Giesu per nostro Saluatore. Venite sorelle a donargli il core . . . il dono che ha fato a la pouera genocha ha tirato li lacrimi de gli ochi *p*er diuotione a molte persone *p*er sentir a sonar a si bel misterio: poi si ricordauano *poi* [underlining in original] della melodia deli Angeli.

36. Undated letter from Federigo to Confaloniera, BA, G. 26 *inf.*, insert 3, n. 21

Però mi è piaciuto estre*mame*nte, che uedo in una uostra [letter], che il giorno della Pentecoste doppo cena andaste a cantare, et a sonare. Quanto faceste bene, et quanto è stato grato a Dio quella discreta, et santa ricreatione. Però fate che io senta che voi lo facciate spesse uolte, massime quando vi trouate haver afaticato. Questa occupatione è megliore che il conuersare taluolta; et è lauda divina cantando voi come sempre fate, cose sacre e tutte spirituali. Quando poi è passata quella poca santa distrattione del doppo disnare, e del doppo cena immediatamente all'hora potete tornare alle uostre contemplationi, e non perdonare a fatica ne a diligenza.

37. Federigo to Confaloniera, G. 26 *inf.*, letter no. 93

Come a discepola mando della carta, acciochè scriuendo facciate quello, che conuiene, e corrisponde al vero nome, cioè di Discepola. Io mando questa carta perche le monache non possano presumere che uoi scriuiate procurando voi stessa d'hauerne. E perchè questa mia lettera è la lettera dei presenti, io ui mando, ancora un canto sopra il salmo: Super flumina Babilonis, il quale è belissimo. Voi se saprete sonarlo, e cantarlo, trouerete che è bello; et le parole sono proprie di chi uorrebbe uolare in alto, come credo, che desiderareste uoi di fare, e quanto prima.

38. Confaloniera to Federigo (*c*.1630)

a. BA, G. 7 *inf.*, fo. 334^r

Poi mi meto a far il liuto cosi con la voce, hora una cosa e hor un altra. E poi cosi cantando e sonando alla mia fogia mi escono a tratto per tratto sospiri grandissimi. O che mi piace tanto questo sentimento di Amore, il qual fa veder che ha bisogno del tutto, insino di doi signi per sfogare. E pensò VS. Ill.ma che non impararei a sonar il uiolino; si per certo che impararei a sonar ancor a gusto. Perche so tutte le cose di simili istrumenti. O giubilo del Amore, che cosa non fa far?! Mi fa sonar di organo sopra un assa, ma [a] tutte queste pare che io sia in sogno. E una di queste domeniche dopo cena, molte di compagnia cosi per ricreatione andauano in camina per dir alla mia fogia, e per la strada incontrando in me, mi pregavano andar con esse loro. E cosi per compiacerle andai ancor io, e come fui la, cominciai a cantare, e cantai un motetto cosi a mente, mentre che loro dauano un pocco di sufragio alla loro fatica, e mentre io cantaua, mi sentiuo ad accender il mio Core, tanto che pareua all'esteriore che fosse una pazarella. E diceuano, [']Si voi aueste beuuto del uino con noi, si potrebe dir che ui auresti ofesa la testa, e che fosse il uino che ui facesse far gusto[']. E io dissi[: 'Voi aueste giusto: e io son restato inubriacha['], e perch'io sfogaua cosi cantando, et erano molte monache.

b. fo. 345^{r-v}

Tornando in proposito del giorno di San Benedetto alle 21 ore si cantaua il uespro in musica, e al secondo salmo mi uenne un sentimento della solenità della Beata Virgine Maria e talmente mi stupe la mente, che pariua nel esteriore che auessi un grandissimo sonno, e quasi non poteuo proferir parola. Pareua che il mio core fosse stato portato al Commando dolcissimo della dolcissima Virgine Maria, e pariua che io uolsi intendere e sapere, come si ne staua quelli giorni auante che il Signore piglia carne umana.

c. fo. 498^{r-v}

O Padre mio Carissimo, quando sarà ch'io vadi a veder quello che alle uolte mi par di udir in spirito quella bella compagnia di Angeli, tanto belli, tanto dolci, o che gioia sarà la mia; si tanto ne sento ora senza saper la uerità questa festa della Beatissima Virgine Maria sentiuo una gioia, una mellodia suauissima, senza ch'io possa acompagnarmi con essi loro. O Dio, o Dio, ancor ch'io, o Padre mio Carissimo, sapessi far quello che fanno loro, io non lo potrei fare. Poi che in quest'istante mi sento priua di forze. Solo questo mi occore fare solo per la suauità di qualche instromento, o uer liuto, che come gli dissi, ch'in tocar li cordi, e sonando questa parola Giesù, mi sentiuo a torrci sentimenti, e cosi restauo senza posser andar inanzi, perche la mente se ne uolaua a Dio, portata da queste parole.

39. Confaloniera to Federigo, (*c.*1630), BA, G. 8 *inf.*, fo. 469^{r-v}

*Pa*d*re* mio Ca*rissi*mo vengo a farli umil*mente Reveren*za et insieme a farli
sapere una Cosa la quale se a Lei non piace è caso saperla *per*che faria in
modo che non si farebe. La cosa è questa; che ui è una Monicha, et è quella
che à insegnato à mi a cantare e sonare, et è sorella del Sig*nor* Antonio
Rusca. Questa monicha sa comporre, e cosi à composto asai motetti, e gli
suoi fratelli gli fano meter in stampa, e gli uogliono dedicar à V.S. Ill.ma per
signo della gratitudine, che a Lei conuiene auere, per la beniuolenza che
mostra al nostro monasterio. Questa compositione è stata molto laudata, e
credo che sara di gusto alli monasterij e cosi questa Giouana è molto spirituale, credo che siano composti con molto spirito; e cosi uorebe dedicarli
a Lei *per*che il nostro Monasterio non à persona che piu ama di Lei, Pero
mi fara Gratia di farmi saper la sua uolunta.

40. 'Coppia della dichiara*tio*ne di Monsig^{r} Fedeli', ASDM XII, vol. 100,
fasc. 3

A di ii xbr. 1631. Per leuar ogni difficoltà intorno al mio decreto già pub-
licato circa la Musica. Mi dichiaro la mia intentione esser stata, ch*e* quando
si tratta de' concerti, alle Messe dei Prelati, et altre solennità a più d'un
Choro, sopraintendano assolutam*ente* le Musiche Anciane di mano in
mano, incominciando dalle Maggiori. Nel resto di Messe, ò siano grando,
ò basse, ouer priuate, et Vespri, quando si canta solo ad un Choro, si faccia
à settimana, et quella à chi tocca la settimana sia quella, chi disponga, et
regga il detto choro, benche n'entrassero in quello più Instrumenti, et si
faccia à Quota, et uoglio che n'entrino tutte due le Sorelle Fissiraghi ciascuna di loro per la sua settimana.

41. S. Marta's nuns to the SCVR, 20 July 1632, ASV, VR, sez. monache,
1632 (set–dic)

Deve p*er* tanto V. Emin*en*za sapere, come già alcuni anni sono naque nel
n*os*tr*o* Monast*er*o un puoco di disturbo nella Musica p*er* causa ch*e* le
Maggiori d'età volevano soprastar' alle minori, con tanto mal termine, ch*e*
la Religione ne restava mal sodisfatta et . . . si rissolve ricorrere
dall'Eminentissimo Sig*nor* Card*in*ale Borromeo n*os*tr*o* Arcivesc*ov*o acciò,
come qu*e*llo, ch'amava teneriss*am*ente questa Religione lui porgesse il rimedio . . . ma p*er* la morte della *felice* me*mor*ia di questo S*an*to Arcivescovo le
maggiori quasi subito hanno procurato di far anular gl'Ordini già detti, con
derisione delle Minori . . . Li superiori esterni qui di Milano, hanno ten-
tato varie strade p*er* accomodar questo negotio . . . ma, una delle Maggiori,
qual'è la Taverna non s'è mai voluto acontentar del ragionnevole, dicendo,
che pretendeva poter haver favor tale in Roma, c'havria conseguito p*er*
favore . . . le minori, quale sono, le Fissiraghe, ch*e* sono di buoniss*i*mi costumi, et M*ol*to virtuose, et si diportanto bene à parer di tutte le Monache,

à finch*e* di nuovo si compiaciano, di ritornar à confirmar gl'Ordini buonissi*mi* del n*ostro* S*an*to Arciv*escov*o.

42. Ginetti's orders to Milan, ASDM XII, vol. 100, fasc. 3

Mo*l*to R*everen*do Sig.re: La S*acra* Congr*egatio*ne uenendo ragguagliata che in coteste mon*aster*io di S*an*ta Marta siano nati alcune differenze tra le monache p*er* causa della musica, m'ha ordinato di scriuere a V.S. che prohibisca che nel med*esi*mo mon*aster*io non si faccia nell'auuenire musica di sorte alcuna, ne circa essa si faccia altra nouità fin ad altro ordine della med*esi*ma S*acra* Congr*egatio*ne la cui mente dunq*ue* saranno le Sue parti di procurare che in ciò uenga puntualm*ente* esseguita. E stia sana. Di Roma à 17. di febr*aio* 1634. Al piacer di V.S. M. Card. Ginetti.

43. Monti's orders, ASDM XII, vol. 100, fasc. 3

R*everen*da come Sorella. Auenga che mo*l*ti giorni sono cotesto Mona*ster*o con supplica di tutte le sorelle sottoscritte, ci habbi fatto instanza, acciò terminassimo alcune differenze nate p*er* causa della Musica con l'autorità n*os*tra, ordinando intorno ad esse quanto hauessimo stimato espedienti p*er* la pace commune, non effettuassimo però all'hora il n*ostro* desidero, ciò faccendo poiche essendo informati che la S*acra* Congr*egatio*ne sopra Vescovi con una lettera del 17 Febr*ar*o 1634 haueua ordinato p*er* causa delle sodette differenze, che p*er* l'auenire, non si faccesse Musica di sorte alcuna, ne circa essa si facesse altra nouità, fin ad'altro ordine della medesima S*an*ta Congr*egatio*ne, stimassimo n*ostro* debbito, dargli parte dell'instanza fatta, et aspettando il n*ostro* sentim*ento*. Hauendo dunque noi rappresentato alla detta S. Congr*egatio*ne non solo il desiderio di coteste sorelle, ma ancora la forma che inteneua [torn] il gouerno, et la sopraintendenza della Musica auanti gli Ordini del Emi*nentissi*mo Sig*no*r Cardinale Borromeo di fel*ice* memoria pubblicati il 24 Agosto 162[0] et insieme significarli il contenuto delli stessi ordini, è piacciuto a*ll*a S*acra* Congr*egatio*ne, che vi ripigle la Musica, ordinando però con la sua lettera de 20 stanti; come siegue[:]

Che la cura, et direttione della Musica sij ripartita in quattro Monache due maggiori, et due minori, cominciando il turno dalle maggiore, et sopraintendo ciascuna quattro Mesi; e con questo, che oltre la parte, che tocca alle maggiori in turno come sopra, esse maggiore habbino di piu la sopraintend*enz*a di essa Musica, nelle solennità del S*antissi*mo Natale, Epifania, Pasque, et Pentecoste, nel giorno della festa di S*an*ta Marta, et in tutte gli altri giorni, ne qual*i* l'Arciuescouo pro tempore, o alcun Cardinale uada a celebrare nella Chiesa del lor Mona*ster*o, ancora che li detti giorni cadano in tutto, o in parte nel turno delle minori. Essendo perciò tale la mente della S. Congr*egatio*ne quale habbiamo significato, con le parole precise della sua lettera, V*ostra* R*everenz*a farà che prontam*ente* si essequisca.

In oltre desiderando noi, che la Santa pace fra cuori religiosi si conserui, essortiamo nelle uiscere di Nostro Signore Gesu Christo tutte le sorelle perite nel Canto, e suono, procurare, che da tale essercitio non sieguano fra loro dissensioni, delle quali tanto gode l'inimico infernale, ma constante pace, et concorde carita, a sembianza de Chori Angelici, indrizzano il talento datoli da Dio benedetto a maggiormente lodarlo, et glorificarlo, et percio

Commandiam che quella Monaca la quale hauerà nel medesimo tempo la cura di gouernare la Musica, indifferentemente si uaglia de sogetti idonei, in modo che ciascuna habbi la sua parte conforme alla sofficienza.

Dall'altra parte qual si voglia perita nella Musica non mancarà d'esseguire prontamente tutto ciò, che gli sarà imposto dalla sopraintendente.

Et perche tal'hora auerra, che per infirmita, ò per altro accidente la Monaca destinata al gouerno della Musica, non possi in tutto il suo tempo attender al carico, ordiniamo, che in tal caso, ella non possi sustituire alcun altra per suplire al mancamento; ma che quella sottentri al gouerno, la quale seguirerà in ordine all' essa impedita, quale doppo che hauerà compito al mancamento della sorella, gouernerà ancora li suoi quatro Mesi, se però il supplimento non fosse stato de tutti li quatro Mesi intieri.

Quando alcuna delle quatro sopraintendenti passasse all'altra uita, ouero per la uecchia indispositione, o altra causa, non potesse, ò non uolesse piu attendere al gouerno, ordiniamo, che dalla Madre Priora, Vicharia, et Diserette si proponghino nel Capitolo delle Monache due, ò tre delle piu idonee all'essercitio, et quella la quale hauerà maggior numero de uoti, quali si daranno con palle secrette s'intenda canonicamente elletta nel luogo della Defonta ouero, di quella, la quale non potrà piu gouernare.

Resta che Vostra Reverenda con ogni uigilanza possibile procuri la pontuale essecutione de soprascritti Ordini, acciò per l'auenire non si suscitano emulationi, et discordie; ma si uiua in perfetta unione, et religiosa Carità, si come speriamo; et fra tanto gli diamo la nostra beneditione. Dal Palazzo Archivescovile il 9 lulio 1635

Cesar Cardinalis Montius Archiepiscopus

44. G. B. Mongilardi, 'Vita Cardinalis Federici Borromaei' (c.1635), BA, Y. 114 *sup*.

Caeterum quae claustralia ferre possent, laeto animo peragerent, patiebanturque, ut psalmodiam facerent musicali concentu, adhibitis etiam organis, seu etiam aliis instrumentis, quae modestiae fines non transcenderent, dicebatque his sacris artibus Sanctimoniales a porta longius arceri, et a saecularibus colloquiis separari, aegreque tulit, cum quis persuadere vellet, ut a musicali cantu Moniales omnes separarentur.

45. Cozzolani, letter to an unnamed Roman protector, ASV, VR, sez. monache, 1659, lug–set

*Reverendissi*mo P*ad*re mio Cole*ndissimo.* Con tutta pontualità e generosità d'animo q*ue*ste Mie Monache hanno obedito alla Sac*ra* Cong*rega*ti*one,* alla Religi*one,* et datto gusto a q*ue*sto Mons*ign*or Arc*ivesc*ovo assicurare nella pre*dilezi*one e prote*zi*one di VS. *Reverendiss*ima alla quale tutte rendiamo molte gr*a*tie confesandoci obblig*atissi*me a tante fatiche sostenute, et a tante diligenze usate in negotio si scabroso. La prego della continua*zi*one dell'istessa prote*zi*one sino alla terminati*one* della causa, acciò resti difesa l'innocenza di tante. E ver*a*m*ente* è caso molto lagrimevole, che quatro ò cinque habbino a mantener in tanta inquietude tutta la Casa. P*er* il presente però s'accerti VS. *Reverendiss*ima che non v'è causa di dolersi mà mi bisogna aggiunto p*er* mantenermi. Mi rimetto a quanto hò scritto al *Reverendissi*mo di costi come già pratico di q*ue*sto governo. Et qui finisco con rivenire VS. *Reverendiss*ima pregandole da n*os*tro Sig*nore* ogni vero bene. Di VS. *Reverendiss*ima Milano li 30 lug*li*o 1659 Divotissma serva nel Sig*nore* D. Chiara Marg*ari*ta Cozzolani Abba*dessa*

46. 'Relatione di quello è successo sin hora in ordine all'imputatione della Monaca Palomera di S.ta Redegonda in Milano', in packet of 5 March 1660, ASV, VR, sez. monache, 1660, feb–mar

[Palomera] fù incolpata di haver violata la clausura, La Madre Badessa [Cozzolani] ne diede parte al suo superiore il P. Abate Melzi Cassinese, questo deliberò che simil delitto non rimanesse impunito quando fosse vero, pensò di participar quello succedeva a Monsig. Arcivescovo, ma riflettando la sua natura, e l'odio irreconcilibile che in tutte le occasioni haveria dimostrato contro la religione Cassinense, e la persona del mede*s*imo Abate in particolare, agitato di molti pensieri rivolse di consultarsi con il Pres*id*ente del Senato suo parente, il quale . . . consigliò che si esami-nassero le Monache . . . il che si fece ne si puose ritrovare maggiore lume che il detto delle due sorelle Vimercati poco amorevoli della incolpata.

47. Unsigned note (*c.*1660), ASDM XII, (S. Margarita), vol. 83, fasc. 2

Maria Calegara Bergamasca virtuosa di sonare è stata acettata in Monasterio con la solita Dote di L. 4000. E pure alle Mani della Collezaria non sono p*er*venuti che L. 1500–, ne si sà se il rimanente gli sia stato condonato *motu proprio* dell'Abbadessa, o pure ella me*des*ima le habbi presse p*er* se, ò consu-mate à suo arbitrio.

48. 'Abusi intorno al Governo spirituale delle Monache di S. Margarita di Milano, e Moderationi da pratticare', ASDM XII, vol. 83, fasc. 1. (*c.*1660)

La musica, e sinfonia instituite p*er* maggior gloria di Dio, et della sua Chiesa, abusandosi dalle Monache di S. Margarita serua di fomento à vizij, di corrutela alle uirtù, e di rovina irreparibile alla buona disciplina. Non capita à questa Città Prelato, Prencipe, Personaggio, o altre persone qualificate, che, subito non si mandino à regolare all'ingressa, e per mezzo de Caualieri, ò altre persone di qualità, prouano in ogni modo di chiamarsi al Monastero, doue in Chiesa, ò Parlatorij si tratengano con canzonette [added: 'amorosi'] profane, sonetti, e madrigali lasciui, discorsi [illegible], atti indecenti, e poi lamenti lontani dalla modestia religiosa.

49. Undated report, (*c.*1660), ASDM XII, vol. 129, fasc. 4

Gli stessi [as in S. Margarita] inconvenienti per questa spetta alla Musica sono in S. Radegonda, Monastero sogetto all'Abbate de Cassinensi di S. Simpliciano, e benchè le musiche & le monache non siano scandalose, sono però causa della rovina spirituale di quel monastero, poiche quanti Prelati, Principi o persone di qualità capitano a Milano, o da se s'incubano per sentire la esquissitezza delle Cantatrici, ò dalle medesme monache per mezzo di Cavallieri sono [added above: si fanno] invitati [e si trattengano in Chiesa] e trattenuti in Chiesa e nelle foristieri [i.e. the external parlours] (trattenimenti di Musica, anche con canzonette amorose, e Madrigali amorosi) con musiche eseguite spirituali et amorose. Quindi nascono poi le amicitie, le carissimanze, et ogni altro disturbo del Monastero, poiche con quest'occasione li carissimi (s'introduscano nell'amicizia) si trattengano sino alle due e tre hore di notte nelle forestieri et alle crati, non possono sicurasi à tempo debito le porte, nella Chiesa i Vesperi si prolongano sino ad una & più hore di notte, et il Concorso di Dame, e Cavallieri è tanto e sale che quella Chiesa sembra più tosto Theatro profano, che luogo consacrato à Dio.

50. ASV, VR, sez. monache, 1661, gen, with 2 copies marked 'lectum'

Eminentissimi e Reverendissimi Signori[:] Carlo francesco Ceva di Milano humilissimo Oratore dell'E.E.V.V. riverentemente l'espone, come desidera far'andare ad imparare meglio di cantare una sua figliola Monaca in S. Radegonda il P. Antonio Cossandi Mastro di Cappella in quella Chiesa di S. francesco virtuosissimo, e di buoni costumi, e sessagenario per maggior'honorevelezza di quel Choro. Ricorre per tanto all'immensa benignità dell'E.E.V.V. humilmente supplicando di degnarsi d'ordinare à quell'Arcivescovo, che conceda licenza al detto P. Antonio Cossandi dell'ordine di Minori Conventuali di S. francesco possa andare ad ammaestrare la detta Monaca in Chiesa dal piccio foro del Torno, che v'è, ò in'altro modo, che giudicherà meglio il detto Monsignore Arcivescovo. Ch'il Tutto, &c.

51. Litta to the SCVR, 9 February 1661, ASV, VR, sez. monache, 1661, feb–apr

Intesasi da me la novità [of the celebration at S. Paolo], quà stava, mandai il mio Vicario Generale al Convento de Theatini acciò pregasse il Padre Silo

Confessore del Sr. Duca, di rapresentarle la proibitione di S. Carlo nelle Concilij Provinciali, di far musiche nelle Chiese esteriori delle Monache . . . Il giorno antecedente alla festa, il Vicario delle Monache, di mia comissione notificò loro [the nuns] la medesima proibitione, spiegandole la Confermatione Apostolica con avvertirle à non contravenirsi; Esse, baldanzose, e ridendo risposero che havevano la licenza, quasi burlandosi di lui, e della proibitione; replicandosi più volte le amonitioni, esse replicarono, che havevano licenza bastante. Io non hò fatta minima dimostratione, ancorche à tutta la Città sia noto d'essersi operato in sprezzo mio.

52. Occasions for music in the *chiese esteriori*, ASV, VR, sez. monache, 1661, feb–apr

Nel Monastero di San Paolo.

1607 Sotto al Governo Ecclesiastico del S.r Cardinal federico Borromeo e nel Temporale Governatore l'Eccellentissimo Sig.r Conte de ficentes Si fecero tre giorni d'Officij funerali con la Musica secolare per la S.ra D.a Anna Visconti Sfondrata.

1620 Tre altri giorni l'Officij funerali per la Sig.ra D.a Sigismonda Sfondrata d'Este con la Musica secolare. Altri tre officij, per la Sig.ra Marchesa Visconti Sfondrata con detta Musica [in margin: D. Pietro de Toledo]

Novembre 1617 Si fecero gli Officij funerali della S.ra Anna Visconte Arconata trè con detta Musica

1620 Si fecero li tre Officij per il S.r Conte Maria Arconati con la Musica come sopra

Nel sudetto anno cantò la sua prima Messa il Reverendo Don Gio: Battista Corradino Musico del Duomo e fu servito di Musica solennissima dalli Musici della medesima Metropolitana

Come similmente L'Officio funerale del Sig. Lodovico Magenta

Sotto al Governo del Sig.r Cardinale Monti

1645 Si cantò l'Officio funerale per la Sig.ra Caterina Coria. Un altro al Cavalier Magenta

Tutti li sudetti Officij si sono cantati nella Chiesa esteriore delle Monache Angeliche di S. Paolo di Milano.

Nota dove gli Eccellentissimi Sig.ri Governatori sono andati con la sua Musica di Palazzo cavata dai libri del Maestro di Cerimonie, e del Maestro di Cappella

Sotto L'Eccellentissimo Sig.r Duca di Feria [in office 1618–25] spesse volte si andava alle Cappucine in Porta Tosa

Sotto L'Eminentissimo S.r Cardinale Albornozzo [1634–5] si andò al Monastero Maggiore.

Sotto *Eccellentissi*mo S.r Marchese di Leganes [1635–6] si andò a *Santa*
Margherita mentre si vestì una Monaca; et al Monastero Maggiore

Sotto L'*Eccellentissi*mo Sig.r Conte di Sirvela [1641–3] si andò al Monastero
della Madalena al Cerchio, et al Monastero Maggiore

Sotto L'*Eccellentissi*mo S.r Marchese di Velada [1643–6] si andò alla
Vittoria, et al Monastero Maggio*re*.

Sotto L'*Eccellentissi*mo S.r Marchese di Carazena [1648–56] si andò al
Monastero Maggiore et alle Capuccine di *San*ta Barbara, et a *San*ta Barbara
[*sic*]

Sotto L'*Emin*entissi*mo S.r Card*inale Trivulzio [1656] alle Capuccine di
Porta Tosa, et al Monastero Maggiore.

Sotto L'*Eccellentissi*mo Sig.r Conte di Fucensaldagna [1656–60] a *San*ta
Marta et al Monastero Maggio*re*

53. Petition addressed 'Alla Santità di Nostro Sig.r Alla cong:ne de
Vescovi, e Reg:ri x Novris 1662 Advocet Agens [illegible]', marked 'lectum', ASV, VR, monache, 1662 (nov–dic)
Beat*issi*mo Padre. Il Capitanno di Giustitia di Milano Dottor Carlo Clerici
Devot*issi*mo Orato*re* di V.S. hà una figlia Monaca professa in Santa
Radegonda di detta Città, quale vorrebbe perfecionarsi nella Musica, e però
il Padre Oratore hà fatto schielta di domenico broglio stimato à proposito
per tutte le parti che si ricercano. Supplica l'Orato*re* V.S. voler concedere
tale licenza al su*detto* Broglio di insegnare nella Chiesa, overo nel Parlatorio
con l'assistenza delle Monache deputate dalla Madre Abbadessa, ordinando
ciò per via di Breve, overo con rimetter il memoriale alla Sacra
Congregat*tione* Di Vescovi, et Regolari, come spera.

54. Petition of 12 January 1663, ASV, VR, monache, 1663, gen–apr
Donna Margherita Zapatta fig*lia* del Gran Cancelliera di Milano d'eta di
anni undeci in dodeci, che si ritrova in educa*tione* nel monasterio di *San*ta
Marta di d*etta* Città presso suor Maria Luisa Gonzaga nipote del d*etto* Aluigi
desiderosa d*etta* fig*liola* d'aprendere la virtù del canto a quale inchina sup-
p*lica* humilm*ente* l'eminenze V*ost*re concederli licenza che possa farsi insegnare da un mastro di consento e sodisfat*tione* di Monsr. Arcivescovo Che il
tutto &c.

55. Litta to the SCVR, 14 February 1663, ASV, VR, monache, 1663,
gen–apr
Al memoriale transmessomi con lettere delli 12 Genaro 1663, dato già da
D. Margarita Zapatta all'EE.V.V. resiste principalmente il Concilio Primo
Provinciale in Quest*a* Chiesa . . . che *Nemini omnino, neque Mari, neque*

Foeminae liceat adire monasterio Monialium docendi causa cantum, quam figuratum vocant . . . Osta in oltre, che il Monastero di S. Martha di questa Città, nel quale dimora la supplicante, hà per particolare Instituo la ritiratezza dalle Grate, e Porta, da quelle monache sin qui con singolare osservanza mantenuto. Onde, quanto è in questo migliore la Disciplina, tanto peggiore ne risultarebbe l'essempio à gl'altri Monasteri, e s'aprierebbe la strada à simili ricorsi, con pregiudicio dell'honore di Dio, mala edificatione de Secolari, e rilassamento delle Regolari Constitutioni.

56. Sebastiano Locatelli, 'Viaggio in Francia . . .' [1664] (Bologna, Biblioteca dell'Archiginnasio, B 1691)

(fo. 41ʳ; 29 April) Per sentire poi cantar diuinamente ci portassimo alle Suore di S. Pietro Martire, le quali conforme l'usanza di questi beati paesi cantano come Angeli.

(fo. 43ᵛ) A di primo Maggio In Milano. Se da tutto l'Vniuerso è riconosciuto per un giorno di giubilo, e d'allegrezza il primo di Maggio, douea anche per noi esser tale, e tanto più che il principio fù di sommo nostra consolatione, per non saper distinguere in S. Radegonda Monastero di Monache, se quelle uoci, che cantauano erano di qua giù, o celesti. Cantarono una Regina Celi, che ben mostrarono hauer imparato da gli Angeli, come si saluta la lor Regina. Quella, che cantò meglio di tutte hauea nome Don'Angiola, che hauendo un petto da Rosignolo, fece trilli, che durarono tanto, che ben parea quell'anima uolesse priuarsi del fiato, per andar à riceuere dalla salutata Madre Maria il premio delle sue fatiche. Tra concorsi à questa melodia u'era il Duca d'Aluita, e molti altri Cauallieri, e con i ringratiamenti, che suseguiro doppo il canto alle madri mostrarono la consolatione prouata in sentire le loro uirtù.

(fo. 46ʳ) Il doppo pranzo tornassimo al Vespro à quelle Monache, ed era cosi piena la Chiesa di Nobiltà, che non ui si potea respirar dal caldo. I forestieri, che discorreuano sopra questa musica, non si uergognauano di dire, che à questa poteua cedere non che quella dell'Imperatore, mà quante se ne fanno in Italia.

(fo. 51 [3 May])
Inuaghito del canto udito alle Suore di s. Pietro Martire il giorno auanti, u'andai à dir messa, e doppo esser stato in Paradiso nel tempo, che cantarono un Motetto concertato con suoni di uiolini, e uiolone, mi donarono una bellissima rama di fiori di seta flossa, che ualeua il suo testone, quale consegnai subito alla mano del Sig. Francesco, che mostro, benche fosse una bagatella un par suo, gradirla assai. Tra quelle cinque suore, che cantarono, ue n'era una, ch'hauea un basso si profondo, che se non l'hauesse veduta con gli occhi miei, haurei dubitato ui fosse un'huomo tra di loro. La gran ferrata, che staua sopra l'Altar maggiore, era aperta fin dal princi-

pio della Messa, ne fanno, come à Bologna, che l'aprono solamente all'eleuatione, e poi subito la chiudono, mà cosi bisogna restasse tutta la matina. Si lamentavano i Compagni perche [io] hauessi tenuto tanto lunga la Messa, ma non so quello hauessero fatto loro, se si fossero uedute inanzi oltre quelle cantauano, tante belle Religiose, e Secolari, che sembrauano un Coro d'Angeli scesi dal Cielo. Le grandi distrattioni, che mi cagionarono l'orecchie, e gli occhi, furono la cagione della mia lunghezza.

(fo. 54) In Milano ci squazza la carne, e i trionfa il lusso, e la uanita. Non cantano inuan le Sirene di quei Monasteri: uogliono si creda esser ueramente Milano sotto il Cielo di Venere. Non per questo dobbiamo credere, non si siano Anima santissime, e de diuotissimi Christiani, Religiosi, e Religiose, perche ogni dritto hà il suo viceoverso; ed in questa Città quelli che sono buoni, sono in uerità molto buoni.

57. C. Pria, 'Relazione del Viaggio fatto dal Ser^mo Sig^re Principe Cosimo Terzo di Toscana L'Anno 1664' (ASF, Mediceo Principato, filza 6383, fo. 50^{r-v})

[Cosimo] Andò a sentire Messa alle Monache Benedettine della Chiesa di Santa Rodegonda Monache Nobili et Ricche virtuose, e particularmente nella Musica, sono di numero circa 140. E regna frà di loro una piccha in questa virtù della Musica, che si sono divise in due parti, non cedendo la prima alla seconda, e daccordo fanno un Mese per ciascuna parte a Cantare e Sonare, à i Riti consueti della Chiesa, e con questa gara virtuosa, hanno fatto progresso tanto grande, che si sono perfezionate nel Suono, che nel Canto come qualsivoglia bravo professore, che è Cosa di Marauiglia. E la picca, e puntualità loro è di tal sorte, che separatamente stanno trà di loro, senza trouarsi mai insieme. E ciascuna parte tiene li suoi strumenti: [long deletion, under which can be read: 'dall'Arcivescovo'] ne mai si fanno servizio in questo interesse; Ma è ben uero che attribuino a fauore e grazia tanto grande, che Sua Altezza fuisse andato alla loro Chiesa per sentire, che uolevano Cantare, hor l'una, e l'altra parte, come se si fussero riunite, che essendone stato auuisato S.A. le volle uisitare, et alla Porta aperta del Monistero, fece lungo discorso con loro, e le ringraziò delle dimostrazioni fatte, in fargli sentire il Canto, dell'una, e l'altra Parte, e con quest'occasione le dette qualche motiuo che migliore sarebbe, l'uniti insieme, à questo dire si mostrono obbediente, e ne feccio la dimostrazione con pregare Sua Altezza che se fuisse con suo gusto, hauerebbe Cantato alla di Lui presenza, per mostrare la stima, et obbedienza che deuono fare de volenta di un tanto Principe. Sua Altezza acconsentando di sentirle volentieri, et alla presenza della Madre Badessa, che se ne compiacque ancora lei, fecero uenire li Strumenti, e cantono Ariette, hor l'una parte hor l'altra, che durono sopra una grossa hora, mostrando il lor ualore, che non si può dire da uantaggio, e particularmente di due una per banda, tanto squisite che non si puol' sentir meglio, con fondame*n*te: à paragone di qualsiuoglia Cantore; S*ua* A*ltezza* ebbe il uanto di hau*e*re riceuto un fauore, non mai più fatto ad alcuno, p*er* la gara che regna tra di loro, E ne dicevo un Contesto Strasordinario, le quali ringrazio con Cortesia e gentilezza p*a*rticolare, e per essere l'ora assai tardi, si licenziò e sene tornò a Casa.

58. 'Relazione del Viaggio fatto dal Ser^{mo} Prn^{pe} Cosimo di Toscana in Lombardia . . .', ASF, MP, filza 6382, fo. 54^{r–v}
Uscito il Sig. Pr*i*ncipe alle 13 . . . fu complementato dal Sig*nore* Co*n*te Fabio Arese Questatore di Milano e cau*aglie*re di S. Iago figlio del Presidente d*e*l Senato . . . seguitandolo nella sua [carozza] fino a S. Rodegonda Monache Benedettine: In questo Monastero, che sono più di 100 Madri si fa professione di Musica, e vi sono 50 Monache fra cantatrici, e Sonatrici di tutta perfezione diuise in due Truppe, con due M*a*dri di Cappella, che non cedendosi fra di loro uanno giornalemente cercando modo di rendersi più abili. Cantò un motetto a coro pieno la Truppa d*e*lla Sig*no*ra Ceua la prima, la 2a quella d*e*lla Sig*no*ra Clariccia, che sono le due Maestre, quali cantono sole tanto bene, che fecero maravuiglia a tutti, et a S*ua* A*ltezza* in particolare, che andò dopo su la porta d*e*l Monastero a ringraziar le Madri, mostrando d'au*e*r auuto sommo diletto, cosa che diede animo loro, e fece che su la porta istessa cantassero ariette mondane à una, à due, e a tre. La Sig*no*ra Ceua in ultimo ne cantò una sul Liuto, che accompagnò diuinamente. Stette S*ua* A*ltezza* quasi due ore a sentirle sempre in piedi, e più u*i* sarebbe stato, se il vespro che si auuicinaua non l'avesse costretto a tornarsene a Palazzo.

59. Nuns at S. Radegonda to the SCVR (*c.*June 1664), ASV, VR, monache, 1664, giu–ago
Ill*ustrissi*mo e Rev*erendissi*mo Sig*nore*. E ridotto ora mai a tal segno la controversia che si trova nel monast*e*ro di S*a*nta Radegona che si puo più tosto stimare un Inferno che luogo dove si stradi il Paradiso; siche D. Bianca Maria Ripa supplicante anco a nome delle sue Compagne che qui vengono sotto scritte ricorono alla protetione di VS. Ill.ma acciò resti servita pigliar quel mezzo che giudicherà più opportuno per la quietudine di tutte, prima che ne partorisca qualche eccesso scandaloso, mentre dalla baldanza di D. Maria faustina Palomera nella quale si ha posto d'oppo d'essergli concesso che canti, che non contenta di questa liberale Carità và seminando col mal parlar hor dell'una hor dell'altra tante Zizanie, che provocano il silentio di tutte. Ill*ustrissi*mo Sig*nore* s'in hora la musica e stato competenza virtuosa delli duoi Partiti di D. Maria Domitilla Ceva e la supplicante, ma di presente muttando faccia dalla persuasiva di d*e*tta Palomera col significare alle Compagne del suo partito Inventioni che non maij sognate dalla supplicante vuole, che fra loro resti un rancore che li porga matteria di mormorare. non

tralasciando di parlar, et opperar indegnamente ne VS. Ill.ma pensi che ciò sij passione perche lei canti nel partito della Ceva, che quando a questa gli mancasserò pari per le sue feste se li somministrarebbe. o come si è fatto in altre occasioni mentre per se stessa merita esser servita, ma ben si mero zelo di vivere in pace; Sapendo la supplicante che non mancherà questa, come non manca di far quanto sà perche arrivi all'orechia di VS. Ill.ma lamente di parlatorio à discredito della supp*licante* che non potendosi di lei far concetto sinistro, nè per sua nascità, ne per l'abito che porta; Protesta a VS. Ill.ma che altro non l'obbliga, che l'esser preciso se vuol continuare nel canto à maggior gloria, et honore di Dio esser li tal volta fortasse valersi di persone virtuose, ma però di boni costumi per haver parole e compositioni nuove, per messe e Vespri, non impiegando il tempo, ne in canzone, ne in altro come sempre che VS. Ill.ma si compiacerà sarà pronta à far constare; siche di nuovo a piedi di VS. Ill.ma ricorre per qualche opportuno rimedio sradicando le malignità di questa Donna che gode di quest'occasione con pessimo fine d'uguagliar l'altre à se stessa, che ancorche sicura, che nol potrà conseguire per diligenza anco col provocare non solo con parole, ma con sguardi, con scherni, et altri modi indecenti col solo fine di mormorar di tutte per non esser sola in mal concetto; sa la supp*licante* che VS. Ill.ma come P*adre* e Pastore non permetterà queste inquietudini, e che ben notto e à VS. Ill.ma che mai habbi ricorso ne in scritto, ne con persuasive d'altri à questo rimedio, ne meno con lettere orbe, ne in altra maniera, e se saranno forsi d'altre Monache, che mal contente dei di lei portamenti l'haveranno fatte per non farsi questa amare da alcuna che per poco tempo, e poi mormorando anche di queste, si disgusta hora con l'una, hora con l'altra, con che à tutte porge matteria di mala volontà, come se ne assicura succederà in breve, anco nel partito ove si trova di presente, che non li perdonerà in prima occasione d'essere maledica la sua absenza e già si conosce tale il suo costume, e poi a qualsivoglia novità vien subito incolpata la supp*licante* senza far lei medesima memoria di quanto à offende alla giornata, si che non sapendo, che rimedio trovarsi non curando questa precetti delle sue superi*ori*, che non mancano col zelo di Carità di far quanto possono. Ha pensato farne consapevole l'autorità di VS. Ill.ma credendo che questa potrà colpire opperando si compiaccia di contentarsi di viver inquiete, e lasciar viver chi non ricerca rinovar le sue, ne antiche, ne moderne piaghe il che spera
Di VS. Ill.ma e Rev.ma Div*otissi*me et Humilissime serve nel sig*nore*
D. Bianca Maria Ripa / D Anna Maria Cittadina / D Antonia Felice Lomazzi / D Teresa Giacinta Ripa / D Regina Vittoria de Laurenzi / D Beatrice Suarez de Qualle / D. Anna Margherita Cozolanna / D. Franc*esca* Marina Merantoli / D. Antonia franc*esca* Clerici / D. Attilia Lomazza / D. Clara Francesca Ripa / D. Anna Teresa Clerici / D. Paola Maria Trecciola / D. Camilla Laudonia Porta / D. Paola Franc*esca* Mercantoli / D. Giovana Margaritta Porta / D. Gio. Alluiggia Pechia.

60. 'Memoriale delle Monache zelanti trasmesso da un ministro regio e ver-ificato", enclosed with Litta's letter of 9 July 1664, ASV, VR, ibid.

Non ponno dimeno le monache di Santa Radegonda (anco per evitare scandali grandissimi vicini a succedere) di recorrere da VS. Ill.ma rapresen-tarle come il giorno di S. Barnaba prossimo passato, e festa seguente del Corpus Domini, Donna Maria faustina Palomera cantò in chiesa al Vespero . . . Ill.mo Sig.re cagione questa cosa un susurro, un ammiratione, e mor-moratione grandissima nel audienza, che in gran numero concorre, men-tre viene fatto particolare invito dal S.r Pietro Paulo Landriano, che frequenta tutte le feste, per sentire questa [Palomera], che non ad altro fine canta. Mà quel che è peggio, ha cagionato nel monastero il Cantare di questa (che punto non è rimessa, che piu che mai baldanzosa, e piena di mille Vanità sene vive, e che mai tralascia di continuamente semminare dis-cordie fra le monache) una revolutione et un bisbiglio tale, che temono di qualche gran Scandalo.

61. Litta to the SCVR, 6 August 1664, ASV, VR, sez. monache, 1664, giu–ago

L'insolenza della Palomera è arrivata tant'oltre, che sia messo il Monastero sottosopra, ed à me stata scritta la congionta lettera, venendo pure avisato per altra parte, che siano per seguire scandali grandi ogni qualvolta *non si sospenda a tutte le Monache di quel Mon[aste]ro la Musica*, che à punto fù orig-ine del delitto della Palomera, e causarà sempre disordini, forse anche più gravi, perche tutta la Gioventù [insert: 'spagnoli Tedeschi Napolitani Zerbini soldati e quanti capitano'] di Milano va del continuo alla Chiesa di esse Monache, e col pretesto d'entrarvi à sentire la Musica.

62. Nuns at S. Radegonda to the SCVR, ASV, VR, monache, 1664, set

1664. a di 31 Agosto in Milano

Faciamo ampla, et indubitata fede, ancho col nostro giuramento di verità noi infrascritte Monache nel Venerando Monastero di Santa Radegonda di Milano. quanto del giorno, nel quale Suor Maria Faustina Palomera Monaca professa nel sudetto Monastero fù liberata dalla prigione, sino al giorno d'hoggi non si è mai portata, ne lasciata vedere in alcuna occasione, ò tempo alla Crate, ne à Parlatorio alcuno, nella porta, mà che sempre se ne obedientamente astenuta in esecuzione dell'iussione, che sopra di ciò teneva; di più attestiamo col nostro giuramento, come sopra, qualmente la detta Suor Maria Faustina, doppo che fù liberata, come sopra, si astenne dal cantare, è suonare, sino à tanto che dal Signore Reverendissimo Padre Abbate Don Pietro Clavarino, con participatione di Monsignor Arcivescovo di Milano fù restituita, è redintegrata à tutte le operazioni, e funzioni, che sogliono fare le altre Monache, fori che à quella di portarsi al Parlatorio, et alla Porta, et in oltre attestiamo con il nostro giuramento, come sopra, che se bene la sude*tta* Suor Maria Faus*ti*na habbia cantato nel Choro interiore della Chiesa, non hà pero mai cantato à voce sola, mà sola*mente* in Choro pieno, ed in concerto con le altre, e che mai per de*tto* suo cantare, sappiamo ne habbiamo sentito à dire, che sia seguito alcun atto di meraviglia nelli Ascoltanti, e molto meno alcuno scandalo in de*tta* Chiesa, ne fuori di essa in alcun tempo; Anzi diciamo, che li disgusti, et evidenti sofferti dalla Suor M*ari*a Faus*ti*na sono (per n*ostr*o credere) cagionati dal non havere ella mai voluto stacarsi del Choro, ove canta, et unirsi à quello di Suor Biancha M*ari*a Ripa, al che fare e stata grand*emente* con diversi mezzi, e persuasioni sollecitate, mà sempre indarno, havendo per questa causa sentiti molti motti, e rimproveri, come noi restiamo pienamente informate et in fede habb*iamo* data la p*res*ente à richiesta della de*tta* Suor M*ari*a Faustina Palomero

Subscript*e* Omnes Infrascripte

D. Francesca Cleonova, Decana, Portiera / D. Anna Luduvica Cachia Guera De*ca*na Maestra delle Novitie / D. Maria Felice Macinona De*ca*na Porti*na*ra / D. Anna Benedetta Stampa / D. Giulia Margheritta Margliana Porti*na*ra / D. M.a Radegonda Greca / D. Maria Vittoria Lampugnana / D. Anglae Prandona / D. Giovanna Lavinia Balsami Porti*na*ra / D. Giulia Allessandra Porti*na*ra Cerbellona / D. Constanza Theresa Paraccicina / D. M*ari*a Franc*es*ca Chioccha Porti*na*ra / D. M*ari*a Luina Perra / D. Anna Aluigia Faronni Porti*na*ra / D. Constanza Vittoria Arcimbolda / D. Laura Maria Balsami / D. Giulia Antonia Lonati Portinara / D. Regina Margaritta Arcimbolda / D. Maria Domitilla Ceva / D. Maria Vestarina / D. Chiara Maria Barnaceggi Portinara / D. Gerolama Felie della Porta De*ca*na, e Portinara / D. Agata Macira Sansona / D. Francesca Luisa Casati Portinara / D. Hieronima Bolona Priora affer*mo* et facio fede con mio giuramento haver visto le sudette monache à soscrire la p*res*ente come sopra
D. Chiara Lavinia Varese affer*mo* et facio fede con il mio giura*mento* haver visto le sudette Monache à sottoscrire la p*res*ente come sopra
D. Lavinia Giuditta Cottica Decana affer*mo* con il mio giuramento haver visto le sudette monache à sottoscrire le p*res*ente come sopra
D. Maria Theresa Faustina Decana Portinara affer*mo* con il mio giuramento haver visto le sude*tte* Monache, à sottoscrire la p*res*ente come sopra

63. C. Vernici to Modena, 26 November 1664, ASMod, Carteggio Ufficiale, Ambasciatori, Milano, busta 114

Il Sig*no*r D. Luigi in sedia . . . visitò il Sig*no*r Cardinale che lo riceve non per anticam*er*a, sin a dove fù portato da segettari; e nella stessa forma partì; il sig*no*r Cardin*a*le vi ha ammessa alla Visita; perche giovedì mattina *Signor Cardinale* dovea celebrar Messa à S. Radegonda, Monast*er*o di molte Monache p*er* udir la Musica, in cui sono cantatrici, che cantano come Angioli, ma s'agitan come Furie, e per ubbidire il sig*no*r Cardin*a*le, il de*tto*

Abb*ate* di S. Simpliciano, ed io, le mandassimo la licenza in scriptù, che le Monache potessero cantare per quella volta, tanto che era da noi stata sospesa sotto gravi pene p*er* accidenti accad*u*ti in mat*eri*a di musica.

64. Vernici to Modena, 25 February 1665, ASMod, ibid.

Dimorano qui tuttavia gli Ser*enissi*mi di Brunswich, trattenuti gli ultimi giorni di Carnevale da q*ue*sta Nobiltà, in Feste, Balli, et Spettatori delle Giostre . . . et hieri furono al Monast*er*o delle Monache di S. Radegonda in Chiesa, con concorso di Nobiltà, oue ambedue gli Cori Musicali d'esso, cantar*o*no uniti (cosa insolita) e trà l'altra, la Ceva, et Clerici, che sono le due famose, con aggradim*en*to, e gusto della loro Altezza. Monsig*no*r Arcivesco*v*o, beneto di sua influenza, si è aperto con l'Abbate di S. Simpliciano et mecon, à fine che trastornassimo l'effetto, uietassimo il canto alle Monache, e l'ingresso della Chiesa a d*e*tti Principi, come Heretici, tanto in ordine al d*e*tto Monast*er*o, quanto di S. Margarita gouer-nati da noi; ma bilanciata la condrene; et i riguardi, e pesate le conuenienze, fossimo d'animo risoluto, ancor che con nostra amarezza, di non usar indis-cretezza, et inciuiltà scandalose, tanto più che essi Principi, douean essere in altri Monasterij sogetti all'Arcivesco*v*o.

65. Unsigned letter, ASV, VR, monache, 1666, gen–feb

Milano . . . 15 Janr*ij* 1666 / Arci*vesco*vo p*er* inf*eri*ore / Per / D. Chiara Margh*ari*ta Cozzolana Monaca nel Monast*ero* di S. Radegonda di Milano: Emin*entissi*mi e R*everendissi*mi S*i*g*no*ri: Sin dall'anno 1618 fù fatta fabricare una cella nel Monast*er*o di S*an*ta Radegonda di Milano p*er* uso di D. Chiara Margherita Cozzolana Monaca professa in d*e*tto Monast*er*o con la dovuta licenza, con conditione però, che in essa Cella fatta à spese de parenti di d*e*tta Religiosa, potesse succedere un altra sua sorella parim*en*te Monaca velata nel med*e*simo, et essendo morta d*e*tta sorella, si supp*li*ca hum*il*m*en*te p*er* parte di d*e*tta D. Chiara Margh*eri*ta ancor vivente à concederle licenza di poter cedere il possesso di d*e*tta Cella successivam*en*te à due sue Nipoti, cioè D. Anna Margh*eri*ta, e D. Giovanna franc*esc*a Cozzolane ambe sorelle Monache, come sopra, pigliando d*e*tta D. Chiara Margh*eri*ta altra Cella del Monast*er*o à luogo di sua professione essendo ella delle mag*gi*ori. Che il tutto, &c.

66. *Regola delle monache di S. Chiara Datali dal Padre S. Francesco, e confirmata da Papa Innocenzo IV. Et alcune osseruationi distinte in dieciotto Capitoli Da praticarsi dalle medesime Monache nelli loro officij per la buona osseruatione di essa Regola. Compillate da vn Religioso dello stesso Ordine.* (Milan, 1670), 'Del Canto, e Cantatrici', Cap. 17 [pp. 119–22]

Se bene nel principio della Religione le Monache non pratticauano il Canto fermo ne figurato, ad ogni modo in progresso di tempo li Superiori

e le Superiore sono venuti in parere d'introdurre e l'vno e l'altro per eccitare alla diuotione i popoli, imitando le Girarchie Celesti che con Chori
musicali laudano la Diuina Maestà, per lo che oltre le Maestra del Choro,
vi saranno le Cantatrici del Canto fermo e figurato, queste del Canto figurato haueranno la loro Maestra, & Organista, la quale ordinarà, e ripartirà
la musica conforme la dispositione delle parti; e doue saranno istromenti si
concordino con le altre, procurando sopra tutto la concordia delli animi
non meno che delle voci, vsando della musica più per mouere à diuotione,
che per eccitare la curiosità, schiuando le armonie profane, e le sinfonie
secolaresche, non meno nel canto che nel suono, fugiendo trà di loro le
partialità, e le diuisioni, e quantunque siano molte le parti che cantino, sia
vno il cuore e l'affetto indrizzato alla gloria di Dio, & al decoro dello stato
religioso: non introducano, ne si permettano Maestri secolari, ò Religiosi
esteriori, che insegnano alle Monache professe à cantare ò sonare, molto
meno alle Nouitie, acciò sotto pretesto di buon fine e del maggior seruitio
di Dio, il Demonio non introduca lo scandalo del Monastero, & in questo
si incarica la conscienza della Madre Abbadessa, & in caso che vi siano secolare in educatione che facciano venire i Maestri secolari, la Madre
Abbadessa inuigli che si troui sempre presente la loro Maestra, e non assis-
tano altre; nel Monastero però sarà lecito à quelle che sanno il Canto fermo,
ò figurato insegnare à quelle Sorelle che haueranno habilità, e desiderio di
impararli; quelle che non voranno cantare il Canto figurato, ò impararlo
non siano obligate; fugiranno le Cantilene, ò motetti troppo longhi specialmente nelle Messe per non causare tedio al Sacerdote, e far perder la
diuotione, e patienza à quelli che ascoltano le Messe, studiando di fuggire
le confusioni acciò non paia la loro Musica vna sinagoga di Hebrei, mà vn
Choro di Angeli.

67. F. Picinelli, *Ateneo dei letterati milanesi* (Milan, 1670), 147

Le Monache di Santa Radegonda di Milano, nel possesso della musica sono
dotate di così rara isquisitezza, che vengono riconosciute per le prime cantatrici d'Italia. Vestono l'habito Cassinense del P. S. Benedetto, e pure sotto
le nere spoglie sembrano à chi le ascolta, candidi, armoniosi Cigni, che, e
riempiono i cuori di marauiglia, e rapiscono le lingue à i loro encomij. Frà
queste Religiose, merita somma vanti Donna Chiara Margarita Cozzolani,
Chiara di nome, mà più di merito, e Margarita, per nobiltà d'ingegno, rara,
ed eccellente, che se nell'anno 1620. iui s'indossò quell'habito sacro, fece
nell'essercitio della musica riuscite così grandi; che dal 1640. fino al 1650.
hà mandato alle stampe, quattro opere di musica, cioè:
Primauera di fiori Musicali à 1.2.3. e 4. voci, dedicata all'Eminentiss.
Cardinal Monti Arciuescouo di Milano 1640
Motetti à 1.2.3. e 4 voci, al Sereniss. Prencipe Mathias di Toscana. Venetia
1642

Scherzi di Sacra Melodia. Venetia 1648

Salmi à 8. voci concertati con Motetti, e Dialoghi à 2.3.4. e 5 voci all'Illustriss. Mons. Badoara Vesc. di Crema. Venetia 1650.

68. Carlo Torre, *Il ritratto di Milano* (Milan, 1674), 338 ff.

[On S. Radegonda]: Benche situata resti quasi nel centro di Milano, tal Clausura, nulladimeno vedesi ornata di Cortili, di vaghi Appartamenti con ampiezza de Giardini, e la loro Chiesa ritrouasi in Nobile Architettura antica con trè Naui . . .

Può dirsi essersi ne' nostri tempi trasportato in questo Monastero il Monte Elicona all'eccellenza delle sue Velate Cantatrici, ouuero che in questa Chiesa volino eleuati spiriti, poiche sentonsi melodie da rapine, e migliori se ne sentiuano gli anni trascorsi ancora. Credetemi, che sebben Roma si gloria di nodrire nouelli Orfei, deue cedere il pregio à queste Lombarde Pieridi, quindi chi sente i loro musicali concenti, restando estatico credeui trasportato alle Stelle non pensando mai, che questi Canti sieno terreni.

69. Maria Domitilla Ceva's singers to the Cassinese superior, 14 November 1675 (ASDM, Carteggio Ufficiale, vol. 92; apparently a copy without the choir's signatures)

Reverendissimo in Christo Padre Signore e Protettore Colendissimo

La fidanza che habbiamo nella carità, e giustizia di VS. Reverendissima ci muoue tutte à pregarla di considerare benignamente le propositioni, che qui esponiam, per darne poi quel giudicio, che le uerra coettato dalla sua equità, e prudenza. Essendo ridotto il nostro coro à tale scarsità, che ci costringe à non cantar molte cose, solo per mancamento di parti, et hauendo inteso, che la Sig.ra Via soprabondaua al Coro della Sig.ra Clerici, è desideraua di uenire nel nostro, per passare con quella unione, è carità, che si ricerca in persone ciuili e religiose, richiedemmo detta Sig.ra Clerici di rilasciarcela, e ne riportammo in risposta, che la prendessimo pure, che essa condiscendeua tanto più volentieri, quanto non ne hauea alcun bisogna. Staua dunque l'affare in questo concerto, quando V.S. Reverendissima per aderire all'antico decreto, che proibisce il passare da un Coro all'altro uietò con espresso commando, alla Sig.ra Via di attentar simil passaggio. In ordine a che preghiamo humilmente V.S. Reverendissima di ponderare i seguenti punti.

Primo che quel Decreto non fù osseruato sotto il gouerno del Reverendissimo Abbate Clauarino, atteso che le SS.re Cozzolani, e Suarez dal Coro di D. Maria Domitilla Ceua passarono all'altro; onde ne uiene per dritta consequenza, che ò il Decreto habbia perduto il uigore, ò se mantiene ancora sua forza debbano le predette SS.re ritornare al Coro antico, ò tralasciar di cantare, che è la pena da quel Decreto, à chi contrauiene intimata.

2.º Che essendosi fatto dal Capitolo Generale un altro Decreto, che proibisca questi passaggi, ciò non ostante, senza consentimento, è saputa di D. M. Domitilla Ceua le fù tolta la Sig.ra Lonati alla quale essa haueua con grandissimo stento insegnato. Dal che potrebbe conchiudersi, che noi sole siamo tenute, e forzate ad osseruare i Decreti, la qual uiolenza di ubbedire ne potiamo temere, ne dobbiamo pur sospettare, quando consideriamo la rettitudine di VS. *Reverendissi*ma indiferente ad ogna persona, e partiale solo del giusto.

3.º Che quel'antico Decreto uiolato dall'altra parte tante uolte con manifesta oppressione, fù annullato per un altro fatto nell'Anno 1669 con l'occasione, che i due Cori amicheuolmente si unirono dicendosi in questo, che quel primo non giouaua al fine della pace, anzi era cagione, che sorgessero difficoltà inestricabili, e uiolente rotture di Pace. Che però ò non si deue stare al primo come annullato, ò standosi al primo deuono ritornare al nostro Coro le tre sopradette, se pure non uuole l'altra parte, che si osseruino tutte due per ferirci con armi doppie, cioè che hora uaglia il primo perche non ritorna a noi la Sig.ra Via, hora uaglia il secondo per tenere le SS.re Cozzolani Suarez e Lonati, e per noi non uagliono ne l'uno ne l'altro.

4.º Che questa Sig.ra Via non è altremente dell'altro Coro, ma di quello di D. Maria Domitilla, essendo stata presa dall Sig.ra Arcimbolda per lei, et hauendo essa dimandata licenza di passare all'altro Coro quando D. Maria Domilla non cantaua, si protestò, che ripigliando ella il Canto, essa ritornerebbe al suo Coro. Onde VS. *Reverendissi*ma uede, che il trattenersi la Sig.ra Via dall'altra parte, non solamente non è osseruanza del Decreto, ma aperta contrauentione al Decreto.

5.º Che D. Maria Francesca presa per Donna Maria Domitilla in questo monistero si come a tutte è palese, andò nel altra parte, e ui è lasciata da la detta D. Maria Domitilla solo per non rompere quella pace, per conservatione della quale adopra tutti i mezzi anche penosi, quantunque in uano.

6.º Che il nostro Coro sminuito notabilmente per l'abandonamento delle 3 prenominate e per altre che per inaspetati accidenti lasciano di cantare non può regger alla fatica, e però conuerrà, ò cadere sotto il peso, ò tralasciare il Canto, con poca riputatione, e stima di questo monastero, quando per la Città, s'intenda, che le une si usurpano l'ingiusto, e le altre non ottengono il giusto, e che si lascia il Canto, perche à questa parte mancano quelli aiuti, che auanzano all'altra.

7.º Che se non si rimedia a questi sconcerti corre gran rischio, che si fomentino amarezze d'animi, disunion di uoler, diuisioni di parte, per euitar le quali furono fatti i decreti, e si sarebbero euitate, se i decreti fossero stati osseruati, cioe se quelle 3 non hauessero dato il primo essempio della trasgressione, o si fosse loro intimata la priuatione del Canto, che è la pena, a chi trasgredisce dall'antico Decreto prescritta.

8.° Finalmente, che o non si osseruano i decreti, e però non si può impedire il passaggio da un Coro all'altro, o se si osseruano deuono ritornare dall'altro Coro a noi, quelle che da noi sono passate all'altro, perche il giogo della legge sia commune, accioche mentre l'altre ne uanno del tutto sciolta noi non siamo forzate a mancare sotto un peso, che non era tutto per noi.

Questi soni i punti principali, che rapresentiamo all'equità di V.S. *Reverendissi*ma inanzi alla quale siamo sicure, che la raggione ha tutto il peso, e favore, che può pretendere dalla sauiezza d'un pronto conoscere, e dalla restitu*tio*ne d'uno religioso uolere. Ella è il Custode delle n*ost*re leggi, e della n*ost*ra pace, e però a lei sola habbiamo uoluto prima riccorrere, perche non desideriamo, se non la pura giustitia, la quale VS. *Reverendissi*ma ne può per l'equità dell'animo, ne deue per l'obbligatione del grado, ne vuole per il rispetto della sua generosa bonta negare ad alcuno. Non è q*ue*sta una priuata passione, ma uoce publica di tante qui sottoscritte, che ricorrono al suo tribunale, implorando quel fauore di cui VS. *Reverendissi*ma è tanto liberale con l'innocenza massimamente oppressa. Ma perche non uogliamo, che lo strido delle querele distolga l'animo suo dalla consideratione delle raggioni, pregandola di nuouo a scorrerle non men con l'occhio, che con la prudenza del suo auertimento, le faciamo profondissima riuerenza. *S*anta Rada*gon*da 14 9bre 1675. Di VS. Reu.ma Diu*otissi*me Obblig*atissi*me Serue, e in *Chris*to figlie

70. List of musicians at S. Radegonda, *c.*1675, ASDM, Carteggio Ufficiale, vol. 92

Al Choro della Sig.ra Ceua

D. Maria Domitilla	Soprano
D. Teresa Giacinta	Soprano
S.a Paola	Soprano
D. Regina Vittoria	Contralto
D. Pauola Maria	Contralto
D. Giouanna Fran.ca	Contralto
D. Bianca Maria	Basso
D. Maria Vittoria	Basso
A sonar l'Organo e Cembali	3
A sonar li violini sono	2
A sonar il Violone	1
A sonar il Chitarone	1

Al Choro della Sig.ra Clerici

D. Antonia Fran.ca	Soprano
D. Giustina	Soprano
D. Ippolita Fran.ca	Soprano
D. Maria Fran.ca	Contralto

D. Anna Marg.ta	Contralto
D. Giulia Antonia	Basso
A sonar l'Organo e Cembali	n.o 3
A sonar li violini	n.o 2
A sonar il Violone	n.o 1
A sonar il Chitarone	n.o 2
D. Gio. Madd.la Via, che uole il passaggio	

71. Pietro Ottoboni to Federico Visconti, ASDM XII, vol. 128, fo. 164

Eminentissimo e reverendissimo Signore mio Osservantissimo
Riceuerà Vostra Eccelenza unita alla presente altra mia con ordine di Nostro Signore [the Pope] di restituire alle Monache di Santa Radegonda il pristino possesso della Musica, ma perche Sua Santità non pretende di coartare l'arbitrio di Vostra Eccelenza quando non concorra pienamente à consolare l'istanze di queste Madri, io le ne porto riuerentemente la notizia, accio possa regolarsi secondo il dettame della sua somma prudenza. Mi so ben lecito di significare all'Eccelenza Vostra che io tengo non piccolo interesse nella sodisfazione delle sudette Madri, et oggi che depende dalla di Lei sola uolontà, mi lusingo che sia per condescendere a quanto uiuamente la supplico, accertandola che per tal grazia io sarò sempre debitore d'un fino riconoscimento alla gentilezza di Vostra Eccelenza, alla quale bacio umilissimamente le mani. Roma 28 8bre 1690
Humilissimo et Devotissimo Servitore
P. Card. Ottoboni

72. Visconti's orders, 9 November 1690, ASDM XII, vol. 45, fo. 188

Per uigore di una lettera data in Roma li 28 8bre poco fa spirato, e scritto dall'Eminentissimo Ottoboni, in nome di Sua Beatitudine, la quale mostrandosi inclinata al presente indulto metter in poter nostro l'arbitrio del Suo uolere, concediamo alla R.R. Madre Superiora, e Monache del Monastero di Santa Radegonda di questa Città, facoltà di usare la musica nelle ore delli diuini ufficij, e delle Messe, che si cantarano nelle loro chiese, e cio con le infrascritte condicioni. Prima che l'uso della Musica come sopra sia loro solamente lecito nelle Solennità della Pasqua, dell'Ascensione, della Pentecoste, del Corpus Domini, della Natività di Nostro Signore, della Circoncisione, et dell'Epifania, nelle feste della B.V.M., della Natiuità di S. Giovanni Battista, di S. Pietro e Paolo Apostoli, nel primo giorno di 9bre dedicato alla festiuita di tutti li Santi, e nelle feste di ciascun Santo del loro Ordine, et in ocasione di uestire, e far professe le Nouizie del lor Monastero; ritterandosi Noi l'amplianza ad altri giorni, se aparera bene. Seconda, che i diuini ufficij siano terminati, prima che si oda il segno dell'Aue Maria solito darsi nel fine del giorno. Terza che in nessun tempo sia loro lecito cantare, o suonare ne Parlatorij ouero nelle porte del

Mon*astero*. Quarta, che non si permetta a Persona secolare di qualunq*ue* grado, e condicione entrare nell'ore, e stare dentro a Cancelli dell'Altare Maggiore nelle ore delli diuini ufficij. Nel resto uogliamo, che la presente concessione sia nulla ipso facto habbia per non fatta in ogni caso, che non si osseruasse alcuna delle sodette conditioni. In Sede dell'Arciue*scov*o di Milano li 9 9bre 1690

73. ASM, Religione, p.a., busta 2221
1714 a di *31* Gen*nai*o da S. Radegonda
Essendo passate a miglior uita D. Antonia Francesca Clerici, e D. Gio*vann*a Gioseffa Caccia ambedue Monache professe di questo Monistero, e mie Cugine di sangue, e sorelle di habito, insigni uirtuose nel canto di musica, le quali haueuano per loro uso un nobil Cembalo da tre registri di singo-lare perfettione; acciocge il medesimo Cembalo resti per seruitio di Dio nella nostra Chiesa, et anche per particolar memoria delle medesime uirtu-ose defonte, ho pensato di applicarlo e destinarlo, come in effetto lo applico, alla Cantoria della musica del nostro Coro, per seruirsene a' suoi tempi sopra di essa in honore di Dio, e decoro del Monistero, quando ui concorra la licenza del mio Reu*erendissi*mo Prelato, quale insieme con D. Antonia Costanza Caccia mia Cugina, supplico del suo beneplacito per tale opera pia, non uolendo in conto alcuno controuenire al uoto della Povertà Religiosa solennemente giurata nella mia Professione: Tanto piu che la M*olto* R*everenda* M*adre* Abbadessa mia Superiora, oltre i soliti aiuti spiritu-ali, dopo la loro morte, ha suffragato le anime di dette mie Cugine defonte con tre Messe cantate, e altrettante basse, con un'Vfficio de' Morti recitato in comune. E per fede della uerità
D. Octauius Abbat. vidit, et attestatur
Io D. Gio. Fran*ces*ca Cozzolana Abba*des*sa Affermo
Io D. Anna Teresa Clerici Affermo
Io D. Ant*oni*a Costanza Caccia

74. Charles Burney, *The Present State of Music in France and Italy* . . . (2nd edn., London, 1773), 107 ff.
[1770] *Sunday, July 22*. This morning . . . I went to the Convent of *Santa Maria Maddalena*; I heard several motets performed by the nuns; it was their feast-day. The composition was by Signor B. S. Martini, who is *Maestro di Capella*, and teaches to sing at this convent. He made me ample amends for the want of slow movements in his mass on Friday, by an *adagio* in the motet of to-day, which was truly divine, and divinely sung by one of the sisters, accompanied, on the organ only, by another. It was by far the best singing, in every respect, that I had heard since my arrival in Italy . . . At my first coming I both hungered and thirsted after music, but I now had had almost my fill; . . . Several of the nuns sung, some but indifferently, but

one of them had an excellent voice; full, rich, sweet, and flexible, with a true shake, and exquisite expression; it was delightful, and left nothing to wish, but duration! . . .

Besides the organ in this convent for the chorusses, there was an organ and harpsichord together, which was likewise played by one of the nuns; and the accompaniment of that instrument alone with the heavenly voice abovementioned, pleased me beyond description, and not so much by what it *did*, as by what it did *not* do; . . . a single note from such a voice as that I heard this morning, penetrates deeper into the soul, than the same note from the most perfect instrument upon earth can do, which, at best, is but an imitation of the human voice.

The music this morning was entirely performed by the nuns themselves, who were invisible to the congregation, and though the church of the convent is open to the public, like a common parish church, in which the priests are in sight, as elsewhere, yet the responses are made behind the altar, where the organ is placed . . . Upon my praising this singing, I was told that there were several convents here in which the nuns sing much better . . . And I was so pleased with this singing, that . . . I ran from the company before the second course was served, in hopes of hearing more of it at the same convent; and was so fortunate as to enter it just as the service was begun, and heard the same motet repeated again by the same nun, and with double delight.

APPENDIX B:
FEMALE MONASTERIES IN THE
DIOCESE OF MILAN, C.1600

Name	Order	Jurisdiction	Size	Liturgy	VR	Deds	DR	Other
A. Urban houses								
Monastero del Bocchetto/ S. Ulderico	B	R to 1646/E	42	A/B 1575		1		
Monastero Maggiore/ S. Maurizio	B	R to 1626/E	133	A/B	1		2	D
S. Agnese	A	E	93		3	1	1	
S. Agostino Bianco (and S. Pietro Martire)	D	E	80				1	
S. Agostino Nero	A	R	97	A	1		2	
S. Anna	A	E						
S. Antonio di Padova	S	R to 1626/E	39					
S. Apollinare	Cl	R to 1730	67		2	2	1	T
S. Barbara	Ca	E		A to 1680				D
S. Bernardino alle Monache	Cl	R	85			2		T
S. Bernardo	D	R	27			1	1	
S. Caterina alla Chiusa	A	E	100		1		2	
S. Caterina in Brera	H	E	19	H			1	
S. Chiara	Cl	R	99			1		
S. Cristina	U	E			1	1		
S. Domenico e Lazaro	D	R	28		1		1	T
S. Erasmo	H	E	15	H				
S. Marcellina	U	E				1		
S. Margarita	B	R	76		3	3		D

Name	Order	Jurisdiction	Size	Liturgy	VR	Deds	DR	Other
S. Maria Annunciata	LC	R	57		I	I		
S. Maria del Cappuccio	A	E				I		
S. Maria del Gesù	Cl	R	87					
S. Maria del Lentasio	B	E	40	A/B				
S. Maria del Soccorso	U	E						
S. Maria della Stella (Consolazione)	S	E	9	A			I	
S. Maria della Vettabia	D	E	53					
S. Maria della Vittoria	D	E	51	R			I	D
S. Maria delle Veteri	D	R	55			I		
S. Maria in Valle	B	E	48		2	I		
S. Maria Maddalena al Cerchio	H	E	44	H	3			D
S. Maria Maddalena in Porta Romana	A	E	23					
S. Marta	A	E	75	A	5	3		D
S. Michele sul Dosso	Ci	R	42	B				
S. Orsola	Cl	R	24		I	3	I	
S. Paolo Converso	An	E	80	R	I	3	I	D
S. Prassede (1)	Ca	E						
S. Prassede (2)	U	E						
S. Radegonda	B	R to 1737	73	B	5+	II	I	
S. Vincenzo	B	R	64		I	2		
B. Extraurban houses								
Abbiategrasso: S. Chiara	Cl		75					
Abbiategrasso: S. Maria Rosa	B		13					
Angera: S. Giuseppe								
Bernaga: S. Gregorio	B		25				I	

Name	Order	Jurisdiction	Size	Liturgy	VR	Deds	DR	Other
Bosto: S. Chiara			50					
Brugora: S. Pietro e Paolo	B		44				1	
Busto Arsizio: S. Maria Maddalena	B						1	
Cannobbio: S. Giustina	A							
Cantello: S. Antonio	A						1	
Cantù: S. Ambrogio	A		10				2	
Cantù: S. Maria	Ci	E from 1581	46		2	1	1	
Cantù: S. Martino			24					
Claro (Ticino): S. Maria	B							
Cremella: S. Pietro	B						2	
Desio: S. Orsola	U							
Gallarate: S. Maria delle Grazie	U							
Gallarate: S. Michele	B							
Lambrugo: S. Maria	B		19					
Lecco: S. Maria Maddalena di Castello	Ci/B		22				2	
Legnano: S. Chiara	Cl		13				2	
Lonate Pozzolo: S. Agata	A		16					
Lonate Pozzolo: S. Michele	A		9				1	T
Magenta: S. Maria della Pace								
Meda: S. Vittore	B		144		2	4		
Melegnano: S. Caterina	U							
Monza: S. Margarita	H		29		1			
Monza: S. Maria Maddalena	B							1

Name	Order	Jurisdiction	Size	Liturgy	VR	Deds	DR	Other
Monza: S. Martino								
Monza: S. Orsola								
Monza: S. Paolo	An						I	
Tradate: S. Sepolchro	B						I	
Treviglio: S. Agostino	A		50				I	
Treviglio: S. Pietro	Cl		19				I	
Varese: S. Antonio	B		9			I		3
Varese: S. Marcellina	U							
Varese: S. Maria sopra Monte	AH		65			I		
Varese: S. Martino	H		13			2		
Varese: S. Teresa	A					I		
Vimercate: S. Girolamo	U					I		
Vimercate: S. Lorenzo	B		2					2

Abbreviations:

Order: A = Augustinian, AH = Ambrosian Hermitess, An = Angeliche, B = Benedictine, Ca = Capuchin, Ci = Cistercian, Cl = Clarissan, D = Dominican, H = Humiliate, LC = Lateran Canoness, S = Servite, U = Ursuline

Jurisdiction: E = Episcopal, R = Regulars

Size (from 1576 *numeri prefissi*)

Liturgy: A = Ambrosian, B = Benedictine, H = Humiliate, R = Roman

VR: Episcopal visitations concerning music

Deds: Number of entire editions or individual pieces dedicated to a nun

DR: Requests to SCVR for dowry reduction or dispensation, 1590–1700

Other: D = Ducal musicians in *chiesa esteriore*, T = request for outside teacher, I = Request for instruments

APPENDIX C:
PRINTED MUSIC DEDICATED TO
NUNS IN THE DIOCESE,
1592–1679

1. Antegnati, Vespers *a 8*, 1592

Salmi a otto voci, di Costanzo Antegnati . . . alle Molto RR.MM. Osservandiss. D. Hortensia Marchi Abbatessa, D. Hieronima Birraga Priora, & Compagne del Monastero di S. Vittore in Meda (Venice: Gardano, 1592)

Dedication: in Gaspari, *Catalogo*, ii. 160

    Domine ad adiuvandum
    Dixit Dominus
    Confitebor
    Beatus vir
    Laudate pueri
    In exitu
    Laudate Dominum omnes gentes
    Laetatus sum
    Nisi Dominus
    Lauda Jerusalem
    Credidi
    In convertendo
    Domine probasti me
    De profundis
    Memento Domine David
    Beati omnes
    Magnificat

RISM A1264

Modern edition: *Laudate pueri* in Kendrick, 'Genres', 915–42

2: Cortellini, Vespers *a 6*, 1595

Salmi a sei voci di Camillo Cortellini . . . (Venice: Vincenti, 1595)

Dedication: ALLA MOLTO ILLVSTRE, ET R.DA DONNA PAOLA ORTENSIA SORBELLONI; *SIGNORA, ET PADRONA OSSERVAN-DISSIMA*. Hauendo deliberato mandar'alla Stampa questi miei Salmi, insieme ancora hò risoluto dedicarli à V.S. molto Illustre, & Reuerenda, si perche co'l fauorirmi di farmi comporre assai volte molte cose, posso immaginarmi, che in parte grate le siano le mie debole compositioni, come anco essendo lei non meno colma di nobiltà, che piena d'ogni virtù di Musica, si nel cantare, come nel sonare, non posso trouare soggetto, che più illustrare e dare forza possi à questi Salmi cosi composti da me in Musica per poterne con essi seruire a Iddio. Resta dunque che lei con la solita sua cortesia di fauorire tanto i virtuosi, voglia con benigno, e sereno occhio riguardare à questa opera, che essendo lei Religiosa, d'essa potra seruirsene se più l'affetto, che l'effetto considererà, che pregandoli da N.S. ogni prosperità humilmente li bascio le mani. Di Bologna il di xxv. d'Agosto 1595. Di V.S. molto Illustre, & Reuerenda Deuotissimo seruitore Camillo Cortellini detto il Violino.

> *Dixit Dominus*
> *Confitebor*
> *Beatus vir*
> *Laudate pueri*
> *Laudate Dominum*
> *In exitu*
> *Magnificat*
> *Laetatus sum*
> *Nisi Dominus*
> *Lauda Hierusalem*

RISM C4161 (reprints of 1609, 1617, and 1618 not considered here)
Modern edition: *Laudate pueri*, Kendrick, 'Genres', 943–56

3. Gallo, Mass and motets *a* 8, 1598
Sacer opus musicum alternis modulis concinendum, liber primus . . . *Authore M.R.D. Josepho Gallo Mediolanensi* (Milan: Tradate, 1598)

> *Veni electa mea*, 'Concentus duplex, continens cantionem la Benvenuta nuncupatam Optimis, venerandisque Christi famulis D.D. Archileae, Angelicaeque Archintis, Monasterij S. Radegundae; sanctitate, virtute, et umilitate osservatissime'
> *Ecce Angelus de caelo*, 'La Galla Concentus duplex vocum, & Instrumentorum. Summe valdeque venerandae D. Maximillaie Biumiae S. Radegondae'
> *Magnificat*, 'Canticum B.M.V. duplici concentu, vocibus instrumentisque; concinendum item multum, observandis DD. Annae Camillae, & Blancae Margaritae Sororibus Vicecomitibus, sacrarum Monialium S. Ursulae Mediolani'

La Mantegazza [Canzona], 'Cantio instrumentis Musicis, alternis mod-
ulis pulsanda. Venerabilibus D.D. Archangelae Mariae Coronae
Sororibus Mantegatijs, praeclarissimi Monasterij S. Agnetis
Mediolani'

RISM G270

4. Soderini, Motets *a 8–9*, 1598

*Sacrae cantiones octo et novem vocibus, liber primus . . . Auctore Augustino
Soderino Mediolanensi* (Milan: Tradate, 1598)

> *Saule, Saule quid me persecutis*, 'In die conv. S. Pauli' (*a 8*): 'Illustrissimae,
> ac Multum Reuerendae D. Angelicae Agathae Sfondratae ex Collegio
> Monialium S. Pauli Mediolani'
>
> *Dic nobis, Maria*, 'In die Resurr. D.N. Jesu Christi Dialogus' (*a 8*): 'D.
> Franciscae Mariae Stampae Religiosissimae Matri Monasterij Sanctae
> Radagundae'
>
> *Vidi Dominum sedentem*, 'In solennitate omnium Sanctorum' (*a 8*):
> 'D. Angelae Catharinae Briuiae, Virgini lectissimae Monasterij Sanctae
> Radegundae'
>
> *Ipsi sum desponsata*, 'In solemnitatibus Virginum novem vocibus':
> 'D. Angelae Catharinae Briuiae, Virgini lectissimae Monasterij Sanctae
> Radegundae'

RISM S3820

Modern edition: *Dic nobis, Maria*, Kendrick, 'Genres', 957–85

5. Vecchi, Falsi bordoni *a 4–8*, 1600

*Falsi bordoni figurati sopra gli otto toni ecclesiastici . . . Magnificat, & Te Deum
laudamus . . . di Orfeo Vecchi Milanese* (Milan: Tini, 1600)

Dedication: Alle Molto ILLVSTRI, ET REVER.^{de} SIGNORE, SVOR
CLARA FRANCESCA, ET CLARA GIERONIMA GOSELINE, ET
CLARA POMPILIA ADDA, nel Signore osseruandissime, Se gl'è vero,
anzi de sapienti tenuto verissimo, che molto riguardevole sij la nobiltà congionta con la virtù, e che l'una e l'altra venghi dalle honorate attioni
aggrandita, ed' illustrata; che merauiglia, s'io scorgendo queste risplendere
nelle SS.VV molto Illustri, come in proprio luogo ardisco presentarli
questo virtuoso dono, ben picciolo à gran meriti suoi, e dedicare la presente
opera mia di Musica à quelle che di cio (oltre l'infinite altre sue virtù) ne
sono intendentissime pregandole insieme ad accetarla con quella grandezza
d'animo, che sogliano le cose maggiori: Et io frà tanto terrommi molto
pago del mio longo studio, quanto intenda questa mia fatica esser stata gra-
dita, e cara alle S.S. loro, alle quali per fine prego da N. Sig. il compimento
de gli alti desiderij suoi. Di Milano li 18. Marzo 1600. Delle molto Illustri
SS.VV. affettionatiss. nel Signore Orfeo Vecchi

Domine ad adiuvandum (a 4). Falsi bordoni del: Primo tono, Secondo tono, Terzo tono alla bassa, Terzo tono all'alta, Quarto tono, Quinto tono, Sesto tono, Settimo tono, Ottauo tono all'alta, Ottauo tono alla bassa

Magnificat, 1. tono, spezzato (*a 4*)

Magnificat, 8. tono, intiero

Domine ad adiuvandum (a 5). Falsi bordoni del: Primo tono, Secondo tono, Terzo tono all'alta, Terzo tono alla bassa, Quarto tono, Quinto tono, Sesto tono, Settimo Tono, Ottauo tono all'alta, Ottauo tono alla bassa

Magnificat, 1. tono, spezzato (*a 5*)

Magnificat, 4. tono, intiero (*a 5*)

Gloria patri (a 8). 1. tono, 2. tono, 3. tono alla bassa, 3. tono all'alta, 4. tono, 5. tono, 6. tono, 7. tono, 8. tono all'alta, 8. tono alla bassa

Falsi bordoni à 8. nel Sicut erat: 1. tono, 2. tono, 3. tono all'alta, 3. tono alla bassa, 4. tono, 5. tono, 6. tono, 7. tono, 8. tono all'alta, 8. tono alla bassa

Domine ad adiuuandum (a 8)

Magnificat 6. tono (*a 8*)

Te Deum laudamus à 4. Primo choro

Te Deum laudamus à 5. Secondo choro

Tre versetti insiemi. à 2. chori.

RISM V1069 + Milan, Biblioteca capitolare della Metropolitana

Modern edition: *Gloria patri octavo tono all'alta a 8,* Kendrick, 'Genres', 986–91

6. *Nova metamorfosi a 5,* book 1

Nova metamorfosi dell'infrascritti autori, opera del R.P.F. Geronimo Cavaglieri . . . (Milan: Tradate, 1600) (madrigal contrafacta and new motets by Lucio Castelnovato)

Dedication: All'Ill. & Reuer. Sor Ottauia Virginia Cattanea Organista meritissima nel Monasterio delle Reuer. Monache di S. Orsola, in Milano. Si come l'ingegnose api nel dolce tempo della Primauera sogliono andar succhiando ne' verdi prati di fresche, e folte herbe: vestiti di vaghi fiori à guisa de bianche perle, verdi smeraldi, e lieti rubini distinti, la celeste ruggiada, per farne quel liquore al gusto humano tanto grato, anchorche dall'istesse non gustato. Così io nel tempo della recreatione son'andato succhiando da molti valent'huomini quel liquore temporale, che al gusto mio, è parso più grato, e soaue, e l'ho conuertito in armonia spirituale con intentione d'adoprarla solo in seruitio mio. Mà essendo gustata questa dolcezza musicale da molti miei amici, e giudicata non men grata, che soaue, mi persuasero non tenerla rinchiusa ne' buchi fra miele, e cera inuolta; mà purgata farne parte à quelli gentili spiriti, che di simil dolcezza volentieri si compiacciono. La onde sapendo io per fama, che V.S. quasi ape celeste ha raccolto da fiori odoriferi primieramente la ruggiada d'ogni Christiana virtù, e poi la perfetta cognitione della Musica, e suoni, Hò giudicato conueniente dedicarla à V.S. come à diligente ape, che à buon'hora con il rimbombo dell'Organo sueglia le compagne à lodar' Iddio, & à raccogliere la ruggiada della celeste gratia, e col silentio le mantiene in consonanza de' suoni, e voci così soaue, che porge diletto, e stupore insieme à quelli che l'ascoltano. Accetti dunque V.S. la presente NVOVA METAMORFOSI con quell'affetto d'animo, con il quale le vien dedicata, e ricordisi di me nelle sue sant'Orationi. Di Milano il dì 20. Maggio, 1600. Di V.S. Ill. e Reuer. Affettionatiss. seruo nel Sig. F. Gieronimo Cauaglieri.

> *Repletur os meum*
> *Exurge gloria mea* (2)
> *Nigra sum sed formosa*
> *Ecce tu pulchra es* (2)
> *Exaudi orationem nostram*
> *Jubilate et exultate Deo*
> *Gaudent in caelis*
> *In canticis et citharis*
> *Immaculata Virgo*
> *Domine ne in furore*
> *Laetamini in Domino*
> *Tentavit Deus Abraham*
> *Veni in hortum meum*
> *Semper laudabo salvatorem*
> *Sana me Domine*
> *Surgens Jesus*
> *Ecce sacerdos magnus*
> *Rorate Coeli*
> *Tulerunt Dominum meum*
> *Isti sunt viri sancti*
> *Ecce dilectus meus*

RISM 1600[11]

7. Vecchi, Penitential Psalms *a 6*, 1601

Orphei Vecchii Mediolanensis . . . In septem Regij prophetae Psalmos vulgò paenitentiales sacrarum modulationum, quae Motecta nuncupantur, & senis vocibus concinuntur, liber quartus (Milan: Tini, 1601)

Dedication: ILLVSTRIS.^{mae} D. ANGELICAE AGATHAE SFON-DRATAE D. COLENDISSIMAE. ORPHEVS VECCHIVS S.P.D. Magna Illustrissime gentis Sfondratae in me non modò officia, sed etiam merita extare fateor, atque ea saepius commemorare summe laudi mihi semper fuit. At cum tot beneficijs respondere me posse diffidam, animum saltem, vtcunq*ue* licet, aliqua ex parte declarare contendam. Tu porrò ex omnibus in mentem vna venisti, quam & iam pridem ex intimo sensu diligo, et verò etiam propter eximiam virtutem singulari quadam obseruantia colo. Et quoniam meis praesertim musicis lucubrationibus, quales quales sint, delectari te scio; accipe nouos hosce ingenij, quod amas, fructus, tenue munus, si vel tua, vel tuorum in me beneficia consideres; magnum verò, si voluntatem; & quoniam, quae tua est incredibilis humanitas, in dantis magis animum, quam in animi donum intueri soles, facilè mihi persuadeo fore, vt hoc quicquid est muneris, tibi gratissimum accidat; & quoties in hunc libellum adijcias oculos, toties ejus habeas testimonium, qui in tuo, tuaeq*ue* familiae Illustrissimae. sic totus aere sit, vt debitis magnitudine oppressus nunquam exire se posse fateatur. Vale. Mediolani xv Martij. M. DCI

> *Domine ne in furore*
> *Beati quorum*
> *Domine ne in furore*
> *Miserere mei Deus*
> *Domine exaudi*
> *De profundis*
> *Domine exaudi orationem*

RISM V1070

Modern edition: 7, *prima pars*, Kendrick, 'Genres', 992–1004

8. Coppini, Madrigal contrafacta *a 5*, book 2, 1608

Il secondo libro della musica di Claudio Monteverde e d'altri autori a cinque voci fatta spirituale da Aquilino Coppini . . . All'Illustriss. Signora Suor Bianca Lodovica Taverna nel Monastero di S. Marta (Milan: Tradate, 1608)

Title-page, partial dedication, and contents in Vogel, i. 520.

> The Ambrosiana copy of this print was destroyed in 1943; the eight Monteverdi contrafacta survive in D-Rp, A.R. 964–84, nos. 48–56; the alto part-book is missing from this manuscript.

Modern edition: *O infelix recessus (Ah dolente partita)*, Kendrick, 'Genres', 1005–22

9. G. P. Cima, Motets *a 1–8*, 1610

Concerti ecclesiastici a una, due, tre, quattro voci . . . Di Gio. Paolo Cima (Milan: Tini & Lomazzo, 1610)

> *Surge propera amica mea* (Concerto in Eco) (CC or TT), 'A D. Paola Ortensia Sorbelloni in S. Vincenzo'

O sacrum convivium (Concerto in Eco) (dedication and scoring as above)

RISM C2229 and 1610⁴

Modern edition: *Surge propera*, Kendrick, 'Genres', 1023–30

10. A. Cima, Motets *a 2–4*, book 1, 1614

Il primo libro delli concerti à due, trè, e 4. voci. Di Andrea Cima . . . (Milan: Lomazzo, 1614)

> *O Domine Jesu Christe*, CCB (B si placet), 'Alla M. Illust. & M. Rever. Madre SOR GIOVANNA MARIA CANEVESA, NEL VENER. MONASTERO DI S. CLARA'

RISM CC2226a

11. Robbiano, Motets *a 2–3*, 1616

Libro primo delli concerti a due et tre voci, di Francesco Robbiano . . . (Milan: Lomazzo, 1616)

> *Congratulamini mihi omnes* (CC), 'All' Illust. & Reu. Sig. Cugina mia osseruandiss. la Sig. Maria Cleofe Castigliona nel Monastero di S. Maria Monte [canto part-book: 'sopra Varese']'

RISM R1786

12. F. Rognoni Taeggio, *Selva de varii passaggi*, 1620

Selva di varii passaggi . . . *Di Francesco Rognoni Taegio* . . . (Milan: Lomazzo, 1620)

> *Quanti mercenarii* [decorated top line of Orfeo Vecchi's contrafactum of Palestrina's *Io son ferito*], 'A Donna Gracia Ottauia Crivelli nel Monastero di S. Margherita'
>
> *Canzon del Mortara passeggiata* [decorated top line of Antonio Mortaro's canzona *La Portia*], 'A Donna Ginepra Criuelli nel Monastero di S. Margherita'

RISM R1942 (modern reprint: Bologna, Forni 1969)

Modern edition: *Quanti mercenarii*, in Kendrick, 'Genres', 1034–42

13. Bellazzi, Mass, Motets, and Litanies, op. 4, 1622

Messa, Motetti, Letanie della B.V., Magnificat, et falsi bordoni . . . *Di Francesco Bellazzo da Vigevano* . . . *Opera Quarta* (Venice: Gardano, 1622)

> *Vox dilecti mei* (CC or TT), 'Alla M. R. Sig. Angela Maria Orrigona nel Venerando Monasterio di S. Martino di Varese' [in T1 'Alla M. Reuerenda Signora Paula Maria Orrigona Organista nel Venerando Monasterio di S. Martino di Varese']
>
> *Missus est Angelus* (CAT), 'Alla Molto Reuerenda Signora Angela Maria Orrigona nel Venerando Monasterio di S. Martino di Varese'

RISM B1721

14. Mangoni, Mass, Vespers, and Motets *a 8*, 1623

Messa, Salmi, Magnificat, Motetti, Falsibordoni, & Gloria patri, con le Letanie della B. Vergine a otto voci in due chori, l'uno puerile, & l'altro voci pari . . . da Gio. Antonio Mangoni . . . Alle Molt'Illustr. & M. Rever. Sorelle del Monastero di S. Pietro in Treviglio (Milan: Rolla, 1623)

Dedication to Aloisia Margarita Panigarola, 'con tutte le sacre Sorelle', in Gaspari, ii. 93

> *Missa Exultate Deo*
> *Deus ad adiuvandum*
> *Dixit Dominus* (Primi Toni)
> *Confitebor* (Secundi Toni)
> *Beatus vir*
> *Laudate pueri* (Quarti Toni)
> *Laudate Dominum omnes gentes*
> *Credidi* (Quinti Toni)
> *Laetatus sum* (Sexti Toni)
> *Nisi Dominus* (Septimi Toni)
> *Lauda Jerusalem* (Octavi Toni)
> *Falsibordoni à 8 & à 4* con Gloria
> *Magnificat* (Secundi Toni)
> *Magnificat*
> *Audivi vocem de Coelo*
> *Exultate Deo*
> *Vox dilecti*
> *O quam suavis est*
> Litany BVM

RISM M360

15. E. Trabattone, Masses and motets *a 4–6*, 1625

Messe, Motetti, Magnificat e Falsibordoni à 4. 5. e 6 . . . di Egidio Trabattone . . . (Milan: Rolla, 1625)

> *Dialogo à 5: Quae est ista* (Canto 1, cleffed C1; Canto 2 [C1]; Canto 3 [C1]; Quinto [C3]; Tenore [C4]), 'Alla Molto Reuerenda SOR PAOLA PRASSEDE GALLA Organista di Santa Christina in Milan'

RISM T1069

16. A. Cima, Motets *a 2–4*, book 2, 1627

Secondo Libro delli Concerti a due, tre e quattro voci di Andrea Cima . . . (Milan: Lomazzo, 1627)

> *Vocem Mariae audivit Elisabeth* (CC or TT [but parts cleffed C1 and C3]). Cantus part-book: 'All'Ill. & M. Reuer. Sor Anna Clemenza Tetoni; Gentilissima Cantatrice, nel Venerando Monasterio, di Santo

Bernardo'; Altus part-book: 'All'Illustr. & Molta Reuer. Sor
Giramma, Gentilissima Cantatrice nel Venerando Monasterio, di
Santo Bernardo'

In te Domine speravi (CC or TT) [in *partitura*: CCB si placet], 'All'Illust.
& M. Reuer. D. Angiola Maria Clerici, Gentilissima Cantatrice, nel
Venerando Monasterio di Santa Redegunda'

O Jesu mi dulcissime (in 'Tavola': *O Jesu Fili mi*): (CA or TA). Cantus part-
book: 'Alla Molto Illust. Signora Anna Arconata'; Altus part-book:
'All'Molt'Illust. & Molt' Reueren. Sor Paola Maria Arconata nel
Venerando Monasterio delle Vetere'

RISM C2226

17. Grancini, Motets *a 1–4*, book 3, 1628

*Concerti a una, due, trè & quattro voci . . . libro terzo. Di Michelangelo Grancini
. . .* (Milan: Lomazzo, 1628)

O anima sanctissima (AC or AT) 'Alla Molto Reuerenda Suor Clara
Virginia Preda Organista Gratiossima nel Monasterio di S. Orsola'

RISM G3400

18. Grancini, Motets *a 1–7*, op. 6, 1631

*Sacri fiori concertati à una, due, tre, quattro, cinque, sei & sette voci . . . opera sesta
di Michel'angelo Grancini . . .* (Milan: Rolla, 1631)

Adjuro vos, filiae Hierusalem (*a 7*: C primo [cleffed G2]; [C secondo]; A
primo [C2]; [A secondo]; Q [C3]; T [C3]; B [C4]), 'All'Illustri, &
Molto RR. Suor Aurelia Maria, & Suor Paola Benedetta Fissiraghi,
Organiste gratiosissime nel Monastero di S. Marta in Milano'

Canzona La Bariola (CATB), 'Alla Molt'Illust. & reuer. Sig. Suor
Antonia Maria Gallina Organista gentilissima, e Suonatrice di Leuto
in San Bernardino di Milano'

RISM G3401

Modern edition: *La Bariola*, Kendrick, 'Genres', 1043–52

19. E. Trabattone, Motets *a 1–4*, book 3, op. 5, 1632

*Il terzo libro de concerti a vna, due, tre e quattro voci. Di Egidio Trabattone . . .
opera quinta . . .* (Milan: Rolla, 1632)

In te Domine speravi (SSSS or TTTT), 'Alla Molto Reverenda Signora D.
ANTONIA FRANCESCA CARCANA Monaca nel Vener.
Monastero di S. Antonino in Varese'

RISM T1071

20. Reina, Mass and Vespers *a 8*, op. 1, 1648

Novelli Fiori Ecclesiastici concertati nell'organo all'uso moderno da Fra Sisto Reina . . . opera prima . . . (Milan: Camagno, 1648)

> Sacramentum Magnum Deum (I: CATB; II: CATB; org), 'A Suor Genevra Francesca Carcana in S. Maria di Cantù'

RISM R1012 and 1648³

21. Reina, Motets *a 1–5*, op. 3, 1651

Armonicae cantiones, una, binis, ternis, quaternis, et quinque vocibus concinendae . . . auctore Fr. Sixto Reina . . . opus tertium (Milan: Rolla, 1651)

> Obstupescite, redempti (C), 'Alla Molt'Illustre, & Reu. Signora, e Patrona singularissima, la Signora Suor Giouanna Antonia Gioseppa Cingarda Cantatrice gratiosissima nel Ven. Monastero di S. Gerolamo in Vimercato'

RISM R1013 + PL–Kj

22. Reina, Motets *a 2–5*, op. 4, 1653

Marsyae et Apollonis de musices principatu certantis . . . praeceptus à Fr. Sixto Reina . . . (Milan: Camagno, 1653)

> Cara vulnera Christi (C, 2Vl), 'All'Illustrissima Signora, e Patrona mia Collendiss. La Signora Donna Candida Aurelia Archinta nel Venerando Monastero di S. Ambrosio di Cantù'
> Surge filia Sion (CCB), 'Alla Molta Ill. et Rever. Signora Donna Candida Maria Campi, Organista gentilissima, e Cantatrice gratiosissima nel Venerando Monastero di S. Ambrosio in Cantù'

RISM R1014 + PL–Kj (T without title-page)

23. Reina, Vespers *a 2–5*, op. 5, 1653

Armonia Ecclesiastica a due, trè, quattro, e Cinque voci. Di Fra Sisto Reina . . . Consecrata All'Illustrissima, & Eccellentiss. Signora Principessa Angelica Luigia Mariana Gonzaga Monacha nel Nobilissimo Monastero di S. Paolo di Milano (Milan: Camagno, [1653])

Dedication: ILL.MA, ET ECC.MA SIGNORA PRINCIPESSA Orfeo nauigando il Mare, acciò dal canto delle Sirene li suoi Compagni non restassero incantati, cantò delli Dei le battaglie, e l'imprese: Onde con la soauità della sua voce oscurò in modo le cantanti Sirene, che sdegnate d'essere da quel Musico superate, gettarono in Mare le cetere. Christo, suauissimo Orfeo (Illustrissima, & Eccellentissima Signora) acciò dal canto del mondo lusinghero, e dal senso fraudelante non siano li huomini allettati, canta anch'egli del suo regno l'essere quando disse *regnum meum non est de hoc mundo*; onde con tal suauità tira à se l'animi di quelli; Si vede in V.S. Illustriss., & Eccellentiss., mentre alle voci di questo celeste Orfeo rendendosi con molto sua gloria, e christianissimo sentimento, per non restar incantata dalla fallacità di questo, fece il felice passaggio dal Stato Regio mondano, oue naquè, à quello oue si troua; Onde hò da credere, che non gli sia per essere, se non di contento il consacrare le presenti cantilene alle glorie del nome di V.S. Illustriss., & Eccellentiss.; non già per aggiongere con questo fatto freggio al cumolo delli altri suoi honori, mà perche da vn'altra armonia fù rapita al Cielo di cotesti chiostri. E quando il mio fallace giudicio peccasse, sperarei, che la melodia, che seco naturalmente porta la musica, regina gouernatrice, e mitigatrice al parere del diuin Filosofo, dell'interne passioni operarebbe in lei questa, quello oprò in Theodosio, Imperatore, qual stando vn giorno grandemente sdegnato, fù dalla soauità della musica affatto radolcito e placato. E se bene in queste cantilene, forse vi sentirà vn'armonia di piombo, nondimeno si toccherà l'oro infocato della mia osseruanza affetuosa, con la quale osseruo i suoi meriti; quindì ammirandoli, me gli rendo deuotissimo, e pieno di deuotione le faccio humilissima riuerenza, pregando Iddio la conserua. Milano li 12. Decembre 1653. Di V.S. Illustriss., & Eccellentiss. Humillissimo, & Deuotissimo Seruo. Fra Sisto Reina.

> *Domine ad adiuvandum a 5*
> *Domine ad adiuvandum a 2* (CA)
> *Dixit a 5*
> *Confitebor a 5*
> *Confitebor a 2* (CA)
> *Confitebor a 3* (CAB)
> *Beatus a 5*
> *Beatus a 4*
> *Laudate pueri a 5*
> *Laudate pueri a 3* (CAB)
> *Laudate Dominum omnes gentes a 5*
> *Magnificat a 5*
> *Letanie della BVM a 5*

RISM R1015

24. Cesati, Sacra melodia *a 2–4*, 1655

Sacra Melodia Divisa In Motetti per Ingressa, Messe et Salmi di N.S. e della B.V. A Due, Tre, e Quattro voci; con Lettanie. Opera prima. Di F. Gio. Battista Cesati Min. Con. Maestro di Capella nell'Insigne Basilica di S. Francesco di Milano. Consecrata All'Ill.ma Sig.ra Sor Corona Maria Madrucci Monaca Professa del Nobiliss.mo Monastero di S. Marta (Milan: Camagno, 1655)

Dedication: Ill.ma Signora sempre col.ma: Non hà la Virtù de Grandi cosi poca forza, che habbia bisogno dello splendore de gli Aui loro, per comparere quello, ch'ella è. Congionto con il valore, e con le dignità de gli Antenati, è vero ch'ella è vna gioia legata in oro: Mà delle gioie moltissime ve ne sono, che si redono à peso, & a prezzo solamente d'oro, perche sono più preziose e vagliono infinitamente più dell'oro, ve ne sono puoche; e queste puoche vanno per le mani, e passano sotto li ochi solamente d'Anime grandi, e di Teste Coronate. Picciola sarebbe la virtù di V.S. Illustriss., quando che all'oro delle porpore e de gli scettri, de i Cardinalati, e de i Principati hereditari di Casa Madrucci, ella non arrecasse à giosa di gioia veramente preziosa, altretanto di pregio, e di splendore, quanto ne riceue. Morte, benche paiano viue, sono le imagini de gli Heroi Madrucci; che adornano le loro, e le altrui Galeria: Mà V.S. Illustr. è vn Colosso viuo, & animato delle loro virtù, Mà più delle sue proprie. Benche rachiusa fra coteste sacre mura, sparge e diffonde per tutta questa Città, anzi per la Italia tutta cosi grande, è cosi soaue la fragranza di vna religiosa santità, che insino le maggiori Regine del Mondo, ha più d'vna volta rapito à vagheggiare cosi bella Gioia, a respirare cosi soaue odore, voglio dire a godere della dolce e santa conuersazione di V.S. Illustriss. Non è chi habbia sensi di pietà, che non desideri fare il medesimo, che non brami tributare al lembo di coteste sue religiose vesti, baci di riuerenza e di diuozione: Mà non possono affissarsi li pipistrelli al sole, ne farsi vulgari, ne anche alla sola vista di tutti gioie si preziose. Compariscono adonque alla presenza di V.S. Illustr. invece mia, questi miei foglij musicali, che recheranno all'orechie di lei pura, e pudica quella melodia, della quale ella tanto si diletta. Anima cosi perfettamente armonizata di virtù, che viuamente rappresenta l'armonia de' Cieli, so' non potrà fare a meno di non gradire vn Tributo, che tutto è armonioso; Mà quando ancor non fosse intieramente armonico ma in qualche parte dissonante, confido ad ogni modo che la gentilezza di V.S. Illust. lo gradirà, se non per diletto, per cortesia almeno. Di tanto riuerente la supplico benche. Di V.S. Illustriss. Milano 4. Settembre 1655. Humilissimo Seruitore. Fra Gio. Battista Cesati Maestro di Capella di S. Francesco

Ingressa *a3 Gaudeamus omnes in Domino* (CTB)
Messa Prima a 3 (CTB)
Ingressa a 3 e 4 de BVM Egredemini filiae Sion
Messa Seconda Concertata a 3 e 4 si placet
Messa Terza Breve a 4
Domine a 4 Concertato
Dixit Dominus sine Intonatione
Confitebor a 2 (CC or TT)
Beatus vir a 4
Laudate Pueri a 3 (CCB)
Laetatus sum a 4
Nisi Dominus a 3 (CCB)
Lauda Jerusalem a 4
Magnificat a 4 (TTCB)
Lettanie Breve della BV a 3–4

RISM *deest*; Aosta, Biblioteca Capitolare di Sant'Orso (A, T, Org)

25. Reina, Motets *a 1–4*, op. 6, 1656

Rose de concertati odori . . . da Fra Sisto Reina . . . Germoglio Sesto
(Milan: Camagno, 1656)

    Quaerens dilectum (CAB), 'A Sor Ottavia Francesca Caldera Monacha
      Professa & Organista in S. Maria delle Vergini della Viggiabbia in
      Milano'
    O anima nimis (CAB), 'A Donna Prassede Caterina Lodi, Monacha &
      Organista in S. Vittore in Meda'
RISM R1016

26. Cazzati, Cantatas *a 1*, op. 20, 1659

*Cantate morali e spirituali a voce sola di Mauritio Cazzati . . . Dedicate
all'Illustrissima Signora Donna Maria Domitilla Ceva, Monaca dell'Insigne
Monastero di S.ta Redegunda di Milano, opera vigesima* (Bologna: Benacci,
1659)

Dedication: ILLVSTRISSIMA SIGNORA SIGNORA, E PADRONA
COLL.MA L'osservanza, quale sempre hò professato verso la Casa di V.S.
Illustrissima m'haurebbe al sicuro fatto conoscere mancheuole dell'obligo
mio, quando in occasione così opportuna, quale è questa di porre alle
Stampe alcune Cantate Morali, e Spirituali, non hauessi fatto leggere in
fonte di queste il nome di V.S. Illustrissima, alla quale mi deuo confessare
obligato, si per essere state altre volte compatite le mie debolezze come
ancora aggradite da V.S. Illustrissima, sicuro che baldanzose si lascieranno
vedere, mentre saranno animate dalle di lei armoniche voci, e veranno
prottette da vna Signora, che vero essemplare della virtù, è lo stupore de
nostri tempi. Accetti per tanto V.S. Illustrissima ciò, che sù l'altare della mia
diuotione riuerentemente li consagro, mentre per rattificarmi di nuouo suo
diuotissimo seruo, non cesso di dichiararmi Di V.S. Illustrissima Diuotiss.
& obligatiss. Seruitore Mauritio Cazzati Bologna li 31. Ottobre 1659.

    La Verità sprezzata (C)
    Per il Giorno di Natale (C)
    Madrigale al Crocifisso (C)
    Peccator pentito (C)
    La Virtù Lacerata (C)
    Absalone (A)
    Peccator Penitente (A)
    Nel Maritirio di S. Stefano (A)
    S. Sebastiano condotto al Martirio (A)
    Per la Festa di S. Tomaso Apostolo (T)
    A S. Gio. dormiente nel seno del Redentore (T)

S. Gioseffo presente alla nascita di N.S. (B)
S. Gioseffo si duole d'hauer perduto il Figlio . . . (B)
Per il Natale di Nostro Signore (B)
Il Ricco Epulone (B)
Aria Morale (B)
Per la Festa de gl'Innocenti (B)
Mondo Fugace (B)
RISM C1609 (modern reprint: Bologna, 1969)

27. Casola, Motets *a 1*, op. 1, 1660

Motetti ecclesiastici a voce sola . . . di Francesco Casola, opera prima (Milan: Camagno, [1660])

    O solemnis solemnitas (C), 'All'Illustriss. Signora Maria Gioconda Figina Monica Virtuosissima nel Ven. Monastero di S. Apolinare'

RISM C1442 + PL–Kj [complete]

28. Caifabri (ed.), Motets *a 2–3*, 1665

Scelta de' motetti da cantarsi a due, e tre voci Composti in Musica da diversi eccellentissimi autori Romani Raccolta dal Molto Rev. Sig. D. Francesco Cavalitti . . . E dati alle Stampe da Gio. Battista Caifabri (Rome: Figl, 1665)

Dedication: Alla Molto Reu.da Madre, Signora e Padrona Coll.ma LA SIGNORA SVOR MARIA VITTORIA RESTA MONICA IN S. APOLLINARE DI MILANO Le continue gratie, che io receuo dalla benignità del Sig. Auocato suo fratello mi obligarebbero ha [*sic*] dedicare a Lui per tributo dell'ossequio mio le presenti Stampe, mà per essere la Musica Arte molto aliena dalla Professione Legale, m'è parso più proprio adattamento con l'istesso atto di gratitudine, e di riuerenza dedicarle a V.S. quale intendo quanto ami, e possegga questa Virtù, benche osseruandissima di vna santa ritiratezza monastica, e veramente esemplare, non curi mostrare al publico il pieno possesso, che' Ella ne tiene. Mentre dunque desidero che queste note (Opere de migliori Virtuosi di Roma) habbino applauso in cotesta Città di Milano per mezzo de Nome che portano in fronte di V.S. la supplico, ad anotare il mio nome nel Catalogo de' più humili serui suoi e della sua Casa, che io come tale sò a V.S. humilissimo inchiono. Di V.S. Molto Reuerenda Deuotissimo, & Humilissimo Seruitore Gio: Battista Caifabri.

    Graziani, *Quam pulchra es* (CC)
    Carissimi, *Salve amor* (CC)
    Stamegna, *O charitas* (CB)
    Corsi, *Domine* (CC)
    Pogliardi, *Jesu mi* (CB)
    Barnabei, *Ecce sacerdos* (CB)
    Benevoli, *Laudate Dominum* (CCA or TTB)

Foggia, *O felix* (CCT)
Graziani, *Justum deduxit* (CCT)
Carissimi, *Suscitavit Dominus* (ATB)
Corsi, *Exaudi Domine* (ATB)
Stamegna, *Bonum mihi* (ATB)
Vincenti, *Paravit in mensa* (CCB)

RISM 1665¹

29. Cazzati, Mass and Vespers *a 4*, op. 37, 1666

Messa, e Salmi a quattro voci con due Violini obligati, e quattro Parti di Ripieno al beneplacito, con altri Salmi à due, e tre voci, Dedicate all'Illustrissima Signora D. Maria Domitilla Ceva Monaca nel Nobilissimo, & Insegno Monastero di Santa Redegunda di Milano. Opera XXXVII. Di Mauritio Cazzati . . . (Bologna: Silvani, 1666)

Dedication: ILLVSTRISSIMA SIGNORA SIGNORA E PADRONA COLLENDISSIMA Le qualità riguardevoli, che sotto il Cielo della virtù la fanno risplendere per vno de gli Astri più luminosi, che non solo alla sua patria porga splendori, mà etiandio alle megliori Città dell'Europa, fanno ch'io torni di nuouo sù l'altare della deuotione à porgerle voti, e sacrificare questo mio, ben che debole parto dell'intelletto, in segno del molto, e gran desiderio, che tengo di farmi conoscere ammiratore del merito suo. Sò, che quanto ardisco dedicarle è piccolo tributo alla infinità del suo merito, ma il rammentarmi, che l'Oceano non isdegna pochi tributi d'acque anche da Ruscelli più piccioli, m'affida del di lei aggradimento, e tanto più quanto consagro Salmi Musicali, a chi Maestra Erudita dell'Armonie non solo le essercita nelle Musiche note, mà ancora appertamente le mostra ne suoi regolatissimi costumi; Accetti per tanto con fronte serena ciò, che dalla mia deuotione le viene affettuosamente offerito, mentre gloriandomi, che in fronte di quest'Opera si legga il glorioso suo Nome, mi soscriuo Bologna li 29. Marzo 1666 Di V.S. Illustrissima Devotis.mo & Oblig.mo Ser.re Mauritio Cazzati

> *Messa concertata a 4* (Kyrie, Gloria, Credo)
> *Domine ad adiuvandum a 2* (AT)
> *Dixit a 4* (CATB, 2 Vl, ripieno)
> *Confitebor a 3* (CTB)
> *Beatus vir a 4* (CATB, 2 Vl, rip)
> *Laudate pueri a 3* (CAB, 2 Vl)
> *Laudate Dominum* (CATB, 2 Vl, rip)
> *Laetatus a 4 da Capella* (CATB, 2 Vl, rip)
> *Nisi dominus a 3* (ATB)
> *Lauda Jerusalem a 4* (CATB, 2 Vl, rip)
> *Magnificat a 4* (CATB, 2 Vl, rip)

RISM C1635

30. Cazzati, Motets *a 1*, book 5, op. 39, 1666

Il Quinto Libro de motetti a voce sola . . . opera XXXIX. Di Mauritio Cazzati . . . (Bologna: Silvani, 1666)

> Qui bella geritis (C or T), 'All'Illustrissima Signora Donna Maria Domitilla Ceua, Monaca Virtuosissima in Sancta Redegunda di Milano'

RISM C1637 (modern reprint: A. Schnoebelen (ed.), *Solo Motets from the 17th Century*, vi, *Bologna II* (New York, 1988))

31. Bagatti, Motets *a 2–4*, book 3, op. 4, 1667

Il Terzo Libro de Concerti Ecclesiastici a due, trè, e quattro voci . . . di Francesco Bagatti . . . Consacrata All'Illustris. Signora Patrona mia Collendiss. La Sig.ra D. Giovanna Maria Visconti Monacha Professa Benedetina nel Nobilissimo Monastero di Santa Maria Valle di Milano (Milan: Camagno, [1667])

Dedication: ILL.MA SIG.RA, E PATRONA MIA COLL.MA: Pongo sotto la protettione di V.S. Ill.ma le musiche di questa mia opera, e le presento à lei per far publica al Mondo la riverentissima mia osseruanza, e la stima, che faccio del suo gran merito, il quale tanto più riluce di alto grado, quanto che è regolato da vn fino, & eccellente intendimento nel sonare l'organo, nella singolarità del cantare, nella particolar maestria del sonare il Violino, & vguale habilità, e merauiglia nel liutto, oltre il considerabile della propria sua origine che in lei risplende si come lei stessa risplende nell'origine medesima, che è de Duchi, e Principi, e di vna nobiltà successiuamente continuata, e conseruata sempre con la prudenza, & attentione, che fù parte propria frà le virtù de suoi grandi, & Antenati, e presentanei parenti, non tralasciando io però qui di commemorare di lei bontà di vita religiosa, che la constatuisce osseruata, e riuerita da tutti; E se milita nel caso l'argomento di che il piacere, & il diletto delle armonie siano preludij di predestinazione ne risulta la consequenza, che V.S. Ill.ma goda parte de felicità in questo Mondo con il probabile acquisto della perfetta nell'altro. Hò ardito di appoggiare su gl'indubitati fondamenti della benignità di V.S. Ill.ma la debolezza delle presenti mie note, affine il credito, & i titoli del suo nome siano per'esser mottiuo di diffesa per farle stimare quelle che in fatti non sono, il che ben intenderò hauer conseguito quando ella con gl'atti, e le dispositioni del suo compatimento, & humanità si degni da auualorarle con l'approuatione, aggradendo il poco per il molto che ambirei di poter renderle in pruoua della fedele, & obligatissima seruitù, e deuotione, che col concorso di tutte le parti dello Spirito, e dell'animo mio; & in qualità di sommo ossequio ho sempre professato a Lei, & all'Illustr.ma sua Casa; La supplico humilmente à riceuere con tutto credito la verità di questi sensi, che escono dall'intimo del core; E posto io in questi immutabili conditioni mi confermo. Di V.S. Illustriss. Milano il 16. Luglio M DCLXVII. Humiliss. & Deuotiss. Seruit. *Francesco Bagatti.*

Ad Caeli Convivium (C, 2 Vl)
Vos Campi Caelestes (C, 2 Vl)
Ad te levavi oculos (CC)
Triumphet in altissimis (CC)
Quid sollicita es anima mea (CA)
Deliciae dilectus (CA)
Salve anima (dialogue) (CA)
O quam suave est (CB)
O quam dulcis (ATB)
O pater pauperum (ATB)
Suspina afflicta (CAB)
Quando Mater saluatoris (ATB)
Salve Regina (ATB)
Accurite populi (CAB)
Quam clamo lumine (CAB)
Laeti gaudentes (CATB)
Festinent hilares (CATB)
Ad cantus mortales (CATB)
Messa Concertante (CATB)

RISM B633

32. San Romano, Motets *a 2–4*, 1668

Cigno Sacro Motetti a piu voci di Carlo Giuseppe Sanromano . . . (Milan: Vigone, 1668)

> *Salve Sponsa Creatoris* (CA or TA), 'All'Illustrissima Sign. la Signora D. Anna Cattarina Archinti Monaca nell'Annonciata di Milano. Mia Signora, e Patrona Colendiss.'

RISM S882

33. Legrenzi, Motets *a 1*, book 1, op. 10, 1670

Acclamationi divote a voce sola di Giovanni Legrenzi Consacrati all'impareggiabil Merito dell'Illustrissima Signora D. Antonia Francesca Clerici Monaca nel Monastero di Santa Redegonda in Milano, Libro Primo, Opera X (Bologna: Monti, 1670)

Dedication: ILLVSTRISSIMA SIGNORA Sig. Patrona Colendisssima. Ardisco di presentare alla virtù luminosa di V.S. Illustriss. queste mie oscurissime Note; fatto nuouo Prometeo nell'ardire, ma confidato nell'esito, di sortire miglior fortuna. Rubbò egli dal Sole la vita al suo parto, e trà'l giaccio, e le fiamme paga l'errore della rapina. Io accosto questi miei parti al Sole delle sue gratie, e da gl'influssi benignisssimi delle di lei impareggiabili doti, spero restino animati, per conseguirne dall'audacia vna pienissima lode. Se V.S. Illustriss. accolgerà i miei voti, che con ossequio le porgo, vedrò tesaurizare le mie ombre splendori di gloria, e risuonare nelle dissonanze mie l'armonie più sonore del Cielo; mentre essa veramente è vn Cielo di gratie, di virtù, e di perfettioni; e mi consacro Bologna li 26. Agosto 1670. *Humiliss. e Deuotiss. Ser. Giouanni Legrenzi.*

Angelorum ad conuiuia (S)	Per il Santissimo
Congratulamini mihi (S)	Per la Beata Vergine
Durum cor (S)	Per ogni tempo
Anima mea (S)	Per ogni tempo
En gentes (S)	Per un Santo
Gaude nunc gaude (S)	Per un Santo
Panis candidissime (A)	Per il Santissimo
Laudibus concino (A)	Per la Beata Vergine
En homo (T)	Per ogni tempo
Plaudite vocibus (T)	Per un Santo
Suspiro Domine (Bar)	Per ogni tempo
Festiui Martires (B)	Per una Santa

RISM L1624 (modern reprint: Bologna, 1980)

34. San Romano, Motets *a 1*, book 1, op. 2, 1670

Il primo libro de motetti a voce sola . . . opera II. Di Carlo Giuseppe San Romano . . . (Milan: Vigone, 1670)

Pangamus hymnum (C or T), 'All'Illustrissima Sig. La. Sig. D. Antonia Mariana de Capitani Monaca in S. Vittore di Meda'

RISM S883

35. Bagatti, Motets, Mass, and Vespers *a 8*, op. 5, 1672

Motetti, Messa e Salmi brevi, e Pieni . . . di Francesco Bagatti . . . Opera Quinta. Dedicata all'Illustriss. Signora e Padrona Colendiss. la Signora Regina Fedele Melzi Monaca professa, celebre Organista, e Cantatrice nel nobilissimo Monastero di S. Bernardino di Milan (Milan: Camagno, 1672)

Dedication: ILL.MA SIG.RA, E PADRONA COL.MA La Musica tanto stimata dagli antichi, e pratticata al parere diuino appresso Giobbe sino dalle sfere celesti (*cap.* 38) *concentum Caelis quis dormire faciet?*, viene tributata dalla mia riuerenza à V.S. Illustrissima come ad vna Sirena innocente, che con le musiche note sà solleuare i cuori à contemplare la luce d'Iddio, non à rubargliela con illetarghirli in sonno fatale. Ed era il douere, che à V.S. Ill.ma consagrassi questo tributo, quando portando ella nelle insegne del suo nobilissimo Casato l'Aquile, mostraua, che lei era vna Musa nouella cantatrice di Pindo appresso Febo, ouero, che Apolline scordatosi de i suoi Cigni canori furato auesse l'augello fulminatore à Gioue. Certo è, che si come ella si porta più sù i vanni della fama, che sù le piume dell'Aquila Melzia al Cielo con il grido delle sue virtù, e della scienza nell'arte

Musicale: così soruola le bassezze terrene con l'abito religioso, inoltratasi al corteggio dell'impiagato Serafino d'Assissi. Dal seguire quest'Angelo terreno forsi ha imparato V.S. Ill.ma à stupore di tutti i Mastri la musica, essendone già Maestra non solo alle sue Suore, mà ancora alla Patria: perche godono sommamente gli Angeli di quest'arte, e ne serono vn soauissimo mottetto al nascere di Cristo, in cui spiccauano marauigliosamente tutti gli artificij musicali, fuorche i sospiri. Dunque à V.S. Ill.ma deuo queste mie fatiche; e se bene và gran disparità frà gli Vsignuoli, e le Cicale, tuttauia non isdegna l'aria anche il canto importuno di queste, perche le vede, e musiche insieme, e suonatrici. Tali appunto sono i miei componimenti, cioè dissimiglianti dal canto delle Filomele; ma per essere sotto al patrozinio d'vna REGINA spero, che acquisteranno prezzo grande dal di lei nome; non potendo io per altro donare cosa di molto valore à chi per la pouertà seguace di Francesco calpestò tutte le ricchezze del Mondo. Si degni V.S. Ill.ma aggradirne l'ossequio, mentre mi sottoscriuo. Di V.S. Ill.ma Milano XXVIII. Nouembre MDCLXXII. Vmiliss., & Deuotiss. Seruitore. *Francesco Bagatti.*

Ad laeta gaudia [all *a 8*]
Laetamur omnes   Motetto per ogni tempo
Messa breve
Domine ad adiuvandum
Dixit Dominus
Confitebor
Beatus vir
Laudate pueri
Laudate Dominum
In exitu
Laetatus sum
Nisi Dominus
Lauda Hierusalem
Credidi
In convertendo
Domine probasti me
De profundis
Memento Domine David
Beati omnes
Confitebor . . . Angelorum
Magnificat I
Magnificat II
Letanie BVM

RISM B634

36. Leonarda, Mass and Vespers *a 2–4*, op. 3, 1674

Messa, e Salmi concertati, & à Capella con Istromenti ad libitum. Di Isabella Leonarda . . . opera quarta . . . (Milan: Camagno, [1674])

 Laetatus sum à 4. voci [CATB; Tenor part-book: 'Laetatus à 3, Canto, Alto e Tenore'], 'Alla Molt'Illustre, & M. Reuerenda Signora Osseruandissima la Signora Donna Gioconda Rosanna Bossi Contralta Eccell. nel Ven. Monastero di Santa Margarita in Milano' [dedication in organ part-book only]

RISM I93

37. Cossoni, Motets *a 2–3*, op. 1, 1678 (reprint)

Il Primo Libro de Motetti a due, e tre voci . . . di Carlo Donato Cossoni . . . Opera Prima, e seconda impressione. All'Illustrissima Signora Sig.ra Maria Vittoria Terzaga Monaca professa nel Monastero del Capuccio di Milano (Milan: Beltramino, 1678)

(first publ. Bologna, 1665).

Dedication: Ill.ma Signora Sig.ra et Padrona Coll.ma Gemono di nouo sotto il torchio le mie fiacchezze; non mai satio di vedermi lacerato dal rabbioso dente di scioperata Critica. Ne per questo mi pentirò già mai di hauer consacrato alla luce questo parto del mio debole ingegno, mentre nell'istesso punto unito con gli splendori del manto di V.S. Illustrissima men chiari compariranno gli miei vergognosi rossori. Perche gli ossequiosi miei accenti gli rimbobassero dall'vdito al cuore acciò gli riuscissero più graditi procurai di Formarli armoniosi; Ne rio Timore il cuore mi turba, che non gli debbono riuscir cari, sapendo quanto l'immensa di lei benignità sij auezza Compattirmi. Sò che ad vn tanto merito se gli richiedono le voci delle Sirene, gli accenti de Cigni, essendo puoco tributo la Melodia di Filomela, & il lamento di Progne, douendosi ad vna gran Dama l'armonia delle Muse, con gli concerti d'Appollo; Mà diuoto seno, Fatto ardito da gli fomenti d'imparigiabil cortesia, non teme dedicarli vn aborto di faticoso sudore. Sotto il Vessillo donque di quella Croce di cui ella tanto si preggia, io n'anderò vittorioso, Sapendo come i miei parti resteranno cheti dai Fulmini della maledicenza. Alla più Canora Musa di questo Felice Parnaso, offerisco la balbezza de miei concerti; Accetti dunque quel puoco, che sà contribuire vna infinita volontà, che mi astringe à perpetua diuotione, mentre con tutta riuerenza immortalmente mi confermo Di V. S. Illustriss. Milano li 30. Marzo 1678. Vmiliss. ser. obligatiss. CARLO DONATO COSSONI.

 O suavis Animantum (SS)
 O superi: Dialogo (SS)
 Alas expandice (CA)
 Funda voces (CB)

    Musa voces (CB)
    Putruerunt: Dialogo (CB)
    O quae monstra: Dialogo (TB)
    Dum clamo (ATB)
    Motior misera (CCB)
    O Maria (ATB)
    O Amor (ATB)
    Quid tibi reddemus: Dialogo de Tobia (CAB)
    Ad lacrimas: Dialogo (CCB)
    Litany BVM (CAB)
RISM C4200

38. Vigoni (ed.), Motets *a 1*, 1679
*Nuova Raccolta de Motetti sacri a voce sola di diversi eccellenti autori. Dati in luce
da Carlo Federico Vigoni . . .* (Milan: Vigone, 1679)
    Angelo Zanetti: *Si Virgo pro nobis* (C or T), 'Al Merito della Molt'Illustre
        Sig.ra La Sig.ra Suor Costanza Francesca Brasca Monaca in S.
        Marcellina di Milano'
    Gerolamo Zanetti: *Palmae aeternae* (C or T), 'All'Illustriss.ma Sig.ra La
        Sig. Donna Daria Violante Piola, Monaca nel Venerando Monastero
        di S. Vlderico detto il Bocchetto, di Milano'
    Paolo Magni: *Ad pugnas, o furie* (C or T), 'Al Cigno piu canoro, per le
        di cui voci s'imparadisa il Mondo, Breue Tributo D'armonioso
        Concerto. Và Consacrando l'ossequioso Autore, All'hor che la Sirena
        de nostri tempi L'ILLVSTRISS. SIG. DONNA ANTONIA
        FRANCESCA CLERICI Monaca Professa in S. Redegonda Si fà
        degna d'ogni più dolce Melodia di Parnasso'
    Giovanni Appiano: *Quid me tentatis, inferi?* (A), 'Alla Virtu et merito
        dell'Illustriss. Sig. Donna Antonia Mariana de Capitani Monaca in S.
        Vitore di Meda'
RISM 1679[1] (reprint of 1681 not considered here)

APPENDIX D: THE WORKS OF SESSA, RUSCA, COZZOLANI, CALEGARI, AND BADALLA[1]

1. [within a frame] / CANORO PIANTO / DI MARIA VERGINE / SOPRA LA FACCIA / DI CHRISTO ESTINTO / Poesia / DEL REVER.MO P. ABBATE GRILLO / RACCOLTA / PER D. ANGELICO PATTO / Academico Giustiniano. / ET POSTA IN MVSICA / DA DIVERSI AVTTORI / Con vn Dialogo, & Madregale Tramutati / da l'Istesso. / *A Vna Voce da cantar nel Chitarone o altri Istromenti simili.* / Nouamente Stampati. / [woodcut of Christ's face] / IN VENE-TIA. / Aere Bartholomei Magni. / M DC XIII.

Di D. Claudia Sessa:
Occhi io vissi di voi [C; on Christ's eyes]
Vattene pur lasciva orechia humana [C; on Christ's ears]

RISM 1613[3]

Editions: *Vattene pur*, in Kendrick, 'Genres', 1031–3; ed. C. Smith, in Glickman and Schleifer (eds.), *Women Composers*, i

2. Sacri Concerti a una, due, tre, quattro e cinque voci. Con salmi e Canzoni Francesi [*etc.*]. Nuovamente dati in luce con la partitura per l'Organo da Suor Claudia Francesca Rusca Monaca nel Monastero di Santa Caterina, a Brera. All'Ill.mo e R.mo Sign. il Signor Cardinale Federico Borromeo Arcivescovo di Milano. In Milano, appresso Giorgio Rolla. 1630.

This edition was held at the Ambrosiana under the call-number X.IX.66 and was apparently destroyed in 1943. But nine motets and two canzonas exist in vocal and instrumental orchestrations by G. F. Ghedini (1892–1965); the reconstructed original versions are forthcoming, ed. M. J. Wasmer and R. L. Kendrick.

Original part-books: ?CATB5, Org

---

[1] All works include basso continuo unless noted.

1. *Salve, regina caelorum* (C or T) (Marian, metamusical)
2. *Consolamini, popule meus* (probably C or T) (Christmas)
3. *Exultate caeli* (C) (Easter)
4. *Tu filia Dei* (C) (Catherine of Alexandria; 25 November)
5. *Veni sponsa Christi* (C or T) (Catherine)
6. *Jesu, dulcis amor meus* (CC) (Christological)
probably missing: other concerti *a 2*
7. *Gaudete gaudio magno* (*a 3*; 2 Canti, vln or cornetto) (Several Martyrs)
probably missing: other concerti *a 3–4*
Missing: *Psalmi (a 4)*: Pss. 109/110/111/112/113?
8. *Omnes gentes* (*a 8*)
9. *Magnificat* (*a 8*)
Missing: *Falsobordoni a 8*; *Gloria Patri a 8*
Canzoni francesi *a 4* (probably complete)
10. *Canzona prima La Borromea*
11. *Canzona seconda*

3. *Primavera de fiori musicali concertati nell'organo a 1, 2, 3 e 4 voci . . .*, Milan 1640 [by Cozzolani]

The Tenor part-book of this work is listed in *Zur Feier des Wohltätenfestes im Berliner Gymnasium zum grauen Kloster* (Berlin, 1856), 7, as among the Gymnasium's holdings; no trace of this or any other copy is known.

4. [part-name] / CONCERTI SACRI / A VNA, DVE, TRE, ET QVATTRO VOCI / Con Vna Messa à Quattro / DI DONNA / CHIARA MARGARITA COZZOLANI / Monaca di Santa Radegunda di Milano, / DEDICATI / AL SERENISSIMO PRENCIPE / MATHIAS / DI TOSCANA / OPERA SECONDA. / [Medici shield] / IN VENETIA [signature letter] / [line] / Appresso Alessandro Vincenti. MDCXXXXII.

Octavo part-books: Canto, Alto, Tenore, Basso, Organo

Dedication: SERENISSIMO PRENCIPE FV costume tall'hora frà gli antichi di consagrare in caratteri d'oro alla Maestà di Gioue quei versi, che nel teatro cantati piaciuti fossero à gli ascoltanti. La gratia, che V.A.S. mi fece già di solleuare questi miei di Musica componimenti dal basso natiuo all'alto de' suoi encomij, quando si degnò con orecchio cortese dar à quegli ricetto fuggitiui nelle mie voci, non mi lascia cercare altro Nume per consagrarglieli, che quello della sua protettione. I caratteri non son già d'oro, ma più che d'oro è il preggio, che lor verrà communicato dall'inestimabil virtù di simil patrocinio. Le offero note chiare, & oscure, ma tutte però fanno chiaro testimonio al Mondo della mia diuota osseruanza, e quanto più sono oscure, corrono più veloci a rendersele tributarie, & schiarirsi insieme allo splendor del suo nome. Sarà questo picciol dono Musicale incontrato dal Choro delle sue molte virtù, che col loro concento, & harmonia si fanno sentire, & ammirare da tutto il Mondo. Quì humilmente m'inchino à V.A.S. pregandole dal Cielo le prosperità douute à suoi meriti, & desideratele da me, che professo viuere eternamente Di V.A. Serenissima Dal Monasterio di S. Radegonda di Milano li 25. Febraro 1642. Diuotissima, & Humilissima Serua D. Chiara Margarita Cozzolani.

a 1:

O quam bonum ò quam iocundum C (Eucharistic)
    free (not Ps. 132)
Ecce annuntio vobis C (Christmas)
    paraphrase of Luke 2: 10–14
Concinant linguae A (Marian praise)
    unknown
    Concordances: F-Pn Vm.¹.1306, voice pb pp. 92–6 and bc pb pp.
    55–6, 'Alto Solo del Sgr Charissimi' (in voice pb only)
O Maria, tu dulcis, tu pia A (Marian intercession)
    loose paraphrase of *Salve regina*

a 2:

Surgamus omnes CC (Marian feast)
    unknown
Bone Jesu fons amoris CC (Christological)
    unknown
Colligite pueri flores CC or TT (Corpus Christi)
    unknown
O dulcis Jesu CC or TT (Christological)
    unknown
Ave Mater dilectissima. Dialogo CA (Easter/Consolation of Mary)
    unknown
Regina caeli AA
    Marian Office antiphon
Salve o Regina AT
    Marian Office antiphon
O mi Domine. Dialogo AT (Anima/Angele penance dialogue)
    unknown
Alma redemptoris mater CB
    Marian Office antiphon
Obstupescite gentes AB
    free; last section sets strophe 1 of *Lauda Sion salvatorem* (Eucharistic)

a 3:

O gloriosa Domina CCB (Annunciation)
    Marian Office hymn, ll. 1–2 as frame for 'Ave Maria', Luke 1: 28 ff.
O quam suavis est Domine ATB (Corpus Christi)
    Magnificat Antiphon, Vespers of Corpus Christi plus free text

Ave Regina Caelorum ATB
Marian Office antiphon

a 4:

Psallite superi. Dialogo CCAA (Assumption)
free frame of Cant. 6: 9 ff. ('Quae est ista?')
Regna terrae CCAB (general; sanctoral?)
Ps. 67: 33–6
Quid miseri? Dialogo CATB (Marian intercession)
unknown; cf. 1619 Grandi setting
Messa (no Benedictus) CATB

RISM C4360

Modern editions: *O dulcis Jesu, Ave mater dilectissima*, and *Ave regina caelorum* in Kendrick, 'Genres' 1053–79, 1089–99; first also in *Women Composers: An Historical Anthology*, ii

5. SCHERZI DI / SACRA / MELODIA / A VOCE SOLA / di Donna / CHIARA MARGARITA COZZOLANI / Monaca in Santa Radegonda di Milano. / DEDICATI / AL REVERENDISSIMO PADRE / DON / CLAVDIO BENEDETTI / DI VERONA / Presidente Generale della Congregatione Cassinense / OPERA TERZA. Con Priuilegio. / [shield] / IN VENETIA Appresso Alessandro Vincenti. 1648

(parte per cantare, [partitura])

Dedication: MOLTO ILL.RE E REVER.MO PADRE MIO COLENDISSIMO. Apena V.P. Reuerendissima si degnò accettare la Presidenza di Nostra Religione, carico ben' douuto à suoi gran' meriti, che tosto per tutto lo sparse con' mille plausi la fama. Ad auuiso si giocondo fiorí vn'allegrezza indicibile ne' cuori di tutti; la onde, per darle anc'io qualche saggio del giubilo, che mi brilla nel petto, hò stimato conueneuole inuiar'alcuni SCHERZI DI SACRA MELODIA A V.P. REVERENDIS-SIMA, come quella, che partialissima dell'Arte, colle rare, e ben concertate qualità dell'animo suo forma sempre all'orecchie del mondo giocondissima armonia. Degni dunque con quella medesima gentilezza, colla quale, ambito Presidente di nostra Religione, reggerà, qual'Orfeo, i' Chori de' nostri cuori, accoglier' parimente questa indegna Operetta, che spera farsi illustre col'ombra de' suoi Splendori, e famosa colla sua fama. E mentre le dedico nella seria Armonia vn riuerente ossequio, ne' trilli vn cuor' bril-lante à suoi cenni, ne' passaggi speditezza nel seruirla, ne gl'intrecci cateni d'oblighi eterni, e nelle molte cadenze mille humilissimi inchini, le priego dal Cielo ogni bramata felicità. à di Primo Settembre. 1648. Di V.P. Molto Illustre, e Reuerendissima Diuotissima, & Humilissima serua D. Chiara Margherita Cozzolani

Contents (all C; all texts non-liturgical and free)

Alleluia, cantemus exultemus (Resurrection)
O Jesu meus amor, mea vita (Christological)
Venite qui esuritis (Eucharistic)
Venite gentes, properate populi (Eucharistic/Corpus Christi)
Venite ad me omnes (Christological/Passion)
O quam tristis est anima mea (Eva/Ave; Eve–Mary)
Ave Maria, Mater Dei (Marian)
Amate ò populi Mariam (Marian)
Succurre, o Diva clemens (Marian intercessory)
Quis mihi det calicem bibere? (Christological meditation)
Venite populi, accurrite gentes (Female saint)
O praeclara dies (Christmas)

RISM C4361

Note: the continuo part to *Venite gentes* existed in the former Königsberg University Library in the manuscript miscellany Crone 13695.[2]

6. [within a frame] / [red:] COROLLARIUM / Geistlicher Collectaneorum / [black:] beruhmter Authorum, so zu denen biszhero / unterschiedenen publicirten vier Theilen ge-/horig und versprochen; / [red:] Nunmehr sampt beygefugten Erraten / [black:] dieselben zu recti-ficieren, gewahret / Von / [red:] AMBROSIO PROFIO, Or-/[black:]gan bey der Kirchen zu S. Elisabeth / in Breslaw. / [part-name] / [line] / Leipzig / [red:] Gedruckt und verlegt durch Timotheum Ritzsch / [black:] Anno M DC XLIX

O dulcis Jesu (from op. 2; CC or TT)   Cozzolani

RISM 1649⁶

7. [part-name] / [red:] SALMI / [black:] A OTTO VOCI / [red:] CON-CERTATI / [black] ET DVE MAGNIFICAT A OTTO / Con vn Laudate Pueri A 4. Voci, & doi Violini, & vn Laudate Dominum / omnes gentes A Voce Sola, & doi Violini, / [red:] MOTETTI, ET DIALOGHI / [black:] A Due, Tre, Quattro, e Cinque voci, / [red:] DI DONNA CHIARA MARGARITA / COZZOLANI. / [black:] Opera Terza. / DEDICATI / [red:] ALL'ILL[black:]MO. [red:] e REVER[black:]MO. / SIG.R PATRONE COL.MO / [red]: MONSIGNOR BADOARO / VESCOVO DI CREMA. / [black:] CON PRIVILEGIO. / [printer's mark] / [red:] IN VENETIA / [black: line] / Appresso Alessandro Vincenti [red:] M.DC.L

[2] As in J. Müller, *Die musikalischen Schätze der Königlichen und Universitätsbibliothek zu Königsberg in Preußen* (Bonn, 1870; repr. 1971), 19. This manuscript does not figure among the holdings of the Königsberg library now in Vilnius, Lithuania; my thanks to Dr. J. Marcinkevicius of the Academy Library (letter of 17 Mar. 1992) and Dr. E. Marcenene of the National Library (letter of 18 Mar. 1992) for their confirmation of this.

NB. Red ink in C1 part-book only

Octavo part-books: I: CATB; II: CATB; Org

Dedication: ILLVSTRISSIMO E REVERENDISSIMO SIGNORE. Sogliono gl'amanti Pastori, mentre dan pascolo alle loro amate Greggie, ricrearle insieme con armonia di suoni, e melodia di Canti. La singolar vigilanza, ardentissimo amore, e benignissima gentilezza di V. S. Illustrissima verso la sua Nobile Greggia, è palese al Mondo non meno del Sole. Onde e per secondar il genio commune degl'ottimi Pastori, e per compir in parte alla gran somma degl'oblighi che tengo alla gentilissima cortesia di V. S. Illustrissima verso di me nel hauer piu volte fauorite, e commendate le mie rozze cantilene: hò voluto comporre, e dedicar al suo gusto, e merito non ordinario la presente armonia. Le parole sono Mottetti diuini già cantati dal Musico Coronato d'Israele al dolce suono di sua Cetra Reale. La melodia, come mio parto, hà non poco del rustico, e boscareccio: acciò in questa parte habbia del pastorale, e perciò proportionata alla metafora; & in quella del Nobile, e Signorile, e però confaceuole alle qualità riguardeuoli di V. S. Illustrissima, e sua Greggia. Tronco il discorso, per non impedir con esso la degna Musica de suoi affari. Solo la Supplico, voglia gradire questo vile, e rozzo tributo di mia seruitù, e con esso vn ampio cuore pieno d'ardentissimi desiderij tutti già concertati a gl'ossequij, & alle glorie di V. S. Illustrissima, a cui mentre prego dal Cielo il fior d'ogni bramata felicità, profondamente m'inchino. di Venetia, à di 24. Marzo 1650. Di V. S. Illustrissima, e Reuerendissima Deuotissima, & Obligatissima Serua D. Chiara Margarita Cozzolani.

Deus in adiutorium (I: CATB; II: CATB)
Office versicle and response
Dixit Dominus
Ps. 109 (in Cassinese liturgy used for Sunday, male and female cursus Vespers)
Confitebor tibi Domine (I: CATB; II: CATB)
Ps. 110 (Sunday and male cursus)
Beatus vir. In forma di Dialogo (I: CATB; II: CATB)
Ps. 111 (Sunday and male cursus)
Laudate pueri (I) (I: CATB; II: CATB)
Ps. 112 (Sunday, male and female cursus)
Laetatus sum (I: CATB; II: CATB)
Ps. 121 (female cursus)
Nisi Dominus (I: CATB; II: CATB)
Ps. 126 (female cursus)
Magnificat (I) (I: CATB; II: CATB)
Magnificat (II) (I: CATB; II: CATB)
Laudate pueri (II) (TT,CC,2Vl)
Laudate Dominum omnes gentes (C,2Vl)

Ps. 116
O quam bonus es (CC)
> free (cf. Porta setting, 1648); Double Intercession; salvation from Christ's wounds and Mary's breasts

Venimus in altitudinem maris (CC)
> unknown; Marian reworking of Matt. 8: 23 ff. (miracle of Jesus calming the sea)

Quis audivit unquam tale? (CCB)
> unknown; Nativity/Epiphany

Venite sodales (ATB)
> Free material and Ecclus. 31: 8–9, the latter employed in Benedictine Vespers for the Chapter of a Confessor not a Martyr; general sanctoral

Gloria in Altissimis (CCAT)
> 'Dialogo fra gli Angeli, e i Pastori, nella Natività di Nostro Signore'; free paraphrase of Luke 2: 10 ff.; Christmas dialogue

Maria Magdalene (CAAT)
> 'Dialogo fra la Maddalena, e gli Angeli, nella Resurretione di N.S.'; free reworking of John 20: 11 ff. with additions from Luke 24: 5 and Cant. 5: 8, 5: 9 ff. with new text

Tu dulcis, ò bone Jesu (AATT)
> unknown; Double Intercession: Jesus and Mary

O Caeli cives. Dialogo (CCCTT)
> free; St Catherine [of Alexandria] dialogue

RISM C4362

Modern editions: *Gloria in altissimis* in Noske, *Saints and Sinners*; *Confitebor*, *Maria Magdalene*, and *O quam bonus* in Kendrick, 'Genres' 1100–1200, 1216–39; *O caeli cives*, ed. Kendrick, in *Women Composers*, ii

8. Cozzolani: Aria 'No, no no che mare'
Listed by Eitner in the library of the Berliner Singakademie, lost.

9. Cornelia (religious name Maria Caterina) Calegari: *Motetti a voce sola* (Bergamo, 1659)
This work is reported by Calvi, *Scena*, after p. 61

10. MOTETTI A VOCE SOLA / *Di D. Rosa Giacinta Badalla Monaca di Santa Redegonda, in Milano.* / DEDICATI / *All'Illustrissimo, & Eccellentissimo Signor* / CARLO VICENZO GIOVANELLI / NOBILE VENETO. / Baron, e Conte di Teleuana, Signore della Pietra di Castel S. Pietro, Caldar, e / Laimburgh, Conte di Moregno, e Carpeneda, &c. / [crest] / [line] / IN VENETIA. APPRESSO Gioseppe Sala. 1684.
Score

[dedication dated 10 July 1684 from S. Radegonda]

[preface to the reader:] AL BENIGNO LETTORE. Dio sà, che incontro sono per hauere, al primo suo comparire alla luce questi miei Componimenti? chi sà, che doppo le strida del Torchio, che han sentito stampandosi, non prouino anco quelle delle male lingue publicandosi? chi sà, che hauendo io creduto d'insinuar ad altri vagezza di cantar questi miei Motetti, non ne tragga io medema stimolo di piangere le mie sfortune? Comunque si sia, io cerco compatimento, non lode. E chi sarà di Cuore così scortese, che dall'acerba mia età (puoco fà uscita dal quarto lustro) voglia pretendere maturezza in quest'arte, che non si perfettiona se non con la longhezza de gl'anni? In ogni caso, io te li presento Benigno Lettore, come saggi. Se sentirò, che non ti dispiaciano, mi farò Cuore di tentare con maggior copia la tua gentilezza. Viui felice.

> *O quali incendio* (C)   Per ogni Tempo
> *Tacete ò languidae armoniae* (C)   Per ogni Santo ò Santa
> *Animae deuotae* (C)   Per ogni Tempo
> *Silentio o carae turbae* (C)   Per la Pasqua di Resurretione
> *Scintillate amicae stellae* (C)   Per il Santo Natale
> *Pane angelico* (C)   Per la Festa del Corpus Domini
> *Non plus vltra* (C)   Per il Santissimo Natale
> *O serenae pupillae* (C)   per ogni Tempo
> *O quam laeta* (C)   Per Santa Rodegonda
> *Non plangete* (C)   Per la Beata Vergine
> *Fugite vmbrae malignae* (A)   Per ogni Santo
> *Totus Mundus* (A)   Per ogni Santo

All textual sources are unknown.

RISM B624/BB624

Modern edition: *Non plangete* in Kendrick, 'Genres', 1242–53; *Pane angelico*, ed. Kendrick, in *Women Composers*, ii

11. *O fronde care, fate l'eco del mio cor*, 'Al qualificato merito dell'Ill.mo et R.mo Sig.re Abb. Camillo Tellier di Louuois'. Explicit: 'Poesia, e Musica di D. Rosa Hiacinta Badalli'

A, 2 Vl or Tpt, 2 Fl or Vl, bc

Location: F-Pn Vm^7.23

12. 'Cantata di Dna Rosa Hiacinta Badalli': *Vuo cercando quella speme* (A, bc)

Location: GB-Lbl, Harley 1273, fos. 44^r–45^v (paper after 1699, in the hand of H. Wanley, according to A. Hughes-Hughes, *Catalogue of the Manuscript Music in the British Museum* (London, 1908), 491)

Text author: unknown (?Badalla)

Modern edition: in Kendrick, 'Genres', 1254–61; also in *Women Composers*, ii

APPENDIX E:
A RECONSTRUCTION OF
BENEDICTINE VESPERS
AT S. RADEGONDA

From the *Rubriche generali del breviario monastico* (Milan, 1614) and from the *Breviarium monasticum* (Venice, 1613), with the specific items found in the latter; the additional responsory and *oratio* for St Radegund are in Lampugnani, *Della vita di S. Radegonda*, 149–50. I have given the items for both Sunday Vespers (I) and for the duplex Common of a single Virgin (II) in full; the specific sanctoral variants (Ia and IIa) list only those items that differ. An asterisk indicates an eight-voice setting in Cozzolani's 1650 collection.

I. *Sunday Vespers* (normal: semiduplex status)

1. Pater noster and Ave Maria
2. Versicle and Respond: Deus in adjutorium/R. Domine ad adiuvandum me★
3. Antiphon: Dixit Dominus domino meo: sede ad dextris meis
   Psalm (109): Dixit Dominus★/Antiphon
4. Antiphon: Fidelia omnia mandata eius: confirmata in seculorum saeculi
   Psalm (110): Confitebor tibi domine★/Antiphon
5. Antiphon: In mandatis: eius cupit nimis
   Psalm (111): Beatus vir★/Antiphon
6. Antiphon: Sit nomen domini: benedictum in saecula
   Psalm (112): Laudate pueri★/Antiphon
7. Chapter (2 Cor. 1: 3–4): Benedictus deus, et pater domini nostri Jesu Christi, Pater misericordium, et Deus totius consolationis, qui consolatur nos in omni tribulatione nostra
8. Responsorium breve: Quam magnificata sunt opera tua domine. V. Omnia in sapientia fecisti. Opera tua domine. Gloria Patri . . . Quam magnificata sunt . . . domine

9. Hymn: Lucis creator optime
10. Verse (said from the Second Sunday after Epiphany to the First Sunday of Lent and from the Third Sunday after Pentecost to the First Sunday of Advent): Dirigatur domine oratio mea
    R. Sicut incensum in conspectu tuo
11. Proper Antiphon for the Magnificat
    Magnificat★/Antiphon
12. Kyrie eleison; Pater noster; Proper *Oratio*
13. Commemoration of the Cross, of Mary, of the Apostles, St Benedict, etc. [possibly replaced by a litany][1]
14. Seasonal antiphon of the BVM[2]

Ia. Variants for the Second Vespers of a Confessor not a Pope (e.g. St William of Vercelli), duplex

3. Antiphon: Domine, quinque talenta tradidisti mihi; ecce alia quinque superlucratus sum.
7. Chapter (Ecclus. 31: 8–9): Beatus vir qui inventus est sine macula, et qui post aurum non abiit, nec speravit in pecunia et thesauris. Quis est hic? et laudabimus eum; fecit mirabilia in vita sua
8. Responsorium breve: Os justi mediabantur sapientium. V. Et lingua eius loquetur
9. Hymn: Iste confessor
10. V. Justum deduxerit Dominus per vias rectas. R. Et ostendit illi regnum Dei
11. Antiphon ad Magnificat: Hic vir despiciens mundum et terram, triumphans, divitias caelo condidit ore, manu
12. *Oratio* for the feast of an abbot: Intercessio nos quaesumus Domine beati N. commendet: ut quod nostris meritis non valemus, eius patrocinio assequamur. Per ipsum Dominum Jesum Christum Filium tuum; qui tecum vivit et regnat in unitate Spiritus Sancti Deus, per omnia saecula saeculorum. R. Amen

II. First Vespers, Common of a single Virgin (Duplex)

1. Pater noster and Ave Maria
2. Versicle and Respond: Deus in adjutorium/R. Domine ad adiuvandum me★

---

[1] This is found only in the *Rubriche generali*.

[2] The *Rubriche generali* (p. 69) state: 'Fuori di choro si dicono [these antiphons] solamente nel fine di Compietà, & nel fine di Matutino detto le laudi. Ma in choro sempre si dicono quando si termina qualche hora per partirsi di choro.'

3. Antiphon: Haec est virgo sapiens; et una de numero prudentium
   Psalm: Dixit Dominus★/Antiphon
4. Antiphon: Haec est virgo sapiens; quam Dominus vigilantem invenit
   Psalm: Laudate pueri★/Antiphon
5. Antiphon: Haec est quae nescivit torum in delicto; habebit fructum in respectione animarum sanctarum
   Psalm (121): Laetatus sum★/Antiphon
6. Antiphon: Veni electa mea; et ponam in te thronum meum, alleluia
   Psalm (126): Nisi Dominus★/Antiphon
7. Chapter (2 Cor. 10: 17–18): Fratres: qui gloriatur, in Domino glorietur: non enim qui se ipsum commendat, ille probatus est, sed quem Deus commendat
8. Responsorium prolix: R. Adiuvabit eam Deus vultus suo. V. Deus in medio eius non commovebitur. Gloria Patri . . . Adiuvabit . . . suo
9. Hymn: Jesu corona Virginum
10. V. Specie tua, et pulchritudine tua. R. Intende, prospere procede, et regna
11. Antiphon ad Magnificat: Veni sponsa Christi, accipe coronam, quam tibi Dominus preparavit in aeternam
    Magnificat★/Antiphon
12. Kyrie, Pater noster, and the following:
    Oratio: Deus, qui inter caetera potentiae tuae miracula etiam in sexu fragili victoriam contulisti, concede propitius ut quae beatae N. natalitia colimus: per eius ad te exempla gradiamur. Per dominum nostrum Jesu Christi, . . .
13. Commemoration of the Cross, of Mary, of the Apostles, St Benedict, etc.
14. Seasonal antiphon of the BVM

IIa. Variants for the First Vespers of St Radegund (11 August) (Here taken from the Common of a Female Saint neither Virgin nor Martyr, with additions from Lampugnani.)

3. Antiphon: Dum esset Rex in accubitu suo; nardus mea dedit odorem suavitatis
   Psalm: Dixit Dominus★/Antiphon
4. Antiphon: In odorem unguentorum tuorum currimus, adolescentulae dilexerunt te nimis
   Psalm: Laudate pueri★/Antiphon
5. Antiphon: Iam hiems transiit, imber abiit et recessit; surge, amica mea, et veni
   Psalm: Laetatus sum★/Antiphon

6. Antiphon: Veni electa mea; et ponam in te thronum meum, alleluia
   Psalm: Nisi Dominus/Antiphon

7. Chapter (Prov. 31: 10–11): Mulierem fortem quis invenit? Procul et de ultimis finibus pretium eius: Confidit in ea cor viri sui, et spoliis non indigebit

8. Responsorium [prolix; taken from Lampugnani]: R. Pulchra facie, sed pulchrior fide, beata es Regina Radegunda, quae regnum mundi, et omnem ornamentum saeculi contempsisti propter amorem Domini nostri Jesu Christi: propterea datum est tibi regnum caelorum.[3] Intercede pro omnibus nobis. V. Specie tua, et pulchritudine tua intende prospere, procede, & regna. Intercede pro omnibus nobis. Gloria Patri . . . Intercede . . .

9. Hymn: Fortem virile pectore

10. V. Specie tua, et pulchritudine tua. R. Intende, prospere procede, et regna

11. Antiphon ad Magnificat: Simile est regnum caelorum homini negotiatori, quaerenti bonas margaritas; Inventa una pretiosa, dedit omnia sua, et comparavit eam
    Magnificat*/Antiphon

12. Oratio (from Lampugnani): Oremus: Clementissime Deus, qui beatam Radegundam caelesti regno terrenum postponere docuisti: da nobis eius intercessione post mortalis vitam, quam suppliciter petimus, pacem, ad aeterna gaudia pervenire. Per Dominum nostrum Jesum Christum . . .

---

[3] Note the centonization of the *responsorium prolix* for the Cassinese use Consecration of a Virgin.

APPENDIX F: TWO COMPOSITIONS BY MILANESE NUNS

1. Chiara Margarita Cozzolani, *O quam bonus es*

2. Rosa Giacinta Badalla, *Non plangete*

-rem et_ pro-du-cet sal-va - to

Allegro

-rem._

Ca-ra di-es, ca-ra di-es_ for-tu-na -

- - - - ta,_

Me ra-pi - te cae - li ae -ter - -

- - ni, me ra-pi-te, me ra-pi-te cae-li ae-ter - -

- ni, iam sunt clau-sae por - tae in - fer -   -   -

- ni, sum con-ten - ta,_ sum_ be - a -   -

- ta, sum con-ten-ta, sum be - a-ta, sum con-ten-ta, sum be -

- a-ta, sum con-ten-ta, sum be - a-ta, sum be-a - ta, sum be - a-ta;

Ca-ra di-es, ca-ra di-es_

for - tu-na -   -   -   -   -

Non_ plus me ten - ta - te,_ no, no, no, non plus me ten - ta - te.

Al - le - lu - ia, al - le - lu - ia,   al - le - lu - ia, al - le - lu -

- ia,   al-le-lu - ia, al - le - lu - ia,_

_ al - le - lu - ia,   al-le-lu-ia, al - le - lu - ia,_

_ al - - - le - lu - ia,

al-le-lu-ia, al - le - lu-ia,_____ al - le - lu-ia,_____

al-le-lu-ia, al - le - lu-ia,___ al - le - lu - ia.

BIBLIOGRAPHY

◇

I. *Manuscript sources*

'Biografia delle monache umiliate di S. Caterina di Brera, anno 1684', BA, Trotti 453.

Untitled necrology from S. Marta, 1558–*c*.1720, BA, G. 150 *sussidio*.

Liber cronaca, S. Vittore in Meda (private collection).

Memorie sacre [S. Mariae] Lambrugensis, ASDM XII, vol. 180.

ALENSOON, JAN, 'Dag-register van een korte Reijs door eenige gedeeltens van Vrankrijk, Italie, Switserland ende Duijtschlaand' [1723–4], Amsterdam University Library, XV-E-25.

BORROMEO, FEDERIGO, *De ecstatibus mulieribus et illusis* (Italian version), BA, F. 26 *inf.*, fos. 1–268.

—— 'Notae in librum Canticum Canticorum Salomonis', ibid., fos. 270–430.

GUENZATI, BIAGIO, 'Vita di Federigo Borromeo', BA, G. 137 *inf.*

LOCATELLI, SEBASTIANO, 'Viaggio in Francia', Bologna, Biblioteca dell'Archiginnasio, B 1691.

[PIZZICHI, FILIPPO], 'Relazione del Viaggio fatto dal Serm° Prn^Pe Cosimo di Toscana in Lombardia', ASF, MP, filza 6382.

PRIA, COSIMO, 'Relazione del Viaggio fatto dal Ser^mo Sigr^e Principe Cosimo Terzo di Toscana L'Anno 1664', ASF, MP, filza 6383.

PURICELLI, GIOVANNI PAOLO, notes on Humiliate history, BA, H. 205 *inf.*

II. *Early printed literature (not including contents of Appendices C and D)*

ANGLERIA, CAMILLO, *La regola del contraponto e della musical compositione* (Milan, 1622; repr. 1983).

ARGELATI, FILIPPO, *Biblioteca scriptorum Mediolanensium* (Milan, 1745).

ARMELLINI, MARIANO, *Biblioteca Benedicto-Casinensis* (Assisi, 1731–2).

BAGLIONE, GIROLAMO, *Sacrae cantiones*, op. 2 (Milan, 1608).

BANCHIERI, ADRIANO, *Lettere armoniche* (Venice, 1628).

BERARDI, ANGELO, *Ragionamenti musicali* (Bologna, 1681).

BONA, VALERIO, *Li dilettevoli Introiti a otto*, op. 18 (Venice, 1611).

Bonomo, Giovanna Maria, *Confusione del cristiano in non corrispondere all'Amore mostrata da Gesù Cristo Sig. N. nella sua acerba Passione, e morte* (Bassano, 1659).

Borromeo, Federigo, *De ecstaticis mulieribus et illusis* (Milan, 1616).

—— *I tre libri delli piaceri della mente cristiana* (Milan, 1625); Latin version as *De christianae mentis jocunditate* (Milan, 1632).

Borsieri, Girolamo, *Soplemento* to P. Morigia, *La nobiltà di Milano* (Milan, 1619).

Breviarium Ambrosianum Caroli S.R.E. Cardinalis Tit. S. Praxedis Archiepiscopi iussu editum (Milan, [1604]).

Breviarium monasticum secundum ritum et morem congregationis Casinensis (Venice, 1600).

Breviarium monasticum Pauli V. Pont. Max. auctoritate recognitum, pro omnibus sub Regula Sanctissimi Patris Benedicti militantibus (Venice, 1613).

Breviarium Romanum ad usum et secundum ritum fratrum ordinis humiliatorum (Pavia, 1621).

Burmeister, Joachim, *Musica poetica* (Rostock, 1606).

Burney, Charles, *The Present State of Music in France and Italy* (London, 1773).

Calvi, Donato, *Scena letteraria de gli scrittori bergamaschi* (Bergamo, 1664).

Campi, Antonio, *Cremona fedelissima città* (Cremona, 1585; repr. Bologna, 1990).

Cantone, Serafino, *Accademia festevole concertata* (Milan, 1627).

Casati, Gasparo, *Sacri concerti a due, tre, e quattro, libro terzo* (Venice, 1640).

—— *Il primo libro de motetti concertati*, op. 1 (Venice, 1643).

—— *Messa e salmi concertati* (Venice, 1644).

—— *Scelta d'ariosi salmi* (Venice, 1645).

Cazzati, Maurizio, *Il secondo libro de motetti a voce sola*, op. 6 (Venice, 1648).

—— *Il sesto libro de motetti à voce sola in Soprano*, op. 63 (Mantua, 1676).

Cigoña, Jusepe, *Entrada en este Estado, y ciudad de Milan de la Reyna Nuestra Señora Doña Maria Anna de Austria* (Milan, 1649).

Cima, Giovanni Paolo, *Partito de ricercari e canzoni francesi* (Milan, 1606).

Cozzi, Carlo, *Messa e salmi correnti*, op. 1 (Milan, 1649).

Della Porta, Francesco, *Motetti a due, tre, quattro, e cinque voci*, op. 2 (Venice, 1645).

—— *Motetti a due, tre, quattro, e cinque voci*, op. 3 (Venice, 1648).

—— *Motetti a due, tre, quattro, e cinque voci*, op. 4 (Venice, 1650).

—— *Salmi da capella a quattro voci*, op. 5 (Venice, 1656/7).

Donati, Ignazio, *Salmi boscarecci* (Venice, 1623).

—— *Il secondo libro de motetti a voce sola* (Venice, 1636).

Fontana Morello, Giovanni Stefano, *Primo libro de sacri concerti* (Milan, 1614).

Gaffurius, Francesco, *Theorica musicàe* (Milan, 1492).

—— *Practica musicae* (Milan, 1496).

GALLONIO, ANTONIO, *Trattato de gli instrumenti di martirio, e delle varie maniere di martoriare usate da' Gentili contro Christiani* (Rome, 1591).

GHIZZOLO, GIOVANNI, *Concerti all'uso moderno a quattro voci* (Milan, 1611).

GRANCINI, MICHELANGELO, *Quinto libro de concerti ecclesiastici*, op. 8 (Milan, 1636).

—— *Novelli fiori ecclesiastici*, op. 9 (Milan, 1643).

GUALDO PRIORATO, GALEAZZO, *Historia di Leopoldo Cesare*, iii (Vienna, 1674).

HELYOT, PIERRE (i.e. Bullot, Maximilien), *Histoire des ordres religieux et militaires* (Paris, 1714–19).

KIRCHER, ATHANASIUS, *Musurgia universalis* (Rome, 1650).

LAMPUGNANI, AGOSTINO, *Della vita di S. Radegonda, che di gran regina si fece monaca di S. Benedetto* (Milan, 1649).

LATUADA, SERAFINO, *Descrizione di Milano* (Milan, 1737).

LODI, EMANUELE, *Breve historia di Meda* (Milan, 1629; repr. 1741).

MAGGI, CARLO MARIA, *I consigli di Meneghino* (Milan, 1697); mod. edn. in Maggi, *Il teatro milanese*, ed. D. Isella (Turin, 1964).

MARINO, GIAMBATTISTA, *La musica. Diceria seconda sopra le sette parole dette da Cristo in croce* (1613); mod. edn. in *Dicerie sacre e La strage de gl'innocenti*, ed. G. Pozzi (Turin, 1960).

—— *La Sampogna* (Paris, Venice, and Milan, 1620); mod. edn. V. De Maldé (Milan and Parma, 1994).

MICHELI, ROMANO, *Psalmi ad officium vesperarum* (Rome, 1610).

Missale Ambrosianum . . . Federici card.lis Borromei . . . iussu recognitum et editum (Venice, 1609).

MORIGIA, PAOLO, *La nobilità di Milano* (Milan, 1595).

—— *Il santuario della città di Milano* (Milan, 1641).

MORTARO, ANTONIO, *Primo libro de canzoni* (Venice, 1600).

NATALI, POMPEO, *Madrigali e canzoni spirituali a due, et a tre voci* (Rome, 1662).

NOVATI, GIOVANNI BATTISTA, *De eminentia Deiparae Virginis Mariae* (Bologna, 1639).

—— *Eucharistici amores ex canticis canticorum* (Milan, 1645).

NUCIUS, JOHANNES, *Musices poeticae* (Neisse, 1613).

Ordo admittendi virgines ad monasterii ingressum . . . Secundum morem Congregationis Cassinensis (Milan, 1607).

PATTA, SERAFINO, *Sacra Cantica Concinenda* (Venice, 1609).

PELLEGRINI, VINCENZO, *Sacer concentus* (Venice, 1619).

PENNA, LORENZO, *Li primi albori musicali* (Bologna, 1672).

PICINELLI, FILIPPO, *Mondo simbolico* (Milan, 1653).

—— *Ateneo dei letterati milanesi* (Milan, 1670).

PONTIO, PIETRO, *Ragionamento di musica* (Parma, 1588).

PUTEANUS, ERYCIUS, *Modulata Pallas* (Milan, 1599; rev. edn. as *Musathena*, Hanover, 1602).

QUANTZ, JOHANN JOACHIM, *Lebensläuffe*, in F. W. Marpurg, *Historisch-kritische Beyträge zur Aufnahme der Musik* (Berlin, 1754), i. 197–266.

Regole delle Monache di S. Chiara (Milan, 1670).

RIGAUD, JEAN-ANTOINE, *Bref recueil des choses rares, notables . . . de l'Italie* (Aix, 1601).

Rubriche generali del breviario monastico (Milan, 1614).

SCALETTA, ORAZIO, *Cetra spirituale* (Milan, 1605).

STEFANINI, GIOVANNI BATTISTA, *Motetti . . . libro primo a due e tre voci* (Milan, 1606).

TORRE, CARLO, *Specchio per l'anime religiose, cioè vita della beata Veronica, monaca del venerabile monastero di S. Marta di Milano* (Milan, 1652).

—— *Il ritratto di Milano* (Milan, 1674/repr. 1714).

TRABATTONE, EGIDIO, *Quarto libro de concerti a due, tre, quattro, e cinque voci*, op. 7 (Milan, 1642).

TURATI, ANTONIO MARIA, *Primi fiori del giardino musicale* (Milan, 1651).

VICENTINO, NICOLA, *Moteta cum quinque vocibus* (Milan, 1571).

VOGT, M., *Conclave thesauri magnae artis musicae* (Prague, 1719).

III. Literature

Acta ecclesiae mediolanensis, 4 vols., ed. A. Ratti (Milan, 1890–7).

BACCHESCHI, EDDY, and CALVESI, MAURIZIO, 'Simone Peterzano', in *I Pittori Bergamaschi: Il Cinquecento* (Bergamo, 1978), iv. 471–558.

BAERNSTEIN, P. RENÉE, 'The Counter-Reformation Convent: The Angelics of S. Paolo in Milan, 1535–1635' (Ph.D. diss., Harvard University, 1993).

BARCIA, FRANCO, *Bibliografia delle opere di Gregorio Leti* (Milan, 1981).

BARTEL, DIETRICH, *Handbuch der musikalischen Figurenlehre* (Laaber, 1985).

BENVENUTI PAPI, ANNA, '*In Castro Poenitentiae': Santità e società femminile nell'Italia medioevale* (Rome, 1990).

BERETTA, RINALDO, *Appunti storici su alcuni monasteri e località della Brianza* (Monza, 1966).

BIANCONI, LORENZO, and WALKER, THOMAS, 'Dalla *Finta Pazza* alla *Veremonda*: Storie di Febiarmonici', *Rivista italiana di musicologia*, 10 (1975), 379–454.

BLOK, ANTON, 'Notes on the Concept of Virginity in Mediterranean Societies', in E. Schulte van Kessel (ed.), *Women and Men in Spiritual Culture, XVth–XVIth centuries* (The Hague, 1986), 27–33.

BONTA, STEPHEN, 'Liturgical Problems in Monteverdi's Marian Vespers', *JAMS* 20 (1967), 87–106.

—— 'The Uses of the *Sonata da Chiesa*', *JAMS* 22 (1969), 54–84.

BORELLA, PIETRO, 'I religiosi e il rito ambrosiano', *Ambrosius*, 22 (1946), 131–7.

—— 'I codici ambrosiani-monastici', *Ambrosius*, 23 (1947), 25–9.

BORROMEO, AGOSTINO, 'La Chiesa milanese del Seicento e la Corte di Madrid', in de Maddalena (ed.), *Millain the Great*, 98–104.

—— 'La storia delle cappelle musicali vista nella prospettiva della storia della chiesa', in O. Mischiati and P. Russo (eds.), *La cappella musicale nell'Italia della Controriforma* (Florence, 1993), 229–37.

BOWERS, JANE, 'The Emergence of Women Composers in Italy, 1566–1700', in ead. and J. Tick (eds.), *Women Making Music: The Western Art Tradition 1150–1950* (Urbana, Ill., 1986), 116–67.

DE BROGLIE, EMMANUEL, *Mabillon et la Société de l'Abbaye de Saint-Germain des Prés* (Paris, 1888).

BUGGE, JOHN, *Virginitas: An Essay in the History of a Medieval Idea* (The Hague, 1975).

BÜLOW, GOTTFRIED VON (ed.), 'Diary of the Journey of Philip Julius, Duke of Stettin-Pomerania, through England in the Year 1602', *Transactions of the Royal Historical Society*, NS 6 (1892), 1–67.

BURATTI, ADELE *et al.* (eds.), *La città rituale: La città e lo Stato di Milano nell'età dei Borromeo* (Milan, 1982).

BURCKHARDT, JACOB, *Die Kultur der Renaissance in Italien* (Basle, 1860).

BURKE, PETER, *The Historical Anthropology of Early Modern Italy: Essays in Perception and Communication* (Cambridge, 1985).

—— *The Italian Renaissance: Culture and Society in Italy* (Princeton, 1986).

—— 'The Renaissance Dialogue', *Renaissance Studies*, 3 (1989), 2–14.

—— 'Historians, Anthropologists and Symbols', in E. Ohnuki-Tienney (ed.), *Culture Through Time: Anthropological Approaches* (Stanford, 1990), 268–83.

BUSNELLI, ROBERTA, 'Il tramonto di un monastero patrizio: Le benedettine di San Vittore di Meda nel Settecento', *ASL* 116 (1990), 147–66.

BYNUM, CAROLINE WALKER, *Holy Feast and Holy Fast: The Meaning of Food to Medieval Religious Women* (Berkeley, 1987).

—— *Fragmentation and Redemption: Essays on Gender and the Human Body in Medieval Tradition* (New York, 1991).

CABIBBO, SARA, and MODICA, MARILENA, *La santa dei Tomasi: Storia di Suor Maria Crocifissa (1645–1699)* (Turin, 1989).

CAFFIERO, MARINA, 'Dall'esplosione mistica tardo-barocca all'apostolato sociale', in Scaraffia and Zarri (eds.), *Donne e fede*, 327–74.

CALVI, GIULIA, 'I Toscani e la Milano barocca', in de Maddalena (ed.), *Millain the Great*, 169–90.

—— (ed.), *Barocco al femminile* (Rome, 1992).

CASTIGLIONE, CARLO, *La chiesa milanese durante il Seicento* (Milan, 1948).

CATTANA, VALERZO, 'Il monachesimo benedettino nella diocesi di Milano dalla fine del Medioevo all'età dei Borromei', *RSCA* 9 (1980), 82–137.

—— 'San Carlo Borromeo e i monaci benedettini: Prime ricerche sull'epistolario carolino', *RSCA* 14 (1985), 111–46.

CATTANEO, ENRICO, 'La religione a Milano dall'età della Controriforma', *Storia di Milano*, xi (1958), 283–331.

—— 'Influenze veronesi sulla legislazione di San Carlo Borromeo', in *Problemi di vita religiosa nel Cinquecento* (Padua, 1960), 123–66.

—— 'Istituzioni ecclesiastiche milanesi', *Storia di Milano*, ix (1961), 507–721.

—— 'Il monachesimo a Milano dalle origini all'età postcarolingia', *RSCA* 9 (1980), 7–29.

—— 'Le monacazioni forzate fra Cinque e Seicento', in Colombo (ed.), *Vita e processo*, 145–95.

CATTIN, GIULIO, 'Tradizione e tendenze innovatrici nella normativa e nella pratica liturgico-musicale della Congregazione di S. Giustina', *Benedictina*, 17 (1970), 254–98.

—— 'I benedettini e la musica', *Schede medievali*, 5 (1983), 393–418.

CAZZAMINI MASSI, FRANCESCO, *Milano durante il dominio spagnolo* (Milan, 1947).

DE CERTEAU, MICHEL, *La Fable mystique, XVIe–XVIIe siècles* (Paris, 1982).

CHABOD, FEDERICO, *Lo Stato e la vita religiosa a Milano nell'epoca di Carlo V* (Turin, 1971).

CHAFE, ERIC T., *The Church Music of Heinrich Biber* (Ann Arbor, 1987).

COAKLEY, JOHN, 'Introduction: Women's Creativity in Religious Context', in Matter and Coakley (eds.), *Creative Women*, 1–16.

COLLETT, BARRY, *Italian Benedictine Scholars and the Reformation: The Congregation of Santa Giustina of Padua* (Oxford, 1985).

COLOMBO, UMBERTO (ed.), *Vita e processo di Suor Virginia Maria de Leyva Monaca di Monza* (Milan, 1985).

COLTURI, GABRIELLA, 'Monache a Milano fra Cinque e Seicento: La storia del monastero di Santa Maria della Consolazione, detto della Stella (1494–1778)', *ASL* 116 (1990), 113–46.

COLZANI, ALBERTO, et al. (eds.), *La musica sacra in Lombardia nella prima metà del Seicento* (Como, 1987).

—— *Tradizione e stile: Atti del II Convegno internazionale di studi sul tema: La musica sacra in area lombardo-padana nella seconda metà del '600* (Como, 1989).

COPPA, SIMONETTA, *Pinacoteca di Brera: Scuole lombarde, ligure e piemontesi, 1535–1706* (Milan, 1989).

CROCE, BENEDETTO, *Storia dell'età barocca in Italia* (Bari, 1929).

CURTIS, ALAN, '*La Poppea Impasticciata*, or, Who Wrote the Music to *L'Incoronazione* (1643)?', *JAMS* 42 (1989), 23–54.

D'AMICO, STEFANO, *Le contrade e la città: Sistema produttivo e spazio urbano a Milano fra Cinque e Seicento* (Milan, 1994).

DE BOER, WIETSE, 'Sinews of Discipline: The Uses of Confession in Counter-Reformation Milan' (Ph.D. diss., Erasmus Universiteit Rotterdam, 1994).

DELFINO, ANTONIO, 'Geronimo Cavaglieri e alcuni contrafacta di madrigali marenziani', in M. T. Rosa Barezzani and M. Sala (eds.), *Luca Marenzio musicista europeo* (Brescia, 1990), 165–216.

DE SANCTIS, FRANCESCO, *Storia della letteratura italiana* (Florence, 1870–1).

DIXON, GRAHAM, *Carissimi* (Oxford, 1986).

DONÀ, MARIANGELA, *La stampa musicale a Milano fino all'anno 1700* (Florence, 1961).

DREVES, GUIDO MARIA, *Analecta hymnica medii aevi*, xxii (Leipzig, 1895).

DRONKE, PETER, *Verse with Prose from Petronius to Dante: The Art and Scope of the Mixed Form* (Cambridge, Mass., 1994).

DURANTE, ELIO, and MARTELLOTTI, ANNA, *Don Angelo Grillo O.S.B. alias Livio Celano: Poeta per musica del decimosettimo secolo* (Florence, 1989).

ELLIS, ALEXANDER J., and MENDEL, ARTHUR, *Studies in the History of Musical Pitch* (Amsterdam, 1968).

EMANS, REINMAR, 'Die einstimmigen Kantaten, Canzonetten und Serenaden Giovanni Legrenzis' (diss., Bonn, 1984).

ERIG, RICHARD, and GUTMANN, VERONICA (eds.), *Italienische Diminutionen: Die zwischen 1553 und 1638 mehrmals bearbeiteten Sätze* (Zürich, 1979).

FABI, MASSIMO, *Biblioteca storica italiana* (Milan, 1854).

FABRIS, DINKO, 'Generi e fonti della musica sacra a Napoli nel Seicento', in D. D'Alessandro and A. Ziino (eds.), *La musica a Napoli durante il Seicento: Atti del Convegno Internazionale di Studi, Napoli, 11–14 aprile 1985* (Rome, 1987), 421–42.

FERRAZZI, MIRELLA, 'Biblioteche e scrittoi benedettini nella storia culturale della diocesi ambrosiana: Appunti ed episodi', *RSCA* 9 (1980), 230–90.

FERRARI, CECILIA, *Autobiografia di una santa mancata*, ed. A. J. Schutte (Bergamo, 1990).

FISCHER, KLAUS, 'Nuove techniche della policoralità lombarda nel primo Seicento', in Colzani *et al.*, *La musica sacra in Lombardia*, 46–50.

DE FLORENTIIS, GRAZIELLA, and VESSIA, GIAN NICOLA, *Sei secoli di musica nel Duomo di Milano* (Milan, 1986).

FORTINI, MARCO, '"Alla Altezza Serenissima di Modena dal Residente in Milano": Ambasciatori, agenti e corrispondenti modenesi nel XVII secolo', in de Maddalena (ed.), *Millain the Great*, 223–41.

Francesco Cairo 1607–1665 (Varese, 1984).

FRANCHINI, FAUSTA, 'Un "concerto di monache" e altri dipinti di Alessandro Magnasco', *Arte antica e moderna*, 34–6 (1966), 232–5.

GAMBI, LUCIO, and GOZZOLI, MARIA CRISTINA, *Le città nella storia d'Italia: Milano* (Rome, 1982).

GASPARI, GAETANO, *Catalogo della Biblioteca Musicale G. B. Martini di Bologna* (Bologna, 1890–1905; repr. 1961).

GEIGER, BENNO, *Magnasco* (Bergamo, 1949).

GIULINI, ALESSANDRO, 'I genitori di Maria Teresa a Milano nel 1711 e 1713', *ASL* 60 (1933), 134–49.

GLIXON, BETH E., and JONATHAN L., *Marco Faustini and Operatic Production in Seventeenth-Century Venice* (forthcoming).

GRASSI, SILVIA, and GROHMANN, ALBERTO, 'La Segreteria di Stato di Sua Santità e la Milano nell'età del barocco', in de Maddalena (ed.), *Millain the Great*, 267–83.

GROTH, RENATE, 'Italienische Musiktheorie im 17. Jahrhundert', in F. Zaminer (ed.), *Italienische Musiktheorie im 16. und 17. Jahrhundert* (Darmstadt, 1989), 307–79.

HABERKAMP, GERTRUD, *Bischöfliche Zentralbibliothek Regensburg: Thematischer Katalog der Musikhandschriften* (Munich, 1989).

HEIMLING, OTTO, 'Der ambrosiano-benediktinische Psalter vom 14.–17. Jh.', *Jahrbuch für Liturgiewissenschaft*, 11 (1931), 144–56.

HOLZER, ROBERT R., ' "Sono d'altro garbo . . . le canzonette che si cantano oggi": Pietro della Valle on Music and Modernity in the Seventeenth Century', *Studi musicali*, 21 (1992), 253–306.

HUGHES, DIANE OWEN, 'Representing the Family: Portraits and Purposes in Early Modern Italy', *Journal of Interdisciplinary History*, 17 (1986), 7–38.

JACKSON, BARBARA GARVEY, *'Say Can You Deny Me': A Guide to Surviving Music by Women from the 16th through the 18th Centuries* (Fayetteville, Ark., 1994).

JEDIN, HUBERT, *Geschichte des Konzils von Trient*, 4 vols. (Freiburg im Breisgau, 1951–75).

—— *Der Abschluß des Trienter Konzils 1562/63: Ein Rückblick nach vier Jahrhunderten* (Münster, 1963).

JONES, PAMELA M., 'Federico Borromeo as a Patron of Landscapes and Still Lifes: Christian Optimism in Italy c. 1600', *Art Bulletin*, 70 (1988), 261–72.

—— 'Bernardo Luini's *Magdalene* from the Collection of Federico Borromeo: Religious Contemplation and Iconographic Sources', *Studies in the History of Art* (Washington, DC), 24 (1990), 67–72.

—— *Federico Borromeo and the Ambrosiana: Art Patronage and Reform in Seventeenth-Century Milan* (Cambridge, 1993).

KAUFMANN, HENRY W., *Nicola Vicentino: Life and Works* (n.p., 1966).

KELLY, JOAN, 'Did Women Have a Renaissance?', in R. Bridenthal and C. Koontz (eds.), *Becoming Visible: Women in the European Past* (Boston, 1977), 137–64.

KENDRICK, ROBERT L., 'Music and Spirituality in Federigo Borromeo's Milan', paper presented at the 57th Annual Meeting, American Musicological Society, Chicago, November 1991.

—— 'The Traditions of Milanese Convent Music and the Sacred Dialogues of Chiara Margarita Cozzolani', in Monson (ed.), *The Crannied Wall*, 211–33.

—— 'Genres, Generations, and Gender: Nuns' Music in Early Modern Milan, *c.*1550–1706' (Ph.D. diss., New York University, 1993).

—— '*Sonet vox tua in auribus meis*: Song of Songs Exegesis and the Seventeenth-Century Motet', *Schütz-Jahrbuch*, 16 (1994), 99–118.

—— 'Four Views of Milanese Nuns' Music', in Matter and Coakley (eds.), *Creative Women*, 324–42.

—— 'La musica nel Santuario di Saronno fra Cinque e Seicento', in M. L. Gatti Perer (ed.), *Il santuario della Beata Vergine a Saronno* (Milan, 1996).

KIRKENDALE, WARREN, *The Court Musicians in Florence during the Principate of the Medici* (Florence, 1993).

KÖCHEL, LUDWIG VON, *Die kaiserliche Hof-Musikkapelle in Wien von 1543–1867* (Vienna, 1869).

KOSKOFF, ELLEN, *Women and Music in Cross-Cultural Perspective* (Westport, Conn., 1989).

KURTZMAN, JEFFREY, *Essays on the Monteverdi Mass and Vespers of 1610* (Houston, 1978).

LADEWIG, JAMES (ed.), *Italian Instrumental Music of the Sixteenth and Early Seventeenth Centuries*, xiii (New York, 1988).

LE BRUN, JACQUES, 'Mutations de la notion de martyre au XVIIᵉ siècle d'après les biographies spirituelles feminines', in J. Marx (ed.), *Sainteté et martyre dans les religions du livre* (Brussels, 1989), 77–90.

LECCISOTTI, TOMMASO, *Congregationis S. Iustinae de Padua O.S.B. Ordinationes Capitolorum Generalium*, pt. 2 (Montecassino, 1970).

LEGG, J. WICKHAM, 'The Divine Service in the Sixteenth Century, Illustrated by the Reform of the Breviary of the Humiliati in 1548', *Transactions of the St. Paul's Ecclesiological Society*, 2 (1890), 273–95.

LOCKWOOD, LEWIS, *The Counter-Reformation and the Masses of Vincenzo Ruffo* (Venice, 1970).

LUPPI, ANDREA, 'Immagine e funzione della musica sacra nella trattatistica di area lombardo-padana nel medio Barocco', in Colzani *et al.* (eds.), *Tradizione e stile*, 29–72.

MCGOWEN, RICHARD A., 'The Venetian Music Printer Giuseppe Sala: New Information Based upon Archival Documents', *Fontes artis musicae*, 36 (1989), 102–8.

DE MADDALENA, ALDO (ed.), *Millain the Great: Milano nelle brume del Seicento* (Milan, 1989).

MAJO, ANGELO, and VIGINI, GIULIANO, *Dizionario della chiesa ambrosiana* (Milan, 1988–93).

MARCOCCHI, MASSIMO, *La riforma dei monasteri femminili a Cremona: Gli atti inediti della visita del vescovo Cesare Speciano 1599–1606* (Cremona, 1966).

—— *La riforma cattolica: Documenti e testimonianze* (Brescia, 1967–70).

—— *I Gonzaga di Castiglione delle Stiviere: Vicende pubbliche e private del casato di San Luigi* (n.p., 1990).

MARCORA, CARLO, 'Due importanti codici della Biblioteca del Capitolo di Gallarate', *Rassegna gallaratese di storia e d'arte*, 17 (1958), 142–53.

—— 'La chiesa milanese nel decennio 1550–1560', *MSDM* 7 (1961), 254–501.

—— 'Lettere del cardinale Federico alle claustrali', *MSDM* 11 (1964), 177–432.

—— 'La biografia del Cardinale Federico Borromeo scritta dal suo medico personale Giovanni Battista Mongilardi', *MSDM* 15 (1968), 125–232.

MARTINI, ALESSANDRO, *'I Tre Libri delle Laudi Divine' di Federico Borromeo: Ricerca storico-stilistica* (Padua, 1975).

MARX, HANS-JOACHIM, 'Die Musik am Hofe Pietro Kardinal Ottobonis unter Arcangelo Corelli', *Analecta Musicologica*, 5 (Cologne, 1968), 104–77.

MASETTI ZANNINI, GIAN LUDOVICO, *Motivi storici dell'educazione femminile (1500–1650)* (Bari, 1980).

—— 'Espressioni musicali in monasteri femminili del primo Seicento a Bologna', *Strenna Storica Bolognese*, 35 (1985), 193–205.

—— 'Composizioni poetiche e trattamenti spirituali per monacazioni benedettine del Settecento', in G. Farnedi and G. Spinelli (eds.), *Settecento monastico italiano* (Cesena, 1990), 581–98.

MATTER, E. ANN, *The Voice of My Beloved: The Song of Songs in Medieval Western Christianity* (Philadelphia, 1990).

—— and COAKLEY, JOHN (eds.) *Creative Women in Medieval and Early Modern Italy: A Religious and Artistic Renaissance* (Philadelphia, 1994).

MATTHEWS GRIECO, SARA F., 'Modelli di santità femminile nell'Italia del Rinascimento e della Controriforma', in Scaraffia and Zarri (eds.), *Donne e fede*, 303–26.

MEDIOLI, FRANCESCA, *L'*'Inferno monacale*' di Arcangela Tarabotti* (Turin, 1990).

MEIER, BERNHARD, *Die Tonarten der klassischen Vokalpolyphonie* (Utrecht, 1974).

MISCHIATI, OSCAR, *Adriano Banchieri 1568–1634: Profilo biografico e bibliografico delle opere* (Bologna, 1971).

—— *Indici, cataloghi e avvisi degli editori e librai musicali italiani dal 1591 al 1798* (Florence, 1984).

—— *La prattica musicale presso i canonici regulari del SS. Salvatore nei secoli XVI e XVII e i manoscritti polifonici della biblioteca musicale 'G. B. Martini' di Bologna* (Rome, 1985).

—— 'Profilo storico della cappella musicale in Italia nei secoli XV–XVIII', in D. Ficola (ed.), *Musica sacra in Sicilia tra rinascimento e barocco* (Palermo, 1988), 23–46.

MODICA VASTA, MARILENA, 'La scrittura mistica', in Scaraffia and Zarri (eds.), *Donne e fede*, 375–98.

MOMPELLIO, FEDERICO, 'La vita musicale in Milano nella prima metà del Cinquecento', *Storia di Milano*, ix. 853–95.

MONETA CAGLIO, ERNESTO T., 'Un *Te Deum* ambrosiano inedito', in C. Alzati and A. Majo (eds.), *Studi ambrosiani in onore di mons. Pietro Borella* (Milan, 1982), 167–72.

MONNERET DE VILLARD, UGO, 'Contributo alla storia delle biblioteche milanesi', *ASL* 45 (1918), 296–301.

MONSON, CRAIG A., 'Elena Malvezzi's Keyboard Manuscript: A New Sixteenth-Century Source', *Early Music History*, 9 (1990), 73–128.

—— 'La pratica della musica nei monasteri femminili bolognesi', in O. Mischiati and P. Russo (eds.), *La cappella musicale nell'Italia della Controriforma* (Cento, 1993), 143–60.

—— *Disembodied Voices: Music and Culture in an Early Modern Italian Convent* (Berkeley, 1995).

—— 'Catholic Reform, Renewal, and Reaction', in J. Haar (ed.), *The New Oxford History of Music*, rev. edn., iv (Oxford, forthcoming).

—— (ed.), *The Crannied Wall: Women, Religion and the Arts in Early Modern Europe* (Ann Arbor, 1992).

MOORE, JAMES H., *Vespers at St. Mark's* (Ann Arbor, 1979).

MORETTI, MARIA ROSA, *Musica e costume a Genova tra Cinquecento e Seicento* (Genoa, 1992).

MONGA, LUIGI, 'Pagine di vita milanese nel diario di un prete bolognese del Seicento', *Libri & Documenti* 14 (1988), 88–95.

MÜNSTER, ROBERT, *et al.*, *Thematisches Katalog der Musikhandschriften der Benediktinerinnenabtei Frauenwörth und der Pfarrkirchen Indersdorf, Wasserburg am Inn, und Bad Tölz* (Munich, 1975).

MURRAY, RUSSELL E., 'The Voice of the Composer: Theory and Practice in the Works of Pietro Pontio' (Ph.D. diss., University of North Texas, 1989).

NEILSON, NANCY WARD, 'A Drawing by Aurelio Luini', *Master Drawings*, 25 (1987), 151–2.

NOSKE, FRITS, *Forma formans* (Amsterdam, 1969).

—— 'Sul dialogo latino del Seicento: Osservazioni', *Rivista italiana di musicologia*, 24 (1989), 330–46.

—— *Saints and Sinners: The Latin Musical Dialogue in the Seventeenth Century* (Oxford, 1992).

NUTTER, DAVID, 'Changing the Instrument for the Music (and Vice-versa): Salomone Rossi's Chitarrone', in C. Gallico (ed.), *Claudio Monteverdi: Studi e prospettive* (Florence, 1996).

O'MALLEY, JOHN, 'Was Ignatius Loyola a Church Reformer? How to Look at Early Modern Catholicism', *Catholic Historical Review*, 77 (1990), 177–93.

ORSINI, PAOLO, 'Il monastero di San Vittore a Meda nell'alto Medioevo', in F. Cajani, *Le vicende del monastero di San Vittore a Meda* (n.p., 1988), 131–203.

OWENS, JESSIE ANN, 'The Milan Part-Books: Evidence for Cipriano de Rore's Compositional Practice', *JAMS* 37 (1984), 270–98.

—— 'Music and the Friars Minor in Fifteenth- and Sixteenth-Century Italy', in *I Frati Minori tra '400 e '500* (Assisi, 1986), 169–88.

—— 'Music Historiography and the Definition of "Renaissance"', *Notes*, 47 (1990), 305–30.

PADOAN, MAURIZIO, 'Sulla struttura degli ultimi motetti vocali-strumentali di Alessandro Grandi', *Rivista internazionale di musica sacra,* 6 (1985), 7–66.

PALISCA, CLAUDE V., 'Die Jahrzehnte um 1600 in Italien', in F. Zaminer (ed.), *Italienische Musiktheorie im 16. und 17. Jahrhundert* (Darmstadt, 1989), 221–306.

PASSADORE, FRANCESCO, 'Le antologie lombarde a voce sola di Carlo Federico Vigoni', in Colzani *et al.* (eds.), *Tradizione e stile,* 221–54.

PATETTA, LUCIANO, *L'architettura del Quattrocento a Milano* (Milan, 1987).

—— *Storia e tipologia: Cinque saggi sull'architettura del passato* (Milan, 1989).

PAVAN, FRANCO, 'La necessità dell'*exemplum*: Gerolamo Borsieri e la musica delle monache milanesi', paper given at the November 1993 Tours Colloquium, 'Les femmes et la musique à la Renaissance'.

PETROCCHI, MASSIMO, *Storia della spiritualità italiana*, ii. *Il Cinquecento e il Seicento* (Rome, 1978).

PICCHI, ALESSANDRO, *Archivio Musicale del Duomo di Como: Catalogo delle opere a stampa e manoscritte dei secoli XVI–XVII* (Como, 1990).

PIOPPI, LUCIA, *Diario 1541–1612*, ed. R. Bussi (Modena, 1982).

POGLIANI, MARCO, 'Contributo per una bibliografia delle fondazioni religiose di Milano', *RSCA* 14 (1985), 157–281.

PORRO LAMBERTENGHI, GIULIO, *Trivulziana: Catalogo dei codici manoscritti* (Turin, 1884).

POWERS, HAROLD S., 'Modal Types and Tonal Categories in Renaissance Polyphony', *JAMS* 34 (1981), 428–70.

PRIZER, WILLIAM F., 'Music at the Court of the Sforza: The Birth and Death of a Musical Center', *Musica disciplina*, 43 (1989), 141–93.

PRODI, PAOLO, *Il cardinale Gabriele Paleotti (1522–1597)*, i (Rome, 1959).

—— 'Borromeo, Federico', *Dizionario biografico degli italiani*, xiii (1971), 30–9.

—— 'A proposito di storia locale dell'età moderna: Cultura, spiritualità, istituzioni ecclesiastiche', in C. Violante (ed.), *La storia locale: Temi, fonti, e metodi della ricerca* (Bologna, 1982), 143–56.

—— 'Riforma interiore e disciplinamento sociale in San Carlo Borromeo', *Intersezioni*, 5 (1985), 273–85.

—— 'Controriforma e/o riforma cattolica: Superamento di vecchi dilemmi nei nuovi panorami storiografici', *Römische historische Mitteilungen*, 31 (1989), 227–37.

PROSPERI, ADRIANO, 'Lettere spirituali', in Scaraffia and Zarri (eds.), *Donne e fede*, 227–52.

PRZYBOŚ, ADAM, *Podróz królwicza Władysława Wazy do krajów Europy Zachodniej w latach 1624–1625 w świetle ówczesnych relacji* (Cracow, 1977).

—— 'Polacchi e lituani di passaggio a Milano nel Seicento', in de Maddalena (ed.), *Millain the Great*, 311–22.

RAYNER, CLARE G., 'The Enigmatic Cima: Meantone Tuning and Transpositions', *Galpin Society Journal*, 22 (1969), 23–34.

REGGIORI, FERNANDO, 'Il monastero di S. Radegonda', *Città di Milano*, 41 (1925), 6–8.

RICCARDI, ANTONIO, 'The Mystic Humanism of Maria Maddalena de' Pazzi', in Matter and Coakley (eds.), *Creative Women*, 212–36.

ROCHE, JEROME, *North Italian Church Music in the Age of Monteverdi* (Oxford, 1982).

—— 'Cross-Currents in Milanese Church Music in the 1640's: Giorgio Rolla's Anthology *Teatro musicale* [1649]', in Colzani *et al.* (eds.), *La musica sacra in Lombardia*, 13–29.

ROLI, RENATO, and SESTIERI, GIANCARLO, *I disegni italiani del Settecento: Scuole piemontese, lombarda, genovese, bolognese, toscana, romana, e napolitana* (Treviso, 1981).

RONCAGLIA, GINO, *La cappella musicale del Duomo di Modena* (Florence, 1957).

RORKE, MARGARET ANN, 'Sacred Contrafacta of Monteverdi Madrigals and Cardinal Borromeo's Milan', *Music and Letters*, 65 (1984), 168–75.

ROSAND, ELLEN, 'The Descending Tetrachord: An Emblem of Lament', *Musical Quarterly*, 65 (1979), 346–59.

ROUGET, GILBERT, *Music and Trance* (Chicago, 1988).

RUBIN, MIMI, *Corpus Christi: The Eucharist in Late Medieval Culture* (Cambridge, 1991).

RUSSO, CARLA, *I monasteri femminili di clausura a Napoli nel secolo XVII* (Naples, 1970).

SABA, AGOSTINO, *Federico Borromeo ed i mistici del suo tempo* (Florence, 1931).

SANNAZZARO, GIOVANNI BATTISTA, 'Nuovi documenti per San Maurizio al Monastero Maggiore', *Civiltà ambrosiana*, 6 (1989), 58–62.

—— *San Maurizio al Monastero Maggiore* (Milan, 1992).

SANTAGIULIANA, TULLIO and ILDEBRANDO, *Storia di Treviglio* (Bergamo, 1965).

SANTAGOSTINO, AGOSTINO, *L'immortalità e gloria del pennello*, ed. M. Bona Castellotti (Milan, 1980).

SANVITO, GRAZIANO, 'Organi, organisti, organari nella diocesi di Novara nel secolo XVII', *Novarien*, 12 (1982), 105–47.

SCARAFFIA, LUCETTA, and ZARRI, GABRIELLA (eds.), *Donne e fede: Santità e vita religiosa in Italia* (Rome, 1994).

SCHAAL, RICHARD, *Die Musikhandschriften des Ansbacher Inventars von 1686* (Wilhelmshaven, 1966).

SCHLEIFER, MARTHA FURMAN, and GLICKMAN, SYLVIA (gen. eds.), *Women Composers: Music by Women through the Ages* (New York, 1995).

SCHRÖDER, FRANZ, *Repertorio genealogico delle famiglie confermate nobili . . . nelle provincie venete* (Venice, 1830).

SCHULZE, STEFAN, *Die Tonarten in Lassos 'Bußpsalmen' mit einem Vergleich von Alexander Utendals und Jacob Reiners 'Bußpsalmen'* (Neuhausen-Stuttgart, 1984).

SCHULZE, WINFRIED, 'Gerhard Oestreichs Begriff "Sozialdisziplinierung" in der frühen Neuzeit', *Zeitschrift für historische Forschung*, 14 (1987), 265–302.

SCOTT, JOAN WALLACH, *Gender and the Politics of History* (New York, 1988).

SEBASTIANI, LUCIA, 'Monasteri femminili milanesi tra medioevo e età moderna', in C. H. Smyth and G. C. Garfagnini (eds.), *Florence and Milan: Comparisons and Relations* (Florence, 1989), ii. 3–15.

SELLA, DOMENICO, 'Premesse demografiche ai censamenti austriaci', *Storia di Milano*, xii, 458–78

—— *Crisis and Continuity: The Economy of Spanish Lombardy in the Seventeenth Century* (Cambridge, Mass., 1979).

—— and CAPRA, CARLO, *Il Ducato di Milano dal 1535 al 1796* (Turin, 1984).

SEVESI, PAOLO, 'Il monastero delle Clarisse in S. Apollinare di Milano (documenti, sec. XIII–XVIII)', *Archivum Francescanum Historicum*, 17 (1924), 338–64, 520–44; 18 (1925), 226–47; and 19 (1926), 76–99.

—— 'Rievocazione dei monasteri delle Clarisse nell'Archidiocesi di Milano', *MSDM* 4 (1957), 212–26.

SHIGIHARA, SUSANNE, 'Bonifazio Graziani (1604/05–1664): Biographie, Werkverzeichnis und Untersuchungen zu den Solomotetten' (diss., Bonn, 1984).

SIGNOROTTO, GIANVITTORIO, *Inquisitori e mistici nel Seicento italiano: L'eresia di Santa Pelagia* (Bologna, 1989).

SILBIGER, ALEXANDER, 'Is the Italian Keyboard *Intavolatura* a Tablature?', *Recercare*, 3 (1991), 81–101.

SIMONSFELD, HENRY, 'Mailändische Briefe zur bayerischen und allgemeinen Geschichte des 16. Jahrhunderts', *Abhandlungen der historischen Classe der Königlich Bayerischen Akademie der Wissenschaften*, 22/2 (1902), 481–575.

SMITHER, HOWARD E., *A History of the Oratorio,* i (Chapel Hill, 1977).

SOBIESKI, JAKUB, *Peregrynacja po Europie, 1607–1613* (Wrocław, 1991).

SOLI, GUSMANO, *Chiese di Modena* (Modena, 1974).

SPINELLI, GIOVANNI, 'Ordini e congregazioni religiosi', *Diocesi di Brescia* (Storia religiosa della Lombardia, 3) (Brescia, 1992), 291–356.

Le stanze del cardinale Monti, 1635–1650 (Milan, 1994).

STEFANI, GINO, *Musica e religione nell'Italia barocca* (Palermo, 1975).

STEVENS, DENIS (ed. and trans.), *The Letters of Claudio Monteverdi* (London and Boston, 1980).

Storia di Milano, 16 vols. (Milan, 1953–62).

STROHM, REINHARD, *Music in Late Medieval Bruges* (Oxford, 1990).

SYAMKEN, GEORG GERRIET, 'Die Bildinhalte des Alessandro Magnasco, 1667–1749' (diss., Hamburg, 1963).

TAMBURINI, LUCIANO, *Le chiese di Torino dal Rinascimento al Barocco* (Turin, 1957).

TIRABOSCHI, GIOVANNI ANTONIO, *Vetera Humiliatorum Monumenta* (Milan, 1766).

TOMARO, JOHN B., 'San Carlo Borromeo and the Implementation of the Council of Trent', in J. Headley and Tomaro (eds.), *San Carlo Borromeo: Catholic Reform and Ecclesiastical Politics in the Second Half of the Sixteenth Century* (Washington, DC, 1988), 67–84.

TOMLINSON, GARY, *Monteverdi and the End of the Renaissance* (Berkeley, 1987).

TROLESE, FRANCESCO G. B., 'Beata Giovanna Maria Bonomo', in R. Zironda (ed.), *Santità e religiosità nella diocesi di Vicenza* (Vicenza, 1991), 145–51.

VERONESE, ALESSANDRA, 'Monasteri femminili in Italia settentrionale nell'alto medioevo: Confronto con i monasteri maschili attraverso un tentativo di analisi "statistica"', *Benedictina,* 34 (1987), 355–416.

VIANELLO, CARLO ANTONIO, 'Il dramma e il romanzo di Suor Paolina dei Conti Pietra', *ASL* 60 (1933), 150–74.

DE VICENTE DELGADO, ALFONSO, *La Música en el Monasterio de Santa Ana de Avila (siglos XVI–XVIII): Catalogo* (Madrid, 1989).

VISMARA CHIAPPA, PAOLA, 'La soppressione dei conventi e dei monasteri in Lombardia nell'età teresina', in A. de Maddalena *et al.* (eds.), *Economia, istituzioni, cultura in Lombardia nell'età teresina* (Bologna, 1982), iii. 481–500.

—— *Per vim et metum: Il caso di Paola Teresa Pietra* (Pavia, 1991).

VLAARDINGERBROECK, KEES, 'Faustina Bordoni Applauds Jan Alensoon: A Dutch Music-Lover in Italy and France in 1723–4', *Music and Letters,* 72 (1991), 536–51.

VOELKER, EVELYN C., 'Charles Borromeo's *Instructiones fabricae et supellectilis ecclesiasticae,* 1577: A Translation with Commentary and Analysis', (Ph.D. diss., Syracuse University, 1977).

Vogel, Emil, *Bibliothek der gedruckten weltlichen Vocalmusik Italiens aus den Jahren 1500–1700* (Leipzig, 1892; repr. 1962).

Voyage de Italie, ed. M. Bideaux (Geneva, 1982).

Walter, Horst, *Musikgeschichte der Stadt Lüneburg* (Tutzing, 1967).

Weaver, Elissa B., 'Spiritual Fun: A Study of Sixteenth-Century Tuscan Convent Theater', in M. B. Rose (ed.), *Women in the Middle Ages* (New York, 1980), 173–206.

—— 'Le muse in convento', in Scaraffia and Zarri (eds.), *Donne e fede*, 253–76.

Wickstrom, John, 'The Humiliati: Liturgy and Identity', *Archivum Fratrum Praedicatorum*, 62 (1992), 195–225.

Winkelmes, Mary-Ann, 'Form and Reform: The Cassinese Congregation and Benedictine Reform Architecture' (Ph.D. diss., Harvard University, 1995).

Wolff, Christoph, 'From Berlin to Lódz: The Spitta Collection Resurfaces', *Notes*, 46 (1989), 311–27.

Wright, Anthony D., *The Counter-Reformation: Catholic Europe and the Non-Christian World* (New York, 1982).

Zanetti, Dante E., *La demografia del patriziato milanese nei secoli XVII, XVIII, XIX* (Pavia, 1972).

Zanzi, Luigi, *Sacri monti e dintorni: Studi sulla cultura religiosa ed artistica della Controriforma* (Milan, 1990).

Zardin, Danilo, *Riforma cattolica e resistenze nobiliari nella diocesi di Carlo Borromeo* (Milan, 1984).

—— 'L'ultimo periodo Spagnolo (1631–1712). Da Cesare Monti a Giuseppe Archinto', in A. Caprioli *et al.* (eds.): *Diocesi di Milano* (Storia religiosa della Lombardia, 10; Brescia, 1990), ii. 575–613.

—— *Donna e religiosa di rara eccellenza: Prospera Corona Bascapè, i libri e la cultura nei monasteri milanesi del Cinque e Seicento* (Florence, 1992).

—— 'Mercato librario e letture devote nella svolta del Cinquecento tridentino: Note in margine ad un inventario milanese di libri di monache', in *Stampa, libri e letture a Milano nell'età di Carlo Borromeo* (Milan, 1992), 135–246.

—— 'Tra continuità delle strutture e nuove aspirazioni di "riforma": La riorganizzazione borromaica della curia arcivescovile', in G. Signorotto and P. Pissavino (eds.), *Lombardia borromaica, Lombardia spagnola (1554–1659)* (Rome, 1995).

Zarri, Gabriella, 'I monasteri femminili a Bologna tra il XIII e il XVII secolo', *Atti e memorie della Deputazione di Storia Patria per le provincie di Romagna*, NS 24 (1973), 133–224.

—— 'Aspetti dello sviluppo degli Ordini religiosi in Italia tra Quattro e Cinquecento: Studi e problemi', in P. Prodi and P. Johanek (eds.),

Strutture ecclesiastiche in Italia e in Germania prima della Riforma (Bologna, 1984), 207–57.

—— 'Monasteri femminili e città (secoli XV–XVIII)', in G. Chittolini and G. Miccoli (eds.), *Storia d'Italia: Annali*, ix: *La chiesa e il potere politico dal Medioevo all'età contemporanea* (Turin, 1986), 357–429.

—— 'Recinti sacri: Sito e forma dei monasteri femminili a Bologna tra '500 e '600', in S. Boesch Gajano and L. Scaraffia (eds.), *Luoghi sacri e spazi della santità* (Turin, 1990), 381–96.

—— *Le sante vive: Profezie di corte e devozione femminile tra '400 e '500* (Turin, 1990).

—— 'Ursula and Catharine: The Marriage of Virgins in the Sixteenth Century', in Matter and Coakley (eds.), *Creative Women*, 237–78.

—— 'Dalla profezia alla disciplina (1450–1650)', in Scaraffia and Zarri (eds.), *Donne e fede*, 177–226.

ZOPPÈ, LEANDRO, *Per una storia di Meda dalle origini alla fine del secolo XVIII* (Meda, 1971).

INDEX

Bold numbers denote references to illustrations. Composers' names are given in parentheses, as are the monasteries to which Milanese nuns belonged.